Lecture Notes of the Institute for Computer Sciences, Social Informatics and Telecommunications Engineering 268

More information about this series at http://www.springer.com/series/8197

Honghao Gao · Xinheng Wang
Yuyu Yin · Muddesar Iqbal (Eds.)

Collaborative Computing: Networking, Applications and Worksharing

14th EAI International Conference, CollaborateCom 2018
Shanghai, China, December 1–3, 2018
Proceedings

 Springer

Editors
Honghao Gao
Shanghai University
Shanghai, China

Yuyu Yin
Hangzhou Dianzi University
Hangzhou, Zhejiang, China

Xinheng Wang
University of West London
London, UK

Muddesar Iqbal
London South Bank University
London, UK

ISSN 1867-8211   ISSN 1867-822X   (electronic)
Lecture Notes of the Institute for Computer Sciences, Social Informatics
and Telecommunications Engineering
ISBN 978-3-030-12980-4   ISBN 978-3-030-12981-1   (eBook)
https://doi.org/10.1007/978-3-030-12981-1

Library of Congress Control Number: 2019932181

This Springer imprint is published by the registered company Springer Nature Switzerland AG
The registered company address is: Gewerbestrasse 11, 6330 Cham, Switzerland

Preface

We are delighted to introduce the proceedings of the 14th European Alliance for Innovation (EAI) International Conference on Collaborative Computing: Networking, Applications and Worksharing (CollaborateCom 2018). This conference brought together researchers, developers, and practitioners from around the world who are interested in fully realizing the promises of electronic collaboration in terms of networking, technology and systems, user interfaces and interaction paradigms, and interoperation with application-specific components and tools.

The technical program of CollaborateCom 2018 consisted of 52 papers, including 33 full papers and 19 short papers in oral presentation sessions at the main conference tracks. The conference sessions were: Session 1, Vehicular Networks; Session 2, Social Networks; Session 3, Information Processing; Session 4, Data Detection and Retrieval and Mobility; Session 5, Parallel Computing; Session 6, Knowledge Graph; Session 7, Cloud and Optimization, Software Testing and Formal Verification; Session 8, Collaborative Computing; Session 9, Social Networks; Session 10, Vehicular Networks, Networks and Sensors; Session 11, Information Processing and Collaborative Computing; Session 12, Mobility and Software Testing and Formal Verification; Session 13, Web Services and Image Information Processing; Session 14, Web Services + Remote Sensing. Apart from high-quality technical paper presentations, the technical program also featured two keynote speeches that were delivered by Dr. Yang Yang from Shanghai Tech University and Dr. Zhi Wang from Zhejiang University.

Coordination with the steering chair, Imrich Chlamtac, and honorary chair, Qing Nie, was essential for the success of the conference. We sincerely appreciate their constant support and guidance. It was also a great pleasure to work with such an excellent Organizing Committee and we thank them for their hard work in organizing and supporting the conference. In particular, the Technical Program Committee, led by our TPC co-chairs, Dr. Muddesar Iqbal and Dr. Xinheng Wang, who completed the peer-review process of technical papers and compiled a high-quality technical program. We are also grateful to the conference manager, Dominika Belisova, for her support and to all the authors who submitted their papers to the CollaborateCom 2018 conference and workshops.

We strongly believe that the CollaborateCom conference provides a good forum for all researchers, developers, and practitioners to discuss all science and technology aspects that are relevant to collaborative computing. We also expect that future CollaborateCom conferences will be as successful and stimulating, as indicated by the contributions presented in this volume.

January 2019

Honghao Gao
Yuyu Yin
Xinheng Wang
Muddesar Iqbal

Conference Organization (CollaborateCom)

Steering Committee

Chair

Imrich Chlamtac   Bruno Kessler Professor, University of Trento, Italy

Honorary Chairs

Qing Nie   Shanghai University, China
Jian Wan   Zhejiang University of Science and Technology, China

Organizing Committee

General Co-chairs

Honghao Gao   Shanghai University, China
Yuyu Yin   Hangzhou Dianzi University, China

Technical Program Committee Co-chairs

Xinheng Wang   University of West London, UK
Muddesar Iqbal   London South Bank University, UK

Workshops Chair

Hui Li   University of Electronic Science and Technology
of China, China

Panels Chair

Liehuang Zhu   Beijing Institute of Technology, China

Demos Chair

Xiaofei Liao   Huazhong University of Science and Technology,
China

Local Arrangements Chair

Yihai Chen   Shanghai University, China

Web Chair

Peng Ren   China University of Petroleum, China

Conference Manager

Dominika Belisova   EAI

Technical Program Committee

Amjad Ali	Korea University, South Korea
Andrei Chernykh	CICESE Research Center
Anwer Al-Dulaimi	University of Toronto, Canada
Bin Cao	Zhejiang University of Technology, China
Bin Zhu	Shanghai Polytechnic University, China
Chekfoung Tan	University of West London, UK
Chen Liu	North China University of Technology, China
Elahe Naserianhanzaei	University of Exeter, UK
Fekade Getahun	Addis Ababa University, Ethiopia
George Ubakanma	London South Bank University, UK
Guobing Zou	Shanghai University, China
Hongchen Wu	Shandong Normal University, China
Hairong Yu	Huazhong University of Science and Technology, China
Haolong Xiang	University of Auckland, New Zealand
Huahu Xu	Shanghai University, China
Imed Romdhani	Edinburgh Napier University, UK
Jian Wang	Wuhan University, China
Jie Cui	University of Science and Technology of China
Jing Liu	East China Normal University, China
Jun Zeng	ChongQing University, China
Junaid Arshad	University of West London, UK
Kai Peng	Beijing University of Posts and Telecommunications, China
Kuangyu Qin	Wuhan University, China
Leila Musavian	University of Essex
Li Kuang	Central South University, China
Liang Chen	University of West London, UK
Lianhai Liu	Central South University, China
Lianyong Qi	Nanjing University, China
Lin Meng	Ritsumeikan University, Japan
Malik Ahmad Kamran	COMSATS University Islamabad, Pakistan
Minzhen Wang	Changchun Institute of Technology, China
Muddesar Iqbal	London South Bank University, UK
Parisa Ffiroozi	University of Mazandaran, Iran
Pengwei Wang	Donghua University, China
Qing Wu	Hangzhou Dianzi University, China
Shaohua Wan	Zhongnan University, China
Shengke Zeng	Xihua University, China
Shizhan Chen	Tianjin University, China
Shunmei Meng	Nanjing University of Science and Technology, China
Stephan Reiff-Marganiec	University of Leicester, UK
Tao Wu	Chengdu University of Information Technology, China
Wanchun	Dou Nanjing University, China

Wei Zheng	Xiamen University, China
Weilong Ding	North China University of Technology, China
Weiwei Lin	Shanghai University, China
Wenbing Chen	Nanjing University of Information Science and Technology, China
Wenmin Lin	Hangzhou Dianzi University, China
Xiao Ma	Beijing University of Posts and Telecommunications
Xiaolon Xu	Nanjing University of Information Science and Technology, China
Xibin Wang	Guizhou Institute of Technology, China
Xu Ma	Xidian University, China
Xue Xiao	Chinese Academy of Sciences, China
Yan Yao	Shanghai Jiao Tong University, China
Ying Chen	Beijing Information Science and Technology University, China
Yingjie Wang	YanTai University, China
Yirui Wu	Hohai University, China
Yiwen Zhang	Anhui University, China
Yu-Chun Pan	University of West London, UK
Yuan Yuan	Michigan State University, USA
Yucong Duan	Hainan University, China
Yueshen Xu	Xidian University, China
Yutao Ma	Wuhan University, China
Yuyu Yin	Hangzhou Dianzi University, China
Yuyu Yin	Shanghai University, China
Zheng Li	Henan University, China
Zhihui Lv	Fudan University, China
Zhizhong Liu	Hohai University, China
Zhongqin Bi	Shanghai University of Electric Power, China
Dongjing Wang	Hangzhou Dianzi University, China
Fu Lu	Tianjin University, China
Hongyue Wu	Shandong University of Science and Technology, China
Qiming Zou	Shanghai University, China
Shahid Mumtaz	Instituto de Telecomunicações
Weimin Li	Shanghai University, China
Wen Si	Shanghai Business School, China
Xiangzheng Zhe	Zhejiang University, China
Xiaoxian Yang	Shanghai Polytechnic University, China
Xindong You	Beijing Institute of Graphic Communication, China
Zhuoyuan Zheng	Guilin University of Electronic Technology, China

Contents

Data, Information and Knowledge Processing

Cloud Technology and Applications

Software Testing and Formal Verification

Collaborative Computing

Meta-Path and Matrix Factorization Based Shilling Detection for Collaborate Filtering

Xin Zhang[1,2], Hong Xiang[1,2(✉)], and Yuqi Song[1,2]

[1] Key Laboratory of Dependable Service Computing in Cyber Physical Society, Chongqing University, Ministry of Education, Chongqing, China
{zhang.x,xianghong,songyq}@cqu.edu.cn
[2] School of Big Data and Software Engineering, Chongqing University, Chongqing, China

Abstract. Nowadays, collaborative filtering methods have been widely applied to E-commerce platforms. However, due to its openness, a large number of spammers attack those systems to manipulate the recommendation results to earn huge profits. The shilling attack has become a major threat to collaborative filtering systems. Therefore, effectively detecting shilling attacks is a crucial task. Most existing detection methods based on statistical-based features or unsupervised methods rely on a priori knowledge about attack size. Besides, the majority of work focuses on rating attack and ignore the relation attack. In this paper, motivated by the success of heterogeneous information network and oriented towards the hybrid attack, we propose an approach DMD to detect shilling attack based on meta-path and matrix factorization. At first, we concatenate the user-item bipartite network and user-user relation network as a whole. Next, we design several meta-paths to guide the random walk to product node sequences and utilize the skip-gram model to generate user embeddings. Meanwhile, users' latent factors are decomposed by matrix factorization. Finally, we incorporate these embeddings and factors to joint train the detector. Extensive experimental analysis on two public datasets demonstrate the superiority of the proposed method and show the effectiveness of different attack strategies and various attack sizes.

Keywords: Shilling detection · Meta-path · Hybrid attack · Heterogeneous information network · Collaborative filtering

1 Introduction

In recent years, with the proliferation of the Internet, a large number of E-commerce platforms are advancing by leaps and bounds, such as Amazon and Taobao. However, due to the wide range of products, it is difficult for users to find what they are truly interested in. Therefore, those platforms use recommender

H. Gao et al. (Eds.): CollaborateCom 2018, LNICST 268, pp. 3–16, 2019.
https://doi.org/10.1007/978-3-030-12981-1_1

system to provide potential personalized products for their customers to alleviate the above information overload problem. And the most prevalent recommended method is collaborative filtering, which recommends items based on purchase behavior of target customer and other customers with similar preference.

Nonetheless, due to the openness of collaborative filtering recommender systems, numerous malicious users (named spammers) can inject biased profiles (namely shilling profiles) into systems to manipulated the recommendation results for authentic users for gaining more profit. Meanwhile, according to various aspirations, some merchants resort to improving the recommendation of their products via increasing the ratings of their own products while another seller endeavor to decrease scores of competitive commodities, and the former called push attack and the latter called nuke attack. Such fraudulent actions are shilling attacks which badly change the recommendation results and affect the decision of the prospective consumers. In consequence, how to detect shilling attacks is a core task of improving the robustness of recommender systems.

Generally, the shilling detection can be regarded as a binary classification problem, which means we need to identify a user is a malicious user (named spammer) or authentic user through his/her profiles. To this end, the main point of this problem is to analyze and model the characteristic of users. Up to now, although dozens of notable works have been down to detect shilling attacks, most of them highly rely on the statistical manners, which may fail in revealing the fine-grained interactions between users and items. Besides, as the collaborative filtering relies on users preference, the relations between users also can make effort to recommendation and attack, but there is little work pay attention to it.

According to above intuition, to dig the interactions between users and items and explore the relations among users for detection, in this paper, we propose a shilling detection algorithm named DMD (Double M Detector). We use the matrix factorization to decompose the user-item rating matrix to obtain the latent factors, while design several meaningful meta-paths based on Heterogeneous Information Network (HIN) according to network characteristics, such as degree, hindex and coreness, to represent users' embeddings of latent relations. Furthermore, joint training the detector via above latent factors to predict the label of users.

The main contributions of this paper are summarized as follows:

- We propose a novel method DMD which exploits the interactions among user-item and user-user based on HIN to detect shilling attacks for collaborative filtering recommender systems;
- We not only focus to detect the rating attacks, but also pay attention to relation attacks, and the proposed DMD is effective for hybrid attacks.
- With extensive experiments on the real-world Amazon dataset and simulated FilmTrust dataset, we evaluate and compare the performance of the method with other methods to show its effectiveness.

The remainder of this paper is organized as follows. Section 2 reviews the related work of shilling detection. Section 3 presents the preliminaries about shilling attack models and the proposed method. The illustration of DMD in detail is shown in Sect. 4. In Sect. 5, we conduct experiments on two datasets. Finally, Sect. 6 concludes the whole paper.

2 Related Work

In collaborative filtering recommender system, the key vulnerabilities derive from the openness of itself and the high reliance on user profiles. To alleviate the shilling attack and reinforce the robustness of collaborative filtering recommender system, many researchers engaged in the field of shilling detection. According to the intent of spammers, to promote items or prevent items from being recommended, attacks can be categorized into two types: the push attack and the nuke attack. As the basic principle of the two kinds of attacks is the same, the most research pays more attention to the push attack.

In the early stage, researchers mainly focused on statistical analysis methods to detect anomalies caused by suspicious ratings. For example, there was some work relied on item average ratings [1] or leveraged Neyman-Person statistical detection theory [2] and so forth. Meanwhile, a lot of research has been undertaken to employ supervised learning for detection, those classifiers are trained through labels information. For instance, a detector based on the average similarity and the Rating Deviation from Mean Agreement (RDMA) metric was presented in [3], a decision-tree based proposed in [4]. More specifically, Williams et al. [5] proposed several generic and attack type-specific attributes, and trained three supervised machine learning algorithms to detect shilling attacks. Recently, Li et al. [6] developed an algorithm, which explored item's popularity degree features; Zhou et al. [7] first used an SVM-based classifier to obtain an amount of suspicious profiles, secondly, removed the genuine profiles from the set via target item analysis method, and Dou et al. [8] proposed a CoDetector model, which jointly decomposes the user-item matrix and the user-user co-occurrence matrix.

Although supervised methods usually could train a good performance detector, it totally depends on labeled samples which increase the number of experts and time consuming to a large extent. Therefore, unsupervised models are utilized in the shilling detection, which are more applicable to real scenarios. The early classical approach is PCASelectUsers [9], which exploited the principal component analysis on the rating records. Lately, Zhang et al. [10] presented a unified framework based on the idea of label propagation, but it requires to set the number of spammers as the initial seed users.

Apart from the above methods, some semi-supervised models have also been explored in shilling detection. A hybrid shilling attack detector was proposed by Wu [11], which collects many detection metrics for selecting features via a wrapper called MC-Relief and the semi-supervised Naive Bayes for classification. In [12], a model based on PU-Learning which relies on a few positive labels and much unlabeled to construct a classifier iteratively was introduced.

The above-mentioned methods all have some limitations: supervised and semi-supervised detection methods are restricted by labeled samples, unsupervised detection methods need some prior knowledge about attacks to guarantee their performance. In addition, some methods are only suitable for detecting known types of attacks, when handling some new or unknown attacks, the performance is poor. Furthermore, most of them focused on rating information rather than relations between users.

3   Preliminaries

3.1   Shilling Attack Models

According to information that attackers used [13], we classify the shilling attack into three broad categories: rating attack, relation attack and hybrid attack. The definitions of those attacks are shown in Table 1.

Table 1. The definition of three types of attack.

Types	Definition
Rating attack	Injecting biased rating profiles to manipulate the recommendation results
Relation attack	Through link farming to influence user's social relationship and distort neighbors' preferences
Hybrid attack	Fusing ratings and relationships to enlarge destructiveness in recommender systems

In the three types of attack, rating attack is a typical and most common forms to affect the recommendation, and despite the fact that relation attack usually aims at social network rather than recommender system, but it can be used as an auxiliary to enhance destructiveness. In consequence, in this paper, we intend to integrate the rating information and users' relationship to detect the shilling attack.

In order to attack the target product and in the same time behave like an authentic user to avoid being detected, spammers always use attack model and generate attack profiles based on knowledge of recommender system. The general rating profile can be divided into four parts. Meanwhile, we combine the relation profile with two segments into the rating profile to form the hybrid profile, which is depicted in Fig. 1. Specifically, the explanation of the above six parts are listed below.

- **Target item** (I^T) indicates the items that spammers design to recommend more often.
- **Selected items** (I^S) are those spammers used to make the relationship with authentic users.
- **Filler items** (I^F) are some items for spammers to disguise themselves as authentic users.

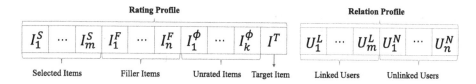

Fig. 1. The general framework of hybrid profile.

- **Unrelated items** (I^{Φ}) stand for items that spammers do not rate, which forms the majority of rating profile.
- **Linked users** (U^{L}) are those users that spammers try to establish a relationship with.
- **Unlinked users** (U^{N}) imply that there is no direct social link between them and spammers, which account for the largest part in relation profile.

In accordance with different attack strategies, rating attack models are categorized into four types, namely random attack, average attack, bandwagon attack and segment attack. Similarly, relation attack models are classified into two categories: random link attack and targeted link attack. Hence, by bridging rating and relation attacks, the hybrid attacks are composed of eight kinds of model: R-random attack, R-average attack, R-bandwagon attack, R-segment attack, T-random attack, T-average attack, T-bandwagon attack and T-segment attack. Table 2 describes these attack models.

Table 2. The features of the attack models.

Models	I^S	I^F	I^T
Random attack	$\emptyset$	randomly chosen items, $r(I_i^F) = r_{random}$	
Average attack	$\emptyset$	randomly chosen items, $r(I_i^F) = r_{mean}$	push: $r(I^T) = r_{max}$
Bandwagon attack	popular items, $r(I_i^S) = r_{max}$	randomly chosen items, $r(I_i^F) = r_{random}$	nuke: $r(I^T) = r_{min}$
Segment attack	like the target item, $r(I_i^S) = r_{max}$	randomly chosen items, $r(I_i^F) = r_{min}$	
Random link attack	U^L: randomly chosen users		
Targeted link attack	U^L: users chosen according to the specific attack plan		

From above table we can make a summary that the target items are always rated the highest rating, the filler items are randomly chosen and rated with different strategies, sometimes, the selected items are not required. As for users, the linked ones are usually chosen randomly but targeted link may according to the specific plan.

3.2   Heterogeneous Information Network

To detect the hybrid attack and motivated the existing studied [14–16], we consider to concatenate the user-item bipartite network and user-user social network as a whole to a Heterogeneous Information Network [17].

Definition 1. **Heterogeneous Information Network**: A graph $H = (V, E, T)$ in which each node v and each link e is tied via their mapping function $\phi(v)V \rightarrow T_V$ and $\phi(e)E \rightarrow T_E$, respectively. Meanwhile, T_V and T_E refer to the types of objects and relations in V and E, and $|T_V| + |T_E| > 2$. This graph H is named HIN. Figure 2 is an illustration of our proposed HIN, where three types of nodes and two types of edge are involved.

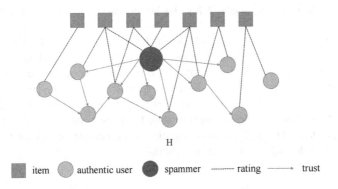

Fig. 2. The heterogeneous information network H.

3.3   Meta-Path

Inspired by the success of network embedding models [15,18], we will design some meta-paths over the HIN to capture the potential characteristics behind spammers.

Definition 2. **Meta-path** [19]: A meta-path scheme P is defined as a path that is denoted in the form of $V_1 \xrightarrow{R_1} V_2 \xrightarrow{R_2} \cdots \xrightarrow{R_{l-1}} V_l$, where $R = R_1 \circ R_2 \cdots \circ R_l$ defines the composite relations from its first type V_1 to the last type V_l.

4   The Proposed Method

In this paper, we propose a meta-path and matrix factorization based method (DMD) to spot shilling attack, and the detection framework of DMD is depicted in Fig. 3.

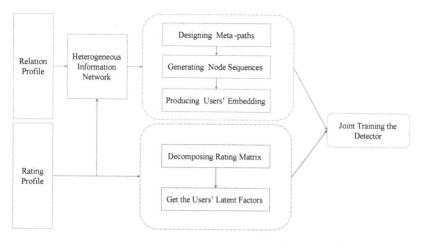

Fig. 3. The framework of DMD

4.1 Exploring Meta-Paths to Get Users' Embedding over HIN

In order to detect the hybrid attack, the user-item bipartite network and user-user social network are cultivated as a whole HIN. For mining anomalous behavior pattern more precisely, we design four meta-paths to model the relations among users according to three network features, as shown in Table 3.

Table 3. The designed meta-paths.

Path	Description
User → Item → User (UIU)	Explore users who rated the same items
User → Degree → User (UDU)	Linked users who have the same degree
User → H-index → User (UHU)	Linked users who have the same Hindex
User → Coreness → User (UCU)	Linked users who have the same coreness

These meta-paths can be used to find a pair of entities that similar but are distant from each other on the original bipartite network and the social network. Furthermore, three network features are used to link users. **Degree** which counts the number of current user linked neighbors, it is the simplest way to measure the importance of a node. **H-index** which was originally used to measure the citation impact of a scholar or a journal [20] and it is defined as the maximum value h such that there exists at least h papers, each with citation count $\geq h$. Here, the H-index of a node is defined to be the maximum value h such that there exists at least h neighbors of degree no less than h. **Coreness** [21] is measured by k-core decomposition [22], and a larger coreness value indicates that the node is more centrally located in the network.

Next, those meta-paths are utilized to conduct random walks to generate a number of node sequences. As most social relations are noisy, we use biased probability to create node sequences. Given a meta-path schema $\mathcal{P} = V_1 \xrightarrow{R_1} V_2 \xrightarrow{R_2} \cdots \xrightarrow{R_{l-1}} V_l$, the transition probability at step i is as follows:

$$p(v^{i+1}|v_t^i, \mathcal{P}) = \begin{cases} \frac{1}{|N_{t+1}(v_t^i)|} & (v^{i+1}, v_t^i) \in rated \\ \frac{\psi(v^{i+1}, v_t^i)}{\sum_{v' \in N_{t+1}(v_t^i)} \psi(v', v_t^i)} & (v^{i+1}, v_t^i) \in trust \\ 0 & (v^{i+1}, v_t^i) \notin E \end{cases} \tag{1}$$

where $v_t^i \in V_t$, $N_{t+1}(v_i^t)$ indicates the V_{t+1} kind of neighborhood of node v_t^i, and

$$\psi(v^{i+1}, v_t^i) = |N_{t+1}(v^{i+1}) \cap N_{t+1}(v_t^i)|. \tag{2}$$

According to the definition, at each step of the random walk, the successor node type is decided by the pre-defined meta-path $\mathcal{P}$ at each step in a random walk. When $V_t = U$ and $V_{t+1} = I$ (or the inverse), the successor node is chosen. However, if $V_t = V_{t+1} = U$ (or the inverse), the successor node is selected by the amount of overlapped neighbors with the current node.

In the next stage, as the collected random walks consist of different types of nodes, we feed it to the heterogeneous Skip-Gram model proposed by [15], for learning node embeddings $X \in \mathbb{R}^{\|V\| \times d}$. Formally, given a meta-path guided node sequence and the current node v^i, the objective function is:

$$\arg \max_{\theta} \sum_{v \in V} \sum_{v_t^n \in C(v^i)} \log p(v_t^n | v^i; \theta), \tag{3}$$

where $C(v^i)$ is the context information of v^i with the window size w and $p(v_t^n|v^i; \theta)$ is defined as a heterogeneous softmax function:

$$p(v_t^n|v^i; \theta) = \frac{e^{x_{v_t^n} \cdot x_{v^i}}}{\sum_{v \in V_t} e^{x_v \cdot x_{v^i}}}, \tag{4}$$

in which x_v is the vth row of X, representing the embedding vector of node v, and V_t is the node set of type t in H.

However, calculating Eq. 4 is still computationally expensive, to accelerate the optimization, we adopt negative sampling [23] for the learning task. Given the type of the node in $C(v^i)$ and the negative sample size M, we randomly select M nodes with the same type label from V for the construction of softmax and then update Eq. 4 by the following objective:

$$\mathcal{O}(X) = \log \sigma(x_{v_t^n} \cdot x_{v^i}) + \sum_{m=1}^{M} \mathbb{E}_{v_t^m \sim P_t(v_t)}[\log \sigma(-x_{v_t^m} \cdot x_{v^i})], \tag{5}$$

where $\sigma(x) = \frac{1}{1+e^{-x}}$ and the sampling distribution $P_t(v_t)$ specified by the node type of v_t^n is a uniform distribution.

4.2 Decomposing Matrix for Users' Latent Factors

Matrix factorization (MF) is a basic method in collaborative filtering which uncovers the latent features underlying the interactions between users and items by mapping both users and items into a low-dimensional latent-factor space [24]. To capture the implicit features in rating profile, we use MF to gain users' latent factors. The objective function of this step is:

$$L = \sum_{u,i} (y_{ui} - p_u^T q_i)^2 + \lambda(\sum_u \|p_u\|^2 + \sum_i \|q_i\|^2), \tag{6}$$

where p_u and q_i indicate user and item latent factors respectively, y_{ui} means the rating record created by user u on item i, and $p_u^T q_i$ is a predictive value. The parameter λ denotes the magnitudes of the latent factors to prevent overfitting.

4.3 Joint Training Based on Above Embeddings

When the node representations are obtained by performing a stochastic gradient ascent method on Eq. 5 and user latent factors are decomposed by Eq. 6, we incorporate them into a random forest model [25], which is an ensemble learning method by constructing a multitude of decision trees at training time and outputting the class that is the mode of the class of the individual trees. After the training, we can obtain the detector to identify spammers from unlabeled users.

Algorithms 1 shows the overall process of our proposed method DMD.

Algorithm 1. DMD

Input: User Label U, user-time rating matrix R, The heterogeneous network
            $H = (V, E, T)$ combined by user-item bipartite graph and user social
            graph, a meta-path schema $\mathcal{P}$, #walks per user n, walk length l,
            embedding dimension X, window size w, #negative samples M
Output: Labels of users to be recognized
1 initialize node embeddings X
2 **for** *user i in V* **do**
3 | **for** $j = 1 \rightarrow n$ **do**
4 | | MP = MetaPathRandomWalk($H, \mathcal{P}, i, l$)
5 | | X = HeterogeneousSkipGram(X,MP,w)

6 **while** *notConverged* **do**
7 | decompose R
8 | update user latent vectors P and item latent vectors Q

9 joint embeddings X and user latent vectors P training the detector DMD based
   on U
10 use DMD to predict user labels

---

5 Experiments

In this section, we present the experimental work. Firstly, two datasets and three metrics will be introduced. Next, we conduct experiments to evaluate the effectiveness of our detector and compare it with other detection methods. Furthermore, several experiments will be done to verify whether the DMD can handle different attacks.

5.1 Datasets and Metrics

We adopt two real-world datasets in experiments: Amazon dataset [26] which includes spammers per se and we extracted user social relationships from candidate groups; FilmTrust [27] is a typical dataset for recommendation without spammers, therefore, we inject spammers based on attack models for detecting. The detailed statistics of those datasets are shown in Table 4. To tune the methods included, we use 80% of the data as the training set and the others as the test set, meanwhile, we randomly select 10% from training set as the validation set.

Table 4. The datasets

Dataset	#Users	#Items	#Ratings	#Relations	# Spammers
Amazon	4,902	21,394	60,000	78,418	1,937
FilmTrust	1,508	2,071	35,479	1,853	0

The experiments were conducted by 5-fold cross validation 10 times, where average values of each set of trials were generated to represent the final results. We adopt the three frequently-used evaluation metrics, i.e., *Precision*, *Recall* and *F-measure* for performance evaluation.

$$Precision = \frac{TP}{(TP + FP)} \tag{7}$$

$$Recall = \frac{TP}{(TP + FN)} \tag{8}$$

$$F - measure = \frac{2 \times Precision \times Recall}{(Precision + Recall)} \tag{9}$$

where P and N represent positive samples and negative samples. The true positive (TP) sample means predicted and actual labels both are positive. If the predicted label is positive, and the actual label is negative, the instance is a false positive (FP) sample. Likewise, false negative (FN) means that the predicted label is negative, but the actual label is positive.

5.2   Experimental Results

Detection Performance. The performance of DMD is compared with DegreeSAD [6], FAP [10], SemiSAD [28] and CoDetector [8]. Among them, DegreeSAD is a supervised method based on popularity degree features, FAP is an unsupervised method via tag probabilistic propagation, FAP is a semi-supervised method. CoDetector, as a supervised method bridging factorization and user embedding, which is the most similar approach to DMD, but it did not explore the social relations. In addition, we inject R-random hybrid attack to the FilmTrust dataset and the rating attack size, rating attack filler size and relation attack size are set to 10%, 5% and 0.2% respectively. The experimental result is shown in Table 5.

Table 5. Performance comparison of our methods and other methods.

	Metric	DegreeSAD	FAP	SemiSAD	CoDetector	DMD
Amazon	Precision	0.7145	0.8931	0.6037	0.8812	**0.9336**
	Recall	0.6184	0.7290	0.6203	0.8915	**0.9084**
	F-measure	0.6626	0.8028	0.6138	0.8863	**0.9208**
FilmTrust	Precision	0.8125	0.8367	0.8333	0.7600	**0.921**
	Recall	0.9286	0.8662	0.7407	0.8636	**0.9347**
	F-measure	0.8667	0.8512	0.7843	0.8085	**0.9269**

We can make the following observations from the table: in all cases, our proposed model DMD outperform all the compared baseline methods. Specifically, on Amazon, the precision, recall and f-measure all reach 90%, and the improvements on them are 4.52%, 1.90% and 3.89%, respectively. On the FilmTrust dataset which injected hybrid attack with random rating and random link, the three metrics all reach highest values, and the precision increases 10.08% and the f-measure increases 6.95%. Therefore, the DMD not only can detect rating attack but also have the ability to handle the relation attack and hybrid attack. In summary, the performance of DMD has a significant advantage over the other four methods, and it shows the effectiveness and robustness of DMD whether in the simulated dataset or real world dataset.

Detection of Simulated Attack. To further demonstrate that our proposed method has good performance to cope with different attack strategies and various attack sizes, we especially attack the FilmTrust dataset manually according to the definition of attack models. As for relation attack, we inject the random link profile with 0.1%, 0.2% and 0.5% link size. For rating attack, the random attack, average attack and bandwagon attack are injected with 5% and 10% attack size. It should be noted that the original users are labeled as normal users and injected ones are spammers. After that, we use DMD to detect those simulated spammers. The results of the experiment are shown in Table 6.

Table 6. Detection results of hybrid attacks on FilmTrust

Link size	Metric	Random		Average		Bandwagon	
		5%	10%	5%	10%	5%	10%
0.1%	Precision	0.9494	0.9081	0.9381	0.933	0.8584	0.8932
	Recall	0.9019	0.8929	0.8903	0.9582	0.8955	0.9007
	F-measure	0.9219	0.8983	0.9068	0.9446	0.8766	0.8969
0.2%	Precision	0.9433	0.921	0.9382	0.9531	0.8876	0.9088
	Recall	0.8259	0.9347	**0.9767**	0.9738	0.9039	0.9263
	F-measure	0.8636	0.9269	0.9553	0.9624	0.8957	0.9167
0.5%	Precision	0.9214	0.8897	0.9192	**0.9724**	0.9269	0.9085
	Recall	0.9167	0.9649	0.8789	0.9757	0.8717	0.9221
	F-measure	0.9162	0.9255	0.8958	**0.9728**	0.8979	0.9144

As shown in Table 6, facing these hybrid attacks, the majority of detection results more than 0.9 and the highest precision, recall and f-measure reach 0.9724, 0.9767 and 0.9728, respectively. As for the different rating attack strategies, the MDM achieve the best performance in average attack detection.

6   Conclusion

In this paper, we proposed a novel shilling detection method DMD based on the meta-path and matrix factorization for collaborative filtering recommender system. Firstly, we incorporate the user-item rating network and user-user relation network as a whole heterogeneous information network and design four meta-paths to capture the undirectly links between users. Afterward, node sequences are produced guided by random walk according to above-mentioned meta-paths. Next, we use the skip-gram model to generate user embedding. In the meantime, we decompose the rating matrix based on matrix factorization to gain the users' latent factors. Finally, using embedding and factors are used to joint train the detector. Experimental results on one real-world public dataset and a simulated dataset show the DMD improve the preference of detecting spammers. In addition, it is not only effective for the rating attack but also has good ability to detect the hybrid attack.

Acknowledgments. The work is supported by the Fundamental Research Funds for the Central Universities (106112017CDJXSYY0002).

References

1. Bhaumik, R., Williams, C., Mobasher, B., Burke, R.: Securing collaborative filtering against malicious attacks through anomaly detection. In: Proceedings of the 4th Workshop on Intelligent Techniques for Web Personalization (ITWP 2006), Boston, vol. 6, p. 10 (2006)
2. Hurley, N., Cheng, Z., Zhang, M.: Statistical attack detection. In: Proceedings of the third ACM Conference on Recommender Systems, pp. 149–156. ACM (2009)
3. Chirita, P.-A., Nejdl, W., Zamfir, C.: Preventing shilling attacks in online recommender systems. In: Proceedings of the 7th Annual ACM International Workshop on Web Information and Data Management, pp. 67–74. ACM (2005)
4. Williams, C., Mobasher, B.: Profile injection attack detection for securing collaborative recommender systems. DePaul University CTI Technical Report, pp. 1–47 (2006)
5. Williams, C.A., Mobasher, B., Burke, R.: Defending recommender systems: detection of profile injection attacks. Serv. Oriented Comput. Appl. **1**(3), 157–170 (2007)
6. Li, W., Gao, M., Li, H., Xiong, Q., Wen, J., Ling, B.: A shilling attack detection algorithm based on popularity degree features. Acta Autom. Sinica **41**(9), 1563–1576 (2015)
7. Zhou, W., Wen, J., Xiong, Q., Gao, M., Zeng, J.: SVM-TIA a shilling attack detection method based on svm and target item analysis in recommender systems. Neurocomputing **210**, 197–205 (2016)
8. Dou, T., Yu, J., Xiong, Q., Gao, M., Song, Y., Fang, Q.: Collaborative shilling detection bridging factorization and user embedding. In: Romdhani, I., Shu, L., Takahiro, H., Zhou, Z., Gordon, T., Zeng, D. (eds.) CollaborateCom 2017. LNICST, vol. 252, pp. 459–469. Springer, Cham (2018). https://doi.org/10.1007/978-3-030-00916-8_43
9. Mehta, B., Nejdl, W.: Unsupervised strategies for shilling detection and robust collaborative filtering. User Model. User-Adap. Interact. **19**(1–2), 65–97 (2009)
10. Zhang, Y., Tan, Y., Zhang, M., Liu, Y., Chua, T.-S., Ma, S.: Catch the black sheep: Unified framework for shilling attack detection based on fraudulent action propagation. In: IJCAI, pp. 2408–2414 (2015)
11. Wu, Z., Wu, J., Cao, J., Tao, D.: HySAD: a semi-supervised hybrid shilling attack detector for trustworthy product recommendation. In: Proceedings of the 18th ACM SIGKDD International Conference on Knowledge Discovery and Data Mining, pp. 985–993. ACM (2012)
12. Wu, Z., Wang, Y., Wang, Y., Wu, J., Cao, J., Zhang, L.: Spammers detection from product reviews: a hybrid model. In: 2015 IEEE International Conference on Data Mining (ICDM), pp. 1039–1044. IEEE (2015)
13. Junliang, Y., Gao, M., Rong, W., Li, W., Xiong, Q., Wen, J.: Hybrid attacks on model-based social recommender systems. Phys. A: Stati. Mech. Appl. **483**, 171–181 (2017)
14. Yuan, Q., Chen, L., Zhao, S.: Factorization vs. regularization: fusing heterogeneous social relationships in top-n recommendation. In: Proceedings of the fifth ACM Conference on Recommender Systems, pp. 245–252. ACM (2011)
15. Dong, Y., Chawla, N.V., Swami, A.: metapath2vec: scalable representation learning for heterogeneous networks. In: Proceedings of the 23rd ACM SIGKDD International Conference on Knowledge Discovery and Data Mining, pp. 135–144. ACM (2017)

16. Song, Y., Gao, M., Yu, J., Xiong, Q.: Social recommendation based on implicit friends discovering via meta-path. In: Proceedings of the 30th International Conference on Tools with Artifical Intelligence (2018)
17. Sun, Y., Han, J.: Mining heterogeneous information networks: principles and methodologies. Synth. Lect. Data Min. Knowl. Discov. **3**(2), 1–159 (2012)
18. Perozzi, B., Al-Rfou, R., Skiena, S.: DeepWalk: online learning of social representations. In: Proceedings of the 20th ACM SIGKDD International Conference on Knowledge Discovery and Data Mining, pp. 701–710. ACM (2014)
19. Sun, Y., Han, J., Yan, X., Yu, P.S., Wu, T.: PathSim: meta path-based top-k similarity search in heterogeneous information networks. Proc. VLDB Endow. **4**(11), 992–1003 (2011)
20. Hirsch, J.E.: An index to quantify an individual's scientific research output. Proc. Nat. Acad. Sci. **102**(46), 16569–16572 (2005)
21. Lü, L., Zhou, T., Zhang, Q.-M., Stanley, H.E.: The h-index of a network node and its relation to degree and coreness. Nat. commun. **7**, 10168 (2016)
22. Dorogovtsev, S.N., Goltsev, A.V., Mendes, J.F.F.: K-core organization of complex networks. Phys. Rev. Lett. **96**(4), 040601 (2006)
23. Mikolov, T., Sutskever, I., Chen, K., Corrado, G.S., Dean, J.: Distributed representations of words and phrases and their compositionality. In: Advances in Neural Information Processing Systems, pp. 3111–3119 (2013)
24. Koren, Y., Bell, R., Volinsky, C.: Matrix factorization techniques for recommender systems. Computer **8**, 30–37 (2009)
25. Liaw, A., Wiener, M., et al.: Classification and regression by randomforest. R news **2**(3), 18–22 (2002)
26. Xu, C., Zhang, J., Chang, K., Long, C.: Uncovering collusive spammers in Chinese review websites. In: Proceedings of the 22nd ACM International Conference on Conference on Information and Knowledge Management, pp. 979–988. ACM (2013)
27. Guo, G., Zhang, J., Yorke-Smith, N.: A novel Bayesian similarity measure for recommender systems. In: IJCAI, pp. 2619–2625 (2013)
28. Cao, J., Wu, Z., Mao, B., Zhang, Y.: Shilling attack detection utilizing semi-supervised learning method for collaborative recommender system. World Wide Web **16**(5–6), 729–748 (2013)

Collaborative Thompson Sampling

Zhenyu Zhu, Liusheng Huang$^{(\boxtimes)}$, and Hongli Xu

University of Science and Technology of China, Hefei, Anhui, China
zzy7758@mail.ustc.edu.cn, {lshuang,honglixu}@ustc.edu.cn

Abstract. Thompson sampling is one of the most effective strategies to balance exploration-exploitation trade-off. It has been applied in a variety of domains and achieved remarkable success. Thompson sampling makes decisions in a noisy but stationary environment by accumulating uncertain information over time to improve prediction accuracy. In highly dynamic domains, however, the environment undergoes frequent and unpredictable changes. Making decisions in such an environment should rely on current information. Therefore, standard Thompson sampling may perform poorly in these domains. Here we present a collaborative Thompson sampling algorithm to apply the exploration-exploitation strategy to highly dynamic settings. The algorithm takes collaborative effects into account by dynamically clustering users into groups, and the feedback of all users in the same group will help to estimate the expected reward in the current context to find the optimal choice. Incorporating collaborative effects into Thompson sampling allows to capture real-time changes of the environment and adjust decision making strategy accordingly. We compare our algorithm with standard Thompson sampling algorithms on two real-world datasets. Our algorithm shows accelerated convergence and improved prediction performance in collaborative environments. We also provide a regret analysis of our algorithm on a non-contextual model.

Keywords: Thompson sampling · Bandits · Collaborative effect · Dynamic clustering

1 Introduction

Thompson sampling has received considerable attention in recent years due to its capability of balancing exploration-exploitation trade-off. The exploration-exploitation trade-off often occurs in online learning problems, where the algorithm tries to balance between exploiting current information to maximize immediate reward and exploring new information that may improve future performance. Theoretical analysis [3,17] and empirical results [6,7,14] revealed that Thompson sampling represents one of the most promising approaches to tackle this problem. It has been successfully applied in a variety of applications, including revenue management [11], Markov decision process [13,23] and recommendation systems [18,20].

© ICST Institute for Computer Sciences, Social Informatics and Telecommunications Engineering 2019
Published by Springer Nature Switzerland AG 2019. All Rights Reserved
H. Gao et al. (Eds.): CollaborateCom 2018, LNICST 268, pp. 17–32, 2019.
https://doi.org/10.1007/978-3-030-12981-1_2

While Thompson sampling is good at balancing exploration-exploitation tradeoff, it may perform poorly in highly dynamic and large-scale applications. In a stationary system, Thompson sampling is an effective and efficient method [24]. Each round, the algorithm applies probability matching heuristic and selects item corresponding to its probability of being optimal. This randomized manner [6] allows Thompson Sampling to continuously explore all possible candidates to accumulate information and explicit the optimal choice in the current context at the same time. However, in nonstationary settings, the environment undergoes frequent and unpredictable changes [12]. In this case, accumulated information of previous rounds becomes irrelevant to future performance. These issues also arise in large-scale settings where it is almost impossible to explore all the items to find the optimal choice. Thus, inferencing the expected reward of items based on a few observations will result in high variance and low accuracy. These drawbacks hinder the practical deployment of Thompson sampling in highly dynamic and large-scale domains [24].

One promising method to address these problems is to leverage on the collaborative effects. The collaborative effects often represent the potential connections between different users and different items in a real-world application. Although integrating collaborative effects into bandit settings has been reported in a series of works [21,22,29], little attention has been paid to incorporating collaboration into Thompson sampling. Previous works focus on applying the collaborative effects to LinUCB [9], a well-studied deterministic contextual bandit algorithm. They use feedback of all users in the same cluster to build a group vector as an estimator of the user vector. The selected item is then determined with upper confidence bound by the group vector. However, we cannot directly apply this strategy to Thompson sampling. Thompson sampling uses a Bayesian heuristic [6], it maintains and updates a posterior distribution of user vector. The distribution of the group vector is not an ideal estimator of the user vector, because it is much more concentrated than the user vector due to the abundance of feedback. Thus, directly applying this strategy will limit the exploration of Thompson sampling and lead to suboptimal performance.

This paper presents a collaborative Thompson sampling algorithm. The algorithm works under the assumption that the feedback of the user can be used to build an unbiased estimator of reward with high variance at the beginning, while the feedback of other users in the same cluster can be a biased estimator of reward with low variance. Combining these estimators to approximate reward may lead to improved prediction accuracy and accelerated convergence. This assumption has been illustrated in previous research [19] on standard statistical problems where the combined estimator outperforms the initial estimators in most cases. In our algorithm, the reward of items is estimated by a compound of both user preference and collaborative information. Specifically, the population of users is dynamically partitioned into clusters based on their similarity. The expected reward is a linear combination of two estimators, the collaborative estimator and the personal estimator. The collaborative estimator is constructed and shared by all users in the same cluster, while the personal estimator is constructed independently by each user. The combination of these two estimators generates a more sophisticated estimator of rewards, which lead to accelerated convergence and improved prediction performance.

We demonstrate that sharing collaborative information among similar users can not only improve the prediction performance of the algorithm but also help to find the optimal item efficiently. We compare our algorithm to standard Thompson sampling algorithm on two real-world datasets. The experimental results show that our algorithm outperforms standard Thompson sampling methods in terms of both prediction accuracy and convergence rate in collaborative environments. We also provide a regret analysis in a standard non-contextual setting.

2   Related Work

Thompson sampling was first proposed in 1933 [27] and has drawn much attention since 2010 [7,26]. It is proved by a series of theoretical analysis [3,17] and empirical evaluations [6,7,14] to be among the most effective bandit policies to tackle complex online problems. Adaptations of Thompson sampling have now been successfully applied in a wide variety of domains, including marketing [25], online advertising [1,15] and recommendation system [18].

Beyond the general settings of Thompson sampling, our work is also closely related to collaborative approaches with dynamic clustering. Clustering at user side or item side to provide collaborative information in bandit settings has been studied in a series of previous works. The work [22] incorporates online clustering into contextual bandit settings to divide users into groups and customizes the bandits to each group. The paper [5] also relies on clustering at the user side, with a constraint condition that once a user consumes an item, the item cannot be recommended to the same user again. The goal of their work is to maximize the number of consumed items recommended to users over time. In [29], the authors developed a collaborative contextual bandit algorithm, in which the adjacency graph is leveraged to share contexts and payoffs among neighboring users. In [21], the authors proposed COFIBA as an extension of [29], in which clustering is performed at both user and item side. They also used sparse graph representation to avoid expensive computation. The most similar work to ours is [8]. In this paper, the authors proposed an online collaborative algorithm to learn the underlying parameters of users and items. They defined the prior distribution of both the user vectors and the item vectors. At each round, the algorithm samples from the posterior distribution of both the user vector and the item vector. The expected reward of item is computed by logistic function with the product of user vector and item vector. Item with the highest expected reward will be selected. After observing the feedback, the posterior distributions of both user vector and item vector are updated with online gradient descent.

Our work shares the same assumption that collaborative effects can be leveraged to share information across users. In our work, we use a compound of both collaborative effects and personal preference to help the users to estimate the expected reward with a few observations.

3   Learning Model

We assume the user preference is parameterized by an unknown vector $\mu_i \in \mathbb{R}^d$ for each user $i \in \mathcal{U}$, where $i = 1, 2, 3, ..., n$ is the set of n users. We follow the settings of standard bandit problem. The parameter u_i of user i determines the payoff of item $j \in \mathcal{C}$ with contextual vector x_j. Formally, the payoff value $r_{i,j}$ is given by a function f and a random variable ϵ:

$$r_{i,j} = f(\mu_i, x_j) + \epsilon_{i,j} \tag{1}$$

Where i is the index of the user, j is the index of the item and ϵ is a zero-mean and bounded random noise. We assume that for any fixed user vector μ_i and contextual vector x_j, $f(\mu_i, x_j)$ is the expected payoff observed by user i for item j.

We model the learning process as a sequential decision problem with T rounds: at each round $t = 1, 2, 3..., T$, for each user i, the algorithm is provided with the set of candidate contents C_t. The contextual information of each content is represent by a vector x_j for $j = 1, 2, ..., |C_t|$. Our task is to select an item $\hat{j}_i^t$ from the candidate pool C_t and recommend to the user i. After that, we will observe the user feedback $r_{\hat{j}_i}^t$. When the user feedback is the behavior whether the selected item is clicked, the payoff is binary. The user feedback is used to evaluate the prediction performance of our algorithm in empirical evaluation, which is represented as the click-through rate $1/(nT) \sum_{t=1}^{T} \sum_{i=1}^{n} r_{\hat{j}_i}^t$ of recommended items over T rounds. The goal of our algorithm is to maximize the click-through rate of the selected items.

For theoretical analysis, the most popular performance measure is the total expected regret. Regret is defined as the gap of reward between the selected item and the optimal item. Total expected regret is formally defined as:

$$\mathbb{E}(\mathcal{R}(T)) = \sum_{i=1}^{n} \sum_{t=1}^{T} E[(r_i^* - r_{\hat{j}_i}^t)] \tag{2}$$

where r_i^* is the reward of the optimal item for user i, and $r_{\hat{j}_i}^t$ is the reward of the chosen item $\hat{j}_i^t$ at round t.

4   Collaborative Thompson Sampling Algorithm

In the learning model, since we do not know the true value of user vector μ^*, we maintain a posterior distribution over the user vector $P(\mu|\cdot)$. The posterior distribution is approximated by a multivariate Gaussian distribution [24] with the diagonal covariance matrix in linear and logistic Thompson sampling algorithms. If we want to exploit the immediate reward, we would choose for user i the item j that maximizes $\mathbb{E}[r_{i,j}|i, j] = \int \mathbb{E}[r_{i,j}|i, j, \mu_{i,j}] P(\mu_{i,j}|\cdot) d\mu_{i,j}$. However, to balance the exploration-exploitation trade-off, Thompson Sampling (TS) uses the probability matching heuristic and chooses for user i an item j according to its probability of being optimal. i.e., with probability [8]:

$$\int \mathbb{I}\big[\mathbb{E}[r_{i,j}|i,j,\mu_{i,j}] = \max_{j'\in C}\mathbb{E}[r_{i,j'}|i,j',\mu_{i,j'}]\big]P(\mu_{i,j}|\cdot)d\mu_{i,j} \qquad (3)$$

The $\mathbb{I}[\cdot]$ is the indicator function. Its value is 1 if the condition holds. The $\mathbb{E}$ donates expectation of rewards in the current context, and the integral denotes expectation over the posterior distribution of user vector. In Thompson sampling, this integral can be estimated by drawing a sample $\tilde{\mu}_{i,j}$ from its posterior distribution $P(\mu_{i,j}|\cdot)$, and calculating its expected reward with $\mathbb{E}[r_{i,j}|\mu_{i,j}] = f(\tilde{\mu}_{i,j},x_j)$ as described in the previous section. The algorithm will choose the item with the largest expected reward. The posterior distribution is then updated according to the feedback of the user (clicked or not). Intuitively, In stationary and infinite time-horizon settings, the algorithm accumulates more information about user preference over time and the posterior distribution of user vector will concentrate around its true μ^*. The optimal choice will be selected with high probability.

The major problem of Thompson sampling is that it has to estimate the expected reward $\mathbb{E}(r_{i,j}|\mu_{i,j})$ on the fly. As described in previous section, the feedback $r_{i,j}$ is determined by user vector $\mu_{i,j}$, contextual vector x_j and a random variable ϵ. Although we assume that the expectation of random variable ϵ is zero, the variance might be large when we try to estimate $\mathbb{E}(r_{i,j}|\mu_{i,j})$ with a few observations. In order to reduce the variance, standard Thompson sampling algorithm has to repeatedly select the same item for users to observe their feedback. Since it runs independent instance for each user, the algorithm converges slowly and is inaccurate in the first few rounds. Accurately estimating the expected reward $\mathbb{E}(r_{i,j}|\mu_{i,j})$ in the current context will help to boost the prediction performance and speed up convergence. To address this problem, we leverage on the collaborative effects. We assume that users may have similar preference and similar behavior, this indicates that the feedback of one user can be used to estimate the feedback of similar users. In other words, the feedback of users in the same cluster can be used to estimate the expected reward $\mathbb{E}(r_{i,j}|\mu_{i,j})$ in the current context. The expected reward is the compound of two different estimators, the personal estimator $\mathbb{E}[r_{i,j}|\mu_{i,j}]$ and a collaborative estimator $\mathbb{E}[r_{i,j}|G_s]$. where G_s is the cluster that user i belongs to.

The personal estimator $\mathbb{E}[r_{i,j}|\mu_{i,j}]$ estimates the reward by user vector $\mu_{i,j}$ which is trained by the user's previous feedback; it is an unbiased estimator of $r^*_{i,j}$. However, it suffers from sparsity of training data. The collaborative estimator $\mathbb{E}[r_{i,j}|G_i]$, on the other hand, is based on the feedback of similar users in the same cluster and is a direct approximation of reward with low variance. But it is a biased estimator of reward $r^*_{i,j}$ since user behavior may not be compatible with cluster behavior.

In our algorithm, both the personal estimator and the collaborative estimator are leveraged to estimate the reward of items in the current context. As a result, collaboration among users can not only capture additional information embedded in user similarity but also help to deal with the data sparsity issues. Both of these effects lead to an improvement of prediction performance and accelerated convergence.

4.1   Algorithm Description

In this section, we use logistic regression as an example to describe our algorithm. Our algorithm stores and updates a posterior distribution $P(\mu_{i,j}|D_t)$ of user vector $\mu_{i,j}$ for user $i \in \mathcal{U}$ and item $j \in \mathcal{C}$ at round t. We assume the prior of μ is a multivariate Gaussian distribution. Due to conjugacy property of normal distribution [24], its posterior distribution $P(\mu_{i,j}|D_t)$ remains normal after any number of rounds. More specifically, if the prior of $\mu_{i,j}$ at round t is given by $\mathcal{N}(\hat{\mu}_{i,j}(t), S_{i,j}(t))$, the posterior distribution at round $t + 1$ is $\mathcal{N}(\hat{\mu}_{i,j}(t + 1), S_{i,j}(t + 1))$.

Our assumption is that the expected reward $\pi_{i,j}$, given contextual vector x_j and user vector $\mu_{i,j}$ is determined by the logistic function $\pi_{i,j} = 1/(1 + \exp{(-\mu_{i,j}^{\mathrm{T}} x_j)})$. And user feedback $r_{i,j}$ is drawn from a Bernoulli distribution parameterized by $\pi_{i,j}$: $r_{i,j} \sim \mathrm{Bernoulli}(\pi_{i,j})$.

As the closed form analysis of logistic regression in Bayesian inference is intractable, we then utilize the Laplace approximation [28] to approximate the posterior distribution of $\mu_{i,j}$ with a Gaussian distribution $\mathcal{N}(u_{i,j}|\hat{u}_{i,j}, S_{i,j})$, where $\hat{u}_{i,j}$ is the mode and $S_{i,j}$ is the Hessian matrix [4,8]. We update $\hat{\mu}_{i,j}^{t+1}$ with online gradient descent $\hat{\mu}_{i,\hat{j}}^{t+1} \leftarrow \hat{\mu}_{i,\hat{j}}^{t} - \eta_t \nabla_{u_{i,\hat{j}}}^{t}$, where

$$\nabla_{u_{i,\hat{j}}}^{t} = S_{u_{i,\hat{j}}}^{t-1}{}^{-1}(\hat{\mu}_{i,\hat{j}}^{t} - \hat{\mu}_{i,\hat{j}}^{t-1}) + (\pi_{i,\hat{j}}^{t} - r_{i,\hat{j}}^{t})x_{\hat{j}}^{t} \tag{4}$$

$x_{\hat{j}}^{t}$ is the contextual vector of the selected item and $r_{i,\hat{j}}^{t}$ is the observed reward and η is the learning rate. We also need to update $S_{u_{i,\hat{j}}}^{t}{}^{-1}$:

$$S_{u_{i,\hat{j}}}^{t+1}{}^{-1} = S_{u_{i,\hat{j}}}^{t}{}^{-1} + \pi_{i,\hat{j}}^{t}(1 - \pi_{i,\hat{j}}^{t})x_{\hat{j}}^{t}x_{\hat{j}}^{t}{}^{\mathrm{T}} \tag{5}$$

Our algorithm also maintains and updates clusters over users $\mathcal{U}$ to approximate the expected rewards of items. This algorithm takes the simple viewpoint that clustering over users is determined by the similarity of their feedback. Each user i maintains a vector l_i and records his click-through rate of all items. If user i and user j are in the same cluster, then $||l_i - l_j||_2^2 < \lambda$, while if i and j are in different clusters then $||l_i - l_j||_2^2 > \lambda$. The clusters are initialized as follows: We first randomly select k items and recommend those items to all users $i \in \mathcal{U}$, the feedback of users on these items can be used to partition users into 2^k clusters. The users with the same feedback are grouped into the same cluster. Each cluster maintains its click-through rate of all items as a vector l_g for $g \in |\mathcal{G}_t|$. We denote by $|\mathcal{G}_t|$ the number of distinct partitions of users $\mathcal{U}$, and work under the assumption that $|\mathcal{G}|$ is significantly smaller than $|\mathcal{U}|$. The clusters $\mathcal{G}_t$ record the current partition of users $\mathcal{U}$ by the similarity of feedback. The clusters are updated each round to estimate the true partition of users.

Algorithm 1. Collaborative Logistic Thompson Sampling

Input:

    Set of users $\mathcal{U} = 1, 2, 3, ..., n$;

    Set of contents $\mathcal{C} = 1, 2, 3, ..., m$;

    Set of contextual vectors $x_1, x_2, x_3..., x_m$

    Hyper-parameter β

Init:

    $\mu_{i,j}^1 = 0 \in \mathbb{R}^d$ and $S_{i,j}^1 = I \in \mathcal{R}^{d \times d}$

    Prior distribution of user vector $\mu_{i,j} \sim \mathcal{N}(\mu_{i,j}^1, S_{i,j}^{1}{}^{-1})$

Initialize user clusters:

Random select k items and recommend them to all users

for each $i \in \mathcal{U}$ **do**

    Suppose user feedback for all k items are $r_{i,1}, r_{i,2}, ..., r_{i,k}$

    The cluster id of user i is $\sum_{0}^{j=k-1} 2^j * r_{i,j+1}$

end for

Recommend contents and update parameters:

for $t = 1, 2, 3..., T$ **do**

    for each $i \in \mathcal{U}$ **do**

        Sampling $\tilde{\mu}_{i,j}^t$ from distribution $\mathcal{N}(\hat{\mu}_{i,j}^t, S_{i,j}^t{}^{-1})$

        Determine the cluster this user belongs to: $\hat{g}_i^t = \arg\max_{g \in \mathcal{G}} ||l_i^t - l_g^t||_2^2$

        for each $m \in \mathcal{C}$ **do**

            Compute personal expected reward $\pi_{i,j}^t = 1/(1 + \exp(\tilde{\mu}_{i,j}^{t\mathrm{T}} x_j))$

            Compute the compound of cluster expected reward and personal

            expected reward: $\mathbb{E}[r_{i,j,t}|i, j, \mu_{i,j}, \mathcal{G}] = \beta l_{\hat{g},j}^t + (1 - \beta)\pi_{i,j}^t$

        end for

        Set $\hat{j}^t = \arg\max_{j \in \mathcal{C}} \mathbb{E}[r_{i,j,t}|i, j, \mu_{i,j}, \mathcal{G}]$

        Recommend content $\hat{j}^t$ to user i and observe payoff $r_{i,\hat{j}}^t$

        Update $\hat{\mu}_{i,\hat{j}}^t$, $S_{i,\hat{j}}^t{}^{-1}$ and the posterior distribution as follows:

        $\nabla_{u_{i,\hat{j}}}^t = S_{i,\hat{j}}^{t-1}{}^{-1}(\hat{\mu}_{i,\hat{j}}^t - \hat{\mu}_{i,\hat{j}}^{t-1}) + (\pi_{i\hat{j}}^t - r_{i,\hat{j}}^t)x_{\hat{j}}^t$

        $\hat{\mu}_{i,\hat{j}}^{t+1} \leftarrow \hat{\mu}_{i,\hat{j}}^t - \eta_t \nabla_{u_{i,\hat{j}}}^t$

        $S_{i,\hat{j}}^{t+1}{}^{-1} = S_{i,\hat{j}}^t{}^{-1} + \pi_{i\hat{j}}^t(1 - \pi_{i\hat{j}}^t)x_{\hat{j}}^t x_{\hat{j}}^{t\,\mathrm{T}}$

        $P(\mu_{i,\hat{j}}|\mathbb{D}(t)) = \mathcal{N}(\hat{\mu}_{i,\hat{j}}^{t+1}, S_{i,\hat{j}}^{t+1}{}^{-1})$

        Update user click-through rate l_i

        Update cluster click-through rate $l_{b_{i,t}}$

    end for

end for

At each round t, collaborative Thompson sampling algorithm first draws a sample $\tilde{\mu}_{i,t}$ from posterior distribution $P(\mu_{i,j}|\mathcal{D}_t)$ and construct the personal estimator of reward $\pi_{i,j} = 1/(1 + \exp(\tilde{\mu}_{i,j}^\mathrm{T} x_j))$. Suppose that at current round t, user i belongs to cluster $\hat{g}$, the click-through rate of items $l_{\hat{g},j}^t$ represents the expected reward in the cluster. The expected reward used in Thompson sampling is a compound of personal estimator and collaborative estimator:

$$\mathbb{E}[r_{i,j}^t|i, j, \mu_{i,j}, \mathcal{G}] = \beta l_{\hat{g},j}^t + (1 - \beta)\pi_{i,j}^t \tag{6}$$

The algorithm will select item $\hat{j}_i = \arg\max_j \mathbb{E}[r_{i,j}^t|i,j,\mu_{i,j},\mathcal{G}]$ to recommend to user i and observe the feedback $r_{i,\hat{j}}^t$. After observing the user feedback $r_{i,\hat{j}}$, the algorithm will update the posterior distribution. The user will be assigned to the closest clusters.

5   Regret Analysis

We consider the special case of two items in a non-contextual setting. There are n users and each user has 2 items to select from. The true reward of item j for user i is $u_{i,j}$. The collaborative Thompson Sampling algorithm assumes that the prior distribution of $u_{i,j}$ is Beta(1, 1). At round t, if the algorithm have observed $S_{i,j}$ successes (reward = 1) and $F_{i,j}$ failures (reward = 0), the posterior distribution of $\mu_{i,j}$ will be Beta$(S_{i,j}+1, F_{i,j}+1)$. At round t, the collaborative Thompson sampling algorithm samples $\tilde{\mu}_{i,j}$ from the posterior distributions of each item, and computes $\hat{\mu}_j = \frac{1}{n}\sum_{i=1}^n \tilde{\mu}_{i,j}$, the selected item for user i is determined by $\hat{j}^t = \arg\max_j \beta\hat{\mu}_j + (1-\beta)\tilde{\mu}_{i,j}$.

Theorem 1. *If* $0 \le |\bar{\mu}_j - \mu_{i,j}| \le \gamma$ *for any* $i \in \mathcal{U}$ *and* $j \in \mathcal{C}$, *where* $\bar{\mu}_j = \frac{1}{n}\sum_{i=1}^n \mu_{i,j}$, *collaborative Thompson Sampling algorithm has expected regret:*

$$\mathbb{E}(\mathcal{R}(T)) = \mathcal{O}(\frac{\ln T}{\Delta} + \frac{\Delta(1-\beta)^2\ln T}{(\Delta+\Delta\beta-4\gamma\beta)^2} + \frac{\Delta(1-\beta)^4}{(\Delta+\Delta\beta-4\gamma\beta)^4} + 18\Delta) \quad (7)$$

Proof. Our proof follows the outline of [2] and only considers one user. The optimal item is the first item. Firstly, we assume that the second item has been selected $L = 24(\ln T)/\Delta^2$ times. The total expected regret before the algorithm selects the second item again is ΔL, where $\Delta = u_1 - u_2$. After the second item has been selected for L times, the following events happen with high probability: the posterior distribution of μ_2 is tightly concentrated around its true value and $\frac{1}{n}\sum_{i=1}^n \tilde{\mu}_{i,j}$ is very close to $\bar{\mu}_j$. Therefore, when we draw a sample $\tilde{\mu}_2$ from its posterior distribution, the value of $\tilde{\mu}_2$ is roughly μ_2. And the value of $\hat{\mu}_j = \frac{1}{n}\sum_{i=1}^n \tilde{\mu}_{i,j}$ is roughly $\bar{\mu}_j$. We then try to estimate how many times the second item will be selected between two consecutive selections of the first item. The selected item is determined by $\hat{j}_t = \arg\max_j \beta\hat{\mu}_j + (1-\beta)\tilde{\mu}_j$. With the above approximations of $\hat{\mu}_j$ and $\tilde{\mu}_j$, we instead estimate how many times we need to sample from the posterior distribution of μ_1 until we get a sample $\tilde{\mu}_1$ that satisfies $\tilde{\mu}_1 > \mu_2 - \beta(\Delta - 2\gamma)/(1-\beta)$.

Using Lemma 6 of [2] for $y = \mu_2 + \Delta/2 - \beta(\Delta - 2\gamma)/(1-\beta)$ and $\Delta' = \frac{\Delta+\Delta\beta-4\gamma\beta}{1-\beta}$, we get a regret bound of:

$$\mathbb{E}(\mathcal{R}(T)) < \frac{24\ln T}{\Delta} + \frac{4\Delta(1-\beta)^2\ln T}{(\Delta+\Delta\beta-4\gamma\beta)^2} + \frac{\Delta(1-\beta)^4}{(\Delta+\Delta\beta-4\gamma\beta)^4} + 18\Delta \quad (8)$$

This regret bound gives us some insight into collaborative Thompson sampling. Firstly, the performance of collaborative Thompson sampling depends on the strength of collaborative effects. If γ is large, it implies that the users have very different preferences and the collaborative effects are very weak. Collaboration among users will result in poor performance in both convergence rate and prediction accuracy. But if the users are carefully clustered and users in the same cluster have similar preference, the algorithm will outperform standard Thompson sampling in terms of prediction and convergence. And also, the optimal value of parameter β is closely related to the strength of collaborative effects.

6 Experiment

To evaluate the performance of our collaborative Thompson Sampling algorithm, we compared our algorithm to standard Thompson sampling algorithm on two real-world large-scale datasets, the Yahoo! front page today module dataset and the Avazu click-through dataset.

6.1 Dataset Description

Yahoo! The first dataset we used to evaluate our algorithm was the Yahoo! front page today module dataset. This dataset was provided by Yahoo! in the "ICML 2012 Exploration & Exploitation Challenge". The dataset contains more than 45 million user visits to the Today Module. The variables recorded in one line are as follows: a timestamp, six user features, one recommended article (id) and its payoff (0 or 1), candidate articles and their features. The recommended article was selected uniformly at random from the candidate article pool. It makes the dataset ideal for unbiased, offline evaluation of exploration-exploitation approaches. Both the users and the articles are associated with a six-dimension feature vector (including a constant feature), constructed using a conjoint analysis with a bilinear model. More detailed description of how this dataset was generated and how the features were extracted can be found in [10].

We preprocessed the Yahoo! dataset to evaluate our collaborative Thompson Sampling algorithm. As the dataset only provides us with user features, we are unable to identify the users by their id. Instead, we performed K-means clustering over visits based on the similarity of user features and summarized their click-through rate of all articles. Each visit was assigned to a cluster, and these clusters were treated as users in our experiment. We then computed the click-through-rate of all articles in a cluster. If an article were never recommended to any user in this cluster, the click-through rate of this article is set to mean of CTR of all visits. In our experiment, if article j is recommended to a cluster i, the payoff $r_{i,j}$ is drawn from a Bernoulli distribution: $r_{i,j} \sim \text{Bernoulli}(\pi_{i,j})$, where $\pi_{i,j}$ is the click-through rate.

Avazu. The Avazu click-through rate dataset was presented by Avazu, which is an international corporation specializing in cross-device advertising. The dataset was provided for an online challenge to build and test models, which aim at predicting the click-through rate of mobile ads. What it contains was divided into two parts, a training set, and a test set. There are over 40 million records in the training set and approximately 4 million records in the test set. We used the training set to build and evaluate our algorithm because we did not know the payoff of the test data. Each line in the training set represents the event of an ad impression on a website or a mobile application. The variables contained in each line can be categorized as follows: id, timestamp, payoff(clicked or not), banner position, three site variables, three app variables, five device variable, and 9 anonymized categorical variables(C1, C14–C21). The payoff was one if it was clicked, and 0 otherwise.

As ID represents a single ad impression, it cannot be used to identify an ad. Instead, we identified the ads with their site variables (site id, site domain, site category) if it is displayed on a website or app variables (app id, app domain, app category) otherwise. We identified the users with the combination of device variables (device id, device IP, device model and C19) rather than device id because most device ids are the same (null). In the Avazu dataset, we had the records of more than 1 million users and 20 thousand ads. However, not all records can be used in the evaluation of our algorithm, as we wanted to compare our algorithm to standard Thompson sampling algorithms in bandit settings in which the goal is to minimize the regret in the long term. If the users were provided with only a few ads, the performance would not be distinguishable among algorithms. Most users only appeared once in the dataset and were not suitable to evaluate our algorithm. In preprocessing, we eliminated the users and ads with less than 1000 records. The number of users and ads end up being 544 and 81 respectively. We used the remaining more than 1 million records in the experiments. However, we found that the dataset is quite sparse, most users were only recommended with few ads. To address this problem, we added one additional impression each ad to each user, and the reward was set to 0.13, which is the mean click-through rate of the remaining impressions. We emphasize that preprocessing did not provide any additional collaborative effects to the dataset, so it can still be used to evaluate the performance of collaborative Thompson sampling.

6.2   Algorithms

To the best of our knowledge, there were no previous works that focus on incorporating collaborative effects into Thompson sampling. To evaluate the prediction performance of our algorithm, we applied collaboration to a set of standard Thompson sampling algorithms.

Beta Thompson Sampling is a non-contextual bandit algorithm. The reward of content j follows a Bernoulli distribution with mean θ. The mean reward of each content is estimated using a Beta distribution because it is the conjugate distribution of Bernoulli distribution.

Linear Thompson Sampling follows the settings of standard contextual linear bandit. The vector parameter u_i of user i determined the payoff of a content $j \in C$

with contextual vector x_j. Formally, the payoff value $r_{i,j}$ is computed by a linear function and a random variable ϵ: $r_{i,j} = \mu_i^T x_j + \epsilon_{i,j}$

Logistic Thompson Sampling works under the assumption that given a contextual vector x_j for content j, the probability that user i click content j is given by $1/(1 + \exp - u_{i,j}^T x_j)$, where $u_{i,j}$ is the user vector to be learned. We used Laplace approximation to approximate the posterior distribution of user vector $u_{i,j}$.

All algorithms require parameter tuning to achieve the optimal performance. There are shared parameters such as the exploration-exploitation tradeoff parameter, the learning rate of rewards. There are also private parameters of each algorithm such as the number of clusters in our algorithm. We tuned standard Thompson sampling algorithm to find the optimal combination of the shared parameter with grid search. The shared parameters were used in both collaborative Thompson sampling and standard Thompson sampling. We then tuned collaborative Thompson sampling to determine their private parameters based on the shared parameters.

6.3   Results

All experiments are aimed at comparing the prediction performance of collaborative Thompson sampling (CTS) and standard Thompson sampling (STS). The shared parameters were determined by standard Thompson sampling via grid search and were used by both CTS and STS. This gives rise to reliable estimation of the actual effect of collaboration under the same experimental conditions.

6.4   Yahoo! Dataset

In this experiment, click-through rate (CTR) was used to evaluate the performance of all Thompson sampling algorithms. CTR was computed in every 200 rounds for each algorithm. We also used the CTR to show the trend of learning procedure.

Performance Comparison. The results on the Yahoo! webscope dataset are presented in Fig. 1. We plotted click-through rate (CTR) of recent 200 rounds (left) and CTR of all rounds (right). The results of standard Thompson sampling are shown with the dotted line and the results of corresponding collaborative Thompson sampling are shown with the full line in the same color.

As we can see, all collaborative Thompson sampling algorithms outperformed corresponding standard Thompson sampling algorithms that do not take collaborative effects into account. All CTSs achieved higher prediction accuracy and accelerated convergence compared to STSs. The results revealed that the ability of CTS to share collaborative information among users allows it to provide an accurate estimation of expected rewards and balance exploration-exploitation trade-off at both the personal level and the system level.

In Fig. 1, We can conclude that collaborative Thompson sampling outperformed standard Thompson sampling in terms of CTR. In these simulations,

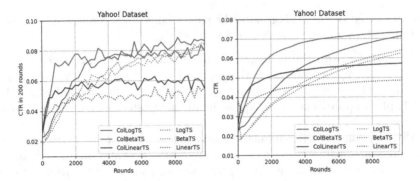

Fig. 1. Plots on the Yahoo! dataset reporting click-through rate (CTR) of all impressions over time, i.e., the fraction of the recommended articles get clicked. Left: CTR in 200 rounds; Right: CTR in all previous rounds (Color figure online)

the performance of Beta TS and Logistic TS was asymptotical to collaborative Thompson sampling. Their CTR of 200 rounds (left) was about the same value with collaborative approaches after 10000 rounds of training and the gap of CTR (right) between CTS and STS was closing over time. These results can be concluded that the collaborative effects accelerate the convergence of Thompson sampling without harming its prediction performance. This finding was consistent with our prediction in regret analysis. For Linear Thompson sampling, the collaborative Thompson sampling consistently achieved better click-through rate. It revealed that incorporating collaborative in a linear setting may help to improve the prediction performance as well.

The CTR of the first relatively small fraction of rounds showed the performance of these algorithms in a cold-start regime. It is shown in Fig. 1 that collaborative Thompson sampling algorithms converge much faster than standard Thompson sampling algorithms. They were able to locate the optimal choice in fewer rounds. Thus, CTSs are more suitable to address the cold start problem. In highly dynamic environments, this property of CTS allows it to accurately estimate the expected rewards of new items and adapt to dynamic changes of environment. Therefore, it is reasonable to expect that our algorithm will perform well in highly dynamic systems with strong collaborative effects such as news recommendation, where new contents regularly become available for the recommendation and the value of news changes over time.

Note that Linear Thompson sampling (blue) performed poorly in terms of click-through rate compared to other algorithms. A possible explanation is that linear TS maintains one user vector for each user to estimate the expected reward of all contents to share knowledge among contents. While the other algorithms maintain independent parameter for each content. The knowledge learned from different contents may conflict with each other. Although Linear Thompson sampling did not perform well in this experiment, they have some advantage over other algorithms. For example, Linear TS converged much faster than Beta TS. Another advantage of Linear Thompson sampling is it is easy to implement because it does not require to approximate the complex distribution of parameters used in logistic regression or sample from the beta distribution.

6.5   Avazu Dataset

In this experiment, regret was used to evaluate the performance of all Thompson sampling algorithms. Regret is the most popular measure in the multi-armed bandit problem. It is defined as the gap of reward between the optimal item and the selected item. Regret was computed in every 100 rounds to show the current performance of algorithms. We also used the total regret to show the performance of our algorithm in the long run.

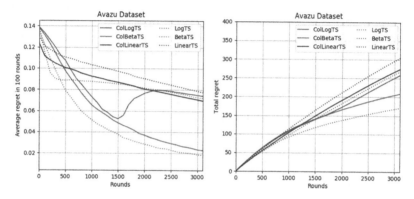

Fig. 2. Plots on the Avazu dataset reporting regret over time. Left: average regret of last 100 rounds; Right: total regret

Performance Comparison. The results on the Avazu dataset are summarized in Fig. 2. We plotted regret of recent 100 rounds (left) and cumulated regret of all rounds (right). The results of standard Thompson sampling were shown with the dotted line, and the results of corresponding collaborative Thompson sampling were shown with the full line in the same color.

As we can see, applying collaborative effects to three standard Thompson sampling algorithms in Avazu dataset revealed different effects. For Linear TS model (blue lines), collaborative Thompson sampling outperformed standard algorithm on both prediction accuracy and convergence rate. Collaborative TS has lower regret in each round and lower total regrets. For Logistic TS model (green lines), the collaborative Thompson sampling also provided slight performance improvement in terms of total regret. These results indicated that applying collaborative effects to contextual settings is profitable in this dataset. However, for the Beta TS model (red lines), collaborative TS did not outperform standard TS. The standard TS converged faster with lower total regret. It indicated that utilizing collaborative in a non-contextual model in this dataset may harm its performance. These effects might result from the sparsity of data. In

Avazu dataset, the ads were identified by their website and application domains rather than their id or contents. Thus many different ads were treated as one. Therefore, users may be recommended thousands of ads impressions without knowing what kind of ads they are. The sparsity of data weakened the collaborative effects among users and ads. Thus collaborative Thompson sampling cannot provide improved performance and accelerated convergence.

These different performances of collaborative TS resulted from the strength of the collaborative effects of these datasets. Although Avazu and Yahoo! dataset are both generated by real online web applications, they are different in the strength of collaborative effects. Firstly, Avazu dataset records the click on ad impressions via mobile apps or websites. The ads are identified by website domain or mobile domain rather than their id. It means that different ads may be identified as the same one in this dataset. In Yahoo! dataset, the articles are identified by their id. Therefore, the collaborative effects of the same article are much stronger. Secondly, for Yahoo! dataset, it is reasonable to predict that certain articles such as breaking news will draw much attention from all users and it is natural to expect that the true value of news can be estimated by feedback of other users. But users may not have the similar preference for ads in Avazu dataset. Thirdly, the Avazu dataset is quite sparse. The users are often recommended with the same ads for thousands of times and no other ads are ever recommended. The sparsity of data weakens the collaboratives effect embedded in the dataset. As our algorithm exploits the collaborative effects of the data, it is reasonable that our algorithm exhibited more significant effects in Yahoo! dataset than Avazu dataset.

To summarize, collaborative TS significantly outperforms standard TS in strong collaborative environments. It is especially effective in the cold-start period. Utilizing the collaborative effects in Thompson sampling results in accelerated convergence and improved prediction accuracy. It makes the algorithm more suitable for dynamic applications with strong collaborative effects. On the other hand, in weak collaborative environments, collaborative TS can still exploit the collaborative effects to improve the prediction accuracy and lower the regret. But in these domains, the users should be carefully clustered to exploit the collaborative information.

7   Conclusion

We introduced collaborative Thompson sampling algorithm. The algorithm exploits collaborative effects to accelerate convergence and improve prediction performance. It works under the assumption that users can be partitioned into groups based on their similarity and users in the same cluster can collaborate to accurately estimate the expected reward of items with a few observations. We carried out empirical experiments on two real-world datasets comparing our algorithm with standard Thompson sampling algorithms. The experiments showed that our algorithm outperformed standard Thompson sampling algorithm in terms of efficiency and prediction accuracy in collaborative environments. Thus, the algorithm is more suitable for dynamic applications with strong collaborative effects. We also provided a theoretical analysis of its total expected regret.

Our algorithm can adapt to any Thompson sampling algorithms and clustering technique in a collaborative environment. One direction of the experimental research is to develop a robust dynamic clustering algorithm to exploit collaborative effects. Another line of theoretical research would be providing regret analysis of collaborative Thompson sampling on contextual settings.

Acknowledgments. This paper is supported by the National Science Foundation of China under Grant 61472385 and Grant U1709217.

References

1. Agarwal, D., Long, B., Traupman, J., Xin, D., Zhang, L.: Laser: a scalable response prediction platform for online advertising. In: Proceedings of the 7th ACM International Conference on Web Search and Data Mining, pp. 173–182. ACM (2014)
2. Agrawal, S., Goyal, N.: Analysis of Thompson sampling for the multi-armed bandit problem. In: Conference on Learning Theory, pp. 39.1–39.26 (2012)
3. Agrawal, S., Goyal, N.: Thompson sampling for contextual bandits with linear payoffs. In: International Conference on Machine Learning, pp. 127–135 (2013)
4. Banerjee, A.: On Bayesian bounds. In: Proceedings of the 23rd International Conference on Machine Learning, pp. 81–88. ACM (2006)
5. Bresler, G., Chen, G.H., Shah, D.: A latent source model for online collaborative filtering. In: Advances in Neural Information Processing Systems, pp. 3347–3355 (2014)
6. Brodén, B., Hammar, M., Nilsson, B.J., Paraschakis, D.: Ensemble recommendations via Thompson sampling: an experimental study within e-Commerce. In: 23rd International Conference on Intelligent User Interfaces, pp. 19–29. ACM (2018)
7. Chapelle, O., Li, L.: An empirical evaluation of Thompson sampling. In: Advances in Neural Information Processing Systems, pp. 2249–2257 (2011)
8. Christakopoulou, K., Banerjee, A.: Learning to interact with users: a collaborative-bandit approach. In: Proceedings of the 2018 SIAM International Conference on Data Mining, pp. 612–620. SIAM (2018)
9. Chu, W., Li, L., Reyzin, L., Schapire, R.: Contextual bandits with linear payoff functions. In: Proceedings of the Fourteenth International Conference on Artificial Intelligence and Statistics, pp. 208–214 (2011)
10. Chu, W., et al.: A case study of behavior-driven conjoint analysis on Yahoo!: front page today module. In: Proceedings of the 15th ACM SIGKDD International Conference on Knowledge Discovery and Data Mining, pp. 1097–1104. ACM (2009)
11. Ferreira, K., Simchi-Levi, D., Wang, H.: Online network revenue management using Thompson sampling (2017)
12. Glaze, C.M., Filipowicz, A.L., Kable, J.W., Balasubramanian, V., Gold, J.I.: A bias-variance trade-off governs individual differences in on-line learning in an unpredictable environment. Nat. Hum. Behav. **2**(3), 213 (2018)
13. Gopalan, A., Mannor, S.: Thompson sampling for learning parameterized Markov decision processes. In: Conference on Learning Theory, pp. 861–898 (2015)
14. Gopalan, A., Mannor, S., Mansour, Y.: Thompson sampling for complex online problems. In: International Conference on Machine Learning, pp. 100–108 (2014)

15. Graepel, T., Candela, J.Q., Borchert, T., Herbrich, R.: Web-scale Bayesian click-through rate prediction for sponsored search advertising in Microsoft's Bing search engine. Omnipress (2010)
16. Johnson, C.C.: Logistic matrix factorization for implicit feedback data. In: Advances in Neural Information Processing Systems, vol. 27 (2014)
17. Kaufmann, E., Korda, N., Munos, R.: Thompson sampling: an asymptotically optimal finite-time analysis. In: Bshouty, N.H., Stoltz, G., Vayatis, N., Zeugmann, T. (eds.) ALT 2012. LNCS (LNAI), vol. 7568, pp. 199–213. Springer, Heidelberg (2012). https://doi.org/10.1007/978-3-642-34106-9_18
18. Kawale, J., Bui, H.H., Kveton, B., Tran-Thanh, L., Chawla, S.: Efficient Thompson sampling for online matrix-factorization recommendation. In: Advances in Neural Information Processing Systems, pp. 1297–1305 (2015)
19. Lavancier, F., Rochet, P.: A general procedure to combine estimators. Comput. Stat. Data Anal. **94**, 175–192 (2016)
20. Li, L., Chu, W., Langford, J., Schapire, R.E.: A contextual-bandit approach to personalized news article recommendation. In: Proceedings of the 19th International Conference on World Wide Web, pp. 661–670. ACM (2010)
21. Li, S., Karatzoglou, A., Gentile, C.: Collaborative filtering bandits. In: Proceedings of the 39th International ACM SIGIR Conference on Research and Development in Information Retrieval, pp. 539–548. ACM (2016)
22. Nguyen, T.T., Lauw, H.W.: Dynamic clustering of contextual multi-armed bandits. In: Proceedings of the 23rd ACM International Conference on Conference on Information and Knowledge Management, pp. 1959–1962. ACM (2014)
23. Ouyang, Y., Gagrani, M., Nayyar, A., Jain, R.: Learning unknown Markov decision processes: a Thompson sampling approach. In: Advances in Neural Information Processing Systems, pp. 1333–1342 (2017)
24. Russo, D.J., Van Roy, B., Kazerouni, A., Osband, I., Wen, Z., et al.: A tutorial on Thompson sampling. Found. Trends® in Mach. Learn. **11**(1), 1–96 (2018)
25. Schwartz, E.M., Bradlow, E.T., Fader, P.S.: Customer acquisition via display advertising using multi-armed bandit experiments. Mark. Sci. **36**(4), 500–522 (2017)
26. Scott, S.L.: A modern Bayesian look at the multi-armed bandit. Appl. Stoch. Models Bus. Ind. **26**(6), 639–658 (2010)
27. Thompson, W.R.: On the likelihood that one unknown probability exceeds another in view of the evidence of two samples. Biometrika **25**(3/4), 285–294 (1933)
28. Wolfinger, R.: Laplace's approximation for nonlinear mixed models. Biometrika **80**(4), 791–795 (1993)
29. Wu, Q., Wang, H., Gu, Q., Wang, H.: Contextual bandits in a collaborative environment. In: Proceedings of the 39th International ACM SIGIR Conference on Research and Development in Information Retrieval, pp. 529–538. ACM (2016)

Collaborative Workflow Scheduling over MANET, a User Position Prediction-Based Approach

Qinglan Peng[1], Qiang He[2], Yunni Xia[1($\boxtimes$)], Chunrong Wu[1], and Shu Wang[3]

[1] Software Theory and Technology Chongqing Key Lab, Chongqing University,
Chongqing, China
xiayunni@hotmail.com
[2] School of Software and Electrical Engineering, Swiburne University of Technology,
Melbourne, Australia
qhe@swin.edu.au
[3] School of information, Liaoning University, Shenyang, China
swang@lnu.edu.cn

Abstract. The explosive increase of mobile devices and advanced communication technologies prompt the emergence of mobile computing. In this paradigm, mobile users' idle resources can be shared as service through device-to-device links to other users. Some complex workflow-based mobile applications are therefor no longer need to be offloaded to remote cloud, on the contrary, they can be solved locally with the help of other devices in a collaborative way. Nevertheless, various challenges, especially the reliability and quality-of-service of such a collaborative workflow scheduling problem, are yet to be properly tackled. Most studies and related scheduling strategies assume that mobile users are fully stable and with constantly available. However, this is not realistic in most real-world scenarios where mobile users are mobile most of time. The mobility of mobile users impact the reliability of corresponding shared resources and consequently impact the success rate of workflows. In this paper, we propose a reliability-aware mobile workflow scheduling approach based on prediction of mobile users' positions. We model the scheduling problem as a multi-objective optimization problem and develop an evolutionary multi-objective optimization based algorithm to solve it. Extensive case studies are performed based on a real-world mobile users' trajectory dataset and show that our proposed approach significantly outperforms traditional approaches in term of workflow success rate.

Keywords: Workflow scheduling · Mobile computing ·
Quality-of-service · Reliability

1 Introduction

Recent years have witnessed a rapid growth and advances of mobile devices, e.g., smart phones, tablet computers, wearable devices, etc., and mobile services.

H. Gao et al. (Eds.): CollaborateCom 2018, LNICST 268, pp. 33–52, 2019.
https://doi.org/10.1007/978-3-030-12981-1_3

Mobile devices are changing the way people access information in their daily lives. In the mobile computing environment, mobile users can exploit nearby resources, e.g., computing resource, data traffic, sensors, etc., through utilizing mobile services shared in a mobile ad hoc network (MANET). MANET is a self-organized local mobile network built by nodes within each other's communication fields.

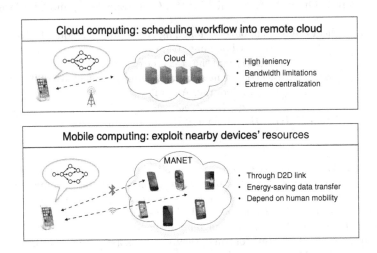

Fig. 1. Mobile computing paradigm.

As illustrated in Fig. 1, the core idea of mobile computing over MANET is sharing. In this paradigm, mobile users are allowed to utilize resources and services shared by other users nearby in a collaborative way, and thus the provisioning capability of involved services is expanded through exploiting direct physical contacts among users. These available resources and services can be shared directly among users in an elastic and on-demand way without time-consuming and energy-requiring communications with pre-existing infrastructure, for example, cellular networks and traditional centralized cloud data centers. Note that, workflow-based mobile applications over MANET (e.g., TensorFlow Lite, Photo editing on mobile, and Online video sharing) usually require huge computational resources and data transfer. Therefore, nearby mobile resources are thus more adept, in terms of timeliness and energy-efficiency, at executing these workflow tasks than remote cloud with the help of device-to-device (D2D) communications such as Bluetooth, Wi-Fi, and NFC. D2D communications are featured by extensively-reduced inter-device delays and energy consumption than traditional cellular networks [3]. It is widely believed to have potential to improve Quality-of-Service (QoS) of mobile services over MANET by providing increased user throughput, reduced cellular traffic, and extended network coverage [5].

However, users in a MANET often have high mobility, which resulting in topological changes in the MANET over time. Under such circumstances, it has become a great challenge how to compose and schedule reliable workflow tasks over a versatile MANET and fulfill users' quality-of-service (QoS) requirements in the meantime.

To cope with aforementioned challenges and concerns, in this study, we propose a predictive reliability-aware mobile workflow scheduling approach over MANET. We first present the concept of mobile resources sharing community and the corresponding mobile resources reliability evaluation method. Then, a gaussian mixture model for user position prediction is used to capture the moving trend of mobile users and make a prediction of resource providers' reliability. Finally, we develop a multi-objective optimization based composition algorithm named MDEWS, the predicted reliability values are feed into this algorithm to yield workflow schedules. The results of experiments conducted on a real-world user movement dataset show that our approach is capable of dynamically capturing the mobility of mobile users and achieving higher success rates of workflows than traditional approaches.

2 Related Work

Workflow scheduling aims to schedule tasks into proper time slice of computing resources at proper time. As a well-known NP-hard problem, extensive studies have devoted into this problem in the past decades. Typically, most workflow scheduling approaches can be classified into two categories in term of computing platform: one is traditional multiprocessor and grid system, another is IaaS cloud which has attracted great attention recent years. In this section, we first review workflow scheduling problems in grid system and IaaS cloud, then discuss the challenges and concerns of scheduling workflow in mobile computing environment.

Grid can be seen as a service-oriented paradigm for resource-intensive applications. In a grid, every resource can be represented as a service and these resources are delivered through a utility computing models based service provisioning. Many heuristics and meta-heuristics based algorithms have been proposed to schedule workflow applications in grid. For example, Maheswaran et al. [10] studied on-line and batch heuristics for workflows scheduling in heterogeneous distributed system, they proposed three heuristics strategies: Min-Min, Max-Min and Sufferage. Topcuoglu et al. [20] presented two algorithms named Heterogeneous Earliest-Finish-Time (HEFT) and Critical-Path-on-a-Processor (CPOP) for workflow scheduling over heterogeneous processors with bounded number. Zhao et al. [16] assign a weight to each node and edge in a workflow, then they use a HEFT algorithm to schedule the tasks of workflow onto heterogeneous machines with bounded number.

Cloud computing is becoming an increasingly popular platform for workflow-based applications such as scientific workflows. Recent years, workflow scheduling in cloud has attracted great attention and extensive efforts have been devoted to this field based on the features of IaaS cloud [17,21,22]. For instance, Mao et al. [11] proposed an auto-scaling workflow scheduling approach, they consider not only user performance requirements but also budget minimization. Abrishami *et al.* [1] extended the Partial Critical Paths (PCP) algorithm for utility grid to IaaS cloud which named Cloud Partial Critical Paths (IC-PCP). The scheduling goal of IC-PCP is minimizing execution cost while meeting deadline constrain. Rodriguez and Buyya [15] presented a static, deadline-constrained, cost-aware workflow scheduling approach based on Particle Swarm Optimisation (PSO). IaaS cloud features such as elastic and unlimited resource provision and VM performance variation are considered in their system model. Li *et al.* [8] proposed a predictive, fluctuation-aware workflow scheduling approach. They consider fluctuant VM performance and use an ARMA (Auto-Regressive Moving Average) model to make a prediction about VMs' future performance to achieve lower SLA (Service-Level-Agreement) violation rate. Zhu *et al.* [24] proposed a evolutionary multi-objective workflow scheduling algorithm named EMS-C, they model the workflow scheduling problem as a multi-objective optimization problem which optimizes both makespan and cost, then a NSGA-II based metaheuristic algorithm is developed to solve it.

It can be seen that most approaches and algorithms are designed for cloud computing environment or grid system. Cloud and grid share the same characteristic of relative stability, and they are usually deployed in permanent data centers or distributed systems. However, these scheduling methods cannot be applied to the mobile computing environment directly because they usually do not consider resource reliability or they just consider constant reliability. In mobile computing environment, the topological structure of an MANET can change at any time and the fluctuation of reliability could be very volatile, which makes them fail to find a reliable schedule. Therefore, to schedule reliable workflow over MANET, approaches which adapt to dynamic mobile computing environment are required. In this paper, we propose a reliability-aware workflow scheduling approach based on user position prediction. To capture the variation trend of reliability, the predicted mobile user positions are used to evaluate the reliability of resource provider, then these reliability values are fed into a multi-objective evolutionary algorithm to generate reliable-aware schedule plans.

3   Preliminaries

3.1   Mobile Resources Sharing Community

A Mobile Resources Sharing Community (MRSC) is a mobile ad hoc network for mobile resources sharing. It is usually constructed by nearby mobile devices and sink nodes. It can be formally described as a 2-tuple $M = (N, C)$, where N is the set of mobile devices and sink nodes in an MRSC, C the set of connections for every communication path. Figure 2 shows an example MRSC established in a coffee shop, where mobile users are within each other's D2D transmission ranges.

An MRSC has three characteristics: (1) locality: A mobile user can perceive available computing resources around and deploy workflow tasks to other mobile devices in the same MRSC, and locality of computing resources can thus

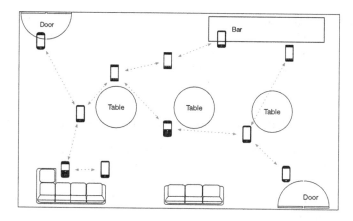

Fig. 2. An MRSC example in a café.

be exploited and utilized; (2) mobility: In an MRSC, it is not uncommon that all computing nodes are constantly moving during task executing time; (3) dynamicity: Mobile users may join or leave an MRSC automatically when they enter or leave a participating user's transmission range.

3.2 Mobile Resource Reliability

It can be seen that scheduling workflow tasks over an MANET is unreliable due to the high mobility of mobile devices. In this paper, the reliability of D2D links between mobile devices in MANET are considered when evaluating the reliability of mobile resource provider [7]. Suppose that there are a total of $|N|$ nodes and $|C|$ connections in an MRSC at time t, the reliability of computing resource provided by provider p for requester r can be calculated as the reliability between these two devices p and r. In an MRSC, each edge has its operational probability ρ, which can be estimated from the received signal strength indicator (RSSI) value or GPS data easily [13]. The state of the MRSC at time t can thus be represented as $S(t) = [S_1(t), S_2(t), ..., S_{|C|}(t)]$, where the i-th element $S_i(t)$ is assigned to 1 if the i-th edge is working at time t, otherwise 0. Thus, the probability of an MRSC being in a given state can be calculated as follows:

$$\mathbf{P}(S(t)) = \prod_{i=1}^{|C|} \rho_i^{S_i(t)} (1 - \rho_i)^{1 - S_i(t)} \tag{1}$$

then the reliability of a D2D link between p and r can be expressed as follows:

$$RL_{(s,d)}[G(t)] = \sum_{all \ S(t)} \phi(S(t), p, r) \mathbf{P}(S(t)) \tag{2}$$

where $\phi(S(t), p, r)$ is the function to identify whether there are available paths between device p and r. If at state $S(t)$, there is at least one path between p and r, then $\phi(S(t), p, r) = 1$, otherwise 0.

It can be seen that the reliability of a resource provider in an MANET varies over time and is closely related to the communication distance between the workflow application requester and the mobile resources providers. A mobile provider currently observed to be available may become unavailable in the near future due to the change in this distance.

3.3 Gaussian Mixture Model for User Position Prediction

A recent study [18] reports that there is a potential 93% average predictability in user mobility. For example, Fig. 3 shows pedestrians' trajectories on a campus. We can clearly see that most trajectories share similarity and regularity patterns. Such similarity, periodicity, and regularity can be formally and properly described with novel methods [2,9,14].

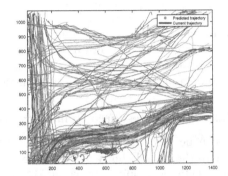

Fig. 3. Trajectories in a campus.

Human trajectories are usually fulfill multiple mobility patterns, depending on the subjective destination, the limit of objective environment, other people's movement and so on. Each pattern within a trajectory can be effectively described by a Gaussian process and the entire trajectories thus corresponds to a Gaussian Mixture Model (GMM).

In a GMM, users' history trajectory data can be described as follows:

$$
\begin{aligned}
U &= \{\Gamma_1, \Gamma_2, ..., \Gamma_n\} \\
&= \{(\overrightarrow{x_1}, \overrightarrow{y_1}), (\overrightarrow{x_2}, \overrightarrow{y_2}), ..., (\overrightarrow{x_n}, \overrightarrow{y_n})\} \\
&= \{\overrightarrow{X}, \overrightarrow{Y}\}
\end{aligned}
\tag{3}
$$

where Γ_i denotes the i-th user's trajectories, $\overrightarrow{X}$ and $\overrightarrow{Y}$ the mapping vector of these trajectories in X and Y directions, respectively. A trajectory $\Gamma_i = (\overrightarrow{x_i}, \overrightarrow{y_i})$ can be expressed as a multiple different Gaussian processes as follows:

$$p(\overrightarrow{x_n}|\lambda) = \sum_{i=1}^{K} \omega_i GP(\overrightarrow{x_n}|\mu_{(x,i)}, \sigma_{(x,i)}) \tag{4}$$

$$p(\overrightarrow{y_n}|\lambda) = \sum_{i=1}^{K} \omega_i GP(\overrightarrow{y_n}|\mu_{(y,i)}, \sigma_{(y,i)})$$

where $GP(\overrightarrow{x_n}|\mu_{(x,i)}, \sigma_{(x,i)})$ denotes the probability function of trajectory Γ_n's X direction in the i-th trajectory pattern, K the number of all trajectory patterns, ω_i the weight of the i-th trajectory pattern with $\sum_{i=1}^{K} \omega_i = 1$, $\mu_{(x,i)}$ and $\mu_{(y,i)}$ the means of the i-th trajectory pattern in directions X and Y, $\sigma_{(x,i)}$ and $\sigma_{(y,i)}$ the covariances of the i-th trajectory pattern in directions X and Y, respectively. We use λ to denote the set of parameters $\{\omega_i, \mu_i, \sigma_i\}$ where $i \in \{1, 2, ..., N\}$. Therefore, the likelihood function of GMM for training set $U = \{\overrightarrow{X}, \overrightarrow{Y}\}$ can be expressed as follow:

$$P(\overrightarrow{X}|\lambda) = \prod_{n=1}^{K} p(\overrightarrow{x_n}|\lambda) \tag{5}$$

$$P(\overrightarrow{Y}|\lambda) = \prod_{n=1}^{K} p(\overrightarrow{y_n}|\lambda)$$

The forecasting process consists three steps: (1) applying a Gaussian Mixture clustering method [23] to trajectory dataset U to obtain K clusters, which correspond to K different trajectory patterns; (2) an expectation-maximization algorithm is applied to estimate parameter λ; (3) forecast a mobile user's future position based on his/her recent trajectory. The prediction process is employed in Sect. 4 to obtain the prediction results of mobile devices' position. Then the reliability of providers is evaluated based on its predicted position is further fed into the optimization formulation to facilitate workflow schedules.

3.4 Proposed Approach Architecture

In an MRSC, each mobile device represent a mobile resource provider which able to provide computing capability to nearby devices. The reliability of mobile resource providers is varying due to the high dynamic of MANET. In order to capture the reliability variations at run-time to realize reliable scheduling, we proposed a user position prediction-based workflow scheduling approach for MANET. As shown in Fig. 4, the process of our approach consists of three typical steps: (1) a workflow template is constructed when a mobile user wants to launch a workflow request. A workflow template usually has multiple tasks and each task can be scheduled to an available mobile resource provider. (2) then, it begins to discover potential providers in the same MRSC. At the same time, the reliability of these providers are evaluated according to its predicted positions. A resource pool which containing available providers is constructed in this step; (3) next, it will decide which provider to select for each task to realize the workflow

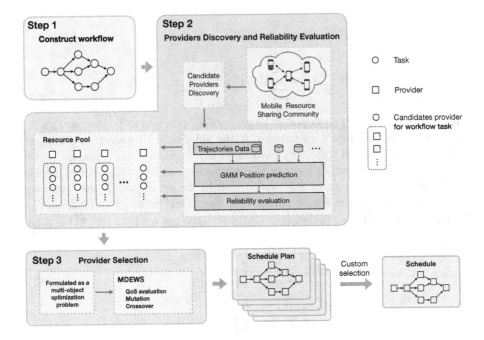

Fig. 4. The process of mobile workflow scheduling.

scheduling with satisfactory reliability and makespan. The decision making is transformed into a multi-objective optimization problem. Then an evolutionary-based algorithm named MDEWS is employed to yield a set of solutions, which are equally optimal from the view of Pareto fronts [4] and can be selected based on user preferences.

4   System Model and Problem Formulation

A workflow application is described by a Directed-Acyclic-Graph (DAG) $W = (T, E)$, where $T = (t_1, t_2, ..., t_m)$ denotes the set of tasks and E the set of edges. Without loss of generality, t_1 and t_m are considered to be the entry and exit tasks, respectively. The edge $e_{i,k}$ indicates that t_k can be executed after t_i is accomplished. $^*t_i$ and t_i^* denote the parent and child sets of t_i, respectively. The workflow

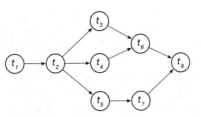

Fig. 5. An example of workflow.

starts and concludes by the entry and exit tasks, respectively. Figure 5 shows an example of sample workflow with 8 tasks. D denotes the user-recommended constraint of the completion time of the workflow, usually specified in SLA documents.

An MRSC supports workflows application through mobile resource providers. These providers are selected from a resource provider pool, $P = \{p_1, p_2, ..., p_n\}$, and at most n providers are required at runtime if no two tasks share the same providers. Providers can be different in their CPU speed, memory, and pricing configurations, and each provider have an available period for tasks. The starting time of tasks is decided by their supporting provider and the completion time of their preceding tasks. If task t_i connects t_k through edge $e_{i,k}$ and they are executed by different providers, the transfer time, $D_{i,k}$, is inevitable because inter-device data and control signal transfer is required. Otherwise, $D_{i,k} = 0$ if both tasks are on the same provider.

Finally, the problem of workflow scheduling over MANET can therefore be formulated as:

$$
\begin{aligned}
Min: \quad & y = f(x) = (1 - \xi(x), \tau(x))^T \\
s.t: \quad & \tau(x) \leq D \\
& x = [x_1, x_2, ..., x_n]^T \in \Theta \\
& x_i^{min} \leq x_i \leq x_i^{max} \quad (i = 1, 2, ..., n)
\end{aligned}
\tag{6}
$$

where $\xi(x)$ and $\tau(x)$ are two functions to identify the estimated reliability and makespan required for schedule x respectively, Θ stands for the decision space (i.e., resource pool).

We use function $w(t_i)$ to identify which provider does task t_i is going to be scheduled into, $\xi(x)$ can thus be aggregated by the reliability of each D2D communication in scheduling plan as follows:

$$
\xi(x) = log \prod_{i=1}^{|E|} RL_{(w(s_i), w(d_i))}[G(t)]
\tag{7}
$$

where s_i and s_i are father and child tasks in edge e_i respectively. The derivation of $\tau(x)$ requires some efforts, $\tau(x)$ can be calculated as the estimated end time of the last task t_m in a workflow:

$$
\tau(x) = d_m
\tag{8}
$$

where d_m denotes the estimated end time of task t_m. We use d_i to denote the estimated end time of task t_i, it can be iteratively calculated as:

$$
d_i = e_i + b_i
\tag{9}
$$

where b_i denotes the estimated start time of executing t_i and e_i the execution time of t_i itself. b_i is decided by the estimated end time of its immediately preceding tasks and the time required for data transfer. Let γ_i denote the estimated time when all earlier tasks scheduled to the same provider to t_i are finished, we have:

$$
\gamma_i = max\{d_j \mid t_j \in {}^*t_i \ \wedge \ w(t_i) = w(t_j)\}
\tag{10}
$$

where $^{*}t_i$ denotes the immediately preceding tasks of t_i, i.e., those which directly connect t_i through edges in the workflow. $w(t_i) = w(t_j)$ indicates that t_i and t_j are scheduled into the same provider.

Note that the dependency constraint requires that a task be executed only if its immediately preceding ones successfully terminate and transfer data. We use y_i to denote the estimated earliest time when the described condition holds for t_i.

$$y_i = max\{d_k + D_{k,i} \mid t_k \in \,^{*}t_i \wedge w(t_k) \neq w(t_k) \} \tag{11}$$

The earliest possible time to execute b_i, can therefore be calculated as:

$$b_i = max\{\gamma_i, y_i\} \tag{12}$$

The first task of a workflow has no preceding task and therefore its estimated ending time is obtained as:

$$d_1 = \delta + e_1 \tag{13}$$

where δ is the time between receiving a workflow request and generating a corresponding schedule.

Since optimal reliability and makespan are two conflicting quality, we consider Pareto domination as the measure of the optimality of candidate solutions. Consequently, for solution $u, v \in \Theta$, u dominates v when:

$$\begin{cases} f_i(u) \leq f_i(v) & \forall\, i \in [1, n] \\ f_j(u) < f_j(v) & \exists\, j \in [1, n] \end{cases} \tag{14}$$

A solution x^{*} is Pareto-optimal if it is not dominated by any other solutions. The set of all Pareto-optimal solutions in the objective space is called a Pareto front. For the workflow scheduling problem, solution u dominates solution v if $\xi(u) \leq \xi(v) \wedge \tau(u) < \tau(v)$ or $\xi(u) < \xi(v) \wedge \tau(u) \leq \tau(v)$.

5   Multi-objective Differential Evolution for Workflow Scheduling

For the problem formulated in last section, methods such as multiple-objective-integer-linear-programming and multi-objective-branch-and-bound can be used for solutions. However, such method are usually considered to be with high time-complexity and thus could be impractical due to the fact that the problem space could be very large (the number of candidate mobile resource providers for one task can be 100+ for some typical cases, e.g., shopping mall and subway station. The number of tasks could be 50+ for some typical complex scientific application, e.g., Montage and Cybershake). In contrast, Multi-objective differential evolution (MODE) has been shown to be a simple yet efficient evolutionary algorithm for multi-objective optimization problems in diverse domains. It is featured by its strong parallelizability of genetic operators and good convergence

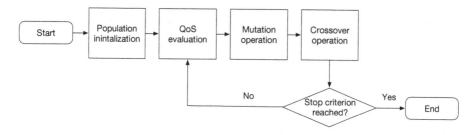

Fig. 6. The process of MDEWS.

properties than other traditional EMO algorithms. For the above problem formulated, we propose an improved MODE algorithm, named MDEWS, short for Multi-objective Differential Evolution for Workflow Scheduling to find solutions.

MDEWS developed in this work is a kind of meta-heuristic procedure similar to the process of natural selection. The process of MDEWS is shown in Fig. 6, it is used to yield high-quality solutions for optimization and searching problems by employing bio-inspired operations, e.g., mutation and crossover. A population of its candidate solutions to an optimization problem keeps evolving toward better solutions.

5.1 Encoding and Population Initialization

In MDEWS, a schedule is expressed as an individual which described by a vector of positive integers. The length of vectors are m, i.e., the number of tasks in a workflow. The i-th entry of the vector, in turn, refers to the mobile provider which i-th task in the workflow is scheduled into. Figure 7 shows the encoding scheme of a schedule and its deployment details for the sample workflow given earlier. In this schedule, task t_1, t_2, t_7 are scheduled into provider p_2 to execute, t_3, t_4, t_8 are scheduled into p_1, t_5 is scheduled into p_3 and t_6 is scheduled into p_4.

MDEWS starts with population initialization. The initial population with y individuals consists of three parts: (1) one individual i_1 with the highest $\xi(i_1)$ regardless of its makespan; (2) one individual i_2 with the shortest $\tau(i_2)$ regardless of its reliability; and (3) $y - 2$ individuals are randomly generated according to the current resource provider pool.

5.2 Mutation

The mutation operator simulates the evolutionary activity that an individual directionally learns from other individuals. To speed up the convergence and optimize the exploration ability, we consider an improved mutation strategy as follows:

$$V_i = X_i + F(X^* - X_i) + \qquad (15)$$
$$F(X^\# - X_i) + F(X_r^1 - X_r^2)$$

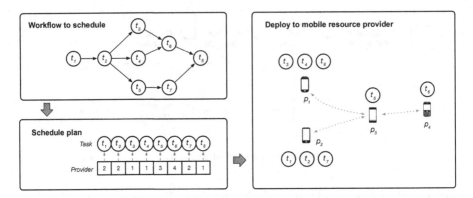

Fig. 7. An example of encoding.

where F is a scale factor, V_i an offspring individual, X_i mutation target, X_r^1 and X_r^2 two random individuals chosen from the current population, X^* and $X^\#$ the individuals randomly chosen from top-k best individuals in the population ordered by their estimated reliability and makespan, respectively, k is set to 15% in this paper. This top-k strategy can accelerate the convergence speed and in the meantime avoiding trapping into local optima. As shown in Algorithm 1, mutation operator first ranks individuals in a population order by its makespan and reliability and get the top 15% best group. Then it chooses base individuals X_r^1 and X_r^2 from current population and target individuals X^* and $X^\#$ from top 15% best group randomly. Finally, mutated individuals are generated by Eq. (15) based on base individuals and target individuals.

The time complexity of ranking all individuals and selecting top 15% best group (as shown lines 1–3 in Algorithm 1) are $O(y \log y)$, mutating all individuals (as shown lines 4–16 in Algorithm 1) is $O(my)$. Generally, m is large than $\log y$, therefore the time complexity of mutation operator is $O(my)$.

5.3   Crossover

The crossover operator simulates the genetic activity that an individual obtains characteristics from other individuals controlled by a crossover rate. As shown in Algorithm 2, the dynamic changing crossover rates are employed to avoid useless crossover operations. The crossover rate in the i-th generation, C_i, is randomly generated from a Gaussian distribution as:

$$C_i = \mathbf{G}(C_m, 0.1) \tag{16}$$

where C_m is calculated from the historical value of C_i, C_m in its first generation is 0.6. We use $\mathbb{C}$ to indicate the set of crossover rates which used in previous generations. C_m thus can be calculated as follows:

$$C_m = w_C \times C_m + (1 - w_C) \times mean_{Pow}(\mathbb{C}) \tag{17}$$

Algorithm 1. Mutation operator

Input: Population X; Task count m; Scale factor F; Resource pool P
Output: Mutated population V;

1: rank individuals in X order by its makespan and reliability
2: $Top_{Rel} \leftarrow$ get top 15% best individuals according to estimated reliability
3: $Top_{Ms} \leftarrow$ get top 15% best individuals according to estimated makespan
4: **for each** individual X_i **in** population X **do**
5:    $X_r^1 \leftarrow$ choose one individual from X randomly
6:    $X_r^2 \leftarrow$ choose one individual from X randomly
7:    $X^* \leftarrow$ choose one individual from Top_{Rel} randomly
8:    $X^{\#} \leftarrow$ choose one individual from Top_{Ms} randomly
9:    $V_i \leftarrow X_i + F(X^* - X_i) + F(X^{\#} - X_i) + F(X_r^1 - X_r^2)$
10:   **for** $j = 1$ **to** m **do**
11:      **if** $V_i[j] < P.LowBounds[j]$ **or** $V_i[j] > P.UpperBounds[j]$ **then**
12:         $V_i[j] \leftarrow$ choose one provider between low bounds and upper bounds of providers randomly
13:      **end if**
14:   **end for**
15:   add V_i into mutated population V
16: **end for**
17: **return** V

---

where

$$mean_{Pow}(\mathbb{C}) = \sum_{i=1}^{|\mathbb{C}|} [\frac{(C_i)^n}{|\mathbb{C}|}]^{\frac{1}{n}} \qquad (18)$$

where w_C is a real value randomly generated from $[0.9, 1]$ and n is set to 1.5 in this paper. The time complexity of crossover operator is $O(my)$.

5.4   Complexity Analysis

The overall computational complexity of our proposed approach can be analyzed by examining its position prediction, population initialization, reliability and makespan evaluation, mutation, crossover and dominance selection. Suppose there are k available mobile resource providers in a MRSC, the time complexity of forecasting all providers' future position is $O(k^2)$. The time complexity of initializing an individual is $O(m)$, and thus population initialization requires $O(my)$ where y is the size of initial population. The reliability and makespan evaluation for each individual has the time complexity of $O(mlog|E|)$ and thus reliability and makespan evaluation for initial population of size y with ω generations has the time complexity of $O(y\omega mlog|E|)$. The time complexity for mutation, crossover, and dominance selection operations are $O(my)$, $O(my)$, and $O(y^2)$, respectively. Consequently, the total time complexity of motion, crossover and dominance selection with ω generations is $O(\omega my) + O(\omega my) + O(\omega y^2)$. Finally, the total time complexity of position prediction, population initialization, reliability and makespan evaluation, mutation, crossover and dominance

---

Algorithm 2. Crossover operator

Input: Population X; Mutated population V; History crossover rate $\mathbb{C}$; Task count
$\quad m$;
Output: Population after crossover operation X';

1: calculate $mean_{Pow}$ according to history crossover rate $\mathbb{C}$ by (18)
2: calculate C_m by (17)
3: calculate crossover rate C_i by (16)
4: **for each** individual X_i in population X **do**
5:     **for** $j = 1$ **to** m **do**
6:       **if** $rand() < C_i$ **then**
7:         $Cv[j] \leftarrow 1$
8:       **else**
9:         $Cv[j] \leftarrow 0$
10:      **end if**
11:    **end for**
12:    **for** $j = 1$ **to** m **do**
13:      $X_i'[j] \leftarrow X_i \wedge (1 - Cv[j]) + V_i \wedge Cv[i]$
14:    **end for**
15:    add X_i' into X'
16: **end for**
17: **return** X'

---

selection is thus $O(k^2) + O(y\omega mlog|E|) + O(\omega my) + O(\omega my) + O(\omega y^2)$. Generally, $mlog|E|$ is large than y, thus the total time complexity of our approach is $O(k^2 + y\omega mlog|E|)$, and such complexity suggests good scalability.

6 Experiments and Analysis

To evaluate the effectiveness of our approach, we conducted experiments on a real-world user trajectory dataset and multiple scientific workflow templates in a wide range of application scenes.

The Stanford Drone dataset [19] is a user trajectory dataset collected from Stanford campus. In this dataset, all pedestrians' movement trajectories in a certain scene are recorded for consecutive periods. We choose *bookstore*, *gates*, *deathcicle*, and *hyang* these four scenes with varying crowd density to conduct our experiments. The aerial views of four scenes are shown in Fig. 8, and we assume that pedestrians within each others' D2D communication distances in the same scene establish an MRSC.

Pegasus project [6] has released a real-world scientific workflow dataset which includes Montage, CyberShake, Sipht and so on. In this dataset, the structure of DAG, size of tasks and data transferring are well recorded. Besides, it also provides a reference execution time of each task. In this paper, we use Montage, CyberShake and Sipht these three most common scientific workflow templates and one randomly generated workflow template to conduct our experiments. The structures of these workflows are shown in Fig. 9.

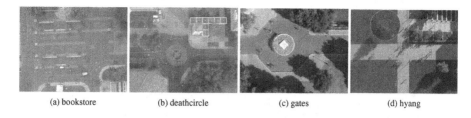

Fig. 8. The aerial view of experiment scenes.

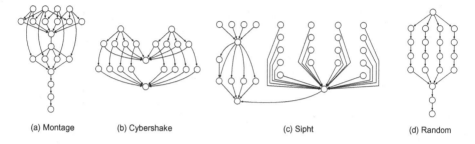

Fig. 9. Workflow templates used for experiment.

We first evaluate the exploitation ability of MDEWS and its peers towards the problem of workflow scheduling. Figure 10 shows the trade-off between reliability and makespan (i.e., pareto fronts) get by MDEWS and it peers. We consider NSGA-II, MOPSO, MOEA\D and SPEA2 as baseline algorithms because they are most widely used methods in solving multi-object workflow scheduling problem. It can be clearly seen that MDEWS can yield better pareto fronts in most cases, NSGA-II performs close to ours, then SPEA2 and MOPSO, MOEA\D cannot get a full pareto front in some cases such as *deathcicle* scene with Sipht workflow and *hyang* scene with Montage workflow and Sipht workflow.

To make a more clear comparison, HV values (a comprehensive evaluation index used to judge a multi-objective optimization method, the higher the better) are used to show the differences between MDEWS and it peers. As shown in Table 1, the ratios are used to offer a clearer comparison, for example, the HV improvement ratio can be calculated as follows:

$$\frac{HV(MDEWS)}{HV(Peer)} - 1 \tag{19}$$

Similarly, the comparison ratio of algorithms' runtime can be calculated as follows:

$$\frac{RunTime(Peer)}{RunTime(MDEWS)} \tag{20}$$

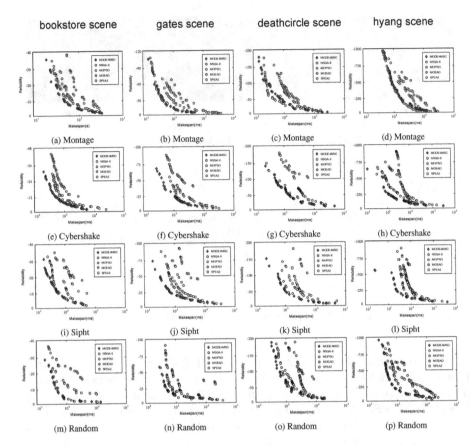

Fig. 10. Trade-off between reliability and makespan for different multi-objective optimization methods.

It can be seen that, MDEWS achieves a higher HV value in most cases. This advantage is achieved in a way that the individuals, with the help of MDEWS, are more likely to learn from a group of other individuals with high reliability and low makespan estimates, rather than learning from a single individual with seemingly highest optimality achieved by traditional algorithms. It also shows that MDEWS achieves higher time-efficiency in all cases (2 times faster than MOPSO on average, 3 times faster than MODE and SPEA2 on average).

We also compared MDEWS with traditional non-prediction-based workflow scheduling algorithms (EMS-C [24], PSO [15], and CEGA [12]) which assume stable resource reliability, in terms of the success rate of workflow execution. As shown in Fig. 11, our proposed approach clearly outperforms non-prediction-based approaches in most cases. To be specific, the success rate achieved by our method is 3.74%, 9.25%, 12.35% and 20.51% higher success rate than EMS-C on average in four scenes, respectively; 5.20%, 9.51%, 12.33% and 23.40% higher than PSO; and 6.05%, 10.94%, 15.02% and 23.07% higher than CEGA. Note that

Table 1. HV and runtime comparison between MDEWS and traditional MOO Algorithms

Scene	Workflow	NSGA-II		MOPSO		MOEA\D		SPEA2	
		HV	Runtime	HV	Runtime	HV	Runtime	HV	Runtime
Bookstore	Montage	−5.81%	1.21	−8.27%	1.51	121.48%	2.43	14.65%	3.04
	Cybershake	−0.47%	1.27	−17.85%	1.62	19.54%	2.68	8.57%	3.28
	Siph	−4.90%	1.31	117.54%	1.69	83.80%	2.93	5.03%	3.43
	Random	1.03%	1.28	13.10%	1.75	117.25%	3.01	61.59%	3.62
Gates	Montage	8.58%	1.13	27.69%	1.51	23.03%	2.06	11.57%	2.73
	Cybershake	10.12%	1.24	21.95%	1.59	61.14%	2.31	8.84%	2.89
	Siph	5.70%	1.25	64.75%	1.65	127.19%	2.94	73.91%	3.41
	Random	8.39%	1.31	36.12%	1.69	117.53%	3.03	42.62%	3.63
Deathcircle	Montage	3.91%	1.07	23.96%	1.54	77.42%	2.13	112.93%	2.63
	Cybershake	7.34%	1.14	77.49%	1.63	132.18%	2.31	16.40%	2.91
	Siph	12.63%	1.19	113.15%	1.65	61.91%	2.53	53.67%	3.13
	Random	6.01%	1.22	124.37%	1.71	143.27%	2.61	22.01%	3.28
Hyang	Montage	−0.24%	1.05	4.76%	1.52	141.57%	2.15	71.87%	2.77
	Cybershake	9.09%	1.12	23.97%	1.53	188.79%	2.26	13.75%	2.90
	Siph	11.75%	1.15	131.06%	1.55	131.22%	2.40	23.77%	3.15
	Random	17.03%	1.20	140.38%	1.59	117.80%	2.51	27.31%	3.32

these four experiment scenes are with vary density of mobile users (*bookstore* about 3428 per km^2, *gates* about 4981 per km^2, *deathcicle* about 6571 per km^2, and *hyang* about 8714 per km^2). The experimental results also show that the more crowded of the mobile users, the better MDEWS performs than traditional non-prediction-based methods.

When the density of mobile users in an MRSC is sparse, there are few resource providers for requester to choice, therefore baseline algorithms perform close to ours. But when the density of mobile users become dense, there will be more resource providers available. Under such condition, traditional non-prediction methods trend to schedule tasks into providers with high reliability and low makespan to meet deadline constrain and QoS requirement. However, as we mentioned earlier, mobile users are keep moving during the resource provisioning, which means that providers which are reliable at the current state are not guaranteed to keep its reliability in the future. In contrast, with the help of user position prediction and reliability evaluation methods, MDEWS prefers to choice those service providers with good expected reliability and acceptable response time. In this way the knowledges and patterns behind users' movement are properly mined to generate more reliable schedules.

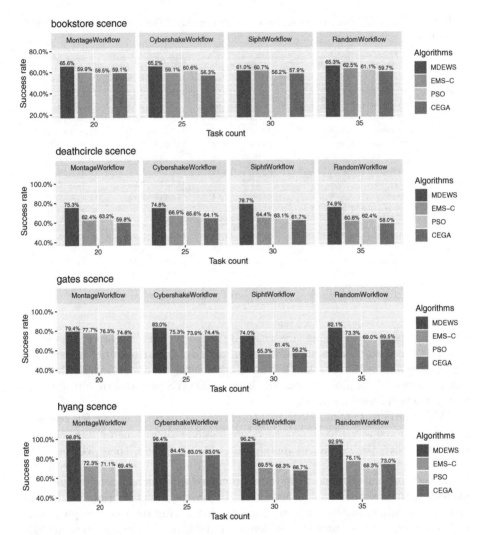

Fig. 11. Success rate comparison between MDEWS and non-prediction-based approaches.

7   Conclusion and Further Work

This paper targets at the problem of unreliable workflow scheduling under the mobile computing environment, and proposed a position-prediction-based mobile workflow scheduling approach in the context of MANET. We evaluate the reliability of mobile resource providers dynamically based on predicted user positions through a Gaussian mixture prediction model. Mobile providers are selected and schedule plans are generated by an evolutionary multi-objective optimization algorithm.

We consider hard deadline in this paper, as future work, we plan to consider soft deadline constraints (where makespan is allowed to exceed a threshold value with a bounded given rate) and introduce corresponding algorithms to generate run-time schedules. Besides, some learning-based method will be employed to achieve a smarter scheduling.

References

1. Abrishami, S., Naghibzadeh, M., Epema, D.H.: Deadline-constrained workflow scheduling algorithms for infrastructure as a service clouds. Future Gener. Comput. Syst. **29**(1), 158–169 (2013)
2. Alahi, A., Goel, K., Ramanathan, V., Robicquet, A., Fei-Fei, L., Savarese, S.: Social LSTM: human trajectory prediction in crowded spaces. In: Proceedings of the IEEE Conference on Computer Vision and Pattern Recognition, pp. 961–971 (2016)
3. Balasubramanian, N., Balasubramanian, A., Venkataramani, A.: Energy consumption in mobile phones: a measurement study and implications for network applications. In: Proceedings of the 9th ACM SIGCOMM Conference on Internet Measurement, pp. 280–293. ACM (2009)
4. Deb, K.: Multi-objective optimization. In: Burke, E., Kendall, G. (eds.) Search Methodologies, pp. 403–449. Springer, Boston (2014). https://doi.org/10.1007/978-1-4614-6940-7_15
5. Giordano, S., Puccinelli, D.: The human element as the key enabler of pervasiveness. In: The 10th IFIP Annual Mediterranean Ad Hoc Networking Workshop (Med-Hoc-Net) 2011, pp. 150–156. IEEE (2011)
6. ISI: Pegasus Project. https://confluence.pegasus.isi.edu (2018). Accessed 26 Aug 2018
7. Kharbash, S., Wang, W.: Computing two-terminal reliability in mobile ad hoc networks. In: Wireless Communications and Networking Conference 2007, WCNC 2007. pp. 2831–2836. IEEE (2007)
8. Li, W., Xia, Y., Zhou, M., Sun, X., Zhu, Q.: Fluctuation-aware and predictive workflow scheduling in cost-effective infrastructure-as-a-service clouds. IEEE Access **6**, 61488–61502 (2018)
9. Liu, S., Cao, H., Li, L., Zhou, M.: Predicting stay time of mobile users with contextual information. IEEE Trans. Autom. Sci. Eng. **10**(4), 1026–1036 (2013)
10. Maheswaran, M., Ali, S., Siegal, H., Hensgen, D., Freund, R.F.: Dynamic matching and scheduling of a class of independent tasks onto heterogeneous computing systems. In: Proceedings of the Eighth Heterogeneous Computing Workshop 1999, (HCW 1999), pp. 30–44. IEEE (1999)
11. Mao, M., Humphrey, M.: Auto-scaling to minimize cost and meet application deadlines in cloud workflows. In: 2011 International Conference for High Performance Computing, Networking, Storage and Analysis (SC), pp. 1–12. IEEE (2011)
12. Meena, J., Kumar, M., Vardhan, M.: Cost effective genetic algorithm for workflow scheduling in cloud under deadline constraint. IEEE Access **4**, 5065–5082 (2016)
13. Microsoft: RSSI. https://msdn.microsoft.com/en-us/library/windows/desktop/ms706828%28v=vs.85%29.aspx (2018). Accessed 26 Aug 2018
14. Qiao, S., Han, N., Zhu, W., Gutierrez, L.A.: TraPlan: an effective three-in-one trajectory-prediction model in transportation networks. IEEE Trans. Intell. Transp. Syst. **16**(3), 1188–1198 (2015)

15. Rodriguez, M.A., Buyya, R.: Deadline based resource provisioningand scheduling algorithm for scientific workflows on clouds. IEEE Trans. Cloud Comput. **2**(2), 222–235 (2014)
16. Sakellariou, R., Zhao, H.: A hybrid heuristic for DAG scheduling on heterogeneous systems. In: Proceedings of the 18th International Parallel and Distributed Processing Symposium 2004, p. 111. IEEE (2004)
17. Schad, J., Dittrich, J., Quiané-Ruiz, J.A.: Runtime measurements in the cloud: observing, analyzing, and reducing variance. Proc. VLDB Endow. **3**(1–2), 460–471 (2010)
18. Song, C., Qu, Z., Blumm, N., Barabási, A.L.: Limits of predictability in human mobility. Science **327**(5968), 1018–1021 (2010)
19. Stanford-CVGL: Stanford Drone Dataset. http://cvgl.stanford.edu/projects/uav_data/ (2018). Accessed 26 Aug 2018
20. Topcuoglu, H., Hariri, S., Wu, M.-Y.: Performance-effective and low-complexity task scheduling for heterogeneous computing. IEEE Trans. Parallel Distrib. Syst. **13**(3), 260–274 (2002)
21. Wu, Q., Ishikawa, F., Zhu, Q., Xia, Y., Wen, J.: Deadline-constrained cost optimization approaches for workflow scheduling in clouds. IEEE Trans. Parallel Distrib. Syst. **28**(12), 3401–3412 (2017)
22. Xia, Y., Zhou, M., Luo, X., Pang, S., Zhu, Q.: Stochastic modeling and performance analysis of migration-enabled and error-prone clouds. IEEE Trans. Ind. Inf. **11**(2), 495–504 (2015)
23. Zeng, H., Cheung, Y.M.: A new feature selection method for Gaussian mixture clustering. Pattern Recogn. **42**(2), 243–250 (2009)
24. Zhu, Z., Zhang, G., Li, M., Liu, X.: Evolutionary multi-objective workflow scheduling in cloud. IEEE Trans. Parallel Distrib. Syst. **27**(5), 1344–1357 (2016)

Worker Recommendation with High Acceptance Rates in Collaborative Crowdsourcing Systems

Mingchu Li[1,2], Xiaomei Sun[1,2], Xing Jin[1,2(✉)], and Linlin Tian[1,2]

[1] School of Software Technology, Dalian University of Technology,
Dalian 116620, China
{mingchul,linlint}@dlut.edu.cn, sunxiaomeijob@mail.dlut.edu.cn,
jinxingdlut@gmail.com
[2] Key Laboratory for Ubiquitous Network and Service Software of Liaoning Province,
Dalian 116620, China

Abstract. Crowdsourcing has emerged as a popular Internet-based collaboration paradigm, in which tasks published by requesters can be economically and efficiently accomplished by crowd workers. To ensure the quality of service (QoS) provided by crowd workers, requesters are more likely to assign tasks to trustworthy workers, therefore, trust have played an important role in the design of worker recommendation mechanisms in crowdsourcing systems. Most existing studies focus on the trust that requesters place on workers, however, which would suffer the low-acceptance problem because crowd workers would refuse to participate in tasks published by low-trustworthy requesters with a great probability. In order to address the low-acceptance problem, in this paper, by using biased matrix factorization, we proposed a novel worker recommendation mechanism which can evaluate mutual trust relationship between requesters and workers. And also, to accurately measure the matching degree between tasks and workers, a comprehensive and practical task matching mechanism has been presented by incorporating time matching, skill matching, payment matching, and location matching. Finally, extensive simulations and real data experiments highlight the performance of our proposed worker recommendation mechanism.

Keywords: Collaborative crowdsourcing · Trust ·
Worker recommendation · Matrix factorization · Task matching

1 Introduction

In recent years, numerous websites and applications have been widely applied in various fields to realize the great potential of the crowdsourcing, including Wikipedia[1], Amazon Mechanical Turk (AMTurk)[2], Gigwalk[3], etc. In

---

[1] https://www.wikipedia.org/.
[2] https://www.mturk.com/.
[3] http://www.gigwalk.com/.

© ICST Institute for Computer Sciences, Social Informatics and Telecommunications Engineering 2019
Published by Springer Nature Switzerland AG 2019. All Rights Reserved
H. Gao et al. (Eds.): CollaborateCom 2018, LNICST 268, pp. 53–74, 2019.
https://doi.org/10.1007/978-3-030-12981-1_4

crowdsourcing systems, participators are required to work collaboratively to accomplish a crowdsourcing task published by a requesters.

One important aspect of crowdsourcing systems is worker recruitment, which directly affects the success of crowd tasks. There are numerous literatures available studying on worker recruitment, which can be generally classified into two methodologies: billboard and worker recommendation.

Billboard. Tasks are distributed on specialized crowdsourcing platforms that crowd workers can participate in their preferred tasks on a first-come-first-served basis. Due to the simplicity of being implemented in practice, the billboard methodology has been widely used in industry filed, for example, AMTurk and Gigwalk. However, the billboard methodology suffers the following two potential disadvantages.

(1) Long time waiting. In large-scale crowdsourcing platforms, a worker need to spend much time on picking a proper task to participate when confronting with numerous and varied tasks. Subsequently, requesters would take a long time to recruit enough workers, which is not allowed for real-time tasks. As illustrated in [17], less than 15% tasks can be completed within one hour in AMTurk.

(2) Low quality service. Due to the open and dynamic nature of crowdsourcing systems, in which there exists various workers with diverse abilities and reliability properties. To guarantee the quality of service (QoS) provided by workers, reputation systems have been naturally introduced in. However, in practice, the deployment of reputation systems encounter the challenge of reputation inflation. As illustrated in [5], workers' acceptance rates (one form of reputation value) on AMTurk are often above 97%, regardless of workers' performances. Therefore, in the billboard methodology, requesters would receive low QoS due to the fact that the truth ability and reliability of workers cannot be clearly figured out.

Worker Recommendation. To address the above two potential disadvantages in billboard, worker recommendation [1–3, 6, 13, 22, 24, 26, 31, 34] has been proposed as the alternative methodology for worker recruitment, in which proper workers will be automatically recommended basing on requesters' requirements. According to existing literatures, the worker recommendation based approach normally consists two parts: task matching and trust evaluation. Task matching part assesses the probability of a worker to complete a specific task, in terms of skills, payments, etc. Trust evaluation part describes the confidence that a requester places on a worker to finish a task expectably. To ensure the QoS, high-trustworthy workers are more likely to be selected as participants.

In bilateral rating crowdsourcing systems, for example, Zhubajie[4] (a famous crowdsourcing platform in China), requesters and workers will rate each other after transactions. Let us consider the following scenario: (1) Requester A trusts worker B by giving a positive rating for her acceptable performance; (2) Due

---

[4] http://www.zbj.com/.

to the delay in payment, B would place a distrust on A by giving a negative rating. Regarding to a new crowd task published by A, B would be unceasingly recommended to A as a potential participant with great probability by using traditional worker recommendation mechanisms which only consider the trust that requesters place on workers. However, due to the distrust that worker B places on requester A, B would refuse to take the task, which will lead a low-acceptance problem of crowd tasks. In order to address the low-acceptance problem, the trust evaluation from workers to requesters should also be studied, however, which has not been considered before in the domain of crowd worker recruitment, to the best of our knowledge.

Our major contributions in this paper are listed as follows.

- We propose a comprehensive task matching mechanism by incorporating time matching, skill matching, payment matching, and location matching. To our best of knowledge, no other previous work has considered in all aspects.
- Basing on biased matrix factorization [12], we firstly propose three methods (Method 1, Method 2 and Method 3) to evaluate the mutual trust relationships between requesters and workers.
- We propose a top-K worker recommendation framework for worker recruitment by combining the proposed task matching mechanism and trust evaluation methods, which also consider the cold start problem.
- We conduct extensive simulations and experiments over a large public dataset to assess the performance of our proposed worker recommendation framework. Results demonstrate that our methods outperform all baselines in terms of trust evaluation and acceptance rates.

The remainder of this paper is organized as follows. In Sect. 2, we give an overview of related work on worker recommendation methodology. In Sect. 3, we present the system model in detail. In Sect. 4, we propose a top-K worker recommendation framework. In Sect. 5, we provide simulations and real data experiments to illustrate the performance of the proposed methods. In Sect. 6, we conclude this paper.

2 Related Work

We particularly review the related work on worker recommendation methodology in terms of task matching and trust evaluation.

Task Matching. In [3], workers and tasks are matched based on an underlying taxonomy that workers' interests are taken into account. Goel et al. [6] consider heterogeneous set of tasks requiring certain skills, and each worker has certain expertise and interests, and then a bipartite graph has been used to represent all the possible assignments between the workers and the tasks. Ye et al. [31] present a context-aware task matching model by incorporating task type and reward amount. Yuen et al. [34] propose a TaskREC framework based on a unified probabilistic matrix factorization to predict the worker-task rating.

Kurve et al. [13] consider the task difficulty and worker skill in the assignment of crowd tasks. In [22], Schnitzer et al. reveal that task similarities act as a key parameter for building a task matching mechanism. Tong et al. [24] study the online mobile micro-task allocation problem in spatial crowdsourcing by considering the time matching and location matching. In CrowdAdvisor [1] framework, five metrics are defined in worker recommendation: Personal Characteristics, Freelancer-Job compatibility, Freelancer-Client compatibility, Freelancer-Team compatibility and Freelancer Motivation. Yuan et al. [33] observe that people usually exhibit different levels of busyness at different contexts in task assignment, and then propose a model to predict people's interruptibility intensity. By using the fuzzy c-Means algorithm, Alsayasneh et al. [2] match workers with personalized and diverse tasks. [20] and [27] consider the timeliness in task matching. In the spatial crowdsourcing scenario, Wang et al. [26] propose an effective heuristic methods to solve the multi-objective optimization in which task coverage is maximized and incentive cost is minimized.

However, these above researches don't study the trust relationship between requesters and workers.

Trust Evaluation. To ensure the QoS provided by crowd worker, reputation and trust mechanisms have been widely used. In [32], Yu et al. propose a social welfare optimizing reputation-aware decision-making approach for task assignment. EndorTrust [28] has been proposed as a reputation system which not only assess but also predict the trustworthiness of contributions without wasting workers' effort. Ye et al. [30] extend their previous work [31] by considering the trust that requesters place on workers, in which random walker algorithm has been adopted. To address the issue of assign reliable workers to nearby tasks in spatial crowdsourcing, Hassan and Curry [7] use semi-bandit learning to reduce the uncertainty of worker reliability. Xiang et al. [29], propose a trust-based mixture of Gaussian processes (GP) model to yield accurate estimations in the presence of various types of misbehaving workers, in which a Bayesian trust framework has been developed to maintain and update trustworthiness of crowd workers. In [9], a new comprehensive model for computing reputation scores of workers has been proposed by considering direct and indirect evaluations expressed by requesters.

However, these above researches don't consider the trust that workers place on requesters, hence they will confront with the low-acceptance problem of crowd tasks.

3   System Model

In this paper, we consider a bilateral rating crowdsourcing system with M requesters and N workers. And each crowd task need multiple workers to participate in, for example, monitoring the traffic [4].

3.1   Task Features

Heterogeneous tasks are studied in our crowdsourcing model, which can be characterized by the following six attributes.

Time Tolerance. Different tasks may have different time tolerance, e.g., some of them need to be finished immediately [23,24]. We use $T_{tolerance} \in [0,1]$ to represent the time tolerance of a certain task, smaller value of $T_{tolerance}$ intuitively denotes the more urgent need to be accomplished. Different from [23,24], we explicitly compute the value of $T_{tolerance}$ by using the following formula:

$$T_{tolerance} = \frac{2}{1 + e^{t_{now} - t_{finish}}} - 1,$$

where t_{now} and t_{finish} stand for the published time of a task and the deadline for calling for workers, respectively, hence, we have $t_{now} < t_{finish}$. The published time can be automatically obtained once a certain task has been distributed, and the deadline would be directly described by the task owner.

Task Type. Heterogeneous crowd tasks [1,3,6,22] are considered in this paper. It is assumed that there are k categories of skills in our model. We use a vector $T_{type} = [t_1, t_2, \ldots, t_k]$ to represent the type of a certain task. Element t_i has a binary value: 1 means the i-th skill is required to finish the given task, otherwise, 0 means the i-th skill is not required.

Skill Level. For a specific task type, heterogeneous skill levels should also be studied [13,18]. We use $T_{level} = [l_1, l_2, \ldots, l_k]$ to represent the requirement of skill level for a certain task. Each element l_i has a continuous value from 0 to 1, the higher value of skill level intuitively carries the greater demand of proficiency in i-th skill, e.g., $l_i \geq 0.9$ means that an expert is required.

In sum, $T_{requirement} = [r_1, r_2, \ldots, r_k]$ has been defined to represent the requirement of skill and skill level of a certain task, simultaneously, where $r_i = t_i * l_i$.

Task Payment. Every worker who finishes a certain task will gain a payment p from the task owner [1,3,5,26,31,34,37]. The payment p will be directly described by the requester once the task is published.

Geographical Location. Regarding to a certain task in spatial crowdsourcing systems [7,23,24,26], the attribute of geographical location should be considered, which has been represented as $T_{geography} = [g_1, g_2]$, where g_1 and g_2 correspond to the longitude and latitude coordinates, respectively.

Number of Workers. Generally, for the crowdsourcing paradigm, multiple workers are needed to complete a complex crowd task [17,18,24,26,31,37]. And in this paper, we use a variable T_n to represent the required number of workers for a certain task.

3.2   Worker Features

Subsequently, heterogeneous worker is studied in our crowdsourcing model, which can be characterized by the following five attributes.

Degree of Busyness. Intuitively, a busier worker would participate in a new task with a smaller probability. Therefore, to develop an efficient worker recommendation mechanism, the degree of busyness for each worker should be evaluated [25,33]. Different from pervious studies, the busyness of a worker is explicitly presented. We use a variable $W_{busyness} \in [0, 1]$ to represent the degree of busyness of a certain worker. The higher value of $W_{busyness}$ implies the much busier the worker will be. Intuitively, a busier worker would participate in a new task with a smaller probability. The degree of busyness can be calculated as:

$$W_{busyness} = \frac{1}{1 + e^{-\alpha_1(n_{task} - \beta_1)}},$$

where n_{task} stands for the number of tasks that the worker has participated in. Parameters α_1 and β_1 are introduced to control the value of $W_{busyness}$. Specially, n_{task} can be set as ∞, if a worker is not online.

Worker Skill. Corresponding to the heterogeneous crowd tasks, the heterogeneity of worker skill is studied [1,3,6,22]. We use $W_{skill} = [s_1, s_2, \ldots, s_k]$ to represent the skill ability of a certain worker. Each element s_i has a binary value: 1 means the i-th skill is owned by the given worker, otherwise, s_i will be fixed as 0.

Skill Proficiency. Regarding to a specific skill, a worker could be an elementary, intermediate, advanced, or expert player [1,21]. We use $W_{proficiency} = [p_1, p_2, \ldots, p_k]$ to represent the proficiency level in each skill for a certain worker. Element p_i has a continuous value from 0 to 1, the higher value of p_i illustrates the greater ability in the use of i-th skill. Based on the data of history transactions, we can formulate p_i as:

$$p_i = \frac{n_j^*}{n_j} \cdot \frac{1}{1 + e^{-\alpha_2(n_j - \beta_2)}},$$

where n_j and n_j^* stand for the number of times to use the j-th skill within previous crowd tasks and the number of acceptance times for using the j-th skill, respectively. Obviously, $\frac{n_j^*}{n_j}$ means the acceptance rate in the use of the j-th skill. And $\frac{1}{1 + e^{-\alpha_2(n_j - \beta_2)}}$ is monotonically increasing with the increase of n_j. Therefore, we get that p_i is proportional to the acceptance rate and practical experience.

In sum, $T_{ability} = [a_1, a_2, \ldots, a_k]$ is defined to represent the skill and skill proficiency of a certain worker, simultaneously, where $a_i = s_i * p_i$.

Bid. We use $W_{bid} = [b_1, b_2, \ldots, b_k]$ to represent the expected bid of a certain worker [1,3,5,26,31,34,37], its element b_i means the expected reward that will be obtained from a requester by using the i-th skill during a crowd task.

Geographical Location. Each worker in our crowdsourcing model has the information of geographical location [7,23,24,26], which can be represented as $W_{geography} = [gw_1, gw_2]$, where gw_1 and gw_2 denote the longitude and latitude coordinates of a certain worker, respectively.

3.3 Trust Relationship

Trust from Requesters to Workers. Generally, in crowdsourcing systems, after worker j finishes a task published by requester i, j would get a positive rating from i, if i is satisfied with j's performance, otherwise, j will get a negative rating. Based on the ratings provided by requesters, we can compute the trust from requesters to workers. Subsequently, a matrix $RW = [rw_{i,j}]_{M,N}$ can be built to represent the trust relationship from requesters to workers, and its element $rw_{i,j}$ denotes the specific trust that requester i places in worker j. The detailed method to compute the trust can be found in the Eigentrust [10,16].

Trust from Workers to Requesters. Due to the open nature of crowdsourcing systems, there also may exist untrustworthy requesters who may refuse to offer payments to workers or be extremely critical on workers' performances, etc. To protect the benefits of workers, the reliability of requesters should also be considered.

In a bilateral rating crowdsourcing system, with the similar procedure in building RW matrix, $WR = [wr_{j,i}]_{N,M}$ matrix can be constructed basing on the feedbacks from workers to requesters over transactions, its entry $wr_{j,i}$ denotes the specific trust that worker j places on requester i.

4 Worker Recommendation Framework

In this section, we discuss the proposed worker recommendation framework in detail in terms of task matching, trust evaluation and top-K recommendation.

4.1 Task Matching

To pick proper workers for a certain task, we firstly propose a comprehensive task matching mechanism by incorporating time matching, skill matching, payment matching, and location matching.

Time Matching. Naturally, to satisfy the time requirement of requesters in completing tasks, an urgent task should be matched with an idle worker.

Given the time tolerance feature $T_{tolerance}$ of a certain task t and the busyness feature $W_{busyness}$ of a certain worker w. As discussed in Sects. 3.1 and 3.2, the higher value of $T_{tolerance}$ means the task can wait more time to be performed, and the lower value of $W_{busyness}$ means the worker has more available time to take a new task. Therefore, the time matching can be qualitatively defined as: $T_{tolerance} - W_{busyness}$. Intuitively, it could be assumed that w can finish t in time if $T_{tolerance} - W_{busyness} > 0$, otherwise, t is not suitable for w to participate in. By normalizing $T_{tolerance} - W_{busyness}$, we can model the time matching as:

$$M_{time} = \frac{1}{1 + e^{-\alpha_3(T_{tolerance} - W_{busyness} + \beta_3)}}, \tag{1}$$

where parameters α_3 and β_3 are used to regulate the value of M_{time}.

Skill Matching. To improve the QoS of crowd tasks, a complex task should be assigned to skilled workers.

$T_{requirement}$ and $W_{ability}$ are given as the skill requirement of a certain task t and the skill ability of a certain worker w, respectively. Considering the fact that there may exist similarity between two different skills, e.g., a worker could has the probability of coding *Python* program if she/he is skilled in writing *C++* program. To have a comprehensive view of workers' ability, we propose a matrix $Corr = [c_{i,j}]_{k,k}$ to represent the similarity of any two skills, its entry $c_{i,j}$ denotes the similarity between i-th and j-th skill. How to build the $Coor$ matrix is out of scope of this paper, one feasible way is to use the clustering technology [14,15,35,36].

We assume a_i as the explicit ability of a certain worker, and a_j is assumed as the implicit ability which has not been used before. Basing on the similarity between tasks, a_j can be updated as:

$$a_j^* = \max_i a_i \cdot c_{i,j}.$$

Thus, a comprehensive ability $W_{ability}^c = [a_1^c, a_2^c, \ldots, a_k^c]$ of worker w over k skills can be proposed, where $a_i^c = a_i$ for explicit ability, and $a_j^c = a_j^*$ for implicit ability. Intuitively, the skill matching m_{skill} can be defined as:

$$m_{skill} = \frac{W_{ability}^c \cdot T_{type}}{T_{requirement} \cdot T_{type}},$$

the higher value of m_{skill} implies the better matching degree. Particularly, $m_{skill} = 0$ means totally mismatching, while $m_{skill} = 1$ means completely matching. By normalizing m_{skill}, we get the skill matching degree as:

$$M_{skill} = \frac{1}{1 + e^{-\alpha_4(m_{skill} - 1 - \beta_4)}}. \tag{2}$$

The term $m_{skill} - 1$ has the similar function as $T_{tolerance} - W_{busyness}$ plays in Eq. (1), a well skill matching M_{skill} will be obtained if $m_{skill} - 1 \geq 0$, otherwise, worker w is regarded as not very suitable for task t.

Payment Matching. The amount of payment plays an important role that workers would like to receive payments from requesters that are not less than their expectation.

Given the task payment feature p of a certain task t and the bid feature W_{bid} of a certain worker w. We use $b = T_{type} \cdot W_{bid}$ to represent the total expected bid of worker w for task t. Intuitively, the difference value $p - b$ can be used to measure the payment matching, the higher value of the difference illustrates the greater probability of w to participate in t. However, this definition of payment matching suffers some vulnerability. Let us consider the following two scenarios.

Scenario 1: The payment $p = 99$ for task t, and the total bid $b = 100$ for worker w.

Scenario 2: The payment $p = 9$ for task t, and the total bid $b = 10$ for worker w.

Obviously, the payment matching in Scenario 1 is better than in Scenario 2, however, $p - b$ obtains the same value 1 in these two scenarios. To address this issue, we revise the payment matching by introducing the total expected bid as the denominator:

$$m_{payment} = \frac{p - b}{b}.$$

By normalizing $m_{payment}$, the skill matching degree can be formally defined as:

$$M_{payment} = \frac{1}{1 + e^{-\alpha_5(m_{payment} - \beta_5)}}. \tag{3}$$

Location Matching. To decrease the cost of moving for involved workers, location matching should be considered.

Given the geographical location $T_{geography} = [g_1, g_2]$ of a certain task and $W_{geography} = [gw_1, gw_2]$ of a certain worker, we can use Euclidean distance to measure the distance between $T_{geography}$ and $W_{geography}$:

$$d = \sqrt{(g_1 - gw_1)^2 + (g_2 - gw_2)^2},$$

the smaller value of d demonstrably illustrates the higher matching in location, and then the location matching $M_{location}$ can be formulated as:

$$M_{location} = e^{-\alpha_6 \cdot d}, \tag{4}$$

which has a continuous value from 1 to 0 with the increasing of d.

Personalized Matching Degree. Different requesters may have different priorities in task matching. For example, requesters who have high demand in QoS would assign more weight to skill matching. In order to propose a personalized matching degree, we introduce a weight vector $W = [w_1, w_2, w_3, w_4]$ which can be directly defined by the task owner, its entries w_1, w_2, w_3 and w_4 denote the weight of M_{time}, M_{skill}, $M_{payment}$ and $M_{location}$, respectively. By using the harmonic mean equation, the personalized matching degree can be obtained:

$$M = \frac{1}{\frac{w_1}{M_{time}} + \frac{w_2}{M_{skill}} + \frac{w_3}{M_{payment}} + \frac{w_4}{M_{location}}} \tag{5}$$

$$s.t. \sum_i w_i = 1$$

4.2   Trust Evaluation

In order to address the low-acceptance problem in traditional worker recommendation mechanisms, in this paper, we firstly develop a novel worker recommendation mechanism by further considering the trust that workers place on requesters.

Background on Matrix Factorization

Due to the data sparsity that each requester have only interacted with a small fraction of the whole workers, and vice versa, therefore, it is a critical problem to inference the trust relationship between unknown requesters and workers. As we know, matrix factorization (MF) [8,12] is one of the most effective recommendation techniques to predict users' unknown preferences from the observed users' preferences, which can be intuitively used to solve the trust evaluation problem in this paper.

Given the RW matrix of dimensions $|M| \times |N|$, the principle of MF based approach is to decompose RW into two low-dimensional matrices: requester-feature matrix $P \in \mathbb{R}^{d \times M}$ and worker-feature matrix $Q \in \mathbb{R}^{d \times N}$, simultaneously. And then, the trust that requester i places on worker j can be predicted by the inner product of requester-specific vector p_i and worker-specific vector q_j, i.e., $\widehat{rw}_{i,j} = p_i^T \cdot q_j$, where $p_i \in \mathbb{R}^d$ and $q_j \in \mathbb{R}^d$ are the i-th and j-th column of P and Q, respectively. By considering requester/worker biases, the basic MF model can be extended to the biasedMF [12]:

$$\widehat{rw}_{i,j} = \mu + b_i + b_j + p_i^T \cdot q_j, \tag{6}$$

where μ is the average trust value in RW, b_i and b_j are the biases of requester i and worker j. We use $\Omega(RW)$ to denote the locations of observed trust rating in RW matrix. The parameters p_i, q_j, b_i and b_j can be learned by minimizing a loss function as follows:

$$\mathcal{L}_{RW} = \frac{1}{2} \sum_{(i,j)\in\Omega(RW)} (\widehat{rw}_{i,j} - rw_{i,j})^2 + \Theta(q_i, p_j, b_i, b_j), \tag{7}$$

where $\Theta(q_i, p_j, b_i, b_j)$ means the regularization term:

$$\Theta(q_i, p_j, b_i, b_j) = \frac{\lambda}{2}(\sum_i \|q_i\|_F^2 + \sum_j \|p_j\|_F^2 + \sum_i b_i^2 + \sum_j b_j^2).$$

where λ is a parameter to control model complexity and to avoid over-fitting. Moreover, with the consideration of implicit ratings, the biasedMF model can be extended to SVD++ [11] which can well improve the predictive accuracy. However, SVD++ is very costly in computing, to balance the accuracy and the run time, in this paper, biasedMF is adopted to design the worker recommendation system.

Matrix Factorization on Both RW and WR Matrices

By considering both RW and WR matrices, we propose a novel worker recommendation mechanism which evaluates mutual trust relationship between requesters and workers, and then address the low-acceptance problem of crowd task.

Depending on the number of shared common feature spaces, our proposed worker recommendation mechanism can categorized into three methods:

Method 1: RW and WR share no common feature space.
Method 2: RW and WR share one common feature space. Without loss of generality, RW and WR are assumed to share a common requester-feature space.
Method 3: RW and WR share two common feature spaces.

Method 1. In this case, as shown in Fig. 1, RW and WR share no common feature space, therefore, we can have the following four feature matrices:

$P \in \mathbb{R}^{d \times M}$: the requester feature matrix of the RW matrix.
$Q \in \mathbb{R}^{d \times N}$: the worker feature matrix of the RW matrix.
$U \in \mathbb{R}^{d \times M}$: the requester feature matrix of the WR matrix.
$V \in \mathbb{R}^{d \times N}$: the worker feature matrix of the WR matrix.

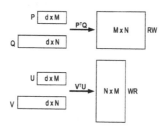

Fig. 1. Method 1.

Similar with the biasedMF model on RW matrix, regarding to WR matrix, the trust that worker k places on requester l can be predicted as:

$$\widehat{wr}_{k,l} = \eta + b_k + b_l + v_k^T \cdot u_l, \tag{8}$$

where η is the average trust value in WR matrix, b_k and b_l are the biases of worker k and requester l. And then, the parameters u_l, v_k, b_l and b_k can be learned by minimizing a loss function as follows:

$$\mathcal{L}_{WR}^{(1)} = \frac{1}{2} \sum_{(k,l) \in \Omega(WR)} (\widehat{wr}_{k,l} - wr_{k,l})^2 + \Theta(u_l, v_k, b_l, b_k). \tag{9}$$

By combining $\mathcal{L}_{RW}$ and $\mathcal{L}_{WR}^{(1)}$, we get an overall loss function for both RW and WR matrices:

$$\mathcal{L}^{(1)} = \mathcal{L}_{RW} + \mathcal{L}_{WR}^{(1)}. \tag{10}$$

In order to obtain a local minimization of the given loss function, we perform the following gradient descents:

$$
\begin{aligned}
\frac{\partial \mathcal{L}^{(1)}}{\partial b_i} &= \sum_{j \in R(i)} e_{i,j}^{RW} + \lambda b_i, & \frac{\partial \mathcal{L}^{(1)}}{\partial b_j} &= \sum_{i \in R^+(j)} e_{i,j}^{RW} + \lambda b_j \\
\frac{\partial \mathcal{L}^{(1)}}{\partial b_k} &= \sum_{l \in W(k)} e_{k,l}^{WR} + \lambda b_k, & \frac{\partial \mathcal{L}^{(1)}}{\partial b_l} &= \sum_{k \in W^+(l)} e_{k,l}^{WR} + \lambda b_l \\
\frac{\partial \mathcal{L}^{(1)}}{\partial p_i} &= \sum_{j \in R(i)} e_{i,j}^{RW} q_j + \lambda p_i, & \frac{\partial \mathcal{L}^{(1)}}{\partial q_j} &= \sum_{i \in R^+(j)} e_{i,j}^{RW} p_i + \lambda q_j \\
\frac{\partial \mathcal{L}^{(1)}}{\partial u_l} &= \sum_{k \in W^+(l)} e_{k,l}^{WR} v_k + \lambda u_l, & \frac{\partial \mathcal{L}^{(1)}}{\partial v_k} &= \sum_{l \in W(k)} e_{k,l}^{WR} u_l + \lambda v_k
\end{aligned}
\tag{11}
$$

Regarding to RW matrix, $R(i)$ denotes the set of workers that requester i has rated, and $R^+(j)$ denotes the set of requesters who have rated worker j. Regarding to WR matrix, $W(k)$ denotes the set of requesters that worker k has rated, and $W^+(l)$ denotes the set of workers who have rated requester l. We use $e_{i,j}^{RW} = \widehat{rw}_{i,j} - rw_{i,j}$ and $e_{k,l}^{WR} = \widehat{wr}_{k,l} - wr_{k,l}$ to denote the trust prediction error from requester i to worker j and from worker k to requester l, respectively.

Method 2. In this case, as shown in Fig. 2, RW and WR share a common requester-feature space, therefore, we can have the following three feature matrices:

$P \in \mathbb{R}^{d \times M}$: the requester feature matrix of the RW and WR matrices.
$Q \in \mathbb{R}^{d \times N}$: the worker feature matrix of the RW matrix.
$V \in \mathbb{R}^{d \times N}$: the worker feature matrix of the WR matrix.

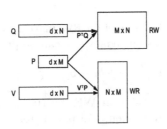

Fig. 2. Method 2.

Subsequently, the trust that worker k places on requester i can be predicted as:

$$
\widehat{wr}_{k,i} = \eta + b_k + b_i + v_k^T \cdot p_i.
\tag{12}
$$

By minimizing a loss function as follows, the parameters p_i, v_k, b_i and b_k can be learned:

$$\mathcal{L}_{WR}^{(2)} = \frac{1}{2} \sum_{(k,i)\in\Omega(WR)} (\widehat{wr}_{k,i} - wr_{k,i})^2 + \Theta(p_i, v_k, b_i, b_k). \qquad (13)$$

By considering both $\mathcal{L}_{RW}$ and $\mathcal{L}_{WR}^{(2)}$, the overall loss function can be formulated as:

$$\mathcal{L}^{(2)} = \mathcal{L}_{RW} + \mathcal{L}_{WR}^{(2)}. \qquad (14)$$

Similarly, gradient descents can be used to achieve the minimization of the given loss function:

$$
\begin{aligned}
\frac{\partial \mathcal{L}^{(2)}}{\partial b_i} &= \sum_{j\in R(i)} e_{i,j}^{RW} + \sum_{k\in W^+(i)} e_{k,i}^{WR} + \lambda b_i \\[1ex]
\frac{\partial \mathcal{L}^{(2)}}{\partial b_j} &= \sum_{i\in R^+(j)} e_{i,j}^{RW} + \lambda b_j, \qquad \frac{\partial \mathcal{L}^{(2)}}{\partial b_k} = \sum_{l\in W(k)} e_{k,l}^{WR} + \lambda b_k \\[1ex]
\frac{\partial \mathcal{L}^{(2)}}{\partial p_i} &= \sum_{j\in R(i)} e_{i,j}^{RW} q_j + \sum_{k\in W^+(i)} e_{k,i}^{WR} v_k + \lambda p_i \\[1ex]
\frac{\partial \mathcal{L}^{(2)}}{\partial q_j} &= \sum_{i\in R^+(j)} e_{i,j}^{RW} p_i + \lambda q_j, \qquad \frac{\partial \mathcal{L}^{(2)}}{\partial v_k} = \sum_{i\in W(k)} e_{k,i}^{WR} p_i + \lambda v_k
\end{aligned}
\qquad (15)
$$

Method 3. In this case, as shown in Fig. 3, RW and WR share two common spaces, therefore, we can have the following two feature matrices:

$P \in \mathbb{R}^{d \times M}$: the requester feature matrix of the RW and WR matrices.
$Q \in \mathbb{R}^{d \times N}$: the worker feature matrix of the RW and WR matrices.

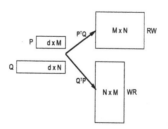

Fig. 3. Method 3.

By using the biasedMF model, regarding to WR matrix, the trust that worker j places on requester i can be predicted as:

$$\widehat{wr}_{j,i} = \eta + b_j + b_i + q_j^T \cdot p_i. \qquad (16)$$

The parameters b_i, b_j, p_i and q_j can be learned by minimizing the following loss function:

$$\mathcal{L}_{WR}^{(3)} = \frac{1}{2} \sum_{(j,i) \in \Omega(WR)} (\widehat{wr}_{j,i} - wr_{j,i})^2 + \Theta(p_i, q_j, b_i, b_j). \tag{17}$$

With the consideration of both $\mathcal{L}_{RW}$ and $\mathcal{L}_{WR}^{(3)}$, we get an overall loss function as:

$$\mathcal{L}^{(3)} = \mathcal{L}_{RW} + \mathcal{L}_{WR}^{(3)}. \tag{18}$$

By using gradient descents, we can obtain a local minimization of the given loss function:

$$
\begin{aligned}
\frac{\partial \mathcal{L}^{(3)}}{\partial b_i} &= \sum_{j \in R(i)} e_{i,j}^{RW} + \sum_{j \in W^+(i)} e_{j,i}^{WR} + \lambda b_i \\
\frac{\partial \mathcal{L}^{(3)}}{\partial b_j} &= \sum_{i \in R^+(j)} e_{i,j}^{RW} + \sum_{i \in W(j)} e_{j,i}^{WR} + \lambda b_j \\
\frac{\partial \mathcal{L}^{(3)}}{\partial p_i} &= \sum_{j \in R(i)} e_{i,j}^{RW} q_j + \sum_{j \in W^+(i)} e_{j,i}^{WR} q_j + \lambda p_i \\
\frac{\partial \mathcal{L}^{(3)}}{\partial q_j} &= \sum_{i \in R^+(j)} e_{i,j}^{RW} p_i + \sum_{i \in W(j)} e_{j,i}^{WR} p_i + \lambda q_j
\end{aligned}
\tag{19}
$$

By using the above three methods, we can predict the trust relationship between requesters and workers, overall, the trust that requester i places on worker j can be described as:

$$rw_{i \to j} = \begin{cases} rw_{i,j} & \text{if } i \text{ has a direct trust with } j \\ \widehat{rw}_{i,j} & \text{otherwise.} \end{cases} \tag{20}$$

And the trust that the worker j places on requester i can be described as:

$$wr_{j \to i} = \begin{cases} wr_{j,i} & \text{if } j \text{ has a direct trust with } i \\ \widehat{wr}_{j,i} & \text{otherwise.} \end{cases} \tag{21}$$

4.3 Top-K Recommendation

Regarding to a certain task published by requester i, we can compute a recommendation score for any participant worker j by combining task matching and trust evaluation as:

$$rs_j = M_j \cdot rw_{i \to j} \cdot wr_{j \to i}. \tag{22}$$

An then, the top-K workers with the highest scores will be recommended to requester i. In order to address the cold start problem, with fixed 10% probability, newcomer workers will be recommended to participated in crowd tasks.

5   Performance Evaluation

In this section, we have implemented simulations and real data experiments to illustrate the performance of the proposed top-K worker recommendation mechanism. Our codes have been built on *Surprise*[5] which is a Python scikit for building and analyzing recommender systems.

5.1   Experimental Settings

Trust Evaluation. Epinions[6] is a well-known publicly data set to illustrate who-trust-whom, which contains: 131828 users and 841372 edges. Each edge has two values: 5 means trust and 1 means distrust. From the original Epinions data set, we randomly extract a subgraph which contains 2000 different users, and 1000 users of them are regarded as requesters, while the rest users are regarded as workers. By only considering weighted edges between requesters and workers, RW and WR can be respectively built. We use 5-fold cross-validation for learning and testing. And each measurement is averaged over 10 instances.

Top-K Worker Recommendation. To conduct our experiments on the proposed top-K worker recommendation mechanism, the task features and worker features are indispensably needed. However, such data sets have not been presented to the public by any existing crowdsourcing platform, as a result, we generate synthetic crowd transactions to evaluate the performance of our mechanisms in terms of acceptance rate.

Table 1. Parameters setting

Parameter	Commentate	Value
M	# of requesters	1000
N	# of workers	1000
k	# of the skills	10
T_n	# of required workers for a certain task	20
α_i	Regulate the value of task matching	1
β_i	Regulate the value of task matching	-1.38
w_i	Weight of task matching	0.25

The base settings that apply for simulations are summarized in Table 1. Considering that there should be a high matching degree (e.g., 80%) if the task feature is exactly matched with the worker feature, hence, α_i and β_i are fixed to be 1 and -1.38 as shown in Table 1. In our simulations, time tolerance $T_{tolerance}$ for

---

[5] https://pypi.org/project/scikit-surprise/1.0.3/.
[6] https://snap.stanford.edu/data/soc-sign-epinions.html.

a certain task follows an uniform distribution $U(0,1)$. Same with other studies [19,29], normal distributions are adopted to realize the settings of the rest task and worker features, e.g., T_{type} and W_{skill}.

The crowdsourcing system is modeled as a discrete time slot system. At the start of each time slot, the features of workers and requesters will be re-initialized. And within one time slot, we assume that each requester will publish a crowd task with a certain probability, e.g., 10%. And the result is averaged over 100 time slots.

5.2   Experimental Results

Results in Trust Evaluation

Baseline Methods. Regarding to trust evaluation, we compare the performance of our proposed mechanisms with the following approaches.

- UserKnn: An user based collaborative filtering method which implements the prediction based on the preferences of similar users.
- ItemKnn: An item based collaborative filtering method which implements the prediction based on item rating similarity.
- Non-biased MF: A basic matrix factorization method.
- Biased MF: An extension of non-biased MF by considering users' biases.

Metrics. Mean absolute error (MAE) and root-mean-square error (RMSE) have been used as the evaluation metrics.

Results. Firstly, we take Method 1 as the example to study the impact of λ on predictive accuracy. As shown in Fig. 4, we tune the parameter λ in the range $\{0.01, 0.02, 0.04, 0.08, 0.16\}$ while fixing $d = 10$, and it is observed that Method 1 achieves the best predictive accuracy with RMSE $= 0.875$ when $\lambda = 0.02$ is adopted. The result clearly illustrates that a proper value of λ can improve the performance on predictive accuracy. Similar results can also be obtained with different settings of d or different methods.

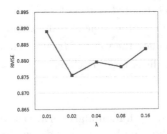

Fig. 4. The impact of λ on predictive accuracy [$d = 10$].

Then, we study the impact of d on predictive accuracy. The result is presented in Fig. 5 in terms of RMSE when Method 1 has been adopted. We tune the parameter d in the range $\{5, 10, 15, 20, 25\}$ while fixing $\lambda = 0.02$. It is indicated that the optimal setting of d is 10, under which case Method 1 achieves the best performance. Moreover, the other settings of λ or methods have similar performance trends.

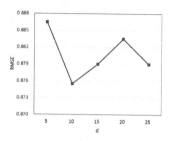

Fig. 5. The impact of d on predictive accuracy $[\lambda = 0.02]$.

Finally, we report the results of our proposed three methods compared to the baselines. The results are obtained based on: $\lambda = 0.02$ and $d = 10$. As shown in Table 2, it is illustrated that our algorithms (Method 1, Method 2, and Method 3) obviously outperform the baselines in terms of RMSE and MAE. Specifically, it is interesting to find that (1) Method 1 achieves the best performance among the three methods, and (2) Method 3 performs better than Method 2. A reasonable explanation for the first finding is that: Method 1 has four explicit feature spaces which can efficiently recover the observed RW and WR matrices. The possible reason for the second finding could be that: Method 3 which simultaneously and unbiasedly consider the RW and WR matrices would has a better prediction than Method 2 which biasedly learns the common requester-feature space.

Table 2. Performance comparison in trust evaluation

	RMSE	MAE
Method 1	0.875	0.475
Method 2	0.975	0.531
Method 3	0.939	0.522
UserKnn	1.092	0.577
ItemKnn	1.082	0.582
Non-biased MF	1.496	1.051
Biased MF	1.047	0.559

Results in Top-K Worker Recommendation

Baseline Methods. The top-K worker recommendation mechanism is a general framework, in which the trust evaluation part can adopt UserKnn, ItemKnn, Non-biased MF and Biased MF, respectively, as the baseline methods.

Metric. Considering the scenario that a worker j has been recommended to a requester i. A valid recommendation instance can be defined as: (1) i accepts to employ j as the participant, meanwhile, (2) j accepts to take i as the employee. And then, the acceptance rate (AR) of a worker recommendation method can be calculated as:

$$AR = \frac{\# \ of \ valid \ recommendation \ instances}{\# \ of \ total \ recommendation \ instances}.$$

In this paper, we adopt the AR as the evaluation metric.

Results. A valid recommendation instance is determined by two factors in our crowdsourcing model: task matching and mutual trust evaluation. An overall matching degree which is derived from Eq. (5) is used as the criterion to measure whether a certain worker is suitable for a specifical task. In experiments, we use the overall matching degree to represent the probability that a certain worker is successfully matched with a published task in respect of task matching. Further, to evaluate the mutual trust between requesters and workers, we introduce a threshold value θ to measure the condition of trust establishment among users: (A) Requester i will trust worker j if $\widehat{rw}_{i,j} \geq 5 - \theta$; (B) Conversely, worker j will trust requester i if $\widehat{wr}_{j,i} \geq 5 - \theta$. In experiment, the mutual trust between requester i and worker j is assumed to be established if condition (A) and condition (B) are both satisfied. Table 3 shows the result of performance comparison in terms of AR, where we tune the parameter θ in the range of $\{4, 2, 1, 0.5, 0.25\}$. It is observed that: (1) AR would gradually decrease with the decreasing value of θ because valid recommendation instances are more difficult to happen if the condition of trust establishment becomes more critical; (2) Due to the better performances in trust evaluation, our proposed algorithms (Method 1, Method 2 and Method 3) evidently have higher values of AR than the baselines especially for the smaller value of θ.

Which part contribute more? In the proposed top-K worker recommendation framework, two parts have been included: task matching and mutual trust evaluation. Definitely, it is necessary to explore which part contributes more on the overall performance. In the following, we introduce:

- OTM: A top-K worker recommendation framework that **O**nly consists the **T**ask **M**atching part.
- OTE: A top-K worker recommendation framework that **O**nly consists the mutual **T**rust **E**valuation part.

The results are presented in Fig. 6 while fixing $\theta = 1$. Obviously, the worker recommendation mechanisms that consider both task matching and trust evaluation significantly perform better than the mentioned compared methods. And,

Table 3. Performance comparison in term of acceptance rate

	$\theta = 4$	$\theta = 2$	$\theta = 1$	$\theta = 0.5$	$\theta = 0.25$
Method 1	0.915	0.844	0.801	0.721	0.547
Method 2	0.915	0.843	0.796	0.696	0.492
Method 3	0.915	0.843	0.794	0.701	0.500
UserKnn	0.915	0.818	0.733	0.603	0.258
ItemKnn	0.915	0.820	0.739	0.615	0.302
Non-biased MF	0.915	0.754	0.589	0.395	0.250
Biased MF	0.915	0.829	0.745	0.624	0.436

OTM with $AR = 0.569$ performs better that OTE with $AR = 0.185$, which illustrates that task matching part plays an more important role than trust evaluation part in the design of worker recommendation mechanisms. Similar results will also be obtained with the different settings of θ.

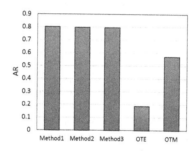

Fig. 6. Performance comparison with OTM and OTE [$\theta = 1$].

6 Conclusion

In this paper, based on biased matrix factorization, we specifically and firstly consider the mutual trust between requesters and workers which can address the low-acceptance problem in traditional worker recommendation mechanisms. Further, a comprehensive task matching mechanism has been proposed by incorporating time matching, skill matching, payment matching, and location matching, no other previous work has considered in all aspects. Extensive simulations and experiments over a large public dataset demonstrate that our proposed worker recommendation methods outperform all baselines in terms of trust evaluation and acceptance rates.

Limitations and Future Work

This paper has the following fundamental limitations.

(i) Requesters and workers considered in this paper are assumed to honestly feedback their opinions, however, which is not true in real-life crowdsensing systems. In our future work, we will further study the reliability of ratings provided by the requesters and workers.

(ii) The fundament of our proposed top-K worker recommendation mechanism is to calculate an overall recommendation score, however, it is difficult to determine the weight of each feature in practice. In our future work, we will use multi-objective optimization to extend this work.

Acknowledgements. The paper is supported by National Nature Science foundation of China under grant Nos.: 61572095 and 61877007.

References

1. Abhinav, K., Dubey, A., Jain, S., Virdi, G., Kass, A., Mehta, M.: CrowdAdvisor: a framework for freelancer assessment in online marketplace. In: ICSE, pp. 93–102. IEEE (2017)
2. Alsayasneh, M., et al.: Personalized and diverse task composition in crowdsourcing. TKDE **30**(1), 128–141 (2018)
3. Difallah, D.E., Demartini, G., Cudré-Mauroux, P.: Pick-a-crowd: tell me what you like, and I'll tell you what to do. In: WWW, pp. 367–374. ACM (2013)
4. Farkas, K., Nagy, A.Z., Tomás, T., Szabó, R.: Participatory sensing based real-time public transport information service. In: PERCOM Workshops, pp. 141–144. IEEE (2014). https://doi.org/10.1109/PerComW.2014.6815181
5. Gaikwad, S.N.S., et al.: Boomerang: rebounding the consequences of reputation feedback on crowdsourcing platforms. In: UIST, pp. 625–637. ACM (2016)
6. Goel, G., Nikzad, A., Singla, A.: Matching workers expertise with tasks: incentives in heterogeneous crowdsourcing markets. In: NIPS (2013)
7. ul Hassan, U., Curry, E.: Efficient task assignment for spatial crowdsourcing: a combinatorial fractional optimization approach with semi-bandit learning. Expert Syst. Appl. **58**, 36–56 (2016)
8. He, X., Zhang, H., Kan, M.Y., Chua, T.S.: Fast matrix factorization for online recommendation with implicit feedback. In: SIGIR, pp. 549–558. ACM (2016)
9. Jabeur, N., Karam, R., Melchiori, M., Renso, C.: A comprehensive reputation assessment framework for volunteered geographic information in crowdsensing applications. Ubiquit. Comput. 1–17 (2018)
10. Kamvar, S.D., Schlosser, M.T., Garcia-Molina, H.: The Eigentrust algorithm for reputation management in P2P networks. In: WWW, pp. 640–651. ACM (2003)
11. Koren, Y.: Factor in the neighbors: scalable and accurate collaborative filtering. TKDD **4**(1), 1–24 (2010)
12. Koren, Y., Bell, R., Volinsky, C.: Matrix factorization techniques for recommender systems. Computer **42**(8), 30–37 (2009)
13. Kurve, A., Miller, D.J., Kesidis, G.: Multicategory crowdsourcing accounting for variable task difficulty, worker skill, and worker intention. TKDE **27**(3), 794–809 (2015)

14. Liu, H., Zhang, X., Zhang, X.: Possible world based consistency learning model for clustering and classifying uncertain data. Neural Netw. **102**, 48–66 (2018)
15. Liu, H., Zhang, X., Zhang, X., Cui, Y.: Self-adapted mixture distance measure for clustering uncertain data. Knowl.-Based Syst. **126**, 33–47 (2017)
16. Lu, K., Wang, J., Li, M.: An Eigentrust dynamic evolutionary model in P2P file-sharing systems. Peer Peer Netw. Appl. **9**(3), 599–612 (2016)
17. Pu, L., Chen, X., Xu, J., Fu, X.: Crowdlet: optimal worker recruitment for self-organized mobile crowdsourcing. In: INFOCOM, pp. 1–9. IEEE (2016)
18. Qiao, L., Tang, F., Liu, J.: Feedback based high-quality task assignment in collaborative crowdsourcing. In: AINA, pp. 1139–1146. IEEE (2018)
19. Rendle, S., Freudenthaler, C., Gantner, Z., Schmidt-Thieme, L.: BPR: Bayesian personalized ranking from implicit feedback. In: Proceedings of the Twenty-Fifth Conference on Uncertainty in Artificial Intelligence, pp. 452–461. AUAI Press (2009)
20. Safran, M., Che, D.: Real-time recommendation algorithms for crowdsourcing systems. Appl. Comput. Inform. **13**(1), 47–56 (2017)
21. Schall, D., Satzger, B., Psaier, H.: Crowdsourcing tasks to social networks in BPEL4People. World Wide Web **17**(1), 1–32 (2014)
22. Schnitzer, S., Neitzel, S., Schmidt, S., Rensing, C.: Perceived task similarities for task recommendation in crowdsourcing systems. In: WWW, pp. 585–590 (2016)
23. Song, T., et al.: Trichromatic online matching in real-time spatial crowdsourcing. In: ICDE, pp. 1009–1020. IEEE (2017)
24. Tong, Y., She, J., Ding, B., Wang, L., Chen, L.: Online mobile micro-task allocation in spatial crowdsourcing. In: ICDE, pp. 49–60. IEEE (2016)
25. Wang, J., Wang, F., Wang, Y., Zhang, D., Lim, B.Y., Wang, L.: Allocating heterogeneous tasks in participatory sensing with diverse participant-side factors
26. Wang, L., Yu, Z., Han, Q., Guo, B., Xiong, H.: Multi-objective optimization based allocation of heterogeneous spatial crowdsourcing tasks. TMC **17**(17), 1637–1650 (2018)
27. Wang, Y., Tong, X., He, Z., Gao, Y., Wang, K.: A task recommendation model for mobile crowdsourcing systems based on dwell-time. In: BDCloud-SocialCom-SustainCom, pp. 170–177. IEEE (2016)
28. Wu, C., Luo, T., Wu, F., Chen, G.: EndorTrust: an endorsement-based reputation system for trustworthy and heterogeneous crowdsourcing. In: GLOBECOM, pp. 1–6. IEEE (2015)
29. Xiang, Q., Zhang, J., Nevat, I., Zhang, P.: A trust-based mixture of Gaussian processes model for reliable regression in participatory sensing. In: IJCAI, pp. 3866–3872 (2017)
30. Ye, B., Wang, Y.: CrowdRec: trust-aware worker recommendation in crowdsourcing environments. In: ICWS, pp. 1–8. IEEE (2016)
31. Ye, B., Wang, Y., Liu, L.: Crowd trust: a context-aware trust model for worker selection in crowdsourcing environments. In: ICWS, pp. 121–128. IEEE (2015)
32. Yu, H., Shen, Z., Miao, C., An, B.: A reputation-aware decision-making approach for improving the efficiency of crowdsourcing systems. In: AAMAS, pp. 1315–1316 (2013)
33. Yuan, F., Gao, X., Lindqvist, J.: How busy are you?: Predicting the interruptibility intensity of mobile users. In: CHI, pp. 5346–5360. ACM (2017)
34. Yuen, M.C., King, I., Leung, K.S.: TaskRec: a task recommendation framework in crowdsourcing systems. NPL **41**(2), 223–238 (2015)

35. Zhang, X., Liu, H., Zhang, X.: Novel density-based and hierarchical density-based clustering algorithms for uncertain data. Neural Netw. **93**, 240–255 (2017)
36. Zhang, X., Liu, H., Zhang, X., Liu, X.: Novel density-based clustering algorithms for uncertain data. In: AAAI, pp. 2191–2197 (2014)
37. Zhang, X., Xue, G., Yu, R., Yang, D., Tang, J.: Truthful incentive mechanisms for crowdsourcing. In: INFOCOM, pp. 2830–2838. IEEE (2015)

Cost-Aware Targeted Viral Marketing with Time Constraints in Social Networks

Ke Xu and Kai Han[(✉)]

School of Computer Science and Technology, Suzhou Institute for Advanced Study,
University of Science and Technology of China, Hefei, People's Republic of China
ustcxk@mail.ustc.edu.cn, hankai@ustc.edu.cn

Abstract. Online social networks have been one of the most effective platforms for marketing which is called *viral marketing*. The main challenge of viral marketing is to seek a set of k users that can maximize the expected influence, which is known as Influence Maximization (IM) problem. In this paper, we incorporate *heterogeneous costs and benefits* of users and *time constraints*, including *time delay* and *time deadline* of influence diffusion, in IM problem and propose *Cost-aware Targeted Viral Marketing with Time constraints* (CTVMT) problem to find the most cost-effective seed users who can influence the most relevant users within a time deadline. We study the problem under IC-M and LT-M diffusion model which extends IC and LT model with time constraints. Since CTVMT is NP-hard under two models, we design a **BCT-M** algorithm using two new benefit sampling algorithms designed for IC-M and LT-M respectively to get a solution with an approximation ratio. To the best of our knowledge, this is the first algorithm that can provide approximation guarantee for our problem. Our empirical study over several real-world networks demonstrates the performances of our proposed solutions.

Keywords: Social network · Influence maximization ·
Time constraints

1 Introduction

Recently, online social networks rapidly increasing to involve billions of active users, which makes it play an important role in daily life. For instance, online social networks such as Facebook, Twitter, have become critical platforms for marketing and advertising. Information and invention can propagate wildly over the network with the help of word-of-mouth effect and we call this marketing *Viral Marketing*. There is an extensively studied problem named Influence Maximization (IM) in viral marketing. It aims to find a seed set of k influential users in a social network so that the number of people influenced by seed set, named *influence spread*, can be maximum.

In their seminal paper, Kempe *et al.* [1] formulated IM as a combinatorial optimization problem and proposed two classical diffusion models, namely, *Independent Cascade* (IC) and *Linear Threshold* (LT) model. However, Chen *et al.*

H. Gao et al. (Eds.): CollaborateCom 2018, LNICST 268, pp. 75–91, 2019.
https://doi.org/10.1007/978-3-030-12981-1_5

[2] considered that IC and LT do not fully incorporate important *temporal* factors that have been well observed in the dynamic of influence diffusion. First, the propagation of influence from one person to another may incur a certain amount of *time delay* and second, the spread of influence may be *time-critical* in practice, i.e., beyond a certain *time deadline*, the spread of influence is meaningless. We conclude the two temporal factors as *time constraints*. They proposed *Independent Cascade with Meeting events* (IC-M) and *Linear Threshold with Meeting events* (LT-M) model to capture the delay of propagation. They studied the IM problem with time constraints under IC-M and LT-M models and proposed some heuristic algorithms.

Unfortunately, except for the time constraints, IM problem still ignores the different cost when select a user into seed set and the different benefit from an influenced user. Nguyen *et al.* [3] extended the IM problem to *Cost-aware Targeted Viral Marketing* (CTVM) problem with the addition of arbitrary costs and benefits above but did not consider the time constraints.

In this paper, we propose *Cost-aware Targeted Viral Marketing with Time constraints* (CTVMT) problem connecting CTVM problem and time constraints together. In our problem settings, every user has his own cost when he is selected into seed set and also has his own benefit when he gets influenced. We aim to find a set of influential users within a predefined budget in a social network such that they can influence the largest number of targeted users when reaching the time deadline. Formally, given a social network G, a budget B and a time deadline T, let each node v_i in G refer to a user and e_{ij} which denotes the edge from v_i to v_j refer to the relationship between users. $c(v_i)$ denotes the cost of v_i and $b(v_i)$ denotes the benefit of v_i. $m(e_{ij}) \in (0,1]$ denotes the *meeting probability* that v_i can meet v_j at any time round t. The CTVMT problem is to identify a seed set $S = \{v_1, v_2, \ldots, v_j\}$ in G, such that (1) the total cost of seed set is within the budget B, i.e., $c(S) = \sum_{v_i \in S} c(v_i) \leq B$, and (2) the users in seed set incur influence spread in G and maximize total benefits when reaching the time deadline T.

CTVMT is more relevant in practice since it considers more realistic factors including time and value. We show that CTVMT problem is NP-hard and propose an algorithm named **BCT-M** to address it. Our algorithm uses the framework of **BCT** algorithm [3] which is an efficient approximation algorithm for CTVM problem. With the help of *Benefit Sampling* (BS) strategies designed elaborately for CTVMT under IC-M and LT-M model respectively, we prove that our algorithm take over guaranteeing a $(1 - 1/\sqrt{e} - \epsilon)$-approximate solution for arbitrary costs and a $(1 - 1/e - \epsilon)$-approximate solution for uniform costs. In summary, the contributions of this paper are as follows.

- We propose the *Cost-aware Targeted Viral Marketing with Time constraints* (CTVMT) problem that consider heterogeneous costs and benefits of users and time constraints, including time delay and time deadline, of influence diffusion. Our problem generalizes other viral marketing problems such as IM, CTVM and time constrained IM.

- We propose a **BCT-M** algorithm using benefit sampling strategies elaborately designed for CTVMT under IC-M and LT-M model. Our algorithm is
  efficient and has the approximation ratio which is $(1 - 1/\sqrt{e} - \epsilon)$ for arbitrary
  costs case and $(1 - 1/e - \epsilon)$ for uniform case.
- We perform extensive experiments on various real-world datasets. The performance of our algorithm demonstrate its efficiency and effectiveness in finding
  higher quality seed set satisfying our constraints.

The remainder of this paper is organized as follows. The related work is
reviewed in the next section. Section 3 introduces preliminary knowledges and
presents the definition of CTVMT problem. In Sect. 4, we present the **BCT-M**
algorithm, and in Sect. 5 we analyze the approximation ratio of our algorithm.
Section 6 presents the experimental study. Finally, the last section concludes this
paper. The key notations used in this paper are given in Table 1.

2 Related Work

Influence Maximization and CTVM. Kempe *et al.* [1] is the first to formulate
Influence Maximization (IM) as a discrete optimization problem. They create two
classical diffusion models, namely, Independent Cascade (IC) model and Linear
Threshold (LT) model. They also prove that IM problem is NP-hard under
these two models. However, because of the monotonicity and submodularity of
$\sigma(S)$, they propose a greedy algorithm to approximately solve it and prove its
approximation ratio is $(1 - 1/e - \epsilon)$.

The major bottle-neck in IM is calculating the influence spread of any given
set and it has been proved to be #P-hard [4,5]. A number of approaches have
been proposed to estimate the influence spread [6–8]. Kempe *et al.* [1] use Monte
Carlo (MC) simulation method which is computationally expensive so that it is
not efficient and scalable. Leskovec *et al.* [9] propose a mechanism named CELF
to accelerate MC method with reducing the number of times required to calculate
influence spread. Chen *et al.* [10] propose two fast heuristics algorithms, namely
DegreeDiscount and PMIA, to select users at each step of the greedy algorithm.

Recently, Borgs *et al.* [11] make a theoretical breakthrough and present an
algorithm for IM under IC model. Their algorithm (RIS) returns a $(1 - 1/e - \epsilon)$-
approximate solution with probability at least $1 - n^{-l}$. In a sequential work,
Tang *et al.* [12] reduce the running time and show that their algorithm is also
very efficient in billion-scale networks. Nguyen *et al.* [3] extend the IM problem
with the addition of assumptions that each user has his own cost and benefit.
Hence, they propose Cost-aware Targeted Viral Marketing (CTVM) problem
and design a BCT algorithm with the help of Reverse Influence Sampling (RIS)
framework. The BCT algorithm is scalable and efficient. Specifically, it has an
approximation ratio of $(1 - 1/\sqrt{e} - \epsilon)$. However, these work above do not consider
the temporal factors in reality.

Influence Maximization with Temporal Factors. Chen *et al.* [2] propose the
time-critical IM problem with two new diffusion models named IC-M and LT-M
model. They incorporate *time delay* denoted by *meeting events* and *time deadline*

of propagation into IM problem, and prove some properties of these two models. They propose two heuristic algorithms, namely MIA-M and MIA-C, for IC-M model and LDAG-M algorithm for LT-M model. Liu *et al.* [13] independently propose time-constrained IM problem and LAIC model to simulate the influence propagation process with latency information. They propose an algorithm based on influence spreading path. However, these two work do not consider the heterogeneous costs and benefits of users and their heuristic algorithms can not provide any approximation guarantee.

Table 1. Table of notations

Notation	Definition
n, n'	The number of users and edges in a network G
e_{ij}	The edge in a network from node v_i to v_j
$b(v_i)$	The benefit of v_i when it is influenced
$c(v_i)$	The cost of v_i when it is selected into seed set
$m(e_{ij})$	The meeting probability of edge e_{ij}
$w(e_{ij})$	The propagation probability of edge e_{ij}
B	The budget of seed set
T	The time deadline of influence propagation
Ω	The sum of all user benefits, $\Omega = \sum_{v \in V} b(v)$
$\sigma_T(S)$	The expected number of influenced users by seed set S
$\mathbb{B}_T(S)$	The feedback benefits of seed set S
$deg_H(S)$	The number of hyperedges incident at some user in S
c	$c = 2(e-2) \approx \sqrt{2}$
k_{max}	$k_{max} = \max\{k : \exists S \subset V, |S| = k, c(S) \leq B\}$
Υ_L^u	$\Upsilon_L^u = 8c \left(1 - \frac{1}{2e}\right)^2 \left[\ln \frac{1}{\delta} + \ln \binom{n}{k} + 2\right] \frac{1}{\epsilon^2}$
Υ_L^c	$\Upsilon_L^c = 8c \left(1 - \frac{1}{2e}\right)^2 \left[\ln \frac{1}{\delta} + k_{max} \ln n + \frac{2}{n}\right] \frac{1}{\epsilon^2}$
Λ_L	$\Lambda_L = \left(1 + \frac{e\epsilon}{2e-1}\right) \Upsilon_L$

3   Preliminaries and Problem Definition

In this section, we will introduce *Independent Cascade with Meeting events* (IC-M) and *Linear Threshold with Meeting events* (LT-M) model [2] briefly as a start. These two models have some useful properties to help us addressing the CTVMT problem. Then we present the definition of the CTVMT problem.

3.1   IC-M and LT-M Diffusion Models

Given a social network denoted by a directed graph $G = (V, E, b, c, m, w)$ in which V is a node set to denote social network users and E is a directed edge set to denote the relationship between users. $|V| = n$, $|E| = n'$ and each node $v_i \in V$ has a cost $c(v_i) > 0$ if v_i is selected into seed set and a benefit $b(v_i) \geq 0$ if v_i is influenced. Each directed edge that from v_i to v_j is denoted as $e_{ij} \in E$, and $m(e_{ij}) \in (0,1]$ denotes the *meeting probability* that v_i can meets v_j at any time t. Furthermore, Each directed edge $e_{ij} \in E$ is associated with an influence weight $w(e_{ij}) \in (0,1]$ which denotes the propagation probability from v_i to v_j, and specifically, keep that $\forall v_j \in V, \sum_{v_i \in V} w(e_{ij}) \leq 1$ for the LT-M model.

Given a network G, a *seed set* $S \subseteq V$ and a *time deadline* T, the influence propagation process in G under the IC-M and LT-M model are following respectively.

Propagation Process Under IC-M Model. The influence propagation under IC-M model happens in round $t = 0, 1, 2, 3, \ldots, T$.

- (*Begining*) At round 0, only the nodes in the seed set S are *activated*. All other nodes stay *inactive*. The cost of activating the seed set is $c(S) = \sum_{v_i \in S} c(v_i)$ and that's all we need to pay.
- (*Propagation*) At round $t \geq 1$, an active node v_i can meet its neighbor v_j with the *meeting probability* $m(e_{ij})$. Only at the first meeting events happened to its inactive neighbor v_j, v_i has the only chance to activate v_j with *propagation probability* $w(e_{ij})$.
- (*Stop Condition*) Once a node becomes activated, it remains activated in all subsequent rounds. The influence propagation process stops when *time deadline T* is reached or no more nodes can be activated.

Propagation Process Under LT-M Model. Firstly, every node $v_i \in V$ choose a *threshold* θ_{v_i} uniformly at random in $[0,1]$ independently. Next the influence propagation happens in round $t = 0, 1, 2, 3, \ldots, T$. LT-M model has the same *Begining* and *Stop Condition* as IC-M model, hence we only introduce the *Propagation* of LT-M to save space.

- (*Propagation*) At round $t \geq 1$, an active node can meet its neighbor v_j with the *meeting probability* $m(e_{ij})$, once the meeting events happened to its inactive neighbor v_j, it's an *effective* active neighbor for v_j. An inactive node v_j can be activated if and only if the weighted number of its *effective* active neighbors reaches its threshold, i.e., $\sum_{\text{effective active neighbor } v_i} w(e_{ij}) \geq \theta_{v_j}$.

The *feedback benefits* of S in G under the IC-M and LT-M model, denoted by $\mathbb{B}_T(S)$, is defined as the expected benefits sum of nodes activated finally including seed set S.

Properties of IC-M and LT-M Models. IC-M and LT-M models are shown in [2] to be equivalent to the reachability in a random graph X. We call it *sample graph with meeting events* hereafter. We will introduce the definition of this random graph of two models respectively.

For IC-M model, its *sample graph with meeting events* is defined as follows. Given a graph $G = (V, E, m, w)$, for every $e_{ij} \in E$, we flip a coin once with bias $w(e_{ij})$, and we declare the edge *live* with probability $w(e_{ij})$ or *blocked* with probability $1 - w(e_{ij})$. Then, for each meeting event (a directed e_{ij} edge and a time step $t \in [1, T]$), we flip a coin with bias $m(e_{ij})$ to determine if v_i will meet v_j at t. All coin-flips are independent. Therefore, a certain set of outcomes of all coin flips corresponds to a *sample graph with meeting events*, denoted by $X = X_M \cdot X_E$, which is a deterministic graph (with all blocked edges removed) obtained by conditioning on that particular set of outcomes, where X_M is a set of outcomes of all *meeting events* and X_E is a set of outcomes of all *live-or-blocked* identities for all edges. Since the coin-flips for meeting events and those for live-edge selections are orthogonal, and all flips are independent, any X_E on top of a X_M leads to a sample graph with meeting events X.

As for LT-M model, for each meeting event, we also flip a coin with bias $m(e_{ij})$ to determine if v_i will meet v_j at t. But for every node $v_j \in V$, we select at most one of its incoming edges at a random, such that the edge is selected with probability $w(e_{ij})$, and no edge is selected with probability $1 - \sum_{v_i} w(e_{ij})$. The selected edge is called *live* and all other edges are called *blocked*. And for the same reason, there is a *sample graph with meeting events* $X = X_M \cdot X_E$ with the same definitions of X, X_E and X_M.

Let $\mathcal{E}_I$ denote the event that I is the true realization of the corresponding random process. By Theorems 2 and 4 in [2], the influence spread of a seed set S equals the expected number of nodes reachable within deadline T from S over all sample graph with meeting events of IC-M and LT-M respectively, i.e.,

$$\sigma_T(S) = \sum_{X \sqsubseteq G} \Pr[\mathcal{E}_X] \cdot |\sigma_T^X(S)| \tag{1}$$

Where $\sqsubseteq$ denotes that the sample graph with meeting events X is generated from G with probability denoted by $\Pr[\mathcal{E}_X] = \Pr[\mathcal{E}_{X_E}] \cdot \Pr[\mathcal{E}_{X_M}]$. And $\sigma_T^X(S)$ denotes the set of nodes reachable from S in X within a deadline T.

Similarly, the *feedback benefits* of a seed set S equals the expected benefit sum of nodes reachable within deadline T from S over all sample graph with meeting events of IC-M and LT-M respectively, i.e.,

$$\mathbb{B}_T(S) = \sum_{X \sqsubseteq G} \Pr[\mathcal{E}_X] \sum_{v \in \sigma_T^X(S)} b(v) \tag{2}$$

And we can get the following theorem easily with some modifications of Theorems 2 and 4 in [2]. We omit the proof of it due to space constraint.

Theorem 1. *The feedback benefits function $\mathbb{B}_T(S)$ is monotone and submodular for an arbitrary instance of the IC-M and LT-M model, given a deadline constraint $T \geq 1$.*

3.2 Problem Definition

We propose the definition of *Cost-aware Targeted Viral Marketing with Time constraints* (CTVMT) problem in this subsection. Informally, CTVMT aims to find a set of user within a budget B in a social network such that its feedback benefits is maximum when time deadline T is reached.

Definition 1 (CTVMT). *Given a budget B and a time deadline T, the Cost-aware Targeted Viral Marketing with Time constraints (CTVMT) problem aims to select a seed set $S \subseteq V$ in a social network $G = (V, E, b, c, m, w)$:*

$$S = \arg \max_{S \subseteq V, c(S) \le B} \mathbb{B}_T(S) \tag{3}$$

where $\mathbb{B}_T(S)$ is the feedback benefits of S in G, i.e., the benefits sum of users activated finally including seed set S.

Unfortunately, the CTVMT problem is NP-hard.

Theorem 2. *The CTVMT problem is NP-hard.*

Proof. The Cost-aware Targeted Viral Marketing (CTVM) problem is NP-hard [3]. It can be regarded as a special case of the CTVMT problem where the *meeting probability* is 1, i.e., $\forall e_{ij} \in E$, $m(e_{ij}) = 1$, and the time deadline is ∞. Hence the CTVMT problem is NP-hard.

4 BCT-M Algorithm

In this section, we present **BCT-M** algorithm to solve the CTVMT problem. We will firstly introduce the RIS approach briefly, which is the foundation of our algorithm. Then we present our **BCT-M** framework [3] and two new sampling algorithms for IC-M and LT-M model respectively, namely **BS-IC-M** and **BS-LT-M** algorithm.

4.1 Summary of the RIS Approach

Reverse Influence Sampling (RIS) is a novel approach for IM to estimate the influence spread of any given nodes set proposed by Borgs *et al.* [11]. We extend the RIS framework under IC-M and LT-M models.

Given $G = (V, E, m, w)$, RIS captures the influence landscape of G through generating a hypergraph $H = (V, \{\varepsilon_1, \varepsilon_2, \dots \})$. Each hyperedge $\varepsilon_j \in H$ is a set of nodes in V and constructed as follows.

Definition 2. *Given $G = (V, E, m, w)$ and a time deadline T, a **random hyperedge** ε_j is generated from G by (1) selecting a random node $v \in V$, (2) generating a sample graph with meeting events $X \sqsubseteq G$ and (3) returning ε_j as the set of nodes that can reach v in X within the time deadline T.*

Node v in the above definition is called the *source* of ε_j and denoted by $\mathbf{src}(\varepsilon_j)$. Observe that ε_j contains the nodes that can influence its source v within time deadline T. If we generate multiple random hyperedges, influential nodes will likely appear more often in the hyperedges. Thus a seed set S that *covers* most of the hyperedges will likely maximize the influence spread $\sigma_T(S)$. Here a seed set S covers a hyperedge ε_j, if $S \cap \varepsilon_j \ne \emptyset$. This observation is captured in the following lemma in [11].

Lemma 1 ([11]). *Given $G = (V, E, m, w)$ and a random hyperedge ε_j generated from G. For each seed set S,*

$$\sigma_T(S) = n \cdot \Pr[S \text{ covers } \varepsilon_j] \tag{4}$$

Time Constrained RIS Framework. Based on the above lemma, the time constrained IM problem can be solved using the following time constrained RIS framework.

– Generate multiple random hyperedges from G using sample graph with meeting events model.
– Use the greedy algorithm for the Max-Coverage problem to find a seed set S that covers the maximum number of hyperedges and return S as the solution.

Nguyen *et al.* [3] extended RIS to estimate feedback benefits $\mathbb{B}(S)$. They modified the RIS framework to find a seed set S that covers the maximum *weighted* number of hyperedges, where the weight of a hyperedge ε_j is the benefit of the source $src(\varepsilon_j)$. Given a seed set $S \subset V$, define a random variable $x_j = b(src(\varepsilon_j)) \times 1_{(S \text{ covers } \varepsilon_j)}$, i.e., $x_j = b(src(\varepsilon_j))$ if $S \cap \varepsilon_j \neq \emptyset$ and $x_j = 0$, otherwise. They showed similar to Lemma 1, that

$$\mathbb{B}(S) = n \cdot \mathbb{E}[x_j] \tag{5}$$

We can also use the same method to extend time constrained RIS framework to estimate feedback benefits $\mathbb{B}_T(S)$, i.e.,

$$\mathbb{B}_T(S) = n \cdot \mathbb{E}[x_j] \tag{6}$$

4.2 BCT-M Framework and Two New Sampling Algorithms

We present **BCT-M** framework which is proposed in [3] and two new sampling algorithms designed for IC-M and LT-M model respectively in this subsection. We note that our algorithm with new sampling algorithms takes over the approximation ratio of **BCT** algorithm. To the best of our knowledge, our algorithm is the first one addressing the CTVMT problem with an approximation ratio.

BCT-M algorithm [3] for the CTVMT problem is presented in Algorithm 1. The algorithm uses **BS** algorithm, either **BS-IC-M** (Algorithm 3) under IC-M model or **BS-LT-M** (Algorithm 4) under LT-M model, to generate hyperedges and **Weighted-Max-Coverage** (Algorithm 2) [3] to find a candidate seed set S following the time constrained RIS framework. The algorithm runs in rounds and after each round, **Weighted-Max-Coverage** algorithm is called to select a seed set $\hat{S}$ within the budget B and stop the algorithm if the degree of $\hat{S}$ exceeds Λ_L. Otherwise, it continues to generate more hyperedges.

The **Weighted-Max-Coverage** algorithm [3] can find a maximum cover within the budget B. It considers two candidates: one is taken from greedy strategy and the other is just a node having highest coverage within the budget, then it return the one with higher coverage. Khuller *et al.* [14] proved that

Algorithm 1. BCT-M

Input: $G = (V, E, b, c, m, w), B, T, \epsilon, \delta \in (0, 1)$.
Output: Seed set S.

1   $\Upsilon_L = \Upsilon_L^u$ for uniform cost and $\Upsilon_L = \Upsilon_L^c$ otherwise ;
2   $\Lambda_L = (1 + \frac{e\epsilon}{2e-1})\Upsilon_L$;
3   $N_t = \Lambda_L, \hat{S} \leftarrow \emptyset$;
4   $H \leftarrow (V, \varepsilon = \emptyset)$;
5   **while** $deg_H(\hat{S}) < \Lambda_L$ **do**
6   **for** $j = 1$ to $N_t - |\varepsilon|$ **do**
7   Generate $\varepsilon_j \leftarrow$ **BS**(G, T) ;
8   Add ε_j to ε.
9     $N_t = 2N_t$;
10    $\hat{S} =$ **Weighted-Max-Coverage**(H, B) ;
11   Return $\hat{S}$.

Algorithm 2. Weighted-Max-Coverage

Input: Hypergraph H and Budget B.
Output: Seed set S.

1   $S \leftarrow \emptyset$;
2   **while** $P = \{v \in V \setminus S | c(v) \leq B - c(S)\} \neq \emptyset$ **do**
3     $v^* \leftarrow \arg\max_{v \in P} \frac{deg_H(S \cup \{v\}) - deg_H(S)}{c(v)}$
4     $S \leftarrow S \cup \{v^*\}$;
5   $u \leftarrow \arg\max_{\{v \in V | c(v) \leq B\}} deg_H(\{v\})$;
6   **if** $deg_H(S) < deg_H(\{u\})$ **then**
7     $S \leftarrow \{u\}$;
8   Return S.

this procedure returns a $(1 - 1/\sqrt{e} - \epsilon)$-approximate cover with arbitrary cost. However, if the node cost is uniform, this algorithm only considers the candidate obtained from greedy strategy and has the approximation factor of $(1 - 1/e - \epsilon)$.

We design two new benefit sampling strategies for IC-M and LT-M model respectively to estimate feedback benefit $\mathbb{B}_T(S)$, and we present these as **BS-IC-M** (Algorithm 3) and **BS-LT-M** (Algorithm 4) algorithm.

BS-IC-M algorithm is designed for generating a random hyperedge $\varepsilon_j \subseteq V$ under IC-M model. We use Breadth First Search (BFS) to find all the nodes can reach source node within time constraints, so we structure two queues to help out. We do some initialization and structure two empty queues firstly (line 1–2). Then we choose the source node with the probability of choosing node v_j is $P(v_j) = b(v_j)/\Omega$ where $\Omega = \sum_{v \in V} b(v)$ (line 3). This is the great deal of difference designed for the **heterogeneous benefits** situation, and we will prove that it is the foundation of the accuracy of the estimation of the feedback benefits. Insert source node v_j into candidate queue Q and insert $t_q = 0$ into

---

Algorithm 3. BS-IC-M

Input: $G = (V, E, m, w), T$.
Output: A random hyperedge $\varepsilon_j \in V$.

1 $\varepsilon_j \leftarrow \emptyset, t_q \leftarrow 0, \Delta t \leftarrow 0$;
2 Two queues $Q \leftarrow \emptyset$ and $Q_t \leftarrow \emptyset$;
3 Pick a node v_j with probability $\frac{b(v_j)}{\Omega}$;
4 Insert v_j into Q and $t_q = 0$ into Q_t ;
5 **while** $Q \neq \emptyset$ **do**
6 | $v_q \leftarrow$ extract the first node in Q ;
7 | $t_q \leftarrow$ extract the first time stamp in Q_t;
8 | Add v_q to ε_j ;
9 | Attempt to select all live-edges e_{iq} with probability $w(e_{iq})$;
10 | **foreach** *edge e_{iq} is selected* **do**
11 | | **if** $v_i \notin Q$ **then**
12 | | | Flip a coin with bias $m(e_{iq})$ until v_i meet v_q and record the number of coin-flips with Δt ;
13 | | | **if** $t_q + \Delta t \leq T$ **then**
14 | | | | Insert v_i into Q and $t_q + \Delta t$ into Q_t ;

15 Return ε_j.

---

time stamp queue Q_t (line 4), then we repeat a loop until Q is empty. In each iteration, we extract the first node in Q as v_q and the corresponding time stamp t_q in Q_t, then add v_q to ε_j (line 6–8). Next, for every edge e_{iq} that can reach v_q, we flip a coin with bias $w(e_{iq})$ to determine if it's *live* (line 9). And for every live-edge e_{iq}, if it hasn't been selected before, we flip a coin with bias $m(e_{iq})$ until v_i meets v_q and we record the number of coin-flips with Δt. If $t_q + \Delta t \leq T$ which means not reach the time deadline, we insert v_i and $t_q + \Delta t$ into Q and Q_t respectively (line 10–14). Finally, when Q is empty, we can get a hyperedge ε_j (line 15).

As for **BS-LT-M** algorithm, it's designed for LT-M model to generate a random hyperedge $\varepsilon_j \subset V$. We also do some initialization and pick the source node with probability $P(v_j) = b(v_j)/\Omega$ (line 1–2). According to the sampling graph with meeting events for LT-M model, we iteratively select node to structure ε_j. Firstly we add source node v_j into ε_j. Then we select at most one of its incoming edges at a random, such that the edge is selected with probability $w(e_{ij})$, and no edge is selected with probability $1 - \sum_{v_i} w(e_{ij})$ (line 5). If edge e_{ij} is selected, then we flip a coin with bias $m(e_{ij})$ until v_i meets v_j and also record the number of coin-flips using Δt and refresh v_j and t (line 6–9). The iteration breaks until v_j has been selected already or $t > T$ (line 3), as well as we choose no edge (line 10–11). Finally, we get a hyperedge ε_j under LT-M model (line 12).

Algorithm 4. BS-LT-M

Input: $G = (V, E, m, w), T$.
Output: A random hyperedge $\varepsilon_j \in V$.

1   $\varepsilon_j \leftarrow \emptyset, t \leftarrow 0, \Delta t \leftarrow 0$;

2   Pick a node v_j with probability $\frac{b(v_j)}{\Omega}$;

3   **while** $v_j \notin \varepsilon_j \wedge t \leq T$ **do**

4   Add v_j to ε_j ;

5   Attempt to select at most one edge e_{ij} with probability $w(e_{ij})$ or no edge with probability $1 - \sum_{v_i} w(e_{ij})$;

6   **if** *edge e_{ij} is selected* **then**

7   Flip a coin with bias $m(e_{ij})$ until v_i meet v_j and record the number of coin-flips with Δt ;

8   Set $v_j \leftarrow v_i$;

9         $t \leftarrow t + \Delta t$;

10   **else**

11   Break;

12 Return ε_j.

---

5   Approximation Analysis

In this section, we prove that **BCT-M** returns a $(1 - 1/e - \epsilon)$-approximate solution for uniform cost version of CTVMT problem and a $(1 - 1/\sqrt{e} - \epsilon)$ solution for the arbitrary cost version under IC-M and LT-M model using corresponding benefit sampling algorithm.

Our proof is following the same way of [3]. They prove the approximation ratio of **BCT** algorithm which is the framework of our algorithm. But with the new benefit sampling algorithms, namely, **BS-IC-M** and **BS-LT-M** algorithm, we need to prove that we can following the same way to get the same approximation ratio. The foundation of their proof is that each hyperedge generated by their sampling algorithm is equivalent to a random sampling using sample graph model to estimate influence spread. So we need to prove the equivalence of random hyperedges generated via **BS-IC-M** or **BS-LT-M** under IC-M or LT-M model respectively.

Lemma 2. *Any hyperedge ε_j generated via **BS-IC-M** or **BS-LT-M** is equivalent to structure a random hyperedge using sample graph with meeting events X under IC-M or LT-M model respectively.*

Proof. We only prove the situation under LT-M model and the other one can easily get using the same method. It's sufficient to prove that for any hyperedge ε_j generated via **BS-LT-M**, there exist at least one sample graph with meeting events X that can also get the same hyperedge with the same source node. It's obviously that we fix the edges in ε_j *live* and for every node $v_j \notin \varepsilon_j$, we select at most one of its incoming edges at a random, such that the edge is selected with probability $w(e_{ij})$, and no edge is selected with probability $1 - \sum_{v_i} w(e_{ij})$. And we also fix the meeting events time stamp in ε_j and flip coin with bias $m(e_{ij})$ for others in time range $t \in [1, T]$. Hence we get a sample graph with meeting events X in which using the same source node of ε_j, we can get the same random hyperedge as ε_j.

We have proved that generate hyperedges via our algorithms is equivalent to structure hyperedges using sample graph with meeting events model. The lemma above clarify that each hyperedge generated by sampling algorithm can be regarded as a random sampling to estimate $\mathbb{B}_T(S)$. And now we prove that selecting source node u with probability $P(u) = b(u)/\Omega$, we can use these hyperedges to estimate $\mathbb{B}_T(S)$ using following equation.

Lemma 3. *Given a fixed seed set $S \subseteq V$, for a random hyperedge ε_j,*

$$\Pr[\varepsilon_j \cap S \neq \emptyset] = \frac{\mathbb{B}_T(S)}{\Omega} \tag{7}$$

Proof.

$$\begin{aligned}
\mathbb{B}_T(S) &= \sum_{u \in V} \Pr_{X \sqsubseteq G}[u \in \sigma_T^X(S)]b(u) \\
&= \sum_{u \in V} \Pr_{X \sqsubseteq G}[\exists v \in S \text{ such that } v \in \varepsilon_j(u)]b(u) \\
&= \Omega \sum_{u \in V} \Pr_{X \sqsubseteq G}[\exists v \in S \text{ such that } v \in \varepsilon_j(u)]\frac{b(u)}{\Omega} \\
&= \Omega \Pr_{X \sqsubseteq G, u \in V}[\exists v \in S \text{ such that } v \in \varepsilon_j(u)] \\
&= \Omega \Pr_{X \sqsubseteq G, u \in V}[\varepsilon_j \cap S \neq \emptyset] \tag{8}
\end{aligned}$$

Lemmas 2 and 3 clarify that our benefit sampling algorithms under IC-M and LT-M model have the properties: (**1**) equivalent to random sampling graph with meeting events model and (**2**) can estimate $\mathbb{B}_T(S)$ effectively. These properties are the same as **BSA** algorithm in [3]. Based on Lemmas 2 and 3 above, we can following the same way of the proof of approximation ratio in [3] directly to get the approximation guarantee of **BCT-M** under two diffusion models. One can get the details by reviewing [3].

Theorem 3 ([3]). *Given a budget B, $0 \leq \epsilon \leq 1$ and $0 \leq \delta \leq 1$. **BCT-M** for **uniform** cost CTVMT problem under IC-M or LT-M model using corresponding benefit sampling algorithm returns a solution $\hat{S}$,*

$$\mathbb{B}_T(\hat{S}) \geq (1 - 1/e - \epsilon)OPT_T \tag{9}$$

with probability at least $(1 - \delta)$.

Theorem 4 ([3]). *Given a budget B, $0 \leq \epsilon \leq 1$ and $0 \leq \delta \leq 1$. **BCT-M** for **arbitrary** cost CTVMT problem under IC-M or LT-M model using corresponding benefit sampling algorithm returns a solution $\hat{S}$,*

$$\mathbb{B}_T(\hat{S}) \geq (1 - 1/\sqrt{e} - \epsilon)OPT_T \tag{10}$$

with probability at least $(1 - \delta)$.

6 Performance Study

6.1 Experimental Setup

Datasets. We use 4 datasets downloaded from [15] in our experiments and we show their properties in Table 2. **Epinions** was generated from a who-trust-whom online social network site Epinions.com. There is an edge from v_i to v_j if v_j trust v_i. **Email** was generated using email data from a large European research institution. There is an edge e_{ij} in the network if person v_i sent person v_j at least one email. **DBLP** construct a co-authorship network where two authors are connected if they publish at least one paper together. In the **YouTube** social network, users form friendship each other and there is an edge between friends. **DBLP** and **YouTube** are undirected, so we do some preprocess to divide one undirected edge into two directed edges with opposite directions. Hence, the total number of edges of these two datasets is twice the initial value.

Table 2. Dataset properties

Property	Epinions	Email	DBLP	YouTube
Type	Directed	Directed	Undirected	Undirected
# of nodes	75,888	265,214	425,877	1,157,806
# of edges initially	508,837	420,045	1,049,866	2,987,624
# of edges finally	508,837	420,045	2,099,732	5,975,248

Graph Parameters. we remark that our solutions are orthogonal to the techniques for generating influence probability [16]. Hence, we consider generating propagation probability in case where the probability on edge e_{ij} is set to be $\frac{1}{N_{in}(v_j)}$, where $N_{in}(v_j)$ is the in-degree of v_j. We generate each user's cost and benefit randomly in $[1, 2]$ with two decimal places. As for meeting probability, we consider two methods of genetating it. (a) **Degree.** The meeting probability on edge e_{ij} is set to be $\frac{N_{out}(v_i)}{N_{out}(v_i)+N_{out}^{max}(v)} + 0.1$, where $N_{out}(v_i)$ is the out-degree of v_i and $N_{out}^{max}(v)$ is the maximum out-degree value. The meeting probability is ranging from $(0.1, 0.6]$. (b) **Random.** The meeting probability on edge e_{ij} is chosen uniformly from the set $\{0.1, 0.2, 0.3, 0.4, 0.5, 0.6\}$. In all experiments, we set $\delta = 0.01$ and $\epsilon = 0.1$.

Performance Measures. We evaluate **BCT-M** algorithm with **BS-IC-M** and **BS-LT-M** sampling algorithm under IC-M and LT-M diffusion model respectively. For each dataset, we conduct experiments under two models respectively with the same graph parameters. We consider two performance measures, (a) **Feedback Benefits.** The benefits sum of all activated users finally. (b) **Runtime.** The runtime of algorithm. All experiments are run on Mac OS X EI Capitan system with Intel Core i5 2.6 GHz DUO core CPU and 8 GB memory.

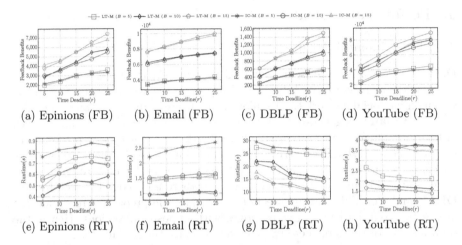

(a) Epinions (FB)   (b) Email (FB)   (c) DBLP (FB)   (d) YouTube (FB)

(e) Epinions (RT)   (f) Email (RT)   (g) DBLP (RT)   (h) YouTube (RT)

Fig. 1. Feedback benefits and runtime vs. time deadline and budget with **Degree** meeting probability (FB: Feedback Benefits; RT: Runtime)

6.2   Experimental Results

We set budget to 5,10,15 and for each budget, we range the time deadline from 5 to 25 rounds, denoted by r, to see the value of feedback benefits and runtime under two diffusion models with degree and random meeting probability respectively. We run 50 times for each budget and time deadline combination. Figures 1 and 2 show the average feedback benefits and runtime of the **BCT-M** algorithm under two diffusion models with degree and random meeting probability respectively.

Feedback Benefits. From Figs. 1 and 2, We can see that feedback benefits with more budget is larger than those with less budget, and it always getting bigger with bigger time deadline under all budget settings for all datasets. This phenomenon prove that given more budget to select seed set and given more time to spread influence, we can get more feedback benefits finally. Besides, We can see that feedback benefits under random meeting probability is a little larger than its corresponding instance under degree meeting probability. We think it is because that degree meeting probability is usually small than random meeting probability in those datasets which has so many nodes and edges.

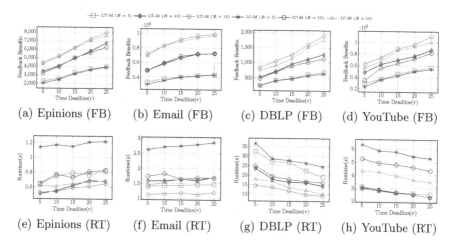

Fig. 2. Feedback benefits and runtime vs. time deadline and budget with **Random** meeting probability (FB: Feedback Benefits; RT: Runtime)

Runtime. From Figs. 1 and 2, we can see that runtime of all settings is reasonable. However, there is an interesting phenomenon that when the combination of budget and time deadline gets bigger, the runtime gets smaller. We consider the reason lies in the **BCT-M** algorithm which iteratively generate *hyperedges* to ensure the approximate accuracy. When budget and time deadline get bigger, the number of iteration gets smaller but also can reach the approximate accuracy, hence the total runtime is smaller than before.

Scalability. The runtime of **BCT-M** algorithm is reasonable even with 10^6 nodes and edges in **DBLP** and **YouTube** datasets. We also study the scalable of this algorithm and it scale well with the graph size. We omit detailed results due to space constraint.

7   Conclusion

In this paper, we incorporate the time delay and time deadline of influence diffusion which is concluded as time constraints as well as heterogeneous costs and benefits of users in a social network in IM problem to propose *Cost-aware Targeted Viral Marketing with Time constraints* (CTVMT) problem. We prove that it's NP-hard and we propose a **BCT-M** algorithm to get a solution with approximation guarantee under IC-M and LT-M model using the corresponding benefit sampling algorithm. Our empirical study over several real-world datasets demonstrates the efficiency and effectiveness of our algorithm.

Acknowledgements. This work is partially supported by National Natural Science Foundation of China (NSFC) under Grant No. 61772491, No. 61472460, and Natural Science Foundation of Jiangsu Province under Grant No. BK20161256, and Anhui Initiative in Quantum Information Technologies AHY150300.

References

1. Kempe, D., Kleinberg, J., Tardos, É.: Maximizing the spread of influence through a social network. In: Proceedings of the Ninth ACM SIGKDD International Conference on Knowledge Discovery and Data Mining, pp. 137–146. ACM (2003)
2. Chen, W., Lu, W., Zhang, N.: Time-critical influence maximization in social networks with time-delayed diffusion process. arXiv preprint arXiv:1204.3074 (2012)
3. Nguyen, H.T., Dinh, T.N., Thai, M.T.: Cost-aware targeted viral marketing in billion-scale networks. In: INFOCOM 2016-The 35th Annual IEEE International Conference on Computer Communications, pp. 1–9. IEEE (2016)
4. Chen, W., Wang, C., Wang, Y.: Scalable influence maximization for prevalent viral marketing in large-scale social networks. In: Proceedings of the 16th ACM SIGKDD International Conference on Knowledge Discovery and Data Mining, pp. 1029–1038. ACM (2010)
5. Chen, W., Yuan, Y., Zhang, L.: Scalable influence maximization in social networks under the linear threshold model. In: 2010 IEEE 10th International Conference on Data Mining (ICDM), pp. 88–97. IEEE (2010)
6. Jung, K., Heo, W., Chen, W.: IRIE: scalable and robust influence maximization in social networks. In: 2012 IEEE 12th International Conference on Data Mining (ICDM), pp. 918–923. IEEE (2012)
7. Ohsaka, N., Akiba, T., Yoshida, Y., Kawarabayashi, K.-I.: Fast and accurate influence maximization on large networks with pruned Monte-Carlo simulations. In: AAAI, pp. 138–144 (2014)
8. Goyal, A., Lu, W., Lakshmanan, L.V.S.: SIMPATH: an efficient algorithm for influence maximization under the linear threshold model. In: 2011 IEEE 11th International Conference on Data Mining (ICDM), pp. 211–220. IEEE (2011)
9. Leskovec, J., Krause, A., Guestrin, C., Faloutsos, C., VanBriesen, J., Glance, N.: Cost-effective outbreak detection in networks. In: Proceedings of the 13th ACM SIGKDD International Conference on Knowledge Discovery and Data Mining, pp. 420–429. ACM (2007)
10. Chen, W., Wang, Y., Yang, S.: Efficient influence maximization in social networks. In: Proceedings of the 15th ACM SIGKDD International Conference on Knowledge Discovery and Data Mining, pp. 199–208. ACM (2009)
11. Borgs, C., Brautbar, M., Chayes, J., Lucier, B.: Maximizing social influence in nearly optimal time. In: Proceedings of the Twenty-Fifth Annual ACM-SIAM Symposium on Discrete Algorithms, pp. 946–957. SIAM (2014)
12. Tang, Y., Xiao, X., Shi, Y.: Influence maximization: near-optimal time complexity meets practical efficiency. In Proceedings of the 2014 ACM SIGMOD International Conference on Management of Data, pp. 75–86. ACM (2014)
13. Liu, B., Cong, G., Xu, D., Zeng, Y.: Time constrained influence maximization in social networks. In: 2012 IEEE 12th International Conference on Data Mining (ICDM), pp. 439–448. IEEE (2012)
14. Khuller, S., Moss, A., Naor, J.S.: The budgeted maximum coverage problem. Inf. Process. Lett. **70**(1), 39–45 (1999)
15. Leskovec, J., Krevl, A.: SNAP datasets: stanford large network dataset collection, June 2014. http://snap.stanford.edu/data
16. Goyal, A., Bonchi, F., Lakshmanan, L.V.S.: Learning influence probabilities in social networks. In: Proceedings of the Third ACM International Conference on Web Search and Data Mining, pp. 241–250. ACM (2010)

17. Nguyen, H.T., Thai, M.T., Dinh, T.N.: Stop-and-stare: optimal sampling algorithms for viral marketing in billion-scale networks. In Proceedings of the 2016 International Conference on Management of Data, pp. 695–710. ACM (2016)
18. Nguyen, H., Zheng, R.: On budgeted influence maximization in social networks. IEEE J. Sel. Areas Commun. **31**(6), 1084–1094 (2013)
19. Ohsaka, N., Yamaguchi, Y., Kakimura, N., Kawarabayashi, K.-I.: Maximizing time-decaying influence in social networks. In: Frasconi, P., Landwehr, N., Manco, G., Vreeken, J. (eds.) ECML PKDD 2016. LNCS (LNAI), vol. 9851, pp. 132–147. Springer, Cham (2016). https://doi.org/10.1007/978-3-319-46128-1_9
20. Mossel, E., Roch, S.: On the submodularity of influence in social networks. In: Proceedings of the Thirty-Ninth Annual ACM Symposium on Theory of Computing, pp. 128–134. ACM (2007)
21. Nguyen, H.T., Nguyen, T.P., Vu, T.N., Dinh, T.N.: Outward influence and cascade size estimation in billion-scale networks. Proc. ACM Meas. Anal. Comput. Syst. **1**(1), 20 (2017)
22. Tang, Y., Shi, Y., Xiao, X.: Influence maximization in near-linear time: a martingale approach. In: Proceedings of the 2015 ACM SIGMOD International Conference on Management of Data, pp. 1539–1554. ACM (2015)
23. Song, C., Hsu, W., Lee, M.L.: Targeted influence maximization in social networks. In: Proceedings of the 25th ACM International on Conference on Information and Knowledge Management, pp. 1683–1692. ACM (2016)

Exploring Influence Maximization in Location-Based Social Networks

Shasha Li, Kai Han$^{(\boxtimes)}$, and Jiahao Zhang

School of Computer Science and Technology/Suzhou Institute for Advanced Study,
University of Science and Technology of China, Hefei, People's Republic of China
{lisa1990,jhcheung}@mail.ustc.edu.cn, hankai@ustc.edu.cn

Abstract. In the last two decades, the issue of Influence Maximization (IM) in traditional online social networks has been extensively studied since it was proposed. It is to find a seed set which has maximum influence spread under a specific network transmission model. However, in real life, the information can be spread not only through online social networks, but also between neighbors who are close to each other in the physical world. Location-Based Social Network (LBSN) is a new type of social network which is emerging increasingly nowadays. In a LBSN, users can not only make friends, but also share the events they participate in at different locations by checking in. In this paper, we aim to study the IM in LBSNs, where we consider both the influence of online and offline interactions. A two-layer network model and an information propagation model are proposed. Also, we formalize the IM problem in LBSNs and present an algorithm obtaining an approximation factor of $(1 - 1/e - \epsilon)$ in near-linear expected time. The experimental results show that the algorithm is efficient meanwhile offering strong theoretical guarantees.

Keywords: Location-based social networks · Influence maximization · Two-layer network model

1 Introduction

Social network is a network system formed by social relations among individual members. Social network analysis is based on informatics, mathematics, sociology, management, psychology and other muti-disciplinary fusion theory to study the mechanism of the formation of various social relations, analyze human behavior characteristics and understand the rule of information dissemination.

As online social networks such as Blogs, Facebook, Twitter have been widely used, they have become important platforms for people to make friends, share ideas and issue advertisements. Therefore, the analysis and research on online social networks have developed vigorously. Among them, one of the most popular topics is the issue of IM which asks for a set of k seed nodes in a network to trigger the largest cascade on a propagation model. A great deal of methods on

© ICST Institute for Computer Sciences, Social Informatics and Telecommunications Engineering 2019
Published by Springer Nature Switzerland AG 2019. All Rights Reserved
H. Gao et al. (Eds.): CollaborateCom 2018, LNICST 268, pp. 92–111, 2019.
https://doi.org/10.1007/978-3-030-12981-1_6

the IM have been extensively studied, because it provides a good way to improve marketing, branding and product adoption.

However, they tend to only consider the influence transmission in online social networks and ignore it in the physical life. In order to break this limitation, we study the issue of IM in LBSNs which considers the influence transmission in both online social networks and the physical world. We conduct our research on the datasets of Gowalla and Brightkite where users' online social relationships and location check-ins are collected. Based on the characteristics of these data, a two-layer network model is proposed. Every user has dual identities: the online and offline nodes. The relationship structure of online nodes is stable while the location of offline nodes changes over time. In this model, users can spread information in two ways: sharing through online social networks or talking to people they meet in the physical world. However, the information does not simply travel through online social networks or the physical world separately. It may propagate from online social networks to the physical world or from the physical world to online social networks, which is called cross propagation.

It is very difficult to study the IM problem in this model for two reasons. First, users' locations changing over time makes it seem impossible to study the offline influence propagation. Second, the cross propagation makes the process of influence spread more complicated. For the first problem, we get the offline influence between any two users by analyzing their historical location records, so as to obtain a stable offline relationship structure. For the second problem, we can use the graph theory to combine online and offline relationship graphs into a stable network structure. Thus a complex two-layer network model becomes a traditional network model. It becomes easy to study the issue of IM in LBSNs with the theory about influence propagation in traditional online social networks. Also, it is clear that the IM in LBSNs is an NP-hard problem, since Kempe et al. [2] have proved the NP-hard nature of IM problem for the traditional network model.

Almost all the studies about IM in LBSNs are based on empirical heuristics without any approximation guarantees. In this paper, we present a fast algorithm for the IM problem, obtaining an approximation factor of $(1 - 1/e - \epsilon)$ in near-linear expected time. The experiments on real-world datasets show that in addition to provable guarantees, our algorithm significantly outperforms node selection heuristics. Therefore, our algorithm is efficient meanwhile offering strong theoretical guarantees.

In summary, the main contributions of this paper are as follows:

- Based on the characteristics of two actual datasets named Brightkite and Gowalla, we propose a two-layer network model. This model is a good illustration of people's online and offline interactions. What's more, it connects two interaction modes very well.
- Through analyzing the network model we build and the real-world datasets, we present an influence propagation model describing how information is transmitted in both online social networks and the physical world. Also we propose several methods to convert a complex two-layer propagation model

to a traditional propagation model. Thus it becomes easy to study the issue
of IM in LBSNs with the theory about influence propagation in traditional
online social networks.

– We present an IM algorithm in LBSNs that runs in near-linear expected time
and returns $(1 - 1/e - \epsilon)$-approximate factor under the propagation model
we describe.
– The experiments we conduct on the real-world LBSN datasets confirm the
effectiveness and efficiency of our proposed algorithm.

The remainder of the paper is organized as follows. The related works are presented in Sect. 2. A two-layer network model and the formulation of the IM in
LBSNs are described in Sect. 3. An influence propagation model is proposed and
the method converting the two-layer propagation model to a traditional propagation model is introduced in Sect. 4. Section 5 provides the corresponding solution
to the IM problem. Section 6 discusses the experiment results, and we conclude
the paper in Sect. 7.

2 Related Wroks

The IM problem was first proposed by Domingos and Richardson [1]. They concluded the problem as an algorithm problem and introduced it into the field of
social network, which caused many scholars to study. Kempe et al. [2] were the
first to formulate influence maximization as a discrete optimization problem and
proved that it is an NP-hard problem. What's more, they also proposed two pio-
neering diffusion models, namely, Independent Cascade (IC) model and Linear
Threshold (LT) model, and designed a greedy algorithm with provable approximation guarantee. However, the algorithm has a serious drawback of high time
complexity. This celebrated work has motivated a lot of work to improve the
greedy algorithm. Leskovec et al. [3] proposed the Cost-Effective Lazy Forward
selection (CELF) algorithm which used the submodularity property of the influence maximization objective to greatly reduce the calculation of approximation.
Goyal et al. [4] presented the CELF++ algorithm which further improved the
calculation speed of the greedy algorithm. Chen et al. [5] also provided a further
improvement to the greedy algorithm that still had a guaranteed approximation.
At last, Borgs et al. [6] created a theoretical breakthrough in time complexity by
using a novel Reverse Influence Sampling (RIS) technique. Their algorithm still
returns a $(1 - 1/e - \epsilon)$-approximate solution with a high probability. Whereafter,
many works try to further reduce the time complexity based on the framework
Borgs et al. [6] provided. Tang et al. [7,8] and Nguyen et al. [9] used highly
sophisticated estimating methods to reduce the number of RIS samples, thus
the time complexity was reduced. The Stop and Stare (SSA) and the Dynamic
Stop and Stare (D-SSA) devised by Nguyen et al. [10] are optimal algorithms for
the IM problem at present. Another direction of research is heuristic algorithms
which have a huge advantage of running time but without any approximation
ratio guarantee. Basic heuristic algorithms are max degree algorithm, distance

centrality algorithm etc. To summarize, it can be seen from the above research status that the research about IM in traditional online social networks is quite mature.

In recent years, location-based social networks have received wide popularity. A great deal of existing works have been done to study LBSNs from multiple aspects. Cranshaw et al. [10] devised a model for predicting friendship between two users by analyzing their location trails. Pham et al. [11] and Zhang et al. [12] utilized people's movement in the real world to derive the influence among nodes. Li et al. [13] investigated the problem of Geo-Social Influence Spanning Maximization: selecting a certain number of users whose influence can maximally cover a targeted geographical region. Zhou et al. [14] carried out the research about IM in O2O model which means to conduct online promotion and bring maximum number of people to consume in the offline shops. Cai et al. [15] studied an event activation position selection problem in LBSN. Yang et al. [16] explored the IM in online and offline double-layer propagation scheme. But they introduced an empirical heuristic method without any approximation guarantees. Thus, the classical influence maximization in LBSNs is still a domain remaining to be researched.

3 Network Model and Problem Definition

3.1 Network Model

User and location are two main subjects that are closely related to LBSNs. Users visit certain locations in the physical world, leaving a corresponding location history. If we connect these locations over time, we can get the trajectory of each user. Based on these trajectories and online social networks users participate in, a network model in the LBSN can be constructed, as illustrated in Fig. 1.

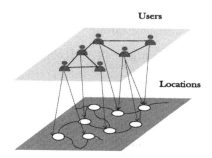

Fig. 1. The network model based on LBSNs

There are two types of nodes: user and location. The edge from the user to the location indicates that the user has accessed the location. The upper layer of the model is a user-user graph which represents the relationships among all users in an online social network. The lower layer of the model is a location-location graph where a point is a location and an edge indicates that a user has visited both nodes successively. In this paper, we assume that information may be transmitted at a certain probability from user u to v, if u and v are friends in the online social network, or u and v meet in the physical world.

In the datasets of Gowalla and Brightkite, users' online social relationships are clear. It is easy to describe the process of information transmission in online social networks. However, only the data of location check-ins is collected in the datasets and the time attribute values for these data are different, so it is difficult to describe the process of information transmission in the physical world. Even if two users are together, it is quite possible that there are certain time and position differences in their check-ins. For example, user u went on a trip with v. When they arrived at a scenic spot A, u posted a check-in. But twenty minutes later, v released another check-in when they arrived at scenic spot B. Considering this situation, within a specific time interval τ, if the distance between two users' check-in locations is less than a certain value r, we assume that they met each other once. we use $u.x$ and $u.y$ to denote the x-coordinate and y-coordinate for the user u. For two users u, v, the Euclidean distance is donated as

$$d(u,v) = \sqrt{(u.x - v.x)^2 + (u.y - v.y)^2}. \tag{1}$$

3.2 Problem Definition

In the aforementioned model we built, the information can be transmitted at a certain probability from user u to v, if u and v are friends in the online social network, or u and v meet in the physical world. In this situation, the problem can be described as follows:

Definition 1 *(Influence Maximization (IM) in LBSNs). Given a graph $G(V,E)$ which represents the structure of online social network, a dataset C which contains check-ins for all users over a given period of time and integer $k \geq 1$, the influence maximization problem is to find a set of nodes S_k containing at most k nodes that maximizes its influence spread, i.e.,*

$$S_k = \arg \max_{S:|S|=k} E[I(S)] \tag{2}$$

4   Influence Propagation Model

In this part, we first describe the online and offline propagation models respectively. In the online propagation model, we can directly adopt the two most basic and widely-studied diffusion models: Linear Threshold(LT) and Independent Cascade(IC) Models proposed by Kempe et al. [2]. In the offline propagation model, the influence rate between any two nodes can be obtained by utilizing their check-ins history. Therefore, we can construct a stable offline social graph. Then we can further adopt the classical propagation models: LT and IC models. Finally, we combine the online and offline propagation models into a traditional propagation model (Table 1, Fig. 2).

Table 1. Main notations used in the paper

Notation	Description
$G(V, E, B)$	A graph G with a node set V and a directed edge set E. Each directed edge has a weight and the set of weights is B
$b_{u,v}^{on}, b_{u,v}^{off}, b_{u,v}$	The weights between nodes u and v in online network, offline network and synthetic network, respectively
$d(u, v)$	The Euclidean distance between nodes u and v
θ_v	The minimum sum of weights of v's active neighbors in order to activate v
d_u	The degree of node u
S_k	A set of seed nodes containing at most k nodes
$I(S)$	The number of nodes S can activate
r	The maximum distance error when two people meet
τ	The maximum time error when two people meet
$m(u, v, d)$	Whether nodes u and v have met on a date d
C_u	A set of all check-ins of node u in a data set
c_u	A member of C_u, namely, $c_u \in C_u$
$m(c_u, C_v)$	Whether the check-in c_u of node u coincides with at least one check-in from the set C_v of node v
C	A set of check-ins

4.1 Online Social Network Propagation Model

We assume that the information travels via the edges of a graph. Each edge (u, v) has a weight which represents the probability that node u affects node v.

The IC model abstracts the independent interaction among people in social networks. Many simple entities are in line with the characteristics of independent transmission, such as the spread of new information in the online network or the spread of new virus among people. In the IC model, we first activate seed nodes to make them infectious, and then the process unfolds in rounds. When node v first becomes infected in step t, it has a single chance to infect each currently uninfected neighbors in step $t + 1$. Until no more nodes are infected, the process finishes. The idea of the LT model is derived from such an assumption: for the unaffected node v, more and more neighbors of v are affected as time goes on. At some point, v may also be affected. In the LT model, we assign a threshold θ_v uniformly at random to each node v from the interval $[0, 1]$. The threshold represents the minimum sum of weights of v's active neighbors to activate v. In addition, it requires each node v to meet a condition: $\sum_{w:neighbor\,of\,v} b_{w,v} \leq 1$. v is activated when the sum of weights of v's active neighbors is greater than $\theta_v : \sum_{w:neighbor\,of\,v} b_{w,v} \geq \theta_v$. The process is over until no more nodes can be infected.

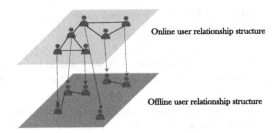

Fig. 2. The influence propagation model based on LBSNs

If we adopt the IC model, we can assign a uniform probability of b to each edge in the graph, such as 0.01 and 0.1. If we adopt the LT model, we can specify a weight of $1/d_u$ for each edge (u, v), where d_u represents the degree of node u. At the same time, we assign a threshold θ_v uniformly at random to each node v from the interval $[0, 1]$. It is worth noting that it is an open question about what model to be adopted and how to allocate weights between nodes. For example, Cai et al. [15] considered the user's interests and the times they received information from neighbors to measure the online influence between nodes.

4.2   Offline Social Network Propagation Model

From the datasets and the network model, we can only get a series of user movements over time at the lower layer of the model. Therefore, it becomes difficult to measure the influence between nodes through these trajectories.

First of all, we might think that the more often two people appear together, the more influence they have. Even when two people are together, they are less likely to submit check-ins at the same time. Also, if they are in a moving state and they submit check-ins one after another at a small time interval, their check-in locations will be somewhat different. Our solution to this problem is as follows: for two users u and v, given a time interval τ and a maximum distance value r, if $d(u, v) < r$, we think that they meet each other.

Next, we introduce several methods to calculate the influence rate between any two nodes.

We measure by days to gather statistic data. Suppose d as a date with a minimum unit of day, we define a function $m(u, v, d)$ which indicates whether node u and v have met on d. If they met on d, $m(u, v, d) = 1$. Conversely, $m(u, v, d) = 0$. It means that in all check-ins of u and v on d, as long as there's a pair of check-ins showing that they met, then $m = 1$, otherwise $m = 0$. Clearly, $m(u, v, d)$ and $m(v, u, d)$ are equal. We represent all the dates in the dataset as a set D and the sum of the dates as $|D|$. $\sum_{d \in D} m(u, v, d)$ is the total number of days on which u and v meet for the dateset D. Thus, $b_{u,v}$(the influence rate between u and v) is $\sum_{d \in D} m(u, v, d)/|D|$. In this way, we can construct a stable undirected graph. Then the IC model can be easily applied above.

We measure by check-ins to gather statistic data. C_u denotes all check-ins of node u in the dataset C. c_u is a member of C_u, namely $c_u \in C_u$. The function $m(c_u, C_v)$ is used to indicate whether the check-in c_u of node u coincides with at least one check-in from the set C_v of node v. $\sum_{c_u \in C_u} m(c_u, C_v)$ is the total number of check-ins in which u meets v for the dataset C_u. We denote the sum of all check-ins in C_u as $|C_u|$. Thus, $b_{u,v}$ (the influence rate of u to v) is $\sum_{c_u \in C_u} m(c_u, C_v)/|C_u|$. Clearly, $b_{u,v}$ is usually not the same value as $b_{v,u}$. In this way, we can construct a stable directed graph. Also, the IC model can be easily applied. Alternatively, we can define $b_{v,u}$ as $\sum_{c_u \in C_u} m(c_u, C_v)/|C_u|$. In this case, node u meets this condition : $\sum_{w neighbor of u} b_{w,u} \leq 1$ which suggests that we can adopt the LT model. Again, we assign a threshold uniformly at random to each node v from the interval $[0, 1]$.

Finally, it's also an open question about how to calculate weights between nodes and what model to be adopted.

4.3   Single Layer Propagation Model

In the two-layer propagation model, people can spread the information in two ways: sharing information through online social networks or talking to people they meet in the physical world. However, the information does not simply travel in online social networks or the physical world separately. Cross propagation makes the process of influence propagation more complicated (Fig. 3).

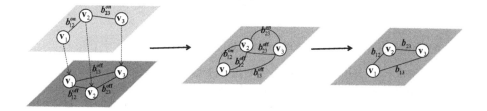

Fig. 3. An example of converting two-layer graph to single-layer graph

Inspired by Yang et al. [16], the two-layer propagation model can be compressed into a single-layer propagation model. For nodes u and v, they can share information by communicating online or talking offline. Therefore, the information can not be spread between u and v, if and only if they don't communicate online, meanwhile, they don't talk offline. Hence, in the resulting single layer model, the weight of u to v is as follows:

$$b_{u,v} = 1 - (1 - b_{u,v}^{on})(1 - b_{u,v}^{off}) \tag{3}$$

We can apply IC model directly in the resulting single layer propagation model. However, we must standardize the incident edges of each node, so that the sum of weights of incident edges is less than or equal to 1, if we want to apply LT model.

5   Our Solution

A single-layer graph has been constructed from the double-layer graph in Sect. 4. Hence, it becomes easy to study the issue of IM in LBSNs with the theory about influence propagation in traditional online social networks. In this section, we formally state the IM problem in traditional online social networks, and present an overview of the RIS framework which is a theoretical breakthrough way to solve the IM problem. Subsequently, our solution to the IM problem will be introduced followed by a summary of approximation and complexity.

5.1   IM Definition in Traditional Online Social Network

Let G be a graph with a node set V and a directed edge set E. Each directed edge has a propagation probability $b(e) \in [0, 1]$. We refer to S as a seed set, and $I(S)$ as the number of nodes that are infected in the end, namely the spread of S. Given the propagation models constructed previously, we formally define the IM problem as follows:

Definition 2 *(Influence Maximization in Traditional Online Social Network). Given a graph $G = (V, E, B)$, a constant $k \geq 1$ and a propagation model, the influence maximization problem is to find a seed set S_k of k nodes at most that maximizes its influence spread, i.e.,*

$$S_k = \arg \max_{S:|S|=k} E[I(S)]$$

5.2   Summary of the RIS Framework

The inefficiency of traditional greedy methods has long been a drawback for IM problem. By using the RIS technique, which is the foundation of the state-of-the art method, the time complexity of algorithms is greatly reduced. The RIS is based on the concept of Random Reverse Reachable set (Random RR set), which is defined below.

Definition 3 *(Random Reverse Reachable set (Random RR set)). Given a graph $G = (V, E, B)$ and a random node $v \in V$, g is a random graph obtained by removing each edge e from G with $1 - b(e)$ probability. The Random RR set is the set of nodes in g that can reach v.*

Borgs et al. [6] proved the following Theorem 1 through mathematical analysis. Theorem 1 provides the theoretical basis for solving the IM problem by the RIS method.

Theorem 1. *Given $G = (V, E, B)$ and a random RR set R from G. For a seed set $S \subset V$,*

$$I(S) = nPr[S covers R]. \tag{4}$$

Theorem 1 implies that we can estimate $E(I(S))$ by estimating the probability of the event S covers R. An example is used to illustrate the process of this method in the Fig. 4. Four random RR sets are generated with sources v_1, v_2, v_3 and v_4, respectively. v_3 appears most frequently among these sets. From the intuitive observation, v_3 is also the most influential node in practice. Based on the above theorem, Borgs et al. [6] proposed a two-step method for IM problem:

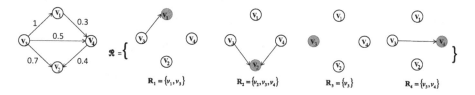

Fig. 4. An example of generating random RR sets for a simple graph.

1. Generate a sufficiently large collection R of random RR sets from G.
2. Use the greedy algorithm of maximum coverage problem to find the seed set with maximum coverage to R.

5.3 SSA and D-SSA Algorithm

So far, the optimal algorithm with approximation guarantee for IM problem is SSA and D-SSA [10], both of which exploit the zero-one estimation theorem [17] to gauge the required number of RR sets. SSA keeps generating RR sets until the generated seed set S is a good approximate solution. The general process of SSA is described as follows:

1. Generate an initial set R of random RR sets with a certain number.
2. Use the greedy algorithm of maximum coverage problem to find a size-k seed set S from R.
3. Generate another set of random RR sets to test whether S is a better approximate solution.
4. If S is a better approximation, terminate the procedure and return S; Otherwise, double the number of random RR sets, and goto Step 2.

In the process described above, the SSA generates two independent sets of RR sets: One is to find the seed set and the other is for estimating the influence of the seed set. It has three parameters ϵ_1, ϵ_2 and ϵ_3. These parameters decide the approximation errors allowed in step 3 and the number of random RR sets generated in each iteration of SSA. They are fixed to $\epsilon_1 = 1/6\delta$, $\epsilon_1 = 1/2\delta$, $\epsilon_3 = \delta/(4(1-1/e))$. However, Nguyen et al. [10] propose to vary them in different iterations to reduce the total number of random RR sets generated. Thus they propose the DSSA algorithm. The general process of DSSA is described as follows:

1. Generate an initial set R of random RR sets with a certain number.
2. Use the greedy algorithm for maximum coverage on R to find a size-k seed set S, along with the number of RR sets in R that overlap S.
3. Generate another set of random RR sets to derive an estimation of S' expected spread and to determine the value of ϵ.
4. Evaluate whether S is a good approximation solution based on the number of RR sets in R that overlap S, the estimation of S' expected spread and ϵ.
5. If S is a better approximation, terminate the procedure and return S; Otherwise, double the number of random RR sets, and goto Step 2.

Nguyen et al. [10] show that SSA and DSSA return a $(1 - 1/e - \epsilon)$-approximate solution with at least $(1 - \delta)$ probability. The details of those algorithms and the analysis of approximation complexity are given in [10].

6   Experiments

6.1   Experimental Settings

All the experiments are run on a PC machine with Intel Core i7 4.00 GHz processor, 16.0G RAM and 64 bit Linux operating system. We carry experiments under IC model on the following datasets and algorithms.

Datasets. We adopt two widely-used LBSNs, Brightkite and Gowalla's datasets in our research. All two datasets are collected from Stanford Network Analysis Project (SNAP) by Stanford University [18,19]. Brightkite was once a location-based social networking service provider where users shared their locations by checking-in. The friendship network was collected using their public API, and consists of 58228 nodes and 214078 undirected edges. we treat it as a directed graph by converting an undirected edge into two opposite directed edges. A total of 4491143 checkins of these users over the period of Apr. 2008 - Oct. 2010 has been collected. Gowalla is a location-based social networking website where users share their locations by checking-in. The friendship network is undirected and was collected using their public API, and consists of 196591 nodes and 950327 edges. we also treat it as a directed graph by converting an undirected edge into two opposite directed edges. A total of 6442890 check-ins of these users over the period of Feb. 2009 - Oct. 2010 has been collected.

Parameter Settings. For simplicity, we assign the same weight b to each edge in the online network model. In the offline network model, we give a distance r and a time interval τ to represent the maximum distance error and the maximum time error respectively when two users meet. The location is measured in degrees so that we use degrees for r. k is the number of seed nodes, varying from 20 to 100 in our experiment. The specific choices of the four parameters b, r, τ and k are shown in Table 2.

Table 2. Experiment parameters

Parameter	Values				
Online influence rate b	0.1	0.01	0.001	0.0001	
Distance error r	0.001	0.0001	0.00001		
Time error τ	0.5 h	1 h	12 h	24 h	
Number of seed nodes k	20	40	60	80	100

Algorithm Compared. On IM experiments, we compare DSSA with three algorithms (TIM [7], IMM [8] and SSA [9]), which are RIS-based algorithms that provide $(1 - 1/e - \delta)$-approximation guarantee.

6.2 Modeling Process

For simplicity, we assign the same weight b to each edge in the online network model. In the offline network model, two methods are introduced to calculate the influence rate between nodes. One is to measure by days for judging whether two users met. The influence rate of two users is obtained by dividing the number of days that they met by the number of days in the dataset. We can get an undirected graph in this way. The other is to measure by check-ins for judging whether two users met. The influence rate of one user u to another v is obtained by dividing the number of check-ins that u met v by the number of u' check-ins in the data set. We can get a directed graph in this way. Finally, we compress the two-layer propagation model into a single-layer propagation model by using Eq. (3). The detailed process is shown in Algorithms 1 and 2. In both algorithms, we represent the graph in the form of an adjacency list.

In the process of modeling, there are three key parameters that affect the comprehensive influence rate of two nodes: uniform influence rate b between nodes in online model, the maximum distance error r and the maximum time error τ when two users meet. In order to compare the effects of different parameters on modeling, we compare the number of edges on the different resulting single-layer graphs and use the DSSA to measure the influence spread by fixing the number $k = 20$ of seed nodes. Figures 5 and 6 show the experiment results of measuring by days on Brightkite and Gowalla during the modeling process. Figures 7 and 8 show the results of measuring by check-ins on Brightkite and Gowalla. In Figs. 5(a), 6(a), 7(a) and 8(a), we change the maximum time error τ from 0.5 h to 24 h. It is obvious that the larger τ is, the more edges it has in the resulting graphs. Also, the larger τ is, the more influence it can achieve in the resulting graphs, which can be learned from Figs. 5(d), 6(d), 7(d) and 8(d). By Eq. (3), the edges in the resulting graph are the union of edges in the online graph and the offline graph. The larger τ is, the more edges we can get in the offline graph. Furthermore, the number of edges in the resulting graph increases.

In Figs. 5(b), 6(b), 7(b) and 8(b), the maximum distance error r is the parameter we want to evaluate, which ranges from 0.00001 to 0.001. A degree of longi-

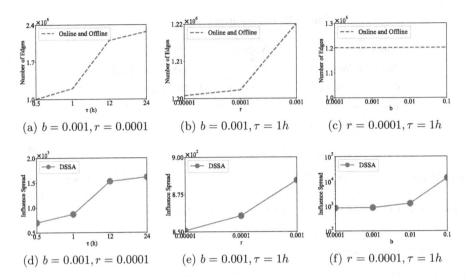

(a) $b = 0.001, r = 0.0001$ (b) $b = 0.001, \tau = 1h$ (c) $r = 0.0001, \tau = 1h$

(d) $b = 0.001, r = 0.0001$ (e) $b = 0.001, \tau = 1h$ (f) $r = 0.0001, \tau = 1h$

Fig. 5. The results of measuring by days on Brightkite

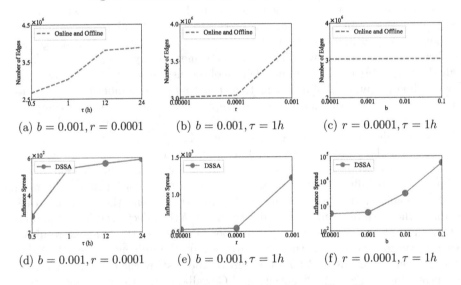

(a) $b = 0.001, r = 0.0001$ (b) $b = 0.001, \tau = 1h$ (c) $r = 0.0001, \tau = 1h$

(d) $b = 0.001, r = 0.0001$ (e) $b = 0.001, \tau = 1h$ (f) $r = 0.0001, \tau = 1h$

Fig. 6. The results of measuring by days on Gowalla

tude or latitude is at most 111.11 km. Thus, 0.001 is at most 111.11 meters, and 0.00001 is at most 1.1111 m. The larger r is, the more edges it has in resulting graphs. Also, the larger r is, the more influence it can achieve in resulting graphs, which can be learned from Figs. 5(e), 6(e), 7(e) and 8(e). For the same reason as the time error parameter, the larger r is, the more edges we can get in the offline graph. Furthermore, the number of edges in the resulting graph increases.

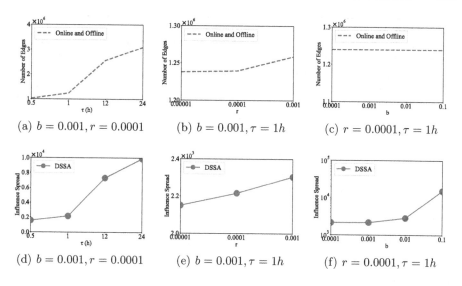

Fig. 7. The results of measuring by check-ins on Brightkite

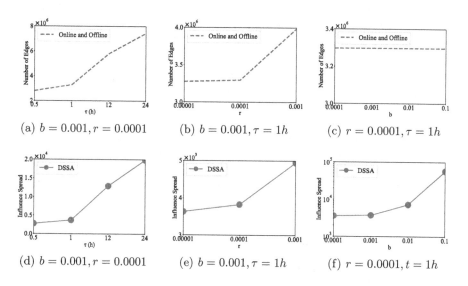

Fig. 8. The results of measuring by check-ins on Gowalla

In Figs. 5(c), 6(c), 7(c) and 8(c), we change the uniform weight b in online social network from 0.0001 to 0.1. The number of edges in the resulting graph remains the same as b increases. But the larger b is, the more influence it can achieve in the resulting graphs in Figs. 5(f), 6(f), 7(f) and 8(f). Different weights b can only change the influence rate between nodes in online graphs, but not change the number of edges in online and offline graphs. Thus the number of

---

Algorithm 1.

Input: an online graph $G^{on} = (V, E^{on}, B^{on})$; a check-ins dataset C; a maximum distance error r; a maximum time error τ;

Output: an compressed single-layer graph $G(V, E, B)$

1: **for** $i = 0 \rightarrow |V|$ **do**
2:     **for** $j = i + 1 \rightarrow |V|$ **do**
3:         $b_{i,j}^{off} \leftarrow MeetDayCount(C, i, j)/|D|$
4:         $b_{j,i}^{off} \leftarrow b_{i,j}^{off}$
5:         $b_{i,j} \leftarrow 1 - (1 - b_{i,j}^{on})(1 - b_{i,j}^{off})$
6:         $b_{j,i} \leftarrow b_{i,j}$
7:         put $b_{i,j}$ and $b_{j,i}$ into B
8:         **if** $b_{i,j} \neq 0$ **then**
9:             put $e_{i,j}$ and $e_{j,i}$ into E
10:         **end if**
11:     **end for**
12: **end for**
13: **return** $G(V, E, B)$

---

edges in the resulting graph remains the same. However, the increase of the online influence can increase the comprehensive influence spread in the resulting graph.

6.3 Comparison Between Online Influence Spread and Online-Offline Influence Spread

In order to evaluate the effect of influence spread in offline physical world, we compare the influence spread in online social network with the influence spread in the online-offline social networks. It can be seen from Figs. 9 and 10 that the number of edges and influence spread increase exponentially due to the effect of oral communication in the physical world. These comparative data show that our research topic is of great practical significance.

6.4 Algorithms Comparison

To show the superior performance of the DSSA we used, we compare it with three other RIS-based algorithms under IC model. Firstly, we compare the quality of the solution returned by all the algorithms. From Figs. 11(b), (d), 12(b) and 11(d), all the algorithms return comparable seed set quality without significant difference. Secondly, we examine the performance in terms of running time of all the algorithms. From Figs. 11(c), (e), 12(c) and (e), DSSA significantly outperforms the other tested algorithms by a huge margin. All of this is due to the fact that the TIM and IMM generate too many RR sets. DSSA overcomes this weakness and commits up to an order of magnitudes speedup.

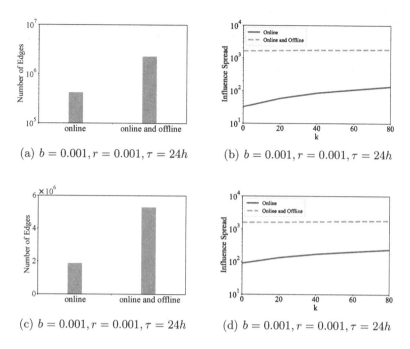

Fig. 9. The results of measuring by days on Brightkite and Gowalla

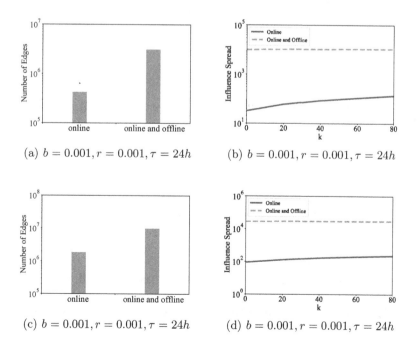

Fig. 10. The results of measuring by check-ins on Brightkite and Gowalla

Algorithm 2.

Input: an online graph $G^{on} = (V, E^{on}, B^{on})$; a check-ins dataset C; a maximum distance error r; a maximum time error τ;
Output: an compressed single-layer graph $G(V, E, B)$

```
 1: for i = 0 → |V| do
 2:     for j = 1 → |V| do
 3:         if i = j then
 4:             continue;
 5:         end if
 6:         b_{i,j}^{off} ← MeetCheckinCount(C, i, j)/|C_i|
 7:         b_{i,j} ← 1 - (1 - b_{i,j}^{on})(1 - b_{i,j}^{off})
 8:         put b_{i,j} into W
 9:         if b_{i,j} ≠ 0 then
10:             put e_{i,j} into E
11:         end if
12:     end for
13: end for
14: return G(V, E, B)
```

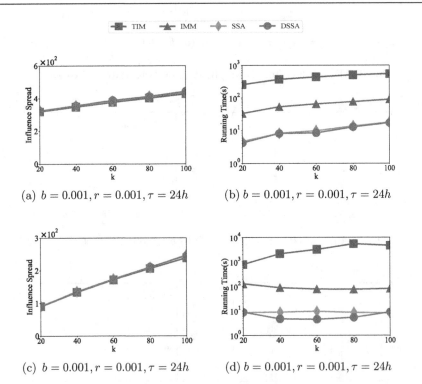

(a) $b = 0.001, r = 0.001, \tau = 24h$

(b) $b = 0.001, r = 0.001, \tau = 24h$

(c) $b = 0.001, r = 0.001, \tau = 24h$

(d) $b = 0.001, r = 0.001, \tau = 24h$

Fig. 11. The results of measuring by days on Brightkite and Gowalla

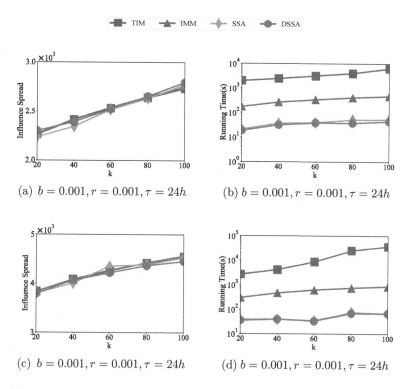

Fig. 12. The results of measuring by check-ins on Brightkite and Gowalla

7   Conclusion

In this paper, we aim to explore the influence maximization in location-based social networks. A two-layer network model and an information propagation model are proposed. Those models are motivated by the fact that influence propagates in both online social networks and the physical world. Also, we formalize the influence maximization problem in LBSNs and present an algorithm obtaining an approximation factor of $(1 - 1/e - \epsilon)$ in near-linear expected time. The experimental results show that the algorithm is efficient meanwhile offering strong theoretical guarantees. Furthermore, we compared the influence spread in the online social network with the influence spread in the online-offline social network and proved the practical significance of our research topic.

Acknowledgements. This work is partially supported by National Natural Science Foundation of China (NSFC) under Grant No.61772491, No.61472460, and Natural Science Foundation of Jiangsu Province under Grant No. BK20161256, and Anhui Initiative in Quantum Information Technologies AHY150300. Kai Han is the corresponding author.

References

1. Domingos, P., Richardson, M.: Mining the network value of customers. In: Proceedings of the Seventh ACM SIGKDD International Conference on Knowledge Discovery and Data Mining, pp. 57–66. ACM, August 2001
2. Kempe, D., Kleinberg, J., Tardos, É.: Maximizing the spread of influence through a social network. In: Proceedings of the Ninth ACM SIGKDD International Conference on Knowledge Discovery and Data Mining, pp. 137–146. ACM, August 2003
3. Leskovec, J., Krause, A., Guestrin, C., Faloutsos, C., VanBriesen, J., Glance, N.: Cost-effective outbreak detection in networks. In: Proceedings of the 13th ACM SIGKDD International Conference on Knowledge Discovery and Data Mining, pp. 420–429. ACM, August 2007
4. Goyal, A., Lu, W., Lakshmanan, L.V.: CELF++: optimizing the greedy algorithm for influence maximization in social networks. In: Proceedings of the 20th International Conference Companion on World Wide Web, pp. 47–48. ACM, March 2011
5. Chen, W., Wang, Y., Yang, S.: Efficient influence maximization in social networks. In: Proceedings of the 15th ACM SIGKDD International Conference on Knowledge Discovery and Data Mining, pp. 199–208. ACM, June 2009
6. Borgs, C., Brautbar, M., Chayes, J., Lucier, B.: Maximizing social influence in nearly optimal time. In: Proceedings of the Twenty-Fifth Annual ACM-SIAM Symposium on Discrete Algorithms, pp. 946–957. Society for Industrial and Applied Mathematics, January 2014
7. Tang, Y., Xiao, X., Shi, Y.: Influence maximization: near-optimal time complexity meets practical efficiency. In: Proceedings of the 2014 ACM SIGMOD International Conference on Management of Data, pp. 75–86. ACM, June 2014
8. Tang, Y., Shi, Y., Xiao, X.: Influence maximization in near-linear time: a martingale approach. In: Proceedings of the 2015 ACM SIGMOD International Conference on Management of Data, pp. 1539–1554. ACM, May 2015
9. Nguyen, H.T., Thai, M.T., Dinh, T.N.: Stop-and-stare: optimal sampling algorithms for viral marketing in billion-scale networks. In: Proceedings of the 2016 International Conference on Management of Data, pp. 695–710. ACM, June 2016
10. Cranshaw, J., Toch, E., Hong, J., Kittur, A., Sadeh, N.: Bridging the gap between physical location and online social networks. In: Proceedings of the 12th ACM International Conference on Ubiquitous Computing, pp. 119–128. ACM, September 2010
11. Pham, H., Shahabi, C.: Spatial influence-measuring followship in the real world. In: 2016 IEEE 32nd International Conference on Data Engineering (ICDE), pp. 529–540. IEEE, May 2016
12. Zhang, C., Shou, L., Chen, K., Chen, G., Bei, Y.: Evaluating geo-social influence in location-based social networks. In: Proceedings of the 21st ACM International Conference on Information and Knowledge Management, pp. 1442–1451. ACM, October 2012
13. Li, J., Sellis, T., Culpepper, J.S., He, Z., Liu, C., Wang, J.: Geo-social influence spanning maximization. IEEE Trans. Knowl. Data Eng. 29(8), 1653–1666 (2017)
14. Zhou, T., Cao, J., Liu, B., Xu, S., Zhu, Z., Luo, J.: Location-based influence maximization in social networks. In: Proceedings of the 24th ACM International on Conference on Information and Knowledge Management, pp. 1211–1220. ACM, October 2015

15. Cai, J.L.Z., Yan, M., Li, Y.: Using crowdsourced data in location-based social networks to explore influence maximization. In: IEEE INFOCOM 2016-The 35th Annual IEEE International Conference on Computer Communications, pp. 1–9. IEEE, April 2016

16. Yang, Y., Xu, Y., Wang, E., Lou, K., Luan, D.: Exploring influence maximization in online and offline double-layer propagation scheme. Inf. Sci. **450**, 182–199 (2018)

17. Dagum, P., Karp, R., Luby, M., Ross, S.: An optimal algorithm for Monte Carlo estimation. SIAM J. Comput. **29**(5), 1484–1496 (2000)

18. Brightkite Database Information from Stanford Network Analysis Project(SNAP). http://snap.stanford.edu/data/loc-Brightkite.html

19. Gowalla Database Information from Stanford Network Analysis Project(SNAP). http://snap.stanford.edu/data/loc-Gowalla.html

Measuring Bidirectional Subjective Strength of Online Social Relationship by Synthetizing the Interactive Language Features and Social Balance (Short Paper)

Baixiang Xue, Bo Wang$^{(\boxtimes)}$, Yanshu Yu, Ruifang He, Yuexian Hou, and Dawei Song

College of Intelligence and Computing, Tianjin University, Tianjin, China
{baixiangxue,bo_wang,rfhe,yxhou,dwsong}@tju.edu.cn,
1575341196@qq.com

Abstract. In online collaboration, instead of the objective strength of social relationship, recent study reveals that the two participants can have different subjective opinions on the relationship between them, and the opinion can be investigated with their interactive language on this relationship. However, two participants' bidirectional opinions in collaboration is not only determined by their interaction on this relationship, but also influenced by the adjacent third-party partners. In this work, we define the two participants' opinions as the subjective strength of their relationship. To measure the bidirectional subjective strength of a social relationship, we propose a computational model synthetizing the features from participants' interactive language and the adjacent balance in social network. Experimental results on real collaboration in Enron email dataset verify the effectiveness of the proposed model.

Keywords: Social relationship · Subjective strength · Interactive language · Balance theory

1 Introduction

To recognize the strength of interrelationships is very essential in online collaboration [1] which have two primary options: The first one is regarding the strength of interrelationships as objective properties, which can be investigated independently of the participants' subjective opinions. The second option is to determine the strength according to two participants' subjective opinions bidirectionally. Recent study [2] indicates that the objective measurement often leads to symmetric values of the interrelationships' properties, while the subjective measurement can leads to asymmetric values, because two participants may have different opinions on their interrelationship's strength. The measurement of this kind of asymmetric and subjective strength is necessary in many social studies. For example, in influence analysis, the possibility of the information spreading is not identical on two directions: the individual who regards their interrelationship is strong will communicate more frequently, while the other individual who regards the interrelationship is weak will do the opposite (Fig. 1).

H. Gao et al. (Eds.): CollaborateCom 2018, LNICST 268, pp. 112–123, 2019.
https://doi.org/10.1007/978-3-030-12981-1_7

Fig. 1. The undirected objective strength and bidirectional subjective strength in social relationship. The undirected objective strength is unable to distinguish the participants' different opinions on each other.

The interaction on the social relationship is an important indicator of the properties of the relationship [3]. To investigate the bidirectional subjective strength of the social relationship, current studies indicate the ability of interactive language in revealing the participants' opinions. The interactive language is the language used by the two participants' for the communication on their relationship. However, the subjective strength in collaboration is not only determined by their interaction on this relationship, but also influenced by the adjacent third-party partners. Wang et al. [2] finds that the interactive language features on a social relationship can be correlated to the neighbor topological features in social network.

To improve the measurement of the bidirectional subjective strength of social relationships, in this work, we propose a computational model synthetizing the features from participants' interactive language and the neighbor topological features in social network. Firstly, inspired by the sociolinguistics, we select four typical interactive language features which indicate the frequency, quantity, quality and emotion of interactive language, respectively. Secondly, according to the balance theory in sociology, we introduce the requirement of the triangle balance among social relationships into the subjective strength measurement. Finally, to combine the proposed language and topological features, we improve an optimization process to derive the bidirectional subjective strength synthetizing the interactive language features and the social balance. The experimental results on real collaboration among Enron email users show that the performance of the proposed model exceed the models using language features independently.

2 Related Work

2.1 Symmetric and Asymmetric Analysis of Social Interrelationships

Many early studies suppose that the properties of interrelationships are symmetric. The concept of the strength of social relationship is firstly explained by Granovetter et al. [4]. The topological features e.g., the balance of the triangular closure, are most widely used to measure the strength of social relationship [5]. In recent studies, behavior feature is popular in measuring symmetric strength of social relationship [6–8]. The content information of social language are also considered, for example Adali et al. [9] applied symbolic words in the interaction, but this work does not involve deeper language features.

There are also some recent studies analyzed the social relationship directionally or asymmetrically in a sense. For directed relationships, Leskovec et al. [10] firstly considered an explicit formulation of the sign prediction problem. West et al. [11] developed a model to predict the polarity of person-to-person evaluations. This work focused on bidirectional evaluation between two individuals which are naturally asymmetric and was an important base of our approach. As an alternation of this work, in this paper, we focus on the bidirectional subjective strength of interrelationship, instead of the bidirectional sentiment evaluation. To distinguish the sentiment evaluation and subjective strength, we replace the sentiment feature with the interactive language features related to the subjective strength, which is inspired by the sociolinguistics. Furthermore, we extend the model on a directed graph instead of the undirected graph.

2.2 Synthesis of Social Language and Social Network Analysis

In recent studies, natural language processing and social networks analysis are often combined to understand the nature of social relationship, user profile or social event. Adali et al. [9] showed that the feature sets from social behavioral information and textual information are practically equivalent in terms of their ability to determine the different types of relationships. Bramsen et al. [12] presented a text corpus-based statistical learning approach to model social power relationships. Thomas et al. [13] capitalized on this insight using an elaboration of the graph-cuts approach of Pang and Lee [14]. Tan et al. [15] used Twitter follows and mentions to predict attitudes about political and social events. Related ideas are pursued by Ma et al. [16] and Huang et al. [17], who add terms to their models enforcing homophily between friends. West et al. [11] developed a model that synthesizes textual and social-network information to jointly predict the polarity of person-to-person evaluations.

Compared with state-of-the-arts works synthesizing the language and network features, we propose to combine the two kinds of features to identify the bidirectional subjective strength of social interrelationship, instead of measuring the strength from an objective view. In the following sections, we will firstly introduce our selection and calculation of the features from the interactive language on social relationships. Then, we will explain our extension of the tradition balance theory in this work, and how to combine the extended balance with the language features in the measuring of the subjective strength.

3 Characterize Subjective Opinions on the Strength of Interrelationship with Interactive Language Features

To describe the individuals' opinions on their interrelationship's strength asymmetrically, some studies choose to use objective features directionally, e.g., the communication frequency in two directions. Though some objective features can be used asymmetrically, they cannot describe the subjective opinions accurately. Therefore, a more reasonable solution is to measure the opinions with subjective features.

Among the available resources, interactive language features are good choices, which are not only closely related to the properties of interrelationship, but also highly descriptive of individuals' opinions. In this section, inspired the theory from sociolinguistics, we propose four typical features of interactive language to measure the subjective strength of social relationship.

3.1 Interactive Language Features from Sociolinguistics

In sociolinguistics, the theory of communicative action [18] proposes to reconstruct the concept of relationship with the communicative act, instead of the objectivistic terms. The linguistic structures of communication can be used to understand the social relationships. Sapir-Whorf hypothesis [19] also supposes that the semantic structure of the language using shapes or limits the ways in which a speaker forms conceptions of the world including the social relationships. In the communication, people's choice of words is always highly depending on their subjective opinions on their interrelationship with the others. The theories inspire us to assume that one's opinion on an interrelationship's strength can impact his language using in communication. Consequently, we can measure the subjective strength of one's relationship according to his language features in interaction. The next problem is which language features should be selected? In sociolinguistics, Holmes [20] introduces four important dimensions to study the language using in social communication:

(1) The solidarity-social distance scale: concerned the solidarity of the individuals' relationship in social communication.
(2) The social status scale: concerned the relative status of the individuals' relationship in social communication.
(3) The formality scale: concerned the formality of language using in different relationships, topics and places.
(4) The referential and affective scale: concerned referential and affective function of the language in social communication.

The first two dimensions concerned the features of social interrelationship from both subjective and objective views. The last two dimensions concerned the features of interactive languages, which are highly related to social interrelationship.

According to Holmes' dimensions, we propose four typical linguistic features of interactive languages to measure an individual's subjective opinion on his interrelationship's strength. The designed features are frequency, length, fluency and sentiment polarity which indicate quantity, quality and emotion of interactive language, respectively. Among the features, the frequency and length are two primary features of language communication, and the fluency and sentiment corresponds to the formality and affective scale mentioned in Holmes' theory, respectively. The following are the detailed explanation of the four features:

(1) The frequency is the times of communication within a period of time, which is supposed to reflect one's intention of the communication on an interrelationship.

(2) The length is the number of the words of interactive language, which is also supposed to reveal one's intention of the communication.
(3) The fluency is the formality and quality of interactive language which is supposed to reveal whether the speaker treats a relationship seriously or not.
(4) The sentiment polarity measures the emotion tendency of interactive language which is supposed to have a positive correlation with the personal opinion on interrelationship, i.e., more positive emotion in interactive language often indicate that the interrelationship is more valuable to the speaker.

It is noted that all these four features can be recognized by the state-of-the-arts natural language processing technologies, which will be illustrated in the experiments in Sect. 5.

3.2 Distinguish the Asymmetry of Opinions from the Asymmetry of Language Habits

Though one's interactive language style is closely related to his opinions on his interrelationships' strength, it is inexact to understand the opinions using the original values of language features directly. Actually, in natural language understanding, the meaning of the language is always not only determined by the content, but also by the context.

The context of the interactive language is very complex. In this work, we focus on how to understand one's opinion more accurately considering his personal habit in language using. For example, suppose A is a very negative person, and he always talks to person B with the language whose sentiment score is negative. But we also know that A talks to everybody very negatively and he talks to B most friendly compared with the others. In this case, if we want to measure the A's opinion on his relationship with B correctly using sentiment polarity score, we need to normalized the scorer according to A's personal language habit, instead of using the original absolute value.

To normalize one's opinion according to his personal language habit, we utilize the strategy in [2]. Given an individual I, we normalize I's each language feature score f with I's personal language habit value $H_f(I)$. $H_f(I)$ is measured by Formula (1), where $f(I, I_i)$ is the feature value f of the language said by I to another individual I_i, and C is the set of all individuals who is in communication with I.

$$H_f(I) = \frac{1}{|C|}\sum\nolimits_{I_i \in C} f(I, I_i) \tag{1}$$

Then $f'(I, I_i)$ is calculated with Formula (2) as the normalized value of $f(I, I_i)$ according to I's personal language habit:

$$f'(I, I_i) = \frac{f(I, I_i) - H_f(I)}{H_f(I)} \tag{2}$$

4   Synthetizing the Language Features and Social Balance to Measure the Bidirectional Subjective Strength

In this section, we formulate a computational model to measure the asymmetric and subjective strength of interrelationship bidirectionally, synthesizing four proposed interactive language features and an extend version of the traditional balance theory.

4.1   Theory of Social Balance and the Extension

Theory of social balance [21] is popular in social network studies. This theory is based on the homogeneity assumption, which states that, in a social triangle, the more similar two individuals' opinions on the third one are, the more positive their interrelationship will be, and vice versa. Figure 2(a) illustrates the balanced and unbalanced triangles in traditional balanced theory, tagging the relationship with '±'. The balance theory is often extended in social relationship studies to meet the requirement of particular task [22]. In this work, for directional measuring, we extend the traditional balance theory to directed triangles according to homogeneity assumption, as shown in Fig. 2(b). In this extended version, all the interrelationships are directed, and four directed interrelationships are considered in the balance identification: the bidirectional relationships between the two participants (i.e., A and B) and two participants' relationships towards the third-party individual (i.e., C). In a directed social triangle, the criterion to identify the balance status is redefined sharing the same principle of the traditional balance theory, i.e., the principle of the homogeneity assumption.

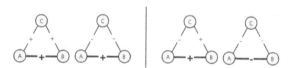

(a) Balanced (left two) and unbalanced (right two) triangles in balance theory

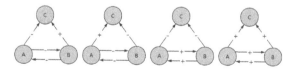

(b) Balanced triangles in extended balance theory

Fig. 2.   Traditional and extended social balance theory on undirected and directed triangles.

4.2   Measuring Bidirectional Subjective Strength

In this work, we modify the model in [11] to deal with the bidirectional subjective strength measurement replacing the sentiment features with interactive language features and extending the undirected graph to directed graph. In the new model, a social network is modeled as a directed graph $G = (V, E, s)$, where V is the set of individuals; E is the directed interrelationships between the individuals; and the real value set $s \in [0, 1]^{|E|}$ is the subjective strength values on each directed interrelationship. A directed triangle $t = \{e_{AB}, e_{BA}, e_{AC}, e_{BC}\}$ is a set of four directed interrelationships in E, and T is the set of all the t in G. $s_t = (s_{AB}, s_{BA}, s_{AC}, s_{BC})$ is the set of the subjective strength values on each interrelationship in t. For each directed interrelationship e, $\{f1_e, f2_e, f3_e, f4_e\}$ is the values of four proposed interactive language features of e, i.e., frequency, length, quality and sentiment. Then, together with the feature of social balance, we can calculate the bidirectional strength with an optimizing process. The process try to find the final strength $s*$ by meeting the linguistic and topological measurement as Formula (3)

$$s^* = \underset{s \in [0,1]^{|E|}}{argmin} \sum_{e \in E, f_e \in \{f1_e, f2_e, f3_e, f4_e\}} c(s_e, f_e) + \sum_{t \in T} d(s_t) \tag{3}$$

In Formula (3), the first term is the linguistic cost representing the difference between the bidirectional strength s_e and the linguistic features f_e which is illustrated as formula (4).

$$c(s_e, f_e) = \lambda_1 (1 - f_e)s_e + \lambda_0 f_e (1 - s_e) \tag{4}$$

In Formula (4), $\lambda_1, \lambda_o \in R_+$ are parameters tuning the costs for higher or lower strength, respectively. The second term is the topological cost representing how unbalanced the triangle is with the bidirectional strength s_t. of four directed edges. This cost is calculated as the difference between s_t and most similar balanced triangle.

The problem in Formula (3) is NP-hard. Adopting the strategy in [11] based on hinge-loss Markov random field, this problem can be relaxed by using sums of hinge loss terms to modify c in Formula (3) over the continuous domain $[0, 1]$ and d in Formula (3) over $[0, 1]^4$. As a result, the hinge-loss Markov random field formulation is equivalent to Formula (3). The relaxation can be illustrated as Formula (5)

$$\widetilde{c}(s_e, f_e) = \lambda_1 ||s_e - f_e||_+ + \lambda_0 ||f_e - s_e||_+ \tag{5}$$

where $||y||_+ = max\{0, y\}$ is the hinge loss. For each $s_t \in [0, 1]^4$, we rewrite $d(s_t)$ as a convex surrogate:

$$\tilde{d}(s_t) = \sum_{z \in \{0,1\}^4} F(s_t, z) \tag{6}$$

where,

$$F(s_t, z) = \begin{cases} t_1 * [1 - f(s_t, z)], & z \text{ is a balanced triangle} \\ t_2 * f(s_t, z), & \text{Other} \end{cases} \tag{7}$$

Here, $t_1, t_2 \in R_+$ are tunable parameters, where

$$f(s_t, z) = \left|\left| 1 - ||s_t - z||_1 \right|\right|_+ \tag{8}$$

where, $||s_t - z||_1 = \sum_{i=1}^4 |s_i - z_i|$ is the degree that s_t different from a directed triangle z. Intuitively, the more the inferred directed triangle strength s_t different from a balanced triangle, the higher the directed triangle costs. Thus, the objective function of optimization problem is the following relaxation of Formula (3) which can be efficiently optimized:

$$s^* = \underset{s \in [0,1]^{|E|}}{argmin} \sum_{e \in E, f_e \in \{f1_e, f2_e, f3_e, f4_e\}} \tilde{c}(s_e, f_e) + \sum_{t \in T} \tilde{d}(s_t) \tag{9}$$

5 Experiments

In this section, we evaluated the proposed model's ability in measuring the bidirectional degrees of individuals' opinions on their interrelationships' strength, i.e., the subjective strength. In particular, we try to use the proposed model to identify the bidirectional subjective strength of the superior-subordinate relationships between Enron email users. We describe the data setting, ground truth and the calculation of the interactive language features of the experiments. Then, we compare the performance of proposed synthetized model with that of the models only using language features.

5.1 Experimental Setup

Data Setting: We utilized the Enron email dataset, which contains 0.5M mails among employees. We retained only those interrelationships where at least 15 emails were sent in each direction. The filtered set contains 1078 interrelationships between 647 individuals. In the filtered set, we obtain the organizational hierarchy of 232 Enron employees provided by Agarwal [23]. From this dataset, 70 pairs of the superior-subordinate relationships are manually exploited consists of 80 nodes and 140 directed edges. We conducted experiments with the proposed model (Formula (9)) synthetizing normalized pair-wise language features (Formula (2)) and directed triangles of interrelationships.

Ground Truth: To find the ground truth of individuals' exact opinions on their interrelationships' strength is difficult. We intuitively make the assumption that in a superior-subordinate relationship, two participants' opinions on their interrelationship are asymmetric. The individual of lower position tend to put more importance on their interrelationship than the individual of higher position does. We use this assumption as the ground truth to evaluate the proposed models' ability in measuring asymmetric opinions on interrelationship's strength in superior-subordinate relationship.

Language Features Calculation: For each directed pair of individuals $<I_i, I_j>$, four linguistic features are calculated with the emails' content sent from I_i to I_j to characterize I_i's opinion on his interrelationship towards I_j as the method in [2]:

(1) "Frequency": average emails count per day from I_i to I_j.

(2) "Length": average words count per email from I_i to I_j.

(3) "Quality": average perplexity score per sentence in the emails from I_i to I_j. Higher perplexity score means lower language quality. The perplexity score is calculated by the SRI language modeling toolkit[1] (SRILM).

(4) "Sentiment": average sentiment score per word in the emails from I_i, to I_j. A sentiment dictionary[2] is used to score the positive, negative and neuter words as 1, −1 and 0, respectively.

5.2   Performance Comparison

In the experiments, given a pair of individuals A and B engaged in a superior-subordinate relationship where A is the one of lower position, score_A and score_B are the degree of A and B's opinion on their interrelationship's strength measured by the proposed model, respectively. If score_A – score_B > threshold, we regard the measurement on this pair to be successful, i.e., the individual of lower position (A) puts more importance on their interrelationship than the individual of higher position (B). We tried the threshold = 0, 0.01, 0.05, 0.1, respectively. The threshold is supposed to tune the model slightly. A too large threshold bring unnecessary manual influence to the model.

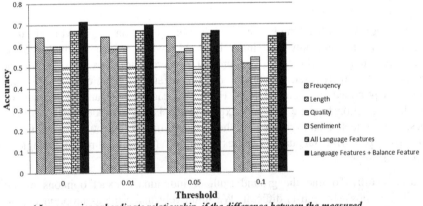

(In a superior-subordinate relationship, if the difference between the measured bidirectional subjective strength exceed the threshold, the measurement is regarded to be successful)

Fig. 3. The performance of single and synthetized models in measuring the asymmetric subjective strength on superior-subordinate relationship in Enron email dataset.

---

[1] http://www.speech.sri.com/projects/srilm/.

[2] http://www.keenage.com/download/sentiment.rar.

The experimental results are shown in Fig. 3. The X-axis is the value of thresholds and the Y-axis is the precision of measurement. In comparison, the results measured by single language features are noted by the names of features, i.e., 'Frequency', 'Length', 'Quality' and 'Sentiment'; the result of proposed model synthetizing only four language features is noted as 'All Language Features'; the proposed model synthetizing language and social balance features is noted as 'Language Features + Balance Feature'.

In Fig. 3, the 'All Language Features' model outperforms all single features on all thresholds. Furthermore, when synthetized with balance feature, the performance of 'Language Features + Balance Feature' model exceeds the 'All Language Features' model. This result illustrates the effectiveness of the proposed model in measuring the bidirectional subjective strength of the social relationships. The key advantage is to synthetize the features from interactive language and social balance.

6 Conclusions

In this paper, we measured bidirectional subjective strength of social relationship in online collaboration, i.e., individuals' asymmetric opinions on their interrelationships' strength, with the help of interactive language features and the balance of social network. According to sociolinguistics theories, we adopted four typical language features to represent one's opinion on their relationships' strength, representing the frequency, length, quality and sentiment of the language. We also extend the traditional undirected balance theory to a directed version to meet the requirement of bidirectional strength measurement.

Synthesizing the designed language and balance features, we extend the state-of-the-arts model to measure the bidirectional subjective strength of social relationship. Using superior-subordinate relationship among Enron email users as ground truth, as a case study, we verified the effectiveness of the proposed model in measuring the asymmetric strength of social relationship from a subjective view. In the experiments, the synthesized model outperformed the baselines using combined or single language features.

Our experimental research illustrate the solution to measure the individuals' asymmetric opinions on their interrelationships' strength, and potentially leads to a promising direction to model the social relationship from a subjective view. In the future work, we will try to profile the opinion on interrelationship with more detailed information using the content of interactive language.

Acknowledgments. This work is supported by National Natural Science Foundation of China (U1736103), National Natural Science Foundation of China (Key Program, U1636203), the state key development program of China (2017YFE0111900) and National Natural Science Foundation of China (61472277).

References

1. Aggarwal, C.C.: Social Network Data Analytics. Springer, Heidelberg (2011). https://doi. org/10.1007/978-1-4419-8462-3
2. Wang, B., Yu, Y.S., Zhang, P.: Investigation of the subjective asymmetry of social interrelationship with interactive language. In: International Conference on World Wide Web (2016)
3. Sundararajan, A.: The Sharing Economy: The End of Employment and the Rise of Crowd-Based Capitalism. The MIT Press, Cambridge (2016)
4. Granovetter, M.S.: The strength of weak ties. J. Soc. **78**, 1360–1380 (1973)
5. Sintos, S., Tsaparas, P.: Using strong triadic closure to characterize ties in social networks. In: Proceedings of the 20th ACM SIGKDD International Conference on Knowledge Discovery and Data Mining, pp. 1466–1475. ACM (2014)
6. Xiang, R., Neville, J., Rogati, M.: Modeling relationship strength in online social networks. In: International Conference on World Wide Web, pp. 981–990. WWW 2010, Raleigh, North Carolina, USA (2010)
7. Zhuang, J., Mei, T., Hoi, S.C., Hua, X.S., Li, S.: Modeling social strength in social media community via kernel-based learning. In: Proceedings of the 19th ACM International Conference on Multimedia, pp. 113–122. ACM (2009)
8. Kahanda, I., Neville, J.: Using Transactional Information to Predict Link Strength in Online Social Networks. In: International Conference on Weblogs and Social Media, ICWSM 2009, San Jose, California, USA (2009)
9. Adali, S., Sisenda, F., Magdon-Ismail, M.: Actions speak as loud as words: Predicting relationships from social behavior data. In: Proceedings of the 21st International Conference on World Wide Web, pp. 689–698. ACM (2012)
10. Leskovec, J., Huttenlocher, D., Kleinberg, J.: Predicting positive and negative links in online social networks. In: Proceedings of the 19th International Conference on World wide web, pp. 641–650. ACM (2010)
11. West, R., Paskov, H. S., Leskovec, J., Potts, C.: Exploiting social network structure for person-to-person sentiment analysis. J. Epr. Arx. (2014)
12. Bramsen, P., Escobar-Molano, M., Patel, A., Alonso, R.: Extracting social power relationships from natural language. In: Proceedings of the 49th Annual Meeting of the Association for Computational Linguistics Human Language Technologies, vol. 1, pp. 773–782 (2011)
13. Thomas, M., Pang, B., Lee, L.: Get out the vote: determining support or opposition from congressional floor-debate transcripts. In: Proceedings of the 2006 Conference on Empirical Methods in Natural Language Processing, pp. 327–335 (2006)
14. Pang, B., Lee, L.: A sentimental education: sentiment analysis using subjectivity summarization based on minimum cuts. In: Proceedings of the 42nd Annual Meeting on Association for Computational Linguistics, p. 271 (2004)
15. Tan, C., Lee, L., Tang, J., Jiang, L., Zhou, M., Li, P.: User-level sentiment analysis incorporating social networks. In: Proceedings of the 17th ACM SIGKDD International Conference on Knowledge Discovery and Data Mining, pp. 1397–1405 (2011)
16. Ma, H., Zhou, D., Liu, C., Lyu, M.R., King, I.: Recommender systems with social regularization. In: Proceedings of the Fourth ACM International Conference on Web Search and Data Mining, pp. 287–296 (2011)
17. Huang, B., Kimmig, A., Getoor, L., Golbeck, J.: A flexible framework for probabilistic models of social trust. In: Greenberg, Ariel M., Kennedy, William G., Bos, Nathan D. (eds.) SBP 2013. LNCS, vol. 7812, pp. 265–273. Springer, Heidelberg (2013). https://doi.org/10. 1007/978-3-642-37210-0_29

18. Habermas, J., McCarthy, T.: The Theory of Communicative Action. Beacon Press, Boston (1985)
19. Sapir, E.: The status of linguistics as a science. J. Lan. 195–197 (1929)
20. Holmes, J., Meyerhoff, M., Meyerhoff, M., Mullany, L., Stockwell, P., Llamas, C., et al.: An Introduction to Sociolinguistics, 4th edn. Routledge, London, New York (2013)
21. Heider, F.: The Psychology of Interpersonal Relations. Psychology Press, London (2013)
22. Wang, B., Sun, Y.J., Han, B., Hou, Y.X., Song, D.W.: Extending the balance theory by measuring bidirectional opinions with interactive language. In: International Conference on World Wide Web (2017)
23. Agarwal, A., Omuya, A., Harnly, A., Rambow, O.: A comprehensive gold standard for the Enron organizational hierarchy. In: Proceedings of the 50th Annual Meeting of the Association for Computational Linguistics, pp. 161–165. Association for Computational Linguistics (2012)

Recommending More Suitable Music Based on Users' Real Context

Qing Yang[1], Le Zhan[1], Li Han[1], Jingwei Zhang[2,3(✉)], and Zhongqin Bi[4]

[1] School of Electronic Engineering and Automation,
Guilin University of Electronic Technology, Guilin 541004, China
gtyqing@hotmail.com, 1217093432@qq.com, 1007060417@qq.com
[2] Guangxi Cooperative Innovation Center of Cloud Computing and Big Data,
Guilin University of Electronic Technology, Guilin 541004, China
gtzjw@hotmail.com
[3] Guangxi Key Laboratory of Trusted Software,
Guilin University of Electronic Technology, Guilin 541004, China
[4] College of Computer Science and Technology,
Shanghai University of Electronic Power, Shanghai 200090, China
zqbi@shiep.edu.cn

Abstract. Music recommendation is an popular function for personalized services and smart applications since it focuses on discovering users' leisure preference. The traditional music recommendation strategy captured users' music preference by analyzing their historical behaviors to conduct personalized recommendation. However, users' current states, such as in busy working or in a leisure travel, etc., have an important influence on their music enjoyment. Usually, those existing methods only focus on pushing their favorite music to users, which may be not the most suitable for current scenarios. Users' current states should be taken into account to make more perfect music recommendation. Considering the above problem, this paper proposes a music recommendation method by considering both users' current states and their historical behaviors. First, a feature selection process based on ReliefF method is applied to discover the optimal features for the following recommendation. Second, we construct different feature groups according to the feature weights and introduce Naive Bayes model and Adaboost algorithm to train these feature groups, which will output a base classifier for each feature group. Finally, a majority voting strategy decides the optimal music type and each user will be recommended more suitable music based on their current context. The experiments on the real datasets show the effectiveness of the proposed method.

Keywords: Music recommendation · Feature selection · User context

1 Introduction

A large number of music existing in different web sites and users' implicit music preferences have presented a big challenge for lean and tailored user services.

© ICST Institute for Computer Sciences, Social Informatics and Telecommunications Engineering 2019
Published by Springer Nature Switzerland AG 2019. All Rights Reserved
H. Gao et al. (Eds.): CollaborateCom 2018, LNICST 268, pp. 124–137, 2019.
https://doi.org/10.1007/978-3-030-12981-1_8

Music recommendation is an important mechanism to provide personalized services for users. Two parts are key to ensure the accuracy of music recommendation, one is how to discover the effective features for recommendations, and the other is the matching strategy between user preferences and different kinds of music. Currently, the popular recommendation strategy for music is to identify users with similar preferences and then to apply collaborative methods for recommendation, which is based on those collected information, for example, which kinds of music users have browsed and listened, namely users' behaviors. It is a good idea to generate the favorite music by applying users' historical behaviors to conclude users' implicit preference, but considering the real user context, such as users' current working state, the most favorite music may be not the most suitable. From the viewpoint of recommendation overfitting and diversification, the recommendation covering users' current context will be more popular and practical, which can help to dig out users' new music preferences.

Collaborative filtering is the most popular recommendation strategy, including user-based collaborative filtering and item-based collaborative filtering, the former focuses on finding a group of similar users and the latter focuses on finding a group of similar items. In fact, collaborative filtering is a transformation from group behaviors to individual characteristics, in which a user or an item is modelled into a vector to show those behaviors that a user has done on items. Obviously, the above model is based on a series of historical behaviors and are more prone to mine the items or users that should be recommended comprehensively, which does not serve for the current context and is also tardy to capture users' interest migration. In order to improve the recommendation effectiveness, this paper proposes the recommendation model covering users' real context and designs a recommendation method based on Naive Bayes model and the Adaboost algorithm. Both users' historical behaviors on music and their current states, including emotional state and working state, etc., are integrated to describe users, and a feature selection process based on the ReliefF algorithm is conducted before recommendation to filter those optimal features for classification training. The Naive Bayes model is introduced to train base classifiers. The Adaboost ensembling algorithm works for integrating each base classifier and recommending those items by a relative majority voting strategy.

This study is organized as following. Section 2 summarizes the work related with music recommendation. Section 3 defines the music recommendation problem serving for users' real context. Section 4 details the proposed recommendation model, including the feature selection and the recommended item generation. Section 5 designs experiments to verify and analyze our method. Section 6 concludes the whole study and discusses the future work.

2   Related Work

With the rapid expansion of digital music and users' diversified amusement requirements, personalized music recommendation has become an important research topic in the fields of recommendation. Compared with recommendation for e-commence, etc., personalized music recommendation are more complex since it not only pays attention on the closeness between user preferences decided by users' historical behavior and music labels or music content, but also is affected by users' real context since one user could like enjoy different styles of music when he/she is in different scenarios. Currently, mainstream recommendation methods include automatical play list generation [14], content-based recommendations [2], collaborative-filter methods [12], context-based methods [19], and hybrid recommendations [18].

Automatical play list generation focuses on those songs that are similar to the chosen seeds to generate a new play list. Baccigalupo [1] presented a Case Base Reuse(CBR) approach to establish a new play list. CBR system retrieves those most relevant music from the Case Base, and then combines them to generate a new play list, in which music is ranked by its relevance to the pre-specified music.

Collaborative filtering methods recommend pieces of music to a user based on music rating, which are contributed by other users with similar taste. To address the data sparsity problem, Huo [9] applied stack denoising auto-encoder to construct content-based model and then proposed deep learning to cooperate with collaborative filtering. Sarwar [15] experimentally evaluated that item-based collaborative filtering can produce high-quality recommendations. Melville [13] put forward an effective framework for combining content-based method and collaborative filtering, which uses a content-based predictor to enhance existing user data and then provides personalized suggestions through collaborative filtering.

Content-based methods compute similarity between songs, and then recommend songs similar to those known favorite songs. Xing [21] proposed and examined a novel approach to generate latent embeddings for podcast items, which utilizes the aggregated information from the text-based features related with the audio items. Kuo [11] presented a personalized content-based music filtering system to support music recommendation based on user preference on melody style. Further, emotional information have also presented their influence on recommendation [10].

Context-based methods take context into consideration, which include time, place, emotion and so on. Gu [8] put forward a context aware matrix factorization model, named AlphaMF, to tackle with the cold start, which uses the matrix factorization for modelling implicit feedback and introduces the linear contextual features for modelling explicit contextual feedback. Wu [20] proposed a context feature auto-encoding algorithm based on regression tree, which can only deal with numerical features. Trajectory data and location information have also been widely considered for recommendation [4,5,23,25].

Hybrid approaches, which consider both music content and other related information for recommendation, are being paid more attention. Yoshii [24] integrated both rating and music content data by a Bayes network to realize recommendation. Donaldson [6] leveraged spectral graph properties of an item-base collaborative filtering as well as acoustic features of the music signal for recommendation. For other recommendation applications, [26] designed a distributed storage and query system for optimizing POI recommendations based on location-constraints. [22] designed a stacked denoising autoencoder model for preprocessing recommendation data and then to improve recommendation performance. Group recommendations are also a popular topic. [16] and [17] studied the problem of the recommendation fairness for package to-group recommendations, which also provided an approximate solutions in reasonable time. [7] proposed a new type of group recommendation, namely personalized recommending event-based groups to users, in which both the linear model for capturing explicit features and matrix factorization model for mining past interactions between users and groups are exploited. [27] designed a Nash equilibrium based item group recommendation approach, in which consumers' preferences for an item group are evaluated from two perspectives, namely the attraction from these customers themselves and the social affection from their friends. [3] conducted extensive experiments to evaluate the influence of recommending accuracy from the rating prediction methods, which shows that the rating prediction for individual users are more effective than for groups on both improving recommendation accuracy and reducing the influence from data sparsity.

3 Problem Definition and Recommendation Model

In this section, music recommendation covering user context is given a formal statement in Definition 1. Music categories are initialized for recommendation, several kinds of user features are considered for matching music categories. The current user context includes users' primary attributes, users' historical behaviors, their current emotional state, etc.

Definition 1. *Music recommendation covering user context. Given a set of music I, a set of music categories C, and a group of users U. Each element $i \in I$ belongs to a subset of P, which is denoted as $i \in c \wedge c \in P \wedge P \subseteq C$. Each element $u \in U$ is described by a series of features, which are namely user context. A user sample can be denoted as a $(l+1)$-tuple, such as $(f_1, f_2, \cdots, f_l, c)$, l is the number of user features and c is to indicate the corresponding music categories that i would like in current context. Music recommendation covering user context tries to find the optimal music categories based on the context of a specific user i and then to recommend the popular music in each found categories to this user.*

Figure 1 presents the music recommendation model covering user context. Figure 1(a) corresponds to U, whose feature set are filtered from $l+1$ into $m+1$ and are presented in Fig. 1(b), c denotes one music category in both Fig. 1(a) and (b). An initial feature selection can help to reserve those features with greater weights. A series of operations will work on the transformed user set, which include enumerating features, learning Bayes classifier, generating recommendation rules, ranking recommended items, etc. Enumerating features tries to find the optimal feature group for the following classification. Here, classifiers exploit the user context to create recommendation rules. A new user can depend on

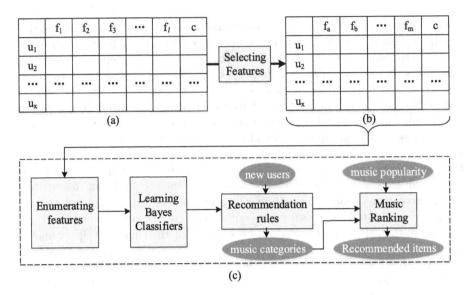

Fig. 1. Music recommendation model

the recommendation rules to obtain his/her related music categories, and then those music in each output category can be recommended to this user on their popularity. The detailed process is presented in Fig. 1(c).

4   Proposed Method

As in Sect. 3, a user u_1 can be denoted as a n-dimensional vector. In order to discover those music categories that u_1 might like on u_1's current states, we design a recommendation rule generation strategy by Bayes classification to find the relationships between users' features and music categories. Those generated recommendation rules can guide to capture both the music categories and the corresponding music that should be recommended to users. Here, we firstly choose the optimal features that are more effective to match users with their favorite music categories. Since music categories need to be represented by multiple labels, we introduce the ReliefF algorithm for the multi-label classification.

4.1   Selecting Features for Ensembling Classification Strategy

Supposing the given data set containing m features and l labels, R^m is the sample feature space and R^l is the sample label space, and the training set can be denoted as $TD = \{(x_1, y_1), \cdots, (x_n, y_n)\}$, $x_i \in R^m, y_i \in R^l$. l is the number of the labels corresponding to music categories. Each feature has a weight, W_A, to indicate its importance for classification, whose updating formula is presented in Formula 7.

$$W_A = \sum_{k=1}^{K} diff(A, T, H_k) \frac{1}{jk} + \sum_{C \notin class(T)} [\frac{p(C)}{1 - p(class(T))}] diff(A, T, M_k(C)) \frac{1}{jk} \tag{1}$$

Here, A is a specific feature, T is a random sample from TD and K denotes the number of T's nearest neighbors. The function, $diff(A, T, H_k)$, is defined in Formula 2 and is responsible for computing the difference between T and the k_{th} nearest neighbor, H_k, which have the same label. $class(T)$ returns the label of T. $M_k(C)$ denotes the k_{th} sample with the label C. $p(C)$ denotes the probability of those samples with the label C. $p(class(R))$ is the probability of the label of sample R. j is just the sampling times. Given a threshold δ, if $W_A > \delta$, the feature A will be retained, otherwise A is removed.

$$diff(A, T, H_k) = \frac{T(A) - H_k(A)}{Max(W_A) - Min(W_A)} \tag{2}$$

Based on the Formula 1, $N(N < M)$ features that are optimal for classification will be obtained. Because each feature can contribute different influence to the classification based on those labels, we try to divide these features into several feature groups on their weight ranking. Namely, the first feature group consists of only the feature with highest weight, the second feature group consists of the features ranked the 1st and 2nd on the weights, etc. Each feature group is inserted a new features that have the highest weight and have not existing in any feature group. For one specific feature group, each feature is considered to be independent and the Bayesian classifier is introduced for classification. Depending on the conditional independence assumption, we have Formula 3, in which S corresponding to the cardinality of one feature group. The posterior probability of every label can be computed as Formula 4.

$$p(X = x | Y = y_i) = \prod_{s=1}^{S} p(X^{(s)} = x^{(s)} | Y = y_i) \tag{3}$$

$$p(Y = y_i | X = x) = \frac{p(X = x | Y = y_i) p(y = y_i)}{\sum_{i=1}^{l} p(X = x | Y = y_i) p(y = y_i)} \tag{4}$$

Since the probability of (x, y_i) can be denoted as $p(Y = y_i | X = x)$, we define the maximum label probability of x_i, G_q, as Formula 5.

$$G_q(x_i) = argmax \; p(Y = y_i) \prod_{s=1}^{S} p(X^{(s)} = x^{(s)} | Y = y_i) \tag{5}$$

Then, we can calculate the error rate of classification err_{qi} as Formula 6, $G_q(x)$ is the classification result. If $err_{qi} > 0.5$, the feature weight distribution can be updated as Formula 7.

$$err_{qi} = \sum_{i=1}^{N} w_{qi} I(G_q(x_i) \neq y_i) \tag{6}$$

$$w_{(q+1,i)} = \frac{w_{qi}}{Z} \exp\left(-\alpha_q y_i G_q(x_i)\right), i = 1, 2, \ldots, N \tag{7}$$

α_q is the coefficient of the $G_q(x)$ and Z is normalization factor that is defined in Formula 8.

$$Z = \sum_{i=1}^{N} w_{qi} \exp\left(-\alpha_q y_i G_q(x_i)\right) \tag{8}$$

The final classifier result is expressed as Formula 9.

$$G(x) = \sum_{q=1}^{Q} \alpha_q G_q(x) \tag{9}$$

4.2 Constructing Initial Recommendation Rules

The above outputs and divides these optimal features into several feature groups, and each feature group are applied to construct a classifier. Given a unclassified sample x^*, we can calculate the probability of each label for x^*. Supposing the current label is y_t, we can obtain the probability of x^* from all the classifiers contributed by the above feature groups, which is defined in Formula 10.

$$P_t(x^*) = \frac{1}{L} \sum_{l=1}^{L} I(G(x^*) = y_t) \tag{10}$$

L is the number of all feature groups and t is the number of labels. We only need to calculate the probability of different labels for x^* and to generate the most probable label for x^* by the majority voting strategy as defined in Formula 11.

$$Y = argmax(P_t(x^*)) \tag{11}$$

4.3 Music Ranking for Recommendation

Now, we can obtain an ordered sequence of labels on users' current context by those constructed Bayesian classifiers and the majority voting strategy. When a new user appears, we can pick the label with the highest score, namely the most suitable music category considering users' real states, to generate the specific music for this user. A list of music will be presented to this user on the music popularity in the chosen music categories, and the music popularity is contributed by the music websites (https://music.163.com/). The detailed recommendation process is presented in Algorithm 1.

5 Experiments

In this section, we designed and carried out experiments on real data sets to verify our proposed recommendation method. All experiments are run on a computer with dual-core CPU @1.90 GHZ and 4 GB memory, and all code is implemented in Python.

Algorithm 1. Music Recommendation Covering Users' Real Context

---

Input U_1: training dataset; U_2: test dataset; L: the number of feature groups; F: a set of features; J: the sampling times; δ: the weight threshold of the selected feature;

Ouput the labels corresponding to music categories.

1: set the weight of each feature to be 0, namely $W_A = 0$
2: **for** $j = 1, 2, ..., J$ **do**
3:　select a sample R randomly, $R \in U_1$
4:　applying Euclidean distance to select k nearest neighbor samples with the same label of R, denoted as H_k, and also select k nearest neighbor samples with different labels of R, denoted as M_k
5:　**for** $A = 1, 2, ..., N$ **do**
6:　　update W_A according to Formula. 1
7:　　**if** $W_A > \delta$ **then**
8:　　　add A to the feature set F
9:　　**end if**
10:　**end for**
11: **end for**
12: divide F into L feature groups
13: **for** $i = 1, 2, ..., L$ **do**
14:　learn a classifier, $G_q(x)$, by the i_{th} feature group on U_1
15:　**repeat**
16:　　apply $G_q(x)$ on U_2 and calculate the error rate err_{qi}
17:　　**if** $err_{qi} \geq 0.5$ **then**
18:　　　update the weight of each feature by Formula. 7
19:　　**end if**
20:　**until** $err_{qi} < 0.5$
21:　calculate the probability of each label by $P_t(x^*)$ and output the label with the highest probability
22: **end for**

5.1 Data Sets and Evaluation Metrics

In order to test the effectiveness of the proposed method, we constructed a data set through our designed questionnaire, which is completed by the friends in WeChat. The whole questionnaire is composed of two kinds of questions, one kind of questions are to let users answer their attributes and current states, the other kind of questions is to let users choose one music category under their current states. The whole data set includes 400 user records, 5 music categories, and all music are crawled from https://music.163.com/. Each user is described by 10 features, which are showed in Table 1.

Three metrics, precision, recall and F1-score are introduced for evaluating recommendation performance, which are presented in Formulas 12 to 14. **Rec-Num** is the number of the recommended music from our proposed model, **RightNum** is the cardinality of the music both recommended by our model and accepted by users. **ExpectedNum** corresponds to the number of all music that should be recommended.

Table 1. User features in data set

f_1	f_2	f_3	f_4	f_5
Emotional state	Times weekly	Character	Gender	Career
f_6	f_7	f_8	f_9	f_{10}
Instrument	Age	Income	History habit	Education

$$Precision = \frac{RightNum}{RecNum} \tag{12}$$

$$Recall = \frac{RightNum}{ExpectedNum} \tag{13}$$

$$F1\text{-}score = \frac{2 * RightNum}{ExpectedNum + RecNum} \tag{14}$$

5.2 Experimental Results and Analysis

Features are key for classification. For the given data set, all features are ranked by **reliefF** algorithm firstly. Then we try different group of features for classification to find the optimal feature group. The combination strategy of features is greedy. Namely, the feature with the greatest weight is considered for classification, and then the feature in the second place is added for classification. All features are considered in order of their weights until the classification accuracy decreases.

We use a 15 cross verification for ranking the features. The data set is divided into 15 parts randomly, for each stage, 14 parts are used for training and one part for testing. The weight of each feature is assigned by the average accuracy contributed by the feature. The detailed experimental results are presented in Table 2, and all weights of the features are presented in Fig. 2, in which **f1** to **f10** correspond to those features in turn in Table 1.

Finding the Optimal Combination of Features. We selected different number of features as input for each Bayes classifier. First, we sorted these features by their weights. Since the music enjoyed by users at different context may be constrained by different features, we set different number of feature groups for experimental verification. Second, we removed the last four features since their weights are small and constructed 5 feature groups, the first group is the combination of f_1 and f_2, the second group is the combination of f_1, f_2 and f_3, etc. Each group of features are used to test their classification performance individually to find the optimal feature group. We carried out the experiment to observe their classification performance of different feature groups, Fig. 3 presents the classification accuracy on different group of features. Obviously, when we consider the five features with the greatest weights, the classification shows the best

Table 2. Experimental results on feature weights

Running times	f_1	f_2	f_3	f_4	f_5	f_6	f_7	f_8	f_9	f_{10}
1	0.171	0.031	0.135	0.124	0.072	0.132	0.162	0.084	0.228	0.071
2	0.176	0.026	0.141	0.123	0.073	0.135	0.167	0.080	0.227	0.079
3	0.169	0.030	0.137	0.120	0.065	0.137	0.169	0.073	0.233	0.073
4	0.173	0.026	0.126	0.126	0.069	0.129	0.172	0.075	0.231	0.064
5	0.166	0.024	0.130	0.133	0.076	0.129	0.163	0.086	0.223	0.072
6	0.162	0.027	0.138	0.127	0.068	0.136	0.168	0.087	0.236	0.071
7	0.170	0.031	0.136	0.129	0.078	0.130	0.171	0.081	0.234	0.075
8	0.173	0.034	0.140	0.123	0.081	0.127	0.173	0.082	0.229	0.069
9	0.164	0.029	0.135	0.114	0.077	0.129	0.172	0.077	0.227	0.073
10	0.170	0.033	0.144	0.122	0.075	0.133	0.164	0.073	0.233	0.082
11	0.169	0.035	0.137	0.129	0.071	0.141	0.168	0.077	0.238	0.087
12	0.171	0.027	0.127	0.130	0.079	0.142	0.163	0.079	0.241	0.075
13	0.175	0.018	0.129	0.128	0.072	0.139	0.168	0.074	0.237	0.072
14	0.177	0.033	0.137	0.117	0.064	0.133	0.172	0.087	0.236	0.073
15	0.171	0.029	0.135	0.124	0.068	0.137	0.169	0.089	0.235	0.071

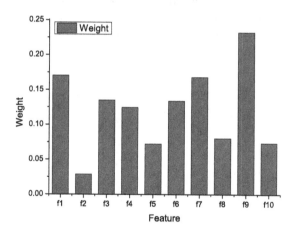

Fig. 2. The weight of each feature

performance. According to Fig. 2, the five features are f_9, f_1, f_7, f_3 and f_6, which will be applied for generating the following recommendation rules.

Generating the Recommended Music. According to the above experimental results, we use the five Bayesian classifiers corresponding to the five specific features to predict the potential music categories for new users. Each classifier

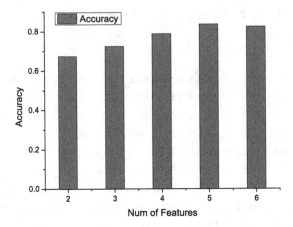

Fig. 3. Accuracy under different group of features.

can output one music category for each user, and we introduce the relative majority voting to conclude the optimal music categories. Those top-k popular music in the output music category are picked for users. Here, the number of the output music categories is set to 2, and k is set to 10. In order to test the effectiveness of the proposed method, we randomly choose the users from the data set and construct different subsets, the user number of each testing data set are 150, 200, 250,300, 350 and 400. The experimental results are presented in Fig. 4.

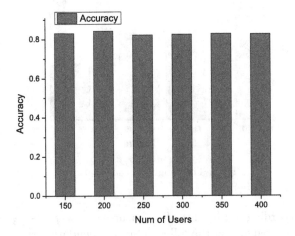

Fig. 4. Accuracy for different number of users.

Conducting Comparison Experiments. We also designed comparative experiments, content-based collaborative filtering, our proposed method

(Adaboost-Bayes) and the Adaboost-Bayes method without considering users' emotions are introduced for the performance comparison on recommendation. For each music categories, five songs are prepared for recommendation, the first two categories are chosen for recommendation, namely 10 songs. The precision, recall and F1-score of three methods are presented in Table 3. Our proposed method, Adaboost-Bayes, outperformed the other two methods, which proved that users' real context have great influence on users' acceptance for the recommended songs.

Table 3. Experimental comparison of different methods

Algorithm contrast	Precision	Recall	F1-score
Collaborate filtering	0.803	0.562	0.645
ABWE	0.742	0.616	0.646
Adaboost-Bayes	0.826	0.578	0.734

6 Conclusions

This study proposes a novel method for music recommendation serving for users' real context, which provides a cooperative mechanism between classification and recommendation. An efficient strategy is designed for guiding classification rules to work for recommendation requirements. Making full use of both users' historical behavior and their current context, the proposed recommendation model uses three functions, namely feature selection, bayes classifying and ensembling strategy for recommendation results, to provide more suitable recommendation. Experiments on real music datasets show the effectiveness of the proposed method. The following work will pay more attention on users' state migration to provide more intelligent recommendation services.

Acknowledgments. This study is funded by the National Natural Science Foundation of China (No. 61462017, 61862013, U1501252, U1711263, 61662015), Guangxi Natural Science Foundation of China (No. 2017GXNSFAA198035), and Guangxi Cooperative Innovation Center of Cloud Computing and Big Data.

References

1. Baccigalupo, C., Plaza, E.: Case-based sequential ordering of songs for playlist recommendation. In: Roth-Berghofer, T.R., Göker, M.H., Güvenir, H.A. (eds.) ECCBR 2006. LNCS, vol. 4106, pp. 286–300. Springer, Heidelberg (2006). https://doi.org/10.1007/11805816_22
2. Basu, C., Hirsh, H., Cohen, W.: Recommendation as classification: using social and content-based information in recommendation. In: Fifteenth National/Tenth Conference on Artificial Intelligence/Innovative Applications of Artificial Intelligence, pp. 714–720 (1998)

3. Boratto, L., Carta, S., Fenu, G., Mulas, F., Pilloni, P.: Influence of rating prediction on group recommendation's accuracy. IEEE Intell. Syst. **31**(6), 22–27 (2016)
4. Chen, T.-Y., Chen, L.-C., Chen, Y.-M.: Mining location-based service data for feature construction in retail store recommendation. In: Perner, P. (ed.) Advances in Data Mining. Applications and Theoretical Aspects. LNCS, vol. 10357, pp. 68–77. Springer, Cham (2017). https://doi.org/10.1007/978-3-319-62701-4_6
5. Dai, J., Yang, B., Guo, C., Ding, Z.: Personalized route recommendation using big trajectory data. In: IEEE International Conference on Data Engineering, pp. 543–554 (2015)
6. Donaldson, J.: A hybrid social-acoustic recommendation system for popular music. In: ACM Conference on Recommender Systems, pp. 187–190 (2007)
7. Gao, L., Wu, J., Qiao, Z., Zhou, C., Yang, H., Hu, Y.: Collaborative social group influence for event recommendation, pp. 1941–1944 (2016)
8. Gu, Y., Song, J., Liu, W., Zou, L., Yao, Y.: Context aware matrix factorization for event recommendation in event-based social networks. In: ACM International Conference on Web Intelligence, pp. 248–255 (2017)
9. Huo, H., Liu, X., Zheng, D., Wu, Z., Yu, S., Liu, L.: Collaborative filtering fusing label features based on SDAE. In: Perner, P. (ed.) Advances in Data Mining. Applications and Theoretical Aspects. LNCS, vol. 10357, pp. 223–236. Springer, Cham (2017). https://doi.org/10.1007/978-3-319-62701-4_17
10. Kim, H.H.: A semantically enhanced tag-based music recommendation using emotion ontology. In: Selamat, A., Nguyen, N.T., Haron, H. (eds.) ACIIDS 2013. LNCS, vol. 7803, pp. 119–128. Springer, Heidelberg (2013). https://doi.org/10.1007/978-3-642-36543-0_13
11. Kuo, F.F., Shan, M.K.: A personalized music filtering system based on melody style classification. In: IEEE International Conference on Data Mining, p. 649 (2002)
12. Mathew, P., Kuriakose, B., Hegde, V.: Book Recommendation System through content based and collaborative filtering method. In: IEEE International Conference on Data Mining and Advanced Computing, pp. 47–52 (2016)
13. Melville, P., Mooney, R.J., Nagarajan, R.: Content-boosted collaborative filtering for improved recommendations. In: Eighteenth National Conference on Artificial Intelligence, pp. 187–192 (2002)
14. Pampalk, E., Pohle, T., Widmer, G.: Dynamic playlist generation based on skipping behavior. In: Proceedings of the International Conference on Music Information Retrieval, ISMIR 2005, London, UK, 11–15 September 2005, pp. 634–637 (2005)
15. Sarwar, B., Karypis, G., Konstan, J., Riedl, J.: Item-based collaborative filtering recommendation algorithms. In: International Conference on World Wide Web, pp. 285–295 (2001)
16. Serbos, D., Qi, S., Mamoulis, N., Pitoura, E., Tsaparas, P.: Fairness in package-to-group recommendations. In: Proceedings of the 26th International Conference on World Wide Web, WWW 2017, pp. 371–379. International World Wide Web Conferences Steering Committee, Republic and Canton of Geneva, Switzerland (2017). https://doi.org/10.1145/3038912.3052612
17. Stratigi, M., Kondylakis, H., Stefanidis, K.: Fairness in group recommendations in the health domain. In: IEEE International Conference on Data Engineering (2017)
18. Tiemann, M., Pauws, S.: Towards ensemble learning for hybrid music recommendation. In: ACM Conference on Recommender Systems, pp. 177–178 (2007)
19. Wang, X., Dou, L.: Social recommendation algorithm based on the context of time and tags. In: Third International Conference on Advanced Cloud and Big Data, pp. 15–19 (2016)

20. Wu, W., et al.: Improving performance of tensor-based context-aware recommenders using Bias Tensor Factorization with context feature auto-encoding. Knowl.-Based Syst. **128**(C), 71–77 (2017)
21. Xing, Z., Parandehgheibi, M., Xiao, F., Kulkarni, N., Pouliot, C.: Content-based recommendation for podcast audio-items using natural language processing techniques. In: IEEE International Conference on Big Data, pp. 2378–2383 (2017)
22. Yang, Q., Yao, X., Jingwei, Z., Zhongqin, B.: Exploiting SDAE model for recommendations. In: the 30th International Conference on Software Engineering & Knowledge Engineering, pp. 11–16 (2018)
23. Yin, H., Sun, Y., Cui, B., Hu, Z., Chen, L.: LCARS: a location-content-aware recommender system. In: ACM SIGKDD International Conference on Knowledge Discovery and Data Mining, pp. 221–229 (2013)
24. Yoshii, K., Goto, M., Komatani, K., Ogata, T., Okuno, H.G.: Hybrid collaborative and content-based music recommendation using probabilistic model with latent user preferences. In: International Conference on Music Information Retrieval, pp. 296–301 (2006)
25. Yu, Z., Tian, M., Wang, Z., Guo, B., Mei, T.: Shop-type recommendation leveraging the data from social media and location-based services. ACM Trans. Knowl. Discov. Data **11**(1), 1 (2016)
26. Zhang, J., Yang, C., Yang, Q., Lin, Y., Zhang, Y.: HGeoHashBase: an optimized storage model of spatial objects for location-based services. Front. Comput. Sci. 1–11 (2018)
27. Zhang, L., Zhou, R., Jiang, H., Wang, H., Zhang, Y.: Item group recommendation: a method based on game theory. In: International Conference on World Wide Web Companion, pp. 1405–1411 (2017)

A Location Spoofing Detection Method for Social Networks (Short Paper)

Chaoping Ding[1], Ting Wu[2], Tong Qiao[2], Ning Zheng[1,2], Ming Xu[1,2(✉)],
Yiming Wu[2], and Wenjing Xia[1]

[1] Internet and Network Security Laboratory,
School of Computer Science and Technology,
Hangzhou Dianzi University, Hangzhou, China
{161050056,nzheng,mxu,161050051}@hdu.edu.cn
[2] School of Cyberspace, Hangzhou Dianzi University, Hangzhou, China
{wuting,tong.qiao,ymwu}@hdu.edu.cn

Abstract. It is well known that check-in data from location-based social networks (LBSN) can be used to predict human movement. However, there are large discrepancies between check-in data and actual user mobility, because users can easily spoof their location in LBSN. The act of location spoofing refers to intentionally making false location, leading to a negative impact both on the credibility of location-based social networks and the reliability of spatial-temporal data. In this paper, a location spoofing detection method in social networks is proposed. First, Latent Dirichlet Allocation (LDA) model is used to learn the topics of users by mining user-generated microblog information, based on this a similarity matrix associated with the venue is calculated. And the venue visiting probability is computed based on user historical check-in data by using Bayes model. Then, the similarity value and visiting probability is combined to quantize the probability of location spoofing. Experiments on a large scale and real-world LBSN dataset collected from Weibo show that the proposed approach can effectively detect certain types of location spoofing.

Keywords: Location spoofing · Social networks · Semantic analysis

1 Introdcution

Several location-based social networks have increased exponentially during the last two decades. The growing popularity of LBSN has brought about the appearance of an economy where users announce. To attract more users, the LBSN provide both virtual or real-word rewards to the user, when a user has certain number of check-in at a venue. Unfortunately, this reward gives users incentives to spoof their location information so that they can check into POI (point of interest) far away from where they really are.

In recent years, the diffusion of location spoofing has stirred debate about the credibility of spatial-temporal data. It can use as an effective countermeasure to protect user privacy, and also has a negative impact on the credibility of LBSN.

© ICST Institute for Computer Sciences, Social Informatics and Telecommunications Engineering 2019
Published by Springer Nature Switzerland AG 2019. All Rights Reserved
H. Gao et al. (Eds.): CollaborateCom 2018, LNICST 268, pp. 138–150, 2019.
https://doi.org/10.1007/978-3-030-12981-1_9

However, these two views cannot have a comprehensive understanding of location spoofing. [1,2] indicated that users make more friends or impress others by claiming a false location in social media. [3] thought the business model of Foursquare make it as a lucrative target to attack by location cheating, a business man may use location spoofing to check into a competing business, and badmouth that business by leaving bad comments. To prevent location spoofing in social networks. Foursquare has adopted the "cheater code" to prevent location spoofing attacks. [4,5] proposed Wi-Fi, QR-code and near field based location verifications solutions to solve location fraud problems. Although above-mentioned measures have been applied, once the user knows the verification mechanism, they can launch location cheating attack.

To further validate and understand the discrepancies between user-generated check-ins and their actual movements. [6,7] quantified the value of geosocial datasets by comparing GPS traces against Foursquare check-ins, they find that a large portion of visited locations are forged. A few researchers have been studying how to detect location spoofing. [8] used tensor decomposition to spot anomalies in the check-in behavior of users. [9] used the Bayesian model to detect location spoofing by using millions of geo-tagged tweets. However, aforementioned approaches only consider check-ins data and ignore the location information contained in the user's microblog text, the method is not suitable for detecting fake check-in that continuously post from the same POI.

Considering the reliability of social network check-in data or the credibility of LBSN, effectively detecting spoofing location check-in data is an urgent problem need to be solved. Thus in this report, we use Sina Weibo[1] to investigate the location spoofing in social networks. Unlike the existing literature, we take both the user-generated content and check-ins data into consideration to detect location spoofing in social networks. Our contributions in this paper are twofold: (1) We introduce a practical way of location spoofing in Weibo, which can easily bypass the current location verification mechanisms. Our finding indicates that the current location verification mechanisms might not sufficient to prevent location spoofing. (2) We develop a novel location spoofing detection approach for quantizing the probability of fake check-in in social network, which can promote the credibility of LBSN and the reliability of spatial-temporal data.

2   Location Spoofing on Sina Weibo

Weibo has already launched a location service called Weibo Place, which allows users to check into special locations in Weibo, the check-in is done by hand, which means a user is able to determine where he/she wants to check in. When users post geo-tagged information, they are actually advertising the place. The check-in data is the concentrated reflection of customers to the POI.

Every check-in on Weibo is associated with a Weibo place page, and the microblogs containing the geo-tags related to the specified POI will display on the same page, the "total people" and "total check-ins" of the POI will also display

---

[1] https://weibo.com/.

on the place page. According to our survey, if users want to share their real location information on Weibo, they can only check in with their mobile phones. But in fact Weibo uses short URL to represent POI, like "http://t.cn/z8Af3JR". As long as users get a URL of POI, he can publish check-in information on any client, which gives the user the possibility of spoof their location.

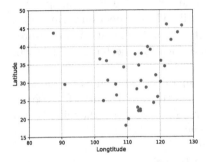

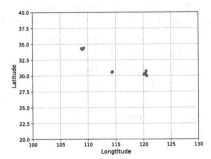

Fig. 1. Spoofing check-in location.   **Fig. 2.** Real check-in location.

To evaluate the location detection mechanisms deployed by Weibo, we reproduce the location spoofing scenario. First, we crawl 30 different venues' short URL throughout China, then we post microblog contained the short URL of POI. In this way, we can check into the same venue at any time interval. And we can also continuously check into different venues that are located far away from each other in just a few minutes. Meanwhile, we model a user to appear as traveling at any speed. Figure 1 shows the check-in location of location spoofing within a few minutes. As we can see in Fig. 1, those venues are scattered pretty far apart and spread over 30 different cities throughout China. Figure 2 shows the recent check-in record of a normal check-in volunteer, and the volunteer's check-in locate in three cities. Obviously, the distance elapsed between two consecutive check-ins cannot be so far in a very short time interval, due to the temporal and spatial constraints. Our experiments show that the location detection mechanisms of Weibo can be bypassed through our method. Unlike Foursquare, Weibo place do not set a limit on the number of check-ins in a given window and the user travel speed between two POI.

3   The Framework for Location Spoofing Detection

In this section, we introduce our approach for location spoofing detection in Weibo. As show in Fig. 3, there are three major parts in our scheme, contend proximity calculation, visiting probability computing and location spoofing estimation.

3.1   Problem Statement

The problem of location spoofing detection is to detect fake check-in data on specified POI. To simplify this problem, we set the detection target POI to the commercial center, we define the commercial center as a heterogeneous structure that consists of parts which are different from each other, including shopping mall, restaurant and so on. For ease of presentation, we use POI, venue, and location interchangeably in this work. Formally, we are given a specified POI V, let $U = \{u_1, u_2, \ldots, u_M\}$ be a set of M users, where each user has the same geo-tag of V. Let $G = \{u_{1g}, u_{2g}, \ldots, u_{Mg}\}$ be a set of the microblog posted by user contained the same geo-tag of V. Our goal is to detect the fake geo-tags of G, the fake geo-tags are generated by user who intentionally falsifying their actual location information. For each POI, we have textual information in terms of geo-tag words, and the regional popularity of V in terms of how many people visited V, the popularity of POI is derived from the "total people" and "total check-ins".

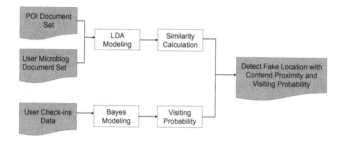

Fig. 3. The framework of location spoofing detection.

We deem that the rating of user launch location spoofing in POI is determined by the visit probability [9], the locational information of user's check-in with a lower visit probability is more likely to be fake. The probability of a user accessing the POI can be inferred by the follow factors: (1) each user's history microblogs contain information related to the POI. As semantic information is embedded in the microblog on LBSN that reflect the relevance of the user to the POIs, e.g., a restaurant name, environment, service, etc. It could help us estimate the probability of a user visiting a venue. (2) each user's history check-ins data associated with the POI can reflect the user's visiting probability at the POI. For these two reasons, we propose a method for location spoofing detection in social media by exploring the user's microblog textual content similarity with the POI and the check-ins data associated with the venue.

3.2   Microblog Textual Content Similarity

As aforementioned, users spoof their location by checking into a POI far away from where they really are so that they can get the rewards, which means those who launch a location cheating attack must be far away from the special POI.

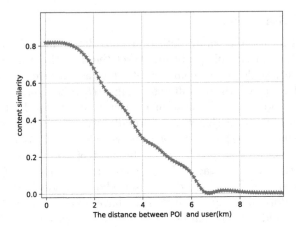

Fig. 4. The user-generated content similarity of different distance.

We observed that the similarity of textual content between the user and POI is inversely proportional to geographic distance. Because user-generated content in social media mainly comes from user's lives in the physical world, the user tends to post content related to the geographically nearby POI. To validate this assumption, we study about 120,000 users sampled from Weibo, the sample consists of users with different distance from POI, we collect microblog generated by those sampled users. In Fig. 4, we plotted the similarity of the user-generated content and the target POI versus distance. We can see that the similarity of the user-generated content and the target POI monotonically decreases with the distance between them. Thus, the content similarity is a key factor to quantize the probability that a user launch location spoofing in the target POI.

For the above reasons, we calculate the similarity between user microblog content and POI information based on topic model, which provides methods to infer the latent topics from visible words, maps textual information corpus to each topic space. We use LDA to model textual information, and then obtain the topic-word probability distribution and document-topic probability distribution from the model, based on this calculate the content similarity by using the symmetric Jensen-Shannon divergence [10] between user u_i and the specified POI.

Topic Models. Unlike the existed similarity calculation method, the similarity calculation based on topic model can mine the latent semantic location information. The LDA model [11] is a popular technique to identify latent information from large document collection. The basic idea of LDA is that every document is represented as the probability distribution of topics, and each topic is represented as the probability distribution of words, the generative process of LDA is as shown in Fig. 5.

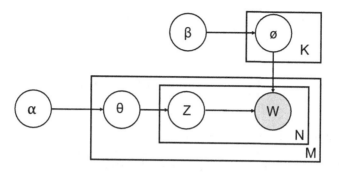

Fig. 5. LDA generation probability diagram.

To explore topics related to POI location of LBSN users, we propose to aggregate each user's history microblog into a user document d_{ui}, let $D = \{d_{u1}, d_{u2}, \ldots, d_{um}\}$, be a set of user document, one document of D is $d_{ui} = \{w_1, w_2, \ldots, w_n\}$, unique N words set of all the associated textual information. We combine all the microblog contained the same geo-tags of specified POI into a POI document d_v. To calculate the similarity between the user microblog and POI, we need to extract more semantic information of a given POI. Thus we crawl the location information matched POI from Meituan[2] to enrich the knowledge of the POI, then we conflate POI information of Weibo with Meituan. In this way, we get each user's microblog documents d_{ui} and the document d_v of POI V. By using LDA model, we get the topic distribution both of the user's microblog and POI. Each user u is associated with multinomial distribution over topic, represented by θ, each location-related topics is associated with a multinomial distribution over textual terms, represented by ϕ, the generation process of LDA model is as follows:

1. For each topic k, a word multinominal distribution ϕ_k is obtained from the Dirichlet (β) distribution.
2. For the document d_{ui} in $D = \{d_{u1}, d_{u2}, \ldots, d_{um}\}$, a topic distribution $\theta_{d_{ui}}$ is obtained from the Dirichlet(α) distribution.
3. For each word w_i in document d_{ui}: (a) extract a topic t from topic multinomial distribution $\theta_{d_{ui}}$. (b) extract a word w_i from word multinomial distribution ϕ_k of the topic.

From the LDA topic model, we can get the probability θ_{ij} that a user i associated with the topic k_j, and the probability distribution ϕ_i of topic i over the number of unique terms N in the dataset. We futher infer the topic distribution η of the specified POI based on the learned user topic term distribution.

---

[2] http://meituan.com/.

Therefore, we can compute the content similarity between the user and POI. According to Fig. 5, the joint distribution probability of all parameters of the whole model is obtained:

$$P(W, Z, \Theta, \Phi \mid \alpha, \beta) = \prod_{n=1}^{N_m} P(w_{m,n} \mid \phi_{z_{m,n}}) P(z_{m,n} \mid \theta_m) P(\theta_m \mid \alpha) P(\Phi \mid \beta) \quad (1)$$

LDA Modelling. In the process of LDA modelling, there are two latent variables that can be inferred from the data: the user level document-topic distribution Θ, and the topic-word distributions Φ. We also need to infer the topic distribution η for the specified POI through the learned model. α and β are super parameter. In this paper, the method used for parameter estimation is Gibbs sampling [12]. Two matrixes can be obtained from Gibbs sampling, the calculation method is as follows:

$$\phi_{k,w} = \frac{n_k^{(w)} + \beta}{\sum_{w=1}^{v} n_k^{(w)} + N\beta}, \theta_{i,k} = \frac{n_i^{(k)} + \alpha}{\sum_{k=1}^{k} n_i^{(k)} + K\alpha} \quad (2)$$

where $n_k^{(w)}$ represents the number of words assigned to topic k, $n_i^{(k)}$ represents the topic observation counts for document d_{ui} of user u_i. N is the number of the unique words and K is the number of topics. Then we infer the topic distribution for POI is: $\eta_{jk} = \frac{n_j^{(k)} + \alpha}{\sum_{k=1}^{K} n_j^{(k)} + K\alpha}$, where $n_j^{(k)}$ is the topic observation count for POI document d_v.

Content Similarity Calculation. After obtaining the document-topic probability distribution and topic-word probability distribution by constructing LDA model, the similarity calculation between user-generated documents d_{ui} and the POI document d_v can be realized by computing the corresponding topic probability distribution. This paper we use the symmetric JS (Jensen-Shannon) distance formula which can measure the distance of probability distribution to calculate the similarity between two documents. It is based on the Kullback-Leibler divergence. By applying Jensen-Shannon divergence to the topic assignment for the documents d_{ui} and document d_v, it will allow us to measure the similarity between the user and the POI. The distance vector $p = (p_1, p_2, \ldots, q_k)$ to $q = (q_1, q_2, \ldots, q_k)$ is computed as follows Eq. (3):

$$D_{js}(p, q) = \frac{1}{2}[D_{KL}(p \| M) + D_{KL}(q \| M)], \quad (3)$$

where $M = \frac{1}{2}(p + q)$ and $D_{KL}(p \| M) = \sum_{j=1}^{T} p_j \log \frac{p_j}{M_j}$ is Kullback-Leibler distance. p represents topic probability distribution of each user's documents d_{ui}, and q represents topic probability distribution of the POI document d_v. Then we define the similarity between the user-generated microblog and the POI information as formula:

$$S(u_i, V) = 1 - D_{js}(p, q) \quad (4)$$

3.3 POI Visiting Probability Based on Bayes Model

In addition to the user's microblog content information and the POI textual information, we have the user's historical check-in data. User's history check-in data can reflect the visiting probability at the POI. Rather than estimate the visiting probability by using historical check-in record directly, we take the popularity of POI into consideration. And use Bayes models to calculate the user's probability of accessing the POI. More concretely, let P(V) represents the visiting probability of user at POI, which can be calculated as the following equation:

$$P(V) = P(A|H) = P(A) \cdot \frac{P(H|A)}{P(H)} \tag{5}$$

where P(A) is the prior beliefs, given a user's historical check-in data, the total number of check-in data is N, and n is the number of user's check-in at POI, then $P(A) = \frac{n}{N}$. P(H) indicates the probability of an arbitrary user check into POI, it can be estimated by the popularity of POI. We can get the "total people" and the "total check-ins" at POI from the POI page, then $P(H) = \frac{total\ people}{total\ check-ins}$. $P(H|A)$ is determined by C_n, C_n is the "total number" check-ins associated with POI. We define $P(H|A)$ as a piecewise function:

$$P(V) = \begin{cases} P(H), & C_n > p \\ P(A), & 0 < C_n \le p \end{cases} \tag{6}$$

where p is the threshold to distinguish the densely populated areas and sparsely populated areas. When $C_n > p$, meaning the POI is a crowded place, human movements P(H) can be barely interfered by the activity of an individual P(A). Therefore, $P(H|A) = $ P(H). When $C_n < $ p, meaning the POI is a sparsely populated area, human movements P(H) can be affected by the activity of an individual P(A). Therefore, $P(H|A) = $ P(A). Ultimately, P(V) can be formulated as follows:

$$P(V) = \begin{cases} P(A), & C_n > p \\ \frac{P(A)^2}{P(H)}, & 0 < C_n \le p \end{cases} \tag{7}$$

For ease of evaluation, we count the total number of check-ins on different densely populated POI in Weibo, the statistical results show that the average number of check-ins on these POIs is no less than 1000, thus we set p = 1000.

3.4 Location Spoofing Detection

Further, to quantize the probability of user's check-in data is fake in social network, we need to consider both (1) the similarity between user-generated content and the target POI information, and (2) the probability of the user accessing the POI. The similarity value can reflect the latent location information between user and POI, and the visit probability reflects the correlation between users and POI. Both the low similarity value and visit probability is more likely to be fake location. Thus we combine the similarity value and visit probability to quantize location spoofing as follows:

$$\vartheta = \lambda * D_{js}(p, v) + (1 - \lambda) * P(V) \tag{8}$$

where ϑ is the quantized value to estimate the probability of spoofing location information. The lower the value of ϑ, the greater the probability of forgery. λ is a factor to balance these two factors.

4   Experiments and Ananlysis

The experiments were performed on real-world social network dataset collected from Weibo. First, we collect all the microblogs containing the geo-tags related to the specified POI, including user ID, microblogs content, Weibo source, microblogs posting time. Then we use the user ID that collect in the specified POI to collect microblogs generated by these sample user, and filter out those users whose historical microblogs is fewer than 20 and check-in data is less than three times on the target POI. Filter out users with less than three check-ins at the target POI for the following two reasons: (1) If the users want to be rewarded by falsifying their location to the target POI, his number of check-ins related to the POI must accumulate to the specified value. (2) We set the specified value to 3, in this case, we can effectively avoid misjudgment of users who have checked into the target once. After applying this filter, we crawled over 2,000 user's historical data, a total of 120,000 microblogs.

There is no formal ground truth to label LBSN user's check-in data in fake. Hence, we invite volunteer to label these users who post fake geo-tags manually according to the forgery features. As mentioned in Sect. 3, if the user's check-in data is legitimate, he can only post the check-in information via the mobile client, and the check-in data should not violate the temporal and spatial constraints. For these reasons, we manually selected the microblogs that contain the target POI geo-tag posted by non-mobile client. And pick out microblogs that obviously violates the space-time constraints. Then we mark those checked-in messages as fake, which can be treated as ground truth.

4.1   Evaluation Metrics

For the evaluation, accuracy, precision, recall and F1-score are the most common used evaluation metrics. Thus in our experiments, we adopt these four metrics defined below to measure performances of our method. Where TP (True Positive) represents the fake geo-tags correctly identified as fake, FP (False Positive) represents the true geo-tags incorrectly identified as fake, TN (True Negative) represents the true geo-tags correctly identified as true, FN (False Negative) represents the fake geo-tags incorrectly identified as true.

$$Accuracy = \frac{|TP| + |TN|}{|TP| + |TN| + |FP| + |FN|}, \qquad Precision = \frac{|TP|}{|TP| + |FP|} \tag{9}$$

$$Recall = \frac{|TP|}{|TP| + |FN|}, \qquad F1 - score = \frac{2 \cdot Precision \cdot Recall}{Precision + Recall} \qquad (10)$$

4.2 Experimental Results

For the probabilistic framework of detecting spoofing location in the dataset, we further need to set the parameter λ in the formulate $\vartheta = \lambda * D_{js}(p, v) + (1 - \lambda) * P(V)$. When $\lambda = 1$, it means that the quantized value ϑ is only determined by the user-generated microblogs, when $\lambda = 0$, it means that the quantized value ϑ is only determined by the user check-in record and $0 < \lambda < 1$ means that the probabilistic framework is determined by these two factors.

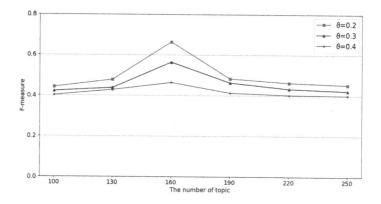

Fig. 6. Relationship between the number of topics and F-measure.

In the LDA modeling process, the accuracy of LDA clustering results will be affected by the number of topics k, so before setting the value of λ, we need to determine the value of k. We use Gibbs sampling algorithm to evaluate parameter, the number of iterations of Gibbs sampling is 2000. According to the empirical value, we set $\alpha = 50/k$ and $\beta = 0.01$. As the topic k and quantized value ϑ will directly affect the precision of LDA model, which will affect the detection result, we determined the value of k and ϑ by experiment, and set $\lambda = 1$. The F-measure is higher, the experiment result is better. As shown in Fig. 6, different number of topics generates different F-measure.

Here the abscissa represents the number of topics, the vertical coordinate represents the value of the F-measure. The change of F-measure with topic K is shown in Fig. 6. Since most of the content similarity values are around 0.6, we set the ϑ as 0.2, 0.3, 0.4. In Fig. 6, we can see that under different values of ϑ, F-measure values change with respect to topic K. When $\vartheta = 0.2$, K = 160, the F-measure reaches the maximum. So the number of topics is determined as 160, and the value of ϑ is determined as 0.2 in our case.

To further investigate the effect of the user-generated microblog and the user history check-in record on the probabilistic framework, we perform the

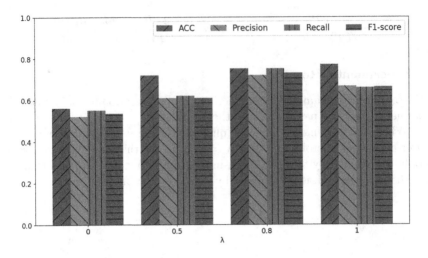

Fig. 7. Accuracy, precision, recall and F1-score with different λ.

experiment by adjusting λ, which controls the weight of this two different factors. Figure 7 shows the experimental results at different λ. When $\lambda = 0$, it means that the experimental result is determined by the user check-in record, and the detection of spoofing location information is based on Bayes Model. When $\lambda = 1$, it means that the experimental result is determined by the user-generated microblogs, and the detection of spoofing location information is based on "LDA+JS". When $0 < \lambda < 1$ means that the experimental result is made by combining both the user-generated microblogs and the user history check-in record, and the detection of spoofing location information is based on "LDA+JS+Bayes Model".

Table 1 shows the experimental results of different methods. We can see that the combination of user-generated microblog and the user history check-in record achieves the highest precision, which means the combination of user-generated microblog compensate the user history check-in record to improve the experimental results. The results demonstrate that we can achieve 20% relative improvement over state-of-the-art approaches, it proves that combining these features together can achieve a better performance.

Table 1. Experimental results of different methods.

Experimental method	Precision Ration	Recall ration	F metic
Bayes model	0.523	0.551	0.537
LDA+JS	0.667	0.660	0.663
LDA+JS+Bayes model	0.724	0.752	0.738

5   Conclusion and Future Work

A method for location spoofing detection in social networks is proposed in this article, and the results show that our approach can detect certain types of spoofing location. Meanwhile, we launch location cheating attack that enables us to check into a venue far away from our real location, and demonstrate the LBS are vulnerable and the true impact of fake locations in social networks.

As the counter measures against location cheating can be bypassed, a method is proposed to detect location spoofing in social networks. Even though our method is to detect the target POI of commercial center, we believe that the method we proposed can open the door to further research in this field. Regarding the future work, we will try to obtain more social context information (e.g., user's social groups) because geographically nearby users are more likely to publish similar geo-related content. The proposed model adopts LDA (based on bag-of-words model) to get the topic distribution of each users and POI, however, it is not based on context. Therefore, extracting location information from POI and user's generated-content by utilizing neural networks (e.g.,Word2Vec [13]) is a part of our future work.

Acknowledgment. This work is supported by the cyberspace security Major Program in National Key Research and Development Plan of China under grant 2016YFB0800201, Natural Science Foundation of China under grants 61572165 and 61702150, State Key Program of Zhejiang Province Natural Science Foundation of China under grant LZ15F020003, Key Research and Development Plan Project of Zhejiang Province under grants 2017C01062 and 2017C01065, and the Scientific Research fund of Zhejiang Provincial Education Department under grant Y201737924, and Zhejiang Provincial Natural Science Foundation of China under Grant No. LGG18F020015.

References

1. Lindqvist, J., Cranshaw, J., Wiese, J., Hong, J., Zimmerman, J.: I'm the mayor of my house: examining why people use foursquare-a social-driven location sharing application. In: Proceedings of the SIGCHI Conference on Human Factors in Computing Systems, pp. 2409–2418. ACM (2011)
2. Patil, S., Norcie, G., Kapadia, A., Lee, A.: Check out where i am!: location-sharing motivations, preferences, and practices. In: CHI 2012 Extended Abstracts on Human Factors in Computing Systems, pp. 1997–2002. ACM (2012)
3. He, W., Liu, X., Ren, M.: Location cheating: a security challenge to location-based social network services. In: 2011 31st International Conference on Distributed computing systems (ICDCS), pp. 740–749. IEEE (2011)
4. Zhang, F., Kondoro, A., Muftic, S.: Location-based authentication and authorization using smart phones. In: 2012 IEEE 11th International Conference on Trust, Security and Privacy in Computing and Communications, pp. 1285–1292. IEEE (2012)
5. Polakis, I., Volanis, S., Athanasopoulos, E., Markatos, E.P.: The man who was there: validating check-ins in location-based services. In: Proceedings of the 29th Annual Computer Security Applications Conference, pp. 19–28. ACM (2013)

6. Zhang, Z., et al.: On the validity of geosocial mobility traces. In: Proceedings of the Twelfth ACM Workshop on Hot Topics in Networks, p. 11. ACM (2013)

7. Wang, G., Schoenebeck, S.Y., Zheng, H., Zhao, B.Y.: "Will check-in for badges": understanding bias and misbehavior on location-based social networks. In: ICWSM, pp. 417–426 (2016)

8. Papalexakis, E., Pelechrinis, K., Faloutsos, C.: Spotting misbehaviors in location-based social networks using tensors. In: Proceedings of the 23rd International Conference on World Wide Web, pp. 551–552. ACM (2014)

9. Zhao, B., Sui, D.Z.: True lies in geospatial big data: detecting location spoofing in social media. Ann. GIS 23(1), 1–14 (2017)

10. Lin, J.: Divergence measures based on the Shannon entropy. IEEE Trans. Inf. Theory 37, 145–151 (1991)

11. Blei, D.M., Ng, A.Y., Jordan, M.I.: Latent Dirichlet allocation. J. Mach. Learn. Res. 3(Jan), 993–1022 (2003)

12. Griffiths, T.L., Steyvers, M.: Finding scientific topics. Proc. Nat. Acad. Sci. 101(suppl 1), 5228–5235 (2004)

13. Goldberg, Y., Levy, O.: word2vec explained: deriving Mikolov et al.'s negative-sampling word-embedding method. arXiv preprint arXiv:1402.3722 (2014)

The Three-Degree Calculation Model of Microblog Users' Influence (Short Paper)

Xueying Sun and Fu Xie[✉]

School of Information Science and Engineering, Shandong Normal University,
Jinan 250014, China
sunxueying@stu.sdnu.edu.cn, 1451850328@qq.com

Abstract. Highly influential social users can guide public opinion and influence their emotional venting. Therefore, it is of great significance to identify high-impact users effectively. This paper starts with the users' text content, users' emotions, and fans' behaviors. It combines the amount of information in the content and sentiment tendency with the fans' forwarding, commenting, and Liking actions. And based on the principle of the three-degree influence, the users' influence calculation model is constructed. Finally, the experimental results show that the three-degree force calculation model is more accurate and effective than other similar models.

Keywords: Three-degree · Microblog · User influence

1 Introduction

Taking the Sina Microblog social networking platform as an example, by September 2017, the number of monthly active users of Microblog was 376 million, increased 27% compared with the same period in 2016, of which China's mobile terminal accounted for 92% and the daily active users reached 165 million, an increase of 25% over the same period of last year. If we can find influential nodes in the network quickly and effectively, it will be better for the government to monitor public opinion and guide them in time. For the business community, it is possible to achieve targeted commercial promotion, advertising marketing, etc. according to the influence nodes in the network. Therefore, the research on the analysis, measurement, modeling, and dissemination of node influence in social networks has a very important theoretical and practical values.

According to the three-degree influence theory, this paper constructed a computing model based on users' blog content and fans' behavior. Firstly, calculate the content of the blog post and measure the amount of content information through the information entropy. Secondly, analyze and calculate the sentiment tendencies of the blog post. In addition, calculate the "forward-comment-like" influence of the user's three-tier. Finally, verify it by crawling data. Results showed that the three-degree influence calculation model proposed in this paper is more accurate and effective than other similar models.

© ICST Institute for Computer Sciences, Social Informatics and Telecommunications Engineering 2019
Published by Springer Nature Switzerland AG 2019. All Rights Reserved
H. Gao et al. (Eds.): CollaborateCom 2018, LNICST 268, pp. 151–160, 2019.
https://doi.org/10.1007/978-3-030-12981-1_10

2   Related Research at Home and Abroad

Research on influence attracted the attention of scholars from all walks of life in the early 20th century. When Triplett [1] studied social promotion theory, he discovered that when a person received attention from others, his/her performance would become more prominent. By the 1950s, Katz et al. [2] found that influence played a very important role in daily life or in political elections. In recent years, with the rise of large-scale social networks such as Microblog, various theories have shown that the distance between people has become shorter and shorter, and the links have become closer and more influential.

Zhang and Tang [3] pointed out three aspects of influence, the first is the individual's influence on one user only, means the ability of affecting other users and the probability of being affected by others; the second one was the influence between the two users of A and B, means A influences B and B influences A; the third is the group influence, which is the most complicated, refers to the influence of a group of multiple users on one user. Shi et al. [4] integrated user behaviors and blog post content and evaluated the predicted users and the influence of the issued microblog through the extraction of behavioral characteristics and content characteristics such as the users' blog posting time and "forward-like" behavior. Chen et al. [5] analyzed users' influence in terms of user behavior and community structure. First, it divided the network into groups. Then, the users' influence was measured from the number of fans of the user and the quality of the fans and the number of communities the user crosses. The authors in [6] evaluated users' influence from two aspects of user behavior and user relationship. First, analyze users' blog post content. Second, improved based on the PageRank algorithm, and calculates activeness for each node. Finally calculate the BRR (Behavior-Relationship Rank) of the node. and sort the nodes based on their value i.e. influence. Xu et al. [7] proposed a new social influence model, the PTIM model, which was an iterative combination of the characteristics of the user's fans and small-world attributes and has achieved relatively good results for all evaluation indicators. Fowler et al. [8] found that the happiness between people could reach a three-degree separation by studying the spread of happiness in social networks, that is the principle of the three-degree influence. The node affects the neighboring node, this is the first-degree effect; it can also affect the neighboring node's neighboring node, which is the second-degree effect; and it also affects the neighboring node's neighboring node of the neighboring node, which is the third-degree effect. The study found that the effect diminished with the separation of time and geography, and the influence beyond three degrees was negligible. In the literature [9,10], through real data experiments on Facebook and SNS, it pointed out that both the intensity of friendship between friends or the intimacy between users have a great impact on user behavior. Through the interaction intensity and intimacy analysis, a richer social graph can be obtained. The above studies on influence started from different aspects and can be roughly divided into three aspects: user relations, behavior, and content of blog post. The dissemination of information was interlocking and complex in the network. As above mentioned [5], attention was paid to the quality of the users' fans. However, the dissemination of information is not merely a forwarding level and can be spread by multiple users.

3 The Three-Degree Calculation Model of Users' Influence

3.1 The Calculation of First-Degree Influence Based on the Content of Information

The more content a microblog user publishes, the greater the amount of information they contain and they are more likely to be forwarded. This article used information entropy to represent how much information the user content contained. For the analysis of the content of the blog post, this paper used the NLPIR semantic analysis system. NLPIR (Natural Language Processing and Information Retrieval Sharing Platform) is a word segmentation system developed by Dr. Zhang Huaping. The more information in the post content, the higher the complexity, the greater the entropy value, and the greater the probability of being followed, browsed, and forwarded. The keyword collection function of the NLPIR semantic analysis system can get the keyword set K, and the keywords' weight in the content also can be obtained.

$$P_i = \frac{W_i}{\sum_{i \in k}^{n} W_i} \tag{1}$$

where W_i refers to the weight of the extracted keywords in the content; and P_i refers to the probability that the $i - th$ keyword appears in the content. The entropy [11] is calculated as follows:

$$E = -\sum_{i \in k} P_i \cdot \log P_i \tag{2}$$

While analyzing the content, we need to consider the topic degree of the blog post, whether the content fits the hot topic. Calculate the similarity of blog post content and topics. For text similarity, we use the cosine similarity to calculate the similarity of blog content and hot topics in this paper.

$$Sim = (content, hottopic) = \cos(K, H) = \frac{\sum_1^n (K_i \times H_i)}{\sqrt{\sum_1^n K_i^2} \times \sqrt{\sum_1^n H_i^2}} \tag{3}$$

In the formula, Ki, Hi refer to the weights of features extracted from the blog post content and feature weights of the current hot topics.

Finally, the influence of the post content can be expressed as:

$$TI = \begin{cases} E(1 + Sim(content, hottopic)), Sim > 0 \\ E, Sim = 0 \end{cases} \tag{4}$$

3.2   The Calculation of Second-Degree Influence Based on Bowen's Emotion

Microblog posts not only contain the views and opinions of users, but also embody their emotions. Therefore, the post's emotions also play a crucial role in the user influence. The study of text sentiment tendencies can be mainly divided into two aspects: the method based on dependency syntax analysis [12–14] and the method based on the term bag model [15–17]. Referring to the methods of these two aspects, the rules for calculating the sentiment orientation of sentences are given below.

Calculation rules 1. Emotional calculation of emotional words. The emotional word is recorded as "*word*", emotional intensity is "*EIntensity*", emotional positive and negative polarity is "*EPolarity*". The calculation is defined as follows:

$$Value(word) = \Theta \times EIntersity(word) \times EPolarity(word), \Theta \in R \quad (5)$$

EIntensity, the emotional intensity, is the original part of speech, and refers to the emotional tendency of the word itself such as "praise", "pampering" which has a clear emotional tendency; *EPolarity*, the positive and negative polarity of emotion is the positive and negative emotional tendency of the word. Θ refers to the harmonic coefficient which is the modified polarity of the word, and it is expressed as an adverb of degree such as "100%" and "compared".

Calculation rule 2. Sentence calculation rules. V is the tendency value of emotional words, and its definition is as follows:

$$Value(sentence) = \sum_{i=1}^{m} V(word) \quad (6)$$

Among them, m refers to the number of emotional words in a sentence, and the emotional tendency of the entire sentence can be obtained by adding up the calculated emotional tendencies of each emotional word.

Calculation rule 3. The emotional value of blog post content is defined as follows:

$$Value(text) = \frac{1}{n-m} \sum_{i=1}^{n} V_i \times W_i \quad (7)$$

Among them, n is the total number of emotional sentences in the blog, and m is the number of sentences in the blog that do not contain emotions. V_i refers to the emotional value of the $i-th$ sentence, and W_i refers to the weight of the $i-th$ emotional sentence in the blog post.

The above calculation can divide the blog into three levels.

$$\begin{cases} Value > posThreshold, Positive\ Emotion \\ negThreshold < Value < posThreshold, Neutral\ Attitude \\ Value < negThreshold, Negative\ Emotion \end{cases} \quad (8)$$

PosThreshold and *negThreshold* are the propensity thresholds for positive emotions and negative emotions, respectively.

3.3   Three-Degree Influence Calculation Based on Fan Behavior

The behavior of fan users on a microblog mainly includes three types: forwarding, liking, and commenting. We use BI to represent behavior-influence, the expression is as follows:

$$BI = U(FI, CI, LI) \tag{9}$$

FI indicates the forwarding influence, which is how many people forwarded the blog post. CI indicates the influence of the comment, i.e., how many people have commented on the blog post. LI is the influence of praise, which is how many people like it.

User v is the fan of u, then $v's$ attention to $u's$ microblogs can be measured by the time difference between u publishing blog posts and $v's$ behavior. Assume that the blog post set posted by u is Mu and the time set is Tu, the blog set forwarded, commented and liked by v is Mv and the time set is Tv. Calculate the time difference of all the actions, and find the mean value. Where the smaller the mean value, the greater attention that v represents for u, the greater the likelihood of $v's$ forwarding. And calculate its variance S^2. The smaller the fluctuation of the variance, the higher the reliability of the mean, and the more stable the attention of v to u.

The specific calculation is as follows:

$$M = \frac{\sum(T_v - T_u)}{N_{vn}} \tag{10}$$

where M is the mean of all time differences; $(T_v - T_u)$ is the time difference for a blog post; $\sum(T_v - T_u)$ is the sum of all time differences; and N_{vu}, which is how many time differences there are.

$$S^2 = \frac{\sum(T_v - M)^2}{N_{vu}} \tag{11}$$

S^2 is the variance of the time difference, and the smaller the variance, the more stable the attention degree. Finally, the variance is translated into the probability that the fan produces behavior. Based on the variance, the frequency of the behavior that generates the behavior should also be taken into consideration.

$$F = \begin{cases} \frac{n}{N}(1 - 0.01S^2), S^2 > 0 \\ 1, S^2 = 0 \end{cases} \tag{12}$$

where n is the total number of fans' actions. N is the total number of users' microblogs.

Therefore, the influences of forwarding, commenting, and liking are calculated as follows, respectively:

$$FI = \sum_{v \in Fan(u)} F_{vu} \tag{13}$$

$$CI = \sum_{v \in Fan(u)} F_{vu} \tag{14}$$

$$LI = \sum_{v \in Fan(u)} F_{vu} \tag{15}$$

We introduced α, β, γ, three parameters that represent the weights of the three types of behaviors, BI was calculated as follows:

$$BI = \alpha FI + \beta CI + \gamma LI \tag{16}$$

The principle of the three-degree influence showed that information was attenuated during propagation, so we introduced an attenuation factor ω, and as the distance increased, the value of the factor will decrease. For content information, emotions, and users' behavior, weighted fusion was based on their relationship. Calculated as follows:

$$SBI = a \cdot (TI \times Value) + b \cdot (\omega_1 BI_1 + \omega_2 BI_2 + \omega_3 BI_3) \tag{17}$$

SBI represents the sum of users' three-degree influence, which is users' influence; TI is the content influence; $Value$ refers to the emotional tendency value; BI_1, BI_2, BI_3 represent the influence of each layer, respectively; and a and b are the weights of the evaluation indicators.

4   Experiments

4.1   Data Collection

Through the Python crawler, the real data set obtained from the API interface provided by the Sina Weibo platform, was to verify the calculation model proposed in this paper. This article has crawled 946 microblogs from the official website of Shandong Normal University from November 2017 to the end of February 2018. There were 66,617 three-layer forwards, comments, and likes, including 5931 pieces of forwarding data, 12,065 pieces of review data, and 48,675 pieces of like data. In addition, we also got the relevant information from 500 hot topics including attributes as content, the number of fans, reading volume, and discussion volume. Before data is used, we has removed the inactive users.

4.2   Data Processing

For the analysis of the content of the blog, we calculated the content information of the blog based on the NLPIR semantic analysis system of the Chinese Academy of Sciences, and calculated the emotional tendency value according to the sentiment calculation rules given above. When calculating fans' attention, we first counted the nicknames of the fans under Microblog, the time when they acted, and the number of microblogs each person interacted with, selected the appropriate time unit, and then got the fans' attention.

Figure 1 shows attention of some fans. The center point of the circle is 0, and it spreads out. The outermost layer is 1. We could see that most of the fans' attention was relatively low, and there were a few fans with high attention.

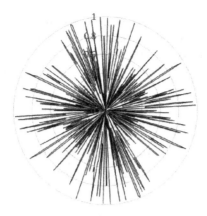

Fig. 1. Attention.

Three weights α, β, γ were introduced when we calculated each layer of users' influence. They represent the proportions of the three types of actions: forward, comment, and like. To calculate three weights, we used the analytic hierarchy process to get $\alpha = 0.539$, $\beta = 0.297$, $\gamma = 0.164$, as Table 1. For the introduced attenuation factor, we obtained that $\omega_1 = 0.136$, $\omega_2 = 0.098$, $\omega_3 = 0.024$ refers to literature [8,18]. According to subjective evaluation method and reference [4,5], a $=0.3$, b $= 0.7$.

Table 1. The value of α,β,γ.

	Like (γ)	Comment (β)	Forward (α)
Like (γ)	1	2	3
Comment (β)	1/2	1	2
Forward (α)	1/3	1/2	1

4.3   Algorithm Comparison

Evaluation Index. The evaluation index adopted in this paper was the coverage rate [19], which was the ratio of the number of nodes affected by the selected user to the total number of nodes in the microblog. The greater the coverage rate, the wider the range of influence that the users spread, and the more people are affected, the greater the influence.

$$Coverage = \frac{The\ number\ of\ affected\ nodes}{Total\ number\ of\ nodes} \times 100\% \qquad (18)$$

Compare. The purpose of the experiment was to prove that the algorithm proposed in this paper had a higher accuracy, so compared it with the PageRank algorithm and BRank algorithm [20], which only considered user behavior and the RBRank algorithm [21] which considered user relationship behavior. The result is shown in Table 2.

Table 2. Comparison between this algorithm and other algorithms.

Algorithm	PageRank	BRank	RBRank	This algorithm
Impact degree	20.9%	23.5%	26.1%	27.1%

From Table 2, we can see that the algorithm proposed in this paper improved the accuracy, but the difference of results was not very obvious. Analyzing the reasons, we believed that Shandong Normal University was the school portal, and the content and emotions conveyed were mainly positive. The fans were mainly students. The composition and structure were unitary, and the influence of fans was limited. Therefore, we needed to select other users with rich attributes to conduct the data acquisition and analysis again.

In the next experiment, we selected Fan Bingbing as a keyword and crawled its data for the past three months. The crawled attributes still included fans' nicknames, profiles, ID, followers, fans, microblogs, blog posts, and release dates. The number of forwarding, comments, number of likes, forwarders nickname, profile, ID, content of forwarded blog, forwarding time, totaled 280,460 items. According to the results of this algorithm, the comparison results are shown in Table 3.

Table 3. Comparison between this algorithm and other algorithms.

Algorithm	PageRank	BRank	RBRank	This algorithm
Impact degree	39.5%	47.6%	56.7%	63%

From Fig. 2, we can see that the RBRank algorithm and the algorithm of this paper had larger influence values than the PageRank and BRank algorithms. It explains that from multiple angles, selecting multiple eigenvalues in combination to evaluate users' influence is much more advantageous than simply calculating users' influence from one aspect. In addition, through the comparison, we found that the coverage rate of the proposed algorithm was the largest, indicating the best effect. Therefore, we reached a conclusion the proposed algorithm considered the users' sentiment content and emotional tendencies as well as the characteristics of the user behavior, expanding the depth of calculations, and calculating the three-degree influence was better.

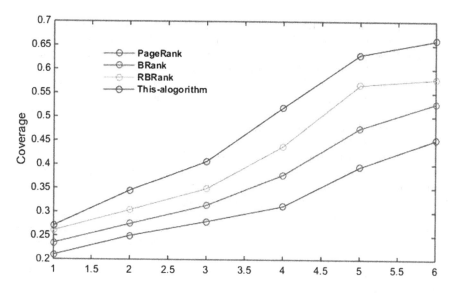

Fig. 2. Comparison between this algorithm and other algorithms.

5 Summary and Further Work

This paper proposed a calculation method based on the users' text content and users' behavior. Through the evaluation of content information and emotional tendency, the overall statistics on the users' forwarding, comments, likes, we constructed a users' influence computing model and improved accuracy. From the above experiment, we could see that selecting different experimental objects would have different effects, and the effect was more significant when the experimental objects were rich in attributes. Therefore, in future work, we will consider adding users' attributes to the calculation model to make the analysis of influence more perfect. Moreover, the cross relationship between fans is not considered in text, we should also be noted in the future work.

References

1. Triplett, N.: The dynamogenic factors in pacemaking and competition. Am. J. Psychol. **9**(4), 507–533 (1970)
2. Katz, E., Lazarsfeld, P.F.: Personal influence: the part played by people in the flow of mass communications. Am. J. Sociol. **21**(6), 1583–1583 (1955)
3. Zhang, J., Tang, J.: A review of social influence analysis. Chin. Sci. Inf. Sci. **47**(08), 967–979 (2017)
4. Shi, C., Tang, J., Hu, Y.: Predicting microblog user influence based on user behavior and blog content. J. Chin. Comput. Syst. **38**(07), 1495–1500 (2017)
5. Chen, Z., Liu, X., Li, B.: Analysis of influence of microblog users communication based on behavior and community. J. Comput. **35**(07), 1–6 (2018)

6. Kang, S., Zhang, C., Lin, Z., Shi, X., Ma, H.: Complexity research of massively microblogging based on human behaviors. In: Proceedings of the International Workshop on Database Technology and Applications, Wuhan, China, 27–28 November 2010, pp. 1–4. IEEE, New York (2010)
7. Xu, D., Liu, Y., Zhang, M., Ma, S.: Research on user influence based on online social network. J. Chin. Inf. Process. **30**(02), 83–89 (2016)
8. Fowler, J.H., Christakis, N.A.: Dynamic spread of happiness in a large social network: longitudinal analysis over 20 years in the Framingham heart study. BMJ **337**, a2338 (2008)
9. Ilić, J., et al.: Proof of concept for comparison and classification of online social network friends based on tie strength calculation model. In: Zdravković, M., Trajnović, M., Konjović, Z. (eds.) Proceedings ICIST 2016 (2016)
10. Al-Ghaith, W.: Understanding social network usage: impact of co-presence, intimacy, and immediacy. Int. J. Adv. Comput. Sci. Appl. **6**(8), 99–111 (2015)
11. Li, R., Zhang, H., Zhao, Y., Shang, J.: Research on automatic abstracting technology of Chinese documents based on topic model and information entropy. Comput. Sci. **41**, 298–300 (2014)
12. Feng, S., Fu, Y., Yang, F., Wang, D., Zhang, Y.: Analysis of Bowen affective tendency based on dependency syntax. J. Comput. Res. **49**, 2395–2406 (2012)
13. Liu, F., Wang, L., Gao, L., et al.: A web service trust evaluation model based on small-world networks. Knowl.-Based Syst. **57**(2), 161–167 (2014)
14. Hu, M., Yao, T.: Chinese micro blog view sentence recognition and evaluation object extraction method. J. Shandong Univ. (Sci. Edn.) **51**(07), 81–89 (2016)
15. Liu, F., Wang, L., Johnson, H., Zhao, H.: Analysis of network trust dynamics based on evolutionary game. Sci. Iranica Trans. E: Ind. Eng. **22**(6), 2548–2557 (2015)
16. Paltoglou, G., Thelwall, M.: A study of information retrieval weighting schemes for sentiment analysis. In: Meeting of the Association for Computational Linguistics, 11–16 July, Uppsala, Sweden, 1386–1395. DBLP (2010)
17. Zhang, H., Li, H., Li, Q.: Research on automatic calculation algorithm of emotional word discovery and polarity weight. J. Chin. Inf. Process. **31**(03), 48–54 (2017)
18. Zhao, J., Liu, Y., Li, X., Wang, M., Mo, S.: The evaluation method of node influence based on the third degree theory. J. Fuyang Teach. Coll. **33**(04), 78–82 (2016)
19. Hou, W., Huang, Y., Zhang, K.: Research of micro-blog diffusion effect based on analysis of retweet behavior. In: International Conference on Cognitive Informatics and Cognitive Computing, pp. 255–261. IEEE (2015)
20. Li, X, Cheng, S., Chen, W., et al.: Novel user influence measurement based on user interaction in microblog. In: International Conference on Advances in Social Networks Analysis and Mining, pp. 615–619. IEEE (2013)
21. Huang, Y., Li, L.: Analysis of user influence in social network based on behavior and relationship. In: International Conference on Measurement, Information and Control, Harbin, pp. 682–686, August 2013

Identifying Local Clustering Structures of Evolving Social Networks Using Graph Spectra (Short Paper)

Bo Jiao[1,2], Yiping Bao[1,3(✉)], and Jin Wang[1,3]

[1] CETC Big Data Research Institute Co., Ltd.,
Guiyang 550008, China
[2] School of Mathematics and Big Data, Foshan University,
Foshan 528000, China
[3] Guizhou Wingscloud Co., Ltd., Guiyang 550022, Guizhou, China
baoyiping@wingscloud.cn

Abstract. The clustering coefficient has been widely used for identifying the local structure of networks. In this paper, the weighted spectral distribution with 3-cycle (WSD3) that is similar (but not equal) to the clustering coefficient is studied on evolving social networks. It is demonstrated that the ratio of the WSD3 to the network size (i.e., the node number) provides a more sensitive discrimination for the size-independent local structure of social networks in contrast to the clustering coefficient. Moreover, the difference of the WSD3's performances on social networks and communication networks is investigated, and it is found that the difference is induced by the different symmetrical features of the normalized Laplacian spectral densities on these networks.

Keywords: Social networks · Clustering coefficient ·
Weighted spectral distribution · Normalized Laplacian spectrum

1 Introduction

Many social networks evolve over time, that is, we need some size-independent metrics to identify different structures of these networks. Small-world presents an important structure of social networks, which is commonly indicated by low path length and high clustering coefficient [1]. The clustering coefficient gives information about local connectivity of evolving networks [1], which quantifies the ratio of the number of triangles composed of a given node and its two neighbors to the maximum possible number of these triangles. The weighted spectral distribution (WSD) is defined on the spectrum of the normalized Laplacian matrix and strongly reflects the distribution of random walk N-cycles in a network [2]. If $N = 3$, Fay et al. indicated that the WSD with 3-cycle (WSD3) and the clustering coefficient can be considered to be similar but not equal [2]. However, their work has not quantificationally studied the WSD3 on evolving networks. In this paper, we will investigate the performance of the WSD3 on evolving social networks and analyze the more sensitive discrimination of the WSD3 on social networks with different sizes. Furthermore, we will compare the performance of the WSD3 on social networks to that on communication networks that is useful for our understanding of the difference between these networks in depth.

© ICST Institute for Computer Sciences, Social Informatics and Telecommunications Engineering 2019
Published by Springer Nature Switzerland AG 2019. All Rights Reserved
H. Gao et al. (Eds.): CollaborateCom 2018, LNICST 268, pp. 161–169, 2019.
https://doi.org/10.1007/978-3-030-12981-1_11

Recently, we indicated that the WSD with 4-cycle (WSD4) provides a sensitive discrimination for networks with different average path length [3]. The path length and clustering coefficient are two critical metrics to measure the small-world structure [1]. Hence, the study of this paper will accelerate the WSD's application for evaluating the small-world structure of social networks.

2   Background (Weighted Spectral Distribution)

Social networks can be modeled by a simple and undirected graph $G = (V, E)$ where V and E respectively denote node set and edge set. Let d_v and n respectively denote the degree of node v and the number of nodes in G. Then, the normalized Laplacian matrix of G can be defined as follows [4]:

$$L(G)(u, v) = \begin{cases} 1 & \text{if } u = v \text{ and } d_v \neq 0 \\ -\frac{1}{\sqrt{d_u \cdot d_v}} & \text{if } u \text{ and } v \text{ are adjacent}. \\ 0 & \text{otherwise} \end{cases} \tag{1}$$

The normalized Laplacian spectrum is composed of all eigenvalues of $L(G)$: $0 = \lambda_1 \leq \cdots \leq \lambda_n \leq 2$. Please note that these eigenvalues are restricted in the range from 0 to 2 [4]. So, the WSD can be defined as follows [2]:

$$W(G, N) = \sum_{i=1,2,\cdots,n} (1 - \lambda_i)^N. \tag{2}$$

Let $\Omega \in \{(2(i-1)/k, 2i/k]\}_{i=1}^{k}$ be equally spaced intervals in $(0, 2]$ and $f(\lambda = \theta)_{\theta \in \Omega}$ be the number of eigenvalues falling in interval Ω where $\theta = (2i-1)/k \in \Omega = (2(i-1)/k, 2i/k]$. Then, the WSD can be transformed into [2]:

$$W(G, N) \approx \sum_{\lambda=0} (1 - \lambda)^N + \sum_{\Omega} (1 - \theta)^N \cdot f(\lambda = \theta)_{\theta \in \Omega}. \tag{3}$$

When $k \rightarrow +\infty$, Eq. (3) goes to Eq. (2).

The multiplicity of the eigenvalue 0 indicates the number of connected components [4], thus only $\lambda_1 = 0$ for the maximum component of a social network. For the maximum component, Eq. (3) can be transformed into:

$$W(G, N) \approx 1 + \sum_{\Omega \subseteq (0,1]} (1 - \theta)^N \cdot f(\lambda = \theta)_{\theta \in \Omega} + \sum_{\Omega \subseteq (1,2]} (1 - \theta)^N \cdot f(\lambda = \theta)_{\theta \in \Omega}. \tag{4}$$

Furthermore, Fay et al. demonstrated that the WSD is equal to the sum over all N-cycles in G [2]:

$$\sum_{i=1,2,\cdots,n} (1 - \lambda_i)^N = \sum_C \frac{1}{d_{u_1} d_{u_2} \cdots d_{u_N}}, \tag{5}$$

where $C = u_1 u_2 \ldots u_N$ denotes all N-cycles in G. Please note that any node in C can appear more than once.

3   The WSD3 in a Deterministic Social Network Model

Deterministic models are useful for the rigorous analysis of graph metrics. First, we choose Chen's deterministic social network model [5] to theoretically analyze the WSD3 because the model captures many properties of social networks, such as skipping the levels, small-world, power-law degree distribution and scaling law between clustering coefficient and degree [5].

3.1   Chen's Model

Let T_{n+1} denote the graph of Chen's model, which can be recursively generated with the increasing of hierarchical levels t from 1 to $n+1$: At level $t = 1$, the graph is composed of only one node 1_1 (main root). At level $t = 2$, two newly added leaf nodes 2_1 and 2_2 are attached to the main root 1_1. At level $t = 3$, each of four newly added leaf nodes $3_j (j = 1, 2, 3, 4)$ is attached to the main root 1_1 and the subordinate root 2_1 for $j = 1, 2$ or 2_2 for $j = 3, 4$. At level $t \in \{4, 5, \cdots, n+1\}$, each of 2^{t-1} newly added leaf nodes $t_j (j = 1, 2, \cdots, 2^{t-1})$ is attached to its $t-1$ roots $(t-k)_{\lceil j/2^k \rceil} (k = 1, 2, \cdots, t-1)$ where $\lceil x \rceil$ rounds the value of x to the nearest integer towards infinity.

3.2   Exact Formula of the WSD3 on Chen's Model

According to Eq. (5), the WSD3 with $N = 3$ can be calculated as:

$$WSD3 = \sum_{v \in V} WSD3(v), \tag{6}$$

$$WSD3(v) = 2 \cdot \sum_{v_1, v_2 \in N(v) \wedge (v_1, v_2) \in E} \frac{1}{d_v \cdot d_{v_1} \cdot d_{v_2}}, \tag{7}$$

where $N(v)$ denotes the set of all nodes attached to node v in simple and undirected graph $G = (V, E)$. For the 3-circle pattern shown in Fig. 1, there are six corresponding circles, namely ABC, ACB, BAC, BCA, CAB and CBA. Specifically, ABC and ACB are two circles starting from node A. Thus, the constant coefficient 2 in Eq. (6) corresponds to two circles vv_1v_2 and vv_2v_1 that start from node v.

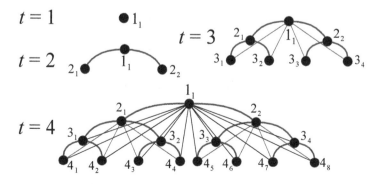

Fig. 1. The generation process of Chen's model.

It is easily to derive the total node number N_{n+1}^T of T_{n+1} and degree d_t of node $t_j(1 \leq j \leq 2^{t-1})$ at level t in T_{n+1}:

$$N_{n+1}^T = \sum_{t=1}^{n+1} 2^{t-1} = 2^{n+1} - 1, \tag{8}$$

$$d_t = 2 \cdot (2^{n-t+1} - 1) + (t - 1), \tag{9}$$

At level t, the connection relationship of t_1 is equivalent to other nodes $t_j(2 \leq j \leq 2^{t-1})$. Thus, we only consider node t_1:

$$N(t_1) = rot(t_1) \cup des(t_1), \tag{10}$$

where $N(t_1)$ includes all nodes attached to node t_1, $rot(t_1) = \{(t-1)_1, (t-2)_1, \cdots, 1_1\}$ is the set of all roots of t_1, and $des(t_1) = \bigcup_{i=1}^{n-t+1} \{(t+i)_1, (t+i)_2, \cdots, (t+i)_{2^i}\}$ is the set of all descendants of t_1. A descendant of t_1 is a node that has a root t_1.

For $\forall k_1 \in rot(t_1)$, we can obtain:

$$N(k_1) \cap N(t_1) = N(t_1)/\{k_1\}, \tag{11}$$

And for $\forall k_j \in des(t_1)$ where k_j is a node at level k,

$$N(k_j) \cap N(t_1) = \left(rot(k_j)/\{t_1\}\right) \cup des(k_j), \tag{12}$$

where

$$rot(k_j) = \left\{(k-1)_{\lceil j/2 \rceil}, (k-2)_{\lceil j/2^2 \rceil}, \cdots, 1_1\right\}, \tag{13}$$

$$des(k_j) = \bigcup_{i=1}^{n-k+1} \left\{(k+i)_{2^i \cdot (j-1)+1}, (k+i)_{2^i \cdot (j-1)+2}, \cdots, (k+i)_{2^i \cdot j}\right\}, \tag{14}$$

According to Eq. (7) and Eqs. (10)–(14), we can obtain:

$$WSD3(t_1) = \frac{1}{d_t} \left[\sum_{k=1}^{t-1} \frac{1}{d_k} \left(\sum_{i=1}^{t-1} \frac{1}{d_i} - \frac{1}{d_k} + \sum_{i=1}^{n-t+1} \frac{2^i}{d_{t+i}} \right) + \sum_{k=t+1}^{n+1} \frac{2^{k-t}}{d_k} \left(\sum_{i=1}^{k-1} \frac{1}{d_i} - \frac{1}{d_t} + \sum_{i=1}^{n-k+1} \frac{2^i}{d_{k+i}} \right) \right], \tag{15}$$

There are 2^{t-1} nodes at level t. Thus, based on Eq. (6),

$$WSD3 = \sum_{t=1}^{n+1} 2^{t-1} \cdot WSD3(t_1), \tag{16}$$

Theorem 1. When $n \to +\infty$, for $\forall \gamma > 1 \land 1 \leq t \leq n+1$,

$$2^{n-t+1} \leq d_t \leq 2^{\gamma \cdot n - t + 3}, \tag{17}$$

where d_t is defined by Eq. (9).

Proof. As is well known, $d_t \geq 2^{n-t+1} + (2^{n-t+1} - 2)$ if $t \geq 1$. When $1 \leq t \leq n$, $d_t \geq 2^{n-t+1}$. When $t = n+1$, $d_t = n \land 2^{n-t+1} = 1 \Rightarrow d_t \geq 2^{n-t+1}$. When $n \to +\infty$, for $\forall \gamma > 1$, $2^{(\gamma-1) \cdot n} \geq n$. Thus, when $n \to +\infty$, for $\forall \gamma > 1 \land 1 \leq t \leq n+1, t-1 \leq n \leq 2^{(\gamma-1) \cdot n} \leq 2^{\gamma \cdot n - t + 1}$. Moreover, we can determine $d_t \leq 3 \cdot 2^{\gamma \cdot n - t + 1} \leq 2^{\gamma \cdot n - t + 3}$. The proof is completed.   □

Additionally, when $n \to +\infty$, with $\gamma \to 1$, we can obtain:

$$2^{n-t+1} \leq d_t \leq 2^{n-t+3}, \tag{18}$$

Using Eqs. (8), (15), (16) and (18), we can determine:

$$\frac{3}{80} \leq \lim_{n \to +\infty} \frac{WSD3}{N_{n+1}^T} \leq \frac{12}{5}, \tag{19}$$

Therefore, the WSD3 of T_{n+1} steadily increases as network size N_{n+1}^T grows.

4   The WSD3 in a Stochastic Social Network Model

Deterministic models cannot capture randomized procedure, so we choose Leskovec's stochastic social network model [6] to numerically analyze the WSD3.

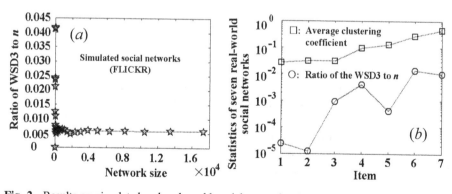

Fig. 2. Results on simulated and real-world social networks. (*a*) WSD3/*n* vs. *n* of Leskovec's model (where *n* is the network size). (*b*) Comparisons of average clustering coefficient and WSD3/*n* on seven real-world social networks (the items of *x*-axis are shown in Table 1).

Leskovec's model [6] has four inputs (namely, $N(t)$, λ, α and β) and three critical processes (namely, node arrival, edge initiation and edge destination selection). The model constructs networks using a recursive method. Specifically, $N(t)$ denotes the number of nodes arriving at step t, λ denotes an exponential distribution parameter predefined for sampling the lifetime of newly arrived nodes, and α, β are two parameters predefined for a special distribution which is used for sampling time gaps between two edge initiation processes of a node. Also, the edge destination selection process is defined by a random-random triangle-closing method. If $N(t) = 0.25^t$, $\lambda = 0.0092$, $\alpha = 0.84$ and $\beta = 0.002$, Leskovec et al. [6] numerically confirmed that the model can generate an evolving system similar to the real-world social network FLICKR (flickr.com). Simulated social networks FLICKR constructed at iteration steps from 1 to 33 are considered in Fig. 2(*a*). Note that, at step 33, the maximum network size is $\sum_{t=1,2,\ldots,33} <N(t)> = 17,300$ where $<N(t)>$ rounds towards the nearest integer of $N(t)$. As shown in Fig. 2(*a*), after 11 iteration steps, when $n > 65$, the ratio of the WSD3 to n tends towards a positive constant that is consistent with Eq. (19). In other words, the ratio WSD3/n is a size-independent metric which can be used for the comparison of social networks with different sizes.

5 The WSD3 in Real-World Social Networks

To analyze the applicability of the WSD3 in realistic social networks, we choose seven real-world networks with different sizes from the Stanford Large Network Dataset Collection [7], as shown in Table 1. Their network sizes span the range from 4,039 to 2,394,385. We sort these networks by the order of increasing average clustering coefficient. The performances of the average clustering coefficient and the WSD3/n in the real-world social networks listed in Table 1 are shown in Fig. 2(*b*), where the average clustering coefficient monotonically grows with increasing item.

Table 1. Real-world social networks.

Item	Description	Node number	Edge number
1	Wikipedia Talk network	2,394,385	5,021,410
2	EU email network	265,214	420,045
3	Slashdot social network, Nov. 2008	77,360	905,468
4	Brightkite social network	58,228	214,078
5	Wikipedia vote network	7,115	103,689
6	Enron email network	36,692	183,831
7	Social circles: Facebook	4,039	88,234

According to the comparisons of Fig. 2(*b*), we can find that the WSD3/n does not monotonically grows and the WSD3/n can commonly provide more sensitive discrimination for the seven different social networks. Both the WSD3/n and the average clustering coefficient pay attention on the triangle structure, but the former is different from the latter in many situations. Based on Eq. (7), the WSD3 located in a given node v quantifies the probability of leaving and returning the node v through two middle nodes for a random walker.

At the same time, we can give the formula of the clustering coefficient located a given node v as follows:

$$ACC(v) = \frac{En(v)}{Total(v)} = 2 \cdot \sum_{v_1,v_2 \in N(v) \wedge (v_1,v_2) \in E} \frac{1}{d_v \cdot (d_v - 1)}, \qquad (20)$$

where

$$En(v) = \sum_{v_1,v_2 \in N(v) \wedge (v_1,v_2) \in E} 1, \quad Total(v) = \frac{d_v(d_v - 1)}{2} \qquad (21)$$

As is well known, $En(v)$ is the number of links between two nodes attached to the node v, and $Total(v)$ denotes the maximum possible number of links between nodes in $N(v)$. The information of node degrees d_{v1} and d_{v2} are included in Eq. (7) but not included in Eq. (20). Also, Eq. (20) shows that the clustering coefficient located in a given node v only reflects the probability of $En(v)$ links existing between two nodes attached to the node v. Hence, the WSD3/n can provide more sensitive discrimination for social networks in contrast to the average clustering coefficient in general that is consistent with the phenomena shown in Fig. 2(b).

6 Difference of the WSD3 on Social and Communication Networks

Existing works [3] indicated that the normalized Laplacian spectral density is quasi-symmetric about one on many communication networks, such as the Interdomain Internet topology. Based on Eq. (4), the quasi-symmetry of the spectral density provides the main reason of that the WSD3/n tends towards zero when n goes to infinity (i.e., the WSD3 almost does not grow with increasing n).

Positive-Feedback Preference (PFP) [8] is an evolving model for Interdomain Internet topologies. The model has three inputs (namely, p, q and δ). Specifically, p and q are two probabilities used to select three different growth mechanisms at the evolving process, and δ is predefined for determining the preferential attachment rule. Zhou et al. [8] numerically found that the model is similar to the realistic Internet system when $p = 0.3$, $q = 0.1$ and $\delta = 0.048$.

We use the PFP model to simulate Internet topologies with increasing network size from 2,000 to 12,000. The WSD3 vs. n of these topologies is exhibited in Fig. 3(a), which shows that the WSD3 of the Internet topology does not grow as n increases. This result is obviously different from that exhibited in Fig. 2(a) (namely, the WSD3 grows sublinearly with increasing n).

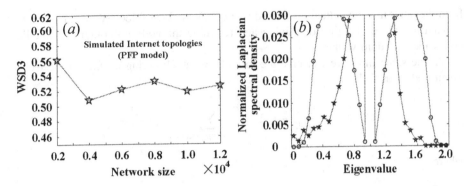

Fig. 3. Difference of the WSD3 on social and communication networks. (*a*) WSD3 vs. *n* of PFP model (where *n* is the network size). (*b*) Comparisons of spectral densities on social and communication networks. ☆: the social network of Item 7 listed in Table 1. O: the Internet topology simulated by the PFP model (having 12,000 nodes).

All eigenvalues of the normalized Laplacian spectrum fall in the range from 0 to 2 [4], so we decompose the range into 31 equally spaced intervals and evaluate the distribution of the eigenvalues falling in the 31 intervals, as shown in Fig. 3(*b*). From Fig. 3(*b*), we can confirm that the spectral density of the Internet topology is quasi-symmetric about one, whereas the spectral density of the social network is obviously asymmetric. Based on Eq. (4), the WSD3 (with $N = 3$) is not far away from one if the spectral density is quasi-symmetric about one because the sum of second and third terms of the right-hand side of Eq. (4) is close to zero. Thus, the asymmetric spectral density of social networks is the main reason for that the WSD3/*n* tends towards a positive constant as *n* goes to infinity.

7 Conclusion

Triangles are important for identifying the local clustering structure of networks. In this paper, we study the performance of a graph spectral metric (i.e., the WSD3) which is defined on the 3-cycle structure. In contrast to the average clustering coefficient, we indicate that the ratio of the WSD3 to network size can provide more sensitive discrimination for the size-independent structure of evolving social networks. Moreover, we compare the performances of the WSD3 on social and communication networks and find that the asymmetric spectral density can provide an effective interpretation for that the WSD3 grows sublinearly with increasing network size. The contributions of this paper are useful for the comparison of social networks with different sizes and are important for our deep understanding of the local clustering structure of evolving social networks.

Acknowledgement. This research has been supported by the Open Fund Project of National Engineering Laboratory for Big Data Application on Improving Government Governance Capabilities.

References

1. Paluck, E.L., Shepherd, H., Aronow, P.M.: Changing climates of conflict: a social network experiment in 56 schools. Proc. Natl. Acad. Sci. **113**(3), 566–571 (2016)
2. Fay, D., Haddadi, H., Thomason, A., et al.: Weighted spectral distribution for internet topology analysis: theory and applications. IEEE/ACM Trans. Netw. **18**(1), 164–176 (2010)
3. Jiao, B., Shi, J., Wu, X., et al.: Correlation between weighted spectral distribution and average path length in evolving networks. Chaos Interdisc. J. Nonlinear Sci. **26**(2), 023110 (2016)
4. Xie, P., Zhang, Z., Comellas, F.: The normalized Laplacian spectrum of subdivisions of a graph. Appl. Math. Comput. **286**, 250–256 (2016)
5. Chen, M., Yu, B., Xu, P., et al.: A new deterministic complex network model with hierarchical structure. Phys. A Stat. Mech. Appl. **385**(2), 707–717 (2007)
6. Leskovec, J., Backstrom, L., Kumar, R., et al.: Microscopic evolution of social networks. In: Proceedings of the 14th ACM SIGKDD International Conference on Knowledge Discovery and Data Mining, pp. 462–470. ACM (2008)
7. Stanford Large Network Dataset Collection. http://snap.stanford.edu/data/. Accessed 19 July 2018
8. Zhou, S., Mondragón, R.J.: Accurately modeling the Internet topology. Phys. Rev. E **70**(6), 066108 (2004)

The Parallel and Precision Adaptive Method of Marine Lane Extraction Based on QuadTree

Zhuoran Li[1,2], Guiling Wang[1,2(✉)], Jinlong Meng[1], and Yao Xu[2]

[1] Beijing Key Laboratory on Integration and Analysis of Large-Scale Stream Data,
North China University of Technology,
No. 5 Jinyuanzhuang Road, Shijingshan District, Beijing 100144, China
wangguiling@ict.ac.cn
[2] Ocean Information Technology Company,
China Electronics Technology Group Corporation (CETC Ocean Corp.),
No. 11 Shuangyuan Road, Badachu Hi-Tech Park,
Shijingshan District, Beijing 100041, China

Abstract. Extracting the marine lane results from the ocean spatial big data is a challenging problem. One of the challenges is that the quality of the trajectory data is quite low, and the trajectory data quality is extremely different in different areas. A parallel and precision adaptive method of marine lane extraction based on QuadTree is proposed to meet this challenge. The method takes advantage of several methods including average sampling, interpolation, removing noise, trajectory segmentation, and trajectory clustering based on GeoHash encoding through the MapReduce parallel computing framework. The preprocessing phase can effectively simplify the big data and improve the efficient of data processing. Based on the QuadTree data structure, a parallel merge filtering algorithm is proposed and implemented used Spark framework. The algorithm performs grid merging on the sparse grid regions, and obtaining a new grid result with different size. The sliding local window filtering algorithm based on the QuadTree is proposed to obtain the marine lane grid set data. Applying the Delaunay triangulation method on the grid data, the multi-precision marine lane results are effectively extracted. The experimental results show that the proposed method can automatically extract multi-precision marine lane using the trajectory data near the coast with high and low grid precision.

Keywords: AIS data · Precision adaptive · Marine lane extraction

1 Introduction

Road-related geographic data is an important part of national basic geographic information and intelligent transportation. It has great application value in smart city building, intelligent navigation, traffic control, and Internet map services. Recent years, with the development of technologies such as mobile sensors and cloud computing, massive trajectory data (also known as crowdsourcing trajectory data) are collected from a large number of vehicles (such as automobiles, ships, etc.). The geographical information of the road is cheaper and faster than the traditional way of acquiring geographic information. However, the data volume of the crowdsourcing trajectory is

H. Gao et al. (Eds.): CollaborateCom 2018, LNICST 268, pp. 170–188, 2019.
https://doi.org/10.1007/978-3-030-12981-1_12

large and there a lot of noisy data that can't reflect the real location of the vehicles. Due to these problems, it is very challenging to extract the geographic information from such crowdsourcing trajectory data and the challenges have attracted more and more researchers' attention.

In the field of urban transportation, the source trajectory data using road geographic information extraction can be collected from the Global Positioning System (GPS) terminal equipment or GPS acquisition center of land vehicles. In the field of maritime traffic, vessel trajectory data is collected from the terminal equipment of the vessel Automatic Identification System (AIS) or the AIS data collection center. Compared with the traditional methods which depend on manual measurement or the high-resolution remote sensing images to extract road information, the acquisition of trajectory data such as GPS and AIS data is cheaper and has higher performance. Since the trajectory data can be classified and analyzed according to different kinds of vehicles, the factual and detailed road information for different kinds of vehicles can be extracted, and the road changing can be reflected in time. Therefore, if the geographic information of the shipping lanes on the sea can be accurately extracted from the crowdsourcing trajectory data, it will have a great prospect.

The source trajectory data has the characteristics of large scale, high noise, and uneven sampling frequency distribution. For example, the original data collected by the global vessel trajectory data for one year is TB level, and almost every vessel's trajectory has wrong sampling data. The sampling frequency of the track points in the offshore area ranges from 5 s to 100 s and in the far-sea area the sampling interval is large ranges from 2 min to 10 min. These pose a challenge for accurately extracting fine marine lane information and it has important research significance.

Compared with vehicles on land such as automobiles, vessels' trajectories are more severely affected by harsh climatic conditions at sea. AIS data's density and quality are unevenly distributed. Therefore, compared with GPS data of vehicles on land, vessel AIS data has higher noise, and the density of AIS data is significantly different in different regions, which poses greater challenges for the extraction and updating of the marine lane. The density and quality of AIS data collecting by the vessel's sensors in the offshore and near shore areas are very different, and the vessel track points in the offshore areas are naturally more densely distributed than far-sea areas. So the fineness of extraction in the offshore areas is also higher than far-sea areas. The distribution of ship trajectory points more densely, and the fineness of the marine lane is higher. Therefore, it is impossible to use a uniform precision to extract the marine lane, and designing a method to uniformly extract the marine lane of different precision in the different areas is necessarily. This paper focuses on solving the difficult problems of unified extraction of the marine lane with different precision from the large-scale, high-noisy, and density uneven data. Aiming at this problem, a QuadTree data structure is proposed. Based on the data structure, a parallel adaptive precision merging and filtering algorithm is designed. It can be used for large-scale crowdsourcing trajectory data and different precision of marine lane recognition and extraction.

Note that the marine lane is an area with attributes such as width and depth. The paper mainly focuses on the plane attribute of the marine lane, and the extracted marine lane information only includes the plane boundary data.

Section 2 of the paper introduces related work. In Sect. 3, the basic concepts throughout the paper are introduced and the problems to be solved are described. Section 4 describes the preprocessing of ship trajectory data. Section 5 describes the basis algorithm for this paper. Including the parallel and precision adaptive marine lane extraction algorithm and so on. The Sect. 6 is the experiment and evaluation. Finally, the paper summary and prospects in the Sect. 7.

2   Related Work

At present, road map information mining from spatiotemporal trajectory big data has become a hot research topic in the research field of big data. There are many research results on extracting the road information from spatiotemporal big data. The GPS data and AIS data is widely used in pattern recognition, predicting route, and anomaly behavior detection, etc. Some researchers focus on extracting road center lines by trajectory data clustering. For the volume of the trajectory data is often very large, there are some works on using parallel computing technologies to simplify trajectory data processing. Edelsbrunner et al. [1] developed an optimal $O(n \ log \ n)$ algorithm that constructs shapes. Brown [2] constructed the K-dimensional Euclidean Voronoi diagram of N points by transforming the points to K + 1-space. Zhang el al. [3] presented a more advanced method for detecting near miss ship collisions. Arguedas et al. [4] performed detection and discovery of such highlighting of frequent lines and breakpoints. He et al. [5] proposed nonlinear optimization method and the results showed that the average classification accuracy is 98.93%. Wu et al. [6] used AIS data to analyze navigational patterns along the waterways. Arguedas et al. [7] had general spatiotemporal characterization and statistical analyses of the traffic systems in some sea areas. Etienne et al. [8] perform a data mining on a huge quantity of mobile object's positions moving in an open space in order to deduce its behaviour. Unusual behaviours such as being ahead of schedule or delayed or veering to the left or to the right of the main route are detected. Vespe et al. [9] provided the basis for robust archives of data to extract main shipping intensities and routes. Pallotta et al. [10] reflected the knowledge discovery process of the Traffic Route Extraction and Anomaly Detection (TREAD) methodology. Wang et al. [11] attempted to tackle the big data issue caused by the AIS data for anomaly detection purposes. Ahmed et al. [12] represented a first comprehensive attempt to benchmark such map construction algorithms. Wang et al. [13] adopted a divide-and-conquer strategy for reconstructing road segments and road intersections separately from raw GPS trajectories. Wang et al. [14] thought GPS probe data can essentially provide information of a traffic condition of a given period, such as travel time estimation, as well as traffic congestion, which directly relates to the distance travelled by a vehicle in that period. Broach et al. [15] developed a multinomial logit (MNL) model to impute travel mode from GPS and accelerometer data. Winden et al. [16] investigated the automatic extraction of eight road attributes: directionality, speed limit, number of lanes, access, average speed, congestion, importance, and geometric offset and developed a supervised classification method (decision tree) to infer them. Costa and Baldo [17] presented a method based on the genetic algorithm for the generation of road maps from trajectories collected with a smartphone. Park et al.

[18] provided a methodology for integrating pedestrian facilities and obstructions information with an existing PND. Hu et al. [19] used area of interest (AOI) has been to describe one kind of POI collections, namely areas that attract and support various human interests and activities. Merry et al. [20] presented a GPU-accelerated implementation of the moving least-squares (MLS) surface reconstruction technique. Mistry et al. [21] built a hierarchy of cavities and protrusions for each polygon and used this hierarchy to check for matching between these geometric features of two polygons. Peethambaran and Muthuganapathy [22] presented a fully automatic Delaunay based sculpting algorithm for approximating the shape of a finite set of points S in R^2. Cheng [23] presented one kind of dynamic positive and negative feedback ACO which differs from existing ACO in two important aspects: (i) positive feedback inner-colony and negative feedback inter-colony, and (ii) parallel implementation on Hadoop, a framework built with iterative Map Reduce model. Aghabozorgi et al. [24] attacked the problem that several different techniques used to cluster time series and sequences by utilizing a novel incremental fuzzy clustering strategy in order to achieve the objective. LI et al. [25] proposed a method of heat factor similarity measurement based on the combination of distance and density of grid heat value. ANMED et al. [12] provided an evaluation and comparison of seven algorithms using four datasets and four different evaluation measures. Yang and Ai [26] presented a new approach to use vehicle trajectory lines to extract road boundary. Kuntzsch et al. [27] inferenced of traffic networks from GPS trajectories. Jiang et al. [28] proposed a thinning-algorithm-based method extract center lines to construct road network in Lujiazui, Shanghai with taxi trajectory data.

Many researchers have achieved many achievements about trajectory big data, but there are still some problems: (1) Most of the researches only extract the center line of the road structure, and do not accurately extract the internal and external boundary information of the road. (2) Most of the researches carry out boundary extraction for trajectory data under some marks of land things, it is not suitable for massive data with uneven distribution of density under a large range. Therefore, this paper focuses on the difficulty of large differences in density of unconstrained big ship data, and establishes a method to remove density differences and construct an effective precision adaptive model for extracting marine lane.

3   Definitions and Problem Description

The paper first gives a few basic concepts, then introduces the framework and working principle of the model.

Definition 1. Vessel Trajectory. Vessel Trajectory T_{vi} is a spatiotemporal point sequence of vessel v_i, which represents the sequence of positions of the vessel over a period of time. $T_{vi} = (v_i, <p_0, p_1, ..., p_N>)$, where v_i represents the maritime mobile service identify (MMSI) of the vessel, $p_j = <x_{i,j}, y_{i,j}, t_j>$ indicates the position of the vessel at a certain moment, t_j is the sampling time, $x_{i,j}$, and $y_{i,j}$ represents the latitude and longitude of the vessel v_i at t_j.

Definition 2. Marine Lane. Marine lane P_{lane} is a two-dimensional polygon representing the area where ships are allowed to sail. $P_{lane} = (p_0, p_1, ..., p_n)$, in which the set of vertices p_i constitutes a polygon P in a clockwise direction.

Definition 3. Empty Hole. Empty hole P_{empty} is a two-dimensional polygon representing the area where ships are not allowed to sail due to obstacles such as reefs and the Government controlled area inside the marine lane. The Empty hole is nested inside the marine lane and does not appear individually. $P_{empty} = (p_0, p_1, ..., p_n)$, in which the set of vertices p_i constitutes a polygon P in a clockwise direction.

Definition 4. Grid. Grid is a rectangular area on a map. By dividing the 2D geospatial through horizontal and vertical direction, the whole geographical area is divided into multi equal rectangular in size, each rectangular being called a grid. Grid can be described by $Grid = (Code, Dsy)$.

$Code$: GeoHash code of grid. $Code$ obtained by GeoHash encoding the location of the grid center including longitude and latitude, it is a string constituted by 0 or 1, and the coding length $|Code|$ represents precision that the grid up to.

Dsy: grid density. Dsy is the number of AIS points in one grid, $Dsy = |\{p|lllon_{grid} < p_{lon} < urlon_{grid}, lllat_{grid} < p_{lat} < urlat_{grid}, p \in P\}|$, p indicates AIS points.

Definition 5. Parent Grid. Parent grid is the grid divided once in the latitude and longitude directions into four sub-grids. The divided grid is called the parent grid of the four sub-grids. For the parent $Grid = \{Code, Dsy\}$, which Code is the prefix of its any sub-grid's $Code$, that is $Code_{par} = subString(Code_{sub}, 0, |Code_{sub}| - 2)$, and the parent grid's density is the sum of four sub-grids' density, that is $Dsy_{par} = \sum Dsy_{sub}$.

Definition 6. Marine Lane Precision. The mean precision of the grid used to extract the marine lane is called the marine lane precision. $Precision_{lane} = \frac{\sum precision_g}{|G|}$, G indicates grid set used to extract marine lane, g is the grid in G.

The main steps of marine lane extraction from vessel AIS trajectory data with large density differences as follows: (1) Obtaining AIS data with specific conditions. (2) Simplifying grid trajectory data use noise data removing, missing data inserting, trajectory data segmentation, sample averaging four preprocessing method and clustering operation. (3) Extracting marine lane grid information extraction, using grid merging algorithm based on QuadTree and dynamic sliding window filtering algorithm to obtain effective marine lane information by grid. (4) Extracting marine lane by Delaunay triangulation and the lane extraction algorithm based on circumscribed circle radius.

In this paper, the problem of marine lane extraction is described as follows: Given AIS trajectory big data collected from the mobile sensors on a large number of vessels, we aim to extract the marine lane information in a certain area of a specific type of vessel. Usually, the vessel reports its position information at different times. These positions can constitute a complete dynamic trajectory sequence. Since the AIS trajectory data is collected by the sensors, there inevitably has error data, missing data and redundant data. And it is difficult to distinguish one vessel's multi trips in a total vessel trajectory sequence. To avoid these problems about data quality, four different preprocessing methods were proposed in this paper. However, the volume of the preprocessed data is still very large. It is difficult to perform marine lane extraction model on it. GeoHash encoding the data is a simplifying method for trajectory data, the neighbor points in position are uniformly simplified into one grid center point. All data points are encoded into GeoHash codes. Then we sum up the data points and can get a set G which is constituted by a large number of grid center points. In our method, we use the size of the grid area to indicate the grid precision of each grid, and use the number of original AIS points within the grid to represent the grid density of this grid. The encoded grid point with *Code* and *Dsy* two attributes can represent original data features effectively. Preprocessing and GeoHash encoding can improve data availability, data neatness, optimize memory usage, and improve efficiency of marine lane extraction model. The precision of marine lane depends on grid precision constituting marine lane. The larger the volume of data in a region, the higher the grid precision and the more significant the grid density in different regions after GeoHash encoding, the higher the precision of the extracted marine lane results and vice versa. However, in different conditions in the far sea and near shore regions, the volume of data collected in different regions is significantly different. If uniform high-precision grid parameters are used for extraction, there will be fine marine lane results in some regions which AIS data volume is proper to the parameters, but other regions are difficult to form effective marine lane. Then in some regions that not proper to the certain uniform parameters, the marine lane produce incomplete phenomena such as channel fracture or loss.

In order to solve the above problems, we firstly merge the sparse grids of different lower densities by the grid merging algorithm based on QuadTree, and then uses the sliding window filtering algorithm to obtain the marine lane grid information. The marine lane extraction algorithm is used to extract the marine lane results. The high-density grid is using to extract a high-precision marine lane. Conversely, the low-density grid is using to extract a low-precision marine lane, and overall the marine lane precision is adaptive.

Figure 1 is an overall architecture figure of parallel and precision adaptive model for marine lane extraction. The data storage layer is responsible for storing all raw AIS data and intermediate process data as well as marine lane extraction results. The core algorithm layer includes AIS data extraction under specific conditions, data preprocessing, and data clustering by Map Reduce parallel computing framework. It can be used once or multiple times median filtering to remove the meaningless isolated grid that may exist in the grid result. The marine lane information extraction process uses the Spark memory distributed computing framework to avoid the memory limitation problem. The marine lane grid information is obtained by the grid merge algorithm based on QuadTree and dynamic sliding window filtering algorithm based on merged QuadTree. Then triangulate the marine lane grid by Delaunay and extract the results by boundary extraction algorithms based on triangle circumcircle radius. The data display layer is responsible for visualizing the upper and lower results of the intermediate and final results, observing the data exception, and providing parameter guidance for the algorithm model.

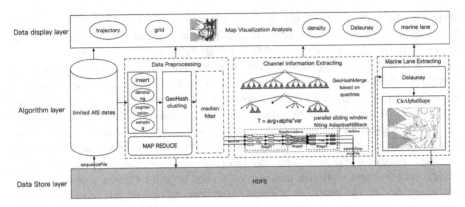

Fig. 1. Framework for marine lane extraction.

4 Trajectory Data Preprocessing

The data collection process is affected by the environment of the vessel, the quality of the telecommunication equipment, and the telecommunication process environment. Therefore, the data inevitably have problems such as data missing and data error and so on. In addition, when the moving vessel is berthed or anchored, the collected data is redundant in the marine lane extraction model. In this paper, we design the missing data inserting, noise data removing, trajectory data segmentation and sampling data averaging four methods to preprocess the original data using the Map Reduce parallel computing framework. The preprocessing can improve the data quality and optimize the extraction results.

The data preprocessing process is described as follows:

(1) Data split, dividing the SequenceFile file in the HDFS storing the original data into m ($m \gg n$, n represents the number of data nodes) data blocks Split, each block is processed by a Datanode.

(2) Map stage, program read data row-by-row, and obtain four attributes of v, x, y, t for each record of data. The field v is the key, and the tuple (x, y, t) is the value, and output form is $<v, (x, y, t)>$.

(3) Reduce stage, each Reduce processes data with the same key v as follows: First, setting the time threshold t_z, the distance threshold d_z and the trajectory number threshold n_z, and sorting the data having the same v by time t. Second step, add p_i in the array list arr_tra, if the distance d between the p_i and p_{i+1} is less than d_z, and the time interval Δt_i is less than t_z, then $i = i + 1$ (add the p_{i+1} to arr_tra), continue to circle this step, otherwise, continue to the third step. Third step, calculate the length N of array list arr_tra, if N is less than n_z, confirming points in the array list arr_tra as noise points, clearing the list, and $i = i + 1$, continue to the second step. Otherwise, confirming the array list arr_tra as a normal trajectory and compute the average distance d between two adjacent points in the array list, execute the fourth step. Fourth step, compute the distance d between the p_j and p_{j+1}, if d_j is less than d, or the difference degree between the longitudes of the two

points is greater than 300 (the two point near east longitude 180° and west longitude 180° respectively, the threshold value can be less than 360° and as large as possible, we assume it to 300), then $j = j + 1$, continue this step. Otherwise, $s = d_s/d + 2$, insert s points between the p_j and p_{j+1}, and add them in the list, then $j = j + 1$, continue to circle this step until traversal list, continue the fifth step. Fifth step, add the elements in the list, and clear the list, then $i = i + 1$, execute the second step until the same v data is traversed. The preprocessed data is output with the field v as the key, the tuple (x, y, t) as the key value, and the form is $<v, (x, y, z)>$.

(4) The preprocessed data is saved in a different text file by v.
(5) Finally, the preprocessed data is obtained. After using the above data processing based on Map Reduce, the overall process was shortened from 40 h to 2 h and 30 min under the cluster experimental conditions described in Table 1.

In addition, we use the GeoHash coding clustering method to simplify the data. GeoHash coding is a classic method of encoding geographic data. This method recursively divides the entire geographical range into multi grid longitude and latitude direction, and obtains a grid map. Each grid corresponds to a GeoHash code, and then falls. Data points in the same raster correspond to the same encoding, and finally the center point of the grid represents all the data in the entire grid. The data set has been simplified by GeoHash clustering.

The GeoHash coding clustering is described as follows:

(1) Data split, dividing data files named by MMSI in HDFS into m' ($m' \gg n$, n represents the number of data nodes) data blocks, each block is processed by one Datanode.
(2) Map stage, Geohash encoding the longitude x and the latitude y of each record of data are extracted as the key, the value corresponds the key is 1, and the form is $<code, 1>$.
(3) Reduce stage, counts grid density as dsy, calculate the center point latitude and longitude C_x and C_y of its corresponding area C, with C_x, C_y and dsy as keys, and $null$ as key value, the form is $<(C\_x, C\_y, dsy), null>$.
(4) Complete GeoHash clustering. All the data is saved by tuple $<C\_x, C\_y, dsy>$.

The distribution of the grid data maintains the original distribution characteristics. In order to make the neighbor grid density more smooth, using the modified median filtering algorithm based on the image processing fuzzy algorithm to process results. Median filtering algorithm removes isolated noise points and makes the density variation trend of all regions smoother and more uniform.

5 Precision Adaptive and Parallel Extraction Algorithm for Marine Lane Based on QuadTree

5.1 Precision Adaptive and Parallel Grid Merging

The trajectory grid data is stored in a QuadTree, and marine lane precision adaptive and parallel merge algorithm merges it automatically based on the traversal method from bottom to up. Grid merging algorithm obtain parent grid unit which has a bigger density value, substitute for the four sub-grids which have smaller density value than merge threshold value. It increasing difference of the local adjacent grid density, so that the overall trajectory grid data performs the apparent difference characteristics between the channel and the non-channel. Therefore, it can establish the precision adaptive marine lane extraction model to extract the marine lane result.

For the grid data processed in Sect. 4, we first create a QuadTree to store data. Each node corresponds to a grid, stores a GeoHash grid with Code and Density value two attributes, except that the root node does not store Code and Density value. The QuadTree is shown in Fig. 2. The principle of QuadTree establishment is from the initial geographical range, and the undivided range is no coding and taken as the root node. Then, the initial range is equally divided into 4 parts through the latitude and longitude direction, and the QuadTree is created. The four nodes of the first layer of QuadTree correspond to the divided geographical regions of the four directions of southwest, southeast, northwest and northeast in the order of coding 00, 01, 10 and 11 respectively. The establishment of the second layer is performed by dividing each divided range of the first layer as above method, and obtaining 16 nodes constructing the second layer. The establishment of subsequent levels as above method too. In general, a QuadTree's layers will not exceed 20 layers, because the grid deviation range of the 20th layer is within 8 meters, which can meet the accuracy requirements of all problem environments. This paper uses the QuadTree structure to store data with the following three advantages: (1) The QuadTree data structure corresponds the principle of GeoHash coding partitioning algorithm, which can reflect the hierarchical relationship and neighbor relationship between geographic grids. (2) In general, creating a QuadTree starting from the entire world geographic range, up to 20 times division can meet the accuracy requirements of all applications, so the QuadTree layer is usually no more than 20 layers, each node of the QuadTree is at most four sub-nodes, the effective nodes avoid the local traversal search spend much time compared the traditional prefix

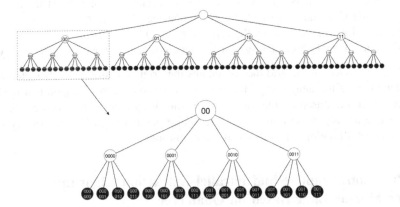

Fig. 2. A QuadTree with 3 layers, each leaf node has coding and density by integer value, not leaf node has coding and 0 density value, while root node has not coding and 0 density value.

tree, so the search efficiency is efficient. (3) For a node, which parent node coding and neighbor nodes coding can be quickly computed through its coding, so its parent and neighbor node can be quickly searched by itself. The algorithm has a lot of search for upper node and surrounding nodes, so using the QuadTree structure improves the efficiency of model.

The core idea of the precision adaptive merging algorithm is that the grid with bigger density value in a certain area has higher grid precision. On the contrary, the grid with smaller density value, the lower the grid precision of the grid. First set parameters of the algorithm: the highest grid precision $bitnum_{max}$ and the lowest grid precision $bitnum_{min}$, and the merge density threshold dsy_t, and then the entire geographic range can be according to the highest grid precision divided into equal sized grids, each grid containing a different number of AIS points, corresponding to the grid density values of the grid. The merging process unit is four sub-grids that belong to same parent grid. If the grid density value of the four sub-grids are lower than the merging density threshold dsy_t, then the four sub-grids are combined into one parent grid, that is, modify the parent grid density value to the sum of the four sub-grids, otherwise, the merge condition is not satisfied and the merging is not performed. The algorithm traverse tree by layer, and judges merging from the highest precision layer. After the first layer traversal is completed, the secondary high-precision layer grid is merged by the method above, and the QuadTree is merged layer by layer. The merge process is completed when the grid has reached the level of the set minimum grid precision. Figure 3 shows a grid which satisfies the merging condition and performs the merge operation. The data structure changes are shown in Fig. 3.

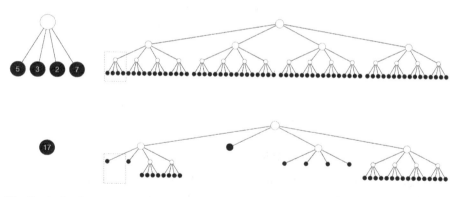

Fig. 3. A simple merge process of a QuadTree with 3 layers, merging start from bottom to top by layer, for one node if four sub-nodes' density value smaller than merge threshold density, then merge to their parent node, set parent node's density to sum of the sub-grids', until one sub-node not smaller than threshold or up to minimum merge layer.

Algorithm 1. Precision adaptive combining algorithm

Input: G: grid data
Output: MG--merged grid data
1: T = initGeohashTrie(G)   *//create a QuadTree T*
2: **for** node in *T* **do**   *// traverse the QuadTree T from bottom to top*
3:      **if** node.depth **in** range(accuracy) **then**
4:          Q.add(node)   *//add a node not below the merge precision*
5: **for** q in Q **do**:   *//traversing queue Q*
6:      **if** (g.subnodes.dsy<maxDsy) **then**
7:          g.dsy = sum(g.subnodes)   *//merged child nodes*
8:          del(g.subnodes);   *//delete child nodes*

The process of the precision adaptive merge algorithm is shown in Algorithm 1: Line 1 establishes a QuadTree T store the grid data.

Lines 2–4 traverse the QuadTree T from bottom to top by layer. If the node layer is not below the set minimum precision and not above the second highest precision range, the node is added to the queue Q.

Lines 5–8 are traversing the queue Q in reverse order, that is, starting from the sub-precision layer, determining whether the grid density values of the four sub-nodes of one node are smaller than the grid density threshold, and if true, set the density value of the node to the sum of all node density values and delete all child nodes, otherwise no operation.

When the grid precision is set high and the geographical range is large at the same time, the number of grid after initialization will more than 2^{40}. If a QuadTree is created to store these data, there will be high memory requirements and program efficiency become low. Aiming at these problems, this paper designs a parallel merging algorithm based on Spark memory-based distributed computing framework technology. The algorithm parallelism is to use the first N bits of GeoHash code as the key value. According to the geographic characteristics of the GeoHash common parent grid with the same prefix code, the algorithm is to divide the geographic range into 2 to N/2 powers. Then computing simultaneously for all divided regions in parallel.

5.2   Parallel Dynamic Sliding Window Filtering Algorithm

The general sliding window algorithm is mostly based on one-dimensional array or two-dimensional matrix data structure. This paper designs a new dynamic local sliding window filtering algorithm based on the above QuadTree structure. The main idea of the window filtering algorithm is to start from the center point of the first window in the upper left, search all the adjacent nodes in the window according to GeoHash code, and then perform local filtering equation in the window. The sliding of the window is the center point of the window. The center point is a sliding object, and the center point of the next window adjacent to it is searched to calculating and filtering until the traversal is completed. If the distance between the center point of the window and the boundary of the window is greater than the distance with the boundaries of the entire range, the boundary points in the window will be out of bounds. In order to avoid the problem of the out-of-bound boundary of the computed neighbor, the distance between selection of the center point with left and up boundary of the entire range is half of the width and height of the window. The range formed by the center point of the window aligned along the entire geographic extent, as the traversal range of the center point of the window.

The idea of local filtering within the window is based on the NiBlack binary filtering method. The filtering threshold is represented by T, and is retained if the center point grid density is greater than the threshold, otherwise discarded. The calculation formula of the filtering threshold T is as follows:

$$T = avg + alpha \times var \tag{1}$$

In Eq. (1), *avg* represents the average density value of all grids in the window, *var* represents the variance density value of all grids in the window, and *alpha* represents the variance correction factor.

When counting the *avg* and *var* of all grids in the window, because the sliding window is constituted of the lowest precision measured grid, the actual one grid may include 4^N higher precision sub-grids. Such grid needs to count all the density values of the actually included higher precision grid. Similarity, for the center point grid, if it is the lowest precision grid, just judging whether it is greater than threshold density value. Otherwise, that is the center point grid actually retains 4^N higher precision sub grids, needing compares every sub-grid with the threshold density value T.

Algorithm 2. AdaptiveNiBlack: local window filtering algorithm based on QuadTree

---

Input: MG--merged grid data
      wwidth--window width
      wheight--window height
Output: FG--filtered grid data
1: **for** node in MG **do**
2:      win = createWin(node,wwidth,wheight); *//initial sliding window*
3:      avg = average(win)
4:      var = var(win)
5:      T = avg + alpha*var   *//calculate the threshold within the window*
6:      **for** hNode in node **do**
7:         **if** hNode.dsy>T **then**
8:            FG.add(hNode)

The process of local filtering of the QuadTree window is shown in Algorithm 2:

The algorithm takes the current node as the center point of the window and creates a window according to the set window size (line 2).

According to the threshold formula, after the local threshold T in the window is calculated, the center point needs to be deeply traversed, and each child node is cyclically judged, and the node whose density value is greater than T is added to the filtered result set FG (lines 6–8).

When the grid precision is set high and the geographical range is global, the algorithm also has high memory requirements and low efficiency due to the large number of grids. Since the geographic range is divided according to the GeoHash coding principle, the data in different grids is locally filtered independently. Therefore, the GeoHash coding prefix is used as the key value to divide the data, and the Spark technique is used to simultaneously run the algorithm on the multi divided parts. Finally, all the filtering results are combined, which improves the efficiency of the algorithm and saves memory space.

5.3 Marine Lane Extraction Algorithm Based on Delaunay

Through the previous two processes, after obtaining the overall filtered grid result, it is equivalent to having obtained the grid points of all the channels. After the grid result is merged and filtered, there may still be uneven distribution on the density of the original data. Therefore, the fuzzy processing algorithm in the image processing technology can be repeatedly used to filter the grid result. That is use the mean value of the surrounding grid density value replaces the density value of the center grid, to achieve the purpose of removing clutter and smoothing the density distribution of the grid result.

Finally, it is necessary to correctly extract the marine lane formed by the adjacent grid from these grid results, and the boundary of the empty hole may exist inside the region where the adjacent grid is located. In this paper, based on the Delaunay triangulation method, the CirAlphaShape marine lane extraction algorithm is designed. The constructed Delaunay triangulation is used to determine the boundary set of the triangle by using the triangle circumscribed circle radius as the judgment condition, and then the marine lane result is extracted from the boundary edge set based on the algorithm.

Algorithm 3. CirAlphaShape: Marine lane extraction algorithm

Input: FG--filtered grid data
             thresCir--circumscribed circle radius threshold
Output: P--marine lane result
1: D = delaunay(FG)   *//FG triangulation*
2: **for** d in D **do**
3:   **if** d.circum>thresCir **then**
4:   E.add(d.edges)   *//d side added to E*
5: P = polygonize(E)   *//E form a set of polygon*

---

6 Experiment and Performance Analysis

6.1 Data Set and Experimental Environment

The data used in this experiment is the AIS data of all cargo ships from June 2016 to July 2016 including China, Malaysia, Singapore, Indonesia and other important ports. AIS data includes vessel's name, call number, MMSI, IMO, ship type, captain, ship width and other static information and accuracy, latitude, longitude, direction, speed and other dynamic information as well as status, destination, ETA for the voyage data, the four columns of MMSI, time, longitude and latitude are used in this paper. The data examples are shown in Table 1. From June 2016 to July 2016, the total amount of AIS data collected by global cargo ships was 510G. After pre-processing, the total data volume was 364G. After encoding and clustering, the data volume was reduced to 5.5G.

The experimental environment of this paper runs in Hadoop cluster environment. The specific configuration of the cluster is shown in Table 2. The data preprocessing process was developed by Map Reduce parallel computing framework. The marine lane information filtering module was developed by Spark memory distributed computing framework. The marine lane extraction process used Python programming language implemented a single process program in the CentOS release 7.0 system.

Table 1. AIS data information table.

MMSI	Longitude	Latitude	Time
412351810	121.000671	30.449981	2016-06-10 12:00:43
412351810	121.000671	30.452728	2016-06-10 12:02:30
…	…	…	…
412351810	121.055603	31.045989	2016-06-10 16:10:58

Table 2. Hadoop cluster configuration table.

IP	Role	CPU	Memory
10.61.2.13	Slave3	Intel Xeon E5620 2.40 GHz	32G
10.61.2.14	Slave4	Intel Xeon E5620 2.40 GHz	32G
10.61.2.17	Slave5	Intel Xeon E5620 2.40 GHz	32G
10.61.2.111	Master	AMD operon(tm) 6128	64G
10.61.2.112	Slave1	AMD operon(tm) 6128	64G
10.61.2.113	Slave2	Intel Xeon E5620 2.40 GHz	32G
10.61.2.123	Slave6	Intel Xeon E5620 2.40 GHz	32G
10.61.2.124	Slave7	Intel Xeon E5620 2.40 GHz	32G
10.61.2.125	Slave8	Intel Xeon E5620 2.40 GHz	32G

6.2 Analysis of Results

The original AIS data is affected by the telecommunication conditions, and there are problems such as data missing, data error, data redundancy, etc. It is difficult to accurately extract the marine lane results directly using original data from the model. After the pre-processing, the preprocessed trajectory data is clean and usable. It is stored in HDFS by vessel. It is impossible to directly extract the boundary of the channel area where a large number of vessels are sailing together. It is necessary to further abstract the data into grid data by GeoHash encoding clustering. This paper compared the parallelization method and the single process method to complete the time performance of the pre-processing module. The result showed that the parallelization method can increase the time performance by more than 5 times on average compared with the single process method.

In order to verify the precision adaptive performance of the proposed method, this paper used the OSTU-based marine lane extraction and the traditional NiBlack-based marine lane extraction for experimental comparison. The OSTU method belongs to the global optimal threshold method, and the optimal threshold is calculated from the overall grid density which can divide all elements into two parts most apparently. The traditional NiBlack is based on the matrix dynamic local window threshold method, which dynamically filters the grid of the same precision to obtain the marine lane information. The AdaptiveNiBlack method performs dynamic local window threshold filtering algorithm based on QuadTree to obtain marine lane information with different grid precision. The Fig. 4 is an experimental comparison of three different methods for marine lane extraction of the same data set.

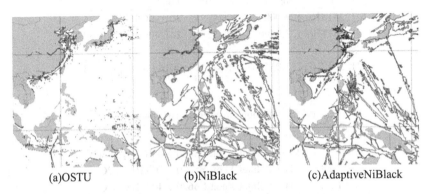

(a)OSTU   (b)NiBlack   (c)AdaptiveNiBlack

Fig. 4. Marine lane extraction result using same AIS data including five important ports Qingdao, Shanghai, Jakarta, Singapore and Sauron by OSTU, NiBlack and AdaptiveNiBlack.

In this paper, the extracted marine lane grid set data is superimposed and compared with the marine lane grid set result extracted by the local single precision algorithm for qualitative evaluation. Two commonly evaluation indicators, namely precision and recall rate, were used to evaluate the experimental results.

$$precision = \frac{grid_{ext} \cap grid_{std}}{grid_{ext}} \tag{2}$$

$$recall = \frac{grid_{ext} \cap grid_{std}}{grid_{std}} \tag{3}$$

The precision and recall indicators calculated as in Eqs. (2) and (3) above, where $grid_{std}$ represents the standard marine lane grid set, $grid_{ext}$ indicates the extraction marine lane grid set.

Quantitative evaluated and analyzed of five important ports in Qingdao, Shanghai, Jakarta, Singapore and Sauron respectively, it can be found in Qingdao, Shanghai and others offshore areas $P_{AdaptiveNiBlack} > P_{OSTU} > P_{NiBlack}$, $R_{AdaptiveNiBlack} > R_{OSTU} > R_{NiBlack}$, in Jakarta, Singapore, Sauron, etc. In the far-sea area, $P_{AdaptiveNiBlack} > P_{NiBlack} > P_{OSTU}$, $R_{AdaptiveNiBlack} > R_{NiBlack} > R_{OSTU}$. Overall, the AdaptiveNiBlack method can adaptively extract more accurate marine lane results in the offshore and near shore areas simultaneously (Fig. 5).

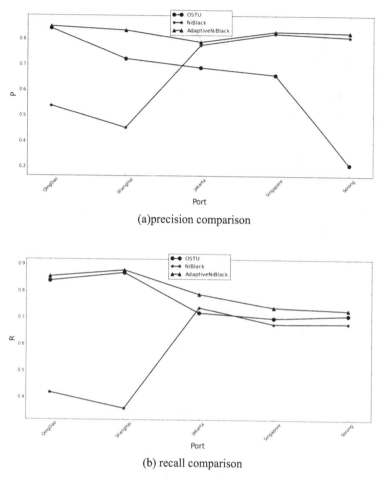

(a)precision comparison

(b) recall comparison

Fig. 5. The precision and recall in the five ports Qingdao, Shanghai, Jakarta, Singapore and Sauron by OSTU, NiBlack and AdaptiveNiBlack.

The AdaptiveNiBlack algorithm consists of four parameters $\{dsy_{max}, dsy_{min}, dsy_{m}, wsize\}$, as shown in Fig. 6. Figure 6(a) is a trajectory grid result after preprocessing in the East China Sea region, and Fig. 6(b) is a parallel merge filter and smoothed result when the parameter value is $\{200, 5, 20, 5 * 5\}$. And Fig. 6(c) is the marine lane results used extraction algorithm to extract.

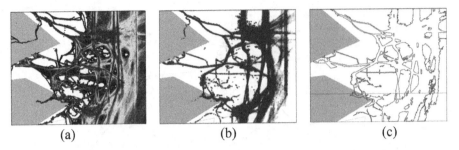

(a)   (b)   (c)

Fig. 6. Marine lane result of east sea of China, (a) is density plot after grid, (b) is density plot after AdaptiveNiBlack filter and once median filter, (c) is marine lane result used CirAlphaShape.

In this paper, we use the weighted optimization method combined with professional experience to find the optimal combination of multiple parameters. As shown in Table 3, when the parameter value is $\{dsy_{max}, dsy_{min}, dsy_m, wsize\} = \{200, 5, 20, 5 * 5\}$, the precision rate of 89.7 and the recall rate of 89.3 can be achieved in the East China Sea region.

Table 3. Quantitative analysis evaluation table.

Number	Precision	Recall	Parameter list
1	63.4	48.3	$dsy_{max} = 100$, $dsy_{min} = 5$ $dsy_m = /$, wsize = 5 * 5
2	78.1	56.5	$dsy_{max} = 200$, $dsy_{min} = 5$ $dsy_m = /$, wsize = 5 * 5
3	85.5	82.4	$dsy_{max} = 100$, $dsy_{min} = 5$ $dsy_m = 20$, wsize = 5 * 5
4	89.7	89.3	$dsy_{max} = 200$, $dsy_{min} = 5$ $dsy_m = 20$, wsize = 5 * 5
5	83.2	86.8	$dsy_{max} = 200$, $dsy_{min} = 5$ $dsy_m = 20$, wsize = 7 * 7
6	79.7	83.8	$dsy_{max} = 200$, $dsy_{min} = 0$ $dsy_m = 20$, wsize = 5 * 5
7	76.7	80.1	$dsy_{max} = 200$, $dsy_{min} = 5$ $dsy_m = 10$, wsize = 5 * 5

In the parameter list of Table 3, dsy_{max} indicates the maximum density value of grid, which is to limit the threshold density value be wrong when the grid with the maximum density, that is, if the grid density value is larger than the dsy_{max}, it is set to dsy_{max}. Dsy_{min} represents the minimum density value for preliminary filtering of a large number of grids with extremely small density values, if the grid density is less than this dsy_{min}, it is realized a noise grid and set to 0. Dsy_m represents the merging judgement density value, dsy_m determines the merging depth of the QuadTree's nodes. $Wsize$ represents the size of dynamic sliding window. By using multiple different sets of parameters to perform experiments, the effectiveness of the precision adaptive parallel extraction algorithm is verified, and has high accuracy and completeness.

7   Conclusion

Based on the data structure of QuadTree, this paper has implemented a parallelized method of precision adaptive extraction of marine lane, which effectively solved the problem that the vessel big data were affected by the environment and the sampling data density is large that resulting in poor marine lane results. The algorithm preprocesses the acquired vessel trajectory big data, and clusters the simplified trajectory data into grid data based on GeoHash coding method, and uses median filtering to smooth the grid result and eliminates discrete points. A parallel merge filtering algorithm has been proposed and implemented based on the QuadTree data structure and Spark technology parallelization. Finally, based on the Delaunay triangulation method, the marine lane results with different precisions have been effectively extracted. The experimental results have shown that the method can automatically identify the marine lane with different fineness and effectively extract the marine lane with different precision.

At the same time, there is still a lot of content that needs to be further improved: (1) This paper only extracts the geometric data of the channel, and other important information such as water depth and weight limit existed in the actual channel remains to be further studied. (2) This paper extracts marine lane of the main channel in a large range, due to the lack of strengthen processing for minor channel caused by minor channel losing, so how to strengthen the minor channel information and join our algorithm is the next research aims.

Acknowledgements. This work is supported by Beijing Natural Science Foundation No. 4172018, National Natural Science Foundation of China No. 61832004, No. 61672042, and University Cooperation Projects Foundation of CETC Ocean Corp.

References

1. Edelsbrunner, H., Kirkpatrick, D., Seidel, R.: On the shape of a set of points in the plane. IEEE Trans. Inf. Theory **29**(4), 551–559 (1983)
2. Brown, K.Q.: Voronoi diagrams from convex hulls. Inf. Process. Lett. **9**, 223–228 (1979)
3. Zhang, W., et al.: An advanced method for detecting possible near miss ship collisions from AIS data. Ocean Eng. **124**(1), 141–156 (2016)
4. Arguedas, V.F., Pallotta, G., Vespe, M.: Automatic generation of geographical networks for maritime traffic surveillance. In: International Conference on Information Fusion, pp. 1–8. IEEE (2014)
5. He, W., et al.: An Internet of Things approach for extracting featured data using AIS database: an application based on the viewpoint of connected ships. Symmetry **9**(9), 186 (2017)
6. Wu, L., et al.: Mapping global shipping density from AIS data. J. Navig. **70**(1), 67–81 (2017)
7. Arguedas, V.F., Pallotta, G., Vespe, M.: Maritime traffic networks: from historical positioning data to unsupervised maritime traffic monitoring. IEEE Trans. Intell. Transp. Syst. **PP**(99), 1–11 (2017)

8. Etienne, L., Devogele, T., Bouju, A.: Spatio-temporal trajectory analysis of mobile objects following the same itinerary. In: Advances in Geo (2010)

9. Vespe, M., Greidanus, H., Alvarez, M.A.: The declining impact of piracy on maritime transport in the Indian Ocean: statistical analysis of 5-year vessel tracking data. Mar. Policy **59**, 9–15 (2015)

10. Pallotta, G., Vespe, M., Bryan, K.: Traffic route extraction and anomaly detection from AIS data. In: COST MOVE Workshop on Moving Objects at Sea (2013)

11. Wang, X., Liu, X., Liu, B., et al.: Vessel route anomaly detection with Hadoop MapReduce. In: IEEE International Conference on Big Data. pp. 25–30. IEEE (2015)

12. Ahmed, M., Karagiorgou, S., Pfoser, D., et al.: A comparison and evaluation of map construction algorithms using vehicle tracking data. Geoinformatica **19**(3), 601–632 (2015)

13. Wang, J., Rui, X., Song, X., et al.: A novel approach for generating routable road maps from vehicle GPS traces. Int. J. Geogr. Inf. Syst. **29**(1), 69–91 (2015)

14. Wang, Y., Zhu, Y., He, Z., Yue, Y., Li, Q.: Challenges and opportunities in exploiting large-scale GPS probe data. Technical report. HPL-2011-109, HP Laboratories (2011)

15. Broach, J., Mcneil, N.W., Dill, J.: Travel mode imputation using GPS and accelerometer data from a multi-day travel survey. In: Transportation Research Board 93rd Annual Meeting (2014)

16. Van Winden, K., Biljecki, F., Van der Spek, S.: Automatic update of road attributes by mining GPS tracks. Trans. GIS **20**(5), 664–683 (2016)

17. Costa, G.H.R., Baldo, F.: Generation of road maps from trajectories collected with smartphone - a method based on Genetic Algorithm. Appl. Soft Comput. **37**, 799–808 (2015)

18. Park, S., Bang, Y., Yu, K.: Techniques for updating pedestrian network data including facilities and obstructions information for transportation of vulnerable people. Sensors **15**(9), 24466–24486 (2015)

19. Hu, Y., Gao, S., Janowicz, K., et al.: Extracting and understanding urban areas of interest using geotagged photos. Comput. Environ. Urban Syst. **54**, 240–254 (2015)

20. Merry, B., Gain, J., Marais, P.: Moving least-squares reconstruction of large models with GPUs. IEEE Trans. Vis. Comput. Graph. **20**(2), 249–261 (2014)

21. Mistry, S., Niranjan, U.N., Gopi, M.: Puzzhull: cavity and protrusion hierarchy to fit conformal polygons. Comput.-Aided Des. **46**(1), 233–238 (2014)

22. Peethambaran, J., Muthuganapathy, R.: A non-parametric approach to shape reconstruction from planar point sets through Delaunay filtering. Comput.-Aided Des. **62**(1), 164–175 (2015)

23. Cheng, X.: Parallel implementation of dynamic positive and negative feedback ACO with iterative MapReduce model. J. Inf. Comput. Sci. **10**(8), 2359–2370 (2013)

24. Aghabozorgi, S., Saybani, M.R., Teh, A., et al.: Incremental clustering of time-series by fuzzy clustering. J. Inf. Sci. Eng. **28**(4), 671–688 (2012)

25. Li, J., Chen, W., Li, M., et al.: The algorithm of ship rule path extraction based on the grid heat value. J. Comput. Res. Dev. **55**(5), 908–919 (2018)

26. Yang, W., Ai, T.: The extraction of road boundary from crowdsourcing trajectory using constrained Delaunay triangulation. Acta Geodaetica et Cartographica Sinica **46**(2), 237–245 (2017)

27. Kuntzsch, C., Sester, M., Brenner, C.: Generative models for road network reconstruction. Int. J. Geogr. Inf. Sci. **30**(5), 1012–1039 (2016)

28. Jiang, Y., Li, X., Li, X., et al.: Geometrical characteristics extraction and accuracy analysis of road network based on vehicle trajectory data. J. Geo-Inf. Sci. **14**(2), 165–170 (2012)

GPU-accelerated Large-Scale Non-negative Matrix Factorization Using Spark

Bing Tang[(✉)], Linyao Kang, Yanmin Xia, and Li Zhang

School of Computer Science and Engineering,
Hunan University of Science and Technology, Xiangtan 411201, China
btang@hnust.edu.cn

Abstract. Non-negative matrix factorization (NMF) has been introduced as an efficient way to reduce the complexity of data compress and its ability of extracting highly-interpretable parts from data sets, and it has also been applied to various fields, such as recommendations, image analysis, and text clustering. However, as the size of the matrix increases, the processing speed of non-negative matrix factorization algorithm is very slow. To solve this problem, this paper proposes a parallel algorithm based on GPU for NMF in Spark platform, which makes full use of the advantages of in-memory computation mode and GPU Single-Instruction Multiple-data Streams mode. The new GPU-accelerated NMF on Spark platform is evaluated in a 4-nodes Spark heterogeneous cluster using Google Compute Engine by configuring each node a NVIDIA K80 GPU card, and experimental results indicate that it is competitive in terms of computational time against the existing solutions on a variety of matrix orders. It can achieve a high speed-up, and also can effectively deal with the non-negative decomposition of higher-order matrices, which greatly improves the computational efficiency.

Keywords: Non-negative matrix factorization · GPU · CUDA · Spark

1 Introduction

Non-negative matrix factorization is a matrix decomposition approach which decomposes a non-negative matrix into two low-rank matrices constrained to have nonnegative elements [4,5]. This results in a reduced representation of the original data that can be seen either as a feature extraction or as a dimensionality reduction technique. The widespread usage of the NMF is due to its ability of providing new insights and relevant information about the complex latent relationships in experimental data sets. Since Lee and Seung's Nature paper [4,5], NMF has been extensively studied and has a great deal of applications in science and engineering. It has become an important mathematical method in machine learning and data mining, and has been widely used in feature extraction, image

© ICST Institute for Computer Sciences, Social Informatics and Telecommunications Engineering 2019
Published by Springer Nature Switzerland AG 2019. All Rights Reserved
H. Gao et al. (Eds.): CollaborateCom 2018, LNICST 268, pp. 189–201, 2019.
https://doi.org/10.1007/978-3-030-12981-1_13

analysis, recommendation systems, pattern recognition, signal analysis, bioinformatics and etc. [6–8]. Unlike other factorization methods (e.g., PCA, ICA, SVD, VQ, etc.), NMF can be interpreted as a parts-based representation of the data because only additive combinations are allowed. In contrast to PCA and ICA, NMF is strictly required that the entries of both resulting matrices are non-negative. Such a constraint is very meaningful in many applications, in which the data representation is purely additive, for instance, the user ratings of e-commerce websites are usually non-negative values, and image pixels are non-negative values.

The main problem of NMF is that the original matrix is usually high-order matrix, which makes the computational complexity very high. Therefore, the parallel algorithm of NMF gradually attracts more attentions, and some parallel NMF algorithms have been proposed. Although the parallelization of NMF can improve the computational efficiency to a certain extent, parallel algorithms should be matched to the machine hardware architecture, and should have strong scalability, that is, the ability to effectively utilize increased processor resources.

Accelerating HPC applications is currently under extensive research using new hardware technologies such as the recent Central Processing Units (CPUs) that are getting multiple processor cores for parallel computing, Graphics Processing Units (GPUs) that process huge data blocks in parallel, hybrid CPUs/GPUs computing that is a very common solution for HPC. GPUs are getting more attention than other HPC accelerators due to their high computation power, strong performance, functionality and low price. The modern GPU is not only a powerful graphic engine, but also a highly parallel programmable processor featuring peak arithmetic and memory bandwidth [10]. They are now used to accelerate graphics and some general applications with high data parallelism (GPGPU) due to the availability of Application Programming Interfaces (APIs), such as Compute Unified Device Architecture (CUDA) and Open Computing Language (OpenCL).

Spark is a distributed in-memory computation framework which was proposed by AMPLab of University of California at Berkeley in 2009, and is based on a framework of processing large amounts of data in memory [12,13]. It supports four programming languages, Scala, Java, Python, and R. Resilient Distributed Datasets (RDD) is a new concept proposed by Spark for data collections. RDD can support coarse-grained write operations [11]. Spark caches a particular RDD into memory, and the next operation can read directly from memory. The data is not written to disk, saving a lot of disk I/O overhead. Experimental performance evaluation confirmed that Spark's performance has increased by dozens or even 100 times compared to Hadoop, which relies on MapReduce model [1] and data being stored in a distributed file system called HDFS, rather than in memory.

Currently, some parallel approaches for non-negative matrix factorization have been proposed, for example, high performance approaches using message passing interface [2], GPU-accelerated approaches [3,9], and Hadoop-based MapReduce approaches [6,7], etc. These approaches mainly utilize the multi-core characteristics of the system, and there is still the potential to improve performance by utilizing memory, CPU and GPU resources together.

This paper proposes a Spark-based in-memory computing model and a GPU-based acceleration model to develop scalable NMF parallel algorithm, which takes advantages of both GPU and in-memory computing, to obtain a highly scalable parallel NMF algorithm. The algorithm can be automatically extended to support the processing of large-dimensional non-negative matrices, so that the algorithm can easily adapt to Internet big data processing.

The rest of the paper is organized as follows. Section 2 introduces the mathematical fundamental of NMF. Section 3 describes the general parallel principle of NMF. Section 4 describes the architecture of GPU-accelerated Spark platform. Section 5 presents GPU-accelerated NMF on Spark. Section 6 presents performance evaluation results, which is followed by the final section concludes the whole paper.

2 Non-negative Matrix Factorization

Non-negative matrix factorization (NMF) seeks to approximate a non-negative $n \times m$ matrix V (in this context, a matrix is called non-negative if all of its elements are non-negative) by a product $V \approx WH$ of non-negative matrices W and H of dimensions $n \times r$ and $r \times m$, respectively, with a given and typically low maximal rank r. Usually, r is chosen to satisfy $r \ll min\{m, n\}$ such that WH can be thought of as a compressed form of the original data. It forms the basis of unsupervised learning and data reduction algorithms with applications to image recognition, speech recognition, data mining and collaborative filtering, etc.

NMF is able to represent a large input dataset as the linear combination of a reduced collection of elements named *factors*. In this way, W contains the reduced set of r factors, and H stores the coefficient of the linear combination of such factors that rebuilds V. NMF iteratively modifies W and H until their product approximates to V. Such modifications, composed by matrix products and other algebraic operations, are derived from minimizing a cost function that describes the distance between WH and V. Lee and Seung presented two NMF algorithms based on multiplicative update rules whose objective functions are *Square of Euclidean Distance* (SED) and *Generalized Kullback-Leibler Divergence* (GKLD), respectively:

$$E(V||WH) = \frac{1}{2} \sum_{i=1}^{m} \sum_{j=1}^{n} \left(v_{ij} - \sum_{k=1}^{r} w_{ik} h_{kj} \right)^2 \tag{1}$$

$$D(V||WH) = \sum_{i,j} \left(v_{ij} \log \frac{v_{ij}}{(WH)_{ij}} - v_{ij} + (WH)_{ij} \right) \tag{2}$$

Then, the objective of NMF is converted to optimize the following: $\min_{W,H}$ $E(V||WH)$ or $\min_{W,H} D(V||WH)$, and *s.t.* $W, H \geq 0$, $\sum_{i=1}^{n} w_{ij} = 1$ $1 \leq j \leq r$.

For the purpose of this paper, we define SED as the objective function, so we have $\min(\|V - WH\|_F^2)$, which leads to the updating rules for matrices H and W:

$$h_{ij} = h_{ij} \frac{(W^T V)_{ij}}{(W^T W H)_{ij}} \tag{3}$$

$$w_{ij} = w_{ij} \frac{(V H^T)_{ij}}{(W H H^T)_{ij}}. \tag{4}$$

3   Parallel Non-negative Matrix Factorization

Before describing our experimental study, we briefly introduce the main existing parallel techniques of NMF. By analyzing Eqs. (1) and (2), we can get the basic principle of iteration calculation of NMF in parallel manner. Matrix operations are performed in blocks. The block-based parallel updating rules for matrices H and W over multi-processes has shown in Fig. 1, and the size of b_m can be adjusted according to the hardware configurations. At the time of initialization, initial W and H are produced. As you see, the size of matrix W is $n \times r$, the size of the matrix block V_j is $n \times b_m$, and the size of the matrix block H_j is $r \times b_m$, and finally the updated matrix block H_j is obtained. As shown in Fig. 1(b), the new matrix H is used to compute the new matrix block W_i, and so on. Matrix H and W are updated alternatively.

It can be seen from the analysis, the original matrix V is equivalent to a read-only variable, which is shared among all processes. With the iteration, matrix W and H need to be synchronized among all processes. The algorithm works by iteratively all-gathering the entire matrix H or W to each processor and then performing the Local Update Computations to update the W_i or H_j.

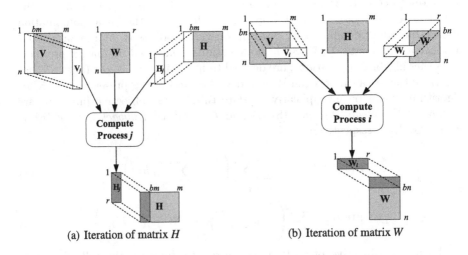

(a) Iteration of matrix H (b) Iteration of matrix W

Fig. 1. Block-based parallel updating rules for matrices H and W over multi-processes.

4   Architecture of GPU-accelerated Spark Platform

4.1   Spark

Conceptually, Apache Spark is an open-source in-memory data analytics cluster computing framework. As a MapReduce-like cluster computing engine, Spark also possesses good characteristics such as scalability, fault tolerance as MapReduce does. The main abstraction of Spark is resilient distributed datasets (RDDs), which make Spark be well qualified to process iterative jobs, including PageRank algorithm, K-means algorithm and etc. RDDs are unique to Spark and thus differentiate Spark from conventional MapReduce engines. In addition, on the basis of RDDs, applications on Spark can keep data in memory across queries and reconstruct automatically data lost during failures. RDD is a read-only data collection, which can be either a file stored in an external storage system, such as HDFS, or a derived dataset generated by other RDDs. RDDs store much information, such as its partitions, and a set of dependencies on parent RDDs called lineage. With the help of the lineage, Spark recovers the lost data quickly and effectively. Spark shows great performance in processing iterative computation because it can reuse intermediate results, keep data in memory across multiple parallel operations.

4.2   Introduction to Architecture

Modern GPUs are now capable of general computing. Due to the popularity of the CUDA on Nvidia GPUs, which can be considered as a C/C++ extension, we will mostly follow CUDA terminologies to introduce GPU computing. Current generations of GPUs are used as accelerators of CPUs and data are transferred between CPUs and GPUs through PCI-E buses. NVIDIA GPU programming is generally supported by the NVIDIA CUDA environment. A program on the host (CPU) can call a GPU to execute CUDA functions called kernel.

GPU is a multi-core processor designed to parallelizable computational intensive tasks. It has very high computational processing power and data throughput. In scientific research and practical applications, the parallelizable computing task modules with less logical processing in the system are often transplanted to the GPU for execution, and a large execution performance improvement can usually be achieved.

However, Spark cluster will slow down when processing extremely large-scale data sets, especially when the node number is not very high. At the same time, more and more developers use GPUs for parallel computing to obtain high throughput and performance. Combing Spark with GPU, the mixed architecture is quickly becoming an emerging technology, which embeds the GPU into Spark, implements CPU/GPU integration, and builds an efficient heterogeneous parallel system.

In the CPU/GPU heterogeneous parallel cluster, the CUDA-based GPU acceleration technology is used, and the Spark computing tasks are accelerated

by GPU. The basic idea is that part of operations of the Spark RDD are transferred to the GPU cores. GPU code execution flows are: (1) copy data from main
memory to GPU global memory; (2) GPU is driven by CPU instructions; (3)
GPU parallel processing in each core; (4) GPU returns results to main memory. According to this idea and combined with Spark workflow, the GPU code
is encapsulated, and then the data is transmitted between Spark Worker and
GPU. The basic principle of Spark-GPU fusion is shown in Fig. 2.

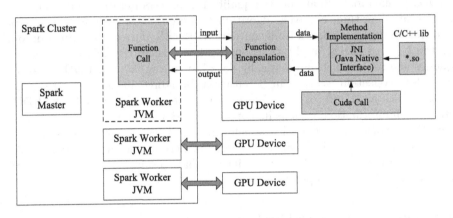

Fig. 2. Architecture of GPU-accelerated Spark platform.

From the perspective of programming language, since the GPU program
is usually developed in C/C++ language, and the Spark platform uses Java
language for program develop, Java's JNI (Java Native Interface) technology
provides a solution to bridge the GPU and Spark, through code encapsulation
to implement interfaces for the Worker to call. Several JNI tools for GPU programming can be used. For example, JCuda[1] is a development kit that provides
bindings to the CUDA runtime, which currently includes multiple packages such
as JCublas, JCufft, JCurand, JCusparse, JCusolver, JCudpp, JNpp, and JCudnn
etc. It is convenient to write GPU programs in Java language. User-defined other
GPU programs written in C/C++ can also be called after being packaged into
Java functions.

For the developers, a bidirectional transmission channel between the main
memory and the GPU global memory should be established. If the operation of
the RDD is transferred to the GPU core, high-speed data transmission between
the main memory and the GPU global memory is required, which is also implemented by function encapsulations, as is demostrated in Fig. 2.

---

[1] http://www.jcuda.org.

5   GPU-accelerated NMF on Spark

5.1   GPU-accelerated NMF

As we demostrated the matrix iterative process in Eqs. (3), (4) and Fig. 1, the main principle of GPU-based parallel NMF is presented in Fig. 3. The basic idea of GPU-based parallel NMF is to design several kernel functions to implement update rules for matrix H and W. H and W are blockwise transferred. In Fig. 3, circled operations denote CUDA kernels, and ".*" and "./" denote pointwise matrix operations, multiplication and division, respectively. Most of the matrix operations can be implemented using the library of Cublas and Cusparse, together with two self-defined operations, dot multiplication and dot division. In order to reduce the programming difficulty, JNI technology is used to transfer the CUDA programs to Java function encapsulations, which are called by Spark executors.

5.2   GPU-accelerated NMF on Spark

Spark has advantages in iterative computing, and GPU has advantages in numerical calculation of vectors and matrices. In the Spark-GPU fusion platform, fast memory read and write, combined with GPU acceleration, can play their respective advantages to improve performance. NMF calculation is started and controlled by Spark driver. The Workers calculate the parallel tasks iterately in a distributed manner. Workers are optimized with the highest speed using the GPU device and running the GPU kernel functions to complete the task. All intermediate results are written to the memory in each iteration, and exchanged among the Workers, and sent to the GPU global memory. Until the iterations are terminated, the tasks are completed and the results are written to HDFS.

The whole algorithm is described in Algorithm 1. The matrix V is broadcasted to all executors, and each worker obtains the corresponding matrix block W_i or H_j from RDD. In the Spark platform, after the Action operator is triggered, all accumulated operators form a directed acyclic graph. Task is splitted into different stages based on different dependencies between RDDs. One stage consists of a series of function execution pipelines. The stages of GPU-accelerated NMF through RDD are listed as follows:

- **Stage 1:** Read and convert matrix W and H, perform `mapPartition` function to update H blocks;
- **Stage 2:** Splice all blocks of H after one iteration through perform a `collect` operation;
- **Stage 3:** Read and convert matrix W and H, perform `mapPartition` function to update W blocks;
- **Stage 4:** Splice all blocks of W after one iteration through perform a `collect` operation, and prepare for the next iteration.

Then, iteratively preform the above four stages. The method of caching data in memory is much faster than in file system for each iteration. When the convergence condition is reached, the matrices updating is terminated, and the results are then written to HDFS.

Algorithm 1. GPU-accelerated NMF on Spark

Input: Original matrix $V_{n \times m}$, low rank r and iteration times $iter$
Input: Context of Spark Environment sc
Input: Number of executors en and number of data partitions pn
Input: Data collection of matrix elements dcM and dcH for matrices M and H
Input: Data collection in the form of RDD $rddM$ and $rddH$ for matrices M and H
Output: Matrices $W_{n \times r}$ and $H_{r \times m}$ after decomposition

1. generate initial W, H by random
2. $dcW \leftarrow W, dcH \leftarrow H$
3. broadcast V
4. **for** $k=1: iter$ **do**
5. $rddH \leftarrow sc.parallelize(dcH, pn)$
6.   //update H
7.   call $rddH.mapPartition(\texttt{mapH})$
8.   **function** mapH(data, result)
9. $X \leftarrow gpu\_multiply(W^T, V)$
10. $WW \leftarrow gpu\_multiply(W^T, W)$
11. $Y \leftarrow gpu\_multiply(WW, data)$
12. $data \leftarrow gpu\_dot\_multiply(data, X)$
13. $result \leftarrow gpu\_dot\_divide(data, Y)$
14. $return \ result$
15.   **end function**
16. $dcH \leftarrow rddH.collect()$
17. $rddW \leftarrow sc.parallelize(dcW, pn)$
18.   //update W
19.   call $rddW.mapPartition(\texttt{mapW})$
20.   **function** mapW(data, result)
21. $X \leftarrow gpu\_multiply(V, H^T)$
22. $WH \leftarrow gpu\_multiply(W, H)$
23. $Y \leftarrow gpu\_multiply(WH, H^T)$
24. $data \leftarrow gpu\_dot\_multiply(data, X)$
25. $result \leftarrow gpu\_dot\_divide(data, Y)$
26. $return \ result$
27.   **end function**
28. $dcW \leftarrow rddW.collect()$
29. **end for**
30. $W \leftarrow dcW, H \leftarrow dcH$

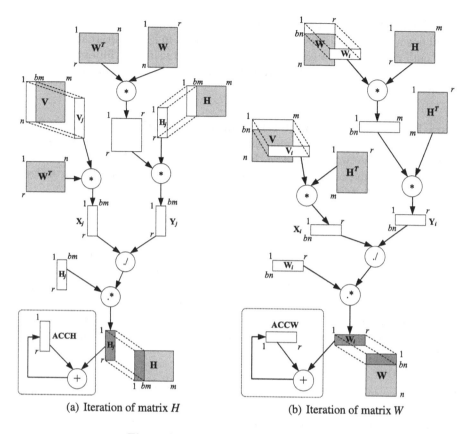

(a) Iteration of matrix H (b) Iteration of matrix W

Fig. 3. GPU implementation of iteration.

6 Performance Evaluations

6.1 Experiment Configurations

For our experiments we have used four n1-standard-4 instances of Google Compute Engine, and each instance is configured with 4 vGPU, 15 GB memory and 100 GB SSD hard disk in asia-east1 district. Each instance is also configured with a NVIDIA K80 GPU with 2496 CUDA cores and 12 GB global memory. In the 4-nodes cluster, 64 bits Ubuntu 16.04 LTS is installed, and other software packages include Hadoop 2.7, Spark 2.3, JDK 1.8 and CUDA 9.0.

6.2 Algorithms for Comparison

Serial NMF. Serial NMF algorithm is performed in a single thread using CPU only. According to the Eqs. (3) and (4), the method of alternately updating W and H are used to obtain the decomposition results by performing multiple iterations.

GPU-based NMF. GPU-based NMF algorithm is also performed in a single thread but with one GPU device support. As you see in Fig. 3, alternately updating W and H are accelerated by GPU, implemented using the library of Cublas and Cusparse, together with two self-defined operations, dot multiplication and dot division.

Spark-Based NMF Without GPU Support. For this algorithm, NMF is computed in a Spark cluster, and each node has no GPU device. Similar to Algorithm 1, in the two stages of $rddH.mapPartition$ and $rddW.mapPartition$, there is no GPU support for the updating of H and W, and only CPU for matrix operations in each iteration.

6.3   Result Analysis

In the experiments, we conducted performance evaluations using four algorithms: (i) Serial NMF, (ii) GPU-based NMF, (iii) Spark-based NMF without GPU support, (iv) Spark-based NMF with GPU support which is proposed in this paper and developed on Spark-GPU fusion platform. We designed three performance comparisons to validate the proposed new algorithm. We select some typical matrix dimensions, and the low rank r is set to 10, the number of iterations is 100.

Performance of GPU Speedup. We performed GPU-based NMF in a single node, and we varied the matrix dimensions as you see in Fig. 4. We measured the computation time, and then we also perform the serial NMF in the same node so

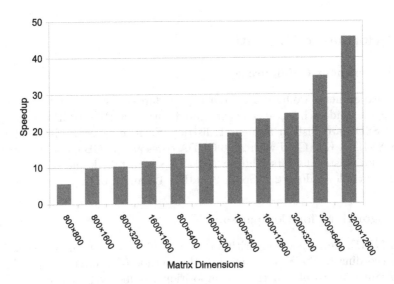

Fig. 4. Performance of GPU speedup.

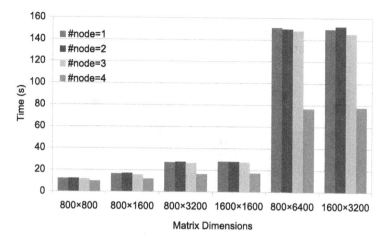

Fig. 5. Performance of NMF on Spark.

as to calculate the GPU speedup to validate the effective of GPU acceleration. The speedup is defined as the ratio of the computation time of the single node serial method to the computation time of the single node GPU method, that is, $Speedup = T_{serial}/T_{gpu\_parallel}$. The speedup varies with matrix dimensions, and we have obtained maximum speedup of 45x for GPU when compared with CPU.

Performance of NMF on Spark. In this evaluation, we started the Spark cluster, and the number of worker nodes is varied from 1, 2, 3 to 4. We varied the matrix dimensions from 800 * 800, 800 * 1600, 800 * 3200, 1600 * 1600, 800 * 6400 to 1600 * 3200, and measured the computation time of NMF in Spark platform, and results are shown in Fig. 5. When the number of nodes is 4, we set the number of Spark executors to 16, and as the increase of the matrix dimensions, the advantages of 4 nodes are becoming more and more obvious. Compared with 3 nodes Spark platform, the computation time of 4 nodes saves about 50% of the time.

Performance of NMF on Spark with GPU Support. In the last evaluation, we started the Spark cluster, the number of nodes is 4, and we varied the matrix dimensions from 6400 * 6400, 3200 * 25600, 6400 * 12800 to 6400 * 25600, and compared GPU support with Non-GPU support. As can be seen from Fig. 6, in the 4-node Spark platform, the computation time of NMF with GPU is smaller than without GPU. When the size of matrix is 6400 * 25600, NMF on Spark with GPU support saves about 10.8% of the time. NMF on GPU-accelerated Spark platform obviously shows execution efficiency.

Due to the mathematical fundamental of NMF and the blockwise-based parallel principle, there are frequent data distributions and data collections among all executors, the communication cost is very high for the NMF on Spark. However, compared with data distributions and data collections, the execution of

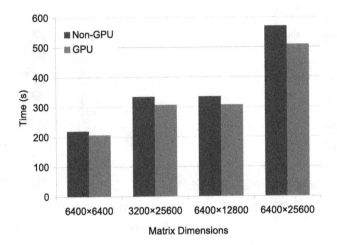

Fig. 6. Performance of NMF on Spark with GPU support.

mapPartition function takes much less time due to the GPU acceleration. From the perspective of time analysis, communication and data exchange are the bottlenecks of NMF parallel algorithm. NMF on GPU-accelerated Spark platform still has great potential for improvement.

7   Conclusion

This paper implements the GPU-accelerated parallel NMF algorithm on Spark platform. Through the performance evaluations, experimental results proved that the combination of Spark-based in-memory computing and GPU has higher execution efficiency. In the heterogeneous CPU/GPU cluster, nodes have large memory resources and GPU multi-core resources, the advantages of distributed storage between nodes and data sharing within nodes should be utilized. This model can effectively improve the parallel computing performance in multi-cores environment. It is an efficient and feasible parallel programming strategy. It can support the processing of ultra-large-scale high-dimensional non-negative matrix factorization, and will further expand the application fields of non-negative matrix factorization. However, the GPU-accelerated NMF algorithm on Spark platform designed in this paper still needs to be improved. First, some improvements can be made to overlap calculations and data transmissions; Second, some optimizations can also be made for non-negative factorization of sparse matrices.

Acknowledgements. This work is supported by the National Natural Science Foundation of China under grant no. 61602169 and 61702181, and the Natural Science Foundation of Hunan Province under grant no. 2018JJ2135 and 2018JJ3190, as well as the Scientific Research Fund of Hunan Provincial Education Department under grant no.16C0643.

References

1. Dean, J., Ghemawat, S.: MapReduce: simplified data processing on large clusters. Commun. ACM **51**(1), 107–113 (2008)
2. Kannan, R., Ballard, G., Park, H.: A high-performance parallel algorithm for non-negative matrix factorization. In: Proceedings of the 21st ACM SIGPLAN Symposium on Principles and Practice of Parallel Programming, PPoPP 2016, Barcelona, Spain, 12–16 March 2016, pp. 9:1–9:11 (2016)
3. Kysenko, V., Rupp, K., Marchenko, O., Selberherr, S., Anisimov, A.: GPU-accelerated non-negative matrix factorization for text mining. In: Bouma, G., Ittoo, A., Métais, E., Wortmann, H. (eds.) NLDB 2012. LNCS, vol. 7337, pp. 158–163. Springer, Heidelberg (2012). https://doi.org/10.1007/978-3-642-31178-9_15
4. Lee, D.D., Seung, H.S.: Learning the parts of objects by non-negative matrix factorization. Nature **401**(6755), 788–791 (1999)
5. Lee, D.D., Seung, H.S.: Algorithms for non-negative matrix factorization. In: Leen, T.K., Dietterich, T.G., Tresp, V. (eds.) Advances in Neural Information Processing Systems, Papers from Neural Information Processing Systems (NIPS), Denver, CO, USA, vol. 13, pp. 556–562. MIT Press (2000)
6. Liao, R., Zhang, Y., Guan, J., Zhou, S.: CloudNMF: a MapReduce implementation of nonnegative matrix factorization for large-scale biological datasets. Genomics Proteomics Bioinf. **12**(1), 48–51 (2014)
7. Liu, C., Yang, H., Fan, J., He, L., Wang, Y.: Distributed nonnegative matrix factorization for web-scale dyadic data analysis on MapReduce. In: Proceedings of the 19th International Conference on World Wide Web, WWW 2010, Raleigh, North Carolina, USA, 26–30 April 2010, pp. 681–690 (2010)
8. Luo, X., Zhou, M., Xia, Y., Zhu, Q.: An efficient non-negative matrix-factorization-based approach to collaborative filtering for recommender systems. IEEE Trans. Ind. Inf. **10**(2), 1273–1284 (2014)
9. Mejía-Roa, E., Tabas-Madrid, D., Setoain, J., García, C., Tirado, F., Pascual-Montano, A.D.: NMF-mGPU: non-negative matrix factorization on multi-GPU systems. BMC Bioinf. **16**, 43:1–43:12 (2015)
10. Mittal, S., Vetter, J.S.: A survey of CPU-GPU heterogeneous computing techniques. ACM Comput. Surv. **47**(4), 69:1–69:35 (2015)
11. Zaharia, M., et al.: Resilient distributed datasets: a fault-tolerant abstraction for in-memory cluster computing. In: Proceedings of the 9th USENIX Symposium on Networked Systems Design and Implementation, NSDI 2012, San Jose, CA, USA, 25–27 April 2012, pp. 15–28 (2012)
12. Zaharia, M., Chowdhury, M., Franklin, M.J., Shenker, S., Stoica, I.: Spark: cluster computing with working sets. In: Nahum, E.M., Xu, D. (eds.) 2nd USENIX Workshop on Hot Topics in Cloud Computing, HotCloud 2010, Boston, MA, USA, 22 June 2010. USENIX Association (2010)
13. Zaharia, M., et al.: Apache spark: a unified engine for big data processing. Commun. ACM **59**(11), 56–65 (2016)

Adaptive Data Sharing Algorithm for Aerial Swarm Coordination in Heterogeneous Network Environments (Short Paper)

Yanqi Zhang[1], Bo Zhang[2($\boxtimes$)], and Xiaodong Yi[2]

[1] State Key Laboratory of High Performance Computing (HPCL),
National University of Defense Technology (NUDT), Changsha, China
zhangyanqi15@nudt.edu.cn
[2] Artificial Intelligence Research Center (AIRC),
National Innovation Institute of Defense Technology (NIIDT), Beijing, China
bo.zhang.airc@outlook.com, yixiaodong@nudt.edu.cn

Abstract. With the development of unmanned aerial vehicle (UAV) systems, multi-UAV cooperation has attracted noticeable attention. In response to the communication constraints faced in UAV swarm coordination, both the lazy and the eager strategies were proposed to enable swarm-wide reliable information exchange to further behavior coordination for UAV swarms. However, these two algorithms are only evaluated in a fixed and homogeneous network scenario. Hence, how to choose the proper information exchange strategy for a UAV swarm in realistic dynamic and heterogeneous network environments remains an open while interesting problem. Therefore, in this paper, we first evaluate the convergence and payload cost of both strategies for robotic swarms in realistic network scenarios. Then we propose a novel online adaptive information exchange strategy by adopting single relay selection schemes to ensure low payload and fast convergence in various network environments. Numerical results reveal our novel strategy performs well across different network scenarios in terms of convergence and payload cost, showing its robustness, adaptive capability and potential applications in UAV swarms.

Keywords: Multi-UAV · Single relay selection ·
Heterogeneous network environments

1 Introduction

With the rapid development of unmanned aerial vehicle (UAV) technology, multi-UAV cooperation has stronger operability, but there are still many

This work is supported by the National Natural Science Foundation of China (No. 91648204, No. 61601486), Research Programs of National University of Defense Technology (No. ZDYYJCYJ140601), and State Key Laboratory of High Performance Computing Project Fund (No. 1502-02).

H. Gao et al. (Eds.): CollaborateCom 2018, LNICST 268, pp. 202–210, 2019.
https://doi.org/10.1007/978-3-030-12981-1_14

challenges to overcome. The restricted communication environments [3,7] can significantly affect the performance of UAV swarm coordination.

Many multi-UAV coordination problems require shared swarm-wide situational awareness. Both the lazy and the eager consensus algorithms were proposed for reliable information exchange to share situational awareness across swarms to converge to an agreed-upon solution for coordination problems depending on distributed UAV-state information [5]. However, these two algorithms are only evaluated in fixed and homogeneous network scenarios. So we first evaluate the performance of both algorithms in realistic network scenarios. According to the performance evaluation of two algorithms in the homogeneous network environments, both algorithms only perform well in simple network environment. However, in reality, the network environments faced by UAV swarms are very complex.

The information exchange strategies in the lazy and the eager algorithms takes two extremes, so we propose an adaptive algorithm that autonomously choose the optimal strategies based on the current network conditions, and we use the single relay selection schemes to optimize the eager strategy.

The remainder of the paper is organized as follows. Section 2 describes the system model, including network model and underlying assumptions, along with the lazy and the eager algorithms. Section 3 details our adaptive data sharing algorithm. The comparative analysis of the performance of three algorithms in different dynamic network environments is presented in Sect. 4. Finally, conclusions are provided in Sect. 5.

2   System Model

2.1   Network Model and Assumptions

It is common to model information exchange between individual UAVs in swarm by directed graph or undirected graph. For a swarm of n UAVs, the network topology is represented by a directed graph with the weighted adjacent matrix $A = [a_{ij}] \in R^{n \times n}$ [12]. a_{ij} denotes the probability of a successful communication between UAV i and j. Although a time-invariant communication model can significantly simplify the consensus problems [9], in reality, the quality of communication links between UAVs in an ad hoc network varies with movements of UAVs. So the network model is described as a time-varying model: $A(t) = [a_{ij(t)}]$. In order to simplify the problem, we abstract the communication model into a synchronous and discretized model. The whole communication process is seen as a series of separate communication rounds.

2.2   Lazy and Eager Consensus Data Sharing Algorithms

In a swarm of n UAVs, each UAV has its own data. To share data across the swarm, request messages and data messages are transmitted until all data are available on each UAV.

The only difference between the information exchange strategy of the lazy and eager algorithm lies in the response to request messages. In the lazy algorithm, an UAV broadcasts a data message only when its own data is requested, so a data message only contains its own data. In the eager algorithm, an UAV broadcasts a data message as long as it has the requested data, regardless of whether the requested data is from itself or through information exchange, so a data message contains all requested data the UAV can provide.

We can regard these two information strategies as schemes of relaying. The "decoding set" here represents a collection of UAVs which contain requested data, including the source UAV. In the lazy algorithm, we choose only one UAV in the "decoding set", namely the source UAV, to transmit data as a relay in a new communication round. In contrast, in the eager algorithm, all UAVs in the "decoding set" serve as relays to forward data. Obviously, the eager algorithm improves the probability that a data message is successfully received in each communication circle, thus accelerating the algorithm convergence. In theory, the eager algorithm can achieve the fastest convergence, while the lazy algorithm requires the lowest message payloads per round. The extreme nature of both strategies limits their applicability to the environment. Experimental results in the fixed and homogeneous network scenarios also prove this point. Both algorithms were tested in MATLAB and SITL [6] simulations with communication packet loss rates of 0.25, 0.50, 0.75 and 0.90 in [5]. The experimental results show: in low-loss communications environments (i.e., 0.25 and 0.50), the eager algorithm converges slightly faster than the lazy algorithm, but the total message payload bytes required by the eager algorithm far exceeds that of the lazy algorithm compared to the difference in convergence; in high-loss communications environments (i.e., 0.75 and 0.90), the eager algorithm is superior to the lazy algorithm in terms of both convergence and total message payload.

In order to adapt to the actual complex communications environments, we design an adaptive algorithm that selects one of these two strategies based on the current instantaneous network conditions in each communication round, and we adopt single relay selection schemes to optimize the eager strategy for reducing payload per round.

3   Adaptive Data Sharing Algorithm

A variety of relay selection schemes are proposed for wireless relay networks. We refer to these selection schemes [8] and choose single relay selection schemes for our adaptive algorithm. Among the existing single relay selection schemes, the nearest neighbor selection scheme [10,11] is adopted by selecting "the nearest relay" with the strongest channel to the source or destination.

Here, we choose a UAV with the strongest channel to the destination for relay forwarding. A method of distributed timers is proposed for distributed relay selection [4]. Each relay listens for pilot signals transmitted from the destination (Clear-to-Send or CTS). Upon receiving CTS, each relay starts a timer, the duration of a timer is inversely proportional to the channel gain. The timer of

Algorithm 1. The adaptive data sharing algorithm

```
1:  swarm ← swarm_uav_ids
2:  data_avail ← {own_data}
3:  repeat
4:     if ∃uav ∈ swarm ⋀ uav ∉ data_avail then
5:        new_data ← NET_RECV_DATA
6:        data_avail = data_avail ∪ new_data
7:        own_request ← swarm \ data_avail
8:        NET_SEND_REQUEST(own_request)
9:     end if
10:    requests ←NET_RECV_REQUESTS
11:    requests ← requests ∩ data_avail
12:    for request ∈ requests do
13:       if  request is for own_data ⋀ PER < PER_th then
14:          data_to_send ← {own_data}
15:       else
16:          single relay selection
17:          update data_to_send
18:       end if
19:    end for
20:    NET_SEND_DATA(data_to_send)
21: until terminated
```

the "best" relay expires first and then the relay sends a flag packet. Other relays will stop their timers once they have received the flag packet.

The information exchange strategy in the adaptive data sharing algorithm is as follows. In each communication round, for the source and the destination UAVs in low-loss communications environments, we use the lazy strategy that the response to a request message is sent by the source UAV; for two UAVs in high-loss communications environments, we use the optimized eager strategy that the response is sent by the chosen relay UAV. The adaptive algorithm expects to approach the eager algorithm in terms of convergence, and approach the lazy algorithm in terms of payloads in a communication round.

The low-loss and high-loss communications environments are determined by the packet loss rate between the source UAV and the destination UAV and the threshold of packet loss rate for the partition is determined by the experimental results at fixed and homogeneous network scenarios.

Two initialization variables are required. The variable *swarm* is a set of UAV identifiers for which data is required. The variable *data_avail* is a set of identifier/data tuples for which the data are obtained. At initialization, the *swarm* set contains all swarm UAV identifiers, the *data_avail* set contains the only identifier/data tuple belonging to the executing UAV.

Two types of messages are transmitted between swarm UAVs: a request message and a data message. A request message contains all UAV identifiers (2-byte unsigned integers) for which the data are required. A data message contains a set of identifier/data (4-byte floating point) tuples. The total per-round message payload bytes required for this implementation is described by Eq. 1:

$$PB = \sum_{i=1}^{n} 2r_i + \sum_{i=1}^{n} 8d_i \qquad (1)$$

where n is the number of swarm UAVs, r_i is the number of UAVs requested by UAV i, an UAV identifier is two bytes, d_i is the number of identifier/data tuples to be sent, and an identifier/data tuple is eight bytes.

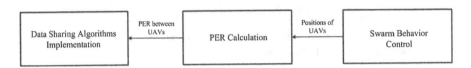

Fig. 1. The three components of the experimental architecture and their relationships. The swarm behavior control module implements different swarm behaviors in Gazebo simulator and sends UAVs' location information to the PER calculation module. The PER calculation module sends the PER information between UAVs to the algorithm implementation module. The algorithm implementation module implements different data sharing algorithms and utilizes the PER information to simulate packet loss in communications.

The algorithm starts with the initialization on the first UAV and ends with the termination on the last UAV in the swarm. At the beginning of each communication round, if the executing UAV does not have identifier/data tuples from all other swarm UAVs, *data_avail* set is updated according to all received data messages since last round. Then a request message is transmitted if there are tuples still missing from the *data_avail* set. In the middle of each communication round, all received request messages are processed. For a request to the executing UAV's own data, if the PER between the executing UAV and the requesting UAV is lower than the PER threshold, then the own data will be send by the executing UAV; if the PER between two UAVs is higher than the threshold, then whether the own data is sent by executing UAV will be determined by the relay selection. For a request to other data obtained through transmission, whether these data are sent by the executing UAV also determined by the relay selection.

The relay selection process is as follows. For each request, the executing UAV starts a corresponding timer. Then wait for timers to stop or interrupt. In the process of waiting, if the executing UAV receives the corresponding flag packet before the timer expires, then interrupt the timer. If no flag packet is received until the timer stops, then broadcast a flag packet to stop timers on other UAVs, thus the corresponding requested data will be sent by the executing UAV. Finally, all UAV tuples selected from the *data_avail* set are sent after all timers have been processed.

4   Experiments

4.1   Experimental Environment

In order to simulate realistic UAV swarm behavior, we choose Robot Operating System (ROS) software framework [2] for development. The swarm-robot communication analysis (SRCA) tool provides the ability to simulate communication channels and packet loss in ROS platform [13], so we use it to simulate lossy communications environments.

The SRCA tool contains three modules: swarm behavior control module, PER (packet error rate) calculation module and packet loss simulation module. The data sharing algorithms are implemented in the packet loss simulation module that simulates packet loss in communications. Swarm behaviors implemented in the swarm behavior control module are used to provide various communications environments. And the PER calculation module simulates communication channels and calculate the PER between any two UAVs. The experimental architecture is shown in the Fig. 1.

In experiments, the threshold of the packet loss rate is set to 0.7, which may be affected by the experimental environment. We choose quadrotor as the UAV model in Gazebo simulator [1]. The communication between UAVs remains synchronized, and after the completion of one communication round, the next round starts.

4.2   Experimental Results and Analysis

We set up experiments in three typical dynamic communications environments to compare and analyze the convergence and total message payload bytes of the three algorithms.

Dynamic Low-Loss Communication Environment. Eight quadrotors are placed equidistantly on the circumference, and the packet loss rate between any two quadrotors is less than 0.7. All quadrotors move radially to the center of the circle, namely that any two quadrotors are in a low-loss communication environment during motion. Figure 2a shows the initial position of the swarm in Gazebo. The triangles on the graph indicate the positions of quadrotors, inside the circle is the range of motion, and the arrows point to the movement directions. Table 1 shows the average number of communication rounds and average total message payload bytes of per UAV required for three algorithms convergence in different realistic communication environment.

The eager algorithm converges slightly faster than the lazy and adaptive algorithms, but the required total message payload bytes exceed that of the lazy and adaptive algorithms. Convergence and required total message payload bytes of the adaptive algorithm is almost the same as that of the lazy algorithm. The performance of the lazy and the eager algorithm in a dynamic low-loss communication environment is consistent with that in a fixed and homogeneous communication environment. The lazy algorithm and the adaptive algorithm behave

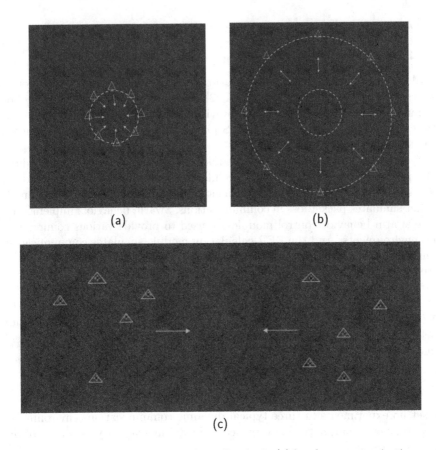

Fig. 2. The initial position of the swarm in Gazebo in (a) low-loss communication environment, (b) high-loss communication environment, (c) mixed communication environment. The triangles indicate quadrotors' positions, the dashed circles show the range of motion, and the arrows point to the movement directions.

Table 1. Experimental results in different realistic communications environments

Environment	Algorithm	Avg convergence rounds	Avg total payload bytes
Low-loss	Lazy	2.23	14.10
	Eager	2.15	74.30
	Adaptive	**2.35**	**15.70**
High-loss	Lazy	1784.28	15967.30
	Eager	96.98	1067.95
	Adaptive	**109.68**	**413.70**
Mixed	Lazy	1129.94	8645.92
	Eager	158.90	1715.00
	Adaptive	**175.10**	**1640.56**

similarly both in convergence and payload bytes because the adaptive algorithm degenerates into the lazy algorithm in this low-loss network environment.

Dynamic High-Loss Communication Environment. Eight quadrotors are placed equidistantly on the circumference, with the packet loss rate of about 0.9 between any two adjacent quadrotors initially. All quadrotors move along the radius until the packet loss rate between two quadrotors on the diameter approaches 0.7 and then moves in the opposite direction. The portion between the two dashed circles in Fig. 2b is the range of motion.

The eager algorithm converges much faster than the lazy algorithm, and the total payload bytes it requires is much lower than the lazy algorithm, which align with the results in the fix and homogeneous network environments. The adaptive algorithm converges a litter slower than the eager algorithm, but it requires lower payload bytes, which proves the effectiveness of the single relay selection method in reducing load.

Dynamic Mixed Communication Environment. Ten quadrotors are divided into two sub-swarms, each with five quadrotors. Two sub-swarms move towards each other until they form a large swarm. The packet loss rate between quadrotors in a sub-swarm is less than 0.7, and the packet loss rate between quadrotors in two different sub-swarms is greater than 0.7. Quadrotors in a sub-swarm are in a low-loss environment, and quadrotors between two sub-swarms are in a high-loss environment. This hybrid communication environment is used to verify the adaptability and effectiveness of the adaptive algorithm. Two arrows in Fig. 2c point to the different movement directions of the two sub-swarms.

The eager algorithm converges fastest, but the adaptive algorithm converges only a little slower, and the lazy algorithm converges the slowest. And the total message payload bytes required for adaptive algorithm convergence is lowest, that of the eager algorithm is next, and that of the lazy algorithm is the highest. The adaptive algorithm proves its effectiveness with the lowest total payloads and the fast convergence that approaches that of the eager algorithm.

5   Conclusion

In this paper, we first evaluate the performance of the lazy and the eager algorithms in dynamic communication scenarios. Then we propose an adaptive algorithm by adopting single relay selection schemes and do simulation experiments in different realistic network environments to compare the performance of these algorithms. Experimental results show the adaptive algorithm converges very close to the eager algorithm and it requires the lower total message payloads in various environments, which reflects its robustness, adaptive capability and potential applications in UAV swarms.

References

1. Gazebo official website. http://www.gazebosim.org
2. Ros official website. http://www.ros.org
3. Bekmezci, I., Sahingoz, O.K., Temel, S.: Flying ad-hoc networks (FANETs): a survey. Ad Hoc Netw. **11**(3), 1254–1270 (2013)
4. Bletsas, A.A.: Intelligent antenna sharing in cooperative diversity wireless networks. Ph.D. thesis, Massachusetts Institute of Technology (2005)
5. Davis, D.T., Chung, T.H., Clement, M.R., Day, M.A.: Consensus-based data sharing for large-scale aerial swarm coordination in lossy communications environments. In: 2016 IEEE/RSJ International Conference on Intelligent Robots and Systems (IROS), pp. 3801–3808. IEEE (2016)
6. Day, M.A., Clement, M.R., Russo, J.D., Davis, D., Chung, T.H.: Multi-UAV software systems and simulation architecture. In: 2015 International Conference on Unmanned Aircraft Systems (ICUAS), pp. 426–435. IEEE (2015)
7. Hauert, S., et al.: Reynolds flocking in reality with fixed-wing robots: communication range vs. maximum turning rate. In: 2011 IEEE/RSJ International Conference on Intelligent Robots and Systems (IROS), pp. 5015–5020. IEEE (2011)
8. Jing, Y., Jafarkhani, H.: Single and multiple relay selection schemes and their achievable diversity orders. IEEE Trans. Wirel. Commun. **8**(3), 1414–1423 (2009)
9. Ren, W., Beard, R.W., Atkins, E.M.: A survey of consensus problems in multi-agent coordination. In: 2005 Proceedings of the American Control Conference, pp. 1859–1864. IEEE (2005)
10. Sadek, A.K., Han, Z., Liu, K.R.: A distributed relay-assignment algorithm for cooperative communications in wireless networks. In: 2006 IEEE International Conference on Communications, ICC 2006, vol. 4, pp. 1592–1597. IEEE (2006)
11. Sreng, V., Yanikomeroglu, H., Falconer, D.D.: Relayer selection strategies in cellular networks with peer-to-peer relaying. In: 2003 IEEE 58th Vehicular Technology Conference, VTC 2003-Fall, vol. 3, pp. 1949–1953. IEEE (2003)
12. Wei, X., Fengyang, D., Qingjie, Z., Bing, Z., Hongchang, S.: A new fast consensus algorithm applied in rendezvous of multi-UAV. In: 2015 27th Chinese Control and Decision Conference (CCDC), pp. 55–60. IEEE (2015)
13. Zhang, Y., Zhang, B., Yi, X.: The design and implementation of swarm-robot communication analysis tool. In: Yuan, H., Geng, J., Liu, C., Bian, F., Surapunt, T. (eds.) GSKI 2017. CCIS, vol. 849, pp. 631–640. Springer, Singapore (2018). https://doi.org/10.1007/978-981-13-0896-3_62

Reverse Collective Spatial Keyword Querying (Short Paper)

Yang Wu$^{(\boxtimes)}$, Jian Xu, Liming Tu, Ming Luo, Zhi Chen, and Ning Zheng

School of Computer Science and Technology, Hangzhou Dianzi University,
Hangzhou, China
{161050040,jian.xu,tuliming,luom,162050110,nzheng}@hdu.edu.cn

Abstract. Recently, Collective Spatial Keyword Querying (CoSKQ),
which returns a group of objects that cover a set of given keywords
collectively and have the smallest cost, has received extensive attention
in spatial database community. However, no research so far focuses on
a situation when the result of CoSKQ is taken as the input of a query.
But this kind of query has many applications in location based services.
In this paper, we introduce a new problem Reverse Collective Spatial
Keyword Querying (RCoSKQ) that returns a region, in which the query
objects are qualified objects with the highest spatial and textual similarity. We propose an efficient method which uses IR-tree to retrieve objects
with text descriptions. To accelerate the query process, a pruning method
that effectively reduces computing is proposed. The experiments over real
and synthesis data sets demonstrate the efficiency of our approaches.

Keywords: Collective Spatial Keyword Querying ·
A set of query objects · Reverse

1 Introduction

Given a set of spatial-textual objects, a query object with a location and a set
of keywords, Collective Spatial Keyword Querying (CoSKQ) is to find a set of
objects such that it covers given keywords collectively and has the smallest cost.
An example application is to find several places that can collaboratively provide
drinking, singing and accommodation to a tourist. In previous works [1,8], the
authors devised both exact and approximate solutions according to different spatial similarities. Then in [7], the authors studied CoSKQ on road network. However, these researches only finish the computation from the user's perspective.
In this paper, we introduce a new problem Reverse Collective Spatial Keyword
Querying (RCoSKQ) to find a region (e.g., influence zone), in which the total
distance between query objects and a user is minimum, and the query keywords
set of the user is a subset of all the keywords of query objects.

Reverse k Nearest Neighbor (RkNN) query has been extensively studied in
spatial database community. Given a set of spatial objects O and a query object,

© ICST Institute for Computer Sciences, Social Informatics and Telecommunications Engineering 2019
Published by Springer Nature Switzerland AG 2019. All Rights Reserved
H. Gao et al. (Eds.): CollaborateCom 2018, LNICST 268, pp. 211–221, 2019.
https://doi.org/10.1007/978-3-030-12981-1_15

a RkNN returns objects in O which take query object as one of k nearest neighbors. In [2,10,11,13], only spatial similarity is considered. Then Reverse Spatial Textual k Nearest Neighbors (RSTkNN) query with both spatial similarity and textual relevance is proposed in [3,5,6,9,12]. However, different with RCoSKQ, only one query object is considered in these researches.

Imagine a case that the government wants to build a residential area in a business district, which includes three facilities, a cinema, a ktv and a Coffee House. In this case, if any user in this region intends to watch movies, sing a song and have coffee, these three facilities cover all the three activities collectively and minimize the accumulated distance to the user. In this example the result is a region in which query objects have the highest influence under combinations of their services. Such a combination consists of text descriptions of query objects. And both spatial proximity and textual similarity are considered in this situation. To the best of our knowledge, we are the first to explore this type of query in which a set of query objects are given in the spatial-textual database domain.

But we face two challenges in this study. The first challenge is how to identify all the keywords sets of query objects which collectively contained by them. The second is how to compute efficiently the influence region of the query objects.

To address these two challenges, we use an IR-tree to retrieve spatial-textual objects. The procedure is divided into two phases. The first phase is to find all the subsets of keywords. An incremental algorithm is presented to improve efficiency, in which query objects are visited one after another. For each existing subset during iteration, it is combined with the keywords of current visited object, and invalid subsets are deleted at the same time. Then in the second phase we use Half-space pruning technology to compute the influence region. Different with studies in [2,12], the input of RCoSKQ is a set of query objects. We develop an efficient spatial pruning method which utilizes both spatial and textual information of the objects.

Our contributions can be summarized as follows: (1) We propose a new query problem, Reverse Collective Spatial Keyword Querying RCoSKQ, and formalize it in the same way with CoSKQ. (2) We propose an efficient method based on Half-space pruning technology. Both textual similarity and spatial proximity are taken into consideration and the region is returned after examining each combination of keywords. An efficient and effective spatial pruning algorithm is proposed which can reduce redundant calculation of generating result region. (3) Extensive experiments are conducted on both real and synthesis data sets to evaluate the efficiency of the proposed algorithm.

The rest of this paper is organized as follows. Section 2 defines some basic concepts. Sections 3 and 4 illustrate our proposed approaches. Section 5 conducts the evaluation on different data sets and analyze of our experimental results. Finally we make a conclusion in Sect. 6.

2   Preliminaries

Assume all objects are located in Euclidean space. Let **O** be a spatial data set consists of m spatial web objects, each object $o \in$ **O** is associated with a tuple $(o.\lambda, o.\psi)$, where $o.\lambda$ is a location and $o.\psi$ is a set of meaningful keywords that describe the object (e.g., the specialties of a restaurant or the sceneries of a scenic spot).

Definition 1. Collective Spatial Keyword Query (CoSKQ) [1]: Given a query q $= (q.\lambda, q.\psi)$, the *Collective Spatial Keyword Querying* (CoSKQ) problem is to find a set S of objects in **O** such that S covers $q.\psi$ and the *cost* of S is minimized.

In this paper, we consider the *sum cost* which is also adopted in [1]. That is,

$$Cost(q, S) = \sum_{k=1}^{N} dist(o_k, q) \tag{1}$$

where N is the number of objects in S, $dist(o,q)$ is the Euclidean distance between q and o_k.

Definition 2. Collective Keyword Set (CKS): Given a set of query objects $Q = \{q_1, q_2, ..., q_n\}$, let Ψ be the set of keywords contained by all the objects in Q (e.g., $\Psi = \bigcup q_i.\psi$), *Collective Keyword Set* is a subset of Ψ contains $|Q|$ different keywords, each keyword is covered by an object of Q, respectively.

Since that in CoSKQ the query's keywords are collectively contained by a group of spatial web objects, we define that each query object covers one keyword and each *CKS* consists of $|Q|$ keywords. For example, there are two query points q_1 and q_2, $q_1.\psi = \{a,b\}$, $q_2.\psi = \{c\}$. The *CKSs* are $\{a,c\}$ and $\{b,c\}$, respectively.

Definition 3. Collective Influence Region (CIR): Given a set of query objects $Q = \{q_1, q_2, ..., q_n\}$, *CKS* is a *Collective Keyword Set* of Q, *Collective Influence Region* is a region if any user in which takes *CKS* as query keywords set, Q will be the result of CoSKQ (Q) which contains $|Q|$ objects.

Definition 4. Reverse Collective Spatial Keyword Querying (RCo SKQ): Given a set of query objects Q, $CKS_Q = \{CKS_1, CKS_2, ..., CKS_k\}$ contains all the *CKSs* of Q. $CIR_Q = \{CIR_1, CIR_2, ..., CIR_k\}$ represents the corresponding *CIRs*. RCoSKQ returns a region R which is the union of all the *CIRs* (e.g., $R = \bigcup CIR_i$).

3   Collective Influence Region Based Algorithm

To the best of our knowledge, none of existing methods can be directly used for RCoSKQ. Most of the existing researches about RkNN and RSTkNN focus only on the situation of a single query object. Some existing researches like

Range Based Query and *Skyline Query* need one point in the result of RCoSKQ as query object, however, the result of RCoSKQ is a region and can not be known in advance. In this section, We propose Collective Influence Region Based Algorithm (CIRB) based on algorithm InfZone [2]. CIRB has two phases. In the first phase, all the *CKSs* of a set of query objects are enumerated. In the second phase, the *CIR* for each *CKS* is computed and all the *CIRs* are combined finally.

3.1   Index Structure

We use IR-tree to retrieve spatial-textual objects. The IR-tree [4] is an R-tree where each node has a reference to an inverted file. Entries of each leaf node are represented in the form (e.mbr,e.inv), where e refers to an object $o \in \mathbf{O}$, *mbr* is the bounding rectangle of a node, and *e.inv* refers to the inverted file of a node. An inverted file contains a vocabulary of all distinct words and a posting list for each word t which means the objects contain the word t. For each non-leaf node, e refers to a child node, *mbr* is the minimum bounding rectangle of all entries of that child node and *e.inv* is the corresponding inverted file which is the union of all the keywords of child nodes.

3.2   The Collective Keyword Set

A straightforward method to acquire all the *CKSs* is to enumerate all possible combinations of keywords of query objects Q and then filter out those are not *CKS*. This method is time consuming and might yield an exponential time complexity in terms of the number of keywords of Q. In order to solve this problem, we propose an incremental enumeration method. In each of the subsequent iterations, for each existing subset, it is combined with the current visited object to generate a new subset. At the same time, the invalid subsets are removed. For example, assume that p_1, p_2, p_3 are a group of query objects, and $\{t_1, t_5\}$, $\{t_2, t_4\}$, $\{t_4, t_6\}$ are the corresponding keywords of query objects. Table 1 illustrates the entire iteration process. Initially, the candidate set $\widetilde{C}$ is empty. Then every query object is visited iteratively and each keyword is used to combine with the existing combinations. In step 4, p_3 is visited and the keywords of p_3 are t_4 and t_6. For the keyword t_4, four combinations are formed (e.g., $\{t_1, t_2, t_4\}$, $\{t_1, t_4, t_4\}$, $\{t_5, t_2, t_4\}$, $\{t_5, t_4, t_4\}$). However, $\{t_1, t_4, t_4\}$ and $\{t_5, t_4, t_4\}$ are not *CKSs* because the duplication of t_4. And at last, there are six qualified sets which consist of three distinct keywords.

Table 1. Optimized enumeration processing

Step	Action	Candidate set
1	Initialization	{}
2	Insert p_1	$\{t_1\},\{t_5\}$
3	Insert p_2	$\{t_1, t_2\},\{t_1, t_4\},\{t_5, t_2\},\{t_5, t_4\}$
4	Insert p_3	$\{t_1, t_2, t_4\},\{t_5, t_2, t_4\},\{t_1, t_2, t_6\},\{t_1, t_4, t_6\},\{t_5, t_2, t_6\},\{t_5, t_4, t_6\}$

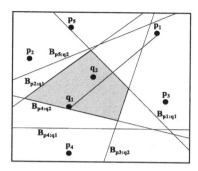

Fig. 1. The Collective Influence Zone

3.3   The Collective Influence Zone

In this phase, the *CIR* for each *CKS* is achieved. In order to compute the result region of RCoSKQ, we compute *CIR* for each *CKS* and then combine all returned regions. The detail procedure of calculating *CIR* is similiar to the basic idea of InfZone [2]. But there are some differences, first we iteratively compute the influence zone *IZone* for each query object. Then, not all of the non-leaf nodes need to be verified whether they will affect *IZone*, only those non-leaf nodes need to be considered whose inverted files contain keywords of query object. After computing *IZone* for each query object, the *CIR* is formed by computing the intersection of *IZones* and the result of RCoSKQ is returned.

Figure 1 shows an example of *CIR*. The *CKS* is {*vegetable, beer*} and the shadow area is the corresponding *CIR*. The formation of the region is based on Half-space pruning. For example, $B_{p1:q1}$ is the perpendicular bisector of the dotted line between q_1 and p_1. The Half-space that contains q_1 is represented with $H_{q1:p1}$ and the half-space $H_{p1:q1}$ is an area for each user in which p_1 is taken as its nearest neighbor with the query keyword *vegetable*. Given q_1 as a query object, $B_{p1:q1}$, $B_{p2:q1}$ and $B_{p4:q1}$ are corresponding perpendicular bisectors because p_1, p_2 and p_4 all cover *vegetable*. In the same way, we get a region formed by $B_{p3:q2}$, $B_{p4:q2}$ and $B_{p5:q2}$. The lemma below shows that the intersection of the two regions is a *CIR*.

Lemma 1. *Given a group of query objects $Q = \{q_1, q_2, ..., q_n\}$ and a corresponding $CKS = \{CKS_1, CKS_2, ..., CKS_m\}$, $\widetilde{R} = \{r_1, r_2, ..., r_n\}$ is a set of regions produced by each q_i and all the spatial objects cover w_i. The intersection of elements of $\widetilde{R}$ is the CIR of Q.*

Proof. Assume $Q = \{q_1, q_2\}$ is a set of query objects, r_1 is a region which is produced by all the half-spaces of q_1 between q_1 and competitors which may have greater influence than q_1. According to Half-space pruning, for any object in r_1, q_1 must be its nearest neighbor compared with competitors. And the region of q_2 is r_2. Let R be the intersection of r_1 and r_2. So each object p in R will take q_1 or q_2 as nearest neighbor under different keywords. Let $Q' = \{p_1, p_2\}$ which *represents another combination. Thus there must be $Cost(p, Q') > Cost(p, Q)$, which proves the region is CIR.*

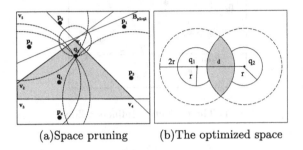

(a)Space pruning   (b)The optimized space

Fig. 2. Optimized pruning method

4   The Optimized Algorithm

The efficiency of the algorithm CIRB decreases dramatically as problem size increases. There are two drawbacks, first each time we compute CIR for every CKS, CIR is initialized with the whole data set. Second, it is time consuming to combine all the CIRs.

In this section, we introduce an effective pruning method which can simplify the CIRB. Same with the algorithm InfZone [2], C_p denotes a circle centered at p with radius equal to $dist(p, q)$, where $dist(p, q)$ is the distance between p and q. The query object q may not be the nearest neighbor of p if an entry intersects with C_p because there may be objects closer to p than q in the entry. In InfZone, it is proved that only the convex vertexes of the unpruned polygon are used to judge whether an entry may influence the region. In Fig. 2(a), only v_1, v_2, v_3 and v_4 are used to construct circles C_{v1}, C_{v2}, C_{v3} and C_{v4}. Any entry intersects with these circles will be used to prune the unpruned polygon. In CIRB, an unpruned polygon is returned for each query object. CIR is returned after intersecting all these unpruned polygons. So we should find that the regions pruned when dealing with the former query objects must not be CIR. However, lots of objects will be used to prune the region which has been pruned before in CIRB.

In our Optimized CIRB algorithm (OCIRB), the unpruned polygon is set to the initial region of current query. When the last query object is processed, the region returned is the CIR of CKS. Figure 2(a) shows an example and the shadow area depicted is the unpruned polygon of q_1. When q_2 is processed, take object p_5 as an example, p_5 will not be visited because no C_v intersects with p_5. In CIRB, the initial region is the whole data set, p_5 intersects with C_{v5} so it is used to prune the region. However, $B_{p5:q2}$ not intersects with the unpruned polygon of q_1 which means the visit of p_5 is redundant.

Now, we analyse the number of facilities used to compute the CIR. We assume that the facilities are uniformly distributed in a unit space and the number of facilities is $|F|$. The expected area of a randomly chosen facility point is $1/|F|$ (the sum of the areas of all the influence zones is 1 [2]). We approximate the influence zone to a circular shape having the same area. In Fig. 2(b), there are two query objects q_1 and q_2 both with radius r. A facility can be ignored if it lies at a distance greater than $2r$ from q_1 or q_2. In CIRB, the area of facilities to be considered is $S_1 = 2\pi r^2$. In OCIRB, for q_2, only objects located in the shadow area will be traversed to compute the CIR. The area needs to be considered is $S_2 = 2r^2 \arccos(d/2r) - 1/2d\sqrt{4r^2 - d^2}$, d is the distance between q_1 and q_2. Note that $d > 4r$ means that there is no CIR of query set $\{q_1, q_2\}$. Thus, for query set $\{q_1, q_2\}$, the amount of calculations for $(S_1 - S_2)|F|$ facilities are pruned off.

5   Experiments

5.1   Setup

Here we use two datasets, namely, GN (extracted from geonames.usgs.gov) and Hotel (extracted from www.allstays.com). Table 2 shows some properties of the two data sets. Several synthesis data sets which are randomly generated. Each object has a location and a set of words.

Table 2. Dataset statistics

Statistics	Hotel	GN
Number of objects	20,790	627,773
Total unique terms	602	102,037
Avg unique terms per object	3.9	3.3

We evaluate the first algorithm CIRB from Sect. 3 which is based on Half-space pruning and the optimized algorithm OCIRB from Sect. 4. Two metrics I/O cost and running time are used to evaluate the performance of our algorithm. The I/O cost is measured as the number of index nodes accessed from the disk. The running time is measured as the time duration from the beginning of the algorithm to the end.

In each experiment, we generate 30 groups of query sets and then report the average I/O cost and average running time. The default numbers of query objects (e.g., $|Q|$) and terms per object (e.g., $|p.\psi|$) are set to 3 and 4, respectively. We first randomly choose an object in database space and then search a set of objects near to the object, a set of query objects is selected from these objects. Both algorithms are implemented in Java and ran on a PC equipped with an Intel 2.1 GHZ Xeon E5-2620 CPU and 16 GB RAM.

5.2   Performance Evaluation

Effect of $|Q|$: In the first set of experiments, we sought to analyze how response time and I/O accesses are impacted by the number of query objects. The experiments are conducted on both real data sets GN and Hotel. The results are reported in Fig. 3. Figure 3(a) and (b) show the effect on response time when varying the number of query objects. As the number of query objects increases, the possible combinations of keywords also increase and more region needs to compute. As OCIRB avoids a lot of unnecessary regions pruning, it outperforms CIRB in both data sets. Figure 3(c) and (d) shows the result of I/O accesses when varying the number of query objects. The I/O accesses increase proportionally with the increase of $|Q|$, as the number of keywords in *CKS* is directly related to the number of query objects which leads to more relevant nodes visited. As a great number of nodes which will not affect the unpruned polygon are ignored, the I/O accesses of OCIRB are much less than CIRB.

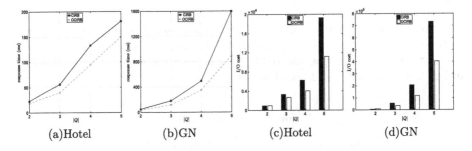

(a)Hotel   (b)GN   (c)Hotel   (d)GN

Fig. 3. The response time and I/O cost on two real data sets

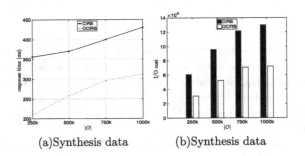

(a)Synthesis data   (b)Synthesis data

Fig. 4. Effect of $|O|$

Effect of datasize $|O|$: This experiment is to evaluate the performance of algorithms both on response time and I/O accesses. Four data sets with cardinalities of 250k, 500k, 750k and 1000k (i.e., 1 million) are randomly generated and the keywords are randomly extracted from the unique terms of GN. The number of query objects in a query is fixed at three. Figure 4(a) shows the result of response time when varying $|O|$. As more related objects are found and may be used to prune the region, the response time of both algorithms increases rapidly. But the OCIRB performs much better than CIRB, the reason is that computing a new region is time consuming and OCIRB eliminates a lot of useless computation. In Fig. 4(b), as the nodes of IR-tree increase when $|O|$ increases, the number of nodes visited augments and more time is spent to traverse IR-tree. Less objects accessed makes OCIRB handle fewer nodes.

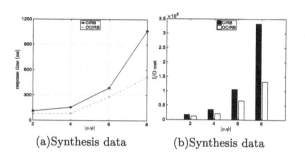

(a)Synthesis data   (b)Synthesis data

Fig. 5. Effect of $|o.\psi|$

Effect of $|o.\psi|$: We further evaluate the response time and I/O accesses of the two methods on synthesis data sets under different number of keywords per object. The sizes of data sets are fixed at 500k and the number of query objects is fixed at three. The $|o.\psi|$ is roughly 2, 4, 6 and 8. Figure 5(a) shows the response time when varying $|o.\psi|$. As $|o.\psi|$ increases, the number of combinations of keywords augments dramatically. In Fig. 5(b), the I/O accesses increase obviously because the number of combinations increases exponentially. The performance is obviously improved in OCIRB because the number of objects processed is reduced.

Effect of data distribution: In Fig. 6, we study the effect of data distribution on both algorithms. U, R and N correspond to Uniform, Real, and Normal

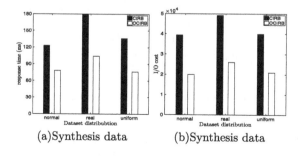

(a)Synthesis data   (b)Synthesis data

Fig. 6. Effect of data distribution

distributions, respectively. The synthetic data sets contain the same number of points as GN, which contains 627,773 points. The keywords of each data set are randomly extracted from the unique terms of GN. Figure 6 demonstrates that OCIRB performs better than CIRB.

6   Conclusion

In this paper, we identified a new problem Reverse Collective Spatial Keyword Querying, named RCoSKQ. A RCoSKQ returns a region in which the query objects will be the best group of objects which have the highest spatial and textual similarity. An efficient algorithm CIRB which based on Half-space pruning is developed and an IR-tree is constructed to retrieve spatial-textual objects. All the *CKSs* of query objects are enumerated firstly, then we compute *CIR* for each *CKS* and combine them together. We also adopt a spatial pruning method, which reduces the number of objects visited, to improve the efficiency of CIRB algorithm. Extensive experiments on both synthetic and real data sets demonstrate the effectiveness of our algorithm.

Acknowledgment. This work is supported by the National Natural Science Foundation of China (No. 61572165), the Natural Science Foundation of Zhejiang Province (No. LZ15F 020003).

References

1. Cao, X., Cong, G., Jensen, C.S., Ooi, B.C.: Collective spatial keyword querying. In: Proceedings of the 2011 ACM SIGMOD International Conference on Management of Data, pp. 373–384. ACM (2011)
2. Cheema, M.A., Lin, X., Zhang, W., Zhang, Y.: Influence zone: efficiently processing reverse k nearest neighbors queries. In: 2011 IEEE 27th International Conference on Data Engineering (ICDE), pp. 577–588. IEEE (2011)
3. Choudhury, F.M., Culpepper, J.S., Sellis, T., Cao, X.: Maximizing bichromatic reverse spatial and textual k nearest neighbor queries. Proc. VLDB Endowment **9**(6), 456–467 (2016)
4. Cong, G., Jensen, C.S., Wu, D.: Efficient retrieval of the top-k most relevant spatial web objects. Proc. VLDB Endowment **2**(1), 337–348 (2009)
5. Fang, H., et al.: Ranked reverse boolean spatial keyword nearest neighbors search. In: Wang, J., et al. (eds.) WISE 2015. LNCS, vol. 9418, pp. 92–107. Springer, Cham (2015). https://doi.org/10.1007/978-3-319-26190-4_7
6. Gao, Y., Qin, X., Zheng, B., Chen, G.: Efficient reverse top-k boolean spatial keyword queries on road networks. IEEE Trans. Knowl. Data Eng. **27**(5), 1205–1218 (2015)
7. Gao, Y., Zhao, J., Zheng, B., Chen, G.: Efficient collective spatial keyword query processing on road networks. IEEE Trans. Intell. Transp. Syst. **17**(2), 469–480 (2016)
8. Long, C., Wong, R.C.W., Wang, K., Fu, A.W.C.: Collective spatial keyword queries: a distance owner-driven approach. In: Proceedings of the 2013 ACM SIGMOD International Conference on Management of Data, pp. 689–700. ACM (2013)

9. Lu, J., Lu, Y., Cong, G.: Reverse spatial and textual k nearest neighbor search. In: Proceedings of the 2011 ACM SIGMOD International Conference on Management of Data, pp. 349–360. ACM (2011)
10. Tao, Y., Papadias, D., Lian, X.: Reverse kNN search in arbitrary dimensionality. In: Proceedings of the Thirtieth International Conference on Very Large Data Bases-Volume 30, pp. 744–755. VLDB Endowment (2004)
11. Wei, W., Yang, F., Chan, C.-Y., Tan, K.-L.: FINCH: evaluating reverse k-nearest-neighbor queries on location data. Proc. VLDB Endowment **1**(1), 1056–1067 (2008)
12. Xie, X., Lin, X., Xu, J., Jensen, C.S.: Reverse keyword-based location search. In: 2017 IEEE 33rd International Conference on Data Engineering (ICDE), pp. 375–386. IEEE (2017)
13. Yang, S., Cheema, M.A., Lin, X., Zhang, Y.: SLICE: reviving regions-based pruning for reverse k nearest neighbors queries. In: 2014 IEEE 30th International Conference on Data Engineering (ICDE), pp. 760–771. IEEE (2014)

Important Member
Discovery of Attribution Trace
Based on Relevant Circle (Short Paper)

Jian Xu[1,2], Xiaochun Yun[1,2,3(✉)], Yongzheng Zhang[1,2], and Zhenyu Cheng[1,2]

[1] Institute of Information Engineering, Chinese Academy of Sciences,
Beijing 100093, China
{xujian,zhangyongzheng,chengzhenyu}@iie.ac.cn
[2] School of Cyber Security, University of Chinese Academy of Sciences,
Beijing 100093, China
[3] National Computer Network Emergency Response Technical Team/Coordination
Center of China, Beijing 100093, China
yunxiaochun@cert.org.cn

Abstract. Cyberspace attack is a persistent problem since the existing of internet. Among many attack defense measures, collecting information about the network attacker and his organization is a promising means to keep the cyberspace security. The exposing of attackers halts their further operation. To profile them, we combine these retrieved attack related information pieces to form a trace network. In this attributional trace network, distinguishing the importance of different trace information pieces will help in mining more unknown information pieces about the organizational community we care about. In this paper, we propose to adopt relevant circle to locate these more important vertices in the trace network. The algorithm first uses Depth-first search to traverse all vertices in the trace network. Then it discovers and refines relevant circles derived from this network tree, the rank score is calculated based on these relevant circles. Finally, we use the classical 911 covert network dataset to validate our approach.

Keywords: Importance rank · Network attribution · Relevance

1 Introduction

According to the report of cybersecurity and cyberwar [11], the cyberspace security is the first class network security problem. In order to expose attackers and their organization behind the scenes, relating these information pieces about the organization community to constitute a trace network for comprehensively profiling the attackers is a very promising means against modern cyberspace threats, such as APT (Advanced persistent threat) [17]. This new emerging threat is a set of stealthy and continuous computer intrusion processes. While generally, it is hard to directly halt these intrusion operations, it is possible to profile the

H. Gao et al. (Eds.): CollaborateCom 2018, LNICST 268, pp. 222–232, 2019.
https://doi.org/10.1007/978-3-030-12981-1_16

attackers as an organization community through continuously monitoring related information pieces about them and to detect their intrusion to certain internet devices by means of seeking for IOCs (Indicators of compromise). Monitoring and mining of the attack network is often a long and ongoing process resulting in a gradual accumulation of information. Over time, as more information is uncovered, new vertices and relations are added [15]. To better facilitate this process, it is significant to distinguish important vertices in the attributional trace network from other relatively less matter ones. Because important vertices in the network are strong relevant to other undiscovered information pieces about the attack organization, and the attributional trace network constituted of information pieces is large, thus processing all these information pieces is inefficient and may lead the investigation to trivial path.

Our paper proposes to rank vertices in an attributional trace network through detecting relevant circles. The effectiveness of this method is demonstrated by applying it to the classical 911 attack dataset. Overall, we make the following contributions.

- We propose relevant circle into ranking vertex importance, derive important measures, such as minimized relevant circles, and propose criterions to score the vertex importance. Relevant circles are effective measurement of relevance among information pieces.
- We implement and explain the key algorithms to rank vertices based on relevant circle, including construction of the network tree, regeneration of relevant circles, deduction of minimized relevant circles and the score algorithm.
- We evaluate the effectiveness of this approach using the 911 covert network dataset. The result shows the key members found by our proposed model are great investigation entry of the covert network. These members lead to more relevant information about the network.

The remainder of this paper is structured as follows: In Sect. 5, we introduce the related researches. Section 2 will present the concept of relevant circle and its derived measures. We implement the corresponding algorithms in Sect. 3. Experiments are conducted in Sect. 4. We finally draw our conclusion in Sect. 6.

2   Method

In this Section, we first introduce the relevance definition, followed by proposing the relevant circle. Minimized relevant circle derived from relevant circle is discussed, and the score rules of rank importance are presented finally.

During the profiling process, information pieces are connected by many means. They may appear in the same context or have been searched in Google by users as a combination. For example, if the information pieces are about people, they may be connected by attending the same conference, living in the same area or they might attend the same college in the past. Two information pieces are relevant when one information piece is being connected to another information piece in a way that makes it necessary to consider the second information piece when considering the first one.

Information pieces are extremely relevant to others especially when the inter relevant relationships form a circle, indicating a strong evidence to confirm the relevance among the vertices residing in this circle. For example, in Fig. 1, network A contains no relevant circle, all vertices in network A are relevant to others through cascading the relevant relationship. While network B contains relevant circles. Every vertex in the relevant circles re-confirms relevance of others.

Sometimes a vertex is located in multiple relevant circles. And one relevant circle is contained in another one. For example, in Fig. 2, circle B is a part of circle A, therefore circle A is not a minimized relevant circle when considering the existing of circle B. On this case, we break relevant circle A into smaller relevant circles B and C, and deduct circle A to circle C. We define that relevant circle B and C are minimized relevant circles. The minimized relevant circle is defined as a relevant circle that is not contained in other relevant circles. It is important to find the minimized relevant circle in the attributional trace network because they influence the rank score of vertices located in them.

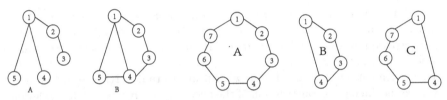

Fig. 1. Relevant circle   **Fig. 2.** Relevant circle deduction

Also there are situations when one vertex performs as the joint of multiple minimized relevant circles. These joint vertices are the central of the organization we are investigating. They may lead to more yet unknown but relevant information pieces if further researches are conducted on them. The more minimized relevant circles one vertex resides in, the more important this vertex becomes. For example, in Fig. 3, there exist three minimized relevant circles, they are 1–2–3–4, 1–4–5 and 1–6–7. Vertex 1 locates in three circles, and vertex 4 in two circles, the rest vertices are in one circle.

What's more, the rank score is also influenced by the size of the minimized relevant circle. Vertices in the smaller circle are assigned with bigger score. Because if the circle size is small, it denotes that these vertices are a compact community with tight connections. In Fig. 3, relevant circle 1–4–5 is smaller than 1–2–3–4, thus vertex 1, 4, 5 are more relevant to each other than vertex 1, 2, 3, 4. These two criterions are efficient to distinguish important vertex from other ones.

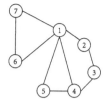

Fig. 3. Multiple circles

We formulate the rank score according to these rules for the importance ranking of vertices. The initial score of each vertex is zero. And the score piles up when a vertex is discovered locating in more relevant circles. The vertex score is calculated according to Formula 1.

$$Score = \sum_{i=1}^{n} \frac{1}{l_i} \qquad l_i \geq 3 \tag{1}$$

Where n is the number of minimized relevant circles that the vertex is found resided in. l_i is the length of the minimized relevant circle and the length is required to be greater than 3. For example, in Fig. 3, vertex 1 is in three minimized relevant circles. And the lengths of these circles are 3, 3 and 4 respectively. Therefore, according to Formula 1, the importance score of vertex 1 is 11/12. And it is the most important vertex in this network.

3   Implementation

In this Section, we present the key algorithms to implement our proposed method. The main process first constructs the network tree. Then, relevant circles are reconstructed from the network tree. Third, relevant circles are further deducted to minimized relevant circles. We finally calculate the rank score of vertices in these minimized relevant circles.

We construct the network tree by means of iteratively calling Algorithm 1. It employs Depth-first search (DFS), and records relevant circles along the searching process. The parent list stores the network tree structure. Algorithm 1 accepts the start vertex and its parent vertex as inputs. It first appends the start vertex into the visited vertex list, then processes every vertex of the start vertex's adjacent vertices excluding the parent vertex. For every vertex, if it is already included in the visited list, it means that the vertex pair (v_{start} and v_i) is contained in a relevant circle and we record this pair into backtrack list for later usage. Otherwise if this vertex is not visited yet, we record the parent-child relation into the parent list, and iteratively call Algorithm 1. This algorithm will guarantee that the search firstly handles vertices in the deepest layer, and then goes back layer by layer to the root vertex.

Algorithm 1. Construct network tree using DFS algorithm

Input: $G(V, E)$, v_{start}, v_{parent}
Output: $parent\_list$, $visited$, $backtrack$
1: $visited.append(v_{start})$
2: $V \leftarrow v_{start}.adjacents$ exclude v_{parent}
3: **if** $V = \emptyset$ **then**
4:     **return**
5: **else**
6:     **for all** $v_i \in V$ **do**
7:         **if** $v_i \in visited$ **then**
8:             $backtrack.append([v_{start}, v_i])$
9:         **else**
10:             $parent\_list.append([v_{start}, v_i])$
11:             $find\_tree\_DFS(G(V, E), v_i, v_{start})$
12:         **end if**
13:     **end for**
14: **end if**

Algorithm 2. Regenerate relevant circles

Input: v_{root}, $parent\_list$, $backtrack$
Output: $circle\_list$
1: **for all** $item \in backtrack$ **do**
2:     $circle \leftarrow \emptyset$
3:     $circle.append(item[0])$
4:     **while** $item[0] \neq item[1]$ **do**
5:         $item[0] = parent\_list(item[0])$
6:         **if** $item[0] \neq v_{root}$ **then**
7:             $circle.append(item[0])$
8:         **else**
9:             $circle.append(item[1])$
10:             $each[0] = each[1]$
11:             $each[1] = v_{root}$
12:         **end if**
13:     **end while**
14:     $circle\_list.append(circle)$
15: **end for**

After the network tree building, Algorithm 2 makes use of network tree information from v_{root}, $parent\_list$, combined with the vertex pairs in backtrack list generated from Algorithm 1 to reform relevant circles. Each item in the backtrack list will be utilized to generate a relevant circle. For each vertex pair in backtrack, the first vertex in the item is pushed into the circle. If the first vertex is not the same as the second vertex, Algorithm 2 will find the parent vertex of the first vertex in the parent list. Then, it will check whether the process is encountered to v_{root}, and push the first vertex into circle if the parent vertex is not the root vertex. Otherwise, it pushes the second vertex, exchanges the first and second vertices, and replaces the second vertex with v_{root}. This loop will continue until the first vertex is the same as the second vertex. The circle stores the relevant circle at this time. Finally, this circle is pushed into the circle list.

Algorithm 3. Deduct circle list

Input: $circle\_list$
Output: $circle\_list$
1: **for all** $circle\ pairs \in circle\_list$ **do**
2:     **if** $circleA \subset circleB$ **then**
3:         break $circleB$ into two small ones
4:         $circleB.update(small\ circle\ that\ is$
            $not\ circleB)$
5:     **end if**
6: **end for**

Algorithm 4. Score

Input: $circle\_list$
Output: $scores$
1: $scores \leftarrow 0$
2: **for all** $circle \in circle\_list$ **do**
3:     **for all** $v_i \in circle$ **do**
4:         $scores(v_i) + = \frac{1}{length(circle)}$
5:     **end for**
6: **end for**

Algorithm 3 will deduct the circle list in order to find the minimized relevant circles. It checks every circle pair in the circle list. If one circle in the pair is a part of the other one, the bigger circle will be broken into two distinguished relevant circles, including the smaller relevant circle. Finally, the bigger circle is updated with the deducted relevant circle. This process will continue running until no circle contains another circle pair in the circle list.

Algorithm 4 calculates the rank score for vertices in the attributional trace network. It initiates the score of all vertices to 0, and then enumerates all the minimized relevant circles in the circle list. For each vertex in the circle, the vertex's score is added by $\frac{1}{length(circle)}$ according to Formula 1.

The variables we used during these implementations are described in Table 1.

Table 1. Variable summary

Module	Variable	Explanation	Type
Construct network tree using DFS	G(V, E)	Store the adjacent vertices of each vertex in the network	Network
	v_start	The start vertex of each running	Vertex
	v_parent	The parent vertex of v_start	Vertex
	$visited$	Keep track of visited vertices	List
Regenerate relevant circles	$parent\_list$	Record the parent-child relations of the network tree	List
	$backtrack$	Record the vertex pairs that may contain relevant circles	List
	v_root	The root vertex where the DFS search begins	Vertex
	$circle\_list$	Record the relevant circles	List

4   Experiment

In this Section, we validate the effectiveness of the method and implementation we proposed using the classic 911 covert network dataset. We first introduce the dataset and its statistical characters, and then preprocess the dataset for the input to be compatible with our implementation. Algorithms in Sect. 3 are experimented to search for the minimized relevant circles through the network, and rank scores of vertices are calculated. We finally demonstrate and discuss the result.

In order to demonstrate the method and its implementations we proposed, we employ the famous network dataset of the terrorists involved in the 911 bombing of the World Trade Centers in 2001. The vertex connection types of this dataset range from 'attend the same school' to 'on the same plane'. It is based on open source intelligence (OSI) such as news reports, and tidied by Krebs [7].

The dataset consists 61 vertices, representing the members who are believed associated to this operation. The whole network is not densely connected, and the density is 0.08, exhibiting the secrecy characteristic of a covert terrorist network. This mitigates the consequence brought when a member is captured or compromised. The statistical characters of this dataset are depicted in Table 2.

228   J. Xu et al.

Despite the connection sparsity, the network diameter is 5, indicating this covert network is organized efficiently. The communication through this network only requires 5 relays in the worst situation. In common cases, the information path is 2.92, which is the average shortest path in Table 2. These characters profile a covert network that although quite invisible, maintains strong communications among its members.

In the original dataset, there exist some incompatible data. Therefore, we preprocess the connections to mitigate the incompatibility. There are 131 connections among these members, of which 64 connections are directed. Because the relevant circle is defined on undirected relations, we consider these directed connections as undirected, and make connections to ensure the relations are bidirection. In the dataset, vertex 32, Rayed Mohammed Abdullah, has connection to itself, and we remove this self loop.

After the dataset preprocess, it contains 61 members and 131 connections. Their relationships are demonstrated in Fig. 4.

Table 2. Dataset summary

Characters	Value
Density	0.08
Avg. degree	4.9
Diameter	5
Avg. shortest path	2.92

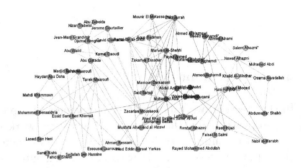

Fig. 4. 911 Covert network (Color figure online)

In Fig. 4, orange circles denote people who were in airplane UA #175 heading to WTC South, green circles denote people who were in airplane UA #93 heading to Pennsylvania, blue circles denote people who were in airplane AA #77 heading to Pentagon, chartreuse green circles denote people who were in airplane AA #11 heading to WTC North and pink circles represent other people who were associated in this event but were not in any hijacked planes.

For the purpose to guarantee the network tree built by Algorithm 1 maintains a shallow tree structure, we utilize the score rank implementations to build the network tree from the vertex of which the degree is the greatest. This vertex is Mohamed Atta with vertex degree as 15. we see him as our topic vertex to start the investigation. This also ensures that these found minimized relevant circles are most around our investigation topic. The rank of these members is depicted in Table 3.

Table 3. Rank result

1	Mohamed Atta	15	Tarek Maaroufi	29	Waleed Alshehri	43	Ahmed Alghamdi
2	Ziad Jarrah	16	Takek Maaroufi	30	Haydar Abu Doha	44	Mohand Alshehri
3	Marwan Al-Shehhi	17	Imad Eddin Baraat Yarkas	31	Mehdi Khammoun	45	Wail Alshehri
4	Ramzi Bin al-Shibh	18	Jerome Courtaillier	32	Ahmed Al Haznawi	46	Bandar Alhazmi
5	Essid Sami Ben Khemail	19	Kamel Daoudi	33	Fayez Ahmed	47	Faisal Al Salmi
6	Abu Qatada	20	Hani Hanjour	34	Ahmed Alnami	48	Lased Ben Heni
7	Said Bahaji	21	Lofti Raissi	35	Raed Hijazi	49	Madjid Sahoune
8	Djamal Benghal	22	Nabil al-Marabh	36	Mamoun Darkazanli	50	Ahed Khalil Ibrahim Samir Al-Ani
9	Zacarias Moussaoui	23	Khalid Al-Mihdhar	37	Osama Awadallah	51	Mohamed Belfas
10	Saeed Alghamdi	24	Agus Budiman	38	Abdussattar Shaikh	52	Abdul Aziz Al-Omari
11	Zakariya Essabar	25	Satam Suqami	39	Abu Walid	53	Ahmen Ressam
12	Mohammed Bensakhria	26	Mounir El Motassadeq	40	Seifallah ben Hassine		
13	Nawaf Alhazmi	27	Rayed Mohammed Abdullah	41	Mustafa Ahamend al-Hisawi		
14	Hamza Alghamdi	28	David Courtaillier	42	Essoussi Laaroussi		

This table includes 53 out of 61 members. 8 members are excluded because they are not found in any minimized relevant circle. From the table, we can figure out that Mohamed Atta is the most important member in this network. It resides in 14 minimized relevant circles, and its rank score is 4. This means the exposure of Mohamed Atta would lead to more relevant information about this covert network. Wikipedia shows that Mohamed Atta is the ringleaders of this attack. The top 3 members, Mohamed Atta, Ziad Jarrah and Marwan Al-Shehhi were 3 leaders separated in three hijacked planes. Although Ramzi Bin al-Shibh, as the fourth important member, did not directly involved in hijacking the planes, wikipedia shows he was a key facilitator of this attack, contributing great to the achievement of this operation. They are all the important members functioning as the perfect investigation entry points for this covert network.

5 Related Work

Vertex importance rank is a well-researched area in SNA (Social Network Analysis) [2,3]. Its optimization as sub research areas are also well established [6,10]. Most of these works are based on the vertex degree and the centricity. While some others are based on the PageRank and the connection importance [14]. Recently, epidemic models are also employed to measure vertex importance. We will introduce these categories respectively in the following.

5.1 Connection-Centric Approaches

Farley presented mathematical analysis of Al Qaeda organization. They used the order theory to quantify the degree to which the organization is still able to work, and determined these important vertices that are needed to be removed in order to neutralize the network [4]. They proposed the break the chains model as to break the connection for separating the important commanders from other vertices in the network.

Taha [12] presented a system called SIIMCO (System for Identifying the Influential Members of a Criminal Organization). It created network from Mobile Communication Data (MCD) and combined the vertex degree and its edge weight to rank the vertex importance. The result of their system showed improvement compared with CrimeNet Explorer [16] and LogAnalysis [5]. Taha also proposed to use the spanning tree of the network for identifying their leaders [13].

5.2 Vertex-Centric Approaches

Memon proposed a vertex centric measure that considers the number of connections incident to vertex along with connection weight. The importance of each vertex is determined by the overall vertex centrality [9].

Butt et al. employed hybrid framework to predict important vertices in the covert network. Their system calculates centrality measures as the features, and hybrid classifiers, such as k-Nearest Neighbors and Support Vector Machine are applied to figure out these key players [1].

5.3 Community-Centric Approaches

Langohr et al. proposed probabilistic similarity measure for vertices, and employed both k-medoids and hierarchical clustering methods to find the community. They regarded the representation of each community as the important vertex [8].

Our approach is different from theirs as we consider the connection structure of the attributional trace network and exploit the inter connection pattern to work as the foundation to rank vertices.

6   Conclusions

In this paper, we proposed a relevant circle-based approach to rank and discover the important vertices in the attributional trace network. The top rank vertices are most relevant to the investigation central, which lead the information trace-back to discover more still unknown relevant information. We also introduced the implementation of pivotal algorithms. Lastly, we demonstrate this method is valuable to mining these key players participating the 911 terrorist crime as a covert network. In further work, we would also like to research on trace networks which are featured by directed relation and connections with weight.

Acknowledgment. This work was supported by the National Natural Science Foundation of China (No. U1736218).

References

1. Butt, W.H., Akram, M.U., Khan, S.A., Javed, M.Y.: Covert network analysis for key player detection and event prediction using a hybrid classifier. Sci. World J. **2014**, 13 (2014). 615431
2. Chitrapura, K.P., Kashyap, S.R.: Node ranking in labeled directed graphs. In: Thirteenth ACM International Conference on Information and Knowledge Management, pp. 597–606 (2004)
3. Dasgupta, S., Prakash, C.: Intelligent detection of influential nodes in networks. In: International Conference on Electrical, Electronics, and Optimization Techniques (2016)
4. Farley, J.D.: Breaking Al Qaeda cells: a mathematical analysis of counterterrorism operations (a guide for risk assessment and decision making). Stud. Conflict Terrorism **26**(6), 399–411 (2003)
5. Ferrara, E., Meo, P.D., Catanese, S., Fiumara, G.: Detecting criminal organizations in mobile phone networks. Expert Syst. Appl. **41**(13), 5733–5750 (2014)
6. Halappanavar, M., Sathanur, A.V., Nandi, A.K.: Accelerating the mining of influential nodes in complex networks through community detection, pp. 64–71 (2016)
7. Krebs, V.E.: Mapping networks of terrorist cells, pp. 43–52 (2002)
8. Langohr, L., Toivonen, H.: Finding representative nodes in probabilistic graphs. In: Berthold, M.R. (ed.) Bisociative Knowledge Discovery. LNCS (LNAI), vol. 7250, pp. 218–229. Springer, Heidelberg (2012). https://doi.org/10.1007/978-3-642-31830-6_15
9. Memon, B.R.: Identifying important nodes in weighted covert networks using generalized centrality measures. In: Intelligence and Security Informatics Conference, pp. 131–140 (2012)
10. Sheikhahmadi, A., Nematbakhsh, M.A., Shokrollahi, A.: Improving detection of influential nodes in complex networks. Physica A Stat. Mech. Appl. **436**, 833–845 (2015)
11. Singer, P.W.: Cybersecurity and Cyberwar: What Everyone Needs to Know. Oxford University Press, Oxford (2014)
12. Taha, K., Yoo, P.D.: SIIMCO: a forensic investigation tool for identifying the influential members of a criminal organization. IEEE Trans. Inf. Forensics Secur. **11**(4), 811–822 (2016)

13. Taha, K., Yoo, P.D.: Using the spanning tree of a criminal network for identifying its leaders. IEEE Trans. Inf. Forensics Secur. **PP**(99), 1 (2017)
14. Wiil, U.K., Gniadek, J., Memon, N.: Measuring link importance in terrorist networks. In: International Conference on Advances in Social Networks Analysis and Mining, pp. 225–232 (2010)
15. Xu, J., Yun, X., Zhang, Y., Sang, Y., Cheng, Z.: NetworkTrace: probabilistic relevant pattern recognition approach to attribution trace analysis. In: 2017 IEEE Trustcom/BigDataSE/ICESS, pp. 691–698, August 2017. https://doi.org/10.1109/Trustcom/BigDataSE/ICESS.2017.301
16. Xu, J.J., Chen, H.: Crimenet explorer: a framework for criminal network knowledge discovery. ACM Trans. Inf. Syst. **23**(2), 201–226 (2005)
17. Wei, Z., Yang, S., Wenwu, C.: A game model of APT attack for distributed network. In: Xhafa, F., Caballé, S., Barolli, L. (eds.) 3PGCIC 2017. LNDECT, vol. 13, pp. 224–234. Springer, Cham (2018). https://doi.org/10.1007/978-3-319-69835-9_21

IoT Networks and Services

Safety Message Propagation Using Vehicle-Infrastructure Cooperation in Urban Vehicular Networks

Xiaolan Tang, Zhi Geng, and Wenlong Chen[✉]

College of Information Engineering, Capital Normal University, Beijing 100048, China
{tangxl,2151002071,chenwenlong}@cnu.edu.cn

Abstract. A soaring number of vehicles in modern cities bring in complicated urban transportation and severe safety risks. After a traffic accident occurs, how to quickly disseminate this alert to other vehicles is very important to avoid rear-end collision and traffic jam. Existing studies mainly use the vehicles travelling in the same direction as the collision vehicles to forward safety messages, which strictly limit the performance improvements. In this paper, we propose a safety message propagation scheme using vehicle-infrastructure cooperation in urban vehicular networks, named SMP. On straight roads, the opposite-lane front vehicles help to relay data when no further collision-lane back vehicles exist, while at intersections, the deployed roadside units create new safety messages with updated dissemination parameters and distribute them in the upstream lanes. The collaboration of vehicles in two directions and roadside units enhances the performances of safety-related applications. Besides, three checking policies are designed to avoid transmission failures and hence save network resources. Simulation experiments show that SMP achieves a high reception ratio and a short propagation delay.

Keywords: Urban vehicular networks · Safety message ·
Vehicle-infrastructure cooperation · Roadside units ·
Transmission checking

1 Introduction

Nowadays, as the number of vehicles in cities sharply rises, the urban transportation becomes more and more complicated. When there is a collision between two vehicles, if the safety message is not propagated to other vehicles immediately, it is probable to result in a multiple-vehicle collision, and the traffic jam thereafter further aggravates the severe transportation states. One of the main application of urban vehicular networks [16] is to improve the driving safety by utilizing communications between vehicles and roadside infrastructures [17].

An urban vehicular network consists of mobile vehicles carrying sensors to sense the vehicle status and the surrounding environments, and roadside units to connect the vehicles to Internet and provide powerful communication or

H. Gao et al. (Eds.): CollaborateCom 2018, LNICST 268, pp. 235–251, 2019.
https://doi.org/10.1007/978-3-030-12981-1_17

computing capabilities [14,19]. Through vehicle-to-vehicle (V2V) and vehicle-to-infrastructure (V2I) communications, a safety message can be disseminated to those vehicles which may be affected quickly [1]. Therefore, the drivers could take actions ahead of time, in order to avoid dangers or jammed roads [10].

Current researches on safety message propagation usually focus on the improvement of MAC protocol rather than the data forwarding among the vehicles and roadside units. Besides, alert messages are often relayed by the vehicles driving in the same lane/direction. However, since the multi-lane multi-direction straight roads and the intersections are very common in modern cities, how to use the vehicles travelling in different directions as well as the stable roadside units deployed at intersections to enhance the alert dissemination, becomes a key problem.

In this paper, we propose a safety message propagation scheme using vehicle-infrastructure cooperation in urban vehicular networks, named SMP. On a straight road, the safety messages are mainly distributed to and forwarded by the vehicles in collision lane, while the opposite-lane vehicles relay data when no more collision-lane vehicle exists in the communication range. In addition, around an intersection, the nearby roadside unit conducts message propagation to upstream lanes in light of divide and conquer method. Meanwhile, in order to reduce the probability of transfer failures, we design several transmission checking policies.

The main advantages of our proposal are listed below. (1) Safety message forwarding by the opposite-lane vehicles helps to extend the dissemination area and accelerate the data propagation. (2) Roadside units create a new safety message for each upstream lane, and start its propagation by V2U communications. Hence the severe problem of bandwidth competition at intersections is addressed. (3) The transmission checking policies avoid the waste of communication resources due to interrupted transmissions.

The remainder of this paper is organized as follows. After surveying the related work, we briefly introduce the network scenario and analyze the problem. Then the transmission checking policies and the safety message propagation algorithms for vehicles and roadside units are discussed in detail. After that, we present and analyze the simulation results, and finally conclude this paper.

2   Related Work

Recently the safety message propagation in vehicular networks becomes a hot research domain because of its important use in intelligent transportation systems (ITSs) [2]. Some studies analyze the performance of safety message propagation and explore the elements affecting the safety applications in vehicular networks [22]. Regarding sparse bidirectional highway scenario deployed with RSUs, Pan and Wu analyze the delivery delay of safety messages with general and decelerating "store-carry-forward" mechanisms [13]. Hafeez et al. analyze the reliability of a dedicated short-range communication (DSRC [8]) control channel (CCH) to handle safety applications in vehicular networks, and design an adaptive algorithm to address DSRC's performance degradation in dense and high-mobility conditions [6]. Dinh and Kim develop information centric networking to disseminate safety information efficiently by exploiting V2V and vehicle-to-road communications [3]. Omar et al. compare IEEE 802.11p standard [15] and a time-division multiple access protocol VeMAC via computer simulations in different highway and city scenarios [12].

Besides, some researchers propose efficient safety message dissemination schemes to enhance the quality of services. For vehicle-safety-related communication services, Ucar et al. combine IEEE 802.11p-based multihop clustering and LTE for safety message dissemination, which achieves a high delivery ratio and a short delay with a small use of the cellular architecture [20]. Ghandour et al. present a cognitive network architecture with spectrum sensing and allocation schemes to dynamically extend control channel used by vehicles for safety-related data transmission [4]. Hassanabadi and Valaee design a sublayer in the application layer of the WAVE stack, which rebroadcasts network coded safety messages to increase the overall reliability of safety application [7]. Based on mobility aware clustering, Gupta et al. improve MAC to support dynamic beacon generations and allow for different data transmission rates [5].

Although a majority of the above work focuses on the link layer protocol, there exists some related work on the higher layers than MAC in safety message propagation schemes. To disseminate time-sensitive event-driven safety warning messages through lossy links, Li et al. propose an opportunistic broadcast protocol to increase reception ratio and accelerate dissemination, and utilize acknowledgements to avoid redundant data transmissions [11]. Wang et al. divide the coverage area of a relay node using regular hexagon equilateral triangle, and set vehicle groups accordingly. They guarantee that only one relay node forwards message in each group and each relay node forwards the same message only once [21].

However, to the best of our knowledge, most of the present researches only utilize the vehicles driving in the same direction as the source of the safety message to forward data. Therefore, the alert dissemination is strictly limited, and hence affects the quality of services. In urban vehicular networks, how to fully utilize a large number of vehicles in different directions and the resource-rich roadside units to improve safety message propagation is our basic motivation.

3   Network Scenario and Problem Statement

For a clear discussion about the problem, we focus on the roads with two lanes in different directions. We assume all the vehicular nodes have the same communication radius CV, and the roadside units have the same communication radius CU. Usually $CU > CV$. The vehicular nodes and the roadside units use omnidirectional antenna to propagate signals. In other words, the signals are disseminated in all the directions, and every node in the communication range can receive this signal theoretically. When a node gets this signal, it decides on whether to receive the data or not by checking the destination field in the packet.

When a vehicle in a collision creates a safety message, it is called the source of this message, and the lane having the collision is called the collision lane. Those vehicles travelling in the collision lane are named collision-lane vehicles, denoted by $S = \{s_1, s_2, ..., s_i\}$, while those vehicles in the opposite lane are called opposite-lane vehicles, denoted by $O = \{o_1, o_2, ..., o_j\}$. For two collision-lane vehicles, along its driving direction, the one in front of the other is called collision-lane front vehicle, while the other is collision-lane back vehicle. Similarly, we have opposite-lane front vehicle and opposite-lane back vehicle.

An instance of safety message dissemination is shown in Fig. 1. When vehicles s_2 and s_3 have a collision, a safety message is generated by and disseminated from s_3 (the source of the safety message). Compared with s_3, s_1 is a collision-lane front vehicle, while s_4 is a collision-lane back vehicle. Similarly, comparing o_1 and o_2, o_1 is opposite-lane front vehicle, while o_2 is opposite-lane back vehicle. Since the crash may lead to a rear-end collision of s_4 or at least slow it down, s_4 should receive the safety message as soon as possible for an immediate reaction. Therefore, s_4 is regarded as one of the destination nodes of this safety message. In this scenario, s_4 receives the data from s_3 by one hop V2V communication.

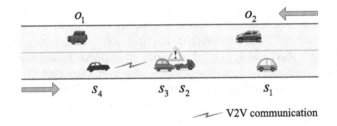

Fig. 1. An instance of safety message dissemination.

From this instance, we get that the safety message dissemination aims to propagate the safety message to those vehicles within a specific distance, whose driving behaviors might be affected by this accident. In specific, in terms of straight roads and intersections in urban road networks, the data dissemination schemes are also different. On straight roads, the safety message propagation aims to deliver the message to the collision-lane back vehicles of the source; in the intersections, the safety message needs to be distributed to those vehicles which might drive into the collision lane. Besides, in order to avoid failed transmissions, we design some policies for transmission validity checking. Next we will introduce these policies first, and then details how to disseminate safety messages on straight roads and in the intersections.

4   Transmission Checking Policies

Since the high velocity results in an unstable inter-vehicle connectivity, it is common that some V2V data transmissions are interrupted when the two communicating vehicles leave each other's communication range. This kind of invalid transmissions occupy the valuable wireless bandwidth, and hence lead to resource wastes. Besides, after transmission failures, vehicles have to reselect some forwarders to continue data relay, which prolongs data dissemination latency. Considering the safety messages require a high quality of service, we design three policies to distinguish the invalid transmissions ahead of time, based on the expected data transmission time, the current distance of the sender and the receiver, and their velocities. Before a vehicular node sends some data, it uses the policies to check this transmission first. If the result is true, it starts to transmit; otherwise, it gives up this transmission.

The transmission checking in safety message dissemination consists of three policies, i.e., the timing checking, the location checking, and the distance checking. If and only if all the three policies return true, the checking result is true; otherwise, it returns false. Next we will give a brief introduction of the time and location checking policies, and then discuss about the distance checking policy in detail.

In the timing checking policy, the vehicle compares the remaining lifetime of the safety message and the expected transmission time. If the safety message has a longer lifetime than the expected transmission time, the checking result is true; otherwise, it is false. In addition, the location checking policy checks the expected location of the receiver when it receives the whole data. If it is within the specific propagation range of this safety message, the policy returns true; otherwise, the result is false. Moreover, the distance checking policy checks whether the two communicating nodes keep in their communication ranges during the expected transmission time. Specifically, it has different rules with respect to the different travelling directions of the sender and the receiver. We will discuss about it in four cases as follows.

(1) Distance checking for transmission between collision-lane vehicles.

From above analysis, we know the collision-lane front vehicles should transmit the safety message to collision-lane back vehicles. On the one hand, for unicast transmission from a vehicle s_i to its back vehicle s_{i+1}. The velocities of s_i and s_{i+1} are v_i^S and v_{i+1}^S respectively, and the current distance between them is $f_{i,i+1}^S$ ($f_{i,i+1}^S \leq CV$). The expected time to transmit the safety message is τ. Based on geometry theory, the distance checking condition is

$$vsgn(v_i^S - v_{i+1}^S) \times [\tau(v_i^S - v_{i+1}^S) + f_{i,i+1}^S] \leq CV, \qquad (1)$$

where $vsgn()$ is a variation of sign function, in which $vsgn(x) = 1$ when $x \geq 0$, and $vsgn(x) = 0$ when $x < 0$. On the other hand, for multicast transmission, take a collision-lane front vehicle s_i sending data to all the collision-lane back nodes in its communication range as an instance. If there exists at least one back vehicle which satisfies the condition (1), then s_i sends data out and the receivers determine whether to obtain the data or not according to their own results of the condition (1).

(2) Distance checking for transmission from collision-lane vehicle to opposite-lane vehicle.

From our SMP scheme below, there only exists unicasting from collision-lane vehicle to opposite-lane vehicle, rather than multicasting. In addition, the collision-lane vehicle is nearer to the source than the opposite-lane vehicle. For example, a collision-lane vehicle s_i wants to send data to an opposite-lane vehicle o_j. Their velocities are v_i^S and v_j^O, and their distance is $f_{i,j}^{SO}$ ($f_{i,j}^{SO} \leq CV$). The lane width is D. After computing the distance between vehicles in different directions, we get the checking condition

$$\sqrt{D^2 + [\tau(v_i^S + v_j^O) + \sqrt{f_{i,j}^{SO}{}^2 - D^2}]^2} \leq CV. \qquad (2)$$

(3) Distance checking for transmission between opposite-lane vehicles.

In SMP, only unicasting from an opposite-lane front vehicle to an opposite-lane back vehicle is supported. Similar with transmission between collision-lane vehicles, the distance checking condition for two opposite-lane vehicles o_j and o_{j+1} with velocities v_j^O and v_{j+1}^O and distance $f_{j,j+1}^O$ is

$$vsgn(v_j^O - v_{j+1}^O) \times [\tau(v_j^O - v_{j+1}^O) + f_{j,j+1}^O] \leq CV. \qquad (3)$$

(4) Distance checking for transmission from opposite-lane vehicle to collision-lane vehicle.

In SMP scheme, this kind of transmission is multicasting from an opposite-lane vehicle to those collision-lane vehicles which are further to the source than the sender. For instance, o_j with velocity v_j^O wants to send message to s_i with velocity v_i^S and their distance is $f_{j,i}^{OS}$. The checking condition is

$$\sqrt{D^2 + [\tau(v_i^S + v_j^O) - \sqrt{f_{j,i}^{OS}{}^2 - D^2}]^2} \leq CV. \qquad (4)$$

When multicasting, if any of the receivers satisfies the above condition, o_j sends this message, and each receiver decides whether to receive it according to its checking result.

5   Safety Message Propagation Scheme

5.1   Safety Message Propagation on Straight Roads

For safety message propagation on straight roads, we propose a propagation scheme using vehicles travelling in two directions. The main idea is to use the collision-lane vehicles to forward the safety message, but when there is a coverage hole (no more collision-lane vehicle can continue data dissemination), the opposite-lane vehicles are utilized to enlarge the coverage area and shorten the propagation delay.

(1) Data propagation algorithm for the collision-lane vehicles.

After the safety message is generated, the source sends this message to all the collision-lane back vehicles in its communication range. In order to propagate the message quickly and efficiently, the farthest collision-lane back vehicle from the source is selected as the next relay. There are two main reasons for this selection. (1) The farthest back vehicle is in the communication range of the current relay node (or the source node), therefore there is no hole (uncovered road segments) in the data propagation. (2) Because of the same communication radius, the communication area of the farthest back vehicle covers that of other back vehicles, which accelerates the dissemination. Other collision-lane vehicles work in the same way as the source.

However, sometimes there may be no collision-lane back vehicles, but exist vehicles in the other lane. Compared with the collision-lane nodes, the opposite-lane vehicles usually meet a new collision-lane vehicle earlier. Therefore, SMP attempts to use the opposite-lane vehicles to achieve a quick propagation. In specific, among all the opposite-lane vehicles in the relay's communication range, the front one is selected as the next forwarder. Since the opposite-lane nodes are not the destinations of the safety message, they only take the role of forwarder. Besides, the front vehicle has a high probability to meet a collision-lane vehicle earlier than others.

The data propagation algorithm for a collision-lane vehicle s_i is shown in Algorithm 1. In the algorithm, $BV(i)$ is the set of collision-lane back vehicles of s_i in its communication range; $OV(i)$ is the set of opposite-lane vehicles in s_i's communication range.

Algorithm 1. Data propagation algorithm for a collision-lane vehicle s_i

---

1 if $BV(i) \neq \emptyset$ then
2 $\quad$ send the safety message to $BV(i)$;
3 $\quad$ select $s_x \in BV(i)$ with max $f_{i,x}^S$ to be the next relay;
4 else
5 $\quad$ if $OV(i) \neq \emptyset$ then
6 $\quad\quad$ select the front $o_y \in OV(i)$ to be the next relay;
7 $\quad\quad$ send the safety message to o_y;
8 $\quad$ else
9 $\quad\quad$ keep going ahead carrying the safety message;
10 $\quad$ end
11 end

An instance of data propagation at a collision-lane vehicle s_3 is shown in Fig. 2. In Fig. 2(a), the source of a safety message s_3 sends the message to its collision-lane back vehicles, including s_4 and s_5. Besides, s_5 is selected as the next relay and continues the data propagation to its collision-lane back vehicles. Another case is shown in Fig. 2(b). The source s_3 has no collision-lane back vehicles in its communication range, but it has two opposite-lane vehicles, i.e., o_1 and o_2. In this case, s_3 sends the safety message to o_1, and then o_1 forwards it to another collision-lane vehicle s_4. According to the triangle theory, in Fig. 2(b), $f_{1,4}^{OS} < f_{2,4}^{OS}$. Therefore, o_1 has a larger coverage of new collision-lane vehicles than o_2, and o_1 is a good next relay.

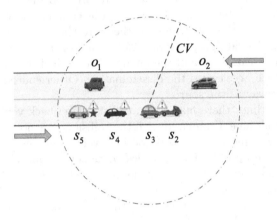

(a) between collision-lane vehicles

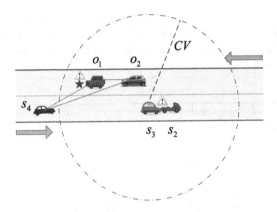

(b) from collision-lane vehicle to opposite-lane vehicle

Fig. 2. An instance of safety message propagation at a collision-lane vehicle.

(2) Data propagation algorithm for the opposite-lane vehicles.

After an opposite-lane vehicle receives a safety message, it carries the message until encountering a new collision-lane vehicle. At this time it forwards the data to all the new collision-lane vehicles, and selects the farthest one as the next relay. Besides, before encountering a collision-lane vehicle, if another opposite-lane vehicle passes the carrier, for a quick propagation, the carrier forwards the message to this passing vehicle.

The data propagation algorithm for an opposite-lane vehicle o_j is shown in Algorithm 2, where $SV(j)$ is the set of newly meeting collision-lane vehicles.

Algorithm 2. Data propagation algorithm for an opposite-lane vehicle o_j

```
 1 if SV(j) ≠ ∅ then
 2     send the safety message to SV(j);
 3     select sₓ ∈ SV(j) with max f_{j,x}^{OS} to be the next relay;
 4     remove the safety message from cache;
 5 else
 6     if o_y passes o_j then
 7         send the safety message to o_y;
 8         select o_y to be the next relay;
 9         remove the safety message from cache;
10     else
11         keep going ahead carrying the safety message;
12     end
13 end
```

Figure 3 illustrates an example of data propagation at an opposite-lane vehicle o_1. In Fig. 3(a), o_1 sends the safety message when encountering new collision-lane vehicles s_4 and s_5. s_4 and s_5 both receive the data, but only s_5 is the next relay. As shown in Fig. 3(b), when o_2 passes o_1, o_1 transmits the safety message to the new next relay o_2. After delivery, the replica in o_1 is removed since o_1 is not a destination of the safety message.

To sum up, SMP disseminates the safety message in the collision-lane back vehicles mainly through collision-lane relays and sometimes through opposite-lane forwarders, which help to increase the coverage and shorten the propagation latency when no further collision-lane relay exists.

5.2   Safety Message Dissemination at Intersections

In urban transportation scenarios, a safety message is forwarded along a straight road segment, and then arrives at an intersection deployed with a roadside unit. Regarding the roadside unit has a stronger communication capability than those vehicular nodes, SMP uses the roadside unit to take charge of the safety message disseminate around the intersection.

Specifically, when a roadside unit receives a safety message from some vehicle, firstly it gets the collision lane, where the safety message is from, by analyzing the collision location in the alert message. Since the safety message only needs to be disseminated in those lanes where the vehicles may drive into the collision lane (called the upstream lanes), the roadside unit finds these lanes according to the geographical information of the intersection.

Then the roadside unit calculates the remaining propagation distance in each upstream lane according to the source location and the overall propagation distance. If the remaining propagation distance is positive, then the roadside unit creates a new safety message for further dissemination in this lane, which takes the roadside unit as its source and the remaining propagation distance as the

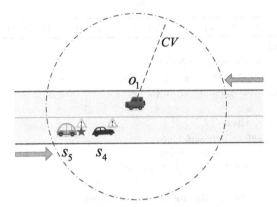

(a) from opposite-lane vehicle to collision-lane vehicles

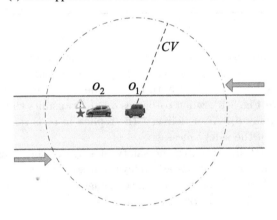

(b) between opposite-lane vehicles

Fig. 3. An instance of safety message propagation at an opposite-lane vehicle.

propagation distance, and has the same warning information as the original safety message. After that, this new safety message is distributed to the vehicles in this lane and in the roadside unit's communication range, among which the farthest one from the roadside unit is selected as the next forwarder. Similar with above analysis, the relay selection helps to accelerate the safety message propagation.

The safety message dissemination algorithm for roadside units is presented in Algorithm 3. LF is upstream lanes; $RD(l)$ is the remaining propagation distance in the lane l; $LV(l)$ is the vehicles in the lane l and in the communication range of the roadside unit; $f_{k,z,l}^{UL}$ is the distance between the roadside unit u_k and the vehicle v_z^l in the lane l.

For a clear presentation, we give an example in Fig. 4. Vehicles can turn left or right at an intersection deployed with a roadside unit u_1. When u_1 gets a

---

Algorithm 3. Data dissemination algorithm for a roadside unit u_k

---

1 find the upstream lanes LF;
2 **for** $\forall l \in LF$ **do**
3   **if** $RD(l) > 0$ **then**
4   generate a new safety message for lane l;
5   **if** $LV(l) \neq \emptyset$ **then**
6   send the new safety message to $LV(l)$;
7   select $v_z^l \in LV(l)$ with max $f_{k,z,l}^{UL}$ to be the next relay in lane l;
8   **else**
9   carry the new safety message;
10   try to send it to vehicles in lane l later;
11   **end**
12   **end**
13 **end**

---

safety message from s_5, it finds three upstream lanes, which are marked with red arrows in the figure. Assume that the remaining propagation distances for all the three lanes are positive, and u_1 creates three new safety messages. Since there are some vehicles in these lanes, u_1 sends the new messages to them. Hence the vehicles d_1^U, d_1^L, d_1^D and d_2^D all receive their messages respectively. Moreover, d_1^U, d_1^L and d_2^D are the next relays in their lanes.

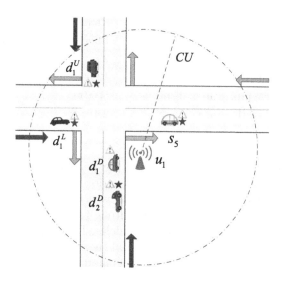

Fig. 4. An instance of safety message dissemination at an intersection.

Overall, in an intersection, SMP utilizes the idea of divide and conquer to replace the original safety message with several new safety messages for different lanes. In each lane, SMP attempts to cover as many vehicles as possible and accelerate data dissemination by multicasting and relay selection.

6   Performance Evaluation

6.1   Network Configurations

To evaluate the performance of our proposal, we take simulation experiments on the opportunistic network environment simulator (ONE) [9,18]. More experiments based on real world data are left to our future work. The network configurations are listed in Table 1 with some discussions below.

Table 1. Simulation environment configuration

Parameter	Value
Roads	5000 m with 2 lanes
Intersection locations	An intersection every 1000 s
Road width	10 m
Vehicle departure interval	4–18 s
Number of roadside units	5
Communication radius of vehicular nodes	300 m
Communication radius of roadside units	500 m
Velocity on straight roads	Random in [60, 110] km/h
Velocity at intersections	Random in [45, 65] km/h
Safety message transmission time	2 s
Lifetime of safety message	120 s
Safety message propagation distance	5000 m
Scenario preparation time	240 s

Since the vehicle density greatly affects the performance of safety message propagation, we conduct experiments in scenarios with different vehicle densities. In order to provide different densities as well as the mobility randomness, we let the vehicle departure interval range from 4 s to 18 s, and select random velocities in a specific range for all the vehicles. Besides, at the beginning of the experiments, we take 240 s to prepare well the scenario with vehicles on the roads. Then simulate a collision at the end of one road, and start safety message propagation.

Considering that our safety message propagation scheme focuses on the higher layers than MAC layer in IEEE 802.11p, SMP can be integrated with those MAC-enhanced protocols. To the best of our knowledge, our proposal is an innovative attempt to fully utilize the vehicles and infrastructures to improve the alert dissemination. Therefore, in the experiments, we select the propagation scheme using only collision-lane vehicles (PCL), the propagation scheme using collision-lane vehicles and opposite-lane vehicles but without roadside units (PBV) as our compared schemes. Comparing the results of PBV and PCL, we can see the advantages of opposite-lane vehicles, while comparing PBV and SMP, we get the performance of roadside units.

We use four criteria, i.e., the reception ratio, the propagation delay, the transmission overhead, and the number of detected failed transmissions. The reception ratio is the ratio of the number of destinations which receive the safety message to the number of all the destinations. A higher reception ratio indicates a better data dissemination. Besides, the propagation delay is the duration from the time when the safety message is generated by its source to the time when it reaches the boundary of the propagation area. A short propagation delay implies a quick response to the accident, and hence works well for urgent events. Moveover, the transmission overhead is the number of safety message transmissions, which shows the communication consumption of the data dissemination. Note that for a multicast transmission with one sender and multiple receivers, we take it as one transmission. Last but not the least, the number of detected failed transmissions directly presents the benefits from the transmission checking policies.

6.2   Simulation Results

The simulation results of the three compared schemes, i.e., PCL, PBV and SMP, are illustrated in Fig. 5.

From Fig. 5(a), we see that when the vehicle density increases (in other words, the vehicle departure interval decreases), SMP keeps a relatively stable reception ratio above 95%, while the reception ratios of PBV and PCL grow from 85% to 98% and from 46% to 87% respectively. The main reasons are as follows. More vehicles bring in more opportunities of V2V communications. Since PCL and PBV only use vehicles to forward data, the advantages of a high density are obvious. By contrast, SMP also utilizes the roadside units with powerful communication abilities to relay data, therefore its reception ratio growth is relatively small. However, compared with PCL and PBV, SMP always has a higher reception ratio in the scenarios with different numbers of vehicles.

As shown in Fig. 5(b), PCL keeps the longest propagation delay 120 s, while PBV shortens its delays from 53 s to 10 s as the vehicle density rises. Actually, in PCL, the safety message does not reach the boundary of the propagation area because of the limited transmissions between collision-lane vehicles. In other words, the warning information is not fully disseminated. After the lifetime 120 s finishes, the messages are out of date and removed from their carriers. Besides, PBV uses the opposite-lane vehicles to disseminate the alerts within the propagation range, and a high vehicle density produces new communication opportunities and hence results in a short delivery latency. It is noteworthy that SMP keeps a stable and short propagation latency at round 20 s, because the roadside units accelerate the data dissemination at intersections.

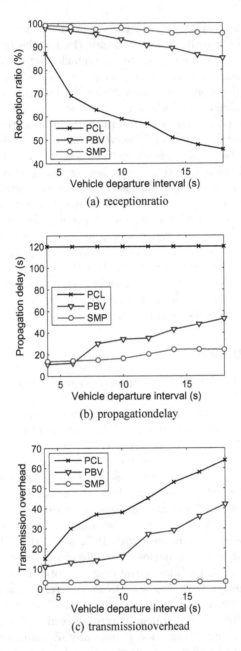

(a) receptionratio

(b) propagationdelay

(c) transmissionoverhead

Fig. 5. Simulation results.

In Fig. 5(c), as the vehicle density decreases, the transmission overheads of PCL and PBV have rapid growths, because the safety message has to be transmitted several times due to the severe inter-vehicle transmission conditions. In comparison, because of the advantages of stable roadside units, SMP has the smallest transmission overhead.

Since the safety message transmission time is short (2 s) in the above experiments, there are few transmission failures. In order to clearly present the performance of our transmission checking policies, we range the safety message transmission time from 2 s to 10 s, and keep the vehicle departure interval to be 8 s. The numbers of detected invalid transmissions in the three schemes are shown in Fig. 6.

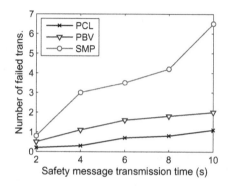

Fig. 6. Results of the number of detected failed transmissions.

We see, in Fig. 6, the numbers of detected failed transmissions in SMP, PBV and PCL rise from less than 1 to 6.5, 2 and 1 individually, when the safety message transmission time ranges from 2 s to 10 s. When transmitting a safety message takes a longer time, it is more probable that the two communicating vehicles travel out of each other's communication range during the data transfer. In particular, SMP with the most communication chances has the most failed transmissions. In one word, the transmission checking policies improve the communication efficiency to some extent, especially when the data transmission takes a long time.

In conclusion, compared with PCL and PVB, our scheme SMP keeps a high reception ratio, a short propagation delay, and a small transmission overhead, in the scenarios with different vehicle densities. Besides, the transmission checking policies have an obvious advantage to avoid invalid transmissions in SMP.

7   Conclusion

For safety applications in urban vehicular networks, we put forward an efficient safety message propagation scheme combining the advantages of vehicles and infrastructures, named SMP. Specifically, on straight roads with two directions, the collision-lane back vehicles are the destinations of the alerts, and the farthest among them is selected as the next relay. If no more collision-lane vehicles can obtain data, the opposite-lane font vehicle is taken as the next forwarder, which helps to shorten the dissemination latency. Besides, at intersections, the roadside units deliver new safety messages with updated information to the upstream lanes. The strong communication capacity of roadside units also improves the warning dissemination. In addition, the transmission checking policies avoid the potential failed transmissions, and thus save resources. Finally the simulation results show that compared with those schemes using only collision-lane vehicles and only vehicles in two directions, SMP has a high reception ratio and a short propagation delay at a small transmission cost.

Although we design several transmission checking policies, there still exist some complex factors affecting the data delivery, such as the bandwidth competition, the packet scheduling, etc. Analyzing these elements may enhance the performance of safety-related services. Besides, the construction and evaluation of an architecture integrating our propagation scheme and new MAC-enhanced protocol also require further study.

References

1. Ali, G.G.M.N., Noor-A-Rahim, M., Chong, P.H.J., Guan, Y.L.: Analysis and improvement of reliability through coding for safety message broadcasting in urban vehicular networks. IEEE Trans. Veh. Technol. **67**(8), 6774–6787 (2018)
2. Bi, Y., Zhou, H., Zhuang, W., Zhao, H.: Safety Message Broadcast in Vehicular Networks. Springer, Heidelberg (2017). https://doi.org/10.1007/978-3-319-47352-9
3. Dinh, N., Kim, Y.: Information-centric dissemination protocol for safety information in vehicular ad-hoc networks. Wirel. Netw. **23**(5), 1359–1371 (2017)
4. Ghandour, A.J., Fawaz, K., Artail, H., Felice, M.D., Bononi, L.: Improving vehicular safety message delivery through the implementation of a cognitive vehicular network. Ad Hoc Netw. **11**(8), 2408–2422 (2013)
5. Gupta, N., Prakash, A., Tripathi, R.: Adaptive beaconing in mobility aware clustering based MAC protocol for safety message dissemination in VANET. Wirel. Commun. Mob. Comput. **2017**(1246172), 1–15 (2017)
6. Hafeez, K.A., Zhao, L., Ma, B., Mark, J.W.: Performance analysis and enhancement of the DSRC for VANET's safety applications. IEEE Trans. veh. Technol. **62**(7), 3069–3083 (2013)
7. Hassanabadi, B., Valaee, S.: Reliable periodic safety message broadcasting in vanets using network coding. IEEE Trans. Wirel. Commun. **13**(3), 1284–1297 (2014)
8. Kenney, J.B.: Dedicated short-range communications (DSRC) standards in the United States. Proc. IEEE **99**(7), 1162–1182 (2011)
9. Keranen, A., Ott, J., Karkkainen, T.: The ONE simulator for DTN protocol evaluation. In: Proceedings of International Conference on Simulation Tools and Techniques (SIMUTools). ACM, Rome, 2–6 March 2009
10. Khan, F.A.: Safety-message routing in vehicular ad hoc networks. Technical report, Georgia Institute of Technology, Atlanta, USA (2013)
11. Li, M., Zeng, K., Lou, W.: Opportunistic broadcast of event-driven warning messages in vehicular ad hoc networks with lossy links. Comput. Netw. **55**(10), 2443–2464 (2011)
12. Omar, H.A., Lu, N., Zhuang, W.: Wireless access technologies for vehicular network safety applications. IEEE Netw. **30**(4), 22–26 (2016)

13. Pan, B., Wu, H.: Analysis of safety messages delivery in vehicular networks with interconnected roadside units. IEEE Access **1**, 1–10 (2017). https://doi.org/10. 1109/ACCESS.2017.2769344
14. Piao, J., McDonald, M., Hounsell, N.: Cooperative vehicle-infrastructure systems for improving driver information services: an analysis of COOPERS test results. IET Intell. Transp. Syst. **6**(1), 9–17 (2012)
15. Rezgui, J., Cherkaoui, S.: About deterministic and non-deterministic vehicular communications over DSRC/802.11p. Wirel. Commun. Mob. Comput. **14**(15), 1435–1449 (2014)
16. Sun, G., Zhang, Y., Liao, D., Yu, H., Du, X., Guizani, M.: Bus trajectory-based street-centric routing for message delivery in urban vehicular ad hoc networks. IEEE Trans. Veh. Technol. **67**(8), 7550–7563 (2018)
17. Tang, X., Hong, D., Chen, W.: Data acquisition based on stable matching of bipartite graph in cooperative vehicle-infrastructure systems. Sensors **17**(6), 1–22 (2017)
18. Tang, X., Pu, J., Cao, K., Zhang, Y., Xiong, Z.: Integrated extensible simulation platform for vehicular sensor networks in smart cities. Int. J. Distrib. Sens. Netw. **2012**(4), 22–26 (2012)
19. Tang, X., Pu, J., Gao, Y., Xie, Y., Xiong, Z.: GPS-based replica deletion scheme with anti-packet distribution for vehicular networks. Comput. J. **58**(6), 1399–1415 (2015)
20. Ucar, S., Ergen, S.C., Ozkasap, O.: Multihop-cluster-based IEEE 802.11p and LTE hybrid architecture for VANET safety message dissemination. IEEE Trans. Veh. Technol. **65**(4), 2621–2636 (2016)
21. Wang, X., et al.: Regular-hexagon-equilateral-triangle area grouping-based broadcast protocol for safety message in urban vehicular ad hoc networks. Int. J. Distrib. Sens. Netw. **13**(1), 1550147716683829 (2017)
22. Yin, X., Ma, X., Trivedi, K.S.: An interacting stochastic models approach for the performance evaluation of DSRC vehicular safety communication. IEEE Trans. Comput. **62**(5), 873–885 (2013)

Predicting Duration of Traffic Accidents Based on Ensemble Learning

Lina Shan, Zikun Yang, Huan Zhang, Ruyi Shi, and Li Kuang[✉]

Central South University, Changsha 410075, China
kuangli@csu.edu.cn

Abstract. Traffic congestion can be divided into recurrent congestion and accidental congestion, and the latter one is usually caused by traffic accidents. It is of great significance to predict the duration of traffic accidents accurately and transfer the results to drivers on the road in time. Most of the existing works utilize traditional, single machine learning model to predict the duration of accident, while the accuracy is not satisfying. In this paper, we firstly construct and extract features from the accident records including description, location, as well as some external information such as weather. We then divide the duration into multiple periods, corresponding to multiple categories. In order to improve the prediction precision of rare categories, we convert the multi-class classification problem into a binary classification problem, constructing multiple XGBoost binary classifiers which are restricted by F1 (harmonic mean) evaluation index. Finally, in order to improve the overall accuracy further, the classification results are integrated by using artificial neural networks. The experiment is conducted on real datasets in Xiamen and employs mean absolute percentage error (MAPE) and root-mean-square error (RMSE) as indicators. The experimental results show the effectiveness of the proposed method and show better performance in comparison with traditional models.

Keywords: The duration of traffic accidents · XGBoost ·
Artificial neural networks

1 Introduction

With the continuous growth of the total number of urban vehicles, the frequency of road traffic accidents has also increased. Prediction about traffic accident is an important part of research on intelligent transportation, since it can help us explore the rules of the occurrence of traffic accidents, control road safety and design suitable strategies. It is an important research issue to predict the duration of traffic accidents effectively and accurately, so that we can schedule the traffic scientifically and reduce the probability of second accidents.

At present, most researches mainly focus on predicting and analyzing the quantity of traffic accidents, including the number of accidents per year, the frequency of accidents at certain places, and the frequency of accidents at specific period. There are only a few studies on real-time traffic accident prediction. Initially, scholars use traditional machine learning methods such as Naive Bayes, KNN, multi-variable linear

H. Gao et al. (Eds.): CollaborateCom 2018, LNICST 268, pp. 252–266, 2019.
https://doi.org/10.1007/978-3-030-12981-1_18

regression and decision trees to predict the traffic accident duration. After taking the diversity of feature attributes in traffic accident data into consideration, scholars fuse different traditional models together which allows different models to handle specific feature attributes to achieve better results. In addition, there are some studies aiming at solving the heterogeneity of traffic accident data, the confidence interval of predicted values, and the probability of second accidents.

However, there are still some shortcomings in existing works: (1) The features are not fully excavated and utilized, for example, the feature that is extracted from accident description is just one-dimensional with some discrete values such as scratching, rear-end collision and running into fixtures, as well, the latitude and longitude are used separately so that the combined feature is lost. (2) The duration of traffic accidents has been proved to follow the log normal distribution, i.e., the data are unbalanced, thus the prediction accuracy of rare categories is not so satisfying. (3) In the aspect of modeling, scholars usually just use single traditional model for prediction, and the overall accuracy is limited.

In this paper, we propose that (1) In the extraction of features, the accident description is encoded as a multi-dimensional vector so that more semantics can be captured, the geographical locations are processed via binning and a reasonable interval is determined through visualization, as well, fusion of isomeric characteristics such as temperature and wind direction. (2) After the feature variable is processed, we should classify the traffic accident duration by training the classifier, and choose XGBoost to classify traffic duration. Then, we convert the accident duration prediction into a multi-binary classification task. We use the accuracy of the evaluation index and recall rate to constrain the model and solve the problem of unbalanced distribution of label training samples, which makes the model more convincing in solving the problem. (3) In order to improve the overall prediction accuracy further, we use neural networks to integrate the prediction results of multiple binary classification models and output the average duration of accidents under this label.

The rest of the paper is organized as follows: Sect. 2 describes the related work of the traffic accidents duration. Section 3 outlines the methods for predicting the duration of traffic accidents. Section 4 gives the experimental verification designs and results. Section 5 summarizes the whole paper.

2   Related Work

In recent years, the problem of predicting the duration of traffic accidents has attracted wide attention of scholars. Related works on the research issue focus on the following aspects: (1) investigating the statistical characteristics of traffic accident data (2) exploring the influence factors which affect the length of accident (3) constructing a proper prediction model.

The analysis of the characteristics of the accident duration distribution in different traffic accident data sets is the first step to build the prediction model. Different prediction models are designed for different distribution characteristics, which is beneficial for improving the accuracy of prediction models. Golob and Recker [1–3] analyzed the durations of the incidents involving large trucks, and demonstrated that the accident duration fits a lognormal distribution. Jones and Chung et al. [4–6] has proved that the accident duration follow a bilogarithmic probability distribution for the accidents on Seattle Expressway. Some researchers find out different distributions in different datasets, such as logarithmic normal distribution, log-logical distribution, Weibull distribution, Gamma distribution, generalized distribution, and etc. [7].

Research during the past few decades has demonstrated that various methodologies and techniques have been employed to analyze and model incident duration, mainly on freeways. These models have determined the relationships between incident duration and influencing variables. The main features that they have found include: accident types [8], severity [9], the number of vehicles involved, time characteristics [10], geography characteristics, weather, etc.

In the perspective of constructing a proper prediction model, many classification methods have been developed to predict the duration of traffic accidents, including decision trees [11], Bayesian network [12], clustering [13], GBDT [14], topic models [15], SVM [16], and etc. For example, Zhan [11] utilizes the M5P tree algorithm for lane clearance time prediction, which has an advantage to deal with categorical and continuous variables and variables with missing values. Yang [12] have proved that Bayesian network has the goodness-of-fit results in traffic dataset when compared with other models. Weng [13] develops a cluster-based lognormal distribution model, and the model can predict the mean and the probability of an accident duration from the base accident information.

Many regression models have also been applied in predicting traffic incident duration. For example, Khattak [17] applies a quantile regression to predict the durations of larger incidents more accurately, since quantile regression can estimate the probability of an incident lasting for a specific duration. He [18] proposed a hybrid tree-based quantile regression method to predict the duration time, and the model has the robustness to outliers, and flexibility in combining categorical covariates. Peeta et al. [19] applied a linear regression model to predict incident clearance time with the time-independent variables.

In recent years, in order to improve the accuracy and efficiency of the prediction model further, many scholars start to use neural networks to predict the duration of traffic accidents. For example, Vlahogianni [20] developed a neural network model for incident duration prediction with single and competing uncertainties, and they improved the generalization power of the prediction models. Wei et al. [21] developed two ANN-based models that sequentially predict traffic accident duration, and the results showed that these models achieve a reasonable prediction. Park [22] introduces Bayesian learning to neural networks for accurate prediction of incident duration, and they updated the network parameters using a hybrid Monte Carlo algorithm.

Compared with these related work that already exists, our main innovations include: (1) In this paper, the multidimensional features coding is used to deal with the accident description characteristics, and the geographical location dealt by points box method. (2) The prediction of accident duration is transformed into a learning task of multiple dichotomies, and the prediction accuracy of rare categories improved by using F1 evaluation index. (3) The prediction results of multiple binary classification models are integrated by using neural network to improve the prediction accuracy.

3 Method

3.1 Problem Definition

Given the data set R = $\{r_1, r_2 \ldots r_n\}$, where r_i denotes the ith traffic accident history, r_i can be represented as a 6-tuple, $r_i = \langle$X, Y, car_number, description, start_time, end_time$\rangle$, where X and Y are the longitude and latitude of the accident location; car_number is the number of vehicles involved in the accident; description is the description of the accident, mainly including the safety and responsibility of the persons involved, and the damage of vehicles; the start_time is the occurrence time of accident; the end_time is the time when the road is clear. The duration of the accident is the end time minus the start time. Some samples are shown in Table 1.

Table 1. Samples of traffic accident dataset

Start time	X	Y	Car number	Accident description	End time
2015/01/01 00:09	118.110169	24.48329	2	A does not ensure safety, B has no fault, the accident results in a right side damage of car A, a left side damage of car B	2015/01/01 00:42
2015/1/1 8:36	118.135313	24.647768	1	A collided with the fixture and an accident occurred, causing damage to the nail tail and right rear corner	2015/1/1 11:09

Given the data set R, and a new accident e = $\langle$start_time, X, Y, car_number, description$\rangle$, based on the historical records, we aim to predict the duration of the new accident, according to the given information including the latitude and longitude of the new accident, the number of vehicles involved, the accident description and the start time.

3.2 Solution

Figure 1 shows a traffic accident duration prediction architecture based on the ensemble learning of XGBoost and ANN, which contains three main steps: **(1) Data preprocessing**: we first process data cleaning, including processing missing data, uniforming format content and removing unreasonable values. Then we analyze the distribution of traffic accident duration and determine reasonable intervals for classification. After that, we construct features for input. **(2) Construct binary classifiers based on XGBoost**: We convert a multi-class classification problem into a multiple binary classification problem. The training set is divided according to the class label, multiple XGBoost binary classifiers are constructed, and parameters for each XGBoost are adjusted by multiple-objective optimization. **(3) Ensemble Learning based on ANN**: Multiple results of binary classification models are integrated based on ANN, so the final category of the predicted duration can be obtained and the average value under the label is output as the prediction value.

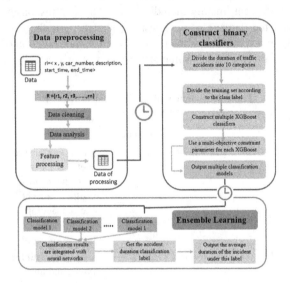

Fig. 1. Architecture of the proposed solution to accident duration prediction

3.3 Data Preprocessing

Data Cleaning and Analysis. The performance of the prediction model is affected by the quality of the data largely. Therefore, we first process the data before constructing features, including removing missing values and unreasonable values, unifying the format content.

The second step is to analyze the distribution of accident durations. The result is shown as Fig. 2. We can see from Fig. 2 that the samples are unbalanced, the accident durations distribute mainly in the range between 6 min to 40 min, accounting for about 70% of the total samples, and the number of samples become fewer and fewer with the increase of duration when the duration is longer than 20 min.

After data cleaning, we can get 39,000 samples approximately. Before we predict the specific minutes of the duration for a target accident, we first try to classify the duration of a target accident into a range, therefore, it is important to divide the durations into multiple ranges reasonably. A primary rule is that we try to make the numbers of accident samples in all ranges are basically equal. We have tried three sizes of each range, which are 5000, 10000 and 20000. For example, when we set the size of each range as 5000, we can divide the durations into [6–13], [14–17], [18–21], [22–25],

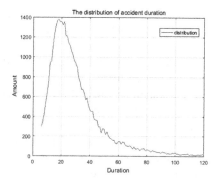

Fig. 2. The distribution of accident duration

[26–30], [31–37], [38–50], [51–109]. We then calculate the average time and variance value in each range. We find that the variance is very large in the last range, since the samples with long duration becomes sparse. Therefore, we aim to divide the last range further, and the division principle is the variances of the subdivisions should be less than a specific threshold value. We have tried three threshold values, which are 10, 15 and 20, and we compare the MAPE values under each threshold respectively, we finally find that the prediction performs the best when the variance threshold is 15. So we divide the last range [51–109] into [51–68], [69–86], and [87–109]. We finally set the division of accident durations as shown in Table 2.

Table 2. Division of traffic accident durations into 10 ranges

Duration time	Amount time	Average	Variance
[6–13]	4984	9.5	4.95
[14–17]	4982	15	2.121
[18–21]	5402	19	2.121
[22–25]	4895	23	2.121
[26–30]	5072	27.5	2.828
[31–37]	4970	33.5	4.243
[38–50]	4885	43.5	8.485
[51–68]	2686	59	12.02
[69–86]	1228	77	12.02
[87–109]	696	97.5	14.09

Feature Processing. In order to prepare for the subsequent algorithms, we then process the original data and integrate external features which affect traffic accidents.

(1) **'start_time':** In addition to the year, month, day, hour, and minute of the accident, we can also get from the original information whether the day is a workday or weekend, whether the time belongs to a peak period or not.

(2) **'car_number'** is the number of cars that are involved in the accident. According to the statistics, the number of accidents involving one car is 3211, that involving 2 cars is 35571, that involving 3 cars and above is 1623. Therefore, the mapping rule is as follows: 1 stands for single-car accident, 2 stands for double-cars accident, 3 stands for multi-cars accident.

(3) **'x'**, **'y'** are the latitude and longitude where the accident occurred. We point the pairs of latitude and longitude into boxes, and Fig. 3(a)–(d) correspond to the binning results under different block sizes, where the area is divided into 5 * 5, 10 * 10, 15 * 15, 20 * 20 blocks respectively. The color of the block represents the average duration time of accidents that occurred within the region. It can be seen from Fig. 3(a)–(c) that the differences of average duration time in adjacent blocks become significant with the increase of blocks, while the number of blocks in Fig. 3(d) increases further, the difference in adjacent blocks is reduced, since the blocks with average duration between 10 to 20 min are missing. Therefore, it is reasonable to set the division size to 15 * 15.

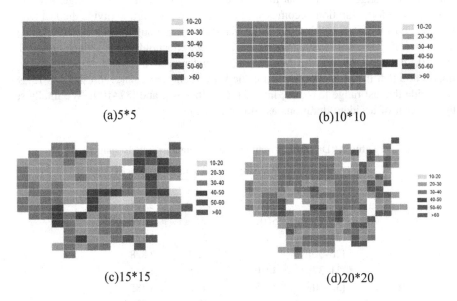

(a)5*5   (b)10*10

(c)15*15   (d)20*20

Fig. 3. Binning results under different block sizes

(4) **'weather':** Weather has been proved to be an important factor that has great impact on occurrence and clearance of accidents [10]. Therefore, we further crawled the weather information in Xiamen in 2015, and Table 3 shows the sample data.
We process the obtained information and define 0–10 °C as cold, 10–20 °C as cool, 20–30 °C as comfortable, and 30 °C or higher as hot. In addition, we classify the weather conditions into 5 categories. Table 4 shows the encoding of temperature and weather feature.

(5) **'description'** describes the main information of accident. It briefly explains the responsible party of the traffic accident, the cause of the accident, the casualties

Table 3. The sample of meteorological dataset

Date	Min_ temperature	Max_ temperature	Weather	Wind direction
2015-01-01	8	15	Cloudy	Northeasterly
2015-01-02	9	18	Cloudy	East
2015-01-03	9	19	Cloudy	North
2015-01-04	9	17	Cloudy	East

Table 4. Encoding of temperature and weather

Parameter	Initial value	Parameter significance
Gamma	0.1	Parameters used to control the post pruning
Maxdepth	12	The depth of the tree
Lambda	2	Regularized term parameter
Subsample	0.7	Random sample training sample

and the vehicle collision. From the description, we can extract four kinds of features, which are responsible party, accident characteristic, vehicle damage grade and accident level. Since the characteristics of an accident in each category may occur at the same time, we employ 13-digit 0–1 coding for the features, and 1 represents that the behavior described on this bit has occurred, in contrast, 0 means not. The meaning represented by each digit is shown in Table 5.

Table 5. The feature coding of accident description

Feature	Coding
Accident responsible party coding [1–3]	1: A no-fault behavior
	2: B no-fault behavior
	3: C no-fault behavior
Accident characteristic coding [4–8]	4: Rear-end
	5: Curettage (vehicle to vehicle)
	6: Curettage (vehicle to person.et)
	7: Bumper
	8: Rollover
Vehicle damage grade coding [9–11]	9: Unilateral damage
	10: Bilaterally damage
	11: Multilateral damage
Accident level coding [12, 13]	12: Vehicle loss
	13: Personal injury

For example, <1000100001010> means that A has no-fault behavior; the accident is caused by the curettage between cars; it leads to the damage on both sides of the vehicle, and it just causes vehicle loss.

3.4 Construct Binary Classifiers

Based on the extracted features and processed data, then we aim to classify the traffic accident duration into a reasonable range first. We choose XGBoost as the classifier. The basic idea is to train multiple weak classifiers for the same training set, and then, these classifiers are combined to form a strong classifier.

As explained in Sect. 3.3, the duration of traffic accidents is divided into 10 ranges, which are [6–13], [14–17], [18–21], [22–25], [26–30], [31–37], [38–50], [51–68], [69–86] and [87–109]. In order to construct an effective classifier, we need to consider the size of training samples under the category tag. The sizes are almost the same for the former 7 categories, while the sizes are less for the latter 3 categories, i.e. the samples are unbalanced for the 10 categories. Therefore, we do not try to classify the duration of a new accident into one of the 10 categories directly, instead, we convert the multi-class classification problem into multiple binary classification problem. Figure 4 shows the construction of multiple binary classifiers. We use the accuracy and recall rate to constrain the model, in order to solve the problem of unbalanced distribution of samples.

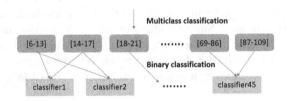

Fig. 4. The process of constructing a binary classifier

As Fig. 4 shows, each classifier performs a binary classification task. For example, we construct the classifier1 which classifies a sample into [6–13] or [14–17], so we pick out the samples in the range of [6–13] and [14–17] to train classifier1. Similarly, we construct the classifier2 which classifies a sample into [6–13] or [18–21], and so on. Every two ranges are formed together as a classification target. In this way, we need to build C(10, 2) classifiers for 10 categories. Then we adjust the parameters of a single XGBoost model to make it perform well in terms of accuracy and recall. Table 6 shows the initial values of the parameters which affect the accuracy and recall rate.

Table 6. Initial setting of parameters

Parameter	Initial value	Parameter significance
Gamma	0.1	Control the post pruning
Maxdepth	12	The depth of the tree
Lambda	2	Regularized term parameter
Subsample	0.7	Proportion of random sampling for training

3.5   Ensemble Learning

After building the 45 binary classifiers, we need to ensemble the results to get the final prediction value. One solution is to take the voting mechanism. For example, when we test a sample, we put it in all the 45 classifiers and count the times it is identified in each of the 10 ranges, then the test sample is deemed to belong to the range with the highest times.

Another solution is that we can train a neural network to ensemble the 45 results. As shown in Fig. 5, the input of neural network is the results of 45 binary classifiers, and n (45)-dimensional feature vector predicted by the learners in first layer is used as the input vector of fully connected neural network classifiers in second layer. According to formula $h = \sqrt{m+n} + \alpha$, we can determine the number of hidden layer nodes in neural network. In the formula, m denotes classifier's output dimension, which is 10 here, and n denotes the input dimension, which is 45, the value of α is generally between 1 to10. The output of this neural network is the label of classification, which is represented as a 10-bit vector, and each bit is 0 or 1. For example, 0100000000 shows the output is the 2nd class. Therefore, we use 45-8-10 three-layer neural network model as the second-layer learner, and the network's activation function is set as sigmod function.

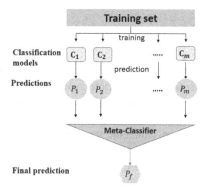

Fig. 5. Process diagram of Stacking

4   Experiments

In this section, we first introduce the evaluation metrics in Sect. 4.1, and then determine the parameters involved in the proposed approach in Sect. 4.2, finally prove its effectiveness and rationality through comparison experiments.

4.1   Evaluation Metrics

We use root mean square error (RMSE) and mean absolute percentage error (MAPE) to evaluate the performance of prediction. The two metrics are defined in formulas (1) and (2), the less RMSE or MAPE, the better performance.

$$RMSE = \sqrt{\frac{\sum (t - \bar{t})^2}{N - 1}} \tag{1}$$

$$MAPE = \frac{1}{N} \sum \frac{|t - \bar{t}|}{t} * 100\% \tag{2}$$

In the formulae, t is the actual duration, $\bar{t}$ is the predicted duration, N is the number of the tests.

For binary classification, we use precision (P) and recall(R) and harmonic mean $(F1)$ as the metrics, and their definitions are shown as formulas (3)–(5), where TP is the number of true positive samples, FP is the number of false positive samples, FN is the number of false negative samples. Since P and R are paradoxical sometimes, F1 is used as well, and the larger F1, the better performance.

$$P = TP/(TP + FP) \tag{3}$$

$$R = TP/(TP + FN) \tag{4}$$

$$2/F1 = 1/P + 1/R \tag{5}$$

4.2   Tuning Parameters

Tuning XGBOOST Classifier Parameters. We take the classifiers that classifies the samples into [22–25] or [51–68] as an example to show the way to tune the parameters of each XGBoost classifier. As mentioned above, multiclass classification can be converted into multiple binary classification, and F1 can be used to evaluate the performance of binary classification. Since the samples in different classes are distributed unevenly, using F1 to tune the parameters of models could have a better performance and be more robust. As shown in Fig. 6(a), when *gamma* is 0.2, F1 reaches the maximum value; when *gamma* is between 0.2 and 0.3, F1 starts to decrease; when *gamma* is larger than 0.3, F1 tends to be unchanged. So we can set *gamma* to 0.2.

After determining the value of gamma, we fix it and start to tune parameter *maxdepth*. As shown in Fig. 6(b), when *maxdepth* starts with 7, F1 gradually increases and reaches the highest point at 10, then starts to gradually decrease and finally becomes stable. So we can determine *maxdepth* as 10.

After fixing *gamma* and *maxdepth*, we begin to tune parameter *subsample*. As shown in Fig. 6(c), when *subsample* is between 0.1 and 0.7, F1 is almost rising, and when *subsample* is larger than 0.7, F1 starts to decrease. So we set *subsample* to 0.7.

Tuning Neural Network Parameters. In the process of training neural networks, choosing a proper learning rate *lr* and the number of iterations *te* is very important, which will often affect the prediction ability of whole network. We can randomly select training data, choose different *lr* and *te*, and calculate corresponding MAPE. The results are shown in Fig. 7. We can see that, when learning rate *lr* is too small, for example, *lr*

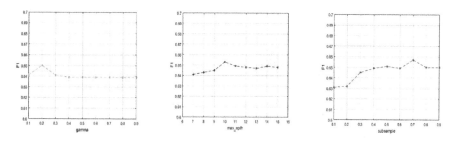

Fig. 6. Tuning parameters in XGBoost

is 0.01 and *te* is 250, or *lr* is too large, for example, *lr* is 1 and *te* is 250, the performance is not so good. When *lr* is 0.5 and *te* is 250, MAPE is the lowest, and the performance of accuracy is the best. So we set *lr* to 0.5 and *te* to 250.

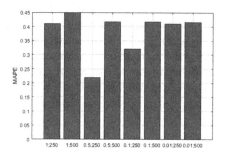

Fig. 7. Tuning parameters in artificial neural network

4.3   Verifying the Effectiveness of the Proposed Solution

Verifying the Effectiveness of the XGBoost Classifiers. In this experiment, we aim to compare our XGBoost classifier with three classical classifiers: random forest, logistic regression and naive Bayes. Figure 8 shows the average MAPE and RMSE of the four models on the whole dataset. It can be seen that the average MAPE of XGBoost is 0.219, and its RMSE is 0.6858. While the MAPE and RMSE values of the other three models are higher than XGBoost, that is to say, their classification performances are worse than XGBoost on our dataset. So we choose XGBoost here.

Verifying the Effectiveness of Converting Multi-class Classification into Binary Classification. In multi-class classification, each class is treated equally. But there are some problems when accuracy is used to evaluate the prediction capability. In our dataset, the data are distributed too unevenly, the accident duration of about 40% training samples falls in the range of [15, 30] minutes. For unbalanced datasets, the prediction accuracy of rare classes is usually more important than that of others. From Fig. 2 we can see, the classes that fall in the range of [0, 15] and [30, +∞] belong to rare classes.

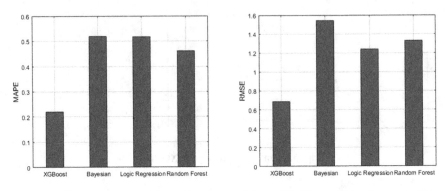

Fig. 8. The comparison of evaluation indexes by different algorithms

In the experiment, we compare the performance of multi-classification and binary classification by using MAPE and RMSE. We divide the duration time into 11 intervals and each interval is 10 min. Figure 9 shows the MAPE and RMSE for each time interval respectively. The red line shows the results for multiclass classification, in which 10 classes are the output in one XGBoost model, and the average value of the predicted class is the predicted duration value; while the black line shows the results for our proposed solution including binary classification and ensemble learning. From Fig. 9 we can see that our proposed solution performs better than multi-classification on the two metrics in each time interval. More importantly, the prediction accuracy of rare classes has been significantly improved.

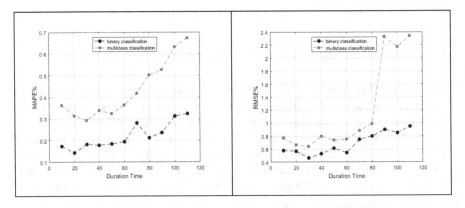

Fig. 9. The comparison between binary classification and multiclass classification

Verifying the Effectiveness of Ensemble Learning. In this experiment, we aim to verify that the neural network is effective for integrating the classification results. We compare our solution with two methods, one is using neural network for prediction directly, and another one is using voting for integrating the classification results. Figure 10 shows the comparison results on MAPE and RMSE for the three solutions.

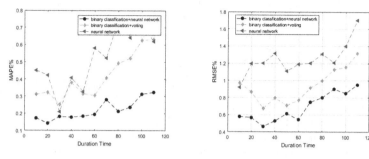

Fig. 10. The comparison between control group and experimental group

From Fig. 10 we can see that the prediction accuracy of our solution is better than the other two methods for each time segment, especially in rare categories, which further indicates the effectiveness of our proposed solution.

5   Conclusions

By using the real accident data in Xiamen, firstly, we deal with the features, such as treatment types of accidents and weather more adequately. Secondly, we convert the multiclass classification problem into multiple binary classification problem based on XGBoost. The conversion can not only reduce the overall prediction error, but also significantly improve the prediction precision of rare categories. Then we use neural network to integrate the prediction results of classifiers in order to reduce the overall prediction error. In the future work, we will study how to deal with the incomplete accident data and predict the reliable accident duration in actual traffic accidents, in addition, we will investigate on predicting traffic flow during accident recovery.

Acknowledgments. The research is supported by National Natural Science Foundation of China (No. 61772560), National Key R&D program of China (No. 2018YFB1003800).

References

1. Giuliano, G.: Incident characteristics, frequency, and duration on a high volume urban freeway. Transp. Res. A: Gen. **23**(5), 387–396 (1989)
2. Golob, T.F., Recker, W.W., Leonard, J.D.: An analysis of the severity and incident duration of truck-involved freeway accidents. Accid. Anal. Prev. **19**(5), 375–395 (1987)
3. Skabardonis, A., Petty, K., Varaiya, P.: Los Angeles I-10 field experiment: incident patterns. J. Transp. Res. Board **1683**, 22–30 (1999)
4. Jones, B., Janssen, L., Mannering, F.: Analysis of the frequency and duration of freeway accidents in Seattle. Accid. Anal. Prev. **23**(4), 239–255 (1991)
5. Nam, D., Mannering, F.: An exploratory hazard-based analysis of highway incident duration. Transp. Res. A: Policy Pract. **34**(2), 85–102 (2000)

6. Chung, Y.: Development of an accident duration prediction model on the Korean freeway systems. Accid. Anal. Prev. **42**(1), 282–289 (2010)
7. Kang, G., Fang, S.-E.: Applying survival analysis approach to traffic incident duration prediction. In: First International Conference on Transportation Information and Safety (ICTIS), Wuhan, China, pp. 1523–1531 (2011)
8. Alkaabi, A.M.S., Dissanayake, D., Bird, R.: Analyzing clearance time of urban traffic accidents in Abu Dhabi, United Arab Emirates, with hazard-based duration modeling method. Transp. Res. Rec. **2229**, 46–54 (2011)
9. Hojati, A.T., Ferreira, L., Washington, S., Charlesa, P.: Hazard based models for freeway traffic incident duration. Accid. Anal. Prev. **52**, 171–181 (2013)
10. Li, R., Guo, M.: Competing risks analysis on traffic accident duration time. J. Adv. Transp. **49**(3), 402–415 (2015)
11. Zhan, C., Gan, A., Hadi, M.: Prediction of lane clearance time of freeway incidents using the M5P tree algorithm. IEEE Trans. Intell. Transp. Syst. **12**(4), 1549–1557 (2011)
12. Yang, H., Shen, L., Xiang, Y., et al.: Freeway incident duration prediction using Bayesian network. In: 2017 4th International Conference on Transportation Information and Safety (ICTIS), pp. 974–980. IEEE (2017)
13. Weng, J., Qiao, W., Qu, X., et al.: Cluster-based lognormal distribution model for accident duration. Transportmetrica **11**(4), 345–363 (2015)
14. Ma, X., Ding, C., Luan, S., et al.: Prioritizing influential factors for freeway incident clearance time prediction using the gradient boosting decision trees method. IEEE Trans. Intell. Transp. Syst. **18**(9), 2303–2310 (2017)
15. Pereira, F.C., Rodrigues, F., Ben-Akiva, M.: Text analysis in incident duration prediction. Transp. Res. Part C **37**(10), 177–192 (2013)
16. Yu, B., Wang, Y.T., Yao, J.B., et al.: A comparison of the performance of ANN and SVM for the prediction of traffic accident duration. Neural Netw. World **26**(3), 271 (2016)
17. Khattak, A.J., Liu, J., Wali, B., et al.: Modeling traffic incident duration using quantile regression. Transp. Res. Rec. J. Transp. Res. Board **2554**, 139–148 (2016)
18. He, Q., Kamarianakis, Y., Jintanakul, K., et al.: Incident duration prediction with hybrid tree-based quantile regression. In: Ukkusuri, S., Ozbay, K. (eds.) Advances in Dynamic Network Modeling in Complex Transportation Systems, pp. 287–305. Springer, New York (2013). https://doi.org/10.1007/978-1-4614-6243-9_12
19. Peeta, S., Ramos, J.L., Gedela, S.: Providing real-time traffic advisory and route guidance to manage Borman incidents on-line using the hoosier helper program. Joint Transportation Research Program, Indiana Dept. Transp., Purdue Univ., West Lafayette, IN, USA. Technical report, 15 2000. http://docs.lib.purdue.edu/jtrp/175/
20. Vlahogianni, E.I., Karlaftis, M.G.: Fuzzy-entropy neural network freeway incident duration modeling with single and competing uncertainties. Comput. Aided Civil Infrastruct. Eng. **28**(6), 420–433 (2013)
21. Lee, Y., Wei, C.-H.: A computerized feature selection method using genetic algorithms to forecast freeway accident duration times. Comput. Aided Civil Infrastruct. Eng. **25**, 132–148 (2010)
22. Park, H., Haghani, A., Zhang, X.: Interpretation of Bayesian neural networks for predicting the duration of detected incidents. J. Intell. Transp. Syst. **20**(4), 385–400 (2016)

A Single-Hop Selection Strategy of VNFs Based on Traffic Classification in NFV

Bo He[✉], Jingyu Wang, Qi Qi, and Haifeng Sun

State Key Laboratory of Networking and Switching Technology,
Beijing University of Posts and Telecommunications, Beijing 100876, China
{hebo,wangjingyu,qiqi,sunhaifeng_l}@ebupt.com

Abstract. Network Function Virtualization (NFV) has become a hot technology since it provides the flexible management of network functions and efficient sharing of network resources. Network resources in NVF require an appropriate management strategy which often manifests as a difficult online decision making task. Resource management in NFV can be thought of as a process of virtualized network functions (VNFs) selection or deployment. This paper proposes a single-hop VNFs selection strategy to realize network resource management. For satisfying quality requirements of different network services, this strategy is based on the results of traffic classification which utilizes Multi-Grained Cascade Forest (gcForest) to distinguish user behaviors on the internet. In the order of VNFs, a network is divided into several layers where each arrived packet needs to queue. The scheduler of each layer selects a layer which hosts the next VNF for the packets in the queue. Experiments prove that the proposed traffic classification method increases the precision by 7.7% and improves the real-time performance. The model of VNFs selection reduces network congestion compared to traditional single-hop scheduling models. Moreover, the number of packets which fail to reach target node in time drops 30% to 50% using the proposed strategy compared to the strategy without the section of traffic classification.

Keywords: NFV · Traffic classification · Resource management · VNFs selection

1 Introduction

The quality of service (QoS) requirements of users rise rapidly such as lower latency, lower packet loss rate and so on. For this reason, networks not only need to enhance bandwidth and capacity, but also require a better scheduling strategy of resources. By separating network functions from traditional hardware, NFV is expected to manage network functions and share network resources more flexibly. Application of NFV has become extensive because more customized network scale and lower capital expenditure are obtained by this technique. In NFV, virtualized network functions (VNFs) which control the creation, configuration, monitor, operation and security of network functions are implemented in software components running on commodity hardware. Services are realized by VNFs in a specific order denominated Service Function Chain

© ICST Institute for Computer Sciences, Social Informatics and Telecommunications Engineering 2019
Published by Springer Nature Switzerland AG 2019. All Rights Reserved
H. Gao et al. (Eds.): CollaborateCom 2018, LNICST 268, pp. 267–283, 2019.
https://doi.org/10.1007/978-3-030-12981-1_19

(SFC). In detail, a traffic packet needs to traverse the nodes which host the VNFs in a specific SFC sequentially. As a result, the strategy of resource management is equal to the strategy of selection and deployment of VNFs.

State-of-the-art efforts about network resource management in NFV are limited to optimizing the algorithms in the interior of network for the purpose that all packets arrive the target node as soon as possible [1–3]. To different kinds of traffic packets, the efforts do not realize the QoS requirements are distinguishing. For example, there is a high demand of online video applications for traffic transmission delay, otherwise it will seriously affect the normal use of network services. By contrast, users do not have urgent requirements of delay when they use File Transfer Protocol (FTP) applications, they need lower packet loss rate instead. Under the existing strategies, significant resources may be occupied by traffic packets of FTP instead of video streaming so that users have bad QoS when watching videos. From this issue, it is natural to think about classifying traffic before scheduling network resource. Then resource scheduling problem is considered to be a combinatorial optimization problem. If a packet can be classified before being transmitted, the delay and packet loss rate requirements of this kind of traffic packet are obtained. Thus the network resource management strategy can exploit the requirements to improve user QoS.

This paper proposes a single-hop selection strategy of VNFs based on traffic classification to schedule network resources in NFV. As the premise of VNFs selection, traffic classification needs to identify the transmission priority of different packets accurately. There have been extensive researches of traffic classification, but they were limited in several specific applications [4–6] or unencrypted packets [7, 8]. In order to distinguish user QoS requirements of different network services, we classify the traffic data according to the user behavior. This categorization achieves covering majority of traffic packets in actual network instead of a few applications. Features of classification are calculated by the arrival times, number and lengths of packets to investigate the differences among user behavior. Unlike traditional features, these selected features can be obtained even the packets are encrypted. As for algorithms of classification, this paper tries deep neural network (DNN) to classify traffic data due to some advantages of multi-layer neural network models in the field of data classification. Besides, a new algorithm called Multi-Grained Cascade Forest (gcForest) [9] which is presented as an alternative to DNN is also employed. In the tasks of giving features, gcForest often obtains better results than DNN.

The proposed VNFs selection strategy divides the network into several layers according to the order of VNFs in SFC. In each layer, each arrived packet needs to queue. Then the packet will be transmitted to a next VNF layer which is selected by the scheduler. VNF layers are selected according to the results of traffic classification with joint consideration of the network real-time bandwidth and computing resources. Experiments prove that the traffic classification method gets higher precision than previous work [10] and improves real-time performance of resource management. Meanwhile, simulation results demonstrate that the VNFs selection strategy reduces the number of packets which fail to meet the QoS requirement under different degrees of network congestion.

2   Related Work

2.1   Traffic Classification

Traffic classification is a hot issue in academic all the time. Instead of many methods based on the port numbers or the payload data of traffic packets in history, more and more researches employ algorithms of machine learning in the last decade. Williams et al. [4] extracted 22 practical flow features for use within IP traffic classification and employed five algorithms of machine learning to classify traffic. Dong et al. [5] selected four flow features for traffic classification and obtained the accuracy up to 95%. But these features only worked well in classifying six kinds of video traffic which the authors selected. Since previous studies only worked offline, Bernaille et al. [7] proposed a method to classify traffic online by observing the first five packets of each TCP connection. But limitation is that the method classifies only several specific TCP applications. Shi et al. [8] realized accurate classification of several kinds of protocol traffic data by means of complex methods to extract features from traffic flows and remove the irrelevant and redundant features later on. Anderson et al. [11] aimed at overcoming two limitations of detection of malicious network traffic: inaccurate ground truth and highly non-stationary data distribution. An enhanced feature set is presented based on the information of Transport Layer Statistics (TLS) sessions.

Most of existing methods to classify traffic employed the statistics algorithms of machine learning like KNN, SVM, decision tree and so on. Some of the latest studies [6, 12] started to utilize some algorithms of deep learning to classify traffic. However, these studies trained features which were still extracted beforehand so they did not take advantage of the ability of neural network models to extract optimal features. Consequently, these studies do not archive overwhelming advantages over the previous ones.

2.2   Network Resource Management in NFV

Purposes of most existing network resource management strategies is to reduce the number of equipment or improve QoS. Tseng et al. [13] carried out several sets of experiments to prove that selecting suitable discontinuous reception parameters can effectively reduce power consumption of nodes. Joe et al. [14] proposed an algorithm of network selection based on Analytic Hierarchy Process (AHP) for predicting power consumption of terminal equipment in the network. Senouci et al. [15] selected suitable network interfaces in a dynamically changing network by utilizing Technique for Order Preference by Similarity to an Ideal Solution (TOPSIS). Park et al. [16] introduced game theory into the field of resource management and proved that different applications can share effective bandwidth by cooperative game. According to whether traffic packets are sensitive to latency or not, Afzal et al. [17] divided them into two classes for scheduling.

In NFV, some studies proposed optimized scheduling algorithms of typical unicast issue by focusing on computing resources of nodes [18] and bandwidth resources of edges [19]. Sun et al. [1] presented a framework which enables network function work in parallel and it reduced latency greatly for real world service chains. More and more studies started to focus on the impact of VNFs on scheduling resources of network. Taleb et al. [2] calculated loss when a VNF breaks down by estimating the number of active/idle user equipment and proposed a network architecture enabled by service resilience-aware mechanisms. For minimizing latency of end-to-end service, Chantre et al. [3] employed the particle swarm optimization technique to solve the redundancy allocation problems. Mestres et al. [20] initiated experiments to prove different VNFs have different curves of resource consumption with the increase of network data even in the same network. Kar et al. [21] tried to solve the problem that optimizing energy-cost with capacity and delay as constraints so that a dynamic placement of SFC heuristic solution was proposed. Gu et al. [22] proposed an algorithm of placement of VNFs for reducing the communication cost with joint consideration of network flow balancing and predetermined network service semantics.

As mentioned above, most of methods to classify traffic are limited to several applications or protocols. Many features of classification are difficult to be extracted from message format information of traffic packets since more and more packets are encrypted. In NFV, many studies about scheduling resources did not realize that QoS requirements of traffic packets are different. Thus, they never thought of utilizing traffic classification technology to identify the transmission priority of different packets.

3 Architecture Overview

In NFV, VNFs need to be deployed in a specific SFC sequentially (e.g. network address translation function requires postprocessing after firewall function). Therefore, selecting and deploying VNFs already become the methods to schedule resources in NFV. For satisfying QoS requirements of different traffic packets better in existing networks, this paper proposes a selection strategy of VNFs based on traffic classification in NFV instead of a strategy of the VNFs placement. However, actual networks are complex because some nodes host one or more VNFs while the others do not. Even the same VNF may be hosted in different nodes. Thus this strategy adopts a fine-gained single-hop mode to cope with complex and variable actual NFV networks. We combine a section of traffic classification at the source node of the network with a section of VNFs selection in the interior of the network. The premise of employing this VNFs selection strategy is that all the VNFs we need are already deployed according to the order in SFC. That is to say, there is at least one path which satisfies the SFC from the source node to the destination node. The architecture of this system is shown in Fig. 1 and described as follows.

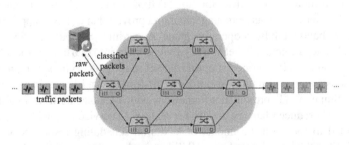

Fig. 1. Illustration of the single-hop selection strategy of VNFs based on traffic classification

Firstly, packets arriving at the source node are sampled and the features of them are extracted and transmitted to an associated server which has a trained model of traffic classification inside. This model distinguishes traffic packets into 8 classes according to user behavior characteristics and QoS requirements, i.e. Browsing, Chat, Audio-streaming, Video-streaming, Email, VoIP, P2P and FTP. These 8 classes are not limited to several specific applications or protocols so that they cover majority of traffic packets in actual networks. This classification coverage is the basis of resource management.

Secondly, the model classifies the input packets and verifies transmission requirements like delay and packet loss rate. According to the classification results, the Differentiated Services Code Point (DSCP) field of every packet is modified as a label.

After being labeled, flow information of the packets is recorded, such as their five-tuple (source IP address, destination IP address, source port number, destination port number, protocol). Then if a new packet which has the same five-tuple is transmitted to the source node, it is labeled as previous ones of this flow and scheduled in this network directly without additional need to be classified.

We emphasize that the transmission time T_i of packet i is obtained by adding the delay time D_e of each edge e and the waiting time W_n on each node n. Let the set E_i represents the set of edges and the set N_i represents the set of nodes which are in the path of packet i passing. During the transmission process, packet i is always checked whether it can continue to be transmitted according to the time t. Thus we have the objective function and the constraint function:

$$T_i = \sum_{e \in E_i} D_e + \sum_{n \in N_i} W_n \tag{1}$$

$$t \geq s_i + d_i \tag{2}$$

where s_i is the start time of the transmission and d_i is the longest transmission time obtained by the QoS requirement. The scheduler of each layer verifies the priority of transmission of each arrived packet by the label in DSCP field. Then this scheduler selects a layer which hosts the next VNF for the packet. The selection process is repeated until the packet reaches the target node.

4 Methodology

4.1 Traffic Classification

On account of that the features selected by many methods only work well in a specific network environment, we extract some features which are calculated by the information of number, lengths and arrival times of packets instead of traditional message format information like protocol and port number. These features can be extracted regardless of whether traffic packets are encrypted. More importantly, traffic classification can identify traffic packets from different applications as the same class by the features. For example, skype and facebook are different applications but both have the VoIP function to generate two-way traffic packets which have short inter arrival times and similar lengths. As a contrast, traffic packets of FTP also have short inter arrival times, but lengths of packets sent forwards are much bigger than packets sent backwards. According to experiments, this paper sets 5 s as the length of flows. The flows consist of two-way traffic packets that have the same five-tuple. Lashkari et al. [10] classified traffic packets by 23 flow features which only based on time. Table 1 exhibits 13 features which we select from these 23 features. Furthermore, considering the bandwidth requirement in the field of resource management and the differences in user behavior, we extract 18 flow features based on number and lengths of packets and show them in Table 2.

Table 1. Features based on time

Basic data	Features
Packets sent forwards	Inter arrival time (mean, min, max, std)
Packets sent backwards	Inter arrival time (mean, min, max, std)
Packets sent in either direction	Inter arrival time (mean, min, max, std)
Flows	Duration

Table 2. Features based on number and lengths of packets

Basic data	Features
Packets sent forwards	Length (mean, min, max, std), bytes and number per second
Packets sent backwards	Length (mean, min, max, std), bytes and number per second
Packets sent in either direction	Length (mean, min, max, std)
Packets sent forwards and packets sent backwards	Ratio of the number of bytes per second, ratio of the number per second

In order to find an optimal classification algorithm, not only common machine learning algorithms such as decision tree, random forest, KNN and SVM, we also employ DNN and gcForest using the same dataset. Compared to common machine learning algorithms, DNN and gcForest performs better in experiments. Therefore, the principles of the two algorithms are elaborated as follows.

Deep Neural Network (DNN). The DNN is especially the neural network with fully connected layers. DNN is an algorithm of supervised learning, which utilizes the fitting function to realize the classification of input data. Each neural node of DNN learns a linear function according to the weight w and the bias b:

$$z = \sum_{i=1}^{n} w_i x_i + b \tag{3}$$

where n is the number of inputs that the neural node receives and x is the value of the corresponding input. Then the result z is input into an activation function for learning nonlinear data better. The activation function we select is Rectified Linear Unit (ReLU):

$$\text{ReLU}(z) = \begin{cases} z, \ z > 0 \\ 0, \ z \le 0 \end{cases} \tag{4}$$

Neural network layers of DNN are divided into three kinds: input layer, hidden layer and output layer. Input layer is used to receive data input to the neural network. Hidden layers can have multiple layers to enhance expressive power of this model. Generally, neural networks with more hidden layers and neural nodes are able to fit more complicated functions. Output layer has multiple output nodes to output predicted results that match the classes of input data. The experiments use five layers to build the model.

The training process of DNN constantly adjusts weight and bias of each neural node to fit the classification function that meets input data better. The evaluation indicator of performance is loss function which we select is cross-entropy cost function:

$$C = -\frac{1}{n} \sum_{i=1}^{n} y \ln a + (1 - y) \ln(1 - a) \tag{5}$$

where y is the expected output result and a is the label. Labels are input into the model with training data as actual output results. Besides, n is the number of outputs and C is the result of loss. Therefore, loss function indicates the gap between predicted results and the actual results. As for optimization function, we select Adaptive Moment Estimation (Adam) to reduce the value of this loss function for obtaining optimal hyper-parameters. Learning rate determines the speed of modifying the parameter to the better value and has a great impact on the performance of neural network. The learning rate we selected is 0.001.

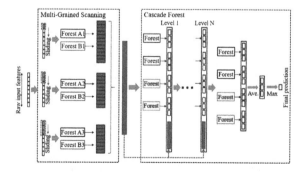

Fig. 2. Architecture of gcForest (Color figure online)

Multi-grained Cascade Forest (gcForest). Multi-Grained Cascade Forest is the improved model of Random Forest [23], which is proposed as an alternative to deep neural networks because its performance is highly competitive in a broad range of tasks. The structure of gcForest is shown in Fig. 2.

The gcForest model consists of two parts: the multi-grained scanning and the cascade forest structure. In the part of multi-grained scanning, sliding windows are used to scan all raw features for forming feature vectors. These feature vectors are used to train completely-random tree forests and random forests to obtain class vectors which are concatenated as transformed features. Random forests contain trees which are generated by choosing the one with the best *gini* value from some randomly selected features for split. And completely-random tree forests consist of regular decision trees. In the part of cascade forest structure, each level composed of different decision tree forests to encourage the diversity which is important to ensemble construction. For example, each level in this structure consists of two random forests (black) and two completely-random tree forests (blue) in Fig. 2. Each level receives information from the preceding level and processes the information by their own forests. Then this level outputs its results to the next level.

Compared to deep neural networks which rely on hyper-parameter tuning, gcForest is much easier to train. In many cases, it works well even using almost same setting of hyper-parameters. The training process of this algorithm is efficient, and users can control training cost according to computational resources available. Moreover, the greatest advantage of gcForest is that the algorithm can obtain a good result in the case of small-scale training data.

4.2   VNFs Selection Strategy

Figure 3 presents an example network in NFV to explain the mechanism of the VNFs selection strategy. A circle with a text represents a node which hosts a VNF and a circle with no text represents a node which only transmits traffic packets. The red and blue lines respectively represent a path which satisfies the order of VNFs in SFC from the source node to the target node. A circle of black dotted lines represents a node which is

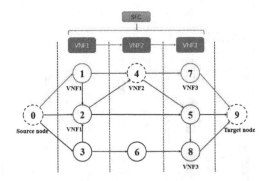

Fig. 3. An example network in NFV. Traffic messages pass through some nodes following the order in SFC from the source node 0 to the target node 9. (Color figure online)

passed through by the both paths. It can be seen that node 0 is the source node and node 9 is the target node.

SFC Layered (SFCL) Model. Considering the characteristic of NFV and the cooperation with traffic classification, a network is divided into layers according to the order of VNFs in SFC. As shown in Fig. 3, traffic packets which are transmitted from source node 0 to target node 9 need to follow the order of VNF1, VNF2 and VNF3 because of the requirement of SFC. Therefore, the network is divided into 5 layers: the source layer, the VNF1 layer, the VNF2 layer, the VNF3 layer and the target layer. Accordingly, the Path1 is divided into node 0, node 1, node 4, node 7, node 9 and the Path2 is divided into node 0, node 2, node 4, node 5, node 8, node 9. What worth mentioning is that node 5 and note 8 are in the same layer in Path2.

Each layer in the network is regarded as an instance object which is represented by a seven-tuple: $\{U, N, X, B, C, K, M\}$. In the seven-tuple, U represents the set of all upper layers of this layer, N represents the set of all next layers of this layer, and X represents the order number of this layer in the path. Besides, B represents the free bandwidth set of edges which connect this layer with its next layers. C represents the congestion degree set of next layers, that is, the numbers of messages waiting to be transmitted in these next layers. Last, K represents a switch that controls this layer whether receives a message from upper layers, M represents the set of messages waiting to be transmitted in the layer. Particularly, an object which has the same index in N, B, C put into correspondence with the same next layer object.

Each message in the network is regarded as an instance object which is represents by a five-tuple: $\{D, S, E, P, R\}$. In the five-tuple, D represents the traffic packet carried by the message, S represents the time when the message enters the network, and E represents the longest transmission time obtained by the result of traffic classification. In addition, P represents the transmission priority of the message, and R represents the probability that the message is transmitted to the next layer which has the best congestion condition.

Scheduling in a Single Layer. Figure 4 shows the scheduling process in a single layer. When a layer receives a message from its upper layer, it first checks whether the time at the moment has exceeded the sum of S and E of the message or not. If the time is exceeded, it means that the message does not reach the target layer within the time delay allowed and it is discarded directly, otherwise the message is put in M of the layer. Then messages of M are sorted by the values of their transmission priorities (P) so that the message which has the largest P is transmitted to one of the next layers. The value of P of message m in layer l is represented by (6).

$$P_m = P_0 + \alpha(E_m + S_m - t) - \beta(L - X_l) \tag{6}$$

where P_0 is the initial transmission priority as the result of traffic classification and t is the time at the moment. L is the number of layers in this network. The values of α and β are determined by conditions of the network so that the scheduler can consider the possibility of this message successfully reaching the target layer in time. If N of the layer has several next layers, each next layer n calculates its own selection priority called SP using (7) in the light of its free bandwidth b_n and congestion degree c_n.

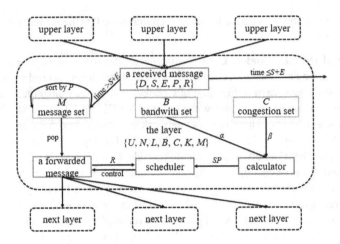

Fig. 4. Scheduling process in a single layer

$$SP = \gamma b_n + \delta c_n \tag{7}$$

where γ and δ are weights of free bandwidth and congestion degree, and their values are determined through experiments. Then the next layers are ranked from high to low according to the values of their SPs. At this time, R of the message is the probability that it being transmitted to the next layer which has the largest SP. Random selection is made according to the 0-1 distribution that matches the value of R. The distribution function of the calculated result x is:

$$P\{x = k\} = p(1 - p)k, \ (k = 0, 1) \tag{8}$$

where p equals to the value of R. Thus the probability of different selection results is:

$$P\{x = 0\} = R \tag{9}$$

$$P\{x = 1\} = 1 - R \tag{10}$$

If x equals 0, the message will be transmitted to this next layer, otherwise the scheduler will continue to make the random selection to decide whether to transmit this message to the next one in the rank of next layers. By that analogy, if only the last next layer is left, the message is transmitted to this remaining next layer directly.

Considering the interference problem in the process of transmitting messages, it is necessary to ensure that each layer receives only one message from its upper layers at any time. Upper layers of the same layer are mutually called interferential layers. After an upper layer of this layer transmits a message to the layer, the switch K is turned off so that interferential layers of the upper layer are banned from transmitting messages to this layer. When the messages are sorted out, K is turned on and the layer continues to receive messages. For example, the layer contains node 1 and the layer contains node 2 are interferential layers because they are both upper layers of the layer contains node 4 in Fig. 3.

5 Experiment and Simulation

5.1 Traffic Classification

We carry out experiments about traffic classification using packets of an open dataset [10]. Firstly, we analyze the impact of lengths of traffic flows on traffic classification. To evaluate the classification performance of different algorithms, we use two metrics: precision (PR) and recall (RC). In [10], authors carried out experiments and obtained the results that 15 s is the optimal length and the highest classification precision is 84.1%. Table 3 exhibits the performance of each algorithm under different lengths of the flows. In addition to SVM, the remaining algorithms get high precisions. The results show that 15 s is also the optimal length, but the performance is close under the same algorithm when employing the new features. Thus traffic classification is no longer restricted by the lengths of flows. Considering the real-time performance of network resource management, we choose 5 s as the length of flow without reducing much classification precision. And the gcForest is the optimal algorithm for traffic classification by these new flow features according to the results in Table 3.

Table 3. Results of length selection in experiments

	gcForest		Random forest		Decision tree	
	PR	RC	PR	RC	PR	RC
5 s	0.9179	0.9164	0.9043	0.9083	0.8839	0.8880
10 s	0.9161	0.9134	0.9069	0.9110	0.8870	0.8914
15 s	0.9190	0.9167	0.9072	0.9119	0.8860	0.8896
20 s	0.9213	0.9205	0.9061	0.9097	0.8858	0.8871
	KNN		SVM		DNN	
	PR	RC	PR	RC	PR	RC
5 s	0.8906	0.8959	0.7594	0.7186	0.8868	0.8830
10 s	0.8866	0.8901	0.7980	0.7272	0.8872	0.8834
15 s	0.8856	0.8919	0.7938	0.7153	0.8836	0.8822
20 s	0.8889	0.8930	0.7555	0.7171	0.8966	0.8933

Figure 5 indicates the performance of the six algorithms under different feature sets. We select three feature sets which are shown in Table 4. It can be seen that the precision of classification obtained by feature set1 is 10% lower than the precision of classification obtained by feature set2. These results prove that when the flows are short, it is correct to add the flow features based on number and lengths of packets to the feature set of classification. At the same time, they also show that the precisions of different feature sets from gcForest is highest. Therefore, gcForest is the best classification algorithm even the feature set changes.

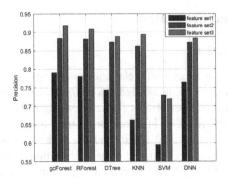

Fig. 5. Precision of different algorithms using different features

Table 4. Different features set

Feature set	Description
Feature set1	Features only based on time
Feature set2	Features based on lengths and number of packets
Feature set3	All features

Figure 6(a) and (b) exhibit the test precisions and recalls of all kinds of traffic. The results show that gcForest and DNN obtain the best performance of recognizing each class of traffic. SVM recognizes several classes of traffic accurately but its overall performance is worse than gcForest. The performance of the traffic classification is satisfactory except some packets originally belong to Chat are wrongly identified as Browsing traffic because some online chat applications run in browsers. Accordingly, the division of traffic classes remains to be optimized.

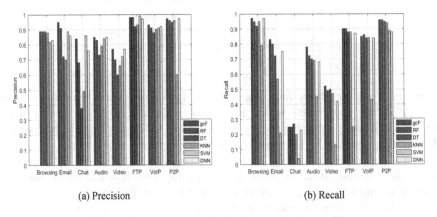

(a) Precision   (b) Recall

Fig. 6. Precision and recall of different kinds of traffic

As for the extra workload of the model with the section of traffic classification, we carry out experiments to evaluate the its impact on real time data transmission. We randomly select 1000 flows from the traffic dataset and measure the total testing time of feature calculation and prediction in the trained classification models. Each flow lasts for 5 s, consisting of the two-way traffic packets which have the same five-tuple. The testing times and precisions of the six trained classification models are shown in Fig. 7. It can be seen that the models classify traffic data quickly and four of them only spend less than 100 ms on 1000 flows. Thus in actual networks, the classification time of a flow is negligible. The proposed scheduling model is feasible due to the section of traffic classification has little impact on real time data transmission.

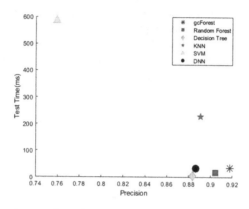

Fig. 7. The testing times and precisions of these classification models using 1000 flows

5.2   VNFs Selection

Considering the diversity and complexity of real networks, we select three networks with different topology: Net1, Net2 and Net3. The networks respectively contain 15, 30, 45 nodes and these three all have some nodes to host VNFs. Two nodes of each network are selected as the source node and the target node. In all three networks, there are several paths which have different bandwidth and congestion from the source node to the target node. And the nodes of these paths are guaranteed to satisfy the order of VNF in SFC. We put data into the source nodes of these networks to simulate the selection process of VNFs.

ATSA [24] and CR-SLF [25] are single-hop models of resource management and they both schedule resources according to the longest transmission time of messages, so they are comparable to SFCL. Differently, SFCL is proposed for working based on the results of traffic classification and it takes the bandwidth and congestion of network into consideration. We made experiments to compare the scheduling performance of the three models in each network. In different network, first we evaluate the length of paths and set longest transmission times of different traffic classes to ensure that all packets have chance to reach the target node. For realizing better user QoS, longest transmission times (LTT) of class with higher transmission priority is shorter. In general, the 8 classes of traffic packets are sorted according to the priority of transmission as a specified order, i.e. VoIP, Video-streaming, Audio-streaming, Chat, Browsing, Email, P2P, FTP. Then the parameters of the model are modified by the topology of each network, such as the coefficients in (6) and (7). Finally, we change speed of data input to cause different degrees of congestion in networks and count the number of packets successfully reached the target node in unit time.

Figure 8(a), (b) and (c) respectively indicate the comparison of scheduling performance obtained by different models in Net1, Net2 and Net3. Experimental message set consists of the 8 classes of messages, each class with 1000 messages. SFCL model works without the section of traffic classification in these experiments. The unlabeled messages are input to the networks in random order. The evaluation indicator of scheduling performance is the Task Unfinished Ratio (TUR). TUR is defined as the ratio of the number of packets that fail to reach the target node before their LTT. The x-axis denotes the speed of data input, namely, the number of messages input per second. And the y-axis denotes that TURs obtained by three models in each network. According to the results, SFCL without section of traffic classification can greatly reduce the TUR compared to the traditional single-hop scheduling models in different network congestion conditions.

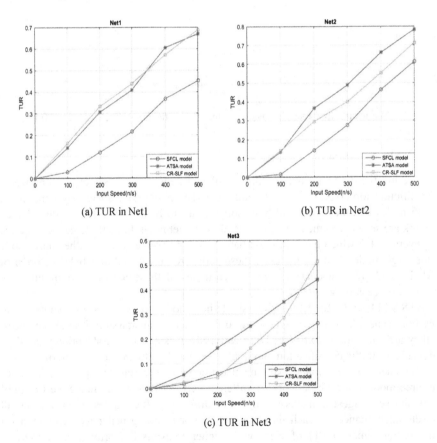

(a) TUR in Net1

(b) TUR in Net2

(c) TUR in Net3

Fig. 8. TURs in different networks under different models

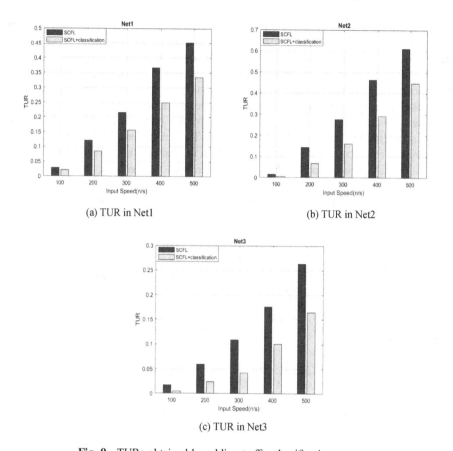

(a) TUR in Net1   (b) TUR in Net2

(c) TUR in Net3

Fig. 9. TURs obtained by adding traffic classification process

The comparisons of the scheduling performance of SFCL model whether to add the section of traffic classification in Net1, Net2 and Net3 are respectively shown in Fig. 9 (a), (b) and (c). Experimental message set is same as before but the messages are labeled after the messages pass through a trained model for classification. Then some parameters of messages are changed for differentiated scheduling, such as transmission priorities. According to the results, TRUs of SFCL decrease by 30% to 50% in different networks after classifying the input traffic packets. Therefore, adding the section of traffic classification is helpful to reduce the TRU and improves user QoS though sometimes the process of classification takes a little time.

6   Conclusion

In this paper, a VNFs selection strategy is proposed to address the problem of scheduling network resources in NFV. The proposed strategy based on a method of traffic classification. This method leverages some flow features based on times, lengths and number of packets to classify different user behaviors on the internet. Results show that the method of classification is no longer restricted by the lengths of flows so that the real-time performance of the resource scheduling strategy is improved. Furthermore, resource management strategy can schedule traffic packets from different user behavior to improve QoS since the method obtains high precision of classification. The gcForest algorithm performs better than other classification algorithms in this task.

The VNFs selection model SFCL proposed by this paper divides the network into layers according to the order of VNFs in SFC. The scheduler of each layer selects a next layer for messages with joint consideration of transmission priority and network congestion. Experiments prove that SFCL can reduce the network congestion effectively compared with the traditional single-hop scheduling models. After adding the section of traffic classification, the number of packets that fail to reach the target node before longest transmission time is reduced by 30% to 50%.

Acknowledgment. This work was jointly supported by: (1) National Natural Science Foundation of China (No. 61771068, 61671079, 61471063, 61372120, 61421061); (2) Beijing Municipal Natural Science Foundation (No. 4182041, 4152039); (3) the National Basic Research Program of China (No. 2013CB329102).

References

1. Sun, C., Bi, J., Zheng, Z., et al.: NFP: enabling network function parallelism in NFV. In: Proceedings of the Conference of the ACM Special Interest Group on Data Communication, pp. 43–56. ACM (2017)
2. Taleb, T., Ksentini, A., Sericola, B.: On service resilience in cloud-native 5G mobile systems. IEEE J. Sel. Areas Commun. **34**(3), 483–496 (2016)
3. Chantre, H.D., da Fonseca, N.L.S.: Redundant placement of virtualized network functions for LTE evolved Multimedia Broadcast Multicast Services. In: 2017 IEEE International Conference on Communications, ICC 2017, pp. 1–7. IEEE (2017)
4. Williams, N., Zander, S., Armitage, G.: A preliminary performance comparison of five machine learning algorithms for practical IP traffic flow classification. ACM SIGCOMM Comput. Commun. Rev. **36**, 5–16 (2006)
5. Dong, Y.N., Zhao, J.J., Jin, J.: Novel feature selection and classification of internet video traffic based on a hierarchical scheme. Comput. Netw. **119**, 102–111 (2017)
6. Lopez-Martin, M., Carro, B., Sanchez-Esguevillas, A., et al.: Network traffic classifier with convolutional and recurrent neural networks for Internet of Things. IEEE Access **5**(99), 18042–18050 (2017)
7. Bernaille, L., Teixeira, R., Akodkenou, I., et al.: Traffic classification on the fly. ACM SIGCOMM Comput. Commun. Rev. **36**(2), 23–26 (2006)
8. Shi, H., Li, H., Zhang, D., et al.: Efficient and robust feature extraction and selection for traffic classification. Comput. Netw. Int. J. Comput. Telecommun. Netw. **119**(C), 1–16 (2017)
9. Zhou, Z.H., Feng, J.: Deep forest: towards an alternative to deep neural networks. In: International Joint Conference on Artificial Intelligence, pp. 3553–3559 (2017)
10. Lashkari, A.H., Gil, G.D., Mamun, M.S.I., et al.: Characterization of tor traffic using time based features. In: International Conference on Information Systems Security and Privacy, pp. 253–262 (2017)

11. Anderson, B., Mcgrew, D.: Machine learning for encrypted malware traffic classification: accounting for noisy labels and non-stationarity. In: The ACM SIGKDD International Conference, pp. 1723–1732. ACM (2017)

12. Shi, H., Li, H., Zhang, D., et al.: An efficient feature generation approach based on deep learning and feature selection techniques for traffic classification. Comput. Netw. **132**, 81–98 (2018)

13. Tseng, C.C., Wang, H.C., Kuo, F.C., et al.: Delay and power consumption in LTE/LTE-A DRX mechanism with mixed short and long cycles. IEEE Trans. Veh. Technol. **65**(3), 1721–1734 (2016)

14. Joe, I., Kim, W.T., Hong, S.: A network selection algorithm considering power consumption in hybrid wireless networks. IEICE Trans. Commun. **91**(1), 1240–1243 (2007)

15. Senouci, M.A., Mushtaq, M.S., Hoceini, S., et al.: TOPSIS-based dynamic approach for mobile network interface selection. Comput. Netw. **107**(2), 304–314 (2016)

16. Park, H., van der Schaar, M.: Bargaining strategies for networked multimedia resource management. IEEE Trans. Signal Process. **55**(7), 3496–3511 (2007)

17. Afzal, B., Alvi, S.A., Shah, G.A., et al.: Energy efficient context aware traffic scheduling for IoT applications. Ad Hoc Netw. **62**, 101–115 (2017)

18. Lukovszki, T., Schmid, S.: Online admission control and embedding of service chains. In: Scheideler, C. (ed.) Structural Information and Communication Complexity. LNCS, vol. 9439, pp. 104–118. Springer, Cham (2015). https://doi.org/10.1007/978-3-319-25258-2_8

19. Jia, M., Liang, W., Huang, M., et al.: Throughput maximization of NFV-enabled unicasting in software-defined networks. In: 2017 IEEE Global Communications Conference, GLOBECOM 2017, pp. 1–6. IEEE (2017)

20. Mestres, A., Rodriгuеznatal, A., Carner, J., et al.: Knowledge-defined networking. ACM SIGCOMM Comput. Commun. Rev. **47**(3), 2–10 (2016)

21. Kar, B., Wu, H.K., Lin, Y.D.: Energy cost optimization in dynamic placement of virtualized network function chains. IEEE Trans. Netw. Serv. Manag. **PP**(99), 1 (2017)

22. Gu, L., Tao, S., Zeng, D., et al.: Communication cost efficient virtualized network function placement for big data processing. In: Computer Communications Workshops, pp. 604–609. IEEE (2016)

23. Breiman, L.: Random forest. Mach. Learn. **45**, 5–32 (2001)

24. Lee, J., et al.: A real-time message scheduling scheme based on optimal earliest deadline first policy for dual channel wireless networks. In: Sha, E., Han, S.-K., Xu, C.-Z., Kim, M.-H., Yang, L.T., Xiao, B. (eds.) EUC 2006. LNCS, vol. 4096, pp. 264–273. Springer, Heidelberg (2006). https://doi.org/10.1007/11802167_28

25. Li, H., Shenoy, P., Ramamritham, K.: Scheduling messages with deadlines in multi-hop real-time sensor networks. In: IEEE Real Time on Embedded Technology and Applications Symposium. pp. 415–425. IEEE Computer Society (2005)

A Stacking Approach
to Objectionable-Related Domain Names
Identification by Passive DNS Traffic
(Short Paper)

Chen Zhao[1,2], Yongzheng Zhang[1,2(✉)], Tianning Zang[1,2], Zhizhou Liang[1,2], and Yipeng Wang[1,2]

[1] School of Cyber Security, University of Chinese Academy of Sciences, Beijing, China
{zhaochen,zhangyongzheng,zangtianning,wangyipeng}@iie.ac.cn
[2] Institute of Information Engineering, CAS, Beijing 100093, China

Abstract. Domain name classification is an important issue in the field of cyber security. Notice that objectionable-related domain names are one category of domain names that serve services such as gambling, pornography, etc. They are classified and even forbidden in some areas, some of these domain names may defraud visitors privacy and property. Timely and accurate identification of these domain names is significant for Internet content censorship and users security. In this work, we analyze the behavior of objectionable-related domain names from the real-world DNS traffic, finding that there exist evidently differences between objectionable-related domain names and none-objectionable ones. In this paper, we propose a stacking approach to objectionable-related domain names identification, VisSensor, that automatically extracts name features and latent visiting patterns of domain names from the DNS traffic and distinguishes objectionable-related ones. We integrate convolutional neural networks with fully-connected neural networks to collaborate features of different dimensions and improve experimental results. The accuracy of VisSensor is 88.48% with a false positive rate of 9.11%. We also compared VisSensor with a public domain name tagging system, and our VisSensor performed better than the tagging system on the identification task of the objectionable-related domain names.

Keywords: Objectionable-related domain name · Traffic analysis · Convolutional neural network

1 Introduction

1.1 Background of Objectionable-Related Domain Names

Domain name system (DNS) is a bridge between the resources on the Internet and the Internet users. The classification of domain names are important

H. Gao et al. (Eds.): CollaborateCom 2018, LNICST 268, pp. 284–294, 2019.
https://doi.org/10.1007/978-3-030-12981-1_20

in the field of cyber security. Many researchers have paid their attentions to this area [5,7,8]. In this paper, we concerned the issue of objectionable-related domain names identification. Objectionable-related domain names are one kind of domain names that related to the objectionable contents such as gambling (e.g. Fig. 1), pornography (e.g. Fig. 2) and other services associated with them (e.g. in Fig. 3, the domain name www.80dytt.com offers pirate medias to attract visitor, and show promotions of ① gambling and ② pornography in its media). The contents of these domain names are harmful for teenager's mental health, and some of these domain names even try to steal users' privacy and property. Current practices on objectionable-related domain names highly rely on manual efforts. However, manual efforts lack of timeliness and cannot fully cover all the active objectionable-related domain names in practice.

Fig. 1. An illegal gambling domain name (01kjz.com). **Fig. 2.** A pornography domain name. **Fig. 3.** A pirate media platform.

1.2   Contributions

In this paper, we propose VisSensor, a stacking based approach to objectionable-related domain names identification. VisSensor collects the DNS answering traffic from the resolver and transforms the traffic into visiting features and name features of domain names, and automatically classifies the domain names appeared in the traffic into objectionable-related ones and none-objectionable ones. Our approach is based on the key insight that the periodical variations of DNS querying traffic are the embodiments of overall visitor behaviors which strongly indicate the services offered by domain names. We leveraged this characteristic for the identification of objectionable-related domain names.

The key novelty of VisSensor lies in the stacking of convolutional neural networks (CNN) and fully-connected neural networks (NN). This combination enables the collaborate of data with different orders of magnitude. VisSensor integrates the identification results based on DNS querying sequences with the results based on the name features. Moreover, VisSensor has outperformed the domain name tagging works aforementioned on the timeliness and completeness using passive DNS traffic.

The key contribution of our work are listed below:

- We propose a stacking based method that can integrate data with diverse orders of magnitude by stacking convolutional neural networks and fully-connected neural networks together. We apply CNN on high dimensional data and fcNN on simple data. And this collaboration evidently improves the overall classification result than any separate sub modules.
- We propose a stacking based approach of objectionable-related domain names identification, VisSensor, which automatically extracts the latent visiting patterns of domain names from the DNS answering traffic and identifies the objectionable-related domain names from the normal ones. VisSensor consists of five parts: data preprocessing module, training module, stacking module, filter and classification module. We build a prototype of VisSensor based on our design, train and test VisSensor on a real-world DNS traffic. The best sub-model of VisSensor achieves an accuracy of 87.47% and the overall results of VisSensor reach an accuracy of 88.48%.
- We compare our VisSensor with the public accessible URL tagging system of McAfee, trustedsource.org, on the task of identifying objectionable-related domain names. The recall and precision of our VisSensor is 85.07% and 90.89% higher while that of Trusted Source is 4.19% and 10.92% which evidently shown the effectiveness of the VisSensor over the state of arts labeling method.

Our arrangement of this paper is listed as followings: in Sect. 2, we are going to talk about our findings in the study of real world domain name visiting traffic; in Sect. 3, we will describe the features we use in the VisSensor; in Sect. 4, we will introduce the classifiers in VisSensor and show the overall design; Sect. 5 will illustrate the experimental results of VisSensor on a real-world DNS data, and compare the results with one of the state of arts applications in domain name tagging; in the last section, we will discuss about the limitation and application of the VisSensor, and provide our opinions on further study of objectionable domain names.

2   Observations

In this section, we provide an intuitive overview on the different visiting patterns of objectionable-related domain names and none-objectionable domain names. Note that we use DNS queries to refer to the DNS querying packets sent by clients that passively recorded on the recursive resolver side. Motived by the previous works [4,6], we design a new way of visualizing DNS queries. Explicitly, we count the queries for every five-minute span, and we illustrate the relative count of each span by the illumination of its corresponding black and white pixel point.

Given a domain name d, assume its five-minute counts in w days are $P = \{p_1, p_2, \ldots, p_{w \times 288}\}$, then the illumination of point p_i can be denoted as:

$$I_i = \lfloor \frac{p_i}{max(P)} \times 255 \rfloor$$

From this equation, we can say that lager queries counts have lager I_is and consequently have brighter pixel points.

We fill all the $I = \{I_1, I_2, \ldots, I_{w \times 288}\}$ into an image. Along the width of an image is 24 h of a day, and along the height represents 14 days of our sampling time. For example, we choose two typical illustrations of domain names to demonstrate the differences between objectionable-related and none-objectionable. As shown in Figs. 4 and 5: *Zompim.com* is the domain name of a live chat software solution company; *5303008.com* is a gambling website and is reported to have potentially harmful software by the Google Chrome. As mentioned above, brighter pixel points indicate higher queries counts. We can see the bright points of normal domain name *zompim.com* gather around the areas that represent the work time (around 8 a.m. to 6 p.m.), while points of gambling domain name are gradually get brighter after working hours and reach the brightest area at around 9 p.m.

Fig. 4. Zompim.com, a normal commercial domain name.

Fig. 5. 5303008.com, a gambling related domain name.

3   Features

3.1   Visiting Features

To quantify a domain name's time sequential accessions, we count the visiting features which compose three kinds of count numbers measured in five-minute grained spans to maintain the visiting details in the passive DNS traffic:

- Query counts denote how many times this domain name is queried;
- Client counts denote how many clients have queried this domain name;
- Network counts denote how many networks that querying clients come from.

We rearrange the arrays of three features into three 14 × 288 matrices. In matrix form, every time span is located between the five-minute span before and latter in the same row, and the time spans on the same column is the same time on different days. And we stacked the three matrices together, making each matrix as one channel of a 3 × 14 × 288 sized domain name visiting features sample.

3.2   Name Features

In our research, we also find that the objectionable-related domain names appear following characteristics: 1. unreadable; 2. the proportion of numbers in the registrable part of domain names (for example, the registrable part of '12345foo.com' is '12345foo', and numbers take up $\frac{5}{8} = 62.5\%$). This finding motivates us to impose the naming features that represent how much a domain name matches with these characteristics. Meanwhile, previous works have shown that objectionable-related domain names distribute unevenly among TLDs (top level domains, the right most label of a domain name; all effective domain name should be registered under a TLD) due to the different regulations of TLDs. For these reasons, we profile the name features in two aspects:

- The percentage of numbers in a domain name's registrable part;
- The index of TLD in the one-hot form.

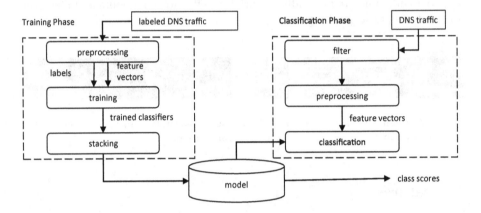

Fig. 6. The overview of VisSensor.

4 The VisSensor

In this section, we present the VisSensor, an ensemble system for classifying domain names into objectionable-related and none-objectionable based on their visiting and name features. We will introduce the core classification model of Vis-Sensor which composed by four classifiers in Sect. 4.1; and we are going to introduce the two phases of VisSensor, the training phase and the classification phase, explicitly in Sects. 4.2 and 4.3. Figure 6 provides an overview of VisSensors.

4.1 Classifiers

In our work, we apply two kinds of neural network classifiers, specifically, fully-connected Neural Network (fcNN) and Convolutional Neural Network (CNN) classifiers. The labels we used are objectionable-related (positive) and none-objectionable (negative), they are known for training purposes.

fcNN Classifiers. FcNN classifiers in VisSensor give objectionable scores according to name features. A fcNN classifier consists of hidden layers with neurons that have learnable weights and biases; each neuron links to all neurons on the previous layer, performs dot product and has an optional non-linearity operation. The fcNN transformed instances on the input end to class scores at the output end.

CNN Classifiers. CNN classifiers aim to extract latent visiting patterns from visiting features and map them to objectionable scores. A CNN classifier is similar to fcNN in the overall structure, but it modified some of the hidden layers into convolutional layers with multi-dimensional neurons that only connect to a small region of the upper layer. The CNN proposed by [9] is able to deal with large scale and high dimensional inputs. Note that we impose dilated convolutional layers [10] in our CNN classifiers to measure the weekly querying characteristics in additional to regular convolutional layers.

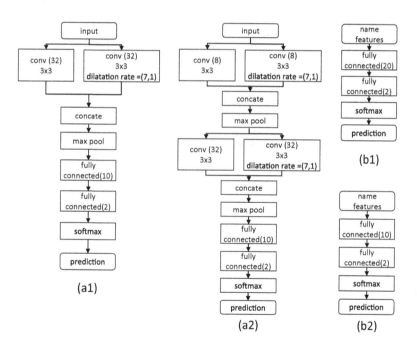

Fig. 7. (a1) the structure of CNN1; (a2) the structure of CNN2; (b1) the structure of fcNN1; (b2) the structure of fcNN2.

4.2   Training Phase

In this phase, we aim to train a stacked model composes the fcNN and CNN classifiers. The model is able to tell the possibility of a domain name to be objectionable-related by giving class scores. First of all, the preprocessing module transforms the labeled DNS traffic into visiting features and name features defined in Sect. 3. Then the training module directs the classifiers to automatically extract the most distinguishing patterns of objectionable-related domain names from visiting and name features. After the classifiers finish training separately, stacking module integrates them together and build an integral classifying model as the output of training phase.

4.3   Classification Phase

In the classification phase, VisSensor classifies arbitrary domain names into objectionable-related and none-objectionable based on the integral model built in the training phase. Firstly, the filter module receives the raw DNS traffic and removes the domain names that do not have enough queries or popular domain names that is irrelevant to objectionable contents (such as Alexa top domain names). The preprocessing module accepts the purified DNS traffic and transforms it into features described in Sect. 3. After that, the previous trained model performs the classification on these features and generates objectionable-related scores for the domain names.

5   Experimental Analysis

5.1   Data Set

Data Collection. The data we use in our research is the passively sampled DNS traffic which is first proposed by Weimer [2], and it became a significant analytic data source of DNS-associated security issues since then [3]. The passive DNS traffic is often collected on the level of resolvers, and it is generated by consecutively sampling the DNS queries and answers between clients and the resolver. Monitoring objectionable-related domain names through passive DNS traffic can significantly improve the timeliness and discover newly appeared objectionable-related domain names when they are visited.

We collect domain name samples by consecutively counting DNS querying answers from a provincial backbone resolver of a major ISP for 14 days (4th August, 2017 to 17th August, 2017). We select the domain names which were queried around 10^3 to 10^7 times in the two weeks, discard the domain names that are either very popular or lack of visiting.

Data Tagging. To label the domain names, we refer to the URL Ticketing System called Trusted Source [1] of McAfee on the Sep. 2017 at first. We refer the categories of domain names given by the Trusted Source rather than the risk levels to ensure the accuracy of tagging. Due to the websites that our targeting domain names hosted, they should be labeled either Malicious, Pornography, Gambling or PUPs (potentially unwanted programs) by the Trusted Source [1]. But we find that a large portion of these domain names are ticketed as Forum/Bulletin Boards or Public Information which might be confused with normal domain names. To guarantee the reliability of our dataset, we manually label 5460 normal domain names and 5661 objectionable-related domain names, and partition them into three sets for training, testing and validation purposes, as shown in Table 1.

Table 1. Domain name samples and partition

Partition	Normal	Objectionable	Total
Training set	2730	2830	5560
Validation set	1365	1416	2781
Testing set	1365	1415	2780
Total	5460	5661	11121

5.2 Experiment Results

With the visiting features and name features of domain names, we separately train four classifiers for the two kinds of features. Specific structures of all classifiers are shown in Fig. 7(b1), (b2), (c1), (c2). For visiting features, we build two CNN classifiers to learn the visiting patterns of domain names. And we use two fcNN classifiers to learn the objectionable-scores from name features. The results of four classifiers are shown as Table 2.

Table 2. Model accuracies

Model	CNN 1	CNN 2	fcNN 1	fcNN 2	Stacked
Valid set	87.03%	86.75%	87.10%	87.25%	-
Test set	87.03%	86.10%	86.66%	87.47%	88.48%

5.3 Comparisons with Trusted Source

The Trusted Source [1] is a URL ticketing system of McAfee that provides the category and risk of a site, it also manually verifies the categories of websites that reported by its users before updating to its databases.

We compare the results of VisSensor with the labels tagged by Trusted Source on the domain names of the testing set, and summarize in the Table 3. We mark the domain names related to gambling, pornography and pirate media as objectionable, and the Trusted Source tickets 4.19% (true positive) those domain names with a total accuracy of 34.37%. While VisSensor can figure out 85.07% objectionable domain names with a false positive rate of 8.23%, which shows a significant improvement upon the state of art of objectionable-related domain name tagging implementation.

Table 3. Comparisons with Trusted Source on the test set

Manual label	Trusted Source		VisSensor		Total
	Normal	Abnormal	Negative	Positive	
Normal	895 (32.31%)	465 (16.79%)	1294 (46.71%)	116 (4.19%)	1410
Abnormal	1353 (48.84%)	57 (2.06%)	203 (7.33%)	1157 (41.77%)	1360
Total	2248	522	1497	1273	2770

6   Related Works

The most common method of domain name classification is domain names tagging, and the typical ways of tagging are blacklists, whitelist and tagging systems. Although the importance of blacklists and whitelists are acknowledged widely in the domain names classification field, many researchers also found that the reliability of these lists are limited. Sinha et al. [11] found that blacklists shown high false positive and false negative rates; Sheng et al. [12] pointed out that blacklists' updating is sometimes not timely, and their coverages varied a lot; Kührer et al. [13] found that 15 public blacklists failed to cover more than 80% of the malicious domain names queried by malwares. Some researchers tried to improve the accuracy of blacklists: Kheir et al. [14] proposed methods that filter legal domain names from blacklists to reduce the false positive rates. Stevanovic et al. built a semi-manual labeling method which tracks the domain names with frequently changed IP addresses and relates the domain names with the reputations of these IP addresses in the blacklists. These works show that the effectiveness of blacklists is questionable.

Meanwhile, the existing tagging systems have some limitations. For example, we have retrieved the data sets on the URL tagging system of McAfee (trustedsource.org) twice, one on Sep. 2017 and the other on July 2018 (shown in Table 4). The objectionable-related domain name should be tagged as 'gambling' or 'pornography' in the Trusted Source. And the identification true positive rates of Trusted Source decreased from 4.56% to 2.74%; some domain names that had been labeled in the 2017 became unverified in 2018. From these results, we can notice that Trusted Source keeps updating its label engines, but its identification of objectionable-related domain names is still need to be further processed.

Table 4. Comparisons with Trusted Source

Manual label	2017-09		2018-07			Total
	Normal	Objectionable	Normal	Objectionable	Unverified	
Normal	3706	1755	3820	1236	404	5460
Objectionable	5402	258	5373	155	133	5661
Total	9108	2013	9193	1391	537	11121

References

1. Customer URL Ticketing System. https://trustedsource.org/sources/index.pl. Accessed 12 July 2018
2. Weimer, F.: Passive DNS replication. In: FIRST Conference on Computer Security Incident, p. 98 (2005)
3. Zdrnja, B., Brownlee, N., Wessels, D.: Passive monitoring of DNS anomalies. In: M. Hämmerli, B., Sommer, R. (eds.) DIMVA 2007. LNCS, vol. 4579, pp. 129–139. Springer, Heidelberg (2007). https://doi.org/10.1007/978-3-540-73614-1_8
4. Antonakakis, M., Perdisci, R., Dagon, D., et al.: Building a dynamic reputation system for DNS. In: USENIX Security Symposium, pp. 273–290 (2010)
5. Bilge, L., Kirda, E., Kruegel, C., et al.: EXPOSURE: finding malicious domains using passive DNS analysis. In: NDSS (2011)
6. Antonakakis, M., Perdisci, R., Lee, W., et al.: Detecting malware domains at the upper DNS hierarchy. In: USENIX Security Symposium, pp. 1–16 (2011)
7. Rahbarinia, B., Perdisci, R., Antonakakis, M.: Segugio: efficient behavior-based tracking of malware-control domains in large ISP networks. In: 2015 45th Annual IEEE/IFIP International Conference on Dependable Systems and Networks, DSN, pp. 403–414. IEEE (2015)
8. Hao, S., Thomas, M., Paxson, V., et al.: Understanding the domain registration behavior of spammers. In: Proceedings of the 2013 Conference on Internet Measurement Conference, pp. 63–76. ACM (2013)
9. LeCun, Y., Jackel, L.D., Bottou, L., et al.: Learning algorithms for classification: a comparison on handwritten digit recognition. Neural Netw.: Stat. Mech. Perspect. **261**, 276 (1995)
10. Szegedy, C., Liu, W., Jia, Y., et al.: Going deeper with convolutions. In: Proceedings of the IEEE Conference on Computer Vision and Pattern Recognition, pp. 1–9 (2015)
11. Sinha, S., Bailey, M., Jahanian, F.: Shades of Grey: on the effectiveness of reputation-based "blacklists". In: 3rd International Conference on Malicious and Unwanted Software, MALWARE 2008, pp. 57–64. IEEE (2008)
12. Sheng, S., Wardman, B., Warner, G., et al.: An empirical analysis of phishing blacklists. In: Sixth Conference on Email and Anti-Spam, CEAS (2009)
13. Kührer, M., Rossow, C., Holz, T.: Paint it black: evaluating the effectiveness of malware blacklists. In: Stavrou, A., Bos, H., Portokalidis, G. (eds.) RAID 2014. LNCS, vol. 8688, pp. 1–21. Springer, Cham (2014). https://doi.org/10.1007/978-3-319-11379-1_1

14. Kheir, N., Tran, F., Caron, P., Deschamps, N.: Mentor: positive DNS reputation to skim-off benign domains in botnet C&C blacklists. In: Cuppens-Boulahia, N., Cuppens, F., Jajodia, S., Abou El Kalam, A., Sans, T., et al. (eds.) SEC 2014. IFIPAICT, vol. 428, pp. 1–14. Springer, Heidelberg (2014). https://doi.org/10.1007/978-3-642-55415-5_1
15. Stevanovic, M., Pedersen, J.M., D'Alconzo, A., et al.: On the ground truth problem of malicious DNS traffic analysis. Comput. Secur. **55**, 142–158 (2015)

Grid Clustering and Routing Protocol in Heterogeneous Wireless Sensor Networks (Short Paper)

Zheng Zhang$^{(\boxtimes)}$ and Pei Hu

College of Software, Nanyang Institute of Technology,
Nanyang 473000, Henan, China

Abstract. In wireless sensor network, sensor nodes usually use batteries to provide energy, and energy consumption have very strict restrictions. High demands about the efficient use of energy are put forward. However typical multi to one communication mode in the wireless sensor network will lead to the uneven consumption of sensor nodes in the whole network. So it will greatly shorten the lifecycle of the entire network. As for this problem this paper optimize the model of heterogeneous chessboard clustering of sensor network and propose a grid clustering mechanism and propose an effective node routing protocol to achieve the goal of prolonging the network lifecycle by balancing the energy consumption of nodes. Simulation experiments show that the grid clustering protocol greatly improves the lifecycle of wireless sensor networks and has better performance compared with LEACH and LRS.

Keywords: Grid clustering · Routing protocol · Heterogeneous · Sensor network

1 Introduction

Recent advances in microprocessor, VLSI and wireless communication technologies have enabled the deployment of large-scale sensor networks where many low-power, low-cost small sensors are distributed over a vast field to obtain fine-grained, high-precision sensing data. These sensor nodes are typically powered by batteries and communicate through wireless channels, and are usually scattered densely and statically.

Sensor nodes usually operate on a nonreplaceable battery. A large proportion of a node'senergy resource is consumed in forwarding data. A major design challenge in sensor networks is to increase the operational lifetime of the network as much as possible by employing energy efficient routing. Many routing protocols have been proposed for sensor networks, such as Directed Diffusion, TTDD, and so on. However, most of the routing protocols did not consider the Uneven Energy Consumption problem in sensor networks. In typical sensor networks, the many-to-one traffic pattern is dominant, a large number of sensor nodes send data to the sink. Thus sensor nodes near the sink have much heavier traffic burden and run out of power much faster than other nodes. The short lifetime of these critical nodes dramatically reduces sensor network lifetime.

© ICST Institute for Computer Sciences, Social Informatics and Telecommunications Engineering 2019
Published by Springer Nature Switzerland AG 2019. All Rights Reserved
H. Gao et al. (Eds.): CollaborateCom 2018, LNICST 268, pp. 295–309, 2019.
https://doi.org/10.1007/978-3-030-12981-1_21

Recently deployed sensor network systems are increasingly following heterogeneous designs, incorporating a mixture of sensors with widely varying capabilities. For example, in a smart home environment, sensors may be powered by AA batteries, AAA batteries or even button batteries. Some recent work starts considering heterogeneous sensor networks. Some paper studied the optimum node density and node energies to guarantee a lifetime in heterogeneous sensor networks, Du presented an energy efficient differentiated coverage algorithm (which can provide different coverage degrees for different areas in a sensor network) for heterogeneous sensor networks. Duarte-Melo and Liu analyzed energy consumption and lifetime of heterogeneous sensor networks.

Clustering-base schemes are promising techniques for sensor networks because of their good scalability and performance. Several clustering-based routing protocols have been proposed for sensor networks, like LEACH, TTDD, and LRS. LEACH and LRS include redundancy in the system by periodically selecting a cluster-head from the sensors in the network. However, these schemes suffer from overhead of frequent re-clustering. In addition, they did not solve the UEC problem near the sink.

2   The Uneven Energy Consumption Problem

Several existing routing protocols based on cluster take into account the problem of uneven energy consumption of nodes. In LEACH and LRS, periodically a cluster head is elected from the sensors to solve the uneven energy consumption in cluster heads. However, these schemes suffer from overhead of frequent re-clustering. Further more, rotating cluster-head among sensors does not solve the uneven energy consumption. Because no matter how to transform cluster-head nodes, the nodes around them always have a lot of communication pressure. Usually these nodes near cluster-head nodes are the key nodes. For example in Fig. 1, the base station node is located in the upper-right corner of the network. All nodes send data packets to the base station nodes by one hop or multi-hops. The sensors within one hop to the base station are the critical nodes and need to relay packets from all other nodes. When all the critical nodes fail, other sensor nodes will be disconnected from the base station, and the sensor network becomes unavailable. The uneven energy consumption problem exists no matter where the base station is located.

For a heterogeneous sensor network, it is reasonable to let the more powerful H-sensors become cluster-head nodes. Each L-sensor sends data to its cluster-head node, and cluster-head nodes forward data to the base station node. If H-sensors have sufficient energy supply, the heterogeneous sensor network solves the uneven energy consumption near the base station. Unfortunately, there is another uneven energy consumption problem in schemes with fixed cluster-head nodes. As for a typical cluster in Fig. 2, cluster-head nodes have a transmission range of r. The nodes within this distance from the cluster-head node are referred to as critical nodes. Every transmission of L-sensors in the cluster to the cluster-head node has to go through these critical nodes. Because these critical nodes are the last hop nodes for every communication link. Hence the critical nodes have the highest burden of tansmission, then these critical nodes will run out of their power much faster than other nodes. When the critical nodes

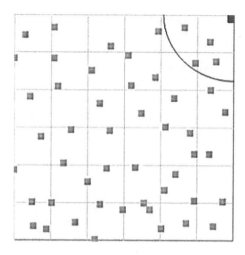

Fig. 1. Nodes near the base station consume more energy

drain out their energy and become unavailable, other L-sensors will not be able to send packets to the cluster head, and the entire cluster becomes unavailable even though the remaining energy in many sensor nodes are still high. The remaining energy in most nodes is wasted.

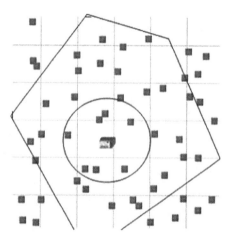

Fig. 2. Typical cluster stricter of sensor network, critical nodes in the circle

Simulation demonstrates the uneven energy consumption among sensor nodes in a cluster. The results are shown in Fig. 3. In the simulation, there are totally 73 sensors in the cluster. The number of sensor nodes that are 1-hop, 2-hop, 3-hop, and 4-hop away from cluster-head node is 7, 22, 29, 15. Each sensors sends to the cluster-head node one packet per second. Each node has a fixed amount of energy, and the nodes die when the energy is run out. The routing protocol used is the greedy geographic routing algorithm. Figure 3 shows the remaining energy in the sensors when all critical nodes run out of energy, where the x-axis signifys the remaining energy percentage. We can see that more than half nodes have higher than 50% energy left from Fig. 3, and this energy will be wasted in a real sensor network. The sum of all the remaining energy is equivalent to 38 sensors with full energy. This simulation demonstrates that there is still the problem of uneven energy consumption with fixed cluster-head nodes.

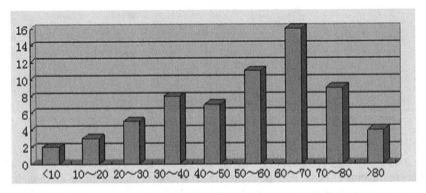

Fig. 3. The remaining energy of sensor nodes

In order to solve the uneven energy comsumption problem and prolong network lifecycle, while at the same improve the performance and measurability of routing mechanism based on clustering. We propose a novel chessboard clustering scheme for sensor network. The details are presented in next section.

3   The Chessboard Clustering Routing Protocol

In this section, we present the Chessboard Clustering routing protocol for heterogeneous sensor networks. We consider a heterogeneous sensor network consisting of two types of nodes: a small number of powerful High-end sensors (H-sensors) and a large number of Low-end sensors (L-sensors). Each sensor node is aware of its own location. Sensor nodes can use location services to estimate their locations, and no GPS receiver is required at each node.

First, we briefly present the idea of our chessboard clustering. The sensor network is divided into several equal-sized cells, adjacent cells are colored with different colors such as white and black. Figure 4 shows the struct of sensor network divided. The H-sensors and L-sensors are uniformly and randomly distributed in the field. Based on location information, H-sensors can determine if it is in a white cell or a black cell. During the initialization phase, only the H-sensors in white cells are active, and the H-sensors in black cells sleep. All L-sensors are active. Clusters are formed around the H-sensors in white cells, and these H-sensors become cluster heads. After a period of time when the H-sensors in black cells wake up and become new cluster heads. The network form a different set of clusters. Previous critical sensors become non-critical sensors, and previous non-critical sensors become critical sensors. Since critical sensors consume much more energy than other sensors, this shift balances the energy comsumption among sensors prolonging the network lifecycle.

Compared with the original chessboard, the improvement of the grid clustering has the following points:

(1) In the initial stage of cluster partition, in order to avoid the broadcast storm of ACK messages, the ACK message interruption mechanism is designed, which reduces the unnecessary forwarding of ACK messages, thus saving the energy cost of nodes.

(2) Based on the black and white grid transformation, a new scheme of partial adjustment of cluster structure based on the real-time congestion degree of communication links is put forward. This scheme improves the flexibility of cluster structure and transformation, reduces the data communication pressure in designated area timely and efficiently, and avoids unnecessary energy consumption of nodes.

(3) Chessboard clustering is used to convert black and white networks passively when the energy of the existing cluster heads is consumed, but it is often unreasonable. Because when cluster head nodes and the surrounding key nodes suddenly decrease in energy, it indicates that the existing cluster structure is no longer suitable for the data transmission pressure of the current communication link, resulting in the excessive consumption of cluster head nodes and key nodes. To solve this problem, the nodes in the grid cluster will monitor the energy usage of cluster heads in real time. When these situations happen, the black-and-white grid transformation will take the initiative to make changes based on the data communication pressure and avoid excessive energy consumption of some nodes.

Fig. 4. Chessboard clustering scheme

3.1 Initial Cluster Formation

The initial division describe the following several steps:

(1) During the initialization phase, all H-sensors in white cells broadcast Hello messages to nearby L-sensors with a random delay. The random delay is to avoid the collision of Hello message from two neighbor H-sensors.
The hello message includes the ID of the H-sensor and its location. The transmission range of the broadcast is large enough so that most L-sensors can receive Hello message from at least one H-sensor.

(2) Then each L-sensor chooses the H-sensor whose hello message has the best signal ratio as the cluster head. Each L-sensor also records other H-sensors from which it receives the hello messages, and these H-sensors are listed as backup cluster heads in case the primary cluster head fails.

(3) If a L-sensor does not receive any hello message during the initialization phase, the node will broadcast an explore message to seek the nearest H-sensor.

(4) When the neighbor L-sensors receive the Explore message, they will response an ack message with a random delay. The ack message includes the location and ID of these L-sensors's cluster head.
A L-sensor will not send ack message again if it receive an ack response from neighbors. This mechanism reduces the number of messages and the comsumed energy.

(5) Then L-sensor can select a cluster-head node based on the ack message. This ensures all L-sensors have a cluster head.

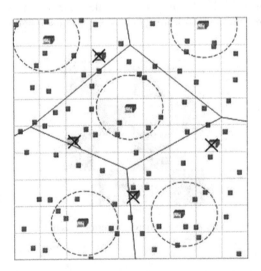

Fig. 5. Shows the initial cluster formation, the rectangle nodes are

Figure 5 shows the initial cluster formation, the rectangle nodes are H-sensors, and the square nodes are L-sensors. The L-sensors within circles are the critical nodes. The H-sensors with a cross are the H-sensors located in black cells, and they are not active until the second half period of the sensor network.

3.2   Re-formation of Cluster

In order to solve the problem of uneven energy consumption of nodes in sensor network, this paper adopts the method of re-formation of cluster while breaking the limit of the traditional cluster structure. The re-formation of cluster can achieve balanced energy consumption of nodes. The tansformation of cluster structure needs certain preconditions that can avoid more additional energy costs from too much transformation of cluster. Usually when the base stations find the following conditions, cluster will re-formate.

(1) The base station will real-time monitor the energy consumption of the working H-sensors. Base station nodes take into account the residual energy of these H-sensors. When the remaining energy is lower than a certain value, the base station node will start the transformation of the cluster.

(2) Base station nodes also monitor the data processing and transmission of communication links and sensor nodes in real time, when there is a high transmission rate of data in one area of the network, it is shown that the sensor nodes in this area have a large number of data to be transmitted to the cluster head nodes. At this point, the base station node will specify a H-sensor as a cluster-head node in the region.

According to the two cases above, the corresponding measures for the two kinds of transformation of clusters are given here. The first one is the black and white grid transformation under the sensor network. It involves the transformation of the cluster structure which is carried out in a whole network range and at a certain time interval. The second one is the adjustment of the cluster structure based on the real-time communication pressure of the communication link in the sensor network, which is the adjustment of the cluster structure in a certain area under the sensor network. The aim is to avoid the effect of uneven energy consumption on nodes of high data communication pressure in the region.

The first cluster transformation: For each active H-sensor in white cells, there is a pairing and sleep H-Sensor in the neighbor black cell. After a period of time, the base station node sends query information to the working H-sensors, asking the remaining energy in the nodes. Based on the overall energy usage of these nodes, the base station will decide whether to go on cluster tansformation. When the transformation is needed, the base station node sends the wake-up message to the H-sensor in the black grid and closes the working H-sensors. The wake-up H-sensors will build their own cluster structure according to the same process. After this transformation of cluster, before the L-sensor as a key node becomes the common node, the original ordinary L-sensor is likely to become a key node, so the transformation of the role can well balance the node energy consumption, to avoid the problem of the entire network failure due to the excessive consumption of energy.

After a series of operations mentioned above, new clustering results are formed in the network. Previously, the H-sensor in white grid was transformed into a sleep state by working state. Instead, the H-sensor in the black grid starts to work as the cluster-head node of the new cluster. Figure 6 gives the results after the grid cluster transformation. As you can see in Fig. 6, as a result of the formation of a completely different set of grid clustering results, most of the previous critical nodes become ordinary nodes with less energy consumption. The reformation of the cluster is equivalent to the reversal of the energy consumption pattern before, so it plays a role in the use of balanced energy.

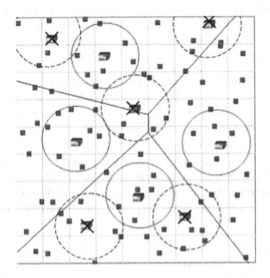

Fig. 6. The results of the grid clustering after the whole cluster transformation

The second cluster transformations: the base station node monitors the communication link in the sensor network in real time. If we find that the data transmission rate in the communication link is higher than the set value, it means that the sensor nodes on the communication link have large amounts of data to transmit to the cluster-head nodes. If these nodes are far away from the cluster head node, it needs a large number of intermediate nodes forwarding data, which leads to unnecessary energy cost of the intermediate nodes, and critical nodes located around the cluster-head nodes will have to bear the pressure of communication more, which leads to the excessive consumption of energy.

In order to solve these problems, the distance between the nodes of these high data transmission rates and their cluster-head nodes needs to be shortened. A simple and feasible method is specifying a nearest cluster-head node which is specially responsible for data transmission of nodes in this area by the base station node, the process of building cluster structure by cluster-head node is the same as that of the initial process of cluster. Only the nodes in this area retain the information of original cluster-head nodes. When the temporary cluster structure is cancelled, these nodes can use these information to establish links with the original cluster head nodes.

The adjustment of the local cluster structure can effectively reduce the data transmission pressure in the above area in a timely and effective way, thereby avoiding unnecessary overhead and uneven use of energy. When the communication link in this area has passed the peak period of the data transmission, at this time the communication pressure of the sensor nodes in the region will be much less. Before the specified cluster head node will be sleeping by the base station node, the sensor nodes in the cluster will re-select the original cluster head node as its cluster head node.

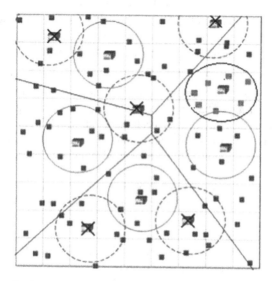

Fig. 7. The result of the adjustment of the local cluster structure (Color figure online)

Figure 7 is the clustering structure of sensor network obtained after second kind of cluster transformation. The red square is used to identify the sensor nodes with high data transmission rate. These nodes are located in the cluster structure represented by the black ellipse. This temporary cluster structure effectively reduces the data communication pressure in the region, thus solving the problem of the imbalance of energy consumption.

3.3 Routing Protocols of Intra-cluster and Inter-cluster

Here we discuss the routing scheme inside a cluster. Each L-sensor sends data packets to its cluster head. Since the location of the cluster head is known from the Hello message, a greedy geographic routing protocol can be used for intracluster routing. A L-sensor sends the data packet to the neighbor that has the shortest distance to the cluster head, and the next node performs the similar thing, until the data packet reaches the cluster head. Since nodes within a cluster are not far away from the cluster head, the greedy geographic routing should be able to route data packets to cluster head with high probability.

Cluster heads know the location of the base station node, and communicate with the base station node via multi-hop transmissions over other cluster heads. If enough number of H-sensors are uniformly and randomly deployed in the network, then with high probability a cluster head can directly communicate with a neighbor cluster head. After cluster formation in the network, each cluster head sends its location information to the base station node. Then the base station node broadcasts the locations of all cluster heads to each cluster head. When a cluster head wants to send data packets to the base station node, it draws a straight line L between itself and the base station node. Line L intersects with several cells, and these cells are denoted as C0, C1, ..., Ck, which are referred to as relay cells. The packet is forwarded from the source cluster head to the sink via the cluster heads in the relay cells. The Inter-Cluster routing scheme is presented in the following. The cluster head initiating the transmission is referred to as source node S.

(1) Based on the location of source cluster-head node S and base station node, the source node determines the relay cells C0, C1, ..., Ck, starting from the cell with node S. S records the relay cells in a cell_list field, which is stored in the header of the packet. The header contains the following fields: session_id, source_id, sink_id and cell_list. session_id plus source_id uniquely determines a data transmission session.

(2) First the data packet is sent from source node S to the cluster head H1 in cell C1. H1 gets the next hop relay cell based on the header information of the packet, where the next hop relay cell is C2. The packet which includes a next_cell field is broadcast to neighbor cluster heads. The neighbor node receives the broadcast packet and compares the next hop relay cell to its own cell. If it matches, it sends the response message to the broadcast node, letting the broadcast node know that it is the cluster head node of next relay cell.

(3) In each of the following forwarding processes, the following steps are carried out in turn. In order to ensure the reliability of each forwarding, every forwarding cluster head node should be responsible for confirming that its next hop forwarding cluster head node can successfully receive packet packets. This security mechanism needs to be implemented by every transmission node, and it needs to monitor whether the packets arrive at the next node in a certain time after the transmission. Of course, if the acknowledgement mechanism on the link is supported by the MAC layer protocol, for example, 802.11 has this function. The security mechanism mentioned above is not necessary. Because, under the MAC layer protocol, every packet that needs to be forwarded is saved in the buffer until the acknowledgement of the receiver is received, so as to prevent the failure of data packet transmission. This acknowledgement mechanism can reduce the impact of channel error.

(4) If a cluster head Hi does not get any acknowledgement within a time period, Hi will re-transmit the data packet to the next hop relay node once. And if the retransmission fails, Hi will find a backup path.

(5) A backup path is set up as follows. The current cluster head draws a straight line between itself and the base station node, and the line intersects with several cells $C_1', C_2', \ldots, C_{k-1}', C_k$. If the next cell is the cell with the failed cluster head, the cluster head will use a detoured path to avoid the cell. Otherwise, the sequence of new cells $C_1', C_2', \ldots, C_{k-1}', C_k$ will be the new relay cells. And the data packet is forwarded to the base station via the new relay cells.

An example of inter-cluster routing is shown in Fig. 8, where cluster head in cell C0 wants to send data packets to the base station, which is the square in the top-right corner. A straight line from the source cluster head to the base station is used to determine the original relay cells: C_o, C_1, C_2, C_3. If the cluster head in cell C2 is not available, the cluster head in cell C1 will use a backup path C_2', C_3 to connect the base station.

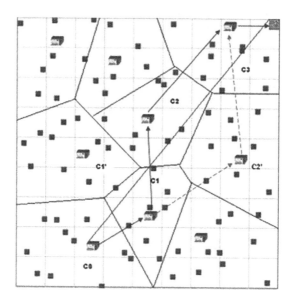

Fig. 8. An example of inter-cluster routing

4   Performance Evaluation of Protocol

We evaluate the performance of the chessboard clustering routing protocol through experiments, and compare chessboard clustering with two other clustering-based routing schemes: LEACH and LRS. LRS is a chain-based 3-level hierarchical protocol proposed. In this protocol, sensor nodes are initially grouped into clusters based on their distances from the base station. A chain is formed among the sensor nodes in a cluster at the lowest level of the hierarchy. Gathered data, moves from node to node, gets aggregated, and reaches a designated leader in the chain. At the next level of the hierarchy, the leaders from the previous level are clustered into one or more chains, and the data is collected and aggregated in each chain in a similar manner.

In the same simulation environment, the performance of the three protocols are compared, the default simulation testbed has 1 base station,1000 L-sensors and 40 H-sensors randomly, uniformly distributed in a 300 m × 300 m area. The transmission range of a H-sensor and a L-sensor is 80 m and 20 m respectively. Both H-sensors and L-sensors hava a fixed amount of energy supply-10 J and 2 J respectively.

4.1 Sensor Network Lifetime

First we compare the network lifetime for different sensor node density. The network lifetime here is defined as the time that no sensor can send packet to the base station. For the fixed 300 m x 300 m routing area, the number of L-sensors in chessboard clustering varies from 500 to 2000 with an increment of 500, while the number of H-sensors remains 40 for all cases. The numbers of L-sensors in LEACH and LRS are always 1.5 times the number of L-sensors in chessboard clustering, varying from 750 to 3000 with an increment of 750. The network lifetimes under the three routing protocols are plotted in Fig. 9, where the x-axis represents the number of L-sensors in chessboard clustering.

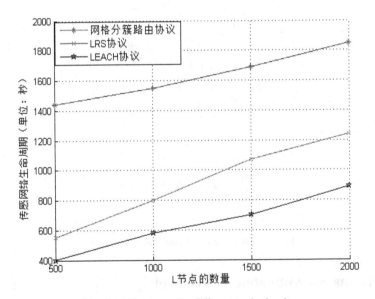

Fig. 9. Lifetime under different node density

As we can see, the network lifetimes under all the routing protocols increase as sensor density increases. With higher node density, more sensors are available to forward packet to the base station, and hence the network lifetime increases. Figure 9 also shows that chessboard clustering has much longer lifetime than both LRS and LEACH. In LRS and LEACH, L-sensors serve as cluster heads in turn to balance node energy consumption and to ensure the availability of cluster heads. However, since L-sensor has limited energy supply, the cluster heads need to re-elected periodically.

Even if each L-sensor only serves as cluster head once, there will be 2000 elections in a 2000-node network.

Each cluster head election introduces large overhead in the network and drains lots of energy from nearby sensor nodes. Large number of cluster head elections cause sensor nodes to die out quickly. Thus, the network lifetimes in LRS and LEACH are much shorter than CC. In CC, the chessboard clustering scheme balances the energy consumption among different L-sensors very well, avoid causing some nodes being out of energy too soon. In addition, only the more powerful H-sensors serve as cluster heads in chessboard clustering, and there is only one election for each H-node, which means there are only 40 elections in total. Thus, in chessboard clustering the overhead from cluster head election is very small. Because of the above two reasons, chessboard clustering prolongs network lifetime.

4.2   Total Energy Consumption

H-sensors have more initial energy than L-sensors, also H-sensors consume more energy than L-sensors for transmitting or receiving data. To fully understand the energy consumption in chessboard clustering, we measure the total energy consumption in the network, including energy spent by both H-sensors and L-sensors. In the experiments, there are 1000 L-sensors in chessboard clustering, and 1500 L-sensors in LRS and LEACH. All the measures are taken before 500 s simulation time, during which the network is connected for all the three routing protocols. The results are shown in Fig. 10. As we can see, the total energy consumption in LRS and LEACH are close to each other, and they are much larger than the total energy consumption in chessboard clustering. In LRS and LEACH, the large number of L-sensors communicate with each

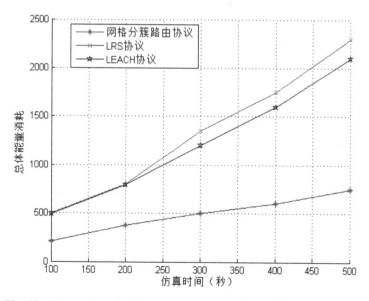

Fig. 10. Comparison of the total energy consumption of the three protocols

other and cause interferences and consume lots of energy, also the frequent re-clustering consumes significant amount of energy. So LRS and LEACH consume more total energy than chessboard clustering.

4.3   Remaining Energy of Node

Figure 11 reports the distribution of the remaining node energy when the sensor net-work became unavailable. The x-axis is the remaining energy in terms of the per-centage of initial L-sensor energy. We can see that most nodes in chessboard clustering have remaining energy below 20%, while in LRS most nodes have remaining energy between 20% and 50%, and in LEACH most nodes have 30% to 70% energy left. Figure 11 shows that chessboard clustering balances the energy consumption among nodes better than both LRS and LEACH, and LRS performs better than LEACH. In typical sensor networks, sensors send packets to the base station via multi-hop com-munications. The failure of any node in the path will cause the route unavailable. If the node energy drain is not balanced well, then some nodes will die too soon and may cause the network disconnected and become unavailable. Besides minimizing the total energy consumption in the network, balancing node energy consumption is also very important for maximizing sensor network lifetime.

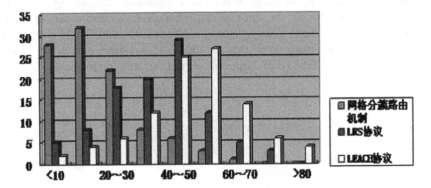

Fig. 11. The distribution of remaining node energy

5   Conclusions

In this chapter, based on the existing chessboard clustering routing protocol, we pro-pose an energy-efficient grid clustering routing protocol, which aims to extend the network lifecycle by balancing the energy consumption of nodes. Because there are a few high performance H-sensors in the heterogeneous sensor network, the energy efficiency of the routing protocol is improved by this isomerism. Simulation experi-ments show that the grid clustering protocol greatly improves the lifecycle of the network. Compared with LEACH and LRS, it has better performance.

References

1. Liu, D., Ning, P.: Establishing pairwise keys in distributed sensor networks. In: proceedings of the 10th ACM Conference on Computer and Communication Security, pp. 52–61 (2003)
2. Jolly, G., Kuscu, M.C., Kokate P., et al.: A low-energy key management protocol for wireless sensor networks. In: Proceedings of the 8th IEEE Symposium on Computer and Communications, pp. 335–340 (2003)
3. Eltoweissy, M., Younis, M., Ghumman, K.: Lightweight Key Management for Wireless Sensor Networks. In: IEEE International Conference on Performance Computing and Communications, pp. 813–818 (2004)
4. Li, J.H., Levy, R., Yu, M.: A scalable key management and clustering scheme for ad hoc networks. In: INFOSCALE 2006, pp. 1–10 (2006)
5. Cheng, B., Sungha, D.: Reduce radio energy consumption of key management protocol forwireless sensor networks. In: ISLPED 2004, Newport Beach, California, US. ACM Press (2004)
6. Benenson, Z., et al.: Realizing robust user anthentication in sensor networks. In: Workshop on Real-World Wireless Sensor Networks, Stockholm, pp. 135–142 (2005)
7. Wang, H., et al.: Elliptic curve cryptography-based access control in sensor networks. Int. J. Secure. Network. **1**(3), 127–137 (2006)
8. Li, X., Lin, Y., Yang, S., Yi, Y., Yu, J., Lu, X.: A key distribution scheme based on public key cryptography for sensor networks. In: Wang, Y., Cheung, Y.-M., Liu, H. (eds.) CIS 2006. LNCS (LNAI), vol. 4456, pp. 725–732. Springer, Heidelberg (2007). https://doi.org/10.1007/978-3-540-74377-4_75
9. Wander, A., Gura, N., Eberle, H., Gupta, V., Chang, S.: Energy analysis for public key cryptography for wireless sensor networks. In: Proceedings of the IEEE PERCOM 2005, pp. 324-328 (2005)
10. Joux, A.: An one round protocol for tripartite Die-Hellman. In: Proceedings of the ANTS4. LNCS, vol. 1838, pp. 385–394 (2000)
11. Zhang, Y., Liu, W., Lou, W., Fang, Y.: Securing sensor networks with location based keys. In: IEEEWCNC05, pp. 1909–1914 (2005)
12. Syed, M.K.U.R.R., Lee, H., Lee, S., et al.: MUQAMI+: a scalable and locally distributed key management scheme for clustered sensor network. Ann. Telecommun. **35**(2), 101–116 (2010)
13. Galbraith, S.D., Harrison, K., Soldera, D.: Implementing the tate pairing. In: Fieker, C., Kohel, D.R. (eds.) ANTS 2002. LNCS, vol. 2369, pp. 324–337. Springer, Heidelberg (2002). https://doi.org/10.1007/3-540-45455-1_26
14. Yarvis, M., Kushalnagar, N., Singh, H., et al.: Exploiting heterogeneity in sensor networks. In: Proceedings of the IEEE INFOCOM 2005, Miami, FL, March 2005
15. Savvides, A., Han, C., Strivastava, M.: Dynamic fine-grained localization in ad-hoc network of sensors. In: Proceedings of the ACM MOBICOM 2001, pp. 166–179 (2001)

GeoBLR: Dynamic IP Geolocation Method Based on Bayesian Linear Regression

Fei Du[1,2], Xiuguo Bao[3], Yongzheng Zhang[1,2(✉)], and Yu Wang[3]

[1] Institute of Information Engineering, Chinese Academy of Sciences,
Beijing, China
{dufei,zhangyongzheng}@iie.ac.cn
[2] School of Cyber Security, University of Chinese Academy of Sciences,
Beijing, China
[3] National Internet Emergency Center, CNCERT/CC,
Beijing, China

Abstract. The geographical location of dynamic IP addresses is important for network security applications. The delay-based or topology-based measurement method and the association-analysis-based method improve the median estimation accuracy, but are still affected by the limited precision (about 799 m) and the longer response time (tens of seconds), which cannot meet the location-aware applications of high-precise and real-time location requirements, especially the position of dynamic IP addresses. In this paper, we propose a novel approach for dynamic IP geolocation based on Bayesian Linear Regression, namely, *GeoBLR*, which exploits geolocation resources fundamentally different from existing ones. We exploit the location data that users would like to share in location sharing services for accurate and real-time geolocation of dynamic IP addresses. Experimental results show that compared to existing geolocation techniques, *GeoBLR* achieves (1) a median estimation error of 239 m and (2) a mean response time of 270 ms, which are valuable for accurate location-aware network security applications.

Keywords: Network security · Dynamic IP geolocation ·
Machine learning · Bayesian Linear Regression

1 Introduction

The ability to accurately identify the geographic of location of an internet IP address has significant implications for network security analysts (e.g. credit card fraud protection), security event forensics and law enforcement [13]. A striking amount of malicious activities have been reported from dynamic IP addresses space, such as spamming, botnets, etc. [18]. Consequently, The dynamic IP geolocation has become increasingly important in finding and preventing fast growing

H. Gao et al. (Eds.): CollaborateCom 2018, LNICST 268, pp. 310–328, 2019.
https://doi.org/10.1007/978-3-030-12981-1_22

network attacks, which can help law enforcement organizations and government agencies to identify the location information or network attack resources of criminals.

The dynamic IP geolocation is a challenging task because of insufficient labelled training data. The variability of the dynamic IP addresses and the excessive size of the dynamic IP addresses network make the task even harder. It is far more challenging to determine an dynamic IP address with fine-grained granularity without information from the Internet Service Provider (ISP).

In this paper, we study the geographic location of dynamic IP addresses, especially, focus on the dynamic behavior of IP addresses assignment [32]. There are two-fold reasons for geolocation inaccuracy. First, the adjustment period of dynamic IP addresses is *ephemeral*, assignment through DHCP protocol. As a result, the same place have observed different IP addresses, even if the observation interval is continuous within a span of 10 to 120 min. Second, the dynamic IP addresses for the same place are *itinerant*—similar IP addresses will be randomly assigned to the same place in consecutive period of time. In other words, dynamic IP addresses do not embed fine-grained information on the device with used one. Consequently, the positioning of dynamic IP addresses and the positioning of devices are intrinsically two different problem.

In existing work towards IP geolocation, Database-driven approaches typically build a database whose geolocation information come from the Whois database [1], DNS [27], user contributions [4], etc. These databases are compiled by combining data from different sources. Database-driven geolocations [1,2,4–7,27] are fast response time. Whereas, such IP/location mappings are very coarse-grained and usually achieve a city-level precision in most cases. Delay measurement based geolocation approaches such as GeoGet [21], Octant [31] and SLG [30], they have (1) high deployment cost, and (2) long response time, which cannot meet the real-time requirement of dynamic IP addresses. Statistical and data mining approaches [9,14,33] are implemented by applying kernel density estimation to delay measurement and using maximum likelihood estimation to distance from landmark. The main purpose of the machine learning approach (GeoCop [29]) is to improve the accuracy and robustness of existing geolocation methods. HG-SOM [17] is an advanced approach for an accurate and self-optimization model for IP geolocation, including identification of optimized Landmark positions. Moreover, the selection of correlated data and the estimated target location requires a sophisticated strategy to identify the correct position. These approaches also cannot meet the demand of fine-grained granularity.

Briefly, our approach, referred to as *GeoBLR*, is based on the fact that most of the IP addresses allocated to the home broadband access adopt dynamic IP address access technology. In this scenario, user end-hosts (such as mobile-phones, pads, laptops, etc.) access the network using wireless technology. The geographical location provided by the APP applications is used as a measurement landmark. Since the distance between the user's mobile phone and the IP access point (AP) is within the coverage of the wireless network, the geographical location within the range may be used as the geographic location of the access IP in the current time period.

The method includes the three phases: First, based on the observation that users are willing to share in location-sharing services by their Global Positioning System (GPS) units, we cluster the location fingerprint at various time periods respectively. Then estimate the candidate landmarks of each IP address. After this phase, we obtain the mappings from each individual IP address to its location candidates. Secondly, we use Bayesian Inference to calculate the maximum posterior probability of candidate multiple landmarks of dynamic IP address, select the geographical location with the highest probability, according to the semantics of the scenario. Next, We use Bayesian Linear Regression to optimization parameters, and correct the trusted landmark database. Finally, based on the mappings obtained from the first two phase, we design an classification model to estimate the mappings from dynamic IP addresses to geographical locations.

Our contribution in this paper is three-fold:

- We propose a novel approach to locate dynamic IP addresses that we call *GeoBLR*. The proposed approach has strong adaptive ability to data, can repeatedly use experimental data, and effectively prevent over-fitting, which can meet the demand of high-precision and real-time positioning.
- We use the largest convex polygon to cover the location area as the candidate set of landmarks, instead of adopting the center point of the *k-means* clustering algorithm, which is consistent with the real IP access scenario.
- We give a formal definition of dynamic IP address geolocation, adding the time attribute to the location description, which is more closer to the real network environment.

The paper is organized as follows: in Sect. 2 discusses related work. Section 3 gives definitions and relevant problem statements. Section 4 explains our algorithm in detail, including mathematical proof, feature extraction and analysis process. Section 5 describes the dataset and presents experimental results and comparative analysis. Finally, draws the conclusions in Sect. 6.

2   Related Work

To evaluate performance of the *GeoBLR* algorithm, we compare against current relevant geolocation approaches.

Database-Driven Geolocation. These approaches try to establish a database with large number of IP/location mapping records, whose geolocation resources come from the Whois database [1], DNS [27], postal addresses from the website [26], user registration records [28]. Such as MaxMind [6], IP2Location [5], Neustar [7] and Digital Element [2]. We will compare geolocation accuracy with both the Maxmind database [6] or the IP2Location database [5]. Both of these databases are commercially available IP lookup packages. Unfortunately, these databases are hard to maintain and keep up-to-date, especially, since it cannot take into consideration dynamic IP assignment.

Data-Mining-Based Geolocation. These approaches try to discover the relationship between location and IP addresses from location-share applications, websites, query-logs and so on. One of the latest data mining-based geolocation technique—Checkin-Geo [24]—can achieve the median error distance to 799 m, which is very prominent. It first obtain that relationship data of "User ↔ Home/office Locations" from the application of some mobile phone application, then obtain the data of "User ↔ Home/office IPs" from the corresponding PC application program, and finally obtains the rule of user activity by machine learning method, and establishes the relationship of "IP ↔ Location" to achieve the target IP location. However, The data resources on which such technologies depend are usually only abundant in a few metropolitan areas and the public cannot access these resources due to privacy concerns. Besides, data mining-based technologies such as [16] are difficult to cover most IP addresses, so they are mapping IP address blocks to the one landmark in order to increase the coverage of IP addresses, which may result in larger positioning errors according to [15]. As compared with previous data-mining-based technologies, Structon [16] uses a new approach to obtaining IP geolocation from the website. In particular, it builds a Geo-IP lookup table and extracts location information using regular expression technique from each page from a large crawler crawling database. Since Structon does not combine delay-based measurement algorithm with the landmarks discovered, it can achieve city-level coarser geolocation granularity. Dan et al. [12] use query-logs-based technology to improve the accuracy of IP address location. It is a supplement and enhancement to the existing IP geolocation database. The main challenges by this technology are: (1) extracting explicit location information in the logs, (2) the query logs are a large scale and belong to CPU-intensive calculation, (3) for a given IP range, multiple candidate landmarks are extracted from the query logs, (4) the metropolises with large influence need to be modified to the surrounding small towns.

Statistical-Based Geolocation. Recent relevant approaches (e.g., [9,14,33]) that find the maximum likelihood probability of geographic location with respect to observed delay-distance measurements. While the construction of the probability distributions varies, e.g., nonparametric kernel density estimators in [14,33], parametric log-normal distributions in [9]) etc., All three methods assume conditional independence between measurements, in order to efficiently calculate the geographic location using the maximum likelihood probability. Spotter [33] leverage a probabilistic approach based on a statistical analysis of the relationship between network delay and geographic distance. [14] regards IP geolocation as classification problem based on machine learning, which makes it possible to incorporate other location information into the framework.

Wireless-Based Geolocation. These wireless-based approaches use GPS, WiFi, cellular and other wireless positioning systems as the source. The GPS-based geolocation method is widely used in mobile phones, computers and various embedded systems. The cellular and WiFi-based location algorithms include Google's My Location [3] and Skyhook [8]. In particular, cellular-based geolocation provides users an estimated location through triangulation, while

Wi-Fi-based geolocation uses Wi-Fi access point as targeted location. These methods require the user's permission to share their locations.

Crowdsourcing-Based Geolocation. These Crowdsourcing-based approaches collect and process data based on crowd-sourcing principles. Ciavarrini et al. [10,11] proposed a method based on the crowd-sourcing principle to use the GPS positioning module in the mobile phone as a landmark. (1) Using the mobile phone as a landmark, its built-in GPS unit has a self-positioning function, (2) Considering the wireless connection in the delay-distance model, (3) Participating in the crowdsourced device through the Portolan platform, not only from the research institutions, it also comes to the real application environment. They also discussed the effects of four different delay-distance models on IP address location errors. Lee et al. [20] propose an IP address database construction method based on location-labelled Internet broadband performance measurement tool, and provide an IP geolocation database based on South Korea's 7-year Internet broadband performance data, which shows fine-grained granularity but only limited to South Korea.

All of the previously mentioned approaches rely on delay-based or topology-based measurements [23,34,35] and a lot of data analysis [22,25], and most methodologies do not take into account the dynamic IP addresses. In such scenarios, the measurement process is neither stable nor reliable. Therefore, this paper presents a novel approach, *GeoBLR*, which uses the location information shared by the user to solve the physical location of dynamic IP addresses and achieves the purpose of (1) a negligible response time and (2) a smaller than existing approaches of median estimation error.

3   Problem Statement

In this section, we present the definitions of relevant concepts and the formalized description of the problem.

Definition 1. *(Location Fingerprint). It is location information containing the spatial location description generated by the mobile device using GPS, cellular and Wi-Fi. A typical location fingerprint ω is a tuple (t, lat, lng, co, c, as), where t is time, lat is latitude, lng is longitude, co is the coordinate system where the latitude and longitude is located, c is the city where it is located, and as is the acquisition method of the location fingerprint (GPS, cellular, Wi-Fi) etc.*

Definition 2. *(Active dynamic IP addresses set $\mathcal{P}$). We define all the dynamic IP address of the broadband access user, does not include the private IP address dynamically allocated within the Network Address Translation (NAT) and the IP address used for the mobile phone.*

Definition 3. *(The landmark set $\mathcal{L}$). It is a geographical location set. A typical geographic location l is a tuple (lat, lng, co, des, r, c, p, n), where lat is latitude, lng is longitude, and co is the coordinate system in which the latitude and longitude is located, des is the semantic description of the location (may be the specific* *building name, or the location description relative to the POI point, or the unit name), r is the community (street level), and c is the city. p is the province or state in which it is located, and n is the country in which it is located.*

Definition 4. *(The coverage area of the largest convex polygon ζ). It is the polygon area covered by the set C of the observed location fingerprints ω_t in a corresponding coordinate system within a period of time t. Its area should cover the C.*

The area (ζ) is a convex polygon, not a circular area formed by the largest diameter in the set C. The convex polygon is more computationally efficient than the area covered by the circular area, and the acquisition of the covered building is more representative than the circular area.

Problem. The geolocation of dynamic IP addresses, given the IP address in the active dynamic IP addresses set $\mathcal{P}$, finds that there may be multiple different dynamic IP addresses in the corresponding geographical location ℓ_t ($\ell_t \in \zeta$) within the time t, and the same IP address may also correspond to different ℓ_t in different time periods t.

4   Bayesian Linear Regression-Based Location

Compared with active measurement, passive data acquisition can effectively reduce the cost of data acquisition, it also introduces some new problems, such as (1) the data "jitter" caused by the hybrid WLAN access and the heterogeneity of the terminal mobile phone. The offset of location fingerprint caused by different operations system, application and driver; (2) data collection depends on the active participation of users, there is regional imbalance, some areas are data intensive, and some areas are sparse. These factors objectively cause measurement errors in IP geolocation. In addition, the configuration strategies of different ISPs, the heterogeneity and diversity of broadband access networks also cause the "last half mile" problem.

In problems where we have limited data or have some prior knowledge that we want to use in our model, the Bayesian Linear Regression approach can both incorporate prior information and show our uncertainty. Bayesian Linear Regression reflects the Bayesian framework: we form an initial estimate and improve our estimate. And as we gather more evidence, our model becomes less wrong. Bayesian reasoning is a natural extension of our intuition.

Since the maximum likelihood estimation always makes the model too complicated to produce a phenomenon of over-fitting, Bayesian Linear Regression can not only solve the over-fitting problem in the maximum likelihood estimation, but also it could make better use of the data sample fully. The training model can effectively and accurately determine the complexity of the model.

Base on the above analysis, the processing flow of our algorithm is shown in Fig. 1. This process can be divided into three phases, which are preprocessing phase, calibration phase and geolocation phase. The complete *GeoBLR* geolocation methodology is presented in Algorithm 1.

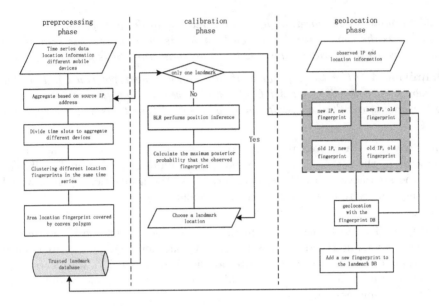

Fig. 1. Flow chart of the proposed *GeoBLR* geolocation process.

Algorithm 1. *GeoBLR* Geolocation Algorithm

Input:
    A set of N record information generated by m mobile devices,
    $\mathcal{T} = \left\{ T_1^{D_1}, T_2^{D_2}, ..., T_m^{D_m} \right\}$, where $T_i^{D_i} = \{s_1, s_2, ..., s_{D_i}\}$

Output:
    The mapping between dynamic IP addresses and landmarks, $\mathcal{P} \longleftrightarrow \mathcal{L}$

1: cluster location fingerprints C from set $\mathcal{T}$, then deriving the convex polygon region
    ζ from C;
2: construct a landmark dataset $\mathcal{L}$ from the convex polygon area ζ,
    $\mathcal{L} = \{\ell_1, \ell_2, ..., \ell_k, ...\ell_n\}$, $(n \geq 3)$;
3: **for** each IP $\in \mathcal{P}$ **do**
4:     train parameters $[\beta_1, \beta_0]$ using Bayesian linear regression on the data set $\mathcal{T}$ to
    maximize the probability of Eq. (8);
5:     obtain the maximum value of posterior probability using Eq. (2),
    associate IP$\leftrightarrow \ell$;
6: **end for**
7: given an IP and observed location fingerprint ω;
8: **if** IP $\in \mathcal{P}$ and $\omega \in \mathcal{L}$ **then**
9:     **return** $\ell \longleftarrow \omega$;
10: **end if**
11: **if** (IP $\in \mathcal{P}$ and $\omega \notin \mathcal{L}$) or (IP $\notin \mathcal{P}$ and $\omega \in \mathcal{L}$) **then**
12:     update the $\mathcal{L}$ and $\mathcal{P}$;
13:     **return** $\ell \longleftarrow \omega$;
14: **end if**
15: **if** IP $\notin \mathcal{P}$ and $\omega \notin \mathcal{L}$ **then**
16:     enter other **procedure** to process;
17: **end if**

4.1   Preprocessing Phase

In the preprocessing phase, data is aggregated by source IP addresses. In the same IP address, the data is divided into multiple time series according to time t. In the same time period, multiple identical mobile device information will appear, and the device information needs to be similarly measurement. We use the bottom-up hierarchical clustering model (DBSCAN algorithm) to compare the device IDs of N records, and the clusters that successfully clustered will enter the next stage. Eventually, N records will be divided into m different devices.

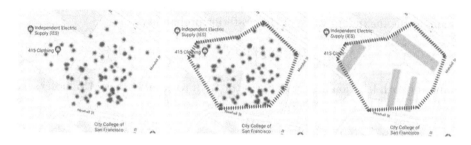

Fig. 2. Mapping between location fingerprints and physical location landmarks.

For multiple records of the same device, the set $T_i = \{s_1, s_2, ..., s_D\}$ is the D records generated by the mobile device i within the time t. We perform density-based clustering on the location fingerprints of these D records, and select a representative position record s_j of the cluster center as the position fingerprint of all the records of the D records. In this step, we mainly remove the abnormal positioning fingerprint, which improves the validity of the data.

Time series data generated for m different mobile devices in time t, i.e., $\left\{T_1^{D_1}, T_2^{D_2}, ..., T_i^{D_i}, ..., T_m^{D_m}\right\}$, extract its location fingerprint set C and draw its largest convex polygon area in the map ζ, the area of the convex polygon should cover all locations of the fingerprint point set ($\zeta \supseteq C$). As shown in Fig. 2.

A collection of location landmarks contained in a convex polygon region $\mathcal{L}$, $\mathcal{L} = \{\ell_1, \ell_2, ..., \ell_k, ...\ell_n\}$, n is the number of landmarks ($n \geq 3$). In this way, the location fingerprint in the collected data is mapped to the physical location, and a trusted database of location fingerprints will be constructed.

4.2   Calibration Phase

In the correction phase, the transformed position fingerprint and source IP are mainly used as input of the positioning algorithm to process the location inference. Considering high-precision and real-time, here we use Bayesian linear regression algorithm, which is very suitable for passively acquired data for its simplicity and high accuracy.

$$P\left(\ell_r|\omega\right) = \frac{P\left(\omega|\ell_r\right) P\left(\ell_r\right)}{\sum_{i=1}^{n} P\left(\omega|\ell_i\right) P\left(\ell_i\right)} \tag{1}$$

$P\left(\ell_r|\omega\right)$ indicates the posterior probability of the occurrence of observing fingerprint, then $P\left(\ell_r\right)$ indicates the prior possibility of a landmark. In the calibration phase, the probability of landmark i and landmark j is not the same $(i \neq j)$ according to the specific context semantics. We will assign a plurality of landmarks in the convex polygon region according to the semantics: $P\left(\ell_r\right) = \rho_r \frac{m}{n}$, which $\sum_{r \in n} \rho_r = 1$, ρ is the weight of the semantics. m is the number of occurrences of the random position ℓ_r in n observations. the value of $\sum_{i=1}^{n} P\left(\omega|\ell_i\right) P\left(\ell_i\right))$ is usually 1, Therefore the estimated location ℓ_k is the one obtaining the maximum value of the posterior probability.

$$\ell_k = \arg\max_r P\left(\omega|\ell_r\right) \tag{2}$$

Supposing each location fingerprint $\omega = (o_1, o_2, ..., o_m)$ and it has M values, then the $P\left(\omega|\ell_r\right) = \prod_{i \in M} P_{o_i|\mathcal{L}}\left(o_i|\ell_r\right)$, bring it into Eq. (2).

$$
\begin{aligned}
\ell_k &= \arg\max_r P\left(\omega|\ell_r\right) \\
&= \arg\max_r \prod_{i \in M} P_{o_i|\mathcal{L}}\left(o_i|\ell_r\right) \propto \ln\left(\arg\max_r \prod_{i \in M} P_{o_i|\mathcal{L}}\left(o_i|\ell_r\right)\right) \\
&= \arg\max_r \ln\left(\prod_{i \in M} P_{o_i|\mathcal{L}}\left(o_i|\ell_r\right)\right) \\
&= \arg\max_r \sum_{i \in M} \ln P_{o_i|\mathcal{L}}\left(o_i|\ell_r\right)
\end{aligned}
\tag{3}
$$

Assuming that the random variable at position ℓ is Y, the position fingerprint ω that can be observed is X, and the observed position fingerprint is a relatively small-scale discrete point. We assume that Y is obtained from a normal distribution and construct a Bayesian Linear Regression model is as follows:

$$y_i = \beta_1 x_i + \beta_0 + \epsilon_i \tag{4}$$

y is the response variable, β's are the weights (known as the model parameters), x's are the values of the predictor variables, and ϵ is an error term representing random sampling noise or the effect of variables not included in the model, $\epsilon \sim N\left(\mu = 0, \sigma^2\right)$.

The likelihood estimate of $ln P_{o_i | \mathcal{L}} \left(o_i | \ell_r \right)$ is:

$$
\begin{aligned}
P\left(Y | X, \beta_1, \beta_0\right) &= \prod_{i=1}^{N} P\left(\beta_1 x_i + \beta_0 + \epsilon_i | x_i, \beta_1, \beta_0\right) \\
&= \prod_{i=1}^{N} P\left(\epsilon_i | x_i, \beta_1, \beta_0\right) = \prod_{i=1}^{N} P\left(\epsilon_i\right) \\
&= \prod_{i=1}^{N} \frac{1}{\sqrt{2\pi}\sigma} e^{\frac{(\epsilon_i - 0)^2}{2\sigma^2}} \\
&= \prod_{i=1}^{N} \frac{1}{\sqrt{2\pi}\sigma} e^{\frac{(y_i - (\beta_1 x_i + \beta_0))^2}{2\sigma^2}} \\
&= \prod_{i=1}^{N} f_o\left(x_i | \beta_1 x_i + \beta_0, \sigma^2\right)
\end{aligned}
\tag{5}
$$

Where $f_o()$ is a function as:

$$
f_o\left(x_i | \beta_1 x_i + \beta_0, \sigma^2\right) = \frac{1}{\sqrt{2\pi}\sigma} e^{\frac{(y_i - (\beta_1 x_i + \beta_0))^2}{2\sigma^2}}
\tag{6}
$$

Here, the likelihood equation can be simplified to:

$$
P\left(Y | X, \beta_1, \beta_0\right) = \prod_{i=1}^{N} f_o\left(x_i | \beta_1 x_i + \beta_0, \sigma^2\right)
\tag{7}
$$

The parameters can be estimated from the sampled data, and the maximum likelihood estimate is:

$$
\begin{aligned}
\hat{L}\left(\beta_1, \beta_0\right) &= \underset{\beta_1, \beta_0}{\arg\max} \prod_{i=1}^{N} f_o\left(x_i | \beta_1 x_i + \beta_0, \sigma^2\right) \\
&\propto \underset{\beta_1, \beta_0}{\arg\max} \sum_{i=1}^{N} ln f_o\left(x_i | \beta_1 x_i + \beta_0, \sigma^2\right)
\end{aligned}
\tag{8}
$$

In a small dataset we might like to express our estimate as a **distribution** of possible values. This is where Bayesian Linear Regression comes in.

4.3 Geolocation Phase

In the geolocation phase, it is very important to be able to form a robust and credible landmark database in the first two phases. The characteristics of dynamic IP addresses are mainly two aspects: (1) the change period is random and irregular, the time when an IP resides in a certain landmark is not fixed; (2) there is a phenomenon of "itinerant", that is, an IP will be repeated at the same landmark position with a certain probability.

In the first two phases, the geolocation of dynamic IP addresses can be corrected for a certain time period t by collecting the time series characteristics of the data in combination with the prior knowledge of the dynamic IP address.

During IP address geolocation, the IP address records that appear within a period of time t are as follows:

(1) It is a new IP address, the location fingerprint is present, it may be the newly assigned IP of the device in the landmark. Then the geographic location of this IP address is the location of the landmark.
(2) It is a newly appearing IP address. If the location fingerprint is also newly observed, it may be a building that is not in the landmark database. In the pre-processing stage and the correction stage, the landmark corresponding to the location fingerprint is added to the trusted landmark database. Continue to observe the subsequent periods of $t+1$ and $t+2$, and if the IP address is not a dynamic IP address, enter the positioning processing of other related categories.
(3) It is a previously located IP address, and the location fingerprint has also appeared, the corresponding landmark is the geographical location of the current IP address.
(4) It is a previously located IP address, and the location fingerprint comes out newly, the dynamic IP address may be obtained by the device in the new landmark. We examine the location fingerprint associated with the IP address in the current time window t, perform the first two phases. Processing and adding the landmark to the landmark database, and the landmark is the geographic location of the current IP address.

5   Experiments

5.1   Data Sets

In order to evaluate our proposed approach, we employ two datasets with information from the Internet Service Provider (ISP), namely, GeoCN2018 and GeoCC2018. These two datasets were collected based on the principle of crowd-sourcing. In order to protect privacy and the legitimacy of research, the sensitive information of user has been processed.

As of 2018, mobile apps (which hides the real name of the app) have over 750 million users. Each user is actually associated with several unique devices, generally, which could be a smart-phone or tablet computer. In the study of this paper, we collected one-month HTTP usage data from May 11, 2018 to June 11, 2018. The volume of our data set is approximately 1.4 TB.

Our one-month dataset covers more than 0.23 million (230,374) IP addresses, The user location collected by Android apps includes two types: coarse-grained location and fine-grained location. The coarse-grained granularity gives the city information of the user, and the fine-grained granularity gives the latitude and longitude coordinates.

We divided 230,374 IP addresses into two data sets, GeoCN2018 in China, GeoCC2018 outside China, The GeoCN2018 dataset contains approximately 760G. The GeoCC2018 database is smaller, with 440G data.

In our one-month data, including *time, url, latitude* and *longitude, ac, Host, User-Agent, city, device ID,* etc. As shown in Table 1.

Table 1. Comparison datasets between GeoCN2018 and GeoCC2018.

Comparison	GeoCN2018	GeoCC2018
Time range	3 consecutive weeks	3 consecutive weeks
IP addresses numbers	6,500	4,000
Dynamic IP addresses numbers	3,000	2,000
Android devices numbers	18,400	10,030
City numbers	1,500	700
latitude & *longitude* numbers	1,302,300	890,345
Coordinate system type	WGS84/GCJ02/DB09	WGS84
Mobile apps numbers	10	6
AC type	2G/3G/LTE/Wi-Fi	3G/LTE/Wi-Fi
Labelled landmark numbers	806	713

Note: The latitude and longitude coordinates are generated by the app and are not the original GPS coordinates, after the user opens the location sharing, if the application accesses the network through Wi-Fi or a cellular (2G/3G/LTE), the background positioning module periodically feeds back the user's location information to the application server. Therefore, it is necessary to calculate the corresponding real physical position in combination with a specific coordinate system and app, namely, GPS "drift" phenomenon.

We have taken a series of steps to protect the privacy of the users involved in the dataset. First, all raw data collected for this study were kept in an ISP data server. Second, our data collection and analysis pipelines were completely managed by two ISP staff. Finally, the ISP staff have made the user identifiers anonymous. The dataset only includes the statistics for the users covered during our study.

5.2 Performance Criteria

– *Error Distance*: We use the error distance—the distance from the measured location to the actual location—to quantitatively evaluate the accuracy of the geolocation.

$$d_{error} \quad = \quad |d_{measurement} - d_{truth}|$$

In consideration of the actual situation, it is difficult to collect dynamic IP addresses with ground-truth locations. Compared with the existing IP geolocation techniques, a dataset with hundreds of IP addresses as sample is fully sufficient to evaluate their technical differences.

- *Response Time*: For dynamic IP geolocation, we use response time as an indicator of the performance of the algorithm. For instance, the response time of m dynamic IP addresses is $t_1, t_1, ..., t_m$, then the *mean* response time is defined as:

$$t_{RT} = \frac{1}{m}\sum_{i=1}^{m} t_i$$

Considering the variability of dynamic IP addresses, response time is an important factor affecting the accuracy of the geolocation algorithm. It usually takes hundreds of milliseconds to tens of seconds to locate a single IP address.

5.3   Implementation Details

In this section, we describe the implementation details. The *GeoBLR* algorithm have implemented in experimental tests. Figure 1 illustrates the algorithm procedure, which consists of four parts:

(1) Preprocessing engine. Implements our candidate landmarks selection strategy described in Definition 4. using the coverage area of the largest convex polygon to get a set of landmarks. Compared to the circular coverage area of the largest diameter, it has lower computational complexity.

(2) Calibration engine. The *GeoBLR* algorithm is deployed on the calibration engine. The aim of Bayesian Linear Regression is not to find the single "**best**" value of the model parameters, but rather to determine the posterior distribution for the model parameters. Here we can observe the two primary benefits of Bayesian Linear Regression: (1) If we have domain knowledge, or a guess for what the model parameters should be, we can include them in our model, unlike in the frequentist approach which assumes everything there is to know about the parameters comes from the data. If we don't have any estimates ahead of time, we can use non-informative priors for the parameters such as a normal distribution. (2) The result of performing Bayesian Linear Regression is a distribution of possible model parameters based on the data and the prior. This allows us to quantify our uncertainty about the model: if we have fewer data points, the posterior distribution will be more spread out.

(3) Landmark database. It stores the landmarks we use, including their IP addresses, location and status information. This database is constantly changing, which means that we need to track the status of the landmarks, and maintain the landmark database dynamically, clean up the landmarks as reported many errors, as well as adding new ℓ as landmarks (described in Definition 3).

(4) Geolocation engine. If a dynamic IP address is done with a fine-grained location, Calibration Engine will check the corresponding landmark and update it in Landmark database.

We also implement two state-of-the-art algorithm, namely, *uCheckin* and *GeoQL*. The *uCheckin* is based on the partial implementation of the Checkin-Geo [24] algorithm, which is mainly a complete-linkage hierarchical clustering method [19]. Due to the lack of the login logs from PCs, we can only implement the "checkin" from location-sharing. The *GeoQL* is based on the algorithmic idea in the paper [12], it is an optimization algorithm based on heuristic rules from the location information of the query logs. Corresponding to the coarse-grained location information in our dataset, we can improve them using *GeoQL*.

We compare *GeoBLR* with IP2Location (download the latest database from the webside), IP2Location is based on database-driven techniques and is also very popular IP geolocation database. Primarily, we compare *GeoBLR* with *uCheckin*. In addition, we also compare *GeoBLR* with *GeoQL*.

We split GeoCN2018 dataset into part-overlapping subsets of 1070, 895 and 743 dynamic IP addresses, for preprocessing, calibration and geolocation, respectively. Compared to the GeoCN2018 dataset, the GeoCN2018 dataset are reserved for preprocessing, calibration and geolocation, while each one sets consists of 600 dynamic IP addresses.

On the GeoCN2018 dataset and GeoCC2018 dataset, we evaluated the error distance distribution and response time of *GeoQL*, *uCheckin* and *GeoBLR*, respectively.

5.4 Results

A. Error Distance
Table 2 gives the *mean, median, max, std.* and *mode* error distance of targets in all the four algorithms. From the experimental results in Table 2, it can be concluded that *GeoBLR* and *uCheckin* have higher precision than *GeoQL* and IP2Location, *GeoBLR* has smaller standard deviation (*std.*) than *uCheckin*, and on the denser GeoCN2018 dataset, the stability of *GeoBLR* experimental results is more than that on the sparse GeoCN2018 dataset.

It is distinctly that IP2Location has the worst estimation precision. The *uCheckin* has better precision and the *GeoBLR* has achieved the best precision. We use the metric *median* error to further compare *uCheckin* and *GeoBLR*. Since the *mean* error can be influenced by abnormal or large errors from few IP addresses, the *median* error is widely used in geolocation systems. The *median* errors of IP2Location, *GeoQL*, *uCheckin* and *GeoBLR* are 13,783 m, 2,700 m, 819 m, and 239 m, respectively. This indicates that *GeoBLR* achieves a median estimation error with an order of magnitude smaller than *uCheckin*, *GeoQL* and IP2Location in most cases. Figure 3a demonstrates the cumulative probability of the error distance from each individual testing IP in the GeoCN2018 dataset. Figure 3b shows the cumulative probability of the error distance from each individual IP address in the GeoCC2018 dataset. It can be drawn from the

Table 2. The results of 4 algorithms on datasets GeoCN2018 and GeoCC2018.

GeoCN2018	GeoBLR	uCheckin	GeoQL	IP2Location
mean error distance	233.47	807.75	2,689.31	19,611.48
median error distance	232	808	2,690	19,688
max error distance	455	1,750	5,336	37,250
std error distance	80.47	282.71	884.55	6,566.98
mode error distance	230	871	1,789	15,105
GeoCC2018	GeoBLR	uCheckin	GeoQL	IP2Location
mean error distance	311.94	801.87	2,701.61	16,828.46
median error distance	297	802	2,726.5	16,788
max error distance	849	1592	5,113	28,716
std error distance	179.92	237.68	893.87	3,843.54
mode error distance	222	859	1,839	18,825

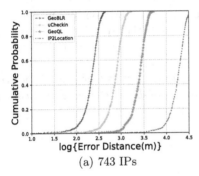 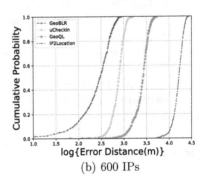

(a) 743 IPs   (b) 600 IPs

Fig. 3. The logarithm of the Error Distances for (a) The 743 IPs in GeoCN2018 Dataset and (b) The 600 IPs in GeoCC2018 Dataset.

comparison of the curves in Fig. 3 that the error range of IP2Location is large, for the dynamic IP address, its application is not significant because the granularity is too coarse. Compared with GeoCC2018 dataset, The GeoCN2018 dataset has a higher density and a more concentrated landmark set. The GeoCC2018 has a lower density but a wider distribution. Our approach is sensitive to the distribution and density of landmarks compared to other approaches (e.g. *uCheckin* and *GeoQL*).

On the GeoCN2018 dataset, the error distance histograms of the three comparison algorithms *GeoBLR*, *uCheckin*, and *GeoQL* are shown in Fig. 4. The error distance distributions of the three algorithms are approximately normal distribution. Its parameter values are similar to calculated values. The error distance of the algorithm *GeoBLR* is concentrated in the interval of 50–350 m, the algorithm *uCheckin* is concentrated between 250–1250 m, and the algorithm *GeoQL* is concentrated in the range of 900–4500 m. Experimental data shows that *GeoBLR* implements fine-grained positioning compared to *uCheckin* and *GeoQL*.

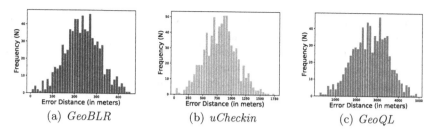

Fig. 4. The histogram of in GeoCN2018 of (a) *GeoBLR*, (b) *uCheckin*, (c) *GeoQL*.

B. Response Time

Obviously, *GeoQL* and IP2Location belong to the database-driven techniques whose IP/Location mappings are precomputed and does not need any delay. Consequently, the response time of *GeoQL* and IP2Location is negligible. On the contrary, our experiments show that *GeoBLR* has a *mean* response time of 309 ms. The major computational overhead for *GeoBLR* comes from the calibration phase, where the computational complexity is large. Our experiments show that the dynamic IP address changes from 1 min to 2 days, and in most cases is 120 min, depending on the specific strategy of the ISP. Therefore, although the response time of database-driven geolocation is negligible, but it is hard to maintain and keep up-to-date frequently, which is not applicable to dynamic IP geolocation. In the Fig. 5a, we observe the response time of 743 different dynamic IP addresses on four different algorithms. Considering that *GeoBLR* algorithm does not calculate all location fingerprints, therefore, the computational complexity is lower than *uCheckin*.

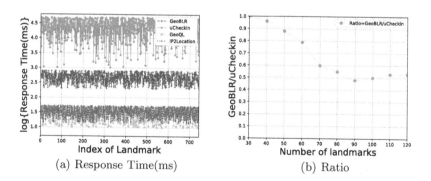

Fig. 5. (a) The logarithm of response time of *GeoBLR* in GeoCN2018 and (b) The ratio between the median error by *GeoBLR* and the one by *uCheckin*.

C. Comparison

We use *ratio* between the *median* error achieved by the *GeoBLR* method and the *median* error achieved by the *uCheckin* method to quantify the impact factors of landmark density. When the number of landmarks is small, the performance of the two algorithms tend to be similar. On the contrary, as the number of land-marks involved in the IP geolocation increases, the performance of the *GeoBLR* method, with respect to the *uCheckin* method, increases as well. When the land-mark density is too large, the performance improvement of the *GeoBLR* method tends to be slow. As shown in Fig. 5b. In fact, Our algorithm relies more on semantic of landmarks than on quantitative of ones.

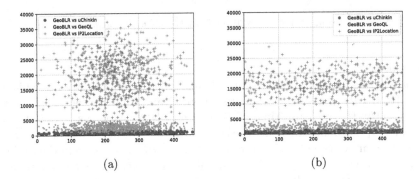

(a)   (b)

Fig. 6. (a) The scatter in GeoCN2018 dataset and (b) The scatter in GeoCC2018 dataset.

On the two different datasets GeoCN2018 and GeoCC2018, we also compared the scatter plot of error distance between our proposed algorithm and the other three algorithms (*uChechin*, *GeoQL*, IP2Location), as shown in Fig. 6. The algorithms with large error distance distribution such as *GeoQL* and IP2Location are affected by the distribution of landmarks, and the position of dynamic IP addresses are more fluctuating, while the algorithm of smaller error distance is more correlated (*GeoBLR* and *uCheckin*). The reason for our analysis is that most of dynamic IP addresses only have one candidate landmark, the final result of the algorithm *GeoBLR* and *uCheckin* tend to be consistent.

6   Conclusion

In this paper, we propose a dynamic IP geolocation method that is based on Bayesian Linear Regression, introducing a time attribute to describe the dynamic IP address in the location information, and using the largest convex polygon cov-erage area to select the candidate landmarks. Our experimental results demon-strate that our method achieves state-of-the-art results (1) error distance 50–300 m, and (2) 100–350 ms response time, which can introduce regularization into the estimation process and prevent the risk of over-fitting of data. It also can be easily extended to leverage other types of information. We believe that results achieved in this scenario are more representative of real-world operating conditions.

Acknowledgment. This work was supported by the National Key R&D Program 2016, 2016YFB080 1300/2016YFB0801304.

References

1. Apnic - query the apnic whois database. http://wq.apnic.net/apnic-bin/whois.pl
2. Digital element. http://info.digitalelement.com
3. Google maps with my location. http://www.google.com/mobile/gmm/index.html
4. Hostip.info. http://www.hostip.info/
5. Ip2location.geolocate ip address location using ip2location. https://www.ip2location.com/
6. Maxmind.detect online fraud and locate online visitors. http://www.hostip.info/
7. Neustar. https://www.home.neustar/
8. Skyhook.location technology and intelligence. https://www.skyhookwireless.com/
9. Arif, M.J., Karunasekera, S., Kulkarni, S., Gunatilaka, A., Ristic, B.: Internet host geolocation using maximum likelihood estimation technique. In: 2010 24th IEEE International Conference on Advanced Information Networking and Applications (AINA), pp. 422–429. IEEE (2010)
10. Ciavarrini, G., Disperati, F., Lenzini, L., Luconi, V., Vecchio, A.: Geolocation of internet hosts using smartphones and crowdsourcing. In: WMNC, pp. 176–183 (2015)
11. Ciavarrini, G., Luconi, V., Vecchio, A.: Smartphone-based geolocation of internet hosts. Comput. Netw. **116**, 22–32 (2017)
12. Dan, O., Parikh, V., Davison, B.D.: Improving IP geolocation using query logs. In: Proceedings of the Ninth ACM International Conference on Web Search and Data Mining, pp. 347–356. ACM (2016)
13. Ding, S., Luo, X., Yin, M., Liu, Y., Liu, F.: An IP geolocation method based on rich-connected sub-networks. In: 2015 17th International Conference on Advanced Communication Technology (ICACT), pp. 176–181. IEEE (2015)
14. Eriksson, B., Barford, P., Sommers, J., Nowak, R.: A learning-based approach for IP geolocation. In: Krishnamurthy, A., Plattner, B. (eds.) PAM 2010. LNCS, vol. 6032, pp. 171–180. Springer, Heidelberg (2010). https://doi.org/10.1007/978-3-642-12334-4_18
15. Gueye, B., Uhlig, S., Fdida, S.: Investigating the imprecision of IP block-based geolocation. In: Uhlig, S., Papagiannaki, K., Bonaventure, O. (eds.) PAM 2007. LNCS, vol. 4427, pp. 237–240. Springer, Heidelberg (2007). https://doi.org/10.1007/978-3-540-71617-4_26
16. Guo, C., Liu, Y., Shen, W., Wang, H.J., Yu, Q., Zhang, Y.: Mining the web and the internet for accurate IP address geolocations. In: IEEE INFOCOM 2009, pp. 2841–2845. IEEE (2009)
17. Hillmann, P., Stiemert, L., Dreo, G., Rose, O.: On the path to high precise IP geolocation: a self-optimizing model. Int. J. Intell. Comput. Res. (IJICR) **7**, 682–693 (2016)
18. Jin, Y., Sharafuddin, E., Zhang, Z.L.: Identifying dynamic IP address blocks serendipitously through background scanning traffic. In: Proceedings of the 2007 ACM CoNEXT Conference, p. 4. ACM (2007)
19. Johnson, S.C.: Hierarchical clustering schemes. Psychometrika **32**(3), 241–254 (1967)
20. Lee, Y., Park, H., Lee, Y.: IP geolocation with a crowd-sourcing broadband performance tool. ACM SIGCOMM Comput. Commun. Rev. **46**(1), 12–20 (2016)

21. Li, D., et al.: IP-geolocation mapping for moderately-connected internet regions. IEEE Trans. Parallel Distrib. Syst. **24**, 381–391 (2012)
22. Li, H., Zhang, P., Wang, Z., Du, F., Kuang, Y., An, Y.: Changing IP geolocation from arbitrary database query towards multi-databases fusion. In: 2017 IEEE Symposium on Computers and Communications (ISCC), pp. 1150–1157. IEEE (2017)
23. Li, M., Luo, X., Shi, W., Chai, L.: City-level IP geolocation based on network topology community detection. In: 2017 International Conference on Information Networking (ICOIN), pp. 578–583. IEEE (2017)
24. Liu, H., Zhang, Y., Zhou, Y., Zhang, D., Fu, X., Ramakrishnan, K.: Mining check-ins from location-sharing services for client-independent IP geolocation. In: IEEE INFOCOM, 2014 Proceedings, pp. 619–627. IEEE (2014)
25. Mun, H., Lee, Y.: Building IP geolocation database from online used market articles. In: 2017 19th Asia-Pacific Network Operations and Management Symposium (APNOMS), pp. 37–41. IEEE (2017)
26. Ng, T.E., Zhang, H.: Predicting internet network distance with coordinates-based approaches. In: Proceedings of Twenty-First Annual Joint Conference of the IEEE Computer and Communications Societies, INFOCOM 2002, vol. 1, pp. 170–179. IEEE (2002)
27. Padmanabhan, V.N., Subramanian, L.: An investigation of geographic mapping techniques for internet hosts. In: ACM SIGCOMM Computer Communication Review, vol. 31, pp. 173–185. ACM (2001)
28. Siwpersad, S.S., Gueye, B., Uhlig, S.: Assessing the geographic resolution of exhaustive tabulation for geolocating internet hosts. In: Claypool, M., Uhlig, S. (eds.) PAM 2008. LNCS, vol. 4979, pp. 11–20. Springer, Heidelberg (2008). https://doi.org/10.1007/978-3-540-79232-1_2
29. Wang, T., Xu, K., Song, J., Song, M.: An optimization method for the geolocation databases of internet hosts based on machine learning. Math. Probl. Eng. **2015**, 17 (2015)
30. Wang, Y., Burgener, D., Flores, M., Kuzmanovic, A., Huang, C.: Towards street-level client-independent ip geolocation. In: NSDI, vol. 11, p. 27 (2011)
31. Wong, B., Stoyanov, I., Sirer, E.G.: Octant: a comprehensive framework for the geolocalization of internet hosts. In: NSDI, vol. 7, p. 23 (2007)
32. Xie, Y., Yu, F., Achan, K., Gillum, E., Goldszmidt, M., Wobber, T.: How dynamic are IP addresses? In: ACM SIGCOMM Computer Communication Review, vol. 37, pp. 301–312. ACM (2007)
33. Youn, I., Mark, B.L., Richards, D.: Statistical geolocation of internet hosts. In: Proceedings of 18th International Conference on Computer Communications and Networks, ICCCN 2009, pp. 1–6. IEEE (2009)
34. Zhao, F., Luo, X., Gan, Y., Zu, S., Cheng, Q., Liu, F.: IP geolocation based on identification routers and local delay distribution similarity. Concurrency Comput.: Practice Exp. e4722 (2018)
35. Zhao, F., Luo, X., Gan, Y., Zu, S., Liu, F.: IP geolocation base on local delay distribution similarity. In: Wen, S., Wu, W., Castiglione, A. (eds.) CSS 2017. LNCS, vol. 10581, pp. 383–395. Springer, Cham (2017). https://doi.org/10.1007/978-3-319-69471-9_28

MUI-defender: CNN-Driven, Network Flow-Based Information Theft Detection for Mobile Users

Zhenyu Cheng[1,2], Xunxun Chen[1,2(✉)], Yongzheng Zhang[1,2], Shuhao Li[1,2], and Jian Xu[1,2]

[1] Institute of Information Engineering, Chinese Academy of Sciences, Beijing, China
{chengzhenyu,zhangyongzheng,lishuhao,xujian}@iie.ac.cn, xx-chen@139.com
[2] School of Cyber Security, University of Chinese Academy of Sciences, Beijing, China

Abstract. Nowadays people save a lot of privacy information in mobile devices. These information can be theft by adversaries through suspicious apps installed in smartphones, and protecting users' privacy has become a great challenge. So developing a method to identify if there are apps thieving users' personal information in smartphones is important and necessary. Through the analysis of apps' network traffic data, we observe that general apps generate regular network flows with the users' normal operations. But information theft apps' network flows have no relationship with users' operations. In this paper we propose a model MUI-defender (Mobile Users' Information defender), which is based on analyzing the relationship between users' operation patterns and network flows with CNN (Convolutional Neural Network), can efficiently detect information theft. Because of C&C (Command-and-Control) server invalidation [33] and system version incompatibility [25], etc., most of the collected information theft apps can't run properly in reality. So we extract information theft code modules from some of these apps, and then recode and compile them into the ITM-capsule (Information Theft Modules capsule) for verification. Finally, we run the ITM-capsule and several normal apps to detect the network flows, which shows our detection model can achieve an accuracy higher than 94%. Therefore, MUI-defender is suitable for detecting the network flows of information theft.

Keywords: Information theft · Network flow · Operation pattern · CNN

1 Introduction

In recent years, smartphones are used more frequently and widely in people's daily life, and people always save lots of personal information in their mobile phones, which has been accompanied with amounts of personal information theft. In the past researches, researchers have done a mint of works to detect

H. Gao et al. (Eds.): CollaborateCom 2018, LNICST 268, pp. 329–345, 2019.
https://doi.org/10.1007/978-3-030-12981-1_23

malwares, especially on the Android system, which becomes the main stream in the market. At present, the typical detections can be classified as signature-based methods [12], content-based methods [2], behavior-based methods [13,16], etc. Although these traditional detection techniques have been widely used in real situations to solve problems, they rarely focus on detecting information theft by network traffic. It has to be noted that some of these detection methods need a priori knowledge, and some have to root the operation system or establish a sand box [29]. For these reasons, we want to develop a flow-based method to detect information theft without any priori knowledge or deeply modifying the system.

With the popularity of multiple wireless interfaces including WiFi and 3G/4G, a smartphone usually keeps persistent Internet connectivity throughout all day. As CISCO [1] reported, mobile traffic data generated by apps had grown 18-fold over the past 5 years. Consequently, collecting and analyzing network traffic became a practicable method for detecting information theft. The analysis of network traffic has been done in traditional areas, such as in personal computers [4,5,8,18,24] and workstation servers [6,11,15]. Recently, it is also applied to mobile devices [3,27,30]. But most of them focused on the questions about how to distinguish the mobile device from the others or how to classify a user's habits of using apps. It is lack of using network traffic data to detect information theft.

In this paper, we propose MUI-defender (Mobile User Information defender) to detect the app that thieves users' private information. We find out that a certain relationship exists between network flows and the user's operation patterns. When an app steals personal information, its network flows' "shape" will be different from normal apps'. So we implement a CNN-driven, network flow-based model to detect information theft, and conduct a series of experiments to validate the capability and accuracy of our work. In general, the contributions of this paper are summarized as follows:

(1) We propose a detection model combining the user's operation patterns and the app's network flows to identify the information theft. The operation patterns include three types: Tap, Swipe and Others. One unit of network flow is defined as one communication session between a client and a server, which is composed of TCP/IP packets.
(2) We design a suitable feature vector model that can be efficiently utilized by CNN (Convolutional Neural Network) to detect information theft network flows. The vector contains the value of calculated DTW (Dynamic Time Wrapping), the weight of the operation pattern and the features extracted from traffic data.
(3) We validate our model by using the real-world apps and ITM-capsule (Information Theft Modules set). Because of C&C server invalidation and system version incompatibility, we design a simulation C&C server and extract information theft code modules to recode them into ITM-capsule for verification. And we achieve an accuracy higher than 94.23%, especially in the outgoing flow type, it is up to 97.12%.

The rest of this paper is organized as follows: In Sect. 2, we discuss some related works around our research topic. The detailed content of our model is described in Sect. 3. We present the performance of the network flows detection in Sect. 4. In Sect. 5, we discuss several limitations and future work, and then we draw conclusions of this paper in Sect. 6.

2   Related Work

Recent studies mostly focused on the suspicious app's behaviors when the app was running in the mobile device. Zhou et al. [34] created a privacy mode to empower users a flexible and fine-grained manner control in apps' information access, and users could dynamically manage the access at app's runtime. Mockdroid [7] was an Android operating system modified by AR Beresford et al., and it allowed users to give an app fake permissions to access privacy resources, after that the system would return null or unavailable information. Enck et al. [13] proposed a system called TaintDroid, which could accurately track the sensitive data and then notify the user when these data left the phone.

Indeed there have been some works which utilized traffic analysis in workstations and web browsers [17,21,32], and few works have been done in mobile devices [3,14,27]. At the first glance, it seems that the traffic analysis of smartphone apps is a simple transformation from the traditional works. While there are some similarities, such as end-to-end communication using IP addresses/ports, the nuances in traffic types and the transmission mode make the traffic analysis distinct between smartphones and traditional devices.

The network level analysis of Android malware behaviors offers complementary methods of characterizing and mitigating malwares. Neasbitt et al. [23] proposed ClickMiner, a tool that reconstructed user-browser interactions from network traces. Stöber et al. [28] extracted some side-channel features from network traffic generated by the most popular apps, such as timing and data volume. They could evaluate whether these information could be used to reliably identify a smartphone. In [20], Liberatore et al. evaluated the effectiveness of naive Bayes and Jaccard, which were based upon classification algorithms to identify encrypted HTTP streams. Conti et al. [9] designed a system that could identify the specific action by using advanced machine learning techniques, when a user was performing on her mobile apps. They further compared their solution with three state-of-the-art algorithms, and the result showed that their solution outperformed others in all of the cases [10]. Shabtai et al. [26] detected deviations of a mobile application's network behaviors, and they presented a behavior-based anomaly detection system that could protect mobile device users and cellular infrastructure companies from malicious applications.

Through summarizing the existing research works above, we know that although there are some studies focusing on network behaviors about the Android malware, it is lack of using the network traffic data to detect information theft. In this paper, we proposed a detection model to determine whether information is leaking through analyzing the relationship between apps' network flows and users' operation patterns.

3   Detecting Through Network Flows with CNN

3.1   Main Idea and Architecture

We know that adversaries always use apps to steal users' personal information, so how to capture and analyse network flows generated by the target app is the first problem. Most of apps generally communicate to severs using SSL/TLS (Secure Socket Layer and Transport Layer Security) for security, which is built on the top of the TCP/IP (Transmission Control Protocol and the Internet Protocol) suite. By using SSL/TLS, most of apps' communication contents can not be acknowledged, while some other information and features can be collected and analyzed. We use Wireshark to capture the mobile internet traffic through the hot spots created by us. Although we can obtain the network flow information as much as we can, the valuable data are just a part of the gained. Hence, we restructure the traffic data and divide them into a time series of packets for different session streams. In this paper, the "network flow" is regarded as a fundamental entity, and we define it as a sequence of TCP/IP packets ordered by time during a single TCP session.

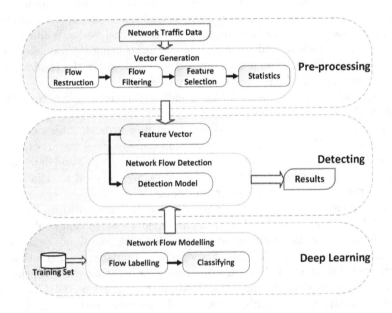

Fig. 1. MUI-defender model

Figure 1 shows the architecture of MUI-defender, which comprises the following phases: (i) "pre-processing", which restructures and filters the captured traffic data to generate the feature vector. (ii) "deep learning", which is based on the training database to establish and train the network flow model. (iii) "detection", which has the ability to determine whether the flow is a information theft flow or not. We detail the "pre-processing" in Sect. 3.2, the "deep learning" in Sect. 3.3 and the "detection" in Sect. 3.4.

3.2 Network Flow Pre-processing Phase

The phase "pre-processing" takes the network traffic data as inputs, and it restructures the traffic to network flows. In this phase, three types of time series are generated: (i) one is obtained by considering the bytes transported by incoming packets only; (ii) another one is obtained by considering bytes transported by outgoing packets only; (iii) a third one is obtained by combining (ordered by time) bytes transported by both incoming and outgoing packets [10]. We apply these time series as an abstract representation of communication between two endpoints.

Figure 2 depicts three examples of different apps' network flows through three cumulative graphs, which represent the three flow types. In each graph, the X-axis represents the flow time series and its unit is the number of packets. The Y-axis respectively represents the incoming traffic, outgoing traffic and complete traffic, whose unit is KB (Kilo Bytes). From these three graphs, we can recognize that the differences among the three instances' flow "shapes" are obvious. First, different flows have different lengths (packet number) in a solitary complete session. Second, the flows' content sizes have marked differences between each other. Third, the ratio of incoming traffic and outgoing traffic is distinct for the different flows. Figure 2a shows that Flow1's incoming traffic is the lowest among the three, and Flow3's is the highest one. On the contrary, Fig. 2b shows that Flow1's outgoing traffic is the highest. As Fig. 2c demonstrates that, Flow1's outgoing traffic is higher than its incoming traffic; Flow2's traffic is balanced; Flow3's incoming traffic is higher than its outgoing traffic. It should be pointed out that we consider the incoming type flow as a negative number sequence in complete series, while the outgoing type flow is considered as a sequence of positive numbers. Intuitively, we want to classify the network flows by learning their "shapes" to detect apps' information theft.

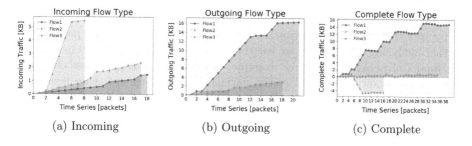

(a) Incoming   (b) Outgoing   (c) Complete

Fig. 2. Network flow types

After the restruction of time series, traffic data filtering is necessary to further improve the data's effectiveness and availability. Hence, a few pre-processing steps have to be performed to generate the corresponding set of time series for each flow: (a) we use a domain filter to select the network flows that belong to the current analyzing app; (b) we continuously filter out the flows by deleting packets which could degrade the precision of our approach (i.e., we filter out ACK, SYN, FIN and retransmitted packets); (c) we limit the flow's duration or length for unified quantitative comparison. All the three pre-processing steps are essential stages before passing the network flows to the detection model. In the following, we will describe these three steps in detail.

Domain Filtering. In order to ensure that we analyze each app independently, we need to identify the traffic data for the same app. There are many different methods which can be used, and we choose the destination IP address as a parameter for the identification. However, an app may communicate with a lot of servers that have different IP addresses (e.g., the servers belong to different web services, databases and so on). To recognize all the individual IP addresses seems impossible, so we only consider the IP addresses clearly identified by their owners, and the WHOIS protocol is used in this work. We also label app's flows that we definitely know which app produces them when we catch them. In addition, we have considered network flows related to the third party services (such as Amazon, Alibaba, Unicom, etc.), which are actually used by some apps [31].

Packet Filtering. Due to network instability, network congestion, or other unpredictable situations, IP packets may be lost, delayed, duplicated, or delivered out of order. TCP discovers and solves these problems by requesting retransmission of lost or delayed packets, and reordering the packets' sequence. In this process, some TCP packets may not carry any valuable data, which can interfere with the analysis. Thus we filter out the packets which are the hinders in our research, such as duplicated packets, retransmission packets, out-of-order packets, etc. Also, the packets tagged with the ACK, SYN, FIN and RST flags are discarded, which have low value in the classification approach (i.e., we abandon the packets generated from the TCP three-way handshake in connection and four-way handshake in disconnection).

Unified Quantification. We choose two ways to quantify a network flow's size: time duration and packet number. A TCP session may contain a series of packets during the connection, so we catch the whole session's packets for further analyzing. Meanwhile, we use the constant number of packets to analyze the model of network flows. For example, in the case of a set of flow data, we select the shortest flow length as the parameter l, then we cut other flows out to pieces with the length of l. After the separation, if a flow piece's length is shorter than l, it will be discarded.

3.3   Deep Learning Phase

Labelling the network flow training data is an essential work that is used to train the models for network flows classification, and we call this stage as "Network Flow Modelling". In order to build the training dataset, we use Wireshark to obtain traffic data through running only one app at a time. After that, we extract and label each network flow from traffic data. Two machine learning algorithms are used to build the flow models: Dynamic Time Warping (DTW) [22] and Convolutional Neural Network (CNN) [19].

Dynamic Time Warping. DTW is an algorithm used in machine learning to measure the similarity between two temporal sequences for time series analysis. DTW has been applied in many situations (e.g., video, audio, and graphic data), and actually if any data can be converted into linear sequences, DTW is able to handle them for analyzing. It is recursively defined as:

$$min\_dtw = MIN(DTW(i-1,j), DTW(i-1,j-1), DTW(i,j-1)) \quad (1)$$

$$DTW(i,j) = local\_distance(i,j) + min\_dtw \quad (2)$$

It should be noted that the implementation of the dynamic time warping is $DTW(s,t)$, while two sequences s and t are strings of discrete symbols. For two symbols i and j (i is in sequence s, j is in sequence t), the $DTW(i,j)$ is defined in terms of the shortest path up to the adjacent symbols, and the $local\_distance(i,j)$ means a distance between the two symbols (e.g., $local\_distance(i,j) = |i-j|$). The calculation of $DTW(s,t)$ is a feature included in the feature vector, which is the preparation work for the next step.

CNN. In machine learning, CNN (or ConvNet) is a class of deep, feed-forward artificial neural networks that has successfully been applied to solve some problems like image recognition. As one of the most popular deep learning algorithms, CNN overcomes the difficulties in feature extraction and is good at extracting local features. These advantages are in line with our vision for the network flow detection, so we choose CNN as our modeling basis. A CNN usually consists of an input and an output layer, as well as multiple hidden layers. The hidden layers typically consist of convolutional layers, pooling layers, fully connected layers and normalization layers, etc. Convolutional layers apply a convolution operation to the input data, passing the result to the next layer. Pooling layers integrate the outputs of neuron clusters at one layer into a single neuron in the next layer. Fully connected layers connect every neuron in one layer to every neuron in another layer, and it is in principle the same as the traditional multi-layer perception neural networks. Figure 3 is the CNN architecture which is designed by us. We set 4 filters with the kernel size of 3, and use the "sigmod" function to squash the single-unit output layer. After training, we take the number 0 as the label of normal flows, and the number 1 as the label of information theft flows.

3.4 Detecting Phase

In the detection phase, we establish a model that uses CNN to learn and classify the network flows. It can determine whether an app is stealing users' information. To better classify network flows with users' operation patterns, we divide them into three categories: Tap, Swipe and Others. The action of Tap is the most

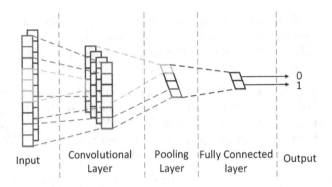

Fig. 3. The architecture of CNN

common operation that people use smartphones (e.g., a user has to tap on the app's icon to start the program). The Swipe is a type of actions by moving the finger on the screen up and down or left and right, and these actions usually happen in browsing web pages or social network information flows. The third type of actions is defined as that happens in other situations, for example, there are no actions on a smartphone (e.g., a user is sleeping without using the phone). In fact, although no actions, some network flows are still generated. Because apps can run in the system's background, and malwares prefer this way to steal information without users' permissions.

Due to the feature vectors generated by pre-processing phase and the flow models generated by deep learning phase, the detection phase could achieve an accurate classification of normal network flows and information theft ones. To better determine the user's operation pattern's influence, we set weights for flows generated by the three categories previously mentioned. Weights could be assigned to grant more importance to some types of flows against others. For example, it is comprehensible to give more weights to the flow produced by the "Others" operation type, while a user almost have no operations on the smartphone. And we give less weights to the flow produced by the Swipe, which indicates that maybe a user is surfing the Internet. At last, we use the CNN to classify network flows. We introduce the detection algorithm which outlined in Algorithm 1. The main idea is that different actions occur in different apps, which generate different classes of network flows, and the algorithm is able to correctly determine the labels of classes for unknown instances.

4 Experiment and Evaluation

In order to assess the performance of our experiment, we also consider several widespread apps in China that have different purposes: QQ, WeChat, Weibo, TouTiao, Evernote, QQMail and BaiduYun. QQ and WeChat are the most popular social network communication apps in China, which are produced by Tencent Inc., and people use them to send messages, photographs and voice messages,

Algorithm 1. Detection of network flows

Require:
>   Training network flows dataset: $F = \{F_0, F_1, ..., F_n\}$
>   Test network flows dataset: $T = \{T_0, T_1, ..., T_n\}$
>   Leader flows: $L = \{L_0, L_1, ..., L_7\}$
>   Weight set of use's operation patterns: $W = \{W_0, W_1, ..., W_n\}$

Ensure:
>   Classified flows: $C = \{C_{Normal}, C_{InformationTheft}\}$

1: **for** $i = 0$ to n **do**
2:      pre-processing F_i
3:      getting feature vector V_i
4:      put W_i into V_i $\{W_i$ is weight of behavior pattern that generates $F_i\}$
5:      **for** $j = 0$ to 7 **do**
6:          $DTW(F_i, L_j)$
7:      **end for**
8:      put MIN(DTW) into V_i
9: **end for**
10: Normalization F {Make the model of CNN}
11: Convolution1D {which will learn 4 filters with kernel size 3}
12: GlobalMaxPooling1D
13: Add a vanilla hidden layer {Dense(),Dropout(),Activation('relu')}
14: Dense(1) {project onto a single unit output layer}
15: Activation('sigmod') {squash with a sigmoid}
16: Classifying F with CNN model into C
17: Detection T using CNN model with C
18: Classifying T into C
19: **return** C

etc. Weibo is a kind of Online Social Networks, in which people can post their statuses, pictures or other something interesting. TouTiao is a news aggregation app, and it supplies personalized information for users and provides new services for connecting people and information. Evernote is an app designed for note-taking and archiving. QQMail is one of the largest email services, and its Android app is at the top of ranking in Chinese market. BaiduYun is a widely used cloud storage service owned by Baidu Inc. All the selected apps use a back-end service to implement the program function, thus they must generate network traffic.

4.1 Hardware and ITM-capsule Configuration

For the assessment of our analysis, we used a Galaxy Note 4 (SM-N9100) smartphone, running the Android 6.0.1 operation system. We used a server computer (Intel Core i7-4790 3.60 GHz with 8 GB DDR3 RAM) to run Windows 7 with two network cards, which simulated a router for receiving network traffic. When communicating with smartphones, the server computer ran Wireshark to catch the traffic packets. And then we created a comma separated files (csv) from Wireshark capture files, in which each row represented a packet. The packet reported time in seconds from Unix epoch, source and destination IP addresses, ports, size in bytes, protocol type, TCP/IP flags and some other information. Because we did not care about the payload, we discarded this part of information. These collected data were used to generate the network flows explained in Sect. 3.2.

In associate with CNCERT/CC (National Computer network Emergency Response technical Team/Coordination Center of China), many information theft app samples were provided for the analysis. In real usage scenarios, we did a lot of work to test and analyze these apps, and we found that almost all of them could not run properly. Some of these apps' C&C servers could not be connected. Some apps could not communicate with them in the original program logic. And some could not be installed on the smartphone because of operating system version incompatibility. In other words, the real information theft apps' life cycles were too short to implement the whole attacking process for analyzing. Therefore, we extracted the information theft modules from these apps and recoded them into ITM-capsule for verification, and designed a simulation C&C server to response the communication requests. ITM-capsule tried to collect the user's information such as the phone identification information, contacts list, call history, short messages, location and Internet records.

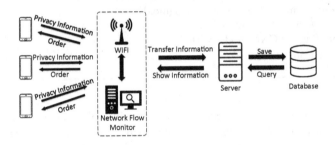

Fig. 4. The process of ITM-capsule running

Figure 4 represents the process of ITM-capsule's communication between smartphones and the server, which is supervised by our network flow monitor. ITM-capsule runs in the Android system, and it uses the HTTP (Hyper-Text Transfer Protocol) to transfer the smartphone user's information. Firstly, it collects phone basic information, and sends the information to the server. Immediately, the server assigns an ID to the smartphone to identify the device, and sends the ID back. Secondly, ITM-capsule adds the ID to all the next transferred contents to ensure the information unity. Then it combines the phone ID with contacts, call history, SMS and so on, to deliver them separately in each new HTTP connection. Finally, when the whole transmission procedure ends, i.e., when it has not receive new data for a long time, the server sends a stop message to the smartphone to finish ITM-capsule's work.

4.2   Operation Pattern and Network Flow Analysis

To analyze the network flows, we installed seven apps from the official market: QQ v6.6.9.3060, WeChat v6.5.6, Weibo v7.3.0, TouTiao v5.3.7, Evernote v7.9.7.1079770, QQMail v5.2.7 and BaiduYun v7.17.0. For each app, we recruited two experimental volunteer and created a new account for each of them. The volunteers simulated the behaviors of users in using the apps, like sending messages, posting statuses, browsing news, etc. To deal with the social network apps, we set several friends or followers for each account. By this way, we avoided configuring the accounts with actual friends or followers, so that we could make sure the experimental environment is pure and under our control.

In order to obtain operation patterns, we developed an app called Action-Catcher that could capture and classify the actions as three categories, which is mentioned earlier in Sect. 3.4. For example, when a user wants to send messages by QQ or WeChat, he has to tap on the app's icon firstly and waits the program to connect the Internet, and then taps on a friend's avatar to open the communicating page and inputs texts or pictures. Finally, he taps on the "send" button to send messages. In the process of the above actions, ActionCatcher can match the "click" action as the Tap type. It is certain that when a user browses news or social network information flows, his finger slides on the screen and ActionCatcher can match these actions as the Swipe type. All these actions can produce network traffic data, so it is important to label the flows with the operation patterns. Since ActionCatcher records the time that actions occurred, we can match them with the network flow time. In the experiment, we limited the volunteers to operate apps in a day (24 h), and then we obtained these sets of flows, which were matched with operation patterns.

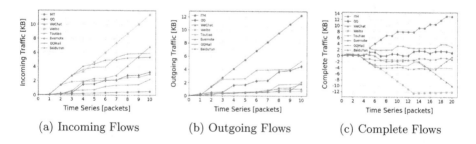

(a) Incoming Flows   (b) Outgoing Flows   (c) Complete Flows

Fig. 5. Apps' network flow types

As mentioned in Sect. 3.2, we could limit the length or use whole duration time of flows to achieve unified quantification. Figure 5 shows the diversity of apps' flow types which are selected with limited length (fixed number of packets). In Fig. 5a, we can find out that within 10 packets, Weibo obtains the most traffic data while ITM-capsule obtains the least. Figure 5b shows that ITM-capsule sends out the most traffic data within 10 packets, and other apps relatively are much less than ITM-capsule, especially Weibo sends the least data. Figure 5c demonstrates the diversity of the complete flow types. From this figure we can find that ITM-capsule's outgoing flow is dominant, and Weibo's incoming flow takes over the majority of traffic data. From each subfigure, we can realize that different apps generate different flow types and their features are different. As a result, we extract the feature vector that contains: the value of DTW, operation pattern with weights, duration, and number of packets, flow length, average packet length, average packet interval for each complete flow, incoming flow and outgoing flow.

To reduce the computation burden of calculating DTW, a leader flow is elected for each app, and these leader flows are representative for their flow type. Giving a class F of flows for one app, which contains the flows $\{f_1, ..., f_n\}$, the leader is the flow f_i that is selected with the minimum overall distance from the other flows of the class, and this can be expressed as a formula:

$$arg\ MIN_{f_i \in F} \left(\sum_{j=1}^{n} DTW(f_i, f_j) \right) \tag{3}$$

The $DTW()$ is declared in Sect. 3.3. Figure 6 shows the comparison between ITM-capsule's network flow and that of other seven apps using the DTW algorithm. The gray-scale image means that when the white line is straighter and smoother in the diagonal, the two flows' "shapes" are more similar and the value of the DTW are smaller. Each subfigure represents ITM-capsule's flow comparison with others', and the three graphs in the subfigure represent DTW calculation of different flow types. For example, Fig. 6b shows the comparison between ITM-capsule's flow and QQ's flow in DTW: The top graph indicates the comparison of incoming flows; The middle one is depicting difference between outgoing flows; The bottom graph shows the complete flows' discrepancy. Since the white line of the Fig. 6b is so tortuous, we can realize that ITM-capsule's flow is very different with QQ's. Indeed, we discover that the flows of ITM-capsule are distinctive with others in Fig. 6.

4.3   Detection Evaluation

For the network flow detection, the captured traffic data were divided into two parts: a training set and a testing set. The training set was used in machine learning phase to train the classifier, while the testing one was used to evaluate the effectiveness of our model and the accuracy of the classifier. As we created two accounts for each app to generate traffic data, we could make sure that the results of the detection do not depend on the specific accounts or users in the process of analysis.

In Table 1, we report detailed results for the accuracy, the precision, the recall, the true positive (TP) rate and the false positive (FP) rate. It demonstrates that different flow types generate different results of detection, and among these types the outgoing flow type gets the best result (97.12% accuracy, 90.45% precision and 94.34% recall). In the analysis, the FP rate of outgoing flow is a little higher

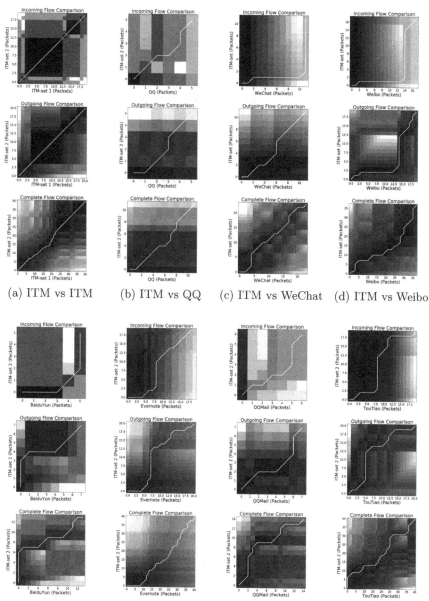

(a) ITM vs ITM   (b) ITM vs QQ   (c) ITM vs WeChat   (d) ITM vs Weibo

(e) ITM vs BaiduYun (f) ITM vs Evernote (g) ITM vs QQMail (h) ITM vs TouTiao

Fig. 6. DTW comparison

than others, while it indicates the model is sensitive about unnormal outgoing flows. This table demonstrates our detection model is in line with the expected results, and the performance is excellent on the network flows detection with CNN.

Table 1. Detection performance

Flow type	Accuracy	Precision	Recall	TP rate	FP rate
Complete	0.9423	0.9213	0.9308	0.9321	0.0842
Incoming	0.9552	0.9249	0.9267	0.9479	0.0768
Outgoing	0.9712	0.9045	0.9434	0.9661	0.1021

5   Discussion

In this paper, we extract and recode information theft code modules into ITM-capsule, and then we use ITM-capsule and several general apps to implement the information theft detection with network flows. The result of the detection demonstrates that the distinction of outgoing flow types between general apps and information theft apps is obvious. If there are some information theft apps could run successfully in reality, we really prefer to use them to verify our detection model. As we mainly focus on the detection of users' information leakage, we do not pay attention to some other classes of malicious flows, for example, the flow data are generated by a suspicious app which is downloading malwares. And considering the convenience of management and the openness of operating system, we only verify our model in Android platform. We need to strengthen the comprehensiveness of our detection model, such as extend its detecting species and system diversity.

Because the detection is conducted after the deep learning, our analysis is inefficient for the detection in real-time, and the timeliness needs to be improved. Although we have achieved a high precision and accuracy, the detection is limited to two classes: normal flows and information theft flows. We plan to investigate more specific classes of network flows, such as flows generated by charges-consuming malwares, remote-controlling malwares, malicious-deducting malwares, etc.

We know that a network flow does not continuously carry valuable data in the packets, and the network flows generated from the same app usually have similar feature parameters. For these reasons, we select CNN for modeling, whose major advantages are local perception and parameter sharing. And it is proved that CNN is suitable for our detection. However, it is lack of comparison with other machine learning methods in this paper, we will perfect this work in the future. In our opinion, the automatic detection needs to be implemented, but CNN needs a training dataset that has to be labeled by people, and automation becomes a limitation of our approach.

6   Conclusion

In this work, we detect network flows to identify the information theft app without deeply modifying the user's mobile device. The model proposed in this paper is able to classify sets of network flows into normal or information theft flows by using the CNN algorithm. As a popular deep learning algorithm, CNN is usually used to analyze multidimensional data, like graphics, audio, etc. But network flows are a kind of one dimension vector data, we modify the input format and the CNN's structure to fit MUI-defender. The result demonstrates that MUI-defender is effective in detecting the network flows generated by information theft apps. In addition, we evaluate the detection model with a series of traffic data, and it shows that our model achieves high accuracy (97.12%), precision (92.13%), and recall (94.34%), etc. These experimental evidences indicate that our model is both efficient and effective to apply in actual detection environments.

Acknowledgement. This work was supported by the National Key Research and Development Program of China (No. 2016YFB0801502), and the National Natural Science Foundation of China (Grant No. U1736218). We are grateful for the assistance from the volunteers. Thanks to their valuable contribution to the experiments in this paper. We also want to thank the reviewers for the thorough comments and helpful suggestions.

References

1. Cisco visual networking index: Global mobile data traffic forecast update, 2016–2021 white paper. https://goo.gl/ylTuVx. Accessed 28 Mar 2017
2. Arzt, S., et al.: Flowdroid: precise context, flow, field, object-sensitive and lifecycle-aware taint analysis for Android apps. ACM Sigplan Not. **49**(6), 259–269 (2014)
3. Atkins, J.B., Dobson, R.W.A.: Monitoring system for a mobile communication network for traffic analysis using a hierarchical approach. US Patent 7,830,812, 9 Nov 2010
4. Barford, P., Kline, J., Plonka, D., Ron, A.: A signal analysis of network traffic anomalies. In: Proceedings of the 2nd ACM SIGCOMM Workshop on Internet measurement, pp. 71–82. ACM (2002)
5. Barford, P., Plonka, D.: Characteristics of network traffic flow anomalies. In: Proceedings of the 1st ACM SIGCOMM Workshop on Internet Measurement, pp. 69–73. ACM (2001)
6. Benson, T., Akella, A., Maltz, D.A.: Network traffic characteristics of data centers in the wild. In: Proceedings of the 10th ACM SIGCOMM Conference on Internet Measurement, pp. 267–280. ACM (2010)
7. Beresford, A.R., Rice, A., Skehin, N., Sohan, R.: Mockdroid: trading privacy for application functionality on smartphones. In: Proceedings of the 12th Workshop on Mobile Computing Systems and Applications, pp. 49–54. ACM (2011)
8. Chandra, R.: Network traffic monitoring for search popularity analysis. US Patent 7,594,011, 22 Sept 2009
9. Conti, M., Mancini, L.V., Spolaor, R., Verde, N.V.: Can't you hear me knocking: identification of user actions on Android apps via traffic analysis. In: Proceedings of the 5th ACM Conference on Data and Application Security and Privacy, pp. 297–304. ACM (2015)
10. Conti, M., Mancini, L.V., Spolaor, R., Verde, N.V.: Analyzing Android encrypted network traffic to identify user actions. IEEE Trans. Inf. Forensics Secur. **11**(1), 114–125 (2016)

11. Deng, J., Han, R., Mishra, S.: Decorrelating wireless sensor network traffic to inhibit traffic analysis attacks. Perv. Mob. Comput. **2**(2), 159–186 (2006)
12. Desnos, A., et al.: Androguard: Reverse engineering, malware and goodware analysis of android applications (2013). google.com/p/androguard
13. Enck, W., et al.: Taintdroid: an information flow tracking system for real-time privacy monitoring on smartphones. Commun. ACM **57**(3), 99–106 (2014)
14. Falaki, H., Lymberopoulos, D., Mahajan, R., Kandula, S., Estrin, D.: A first look at traffic on smartphones. In: Proceedings of the 10th ACM SIGCOMM Conference on Internet Measurement, pp. 281–287. ACM (2010)
15. Fusco, F., Deri, L.: High speed network traffic analysis with commodity multi-core systems. In: Proceedings of the 10th ACM SIGCOMM Conference on Internet Measurement, pp. 218–224. ACM (2010)
16. Grace, M., Zhou, Y., Zhang, Q., Zou, S., Jiang, X.: RiskRanker: scalable and accurate zero-day android malware detection. In: Proceedings of the 10th International Conference on Mobile Systems, Applications, and Services, pp. 281–294. ACM (2012)
17. Hintz, A.: Fingerprinting websites using traffic analysis. In: Dingledine, R., Syverson, P. (eds.) PET 2002. LNCS, vol. 2482, pp. 171–178. Springer, Heidelberg (2003). https://doi.org/10.1007/3-540-36467-6_13
18. Lakhina, A., Papagiannaki, K., Crovella, M., Diot, C., Kolaczyk, E.D., Taft, N.: Structural analysis of network traffic flows. In: ACM SIGMETRICS Performance Evaluation Review, vol. 32, pp. 61–72. ACM (2004)
19. LeCun, Y., Bottou, L., Bengio, Y., Haffner, P.: Gradient-based learning applied to document recognition. Proc. IEEE **86**(11), 2278–2324 (1998)
20. Liberatore, M., Levine, B.N.: Inferring the source of encrypted HTTP connections. In: Proceedings of the 13th ACM Conference on Computer and Communications Security, pp. 255–263. ACM (2006)
21. Mah, B.A.: An empirical model of HTTP network traffic. In: Proceedings of Sixteenth Annual Joint Conference of the IEEE Computer and Communications Societies. Driving the Information Revolution, INFOCOM 1997, vol. 2, pp. 592–600. IEEE (1997)
22. Müller, M.: Information Retrieval for Music and Motion, vol. 2. Springer, Heidelberg (2007). https://doi.org/10.1007/978-3-540-74048-3
23. Neasbitt, C., Perdisci, R., Li, K., Nelms, T.: ClickMiner: towards forensic reconstruction of user-browser interactions from network traces. In: Proceedings of the 2014 ACM SIGSAC Conference on Computer and Communications Security, pp. 1244–1255. ACM (2014)
24. Qadeer, M.A., Iqbal, A., Zahid, M., Siddiqui, M.R.: Network traffic analysis and intrusion detection using packet sniffer. In: Second International Conference on Communication Software and Networks, ICCSN 2010, pp. 313–317. IEEE (2010)
25. Schmidt, A.D., et al.: Enhancing security of Linux-based Android devices. In: Proceedings of 15th International Linux Kongress. Lehmann (2008)
26. Shabtai, A., Tenenboim-Chekina, L., Mimran, D., Rokach, L., Shapira, B., Elovici, Y.: Mobile malware detection through analysis of deviations in application network behavior. Comput. Secur. **43**, 1–18 (2014)
27. Sommer, C., German, R., Dressler, F.: Bidirectionally coupled network and road traffic simulation for improved IVC analysis. IEEE Trans. Mob. Comput. **10**(1), 3–15 (2011)

28. Stöber, T., Frank, M., Schmitt, J., Martinovic, I.: Who do you sync you are?: smartphone fingerprinting via application behaviour. In: Proceedings of the Sixth ACM Conference on Security and Privacy in Wireless and Mobile Networks, pp. 7–12. ACM (2013)

29. Tan, D.J., Chua, T.W., Thing, V.L., et al.: Securing Android: a survey, taxonomy, and challenges. ACM Comput. Surv. (CSUR) **47**(4), 58 (2015)

30. Tang, D., Baker, M.: Analysis of a local-area wireless network. In: Proceedings of the 6th Annual International Conference on Mobile Computing and Networking, pp. 1–10. ACM (2000)

31. Wei, X., Gomez, L., Neamtiu, I., Faloutsos, M.: Profiledroid: multi-layer profiling of android applications. In: Proceedings of the 18th Annual International Conference on Mobile Computing and Networking, pp. 137–148. ACM (2012)

32. Yu, S., Zhao, G., Dou, W., James, S.: Predicted packet padding for anonymous web browsing against traffic analysis attacks. IEEE Trans. Inf. Forensics Secur. **7**(4), 1381–1393 (2012)

33. Zhou, Y., Jiang, X.: Dissecting android malware: characterization and evolution. In: 2012 IEEE Symposium on Security and Privacy (SP), pp. 95–109. IEEE (2012)

34. Zhou, Y., Zhang, X., Jiang, X., Freeh, V.W.: Taming information-stealing smartphone applications (on Android). In: McCune, J.M., Balacheff, B., Perrig, A., Sadeghi, A.-R., Sasse, A., Beres, Y. (eds.) Trust 2011. LNCS, vol. 6740, pp. 93–107. Springer, Heidelberg (2011). https://doi.org/10.1007/978-3-642-21599-5_7

Delayed Wake-Up Mechanism Under Suspend Mode of Smartphone

Bo Chen[✉], Xi Li, Xuehai Zhou, and Zongwei Zhu

University of Science and Technology of China, Hefei 215123, China
chenbo2008@ustc.edu.cn

Abstract. In this paper, the impact of Suspend/Resume mechanism on the power consumption of smartphone is investigated. When the operating system (OS) is in suspend mode, many trivial (less urgent) network packets will always wake up system, making OS frequently switch from suspend mode to resume mode, thus causing a high power consumption. Based on this observation, an novel optimization mechanism was proposed to delay wake-up system and prolong the duration of suspend mode so as to reduce power consumption. This novel method not only reduces the power consumption of WiFi components, but also reduces the power consumption of the total components. To verify the effectiveness of the novel mechanisms, we implemented such proposed mechanism on Huawei P8 platform, and carried out relevant experiments. The results showed that the proposed mechanism can effectively decrease power consumption by more than 7.63%, which indicates the feasibility of the proposed mechanism.

Keywords: Android · Power Save Mode · Suspend/Resume Mode

1 Introduction

With the development of mobile network communications, smartphone has become an important part of our daily life. With the successful development of battery-based personal mobile devices, low power consumption has become a major trend in the development of smartphone. The problem of high power consumption is becoming more and more serious, which has been widely concerned by researchers and scholars in various fields [1–3]. From the point of view of power management, there are mainly two mechanisms controlling the power consumption, i.e. Dynamic Voltage and Frequency Scaling (DVFS) and Suspend/Resume (or sleep/active) method. DVFS method is a low-energy consumption mechanism supported by hardware, which dynamically adjusts the voltage for processor implementation and decreases the system power consumption by extending operation time of the tasks. Suspend/Resume (or Sleep/Active) method brings the CPU to various low-power states when there are no activities scheduled in the systems. For instance on android OS, to reduce the power consumption, Suspend/Resume mechanism can make the android kernel suspended, and thus all components (DSP/bluetooth/Radio, etc.) are suspended simultaneously.

In general, after the android OS has stayed in suspend mode for a period of time, some external events (Timer/signal/hardware interrupt. etc.) will make the smartphone switched to resume mode. A number of experiments show that small amounts of trivial

© ICST Institute for Computer Sciences, Social Informatics and Telecommunications Engineering 2019
Published by Springer Nature Switzerland AG 2019. All Rights Reserved
H. Gao et al. (Eds.): CollaborateCom 2018, LNICST 268, pp. 346–355, 2019.
https://doi.org/10.1007/978-3-030-12981-1_24

network packets transmission can frequently 'wake-up' the system and make the smartphone switched to resume mode. Therefore the WiFi component will be woken up to resume mode to receive the network packets, and thus more power consumption will be consumed. In fact, a delay processing of trivial network packets transmission is possible.

In this paper, an optimization mechanism was proposed to realize delayed "wake up" mechanism of smartphone under the suspend mode. Such mechanism will delay system resuming in a certain interval of time, and process all the buffered network packets transmission at one time. In this way, it can effectively reduce the power consumption of smartphone.

2 Suspend & Resume Mechanism

Suspend & Resume mechanism [4] is a huge function provided by Linux kernel to decrease the power consumption of mobile devices. Suspend & Resume mechanism will try to put the system into a sleep mode as soon as possible while executing no task for saving more power consumption.

However, WiFi component or CPU will hold the Wake lock of the 'Suspend' mode, then the system will not be suspended. On the other hand, when system is in the suspend mode, the packets transmission of WiFi network or the interruption of Timer will resume the system to handle the relevant operations. In this case, the trivial external events will always wake up the system and eventually switch the smartphone to Suspend mode again. Such repeated process will consume more power consumption.

2.1 Impact of Network Transmission on Power Consumption

A large number of experiments have shown that the transmission of network packets has a great influence on the power consumption when Android OS is in suspend mode. As shown in the Fig. 1, the lower part represents the packets transmission in suspend mode, while the upper part represents the switching of mode caused by packets transmission of Android OS. It can be seen that, when the network packets arrived at Access Point (AP), the WiFi component woke up the system to receive the network packets, and after a period of time, the system was switched back to suspend mode again.

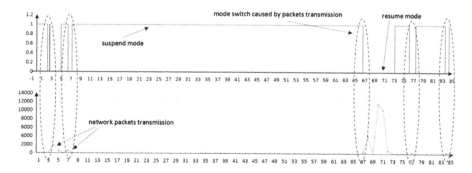

Fig. 1. Impact of network transmission behavior on suspend/resume mode switching

It can be known that frequent transmission of less urgent packets has a great impact on power consumption. Based on this, an optimization mechanism was proposed to decrease the power consumption of WiFi component while delaying the resuming of all hardware components, also in order to decrease the power consumption of total device.

2.2   IEEE PS-POLL Mechanism

From the aspect of WiFi component, focus was paid on whether delayed transmission of packets could affect the original network protocol.

For WiFi network, when a client station (smartphone) is set to Power Save mode, some of the transceiver equipment will be shut down to conserve power. Considering the communication behavior, when the WiFi components are in PS mode, Access Point (AP) will periodically send the beacon frame to smartphone to indicate in the frame whether there are any data reaching the AP. If there are no packets reaching AP, the TIM field is set to 0 (TIM = 0). When some packets have reached AP, the TIM is set to 1. Then, smartphone will send PS-Poll frame [5] to AP, which indicates that the smartphone has been woken up to receive data, as shown in Fig. 2.

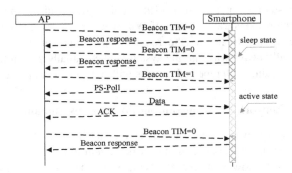

Fig. 2. The behavior of router retrieves network packets

It has been proved that the proposed mechanism will delay sending the PS-POLL frame to AP without affecting the original network protocol.

2.3   Related Works

In the past decade, a lot of researches have been conducted on reducing the power consumption and increasing the energy efficiency. For example, Niranjan [6] conducted a classical measurement study of the energy consumption characteristics of 3G, GSM, and WiFi, and developed energy consumption model for each technology. Based on this model, they developed TailEnder, a protocol that reduces energy consumption of common mobile applications. By revisiting one of the most comprehensive WiFi power models [7], Swetank re-evaluated the model for the current generation of smartphones equipped with both 802.11g and 802.11n NICs, and found that such model remained valid for a wide range of devices and network types, although the model parameters exhibited different trends compared with the ones reported in the original paper.

Another interesting work is to optimize network protocol and thus reduce energy consumption [8–10]. In [11], the impact of network protocol on the power consumption was studied [11]. The author examined the TCP and UDP protocols with screen on and off, while the smartphones forwarded the packets to an Access Point. The findings were obtained using 802.11n/ac wireless cards, which is of great guidance value.

3 Delay Wake-Up Mechanism

According to the above content, non-urgent network packets will increase the power consumption. Therefore, an optimized mechanism was proposed in this work to delay the wake-up of the system and make the Android OS late switched to resume mode. It can be seen from the Fig. 3 that the response beacon has been delayed by the 3 beacon intervals.

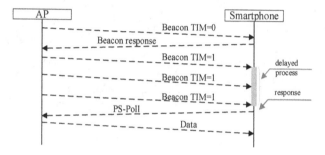

Fig. 3. The delay transmission behavior of router retrieves network packets based on PS-Poll mechanism

3.1 Suspend & Resume Operation of Android OS

When the system is in suspend mode, kernel will execute a big loop program to wait for the external interrupt events or signals. When an external event is arrived, the system will wake up all the sub-components and call the corresponding interrupt handlers to handle the event. The switching operation from resume mode to suspend mode is as follows (Fig. 4):

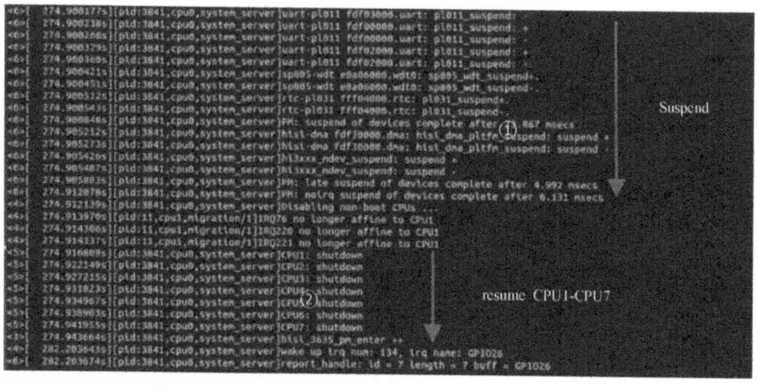

Fig. 4. Switch operation flow of Suspend mode

As shown in Fig. 3, almost all hardware components are suspended in the first step. It can be seen that the last operation is to shutdown all CPU except CPU0, which will execute a big loop task for handling the external events/signals. That is the suspension flow of the android OS.

Similarly, when an external interrupt event is received (*irq name:GPIO26, actually it is an WiFi interrupt which means AP has received packets*), the system will be woken up. The total suspend time is about 7.27 (282.20–274.94) s.

After that, the system will resume all components (first the CPU1–CPU7 and then the other hardware components), as shown in Fig. 5.

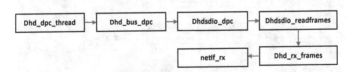

Fig. 5. Switch operation flow of Resume mode

To prolong the duration of suspend mode, the proposed mechanism will delay the wake-up of the system when the external interrupts are detected (for instance, the interrupt generated by the WiFi component, which is quite rightly our concern).

3.2 Resume Operation of Android OS API

The trace of the function call is investigated when the system receives an external interrupt event. As shown in Fig. 6, after the WiFi component receives the interrupt, and the interrupt handler function (*Dhd_dpc_thread()*) is invoked. Finally, the driver calls *netif_rx* to invoke the handler for the upper network protocol layer.

```
Dhd_dpc_thread → Dhd_bus_dpc → Dhdsdio_dpc → Dhdsdio_readframes
                                                      ↓
                netif_rx ← Dhd_rx_frames
```

Fig. 6. Trace of API for Resume operation

3.3   Implementation of Delayed Wake-up Operation

To accomplish the delayed switching from suspend mode to resume mode, the proposed mechanism delays the response to the WiFi interrupt event, which leads to a delay in sending the PS-POLL frame and rebooting the CPU.

The implementation process of WiFi interrupt handler is as follows:

```
/kernel/drivers//bcm/wifi/driver/bcmdhd/dhd_linux.c

/*Run until signal received*/

  While(1) {

     if (!binary_sema_down(tsk))  {

    if (responese_number > 0)

      if(dhd->pub.sus ==1)
```

After WiFi network receives interrupt signals, the wake-up of system will be delayed for a while. The wait_ queue() mechanism is used to implement such delay operation. This mechanism makes processes wait for the occurrence of a particular event. In the implementation process, when the delay time is up, CPUs will be rebooted firstly, as shown as below.

```
/kernel/net/core/dev.c

  void __ref enable_nonboot_cpus(void)

  {

      int cpu, error;

      int my_f, my_f_s;

      my_f = get_my_flag(0);

      my_s=get_my_flag_s(0);

      if(my_f_s == 1);

      .....

  }
```

3.4 Delay Time Setting

To set the delay time more reasonably, we need to balance between the performance and the user experience. If the delay time is set to be relatively large, a lower power optimization effect can be realized, but the user's interactive experience will be negatively affected. A too long delay time will lead to the loss of network packets or even multiple re-transmission. To obtain an appropriate delay time, we evaluated the communication behaviors of the different apps such as *WeChat*, *QQ*, *Microblog*, and analyzed the interval between the packet's arrival of the combination of apps (see the last line in the table below):

Table 1. Time distribution of the interval between the packet's arrival

APP	1–6 (s)	6–10 (s)	>=10 (s)
MicroBlog	30.45%	8.69%	60.86%
Wechat	30.59%	15.78%	53.63%
QQ	39.39%	12.13%	48.48%
QQ+Wechat+MicroBlog	56.53%	15.21%	28.26%

From the Table 1, it can be seen that for *Wechat* alone, more than 53.63% of packets will arrive within 10 s. However, for the composite behaviors of the last line (QQ+Wechat+MicroBlog), more than 56.53% of the network packets will arrive within less than 6 s. Thus, to balance between the performance and user experience, the delay time is respectively set to be 1/3/5/10 s.

4 Evaluation

The proposed mechanism is implemented on the Huawei-P8 platform on which the rooted Android 6.0 OS has been installed, and BCM4334 chipset is used as WiFi connector. In this chapter, the power consumption is calculated by the power model of smartphone, and the experimental setting and result analysis are presented.

4.1 Power Model of Smartphone

Apktool tool is used to extract the *power_profile.xml* file from the kernel directory of / framwork-res/res/xml/. The format is *<item name = "wifi.on"> 0.06 </item>*, *<item name = "wifi.scan"> 100 </item>, etc.* Then, the power consumption can be calculated by such hardware parameter when Android OS is in suspend or resume mode.

Nearly all hardware components are suspended except one CPU core when android OS enters Suspend mode. This indicates that the power saving is not only for WiFi component, but also for the other components. The power consumption is calculated using the formula as below.

$$E_{total} = E_{cpu} + E_{Bluetooth} + E_{WiFi} + E_{Dsp} + E_{Radio}$$

By dividing the total power consumption of smartphone into five parts, it is possible to separately calculate the power consumption of each component.

- *CPU parameters relevant to power consumption*

When Android OS enters suspend mode, there is only one CPU core executing the operation which is the necessarily needed by kernel. For example, it will execute the periodic task to detect (external) events and wake-up the system. Thus, the power consumption under each working mode should be calculated separately. The rough formula for calculating power consumption of the CPU is as below:

$$\begin{cases} E_{cpu\_resume} = Time_{cpu\_resume} \times Power_{cpu\_resume} \times 8 \\ E_{cpu\_suspend} = Time_{cpu\_suspend} \times Power_{cpu\_suspend} \end{cases}$$

- *WiFi parameters relevant to power consumption*

For WiFi component, when OS enters suspend mode, *<item name = "wifi. on">* 0.06 *</item>* can be used to calculate the power consumption. When OS stays in resume mode, *<item name = "wifi.active">* 97 *</item>* can be used to represent the WiFi power parameter.

As an analogy, the power consumption of each component is shown in Table 2.

Table 2. Time distribution of suspend/resume mode

	CPU	WiFi	DSP	Bluetooth	Radio
Suspend (mAh)	348.3	97	91	116	117
Resume (mAh)	3	0.06	0	2.8	37.5

4.2   Experimental Setting and Experimental Result Analysis

Finally, to verify the effectiveness of the proposed mechanism, comparison experiment was carried out to study the influence of delay time on smartphone performance and packet loss.

A network application was designed based on the C/S architecture. The time for sending and receiving the network packets was collected, respectively. The packet delay (the end-to-end delay between selected packets in a flow with any lost packets) and the packet loss (the failure of transmitted packets to arrive at their destination) were calculated. The statistical results are shown as follow (the packet is sent 100 times at a random time interval).

The delay time was set to 1 s, 3 s, 5 s and 10 s, respectively. Then, the sending and receiving time of packets as well as the duration of suspend mode and resume mode were collected. The proposed mechanism was evaluated from mainly three aspects: (1) the duration of suspend mode and resume mode. (2) the packet transmission delays. (3) the performance gains.

For the first aspect, the statistical result is showed in Fig. 7. When no delay time was set, the duration of suspend mode accounted for 76.38% of total working time. When the delay time was 1 s, the duration of suspend mode accounted for 85.31% of total working time. When the delay time was 10 s, the duration of suspend mode accounted for 91.75% of total working time.

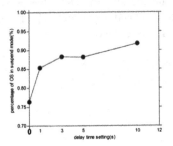

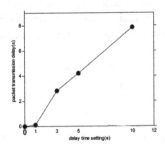

Fig. 7. Percentage of OS in suspend mode

Fig. 8. Packet transmission delay after using new mechanism

For the second aspect, the statistical result is showed in Fig. 8. When no delay time was set, there was almost no delay. When the delay time was 1 s, the packet was delayed by 0.12 s. When the delay time was 10 s, the packet was delayed by about 7.86 s. This indicates the average time from end to end in the proposed mechanism is significantly larger than before.

For the third aspect, the performances of each APP alone and combination of APPs (QQ+Wechat+MicroBlog) were tested, and the statistical result is shown in Fig. 9. When the delay time was set to 1 s, the energy saving was less 6.92%. When the delay time was set to 3 s, the percentage of energy saving was between 4.72% to 15.32%. When the delay time was set to 10 s, the energy saving was between 30.19% to 37.96%.

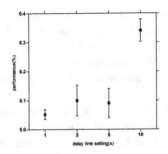

Fig. 9. Percentage of power saving after using proposed mechanism

5 Conclusion and Prospect

When android OS is in suspend mode, unexpected external network packet transmission will cause the system to switch from suspend mode to resume mode, and thus leading to more energy consumption. For this reason, an optimization mechanism was proposed in this study to delay receiving WiFi packet, and prolong the duration of suspend mode. According to the experiment data, it can be known that the proposed mechanism can effectively reduce the power consumption and has high feasibility.

Acknowledgments. This work was supported by the Suzhou Scientific Research Program (No.: SYG201731), and the National Natural Science Foundation of China (No.: 61772482, 61303206).

References

1. Ding, N., Hu, Y.C.: GfxDoctor: a holistic graphics energy profiler for mobile devices. In: Proceedings of the Twelfth European Conference on Computer Systems, pp. 359–373. ACM (2017)
2. Chen, B., Li, X., Zhou, X., et al.: Towards energy optimization based on delay-sensitive traffic for wifi network. In: 2014 IEEE International Conference on Ubiquitous Intelligence and Computing and IEEE International Conference on and Autonomic and Trusted Computing and IEEE International Conference on Scalable Computing and Communications and ITS Associated Workshops, pp. 252–259. IEEE (2015)
3. Li, H., Chen, L.: RSSI-aware energy saving for large file downloading on smartphones. IEEE Embedded Syst. Lett. **7**(2), 63–66 (2015)
4. Ding, N., Wagner, D., Chen, X., Hu, Y.C., Rice, A.: Characterizing and modeling the impact of wireless signal strength on smartphone battery drain. In: Proceedings of ACM SIGMETRICS (2013)
5. Swain, P., Chakraborty, S., Nandi, S., Bhaduri, P.: Throughput analysis of the IEEE 802.11 power save mode in single hop ad hoc networks. In: Proceedings of ICWN (2011)
6. Balasubramanian, N., Balasubramanian, A., Venkataramani, A.: Energy consumption in mobile phones: a measurement study and implications for network applications. In: Proceedings of the 9th ACM SIGCOMM Conference on Internet Measurement, pp. 280–293. ACM (2009)
7. Saha, S.K., Malik, P., Dharmeswaran, S., et al.: Revisiting 802.11 power consumption modeling in smartphones. In: IEEE International Symposium on A World of Wireless. IEEE (2016)
8. Serrano, P., Garcia-Saavedra, A., Banchs, A., Bianchi, G., Azcorra, A.: Per-frame energy consumption anatomy of 802.11 devices and its implication on modeling and design. IEEE/ACM Trans. Netw. (ToN) **23**(4), 1243–1256 (2014)
9. Rice, A., Hay, S.: Decomposing power measurements for mobile devices. In Eighth Annual IEEE International Conference on Pervasive Computing and Communications (PerCom), pp. 70–78, March 2010
10. Kim, S., Kim, H.: An event-driven power management scheme for mobile consumer electronics. IEEE Trans. Consumer Electron. **59**(1), 259–266 (2013)
11. Saha, S.K., Deshpande, P., Inamdar, P.P., Sheshadri, R.K., Koutsonikolas, D.: Power-throughput tradeoffs of 802.11n/ac in smartphones. In: Proceedings of IEEE INFOCOM (2015)

Mobile Data Sharing with Multiple User Collaboration in Mobile Crowdsensing (Short Paper)

Changjia Yang[1,2], Peng Li[1,2(✉)], Tao Zhang[3], Yu Jin[1,2], Heng He[1,2],
Lei Nie[1,2], and Qin Liu[4]

[1] College of Computer Science and Technology,
Wuhan University of Science and Technology, Wuhan, Hubei, China
lipeng@wust.edu.cn
[2] Hubei Province Key Laboratory of Intelligent Information Processing
and Real-time Industrial System, Wuhan, Hubei, China
[3] Department of Computer Science, New York Institute of Technology,
New York, USA
[4] School of Cyber Science and Engineering, Wuhan University, Wuhan, Hubei, China

Abstract. With the development of the Internet and smart phone, mobile data sharing have been attracted many researcher's attentions. In this paper, we investigate the mobile data sharing problem in mobile crowdsensing. There are a large number of users, each user can be a mobile data acquisition, or can be a mobile data sharing, the problem is how to optimal choose users to collaborative sharing their idle mobile data to others. We consider two data sharing models, One-to-Many and Many-to-Many data sharing model when users share their mobile data. For One-to-Many model, we propose an OTM algorithm based on the greedy algorithm to share each one's data. For Many-to-Many model, we translate the problem into the stable marriage problem (SMP), and we propose a MTM algorithm based on the SMP algorithm to solve this problem. Experimental results show that our methods are superior to the other approaches.

Keywords: Crowdsensing · Mobile data sharing ·
Multiple users collaboration · Stable marriage problem

1 Introduction

In recent years, with the popularization and development of mobile technology, everyone has one or more mobile terminals, such as mobile phone, tablet, laptop

This work is partially supported by the NSF of China (No. 61502359, 61602351, 61572370, and 61802286), the Hubei Provincial Natural Science Foundation of China (No. 2018CFB424), and the Wuhan University of Science and Technology Innovative Entrepreneurship Training Program (17ZRA118).

H. Gao et al. (Eds.): CollaborateCom 2018, LNICST 268, pp. 356–365, 2019.
https://doi.org/10.1007/978-3-030-12981-1_25

and so on. Each users have their data plan per month to use mobile terminals surf on the Internet. However, the mobile data usage of each user per month is uncertain. Some users may use little per month, but others may be completely inadequate. Therefore, some users could use redundant mobile data to share with others who need data. The mobile data sharing users sell their data to the mobile data requesters, and obtain some reward. In the other hand, the mobile data requesters could take less money to buy mobile data.

In the data sharing systems, users who need data are data request users (DR users for short), and users who share data are data sharing users (DS users for short). In crowded places, such as a train, airport, shopping center, etc, the mobile DS users has a coverage area, and the mobile DR users can obtain shared data only within the coverage area of any DS users. If there are lots of DS users, the data sharing coverage will expand to a larger area. Similarly, If there are lots of DR users, the DS user can share his data easily, and do not limit the fixed position, as long as the DR users is nearby. Therefore, to some extent, it is win-win to mobile data sharing users and requesters. As shown in Fig. 1, there are four mobile DS users, DS1, DS2, DS3 and DS4, and three DR users, DR1, DR2 and DR3. There are two data sharing models. One data sharing model is One-to-Many model, that is, a DS user can find multiple DR users simultaneously, and choose one DR users to share the mobile data, such as DR1, DR2, DR3, DS2 group. The other data sharing model is Many-to-Many model. In this model, any DR users can find multiple DS users simultaneously, and any DS users will cover multiple DR users, such as DS2, DS3, DR2, DR3 group. Moreover, the group DR1 can obtain DS1,DS2 shared signals at the initial location 1. When DR1 moves to location 2, he can not get a shared signal, and when DR1 moved to location 3, he get the shared signals from DS4.

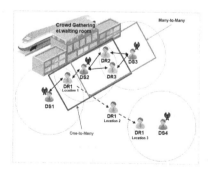

Fig. 1. Mobile data sharing example.

Nowadays, there are some researches focus on the mobile data sharing and trading. Yu et al. [1] investigated the data trading and introduced a trading platform that matches the market supply and demand. Jiang et al. [2] proposed a quality-aware data sharing market, where the users sell data to data requesters. Ma et al. [3] proposed how to develop a shared WiFi operation strategy to motivate users to participate. However, they did not propose how to matching optimal users among two groups. In this paper, different models are divided according to different user groups, and solved how to match the two kinds of users in the same range. The main difference between this paper and previous research is that two algorithms are proposed to match two kinds of data sharing model. Overall, the contributions of this paper are summarized as follows:

- We considering two data sharing models, One-to-Many and Many-to-Many data sharing model when users share their mobile data. Then, we formulate this two kind of data sharing models.
- We propose an OTM algorithm to solve the One-to-Many data sharing problem based on the greedy algorithm, which greedy choose the optimal users to sharing the mobile data. Then, we translate the Many-to-Many data sharing problem into a stable marriage problem (SMP), and we propose a MTM algorithm base on the SMP algorithm.
- We conduct extensive simulations over different environments to evaluate the performances of the proposed algorithm. Simulation results show the proposed algorithms is superior to the traditional algorithms.

2   Related Work

In the sharing economy, such as sharing bicycles [4], it has adopted a shared model. Ma et al. [5] proposed a framework of independent service sharing coordination, which sharing of spectrum and radio access networks (RANs). Ferrari et al. [6] described a unifying optimization framework to share backhaul network resources across different operators and wireless platforms.

Mobile crowdsensing (MCS) is a new paradigm of sensing by taking advantage of the rich embedded sensors of mobile user devices [7]. Zhu et al. [8] provided a (reverse)VCG Auction at each time slot the user is trusted to disclose the address of the information, where SP is the auctioneer (buyer), and the user is the bidder (seller).

Wang et al. [9] proposed a VM allocation mechanism based on stable matching. He et al. [10] proved that the allocation problem is NP-hard between tasks and users in crowdsensing, and devised an efficient local ratio based algorithm (LRBA) to solve. Gu et al. [11] studied matching theory for wireless networks and analyzed three classic matching problems. Different from the previous study, we studied One-to-Many case and Many-to-Many case in the sharing model.

3   System Model and Problem Formulation

3.1   System Model

In the system, we set three types of role: mobile data sharing users (DS for short), mobile data requester (DR for short), Services Platform (SP for short). DS users share their mobile data to DR users, and DR users get the mobile data which DS users share, and the SP is used to guarantee the fairness of the transaction. When the DR users is covered by the DS users, and the required data and the data download tolerance time of the DR users are satisfied, the optimal DS user is selected, and DS users share data for DR users, and DR users pay DS users rewards. SP is used to ensure the reliability of the transaction, at the same time, record the relevant transaction information, and constrain DR users and DS users according to certain rules.

We consider two sharing model, One-to-Many (OTM for short) sharing models and Many-to-Many (MTM for short) sharing models. For OTM model, there is only one DS user (or DR user) and multiple DR users (or DS users), the DS user (or DR user) choose an optimal DR user (DS user). For MTM model, there are multiple DS user and multiple DR users, the system should choose an optimal match between DR user and DS user.

3.2 One-to-Many Sharing Problem

We consider One-to-Many sharing problem firstly. No loss of generality, we consider that there is only one DS user and multiple DR users. Let $\mathbb{R} = \{R_1, R_2, ..., R_n\}$ as the set of DR users, and n is the number of DR users. We denote f_i as the required data size of DR users R_i, and denote t_i as the data download tolerance time when DR users R_i downloads the required data. As different sharing data users have different hardware and different configurations, they could offer different network speeds to DR users. We set V as the available sharing network speed of DS users, and set F as the sharing data size of DS user. Then, the sharing network speed should be more than the data download network speed of the DR users. Let x_i represents whether the DS user choose the DR users R_i to share his data. We define variance $\{Q(x) = |F - f_i * x_i|, 1 \leq i \leq n\}$ as the matching degree, which indicates the matching result of DS user and DR user R_i. The matching degree $Q(x)$ is the closeness degree to which sharing data and acquiring data. The smaller the $Q(x)$, the better matching stability and the smaller the sharing data gap of DS users and DR users. Conversely, the larger the $Q(x)$, the worse matching stability.

In order to achieve data sharing, our One-to-Many sharing problem is that: When DR users within the coverage of one DS user, and DS user meets the DR user R_i data download tolerance time t_i, how to choose the optimal DR users, making DS users and DR users matching degree are minimal? Therefore, our One-to-Many sharing problem is to minimize the total matching degree, that is:

$$\min Q(x) = \sum_{i=1}^{n} |F - f_i * x_i| \tag{1}$$

subject to:

$$V \geq x_i * f_i / t_i \tag{2}$$

$$x_i \in \{0, 1\}, 1 \leq i \leq n \tag{3}$$

Constraint (2) denotes that the sharing network speed should be more than the data download network speed of the DR users. Constraint (3) guarantees that x_i only choose 0 or 1.

3.3 Many-to-Many Sharing Problem

For Many-to-Many sharing problem. There are multiple DS users and multiple DR users. For DR users, the notations is the same as the One-to-Many sharing problem. For DS users, we denote $\mathbb{S} = \{S_1, S_2, ..., S_m\}$ as the set of DS users, and m is the number of DS users. As different sharing data users have different hardware and different configurations, they could offer different network speeds to DR users. We set V_i as the available sharing network speed of DS users S_i, and set F_i the sharing data size of DS users S_i. We use a failure rate r to indicate the failure rate of the matching result, the smaller the r, which indicates that few users have not been matched to. Relatively, the smaller the r, indicating that the more successful matches are. We use $\mathbb{R}'$ as the successful matching set, and $|\mathbb{R}| - |\mathbb{R}'|$ is the number of failure matching set. Then, the failure rate is $r = \frac{|\mathbb{R}| - |\mathbb{R}'|}{|\mathbb{R}|}$. In this problem, we also want the failed matching set is a little less. We set y_j represents whether the DS user S_j sharing his data to the DR users. Therefore, our Many-to-Many sharing problem is that: When DR users within the coverage of DS users, and DS user S_j meets the DR user R_i data download tolerance time t_i, how to choose the optimal DS users and DR users to match, making the failure rate and matching degree are minimal? Therefore, our Many-to-Many sharing problem is:

$$\min Q(x) = \frac{|\mathbb{R}| - |\mathbb{R}'|}{|\mathbb{R}|} * \sum_{i=1}^{n} \sum_{j=1}^{m} |F_i * y_j - f_i * x_i| \tag{4}$$

subject to:

$$v_j y_j \geq x_i * f_i / t_i \tag{5}$$
$$x_i, y_j \in \{0, 1\}, 1 \leq i \leq n, 1 \leq j \leq n \tag{6}$$

Constraint (5) denotes that the sharing network speed of DS user y_j should be more than the data download network speed of the DR users x_i. Constraint (6) guarantees that x_i and y_j only choose 0 or 1.

4   Our Solution

In this section, we first give the define of data matching ratio and its calculation formula. Then, we propose One-to-Many Greedy Algorithm and Many-to-Many Match Algorithm to solve the above problems. In order to better solve the above problems, we define some notations. First, We define a cost rate C of DR users to measure the matching results. Cost rate C represents the ratio of unmet data requirements to total data requirements for DR user in a successful match. If data requirements is met for DR user, we set the cost rate C as 0. That is:

$$C_i = \begin{cases} (f_i - F_i)/f_i, f_i > F_i \\ 0, f_i \leq F_i \end{cases} \tag{7}$$

Then, we define data matching ratio φ, it also gains rate of DS users. It determines the order of DS users to select DR users. φ_i is the proportion of DR user R_i data size f_i and DS user S_i data size F_i. If $f_i \geq F_i$, the ratio φ_i is 1. That is:

$$\varphi_i = \begin{cases} 1, f_i \geq F_i \\ f_i/F_i, f_i < F_i \end{cases} \tag{8}$$

4.1   One-to-Many Solution

We propose Algorithm 1 based on Greedy Algorithm. In Algorithm 1, we greedy find the maximum data matching ratio and find the optimal DR user to acquire data in each step.

Algorithm 1. One-to-Many Greedy Algorithm (OTM)

Input :
    $\mathbb{R}$: DR user set, S: a DS user.
Output :
    $SelectedDR$: Selected DR user.
1: begin
2:   $SelectedDR \leftarrow \varnothing$, $SecondSelectedDR \leftarrow \varnothing$, TAG $\leftarrow 0$, isNotFirstSelected $\leftarrow$ true, $Max(\varphi) \leftarrow 0$;
3:   sort ($\mathbb{R}$) by the merging algorithm according to f;
4: **while** $TAG \leq |\mathbb{R}|$ **do**
5:    $Tem(\varphi) \leftarrow$ the data matching ratio (DS user , the TAG'th DR user);
6:    **if** $Tem(\varphi) > Max(\varphi)$ **then**
7:      $Max(\varphi) \leftarrow Tem(\varphi)$;
8:      **if** isNotFirstSelected **then**
9:        isNotFirstSelected $\leftarrow$ false;
10:     **else**
11:       $SecondSelectedDR \leftarrow SelectedDR$;
12:     **end if**
13:     $SelectedDR \leftarrow$ the TAG'th DR user;
14:    **end if**
15:    **if** $Max(\varphi) \geq 1$ **then**
16:     break;
17:    **end if**
18:    TAG $\leftarrow$ TAG+1;
19: **end while**
20: **if** $|F \text{ - } f_{SecondSelectedDR}| \leq |F \text{ - } f_{SelectedDR}|$ **then**
21:   SelectedDR $\leftarrow$ SecondSelectedDR;
22: **end if**
23: **return** SelectedDR;
24: end;

---

362   C. Yang et al.

In the algorithm, we sort the DR users according to f. When the data download tolerance t of DR user was met by the DS user, we calculate the matching ratio φ. When the matching ratio φ is 1 or greater, and stop. Suppose r_1 and r_2 are optimal and suboptimal elements of $\mathbb{R}$ set, we could derive to two matched pairs (S, r_1) and (S, r_2). and choose the pair to match that the least sharing data gap between DS users and DR users pair.

4.2 Many-to-Many Solution

In the problem, we can abstract the DR user as the male, the DS user as the female, each DS user sort to the DR users according to the data matching ratio. In turn, each DR user will have a preferred order to DS users based on similar principle. We assume that the number of DR users equals the number of DS users, that is classic SMP problem. When the number of DS users and

---

Algorithm 2. Many-to-Many Match Algorithm (MTM)

Input :
    $\mathbb{R}$: DR user set, $\mathbb{S}$: DS user set.
Output :
    $\mathbb{R}'$: the successful matching set.
1: begin
2: sort($\mathbb{R}$) and sort($\mathbb{S}$) by merging algorithm according to f and F;
3: Initialize all $m \in \mathbb{R}$ and $w \in \mathbb{S}$ to be free;
4: **while** some DS users w is free and $\exists$ DR user m is free **do**
5:    $w :=$ first DS user on $\mathbb{S}$ list;
6:    Calculate a preference ranking set SR for w ;
7:    **if** $|SR| \geq 1$ **then**
8:       suppose r_1 and r_2 of SR set can be matched to w, two pairs (DS, r_1) and (DS, r_2) can be matched;
9:    **end if**
10:   **if** the optimal matching user of r_1 is not w **then**
11:      suppose optimal user is s_1 and sub optimal user is s_2, two pairs (r_1, s_1) and (r_1, s_2) can be matched;
12:   **end if**
13:   Choose the pair as successfully matched that $|F - f|$ is least among the pairs, w as a successful matching DS user, m as a successful matching DR user;
14:   **if** some DR user p is matched to w **then**
15:      assign p to be free;
16:   **end if**
17:   assign m and w to be matched to each other;
18:   **for** each successor m of $\mathbb{R}$ list and w of $\mathbb{S}$ list **do**
19:      delete the pair(m,w);
20:      join the pair (m,w) to set $\mathbb{R}'$;
21:   **end for**
22: **end while**
23: **return** $\mathbb{R}'$;
24: end;

the number of DR users are not equal, this problem becomes an SMI (stable Marriage with incomplete list) problem [12]. When the number of DS users and the number of DR users are not equal, if there are no matching users in each round, waiting for the next round to match.

We propose the Algorithm 2 to match the DS users and DR users based on SMP algorithm. In this algorithm, the optimal matching users is selected iteratively. Firstly, DR users are sorted according to the required data size, and DS users are sorted according to the shared data size. Secondly, we calculate a preference ranking set SR of each DS user according to matching ratio 8. If the size of SR greater than or equal to 2, we could further infer the matching result. Suppose r_1 and r_2 are optimal and suboptiaml elements of SR set, S_1 is the first elements of DS users. We could derive to two matched pairs (S_1, r_1) and (S_1, r_2). In the same way, we could get another two pairs (R_1, s_1) and (R_1, s_2), where s_1 and s_2 are optimal and suboptiaml elements of preference ranking set of DR user R_1. Finally, we choose the least sharing data gap between DS users and DR users pair. Repeat the above steps until the matching is finished.

5   Performance Evaluation

Here, we evaluate the performance of the proposed algorithm and conducted a simulation experiment in One-to-Many case and Many-to-Many case respectively by setting different numbers of users. In the experiment, the cost rate C and matching degree $Q(x)$ between DS user and DR user are compared and analyzed. We compare several algorithms as follows.

Common Matching Algorithms(COM): In this algorithm, a DS user is selected from $\mathbb{R}$, and matched with a DR user when the data download tolerance t of DR user was met by the DS user. **Stable Matching Problem(SMP):** In this algorithm, according to the classical SMP algorithm [12], each DS user find a preference ranking set SR to DR users according to matching ratio φ, and each DS user selects the first DR user that no matched from its preference SR set to match. **Random Matching Algorithms(RM):** In this algorithm, a DS user of $\mathbb{S}$ is matched to a DR user that selected randomly from $\mathbb{R}$ when the data download tolerance t of DR user was met by the DS user.

According to Eqs. (7) and (8), we calculate the gains rate of DR users through by $(1 - C)$, so, the sum of gians rate of DS users and DR users can be expressed by $B = (\varphi_i + (1 - C))$. We mainly compare the sum of gains rate B and the matching degree $Q(x)$.

5.1   One-to-Many Simulation

In the One-to-Many experiment, we simulated a DS user and 5 to 15 DR users respectively. We calculate the sharing data gap of DS user and DR user, then, compare the value of $Q(x)$. After each case is simulated 100 times, then solve the average value. The sum of gains rate result of users are shown as Fig. 2, the matching degree result are shown as Fig. 3.

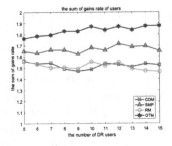

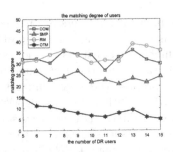

Fig. 2. The sum of gains rate of users.   **Fig. 3.** The matching degree of users.

In the One-to-Many case, we know that the sum of the algorithm gains is the highest in Fig. 2. From Fig. 3, we can see that the matching degree $Q(x)$ of our algorithm is the smallest and the matching result is the most stable.

5.2 Many-to-Many Simulation

In the Many-to-Many experiment, we simulated 50 DS users and 10 to 100 DR users respectively. The sum of gains rate result of users are shown as Fig. 4, the matching degree result of users are shown as Fig. 5.

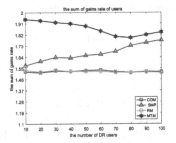

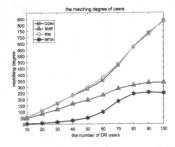

Fig. 4. The sum of gains rate of users.   **Fig. 5.** The matching degree of users.

In the Many-to-Many case, the number of DS users greater than the number of DR users or less, we know that the sum of the MTM algorithm gains is the highest and the matching degree $Q(x)$ is the lowest. We can see that our algorithm has the optimal overall gains and the most stable matching result.

We can know that the sum of our algorithm gains is the highest and the matching degree $Q(x)$ is the lowest. By improving social welfare, the user's income is increased or the user's cost is reduced. The matching degree $Q(x)$ is lowest, the matching result is the most stable, and the benefits of DS users and the costs of DR users are balanced. So, our proposed algorithms is superior to the other approaches.

6   Conclusions

In this paper, we investigate mobile data sharing problem based on multi users Collaborative and crowdsening. To solve the problem, we introduced two mobile data sharing models, One-to-Many model and Many-to-Many model. Basic these two models, we proposed two algorithms to solve the mobile data sharing problem. Extensive simulations show that the performance of our proposed algorithms is superior to the other approaches.

References

1. Yu, J., Man, H.C., Huang, J., Poor, H.V.: Mobile data trading: behavioral economics analysis, algorithm, and app design. IEEE J. Sel. Areas Commun. **35**(4), 994–1005 (2017)
2. Jiang, C., Gao, L., Duan, L., Huang, J.: Scalable mobile crowdsensing via peer-to-peer data sharing. IEEE Trans. Mobile Comput. **17**(4), 898–912 (2018)
3. Ma, Q., Gao, L., Liu, Y.F., Huang, J.: Economic analysis of crowdsourced wireless community networks. IEEE Trans. Mobile Comput. **16**(7), 1856–1869 (2017)
4. Bao, J., He, T., Ruan, S., Li, Y., Zheng, Y.: Planning bike lanes based on sharing-bikes' trajectories. In: Proceedings of the 23rd ACM SIGKDD International Conference on Knowledge Discovery and Data Mining (KDD), pp. 1377–1386. ACM (2017)
5. Ma, L.Y., Wei, S.W., Chang, S.C., Su, H.C., Wang, C.N., Chang, R.Y.: Independent coordination for sharing spectrum and small cells. In: International Conference on Control, Decision and Information Technologies, pp. 959–965 (2018)
6. Ferrari, L., Karakoc, N., Scaglione, A., Reisslein, M., Thyagaturu, A.: Layered cooperative resource sharing at a wireless SDN backhaul. In: Proceedings of the IEEE International Conference on Communications Workshops (ICC Workshops), International Workshop on 5G Architecture (5GARCH), pp. 1–6 (2018)
7. Yang, D., Xue, G., Fang, X., Tang, J.: Incentive mechanisms for crowdsensing: crowdsourcing with smartphones. IEEE/ACM Trans. Netw. **24**(3), 1732–1744 (2016)
8. Zhu, X., An, J., Yang, M., Xiang, L., Yang, Q., Gui, X.: A fair incentive mechanism for crowdsourcing in crowd sensing. IEEE Internet Things J. **3**(6), 1364–1372 (2017)
9. Wang, J.V., Fok, K.Y., Cheng, C.T., Chi, K.T.: A stable matching-based virtual machine allocation mechanism for cloud data centers. In: 2016 IEEE World Congress on Services (SERVICES), pp. 103–106 (2016)
10. He, S., Shin, D.H., Zhang, J., Chen, J.: Near-optimal allocation algorithms for location-dependent tasks in crowdsensing. IEEE Trans. Veh. Technol. **66**(4), 3392–3405 (2017)
11. Gu, Y., Saad, W., Bennis, M., Debbah, M., Han, Z.: Matching theory for future wireless networks: fundamentals and applications. IEEE Commun. Mag. **53**(5), 52–59 (2015)
12. Alhakami, H., Chen, F., Janicke, H.: SMP-based service matching. In: Science and Information Conference (SAI), pp. 620–625. IEEE (2014)

Exploiting Sociality for Collaborative Message Dissemination in VANETs

Weiyi Huang[1,2], Peng Li[1,2(✉)], Tao Zhang[3], Yu Jin[1,2], Heng He[1,2], Lei Nie[1,2], and Qin Liu[4]

[1] College of Computer Science and Technology,
Wuhan University of Science and Technology, Wuhan, Hubei, China
lipeng@wust.edu.cn
[2] Hubei Province Key Laboratory of Intelligent Information Processing
and Real-time Industrial System, Wuhan, Hubei, China
[3] Department of Computer Science, New York Institute of Technology,
New York, USA
[4] School of Cyber Science and Engineering, Wuhan University, Wuhan, Hubei, China

Abstract. Message dissemination problem have attracted great attention in vehicular ad hoc networks (VANETs). One important task is to find a set of relay nodes to maximize the number of successful delivery messages. In this paper, we investigate the message dissemination problem and propose a new method that aims at selecting optimal nodes as the collaborative nodes to distribute message. Firstly, we analyze the real vehicle traces and find its sociality by extracting contacts and using community detecting approach. Secondly, we propose community collaboration degree to measure the collaborative possibility of message delivery in the whole community. Moreover, we use Markov chains to infer future community collaboration degree. Thirdly, we design a community collaboration (CC) algorithm for selecting the optimal collaborative nodes. We compare our algorithm with other methods. The simulation results show that our algorithm performance is better than other methods.

Keywords: Message disseminations · VANETs ·
Community collaboration degree

1 Introduction

With the development of vehicular ad hoc networks (VANETs), there are more and more message dissemination applications in VANETs. Message dissemination problem is a difficult problem in VANETs, as it is hard to find a set of nodes

This work is partially supported by the NSF of China (No. 61502359, 61602351, 61572370, and 61802286), the Hubei Provincial Natural Science Foundation of China (No. 2018CFB424), and the Wuhan University of Science and Technology Innovative Entrepreneurship Training Program (17ZRA118).

H. Gao et al. (Eds.): CollaborateCom 2018, LNICST 268, pp. 366–385, 2019.
https://doi.org/10.1007/978-3-030-12981-1_26

to maximize message deliver ratio. Moreover, it is also an interesting problem as the messages are timely disseminated based on designed scheme in VANETs.

Due to the delay and opportunity of VANETs, data forwarding between nodes plays an important role in which the information exchange between nodes in the network. The routing schemes have been widely investigated [1]. Some papers consider sociality-based routing, others consider geographic-based routing. Generally speaking, geographical routing considers hot spots, but ignores the internal correlation between nodes. Although messages is easy to disseminated in hot areas, it is hard to diffuse in non-hot areas, resulting in low forwarding efficiency in some areas. Sociality-based forwarding is concerned about the nodes correlation compared with geographical routing. It takes the contacts between nodes as the link, and measures the probability, frequency of contact, etc. These factors determine which nodes are suitable as forwarding nodes. In this paper, we present a new message forwarding scheme that help forward messages to a destination. Our scheme exploits the vehicles moving pattern based on vehicular sociability.

In order to study the rule of nodes in community, we analyze the real taxis history trace and construct the contact graph. Further, we characterize the contact of nodes. Based on our analyses, we formulate two definitions: delivery probability and community collaboration degree. The delivery probability measures the possibility of a node forwarding messages to another node. The community collaboration degree measures a node's contribution to the community. Our scheme has several advantages as compared with existing approach. First, in our scheme, the delivery probability of nodes considers two factors: direct delivery and indirect delivery. Whether a node chooses to deliver directly messages or indirectly messages depends on the direct delivery probability and the indirect delivery probability. Second, in previous papers, only the contact between nodes is considered, but we present the community collaboration degree to measure the relationship between a community and its nodes.

The contributions of this paper are as follow:

- We formulate the message dissemination problem in VANETs, which selects the optimal collaborative nodes based on delivery probability and community collaboration degree, and prove it to be a NP-hard problem.
- Our paper analyzes real vehicle traces and exploits the sociability of vehicles. On the basis of the delivery probability, we also consider the relationship between the total number of forwarding messages in a community and the number of messages which are forwarded by a node.
- We purpose an scheme based on delivery probability and community collaboration degree, for solving the message dissemination problem in VANETs, which predicts delivery probability and community collaboration degree by utilizing the Markov model in the next slot to select a set of nodes to forward messages. Based on the purposed scheme, we design the CC algorithm to measure those nodes with high delivery probability and community collaboration degree, and then choose the optimal nodes as the collaborative nodes.

– We perform experiments to validate the effectiveness of our scheme and other methods. The experimental results show that our scheme has better performance than prophet in terms of delivery ratio, average delay and delivery cost.

The remainder of this paper is organized as follows. Section 2 gives the related work. Section 3 describes the system and defines the problem. Section 4 investigates vehicular sociality. In Sect. 5, we design the scheme based on community collaboration degree. Section 6 describes performance evaluation. Finally, we give our conclusion and outline the directions for future work in Sect. 7.

2   Related Work

Message dissemination is a key component of vehicular ad hoc networks (VANETs). Many schemes have been developed for VANETs, which are different in their protocols characteristics, frame of network [1]. There are many protocols investigated in previous literature [2–4]. The epidemic is used to relay messages by flooding or restricted flooding [5]. FirstContact [3] is a single-copy routing protocol, which consumes only a little buffer and delivery cost. However, forwarding only one copy may cause messages transmission failure, so the performance of this protocol in delivery ratio and delay will be worse than multiple copy protocols. Baiocchi et al. [4] presented an analytical model to evaluate the performance of the distributed beaconless dissemination protocols in VANETs. However, the beaconless protocols may produce occurrence of duplicated message transmissions.

Recently, there are some researches based on social structure [6–13]. In [11], authors presented SimBet, an algorithm for forwarding data in delay-tolerant MANETs based on the node's centrality to choose the next forwarding node. They predicted the delivery by estimating the centrality of the node. They have demonstrated through real trace data that SimBet had better delivery performance compared with epidemic. Also, SimBet achieves the goal that finding a route due to the low connectivity of the sending and receiving nodes. In [12], it introduced a centralized heuristic algorithm to learn delivery probability of different paths and choose the best path. Instead of [12], the work of [13] focused on buffer management and messages schedule. The later the message is created, the higher priority it gets. In contrast, our strategy does not focus on buffer management, but we consider buffer size in the simulation experiment. Besides the delivery probability, we also consider the proportion of node forwarding numbers in the overall forwarding numbers of the community.

Moreover, the game theory based routing protocol is also emerging. There have been many articles published on the theory. Abdelkader et al. [14] proposed a distributed game theoretic approach that computes a node utility function to achieve fair cooperation. Compared with other DTN protocols in performance, this approach shows that fairness among the nodes is improved, and delivery cost is reduced. Cai et al. [15] presented an efficient incentive compatible routing protocol (ICRP) with multiple copies for two-hop DTNs based on the algorithmic game theory. The protocol considered the behaviors of selfish nodes that did not forward other nodes' messages and rely on the nodes to forward its own messages. Besides, the optimal sequential stopping rule and Vickrey Clarke Groves auction strategy are also adopted for selecting optimal relay nodes. Further, they proposed the realistic probability model to find the optimal stopping time threshold and optimizes selection of relay nodes.

In addition, we have noticed some interesting studies [16–21] about message dissemination. He et al. [19] first proposed a store-and-forward framework with extra storage to solve the scalability and high-mobility issues. Then he proposes an optimal link strategy based on the dependence of the delay components. The experimental results show performance of the proposed solution is much higher in delivery ratio compared with the state-of-the-art solutions. Li et al. [20] presented an scheme to ensure the minimal budget to deliver the message to the vehicle in a given geographical area and a given a piece of a message. Further, they considered to utilize the optimal RSUs to forward the message based on the proposed quadtree model. Bi et al. [21] proposed an urban multi-hop broadcast protocol which aimed at delivering emergency messages so that lowering transmission delay and reducing message redundancy.

Although, there are plenty of different approaches in message dissemination, most of them are probably limited to a specific traffic scenarios including the topological structure of street, vehicle speed, etc. Our work aims to propose the message dissemination problem and design a scheme about how to select the optimal collaborative nodes, which is independent of specific scenarios. Compared with [5,22], our scheme considers the proportion of forwarding numbers of a node in the whole community besides delivery probability. Then, we utilize Markov chains to infer the future nodes forwarding states.

3   System Description and Problem Definition

3.1   System Description

In the traditional urban vehicular network, infrastructures are often used as relay nodes for message dissemination because it has larger coverage and longer service time. However, it is difficult to deploy them on a large scale due to its high price and deployment costs. Besides, the dissemination effect is not ideal since it is hard to move flexibly when it is built, which results in a large coverage blind area throughout the network. By using the short-distance communication technology of on-board equipment such as Bluetooth and WiFi, vehicles can become "mobile infrastructures" to accomplish dynamic transmission. Although they only have a small transmission range and short working cycle, they can rely on quantity advantage to compensate for the coverage blindness caused by the infrastructures to some extent.

In urban environment, we can divide dynamic nodes into potential collaborative nodes and high quality collaborative nodes according to whether they are willing to participate in forwarding messages. In general, potential collaborative nodes such as pedestrians, shared bikes, private cars, often request to other nodes for forwarding its own data in buffer but do not always forward data from other nodes for privacy reasons. High quality collaborative nodes are voluntary to forward messages and have a wide range of movement than pedestrians, private cars or shared bikes. These public vehicles cannot refuse to provide forwarding services for privacy reasons. Nevertheless, the number of such high quality collaborative nodes is significantly smaller than the former. Therefore, the research focuses on the potential collaborative nodes.

We assume that there is a potential collaborative node i, if it helps forward the message of node a, then i becomes the collaborative node of node a. However, potential collaborative nodes may be less likely to forward messages for their own reasons and just send their own requests to other nodes. In order to allow more potential collaborative nodes to participate in the forwarding service, we consider to give the nodes that are willing to be collaborative nodes a certain reward to inspire more potential collaborative nodes to participate in the forwarding service. The main advantages of utilizing potential collaborative nodes for message dissemination lies in two aspects. On the one hand, it effectively reduces the deployment and forwarding costs compared with fixed infrastructures. On the other hand, it can increase the likelihood of successful messages delivery based on its high mobility.

3.2   Problem Definition

We consider disseminating message within a given budget. Due to the time to live of messages, it is of great importance to be timely forwarded before they are out-of-date. We define our message dissemination problem as follows:

Definition 1. *In the case of giving the budget B and reward r for inspiring vehicles to disseminate messages in VANETs, how to choose the optimal potential collaborative nodes so that the number of successful delivery messages is maximized?*

The formulation of above problem is shown as follows:

$$max\,D(x) = \sum_{i=1}^{n} (x_i * m_i) \qquad (1)$$

subject to

$$\sum_{i=1}^{n} (x_i * r_i) \leq B \qquad (2)$$

$$x_i \in \{0, 1\}, 1 \leq i \leq n \qquad (3)$$

where n represents the total number of nodes in the network. x_i indicates whether the node is the collaborative node. If $x_i = 1$, it indicates that this node is the destination. Otherwise, it is not. m_i represents the number of messages that destination has received. Constraint (2) denotes that the total rewards should be less than the given budget B, where r_i represents the reward for inspiring node i to be a collaborative node.

Our message dissemination problem can be modeled as the budgeted maximum coverage problem [23]. We have the following theorem to prove it,

Theorem 1. *The message dissemination problem is NP-hard*

Proof. We can construct the contact graph $G(N, E)$ from the known traces of vehicles, where N is the set of nodes and E is the set of edges. Each node in the network represents a vehicle and each edge indicates that there is at least one communication within the period of time. We assume that $C = \{c_1, c_2, ..., c_n\}$ indicates potential collaborative nodes set with correlative rewards $\{r_i\}_{i=1}^n$, $n = |N|$. Similarly, $M = \{m_1, m_2, ..., m_n\}$ indicates a set with correlative the number of received messages. Our goal is to find a set $C' \subseteq C$, such that the number of successful delivery messages are maximized and rewards does not exceed a given budget B. Accordingly, we reduce the message dissemination problem to a budgeted maximum coverage problem, which is a classical NP-hard problem.

4   Scaling Vehicular Sociality

In order to understand the pattern of vehicular mobility and design message dissemination schemes, it is of great importance for us to study historical data in terms of frequency of contacts. After obtaining the messages to be forwarded (which can be implemented by V2V or V2R communication), the vehicle continues to drive along its own path. When two vehicles encounter within the communication range, they can contact with each other but not for long. The sociality between vehicles can be found in a large number of such short and frequent contacts.

4.1   Observation of Hot Spots

We collect the GPS trace of taxis in Shanghai, which is collected between Feb. 1 and Feb. 7, 2007. Due to the interference and loss of wireless signals, we amend the drifted GPS data. Figure 1 is the heat map formed in different time periods after processing the GPS data of 4,316 taxis. As can be seen from the figure, the heat of the whole area is relatively low at 8 a.m., because the majority of office workers travel during this period. At 12 o'clock, the heat increased significantly, and there was a trend that the dispersed heat areas are linked together. Obviously, present vehicle activity is more frequent than 8 o'clock. By 22 o'clock, the heat has dropped compared with 12 o'clock. After analyzing the vehicle trajectory for 7 days, we find that the movement pattern of vehicles presents a concentration and periodicity. On the whole, the areas with large traffic flow are concentrated in Jing 'An district, Xuhui district, Putuo district, Hongkou district, Pudong new area and Minhang district.

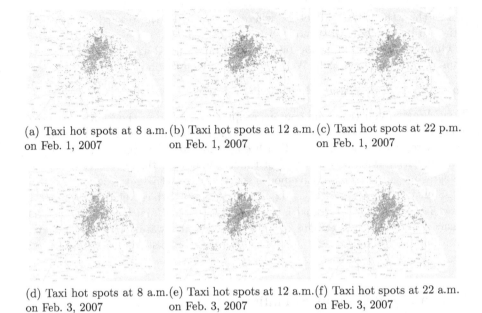

(a) Taxi hot spots at 8 a.m. (b) Taxi hot spots at 12 a.m. (c) Taxi hot spots at 22 p.m.
on Feb. 1, 2007   on Feb. 1, 2007   on Feb. 1, 2007

(d) Taxi hot spots at 8 a.m. (e) Taxi hot spots at 12 a.m. (f) Taxi hot spots at 22 a.m.
on Feb. 3, 2007   on Feb. 3, 2007   on Feb. 3, 2007

Fig. 1. Observation of hot spots in Shanghai

4.2   Constructing Social Structures

We use the Shanghai taxi data set including GPS data on Feb. 20, 2007. This
information includes the following fields: ID, TaxiID, Longitude, Latitude, Speed,
Angle, DateTime, status, etc. The granularity of reports is one minute for taxies
with passengers and about 15 s for vacant ones.

We first extracted effective V2V communication, as known as contact based
on literature [24] and generated the contact graph accordingly. Many literatures
have put forward different opinions on the weight of the edge of contact graph.
For example, the age of last the contact frequency [25], contact [26], contact ratio
[8]. We choose vehicle contact frequency as the weight measurement method of
the edge. For the contact graph, each node in the network represents a vehicle,
and each edge represents the contact frequency between two vehicles. Then, we
get social structure by using fast unfolding algorithm [27] find community and
calculate the corresponding modularity [28] defined as

$$Q = \frac{1}{2m}[\sum_{ij} A_{i,j} - \frac{k_i k_j}{2m}]\delta(c_i, c_j) \qquad (4)$$

where m is the total number of edges. If there is an edge between node i and j,
$A_{i,j}$ is the weight of edge between node i and j. Otherwise, $A_{i,j} = 0$. k_i and k_j
are the degrees of node i and j, respectively. c_i and c_j are the community where
node i and node j belong, respectively. If c_i is equal to c_j, $\delta(c_i, c_j) = 1$ and zero
otherwise.

Figure 2a illustrates a contact graph using Shanghai taxi trace on Feb. 20, 2007, which contains 1127 vehicles. Obviously, there is a clear community structure. The modularity is 0.845. Figure 2b shows the community distribution on Feb. 21, 2007. The modularity is 0.85. Obviously, the relationship of some communities is pretty close. These nodes of close communities should naturally become relay nodes for forwarding messages. Besides, we observe that although different vehicles had different trajectories, vehicles present a stable community relationship.

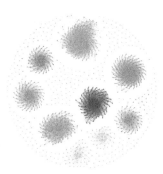 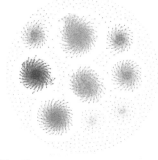

(a) Community distribution of 1127 taxis on Feb. 20, 2007.   (b) Community distribution of 1152 taxis on Feb. 21, 2007.

Fig. 2. Contact graph extracted from Shanghai taxi trace.

4.3 Analyzing Centrality on Social Structures

Through the collected data and the above community analysis, we obtain the degree distribution of Shanghai taxi in Fig. 3a and calculate the average degree of contact graph. The result is 21.514. Then, we plot the Cumulative Distribution Function (CDF) of degree centrality and closeness centrality in Fig. 3b and c.

It can be seen that node degrees are almost concentrated within 30, which is illustrated from CDF of degree in Fig. 3b and c as well. For any one of these vehicles, it is almost impossible to meet more than one third of the vehicles in a day. Besides, we have some significant findings from Fig. 3b and c. First, both the degree centrality and closeness centrality are effective metrics that distinguish part of vehicles with centrality. Second, in vehicle degree centrality graph, the curve that vehicle degree is more than 30 flattens out and grows slowly. That means the proportion of vehicles whose degree is more than 30 is much less than that within 30. A similar case can be confirmed from vehicle closeness centrality graph.

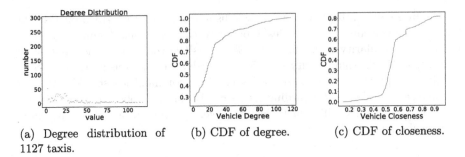

(a) Degree distribution of 1127 taxis.   (b) CDF of degree.   (c) CDF of closeness.

Fig. 3. Degree distribution and CDFs of degree, closeness in contact graph constructed from GPS data of Shanghai taxis.

5   Community Collaboration Scheme Design

From the above analysis, we can see that the node movement has sociality. A pair of nodes that have met are likely to meet again in the future. In this section, we study the delivery probability between nodes and the contribution of nodes to the community, and predict future delivery probability and contribution changes by using Markov chain models.

Using potential collaborative nodes as the relay nodes of message dissemination has two advantages. First, the high dynamic of vehicle movement makes the selection of relay node flexible and changeable. Although, the average delay by infrastructure is lower than V2V or V2R (if there are enough infrastructures deployed), the total budget will greatly increase. Moreover, since the infrastructure is located in a fixed location, V2R communication should be ensured for the data transmission of the "last kilometer" if there are places where data cannot be delivered directly. Second, the vehicles, as mobile nodes, keep moving and contact with more vehicles, which will naturally spread data more rapidly. In contrast, infrastructure can only provide data with vehicles passing through its range due to its fixed location.

5.1   Delivery Probability and Community Collaboration Degree

Although, there were many studies based on degrees and closeness, these studies are based on a fact that all the nodes in a network is voluntary to open its own on-board equipment for other nodes for forwarding messages. However, it is unrealistic. Many vehicles do not want to participate in forwarding messages for privacy reasons. For dynamic networks, we denote the number of contacts between node a and node b as $E_a(b)$, where a or b represents anyone of nodes. Therefore, we get the total number of contacts as follows:

$$N = \sum_{a \in \Omega} \sum_{b \in \mu_a} E_a(b) \tag{5}$$

where μ_a denotes the set of contact of node a, Ω denotes the all nodes in the network. In the opportunity network, the node carrying the messages has two ways to deliver the messages to the destination, one is direct delivery and another is indirect delivery. For a and b, we have the definition:

Definition 2. Direct Delivery Probability: *The probability that node a delivers messages directly to node b, denoted by $DD_a(b)$.*

It is calculated as:

$$DD_a(b) = \frac{E_a(b)}{N} \tag{6}$$

Definition 3. Indirect Delivery Probability: *The probability that node a delivers messages by relay nodes to node b, denoted by $ID_a(b)$.*

It is calculated as:

$$ID_a(b) = \sum_{k \in \mu_a, k \neq b} \left(\frac{E_k(b)}{N} \cdot \frac{E_a(k)}{E_a} \right) \tag{7}$$

$$E_a = \sum_{i,j \in \mu_a, i \neq j} E_i(j) \tag{8}$$

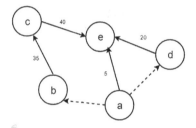

Fig. 4. Messages delivery process.

Here, we give a example. As shown in Fig. 4, we assume that node a encounters node b and node d, node a is going to deliver messages to node e. The total number of encounters between node a and other nodes is $N = E_a(e) + E_b(c) + E_c(e) + E_d(e) = 100$. For node a delivering messages to node e, we have two ways: direct delivery and indirect delivery. If delivered directly, its delivery probability is $DD_a(e) = 0.05$. We observed that if node a delivers the message to b and b indirectly delivers the message to e, its delivery probability $ID_a(e) = max\{ID_b(e) = 0.35 * 0.4, DD_d(e) = 0.2\}$ was higher than $DD_a(e)$. Intuitively, node a is more likely to forward messages to d rather than to b or directly delivering.

Definition 4. Delivery Probability: *The ratio of the number of contacts between a and b to N, denoted by $P_a(b)$.*

Given any two nodes, they are affected by both the direct delivery probability and the indirect delivery probability. Here we define the delivery probability of node a to node b:

$$P_a(b) = \alpha DD_a(b) + (1 - \alpha)ID_a(b), 0 < \alpha < 1 \tag{9}$$

This probability determines whether the node is significantly affected by the direct delivery probability or the indirect delivery probability. When a node carrying messages encounters multiple nodes and these nodes are qualified for forwarding messages, it is natural to select a node with a high delivery probability as the collaborative nodes. However, the following scenario may occur: We assume that node a encounters node b, c and d, and these three encountered nodes are qualified for forwarding. If the delivery probabilities of the three nodes are $E_a(b) > E_a(c) > E_a(d)$. We should give priority to node b as the collaborative node based on delivery probability. Nevertheless, if node b does not forward or rarely forward messages from other nodes before compared with node c and d, the number of messages forwarded by node b is relatively small compared with the total number of messages forwarded by the whole community. In other words, node b contributes less to community in forwarding messages. Besides, the vehicle will forward messages from multiple nodes on the way, it may be better to select c or d from the perspective of the whole community. In order to study the above situation, we have the following definitions.

Definition 5. *Node Request Numbers*: *The number of messages that node a wants node b to forward, denoted by $Q_a(b)$.*

Definition 6. *Node Forwarding Numbers*: *The number of messages that node a forwards messages from request of node b, denoted by $R_a(b)$.*

Based on Definitions 5 and 6, we have a conclusion that if two nodes forward messages for each other, we think that these two nodes are collaborative. If anyone of them only sends the request and does not forward messages from another node, we think such selfish node should not have priority in forwarding data. Further, we get define the community collaboration degree to measure the importance that a node to the whole community.

Definition 7. *Community Collaboration Degree*: *The total node forwarding numbers of a node a to any node b in a community divided by the sum of the node request numbers and node forwarding numbers, denoted by CS_a.*

$$CS_a = \frac{\sum_{b \in \mu_a} Q_a(b)}{\sum_{b \in \mu_a} (R_a(b) + Q_a(b))} \tag{10}$$

Intuitively, if a node has a high community collaboration degree, this node forward more messages from other nodes than. We should regard it as a collaborative node.

5.2 Inferring Future Delivery Probability and Community Collaboration Degree

As we study how to select the optimal collaborative node in potential collaborative nodes set, we prefer to estimate the delivery probability and community collaboration degree utilizing Markov chain model. In Markov chain model, the current state of the process only depends on a certain number of previous values of the process, which is the order of the process. In order to capture the community collaboration degree dynamics in the network, we divide time into slot of equal length δ. It is great important that measuring the length of δ. If δ is relatively short, we can observe the community collaboration degree dynamics between consecutive time slots but at the same time more random factors would involve in the observations which makes it hard to capture the correlations of community collaboration degree. If δ is relatively long, we find it stable, but lose the dynamics.

For each node i, we examine the number of contacts of each node in a series of contact graphs like Fig. 2 and get a sequence of the number of contacts. After discretizing continuous measures, we get a finite state space of contacts named as Θ_c. Let any state $s \in \Theta_c$ and $m \in \Theta_c^k$, where k is the number of order and $m = \{m_1, m_2, ..., m_k\}$. We denote n_{ms}^c as the number of times that state m equals to state s in a given sequence and n_m^c as the number of times that state m is observed. Therefore, we get the estimation of the state transition probability of contacts when state $m = \{m_1, m_2, ..., m_k\}$ transfers to state $\{m_2, m_3, ..., m_k, s\}$ as follows:

$$p_{ms}^c = \frac{n_{ms}^c}{n_m^c}, n_m^c > 0 \tag{11}$$

Besides, we get a series of requests and forwarding and conduct the state transition probability of requests and forwarding. We denote any state $s' \in \Theta_q$ and $m' \in \Theta_q^k$, where Θ_q is the finite state space of requests. Also, Θ_r is the finite state space of forwarding, any state $s'' \in \Theta_r$ and $m'' \in \Theta_r^k$. $n_{m's'}^q$ is the number of times that state m' equals to state s' in a given sequence of requests and $n_{m'}^q$ is the number of times that state m is observed. Also, $n_{m''s''}^r$ is the number of times that state m'' equals to state s'' in a given sequence of forwarding and $n_{m''}^r$ is the number of times that state m'' is observed in the sequence.

$$p_{m's'}^q = \frac{n_{m's'}^q}{n_{m'}^q}, n_{m'}^q > 0 \tag{12}$$

$$p_{m''s''}^r = \frac{n_{m''s''}^r}{n_{m''}^r}, n_{m''}^r > 0 \tag{13}$$

For any node i in the network, we have the estimated number of contacts in the next slot as follows:

$$E_i'(j) = \sum_{s \in \Theta} p_{ms}^c \cdot s \tag{14}$$

Besides, the estimated number of requests and forwarding calculate as follows:

$$Q'_i(j) = \sum_{s' \in \Theta_q} p^q_{m's'} \cdot s' \tag{15}$$

$$R'_i(j) = \sum_{s'' \in \Theta_r} p^r_{m''s''} \cdot s'' \tag{16}$$

5.3 Choosing the Collaborative Nodes

The collaborative message dissemination problem has been proven to be NP-hard in Sect. 3. Therefore, we give our community collaboration (CC) algorithm based on greedy heuristics. Algorithm 1 shows our Community Collaboration (CC) Algorithm. Given the information, our scheme greedily selects the collaborative nodes with the higher delivery probability and the community collaboration degree. Specifically, when a node carrying messages meets one or more nodes, we compare the delivery probability between it and the destination and the delivery probability between the encountered node and the destination. If the delivery probability of the encountered node is higher than itself, then we further compare their community collaboration degree. Here, we consider two types of collaborative nodes. For potential collaborative nodes, we believe that they will provide forwarding services by giving certain rewards.

Algorithm 1. Community Collaboration (CC) Algorithm

Input: All nodes set Ω, Request list R_i of node i, Contact set C_i of node i
Output: Forwarding set $G = \{G_1, G_2, ..., G_n\}$, $n = |\Omega|$

1: Begin
2: $G = \varnothing$
3: **while** $\Omega \neq \varnothing$ **do**
4:　　node i transmit NCT_i to nodes it encounters and request NCT
5:　　select node i from Ω and node j from C_i
6:　　**for** any destination node k in request list R_i **do**
7:　　　　**if** $P_i(k) < P_j(k)$ **then**
8:　　　　　　**if** $CS_i < CS_j$ **then**
9:　　　　　　　　Inform node i to add j to candidate set $G_i(k)$
10:　　**if** node i received NCT_j from j **then**
11:　　　　$G_i(k) = G_i(k) \bigcup j$
12:　　　　$\Omega = \Omega \setminus \{j\}$
13: **for** destination k in request R_i **do**
14:　　select $max(P_i(k)/CS_i)$ node in $G_i(k)$
15:　　$G_i(k) = G_i(k) \bigcap max(P_i(k)/CS_i)node$
16:　　$G_i = G_i \cup G_i(k)$
17: **return** G_i
18: End

For high quality collaborative nodes, we believe that these public vehicles cannot refuse to provide forwarding services for privacy reasons. Therefore, we do not pay more attention to high quality collaborative nodes.

To implement our algorithm, we use two tables, node contact table (NCT) and request list table. Node contact table saves updateId field, the list of contact nodes, contact numbers, forwarding numbers, request numbers and request list table saves destinations, data, isForwarded field and keepingTime field. When the node a carrying message meets node b, a sends its contact table and request list table to b. After receiving the contact table of a, b will calculate which messages are appropriate to forward to itself and inform node a. Node a will update the records of corresponding node after receiving it. When the node contact table changes, the updateId field for the node that corresponds to the changed node is updated. New record will override the previous record. When two nodes exchange table information, if the updateId of the same node is different, the record behind the timestamp should be adopted.

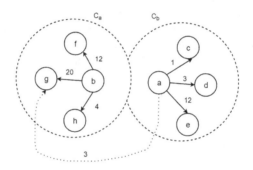

Fig. 5. Cross-community forwarding.

Our algorithm starts with the meeting of two nodes. As shown in Fig. 5, C_a and C_b denotes two communities. Assuming that there are only two communities and node a encounters node b, $\alpha = 0.5$. it starts timing when sending its own NCT to node b and waits for receiving NCT from node b. The total number of contacts $N = E_a(c) + E_a(d) + E_a(e) + E_a(g) + E_b(f) + E_b(g) + E_b(h) = 55$. If node a will deliver messages to node g, the direct delivery probability between node a and node g is $DD_a(g) = E_a(g)/N = 0.055$ and indirect delivery probability $ID_a(g) = E_b(g)/N = 0.364$. $P_a(g) = 0.055 * 0.5 + 0.364 * 0.5 = 0.21$ and $P_b(g) = 0.5 * DD_b(g) + 0.5 * ID_b(g) = 0.5 * 0.36 + 0 = 0.18$. Therefore, node a has a higher delivery probability than node a, and node a should deliver directly it to node g instead of forwarding the data to node b. If $P_a(g) < P_b(g)$, we check how many source nodes of messages in the request list of nodes a and b are themselves, which is the number of requests. And the number of messages forwarded by the node itself, that is, the forwarding amount. If the community collaboration degree of node b is higher than that of node a, then node b will send its own NCT. It will stop the calculation if the update of its own NCT

has not finished within the contact threshold. If node a receives NCT_b from the node b, it will update its own NCT. Then, each destination in the request list is forwarded accordingly.

6   Performance Evaluation

We use the Opportunistic Network Environment (ONE) simulator [29], an effective tool developed by Java. This simulator can simulate the movement of nodes and can evaluate various network parameters. It is designed for Delay Tolerant Networks (DTNs), and also suitable for VANETs. The performance of our scheme is measured and compared with other two schemes: Epidemic [5] and Prophet [22].

6.1   Simulation Setup

In our experiment, we adopt the city of Helsinki as simulation scenario, which is a rectangle of size $5 * 4 \, \text{km}^2$. Nodes move according to the Shortest Path Map Based Movement model, map-based movement model that uses Dijkstra's algorithm to find shortest paths between two random map nodes. Though the working day movement model [30] is best for simulating the movement pattern of vehicles, since it simulates the real activities of human being such as working at office, sleeping at home and visiting some places. In fact, compared with the working day movement model, the Shortest Path Map Based Movement model dilute the influence of node movement pattern with time. In turn, we can observe the nodes forwarding in a long time. Considering the simulation time, we have omitted the differences of day and night. The simulation run lasts for 10 h and messages are created after the first 2 h. In order to avoid accidental factors, each simulation is repeated 5 times with random nodes. Other parameters are specified in the Table 1. Here, the participation rate represents the maximum proportion of collaborative nodes in the network. It means that the ratio of the number of collaborative nodes and the total number of nodes should not exceed that value.

We compare our CC algorithm with Epidemic [5], Prophet [22]. The epidemic scheme indicates that random pair-wise exchanges of messages ensure eventual message delivery among mobile nodes in the range of communication. The goal of epidemic is to maximize message delivery ratio and minimize message delay. The prophet generates a delivery predictability sequence from history traces. That can calculate how likely it can relay a message to the destination. The metrics used to compare above schemes are listed as follows:

- **Delivery Ratio**: The ratio of messages successfully delivered to destination to all messages generated.
- **Average Delay**: The average duration that each message is successfully delivered.
- **Delivery Cost**: The ratio of the total number of message packets in a network to the number of source packets created.

Table 1. Simulation setting

Network area	$5 * 4\ \mathrm{km}^2$
Simulation time	10 h
Transmit speed	2 Mbps
Transmission range	200 m
Number of node	240
Package size	50 KB ~ 1 MB
Messages TTL	1 h
Participation rate	0.8
α	0.5

6.2 Impact of the Number of Vehicles

We first show that how the number of vehicles impacts the performance of the different schemes. As shown in Fig. 6a, as the number of vehicles increases, the delivery ratio of three schemes grows smoothly. The epidemic has the highest delivery ratio in three schemes. This is because the main idea of epidemic is that a node will forward messages from them when it meets other nodes. This scheme can get the higher delivery ratio than other schemes, but the loss packet rate will increase due to network congestion, resource exhaustion and other reasons when the number of copies reaches a certain number. Our scheme is higher than prophet in delivery ratio. Figure 6b show that the average delay lowers as the number of vehicles. The CC algorithm is 6% lower than prophet in delivery delay. Compared with prophet, our scheme not only considers the delivery probability, but also considers the contribution of a node to the community. As for Fig. 6c, we can see that a message which is successfully forwarded requires multiple copies. Our scheme is 7% lower than prophet in delivery cost.

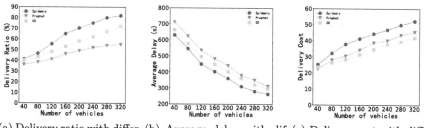

(a) Delivery ratio with different number of vehicles. (b) Average delay with different number of vehicles. (c) Delivery cost with different number of vehicles.

Fig. 6. Impact of the number of vehicles.

6.3   Impact of Message Time to Live

Figure 7 shows that how the message time to live impacts the performance of the different schemes. As shown in Fig. 7a, the epidemic has the highest delivery ratio in three schemes. Compared with prophet, our algorithm is higher than prophet in delivery ratio. This is because the effective preservation period of messages becomes longer as the increase of TTL, so that there are more opportunities to contact other nodes, which naturally increases the chance of forwarding. In Fig. 7b, our algorithm is 7% lower than prophet in delivery delay. Although our algorithm is less than epidemic, which takes the method of forwarding messages as soon as a node encounters another. As a result, there exist a large number of copies in the network and they waste cache resources. That may cause network congestion. As for delivery cost, our algorithm is 8% lower than prophet and also lower than epidemic in Fig. 7c.

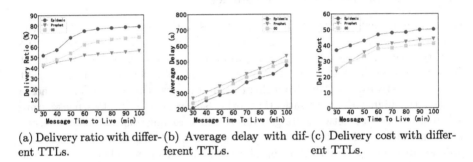

(a) Delivery ratio with different TTLs. (b) Average delay with different TTLs. (c) Delivery cost with different TTLs.

Fig. 7. Impact of the message time to live.

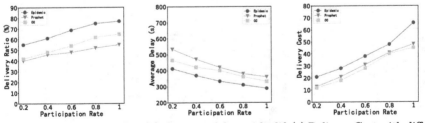

(a) Delivery ratio with different participation ratio. (b) Average delay with different participation ratio. (c) Delivery Cost with different participation ratio.

Fig. 8. Impact of the participation ratio.

6.4   Impact of Participation Ratio

Figure 8 shows the participation rate to change the number of collaborative nodes in the network and compare the changes of three metrics. In Fig. 8a, we can see that the delivery ratio increases as the participation rate increases. When the participation rate reach 1.0, the delivery ratio reaches a maximum. Because there is no privacy node in the network at maximal participation rate. All nodes voluntarily forward messages from other nodes with rewards. Our algorithm has higher delivery ratio compared with prophet, although it is lower than epidemic. Figure 8b show the average delay of three schemes. Our algorithm is 8% higher than prophet. The epidemic has the lowest delay, because its forwarding strategy like flooding that sacrifices space for time. Also, Fig. 8c show that delivery cost of three schemes increase as the participation rate increases. Our algorithm is 9% higher than prophet. If there are many potential collaborative nodes, the delivery ratio of the whole network is relatively low, and there are fewer forwarding nodes, so delivery cost is relatively low. When the participation rate increases, there are fewer potential collaborative nodes and higher forwarding frequency, so the delivery cost increases.

7   Conclusion

In this paper, we study the message forwarding based on community collaboration degree in VANETs. We find that there is a clear social structure within the network by analyzing the real traces of taxis. That inspires us to combine the community into scheme. Firstly, we define the delivery probability including direct delivery probability and indirect delivery probability and community collaborative nodes. Secondly, we purpose our CC algorithm to improve the delivery ratio and lower the delivery delay and delivery cost. The results show effectiveness of our methods under different environments. As a future work, we will study how to choose collaborative nodes in a hybrid vehicular networks.

References

1. Altayeb, M., Mahgoub, I.: A survey of vehicular ad hoc networks routing protocols. Int. J. Innov. Appl. Stud. **3**(3), 829–846 (2013)
2. Ramanathan, R., Hansen, R., Basu, P., Rosales-Hain, R., Krishnan, R.: Prioritized epidemic routing for opportunistic networks. In: International MobiSys Workshop on Mobile Opportunistic Networking, pp. 62–66 (2007)
3. Cao, Y., Sun, Z.: Routing in delay disruption tolerant networks: a taxonomy, survey and challenges. IEEE Commun. Surv. Tutorials **15**(2), 654–677 (2013)
4. Baiocchi, A., Salvo, P., Cuomo, F., Rubin, I.: Understanding spurious message forwarding in vanet beaconless dissemination protocols: an analytical approach. IEEE Trans. Veh.Technol. **65**(4), 2243–2258 (2016)
5. Vahdat, A., Becker, D.: Epidemic routing for partially-connected ad hoc networks. Master thesis (2000)
6. Boldrini, C., Conti, M., Passarella, A.: Social-based autonomic routing in opportunistic networks. Auton. Commun. **15**(1), 31–67 (2009)

7. Conti, M., Kumar, M.: Opportunities in opportunistic computing. Computer **43**(1), 42–50 (2010)
8. Zhu, H., Dong, M., Chang, S., Zhu, Y., Li, M., Shen, X.S.: ZOOM: Scaling the mobility for fast opportunistic forwarding in vehicular networks. In: 2013 Proceedings IEEE INFOCOM, pp. 2832–2840. IEEE (2013)
9. Pujol, J.M., Toledo, A.L., Rodriguez, P.: Fair routing in delay tolerant networks. In: INFOCOM, pp. 837–845 (2009)
10. Fraire, J., Finochietto, J.M.: Routing-aware fair contact plan design for predictable delay tolerant networks. Ad Hoc Netw. **25**, 303–313 (2015)
11. Daly, E.M., Haahr, M.: Social network analysis for routing in disconnected delay-tolerant MANETs. In: ACM Interational Symposium on Mobile Ad Hoc Networking and Computing, pp. 32–40 (2007)
12. Liu, Y., Wu, H., Xia, Y., Wang, Y., Li, F., Yang, P.: Optimal online data dissemination for resource constrained mobile opportunistic networks. IEEE Trans. Veh. Technol. **66**(6), 5301–5315 (2017)
13. Hsu, Y.F., Hu, C.L.: Enhanced buffer management for data delivery to multiple destinations in DTNs. IEEE Trans. Veh. Technol. **65**(10), 8735–8739 (2016)
14. Abdelkader, T., Naik, K., Gad, W.: A game-theoretic approach to supporting fair cooperation in delay tolerant networks. In: Vehicular Technology Conference (2015)
15. Cai, Y., Fan, Y., Wen, D.: An incentive-compatible routing protocol for two-hop delay-tolerant networks. IEEE Trans. Veh. Technol. **65**(1), 266–277 (2016)
16. Liu, B., et al.: Infrastructure-assisted message dissemination for supporting heterogeneous driving patterns. IEEE Trans. Intell. Transp. Syst. **18**(10), 2865–2876 (2017)
17. Lin, Y.Y., Rubin, I.: Integrated message dissemination and traffic regulation for autonomous VANETs. IEEE Trans. Veh. Technol. **66**(10), 8644–8658 (2017)
18. Liu, B., Jia, D., Wang, J., Lu, K., Wu, L.: Cloud-assisted safety message dissemination in VANET-cellular heterogeneous wireless network. IEEE Syst. J. **11**(1), 128–139 (2017)
19. He, J., Cai, L., Cheng, P., Pan, J.: Delay minimization for data dissemination in large-scale vanets with buses and taxis. IEEE Trans. Mobile Comput. **15**(8), 1939–1950 (2016)
20. Li, P., Zhang, T., Huang, C., Chen, X., Fu, B.: RSU-assisted geocast in vehicular ad hoc networks. IEEE Wireless Commun. **24**(1), 53–59 (2017)
21. Bi, Y., Shan, H., Shen, X.S., Wang, N., Zhao, H.: A multi-hop broadcast protocol for emergency message dissemination in urban vehicular ad hoc networks. IEEE Trans. Intell. Transp. Syst. **17**(3), 736–750 (2016)
22. Lindgren, A., Doria, A., Schelén, O.: Probabilistic routing in intermittently connected networks. ACM SIGMOBILE Mobile Comput. Commun. Rev. **7**(3), 19–20 (2004)
23. Khuller, S., Moss, A., Naor, J.: The budgeted maximum coverage problem. Inf. Process. Lett. **70**(1), 39–45 (1999)
24. Zhu, H., Li, M., Fu, L., Xue, G., Zhu, Y., Ni, L.M.: Impact of traffic influxes: revealing exponential intercontact time in urban VANETs. IEEE Trans. Parallel Distrib. Syst. **22**(8), 1258–1266 (2011)
25. Li, Z., Wang, C., Yang, S., Jiang, C., Stojmenovic, I.: Space-crossing: community-based data forwarding in mobile social networks under the hybrid communication architecture. IEEE Trans. Wireless Commun. **14**(9), 4720–4727 (2015)

26. Dubois-Ferriere, H., Grossglauser, M., Vetterli, M.: Age matters: efficient route discovery in mobile ad hoc networks using encounter ages. In: Proceedings of the 4th ACM International Symposium on Mobile Ad Hoc Networking and Computing, pp. 257–266. ACM (2003)
27. Blondel, V.D., Guillaume, J.L., Lambiotte, R., Lefebvre, E.: Fast unfolding of communities in large networks. J. Stat. Mech. **2008**(10), 155–168 (2012)
28. Newman, M.E.J.: Modularity and community structure in networks. Proc. Natl. Acad. Sci. **103**(23), 8577–8582 (2006)
29. Keränen, A., Ott, J., Kärkkäinen, T.: The one simulator for DTN protocol evaluation. In: International Conference on Simulation Tools and Techniques, p. 55 (2009)
30. Ekman, F., Karvo, J.: Working day movement model. In: ACM SIGMOBILE Workshop on Mobility Models, pp. 33–40 (2008)

An Efficient Traffic Prediction Model Using Deep Spatial-Temporal Network

Jie Xu[1,2(✉)], Yong Zhang[1,2], Yongzheng Jia[3], and Chunxiao Xing[1,2]

[1] Department of Computer Science and Technology, Tsinghua University,
Beijing, China
xuj15@mails.tsinghua.edu.cn,
{zhangyong05,xingcx}@tsinghua.edu.cn
[2] Research Institute of Information Technology,
Beijing National Research Center for Information Science and Technology,
Beijing, China
[3] Institute of Interdisciplinary Information Sciences, Tsinghua University,
Beijing, China
jiayz13@mails.tsinghua.edu.cn

Abstract. Recently years, traffic prediction has become an important and challenging problem in smart urban traffic computing, which can be used for government for road planning, detecting bottle-neck congestions roads, pollution emissions estimating and so on. However, former data mining algorithms mainly address the problem by using the traditional mathematical or statistical theories, and they were impossible to model the spatial and temporal relationship simultaneously. To address these issues, we propose an end-to-end neural network named C-LSTM to predict the traffic congestion at next time interval. More specifically, the C-LSTM is based on CNN and LSTM to collectively capture the spatial-temporal dependencies on the road network. Inspired by the procedure of handling the image by CNN, the city-wide traffic maps are first converted into a series of static images like the video frame and then are fed into a deep learning architecture, in which CNN extracts the spatial characteristics, and LSTM extracts the temporal characteristics. In addition, we also consider some external factors to further improve the prediction accuracy. Extensive experiments on reality Beijing transportation datasets demonstrate the superiority of our method.

Keywords: Road network · Traffic prediction · Residual · CNN · LSTM

1 Introduction

Road traffic prediction has become an interesting and challenging issue recently years, which is very important for the government in city managing, such as road planning, detecting the bottle-neck congestions roads, estimating the pollution emissions and so on. However, traditional traffic prediction studies were mainly based on statistical theory or mathematical theory, whose scalability and migration were poor, and they also tended to ignore the dynamic changes of each road segment, thus neglect the whole city-wide dependencies. Fortunately, with the great achievement of deep

© ICST Institute for Computer Sciences, Social Informatics and Telecommunications Engineering 2019
Published by Springer Nature Switzerland AG 2019. All Rights Reserved
H. Gao et al. (Eds.): CollaborateCom 2018, LNICST 268, pp. 386–399, 2019.
https://doi.org/10.1007/978-3-030-12981-1_27

learning in computer vision and natural language processing domains [1, 2], numerous researchers also implement the deep learning techniques to address the road trans- portation problems [3, 4, 5, 6, 7], since the deep learning can theoretically model complex nonlinear relationship. However, they have following disadvantages: In [7], they simply divided the historical data into categories groups and then fused them directly, lacking of theoretical proof for periods changes and an in-depth description for the temporal characteristics. In [4], they did not consider the impact of external factors (weather, Chinese festivals, etc.) on traffic flow, and the histories time sequences trajectories were too small.

In this paper, we predict the road traffic at next interval by using convolutional neural networks (CNN) and long short-term memory (LSTM) [8] to capture complex spatial and temporal nonlinear correlation, that means given a set of historical traffic data through a time period, the deep learning structure treats the traffic volume and flow as pixel values within a series of image, and predicts the traffic image like a motion- prediction issue. CNN and LSTM are applied to hierarchically learn the spatial- temporal relationship. There are three characteristics in the traffic trajectories data [6, 7]. (1) Spatial characteristic. A road traffic conditions will affect the relative link road traffic, for example, traffic accidents on overpasses may affect many connected roads traffic. At the other hand, the residential areas traffic perhaps affects the corresponding commercial areas traffic, the reverse is the same. (2) Temporal characteristic. Traffic conditions vary greatly with seasonal changes, or from rush hour to midnight, or from weekdays to weekend. (3) External factors, such as weather condition, time-of-day, day-of-week and Chinese festivals which are proven to be promising impact factors. In summary, the contributions of this work are summarized as follows:

First, in this paper, we illustrate how a road network traffic condition can be transferred to a image-related heat map (in particular, CNN and LSTM related), which is helpful for deep learning methods to describe the road traffic features.

Second, we propose an end-to-end combination model named C-LSTM which is comprised of CNN and LSTM to sketch the road network traffic image characteristic. CNN utilize the strengthen to capture the spatial characteristic, while LSTM capture the temporal characteristic of traffic map. In order to make the model fully close to reality, we fuse the external factor such as weather and time metal date, which can obvious improve forecasting effectiveness.

Third, we conduct extensive experiments on real datasets, and results show the high convergence rate and advancement of the our approach.

The rest of this paper is organized as follows: We propose the related work in Sect. 2, then model the problem and illustrate our algorithm in Sect. 3. Experimental results are discussed in Sect. 4. The conclusions are summarized in Sect. 5.

2 Related Work

There are some previously existing works on predicting time series movements [9] based on the history trajectories, the approaches can be classified into mainly two categories: traditional algorithms and deep learning algorithms.

2.1 Traditional Prediction Algorithms

Shu et al. [2] proposed an adapted traffic prediction methods named FARMIMA, the dependencies in the network traffic can be divided into two kinds, i.e., long-range and short range dependence. They adjusted an indicator parameter named weight bias for short and long range dependence by congregating on standard autoregressive integrated moving average. Clark et al. [10] designed an intuitive method for forecasting the traffic by using a pattern matching technique that exploited the three-dimensional nature of the traffic state. The approach was a multivariate extension of nonparametric regression and can be easily understood by the practitioners. However, they neither took consideration of the main factors of traffic conditions, nor considered the interaction among different city-wide regions. Min et al. [11] proposed a framework which took into account the spatial characteristics of a road network, that can reflect not only the distance but also the average speed on the road segment, they also involved incorporating weather, incident data, current or planned roadwork into the forecasting model. However, all above algorithms fail to depict the spatial and temporal relationship simultaneously.

2.2 Deep Learning Algorithms

Recently, a series of studies applied CNN and LSTM to capture spatial and temporal dependencies and achieved great success [3, 4, 5, 6, 12]. Ke et al. [6] proposed a one end to end convolutional and multiple LSTM network named FCL-NET to address these three dependencies for short-term passenger demand forecasting. The evidence from benchmark models proved that spatial-temporal correlations in models can greatly improve the predictive accuracy. Zhang et al. [7] introduced a deep learning methods based on CNN named ST-ResNet for citywide crowd flows prediction. They divided the historical data into three categories, i.e., closeness, period, trend data, which depicted the denoting recent time, near history and distant history respectively. The residual unit were applied for training super deep neural networks. Yu et al. [4] designed a novel deep architecture with CNN and LSTM, namely, spatiotemporal recurrent convolutional networks (SRCNs) for traffic prediction. They divided the road network into many grids whose average velocity represented the each grid velocity in specified timestamp, that can retain the fine-scale structure of a transportation network, but they didn't consider the extensive features. Wang et al. [3] proposed an end-to-end deep learning framework named DeepTTE to estimate the travel time of the whole path directly, in which the geographic information were integrated into the classical geo-convolution, which was capable of capturing spatial correlation. Their method was novel and worked well for depicting vehicle trajectories. Zhang et al. [14] presented a deep spatial-temporal neural networks named FCN-rLSTM to sequentially count vehicles from low quality videos on road network, that model connected fully convolutional neural networks (FCN) with LSTM in a residual learning fashion, and enabled the processing to refine the feature representation and implement a novel end-to-end trainable mapping from pixels to vehicle count.

3   Traffic Prediction Based on Deep Learning

3.1   Preliminaries

Definition 1 Road network G = (V, E), which is used to model a road network, where a vertex set V is associated with a geographical position, including the longitude and latitude, a vertex set E is defined for the edges between two positions. The road network is divided into multiple same size grids (e.g. 10 * 10 m), where the velocity in each region is regarded as the same.

Definition 2: Average velocity V_{ij}^t is defined as the average ratio of travel distance to travel time in i * j region according to the road links condition at specified timestamp t, in our paper, the length of the time interval is set as 30 min.

Definition 3: Velocity heat map. Give a set of historical trajectories, we can treat the velocity as pixel values in one grid, and mark different colors according to different velocities. By doing so, the whole velocity heat map can be built based on the road network and can be denoted as V(R, t) at time t. As in Fig. 1, the left figure represents the whole traffic status, the different colors lines on the road represent different velocities, the right figure represents how the velocity of each region is mapped and colored in corresponding region.

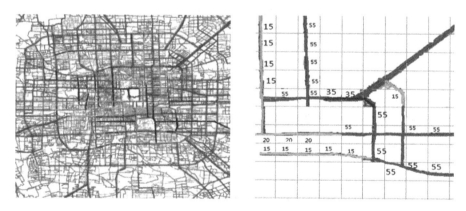

Fig. 1. Velocity heat map

Problem: Give a time series of historical road trajectories maps V(R, t − 3), V(R, t − 2), V(R, t − 1), our goal is to predict the next V(R, t).

3.2   Framework of C-LSTM

Figure 2 presents the architecture of C-LSTM, which is comprised of three major components [13]. For geographic problems, the key spirit is how to transform the problem into a sequence of 2D image, i.e., velocity heat map, which is similar with the video frame, the image itself has natural spatial and temporal attributes which is

associated with CNN and LSTM. The strength of CNN is to outline spatial characteristic, on the other hand, for traffic information, intuitively, we can find that traffic
conditions vary with rush hours and midnight, weekdays and weekend, using RNN
(recurrent neural network) to describe temporal series characteristics has achieved great
success. In this paper, we utilize the CNN and LSTM to jointly predict traffic in a
residual fashion, such combination leverages the strengths of Resnet (Deep residual
network) [15] for pixel-level description and the strengths of LSTM for learning
temporal dependencies, we further aggregate the external components to describe the
influence of complex external factors.

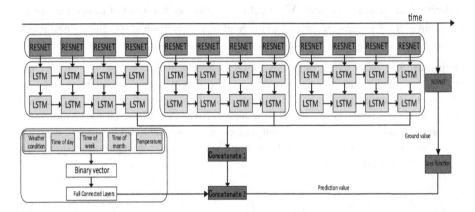

Fig. 2. Framework of C-LSTM

Steps for Model: The trajectories data are divided into three groups according to time
axis, denoting as recent time, week period, and month period respectively. In theory,
shallow CNN can capture near-distance features, and deep CNN can capture far away
area information, thus each image characteristics can be exacted by a convolutional
neural network with the residual units [4, 16]. To predict the heat map V(R, t), then the
LSTM capture the temporal sequences, the output of each group of CNN is used as the
input of LSTM. Theoretically, more stacked LSTM layers can overcome the vanishing
gradient and exploding gradient problems [17], in our model, the LSTM model was
stacked by two to four layers.

For external component, the external factors are collected and organized at the same
time interval, such as weather, time of day, time of week, etc. External factors are first
transfer to binary vector and feed into full connected layers, whose output are fused
with the output of LSTM. Finally, the aggregation is mapped into one-dimensional
vector whose value is restrict within [−1, 1], by steadily narrowing the loss function to
convergence status.

3.3 Spatial Characteristics Captured by CNN

The convolution neural network (CNN) has achieved great success in extracting features. In the road network structure, a snapshot of network traffic flow at specified time

can be seen as a 2D image, the traffic conditions on a road not only affect the most adjacent area, but also have potential impact on more distant regions. CNN is good at processing image and video frame with both near distance and far away distance correlations, the input for CNN is a tensor for sequence 2D heat map at a pixel level, the value is converted from −1 to 1 with normalization technique.

In ours study, the deep convolution neural networks is firstly constructed to capture the spatial relationships in the heat road traffic image. As in Fig. 2, we use zero padding to the end of the boundaries of city. The regular transformation at each CNN layer is defined as follows:

$$O_k^l = f(w_k^{l-1} * O_k^{l-1} + b_k^{l-1}) \tag{1}$$

Where the $f(\cdot)$ denotes an activation function and $*$ denotes the convolutional operation, which usually is a nonlinear activation function. The w_k^l presents weight parameters matrix, the O_k^l represents the output of the k filter for l-th layer, in our study, the activation function is tanh (x).

From [7], near spatial dependencies can be seized by the shallow CNN, however, since one convolutional layer can only figure out near characteristic because of the limitation of kernel size, we need design deep CNN layers, e.g. 50 layers, to capture the distance dependencies. However, it is also well-known that very deep convolutional networks exposed a degraded problem, the accuracy becomes saturated and inaccurate, and more deep layers may generated higher error.

In this paper, the residual method is employed to train the CNN. The Resnet take advantage of a connection method named "shortcut connection", and bottleneck design, whose purpose is to reduce the number of calculations and parameters. As in Fig. 3, shortcut connections are inserted with the plain network [15] by residual blocks. The right figure is called "bottleneck building design". To reduce the number of parameters, the first 1×1 convolution reduces the 256-dimensional to 64-dimension, and then recovers at the end through a 1×1 convolution with 64 filters. For plain

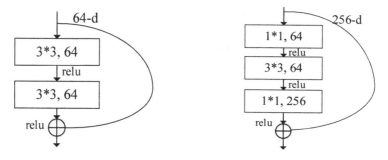

Fig. 3. Residual unit

network, it can be applied in networks of 34 layers or less as in left Fig. 3, and shortcut for bottleneck design is usually implemented in deeper networks like 50/101/152.

The updating rule of our residual layer can be expressed as:

$$X_k^{l+1} = X_k^l + F(X_k^l, \theta_k^l) \tag{2}$$

Where $F(\cdot)$ is the residual function as presented in Fig. 3. After convolution, max-pooling is applied to select remarkable features, and fully connected layer is to generate the class scores for different features at each interval t, the output features vector $X \in R^{1000}$ is fed as the LSTM input.

3.4   Temporal Characteristics Captured by LSTM

Intuitively, for the road network velocity, such as the rush hour and midnight of the day, the heat map shows a periodicity changes, similar phenomena occur in the time of week and time of month. For example, 5 pm, on Monday in June, the traffic condition is similar to 5 pm, on Monday in July.

The one of most successful model for handling time sequential is RNN (recurrent neural network), which is a repeated structure and the output of a neuron can be used as the input for the next neuron unit. The main components can be concluded as $s_t = f(Ws_{t-1} + Ux_t)$, where the $f(\bullet)$ function is usually a nonlinear function and x_t is the input at time t. However, RNN can only process a certain length of sequence, if the time interval is too large, there may be gradient disappearance or exploding gradient problem, and the effectiveness becomes poor. Consequently, the LSTM based on processing the long-term information method is introduced [18], which is a special structural variant of RNN. The LSTM designs one forget gate, one input gate, and one output gate. The gates record and pass the information through the units. In this way, this gate can memorize the information that needs to be saved, or drop redundant and irrelevant one. The structure parameters for all gates are same and shared through whole steps.

At each time interval, LSTM takes time series C_t as an input, and then all information is accumulated to memory cell, the architecture of LSTM is defined as follows:

$$f_t = \delta(W_{fh}h_{t-1} + W_{fx}x_t + b_f) \tag{3}$$

$$i_t = \delta(W_{ih}h_{t-1} + W_{ix}x_t + b_i) \tag{4}$$

$$\widetilde{C}_t = tanh(W_{Ch}h_{t-1} + W_{Cx}x_t + b_C) \tag{5}$$

$$C_t = f_t \circ C_{t-1} + i_t \circ \widetilde{C}_t \tag{6}$$

$$o_t = \delta(W_{oh}h_{t-1} + W_{ox}x_t + b_o) \tag{7}$$

$$h_t = o_t \circ tanh(C_t) \tag{8}$$

Where the W_f, W_i, W_c, W_o are the weight parameters matrices and the b_f, b_i, b_c, b_o are the biases values of the three gates, the δ denotes the non-linear activation function. In our case, the LSTM with CNN are combined to jointly learn traffic velocity heat map.

Furthermore, it has been shown that multiple stacked LSTM layers are more efficient to increase the model capacity compared with a single LSTM layer. In our model, the input sequence of the LSTM is the features (i.e. 1000 dimension) outputted by the last layer of Resnet. For different temporal period, the number of time series is set 3, 3, 4 respectively. The three different CNN-LSTM units are integrated by using the fusion methods as follows:

$$X_t^{Lstm} = W_{h1} \circ h_t^h + W_{h2} \circ h_t^d + W_{h3} \circ h_t^m \tag{9}$$

Where the $h_{t+1}^h, h_{t+1}^d, h_{t+1}^m$ represent the hour dependencies, day dependencies, week dependencies respectively, $\circ$ is Hadamard product.

3.5 The Structure of External Factors

Traffic flows can be affected by many complex external factors, such as weather and event. For instance, rainy days are usually more congested than usual, and road is more prone to have high level crowd [19], etc. In our implementation, we mainly consider weather condition, day-of-hour, time-of-week, and day-of-month. Note that these property values cannot be directly fed into CNN, we embed the weather condition as $X \in R^{16}$, time-of-hour as $X \in R^{24}$, day-of-week as $X \in R^7$, and day-of-month as $X \in R^{12}$ by using the hot coding to transform each categorical attribute into a vector, then concatenate the individual vectors into a integrated vector, further feed them into a full FC connection layer to reduce the dimension of spatial-temporal features [20]. The output of LSTM is fused with the external component. The definition is formulated as follows:

$$\widetilde{Y}_t = \sigma(W_{Lstm} \circ X_t^{Lstm} + W_{ext} \circ E_{ext}) \tag{10}$$

$\sigma(\cdot)$ is a sigmoid function defined as $\sigma(x) = 1 = (1 + e^{-x})$, W_{Lstm} and W_{ext} are two learnable parameter sets. For the actual value of traffic heat map at time interval t, we also capture the feature using the same Resnet architecture, and then fed them into FC layers, whose output is Y_t, and the dimensions is equal to the X_t^{Lstm}. In this paper, recall that our goal is to predict road congestion at the next time interval t, we need to reduce the error between the actual value and the predicted value within a reasonable deviation during training process, thus the loss function is defined as follows:

$$L(\theta) = \left\| Y_t - \widetilde{Y}_t \right\| \tag{11}$$

Where θ are all learnable parameters needed to be trained. We continuously adjust the parameter sets by Tensorflow until loss function converges.

4 Experiments and Discussions

4.1 Dataset

Datasets: We use two real historical data set [21] in Beijing road which contains about 330,000 vertices and 440,000 edges, the **Taxi data**, which contains about 180,000 trajectories generated by more than 7,000 public taxicabs, the **Ucar data**, which contains about 480,000 trajectories generated by more than 5,000 public taxicabs. Those abnormal records are first filtered out, and the map matching algorithm is employed to locate the deviated GPS data to the road network, the vehicle velocity maps are converted to a congestion heat map at every 15 min interval.

Meteorological data: We record the Beijing weather data from Beijing Meteorological Bureau to incorporate the impacts on the road traffic. The weather conditions are divided into 16 types: normal days, rainy, sunny, snowy, overcast, cloudy, sleety, Foggy etc. [22]. For example, we choose the following nine features, e.g. 2016-06-09, the Chinese Dragon Boat Festival, 10 am, hourly temperature, rain, wind speed, as one hot-encoded vector that denotes external factors.

4.2 Parameters Setting

Parameters setting: The parameters are described as follows. In the Resnet component, first, the global road network is divided into small equal region with size 10 * 10 m, the layers of Resnet is set as 32/50/101, with core kernel size 3 * 3, the dimensional of time series C_t for LSTM is set as 1000. Our model is implemented with Python 2.0. We adopt Adamax optimization algorithm to train the parameters, the learning rate is 0.1, the weight of loss is 0.01. The embedding function converts the raw data to the range of [0, 1] by using max-mix normalization, the formula is defined as follows:

$$Xnorm = \frac{X - Xmin}{Xmax - Xmin} \tag{12}$$

4.3 Baseline Algorithms

To demonstrate the validity of our model, we compare it with 6 baseline methods, including:

ARIMA [2]: ARIMA means AutoRegressive Integrated Moving Average, which is a class of statistical models and can captures a suite of different standard temporal structures in time series data, leverage the dependency between an observation and some number of lagged observations with a residual error.

GBDT: GBDT is a machine learning technique for regression, classification and sorting tasks by ensemble multiple weak learners, usually decision trees. It belongs to ensemble learning.

SRCNS: SRCNS is a spatiotemporal recurrent convolutional networks, which inherit the advantages of deep convolutional neural networks (DCNNs) and the long short-term memory (LSTM) neural networks, the DCNN captures the spatial dependencies, and LSTM captures the temporal dependencies.

DMVST-Net: DMVST-Net is a deep multi-view spatiotemporal network. To model spatiotemporal relationships [5], they construct a region map based on the similarity of demand patterns for modeling related but distant areas.

FCL-Net [6]: FCL-Net is a fusion convolutional long short-term memory network to forecast an on-demand ride service, this model is stacked and fused by convolutional operators, LSTM layers, multiple conv-LSTM layers. A tailored spatially random forest is utilized to score the variables for feature selection.

ST-ResNet [7]: In ST-ResNet, the historical data was divided into three categories, they leveraged the residual neural network framework to model the time tightness, period and trend characteristics of crowd traffic respectively, and also added external attribute information such as weather, time of day, time of month, time of week. In this paper, the above algorithms are all implemented under the same equipment and environment.

4.4   Evaluation Metric

In our study, the Mean Absolute Percentage Error (MAPE) and Root Mean Square Error (RMSE) are employed as evaluation metric, the definitions are as follows:

$$MAPE = \sum_{t=1}^{n} \left| \frac{y_t - \tilde{y}_t}{y_t} \right| * \frac{1}{n} \tag{13}$$

$$RMSE = \sqrt{\frac{1}{n} \sum_{t=1}^{n} (y_t - \tilde{y}_t)^2} \tag{14}$$

Table 1. Performance comparisons

Model	Taxi		Ucar	
	MAPE	RMSE	MAPE	RMSE
ARIMA	0.32	51	0.28	47.25
GBDT	0.278	43	0.257	39.41
SRCNS	0.243	39	0.214	35.47
DMVST-Net	0.196	28.74	0.176	24.19
FCL-Net	0.174	24.68	0.154	26.56
ST-ResNet	0.157	18.4	0.137	13.61
Ours	**0.123**	**13.34**	**0.104**	**8.76**

Where y_t is the predictive value, the $\tilde{y}_t$ is the actual value. To verify the effectiveness of C-LSTM, we compare it with several state-of-the-art methods, the results are shown in Table 1.

From the Table 1, we can see that the MAPE and RMSE of the ARIMA perform poor results(i.e., has a MAPE of 0.32 and RMSE of 51, respectively), which means that the simple traditional prediction method cannot effectively describe the spatial-temporal information. The effect of DMVST-Net and FCL-NET is similar, and achieves better performance than ARIMA and GBDT, the comparison shows that deep learning methods can work. The ST-ResNet shows a good performance, however, it does not illustrate the time dependencies very well. Our algorithm significantly out-performs above mentioned methods with the lowest MAPE (0.123% and 0.104%) and RMSE (13.34 and 8.76) on two datasets, it verifies the superiority and feasibility of the our approach, as our algorithm further exploits LSTM and takes account of the influence of external factors.

4.5   Effectiveness of Resnet

In this section, we compare the model performances with different Resnet varieties, the traditional AlexNet [23] network is used to replace the Resnet. We can observe that the result of the replacement is not as well as Resnet. On the other hand, we compare different Resnet variants with respect to different number of layers [15], i.e., 34/50/101.

Table 2. Experimental results with different CNN variants

Model	Taxi		Ucar	
	MAPE	RMSE	MAPE	RMSE
AlexNet	0.235	17.63	0.215	14.86
Resnet 34	0.176	15.89	0.164	11.34
Resmet 50	0.153	15.14	0.132	9.72
Resmet 101	**0.123**	**13.34**	**0.104**	**8.76**

The results are shown in Table 2, we can see that as the layers increases, the values of MAPE and RMSE decay, the Resnet 101 decreases 36% and 22% for MAPE and RMSE respectively comparing with Resnet 34 for Ucar dataset.

4.6   Effectiveness of LSTM

In our article, for different sequence length for LSTM, we mainly consider the number of days in one week and the number of hours in one day. In fact, Multiple layers of LSTM are added, such as Layers 3 and 4, to evaluate the effect. The results reveal that the effect of the 3 and 4 layers are better than that 2 layers, but the increasing trend is not obvious. In addition, we set $(d_1, d_2, d_3) = (3, 5, 7)$, and $(h_1, h_2, h_3, h_4) = (2, 4, 8, 16)$ which indicates that traffic speeds are predicted from the previous (3, 5, 7) days and (2, 4, 8,16) hours based on historical data by fixing the number of other two LSTM hidden units components respectably. As in Table 3, we observe that the layers-h-8 yields the lowest MAPE and RMSE, which demonstrates when the historical data length goes larger, the prediction error decreases. However, for layers-h-16, it no

Table 3. Experimental results with different hidden units of LSTM.

Model	Taxi		Ucar	
	MAPE	RMSE	MAPE	RMSE
Layers-d-3	0.139	16.78	0.121	11.34
Layers-d-5	0.135	15.67	0.116	10.67
Layers-d-7	0.127	14.32	0.112	9.87
Layers-h-2	0.153	16.89	0.137	13.24
Layers-h-4	0.147	14.78	0.119	10.14
Layers-h-8	**0.123**	**13.34**	**0.104**	**8.76**
Layers-h-16	0.148	15.64	0.121	10.24

longer displays remarkable results, we find that it tends to overfit the training data and thus exhibits the slightly degrades prediction performance.

4.7 Effectiveness of Attribute Component

In our article, we mainly leverage external influence conditions, but in fact, each external condition is not always available at the same time. The whole external information component is removed first, the rustles decrease nearly 30%. Second, we choose frequently-used available external conditions as attribute information, excluding partly uncommon factors such as temperature, wind speed, humidity, etc., the results display that the prediction error increases, but the degree is not large, this finding confirms that the weight of external factors are different.

5 Conclusions

In this paper, we propose a novel deep learning end-to-end model method based on CNN and LSTM model for predicting the future traffic flow based on real historical traffic data. The method inherits the strength of both CNN and LSTM, and transform historical data into heat map firstly, then employ CNN to extract the spatial features, further utilize LSTM to capture the temporal characteristic. To validate the effectiveness of the proposed C-LSTM, six previous prediction approaches are exploited to compare the results by extensive experiments in terms of RMSE and MAPE, the results show that our method can effectively deal with spatiotemporal and spatial information, and demonstrate the superiority of our methodologies.

The key spirit of this paper is how to transform the historical trajectories data on road network into a heat map, and then take advantage of the deep learning method as the domain of video frame research, which can be used for these similar types transportation problem, such as taxi demand, traffic flow, POI (Point Of Interest) prediction and so on. For future work, we plan to (1) add some other mechanisms, such as attention mechanism, to improve the effectiveness in time sequence learning task, (2) consider incorporating the road semantic information for deep learning model,

(3) apply machine learning to interdisciplinary areas such smart transportation and economics disciplines.

Acknowledgments. This research was financially supported by NSFC (91646202), the National High-tech R&D Program of China (SS2015AA020102), Research/Project 2017YB142 supported by Ministry of Education of The People's Republic of China, the 1000-Talent program, Tsinghua University Initiative Scientific Research Program.

References

1. Krizhevsky, A., Sutskever, I., Hinton, G.E.: ImageNet classification with deep convolutional neural networks. In: Advances in Neural Information Processing Systems, pp. 1097–1105. Hinton (2012)
2. Shu, Y., Jin, Z., Zhang, L., et al.: Traffic prediction using FARIMA models. In: IEEE International Conference on Communications, ICC 1999, vol. 2, pp. 891–895. IEEE (1999)
3. Wang, D., Zhang, J., Cao, W., et al.: When will you arrive? Estimating travel time based on deep neural networks. In: AAAI (2018)
4. Yu, H., Wu, Z., Wang, S., et al.: Spatiotemporal recurrent convolutional networks for traffic prediction in transportation networks. Sensors **17**(7), 1501 (2017)
5. Yao, H., Wu, F., Ke, J., et al.: Deep multi-view spatial-temporal network for taxi demand prediction. arXiv preprint arXiv:1802.08714 (2018)
6. Ke, J., Zheng, H., Yang, H., et al.: Short-term forecasting of passenger demand under on-demand ride services: a spatio-temporal deep learning approach. Transp. Res. Part C Emerg. Technol. **85**, 591–608 (2017)
7. Zhang, J., Zheng, Y., Qi, D.: Deep spatio-temporal residual networks for citywide crowd flows prediction. In: AAAI, pp. 1655–1661 (2017)
8. Xingjian, S.H.I., Chen, Z., Wang, H., et al.: Convolutional LSTM network: a machine learning approach for precipitation nowcasting. In: Advances in Neural Information Processing Systems, pp. 802–810. MLA (2015)
9. Zheng, Y.: Trajectory data mining: an overview. ACM Trans. Intell. Syst. Technol. (TIST) **6** (3), 29 (2015)
10. Clark, S.: Traffic prediction using multivariate nonparametric regression. J. Transp. Eng. **129** (2), 161–168 (2003)
11. Min, W., Wynter, L.: Real-time road traffic prediction with spatio-temporal correlations. Transp. Res. Part C Emerg. Technol. **19**(4), 606–616 (2011)
12. Song, X., Kanasugi, H., Shibasaki, R.: DeepTransport: prediction and simulation of human mobility and transportation mode at a citywide level. In: IJCAI, vol. 16, pp. 2618–2624 (2016)
13. Liao, S., Zhou, L., Di, X., et al.: Large-scale short-term urban taxi demand forecasting using deep learning. In: Proceedings of the 23rd Asia and South Pacific Design Automation Conference, pp. 428–433. IEEE Press (2018)
14. Zhang, S., Wu, G., Costeira, J.P., et al.: FCN-rLSTM: Deep spatio-temporal neural networks for vehicle counting in city cameras. In: 2017 IEEE International Conference on Computer Vision (ICCV), pp. 3687–3696. IEEE (2017)
15. He, K., Zhang, X., Ren, S., et al.: Deep residual learning for image recognition. In: Proceedings of the IEEE Conference on Computer Vision and Pattern Recognition, pp. 770–778 (2016)

16. Ma, X., Tao, Z., Wang, Y., et al.: Long short-term memory neural network for traffic speed prediction using remote microwave sensor data. Transp. Res. Part C Emerg. Technol. **54**, 187–197 (2015)
17. Hochreiter, S., Schmidhuber, J.: Long short-term memory. Neural Comput. **9**(8), 1735–1780 (1997)
18. Gers, F.A., Schmidhuber, J., Cummins, F.: Learning to forget: continual prediction with LSTM (1999)
19. Wang, J., Gu, Q., Wu, J., et al.: Traffic speed prediction and congestion source exploration: a deep learning method. In: 2016 IEEE 16th International Conference on Data Mining (ICDM), pp. 499–508. IEEE (2016)
20. Zheng, Y.: Methodologies for cross-domain data fusion: an overview. IEEE Trans. Big Data **1**(1), 16–34 (2015)
21. Ta, N., Li, G., Zhao, T., et al.: An efficient ride-sharing framework for maximizing shared route. IEEE Trans. Knowl. Data Eng. (TKDE) **30**, 219–233 (2017)
22. Tong, Y., Chen, Y., Zhou, Z., et al.: The simpler the better: a unified approach to predicting original taxi demands based on large-scale online platforms. In: Proceedings of the 23rd ACM SIGKDD International Conference on Knowledge Discovery and Data Mining, pp. 1653–1662. ACM (2017)
23. Krizhevsky, A., Sutskever, I., Hinton, G.E.: ImageNet classification with deep convolutional neural networks. In: Advances in Neural Information Processing Systems, pp. 1097–1105 (2012)

Data, Information and Knowledge Processing

Assessing Data Anomaly Detection Algorithms in Power Internet of Things

Zixiang Wang[1], Zhoubin Liu[1], Xiaolu Yuan[2], Yueshen Xu[3],
and Rui Li[3(✉)]

[1] State Grid Zhejiang Electric Power Research Institute, Hangzhou 310000,
Zhejiang, China
{wangzixiang, liuzhoubin}@zj.sgcc.com.cn
[2] RUN Corporation, Wuxi 214000, Jiangsu, China
rubin0513@gmail.com
[3] Xidian University, Xi'an 710071, Shannxi, China
{ysxu, rli}@xidian.edu.cn

Abstract. At present, the data related to the Internet of Things has shown explosive growth, and the importance of data has been greatly improved. Data collection and analysis are becoming more and more valuable. However, a large number of abnormal data will bring great trouble to our research, and even lead people into misunderstandings. Therefore, anomaly detection is particularly necessary and important. The purpose of this paper is to find an efficient and accurate outlier detection algorithm. Our work also analyzes their advantages and disadvantages theoretically. At the same time, the effects of the data set size, number of proximity points, and data dimension on CPU time and precision are discussed. The performance, advantages and disadvantages of each algorithm in dealing with high-dimensional data are compared and analyzed. Finally, the algorithm is used to analyze the actual anomaly data collected from the Internet of Things and analyze the results. The results show that the LOF algorithm can find the abnormal data in the data set in a shorter time and with higher accuracy.

Keywords: Anomaly detection · Internet of Things · LOF

1 Introduction

The application of the Internet of Things technology in the power industry is the result of the development of information and communication technology to a certain stage. The Internet of Things integrates communication, information, sensing, automation and other technologies. It deploys a wide range of intelligence with certain perception, computing and execution capabilities in all aspects of power production, transmission, consumption and management. It can sense equipment, adopt standard protocol based on IP, realize reliable transmission of information security, cooperative processing, unified service and application integration through power information communication network, thus realize holographic perception, interconnection and seamless integration in the whole process of power grid operation and enterprise management. The construction of power Internet of Things can effectively integrate communication infrastructure resources and power system infrastructure resources, improve the level of

H. Gao et al. (Eds.): CollaborateCom 2018, LNICST 268, pp. 403–416, 2019.
https://doi.org/10.1007/978-3-030-12981-1_28

power system information, improve the efficiency of existing power system infrastructure, and provide important technical support for power grid generation, transmission, transformation, distribution and power consumption.

2   Angle-Based Anomaly Detection (ABOD)

At present, there are many kinds of abnormal data detection algorithms, and each method faces some problems which are suitable for different scenarios. For example, anomaly detection algorithms based on statistics generally need to know the model of a given data set, the distribution parameters and the expected number of anomaly data objects. However, these parameters are very difficult to obtain [1–3]. Distance-based abnormal data detection algorithms [4–6] have good effects on the detection of high-dimensional data, but the relevant parameters must be set in advance, and the setting of parameters is related to the detection results of the entire abnormal data object, and the detection of abnormal data based on distance is only to detect the global data. When detecting abnormal data objects, the whole data set must be scanned frequently, and it is a difficult problem for the rapid mining of data flow. Density-based anomaly data detection algorithms [7, 8] are for local anomaly data object detection, and they have great dependence on the nearest, index data structure and other methods, high computational complexity.

In view of the above situation, Kriege et al. [9] proposed an outlier detection algorithm based on angle to mine outlier data objects in high-dimensional data sets. At the same time, Pham and others proposed a new outlier detection algorithm based on angle analysis [10]. The basic principle is to compare the angle variance between each data object and other data objects in the hyperplane. The smaller the variance, the farther away from the center point. In the high-dimensional massive data space, the angle is more stable than the distance calculation, moreover, the method based on the angle distribution will not deteriorate substantially [11].

According to the method based on angle distribution proposed by Kriegel and others to calculate the anomalies of each data object, the distribution of a 2-dimensional cube on the plane is shown in Fig. 1 above. Point P is a normal point (see Fig. 1(a)). Since all the other points are distributed in all directions around it, the angles of point P and any point are not uniform, so these angles fluctuate more, that is, the angular variance of point P is larger. Therefore, for other points, the greater the angular variance of a point, the greater the likelihood that the point will be normal.

If point P is outside the cluster (see Fig. 1(b)), each angle is made up of point P and arbitrary points. Because all the other points are in a specific direction of P, the size of these angles is very close. Moreover, the angular fluctuation is also small, that is, the angle variance of point P is small. For other points, if the angular variance of a point is smaller, then this point is more likely to be an outlier.

As is known above, when the variance of the angle is between the two, it can be seen as a boundary point (see Fig. 1(c)). Therefore, we can use the variance of the angle to obtain the abnormality of each point, to distinguish normal points, outliers and boundary points.

Based on the above idea, Pham and others put forward the concept of anomaly factor based on angular distribution. The specific definitions are as follows:

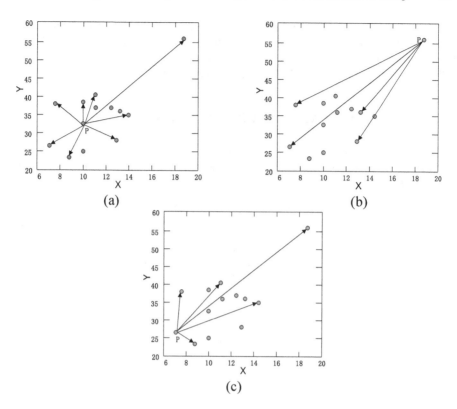

Fig. 1. Distribution of the data set

Given a data set, and a sample point, randomly select a sample point, and have different vectors and angles between them, then all variance angular distribution anomaly factor VOA (p), i.e.,

$$VOA(\mathrm{p}) = VOA[\Theta_{apb}]$$
$$= \mathrm{MOA}_2(\mathrm{P}) - (\mathrm{MOA}_1(\mathrm{P}))^2 \tag{1}$$

$$MOA_1(\mathrm{p}) = 2\frac{\sum\limits_{a,b \in S \setminus \{p\}, a \neq b} \Theta_{apb}}{(\mathrm{n}-1)(\mathrm{n}-2)} \tag{2}$$

$$MOA_2(\mathrm{p}) = 2\frac{\sum\limits_{a,b \in S \setminus \{p\}, a \neq b} \Theta_{apb}^2}{(\mathrm{n}-1)(\mathrm{n}-2)} \tag{3}$$

In the upper form, they are the 1-order matrix and the 2-order matrix of point P respectively. Therefore, VOA has no parameters. Therefore, this method is suitable for unsupervised anomaly data monitoring algorithm [12, 13]. ABOD algorithm prototype algorithm calculates VOA of each data point, and returns the minimum m points in VOA as the anomaly data points to be mined. At the same time, the time complexity of the prototype algorithm is illustrated, where D is the dimension of the dataset, and N represents the number of data sets. Because its time complexity is cubic time complexity, it will be very difficult to mine high-dimensional massive abnormal data [14, 15].

3   An Approximate Algorithm Based on ABOD

Because the time complexity of ABOD is cubic, in order to avoid such a high time complexity, we propose a near-linear time complexity algorithm to estimate the angle variance of each data point.

(1) We first approximate estimate the first order matrix.

$$
F_1(p) = \frac{2}{(n-1)(n-2)} \left(2\pi \sum_{\substack{a,b \in S \setminus \{p\} \\ a \neq b}} E\left[X_{apb}^{(i)}\right] \right)
$$

$$
= \frac{2\pi}{(n-1)(n-2)} \sum_{\substack{a,b \in S \setminus \{p\} \\ a \neq b}} \left(E\left[X_{apb}^{(i)}\right] + E\left[X_{bpa}^{(i)}\right] \right)
$$

$$
= \frac{2\pi}{(n-1)(n-2)} \left| L_p^{(i)} \right| \left| R_p^{(i)} \right| \tag{4}
$$

The set $L_p^{(i)} = \{x \in S \setminus \{p\} | x \cdot r_i < p \cdot r_i\}$ and set $R_p^{(i)} = \{x \in S \setminus \{p\} | x \cdot r_i \rangle p \cdot r_i\}$ are composed of points on both sides of the P point.

(2) We further estimate the two-order matrix.

$$
MOA_2(p) = \frac{2}{(n-1)(n-2)} \sum_{\substack{a,b \in S \setminus \{p\} \\ a \neq b}} \Theta_{apb}^2
$$

$$
= \frac{2}{(n-1)(n-2)} \sum_{\substack{a,b \in S \setminus \{p\} \\ a \neq b}} \left(\Theta_{apb}^2 + \Theta_{bpa}^2 \right)
$$

$$
= \frac{4\pi^2}{t(t-1)(n-1)(n-2)} \left(\sum_{i=1}^{n-1} \sum_{j=1}^{n-1} E\left[P_{ij}^2\right] - \frac{t}{\pi} \sum_{\substack{a,b \in S \setminus \{p\} \\ a \neq b}} \Theta_{apb} \right)
$$

$$
= \frac{4\pi^2}{t(t-1)(n-1)(n-2)} \left(E\left[\|P\|_F^2\right] - \frac{t(n-1)(n-2)}{2\pi} MOA_1(P) \right)
$$

$$
= \frac{4\pi^2}{t(t-1)(n-1)(n-2)} E\left[\|P\|_F^2\right] - \frac{2\pi}{t-1} MOA_1(p) \tag{5}
$$

Based on the above formula, we can estimate $MOA_2(p)$:

$$F_2'(P) = \frac{4\pi^2}{t(t-1)(n-1)(n-2)} \|p\|_F^2 - \frac{2\pi}{t-1} F_1(p) \tag{6}$$

The time complexity of FAST-ABOD has been greatly improved for ABOD.

4   An Improved Algorithm Based on Filter-Refinement

From above section, we can see that FAST-ABOD is more sensitive to the dimension of data. What's more, we find that abnormal data from ABOD is always those data points with the highest ranking, and ABOD always has a lower bound [16]. Therefore, based on the above analysis, we can select the lower bound of the angle variance anomaly factor from L candidate outliers and correct it until no point in the candidate list has an angle variance anomaly factor smaller than the corrected one.

Therefore, we get a more accurate $MOA_1(p)$ unbiased estimator:

$$F_1(p) = \frac{2\pi}{t(n-1)(n-2)} \sum_{i=1}^{t} \left| L_p^{(i)} \right| \left| R_p^{(i)} \right| \tag{7}$$

The last two order matrix $F_2(p)$ is estimated to be:

$$F_2(p) = \frac{4\pi^2 \left(\sum_{i=1}^{t} AMS\left(L_p^{(i)}\right) AMS\left(R_p^{(i)}\right) \right)}{t(t-1)(n-1)(n-2)} - \frac{2\pi F_1(p)}{t-1} \tag{8}$$

The vectors $AMS(L_p^{(i)})$ and vectors $AMS(R_p^{(i)})$ are estimated by product domain AMS Sketch. And there are:

$$\|P\|_F^2 = \left(\sum_{i=1}^{t} AMS\left(L_p^{(i)}\right) AMS\left(R_p^{(i)}\right) \right)^2 \tag{9}$$

Therefore, for the first L outlier data points, we propose the following methods to find the first L outlier data objects:

1. (Filtering Process) For each point in the region D, find k points (e.g. k nearest points) that have the greatest impact on it.
2. Calculate the LB-ABOF value of each point.
3. The LB-ABOF of each point calculated by 2 will be arranged in ascending order and coexist in the candidate column.
4. (Correction Process) Calculate the true ABOF of the first L objects in the candidate column, delete them from the candidate column and insert them into the result column.

5. Calculate the ABOF value of the next object in the candidate column and delete it from the candidate column. If the ABOF value of the next object is smaller than the maximum ABOF value in the result column, interchange the object corresponding to the maximum ABOF value in the result column, remove the point from the result column, and insert the next object into the result column.
6. If the largest ABOF value in the result column is smaller than the smallest approximate ABOF value in the candidate column (that is, LB-ABOF), the algorithm terminates; otherwise, step 5 is executed.

The LB-ABOD algorithm combines the scalability of Fast ABOD on data scale and the robustness of ABOD in dimensionality. The time complexity of the filtering process is (same as FAST-ABOD), and the time complexity of the correction process is, where n is the number of corrected data points. Therefore, the acceleration effect of ABOD depends on the value of the lower bound and the number of final corrected object points n. In practice, the running time of LB-ABOF is very unstable, which is closely related to the number of neighboring points (kNN).

5   Performance Analysis

5.1   The Influence of the Number of Adjacent Points (KNN)

All the above algorithms are implemented in C# language on Visual Studio 2016 development platform, and all the experiments are implemented on a PC running Windows 10 64bit operating system.

Due to the unsupervised nature of the actual collected data sets of power sensor networks, we cannot determine whether the abnormal data detected by the above algorithms are abnormal data in the real sense. In order to compare the performance and accuracy of the above detection algorithm more comprehensively, we randomly generated a number of different dimensions of the data set. Generation rules are: using time as random number seed to generate dimension D data sets, by controlling the range of random numbers to generate outliers and normal points. There is one outlier per 50 points in the generated dataset (here we call each table item of the dataset a "point").

This experiment will test the performance of the algorithm based on the above dataset. Therefore, we will use the precision and recall to evaluate the performance of the algorithm.

The precision ratio (precision) is an index to measure the signal-to-noise ratio (SNR) of a retrieval system, that is, the percentage of the relevant literature detected and the total literature detected. It is generally expressed as: precision ratio = (retrieves the total amount of information/information retrieved) × 100%. The retrieval language with strong generality (such as upper class and upper subject word) can improve the recall rate, but the precision rate decreases.

Recall rate (recall rate) is a measure of a retrieval system from the collection of relevant documents to detect the success of an indicator, that is, the number of relevant documents detected in the retrieval system and the total amount of relevant literature ratio. It is generally expressed as: recall ratio = (the total amount of relevant information retrieved/the relevant information in the system) × 100%. The retrieval language with strong generality (such as upper class and upper subject word) can improve the recall rate, but the precision rate decreases.

We hope that the higher the precision, the better the recall. But in fact, this is not the case. In some extreme case, we only detected an abnormal result, and it was accurate. Well, we can say that the precision rate is 100%, but the recall rate is very low. Conversely, when we return all the data, our recall rate is very high, but the precision rate is very low.

As a result, when we want both of them to be very high, we use F1 (F-score) to measure the equilibrium point, where $P(Precision) = \frac{A}{A+B}$, $R(Recall) = \frac{A}{A+C}$, and $F1 = \frac{2PR}{P+R}$.

In order to study the effect of the number of neighboring points on the performance of each algorithm, we tested 1000 data objects with 50 dimensions. According to the simulation test data set generation rules, there are 20 outliers.

For Fast ABOD and LB-ABOD, the theory holds that the former top K object is an outlier. For LOF algorithm, the theory holds that when the local reachable density of P is much smaller than that of its neighbors, P is an outlier. Because of the different data sets, it is difficult to have a unified definition of k, that is, it is difficult to determine a unified value, and the size of K has a greater impact on the detection results. For convenience of comparison, we calculate the LOF values of each point and sort them. The top K points with the largest LOF values are treated as outliers. Top K must be specified here. Because we know in advance which points are outliers, we set the number of outliers to be detected in the program (Top K) equal to the number of real outliers in the data set. Therefore, in this section, for FAST-ABOD, LB-ABOD, and LOF, the precision equals the recall equals its harmonic mean (precision = recall = F-Score).

Table 1. Relationship between CPU time and kNN ($N = 1000$, $D = 50$, $Top\ K = 20$)

(kNN)	CPU time (s)			Precision		
	LB-ABOD	Fast ABOD	LOF	LB-ABOD	Fast ABOD	LOF
100	2217.6	28.45	5.53	1	0.85	1
200	2280.5	101.22	13.26	1	0.95	1
300	2396.3	224.63	26.51	1	0.95	1
400	2555.2	397.32	44.87	1	0.95	1
500	2751.1	618.87	68.7	1	1	1
600	882.5	910.93	103.19	1	1	1
700	1139.7	1236.38	137.79	0.5	1	1
800	1459.4	1609.21	177.8	0.5	1	1

From Table 1, we can see that the CPU time of LB-ABOD decreases with the increase of KNN, while the CPU time of Fast-ABOD and LOF both go to a larger direction with the increase of KNN. At the same time, for their precision LOF has always maintained an efficient precision of 100%, on the contrary, LB-ABOD, and FAST-ABOD are not so ideal precision.

Figure 2 shows the influence of the number of adjacent points kNN on the performance of the algorithm. As can be seen, for Fast-ABOD, the CPU time increases exponentially with the increase of kNN, while the growth of LOF is relatively flat (Fig. 2(a), (b)).

Compared with Fast ABOD, LB-ABOD maintained 100% precision at fewer proximity points, which corresponded to several times the CPU time of FAST-ABOD under the same conditions (Fig. 2(a)); at that time, LB-ABOD had a CPU time of

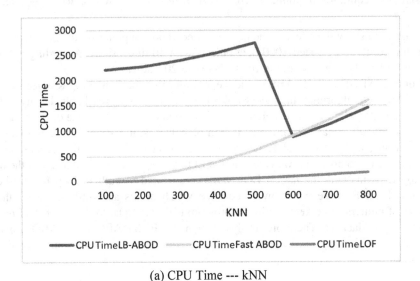

(a) CPU Time --- kNN

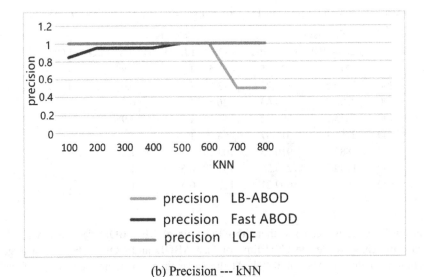

(b) Precision --- kNN

Fig. 2. Influence of kNN on algorithm performance ($N = 1000$, $D = 50$, $TopK = 20$)

2217.6 s, 78 times that of Fast ABOD (28.45 s). This is because when the kNN is relatively small, the LB-ABOF calculated by each object is negative, and there is no object in the candidate column whose LB-ABOF is greater than that of the object in the result column. At this point, the ABOF value of each object needs to be computed, and LB-ABOD degenerates into ABOD algorithm, so its running time is longer. When the kNN increases to 60% of the data set size, the run time of LB-ABOD drops sharply, and then the CPU time continues to increase with the increase of the kNN, and the CPU time of LB-ABOD is less than that of Fast ABOD under the same conditions (Fig. 2 (a)). This is because, when the LB-ABOF value of each object is positive, the correction process starts to work: the algorithm terminates when the largest ABOF in the result column is less than the smallest LB-ABOF in the candidate column. KNN continues to grow, and the LB-ABOF computing time of each object increases, so its CPU time continues to grow.

From the above discussion, the value of kNN is very important for LB-ABOD: kNN is too small, the operation efficiency of the algorithm is too low (ABOD); kNN is too large, while increasing the operation time will reduce the accuracy (Fig. 2(b)). Therefore, in practical applications, it is necessary to find a suitable balance between CPU time and accuracy, that is, the "balance point" of the minimum CPU time of LB-ABOD in Fig. 2(a). This needs to be analyzed according to the characteristics of different data sets. In this section, it is more appropriate for kNN to take about 60% of the dataset scale.

Figure 3 shows the relationship between algorithm accuracy and kNN, where Fig. 3(c) is a partial amplification of Fig. 3(b). Obviously, when the number of adjacent points is too small, it will seriously affect the accuracy of LOF; with the increase of the number of adjacent points, the precision of LOF increases gradually; when the number of adjacent points increases to a certain degree (in this case, $kNN = N/40 = 25$), the precision of LOF reaches 100%, and then it remains unchanged at this level.

Compared with LOF, the precision of Fast ABOD fluctuates greatly. When the number of adjacent points is small, the precision increases with the increase of kNN. When kNN reaches a certain size ($kNN = 50$), the precision decreases; then, with the increase of kNN, the precision increases gradually (Fig. 3(b), (c)). The above situation is more evident in the higher dimensional data set (Fig. 3(d)).

There are many reasons for the instability of the above-mentioned Fast ABOD precision: when the number of adjacent points is small ($kNN = N/200 = 5$), the precision is low because of the small number of samples compared; when the number of adjacent points is large ($kNN = N/2 = 500$), the Fast ABOD approximates to the ABOD algorithm, so the precision is high.

Considering the case shown in Fig. 4, it shows the effect of different proximity values on the results of Fast ABOD detection in a two-dimensional plane. When the number of kNN is small ($kNN = 6$), point P is an outlier relative to its proximity (Fig. 4(a)); however, as the number of proximities increases, the proximity of point P appears in all directions around it, and then P is no longer an outlier relative to its proximity (Fig. 4(b)). This also explains why the precision of Fast ABOD in Figs. 3, 4 and 5 increases first and then decreases as the number of near points (kNN) increases. It can be seen that another disadvantage of Fast ABOD is that it is sensitive to the number of adjacent points, and the algorithm is unstable.

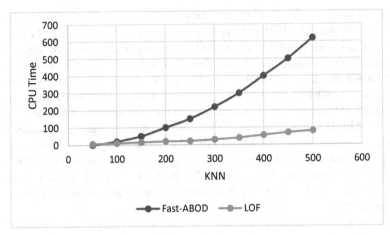

(a) *CPU Time—kNN (N=1000, D=20)*

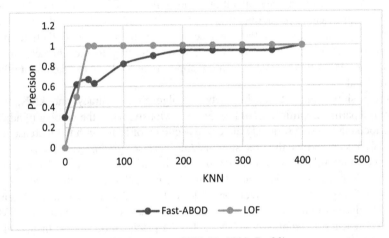

(b) *Precision—kNN (N=1000, D=20)*

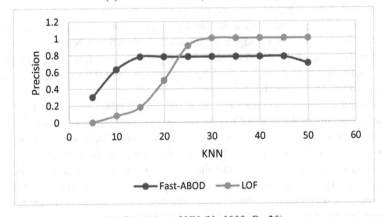

(c) *Precision—kNN (N=1000, D=20)*

Fig. 3. The relationship between kNN and Fast ABOD or LOF performance

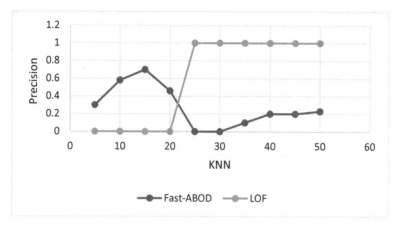

(d) *Precision—kNN (N=1000, D=50)*

Fig. 3. (*continued*)

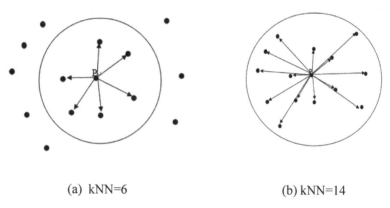

(a) kNN=6   (b) kNN=14

Fig. 4. The influence of the proximity points on the two-dimensional plane to the determination of outliers

5.2   Influence of Top K on Algorithm Accuracy

Let N = 1000, in which there are 20 outliers; data dimension D = 20; for LB-ABOD, take the number of near points kNN = 650; for Fast ABOD, LOF, kNN = 100, get the relationship between topK and algorithm precision, recall, F-Score as shown in Table 2.

Figure 5 is an intuitive display of Table 2. When topK is less than the number of outliers in the data set (topK < Outlier = 20), the precision of FAT ABOD and LOF is 100%, and the recall and F-Score are increased with the increase of topK. For LB-ABOD, the precision of F-Score is decreased with the increase of topK. When topK is greater than Outlier, for LOF, because it has found all the outliers, the increase of topK

Table 2. Influence of topK on algorithm accuracy ($N = 1000$, $D = 20$, $Outlier = 20$)

topK	Accuracy								
	LB-ABOD			Fast ABOD			LOF/ABOD		
	P	R	F	P	R	F	P	R	F
10	1	0.5	0.67	1	0.5	0.67	1	0.5	0.67
15	0.67	0.5	0.57	1	0.75	0.86	1	0.75	0.86
20	0.5	0.5	0.5	0.85	0.85	0.85	1	1	1
25	0.44	0.55	0.49	0.72	0.9	0.8	0.8	1	0.89
30	0.37	0.55	0.44	0.6	0.9	0.72	0.67	1	0.8

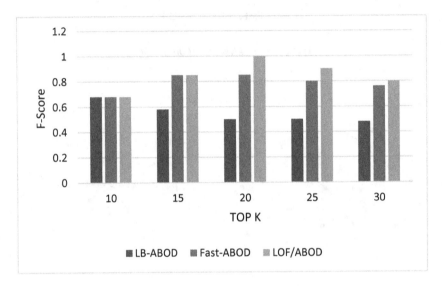

Fig. 5. The influence of topK on F-Score

is meaningless (recall = 1 and remains unchanged), but leads to the decrease of precision; for Fast ABOD, for LB-ABOD, the precision is gradually increased, but the increase of precision is far less than the decrease of recall. In general, its F-Score is decreasing. In summary, to detect outliers in the most efficient and accurate way (i.e. when F-Score is maximum), the size of topK must be equal to the number of real outliers in the data set.

6 Conclusion

The main work of this paper is to compare the application of different anomaly detection algorithms in anomaly data detection of power Internet of Things. Its data is mainly the data of electric power sensor network. Our goal is to improve the running time and efficiency of the algorithm on the basis of obtaining a suitable algorithm. It can adapt to the high-dimensional data acquired by the system. After our algorithm implementation, the CPU time of ABOD increases exponentially with the size of data set N, and the dimension increases linearly. The algorithm has high accuracy, but its time complexity is too high to be suitable for practical application. FAST ABOD and LB-ABOD are the improvements of ABOD algorithm, showing good results. The CPU time of LOF is approximately linear to data size N, and has a linear relationship with data dimension D. It can achieve very high accuracy only by taking fewer proximity points, and the ratio of CPU time to dimensionality remains unchanged, and it can still maintain very high accuracy in high-dimensional data.

Acknowledgement. This work is partially supported by Project No. 5211DS16001R of State Grid Zhejiang Electric Power Co., Ltd. This work is also supported by the National Natural Science Foundation of China (NSFC) under Grant No. 61502374.

References

1. Lyu, L., Jin, J., Rajasegarar, S., et al.: Fog-empowered anomaly detection in IoT using hyperellipsoidal clustering. IEEE Internet of Things J. **4**(5), 1174–1184 (2017)
2. Kriegel, H.-P., Schubert, M., Zimek, A.: Angle-based outlier detection in high-dimensional data. In: KDD, Las Vegas, Nevada, USA (2008)
3. Breunig, M.M., Kriegel, H.-P., Ng, R.T., et al.: LOF: identifying density-based local outliers. In: ACM MOD, Dallas, TX USA (2000)
4. Taghizadeh, M.J., Parhizkar, R., Garner, P.N., Bourlard, H., Asaei, A.: Ad hoc microphone array calibration: euclidean distance matrix completion algorithm and theoretical guarantees. Sig. Process. **170**, 123–140 (2014)
5. Zarpelão, B.B., Miani, R.S., Kawakani, C.T., et al.: A survey of intrusion detection in Internet of Things. J. Netw. Comput. Appl. **84**, 25–37 (2017)
6. Trihinas, D., Pallis, G., Dikaiakos, M.D.: ADMin: adaptive monitoring dissemination for the internet of things. In: IEEE Conference on Computer Communications, INFOCOM 2017, pp. 1–9. IEEE (2017)
7. Gregg, D., David, U.: Parameterizing dose-response models to estimate relative potency functions directly. Toxicol. Sci. **129**, 447–455 (2012)
8. Liu, C.-S.: Reconcile the perfectly elastoplastic model to simulate the cyclic behavior and ratcheting. Int. J. Solids Struct. **43**(2), 222–253 (2005)
9. Kriegel, H.P., Zimek, A.: Angle-based outlier detection in high-dimensional data. In: Proceedings of the 14th ACM SIGKDD International Conference on Knowledge Discovery and Data Mining, pp. 444–452. ACM (2008)
10. Lu, Y., Qin, X.S.: Multisite rainfall downscaling and disaggregation in a tropical urban area. J. Hydrol. **509**, 55–65 (2014)
11. Le Grand, S., Götz, A.W., Walker, R.C.: SPFP: speed without compromise—a mixed precision model for GPU accelerated molecular dynamics simulations. Comput. Phys. Commun. **184**(2), 374–380 (2013)
12. Polišenská, K., Chiat, S., Comer, A., McKenzie, K.: Semantic effects in sentence recall: the contribution of immediate vs delayed recall in language assessment. J. Commun. Disord. **52**, 65–77 (2014)
13. Feng, D.-C., Chen, F., Xu, W.-L.: Detecting local manifold structure for unsupervised feature selection. Acta Automatica Sinica **40**, 2253–2261 (2014)

14. Zhou, M., Wang, Y., Srivastava, A.K., et al.: Ensemble based algorithm for synchrophasor data anomaly detection. IEEE Trans. Smart Grid (2018)
15. Li, W., Mahadevan, V., Vasconcelos, N.: Anomaly detection and localization in crowded scenes. IEEE Trans. Pattern Anal. Mach. Intell. **36**(1), 18–32 (2014)
16. Erfani, S.M., Rajasegarar, S., Karunasekera, S., et al.: High-dimensional and large-scale anomaly detection using a linear one-class SVM with deep learning. Pattern Recogn. **58**, 121–134 (2016)

PARDA: A Dataset for Scholarly PDF Document Metadata Extraction Evaluation

Tiantian Fan[1,2], Junming Liu[1,2], Yeliang Qiu[1,2],
Congfeng Jiang[1,2(✉)], Jilin Zhang[1,2], Wei Zhang[1,2], and Jian Wan[2,3]

[1] School of Computer Science and Technology, Hangzhou Dianzi University,
Hangzhou 310018, China
{ttfanx,jmliu,qiuyeliang,cjiang,jilin.zhang,
maghero}@hdu.edu.cn
[2] Key Laboratory of Complex Systems Modeling and Simulation,
Ministry of Education, Hangzhou 310018, China
wanjian@zust.edu.cn
[3] School of Information and Electronic Engineering,
Zhejiang University of Science and Technology, Hangzhou 310023, China

Abstract. Metadata extraction from scholarly PDF documents is the fundamental work of publishing, archiving, digital library construction, bibliometrics,
and scientific competitiveness analysis and evaluations. However, different
scholarly PDF documents have different layout and document elements, which
make it impossible to compare different extract approaches since testers use
different source of test documents even if the documents are from the same
journal or conference. Therefore, standard datasets based performance evaluation of various extraction approaches can setup a fair and reproducible comparison. In this paper we present a dataset, namely, PARDA(Pdf Analysis and
Recognition DAtaset), for performance evaluation and analysis of scholarly
documents, especially on metadata extraction, such as title, authors, affiliation,
author-affiliation-email matching, year, date, etc. The dataset covers computer
science, physics, life science, management, mathematics, and humanities from
various publishers including ACM, IEEE, Springer, Elsevier, arXiv, etc. And
each document has distinct layouts and appearance in terms of formatting of
metadata. We also construct the ground truth metadata in Dublin Core XML
format and BibTex format file associated this dataset.

Keywords: Metadata extraction · Dataset · Performance evaluation ·
Document analysis

1 Introduction

Metadata of a scholarly document, including title, authors, affiliation, author-affiliation-
email matching, publishing date, journal information(name, volume, issue) or conference information(conference name, location, date), is the key data for document
analysis and digital library construction. Researchers proposed various approaches to
extract metadata from different domains [1, 2]. However, different scholarly documents
have different sections containing the metadata, with different formatting styles and

H. Gao et al. (Eds.): CollaborateCom 2018, LNICST 268, pp. 417–431, 2019.
https://doi.org/10.1007/978-3-030-12981-1_29

layouts. For example, some documents have headers, some have equations and special symbols in title, some have single-column authorship, some have multi-column authorship, others may have marks preceding or after the authors or affiliations. In some extreme cases, paper title may have different font type, font size and subtitle. This makes it impossible to compare different extraction approaches since they use different dataset with different formatting layouts [3].

As for the automatic metadata extraction, the extraction approaches usually aim to achieve the following goals:

(1) High accuracy. Accuracy is the basic goal and the most important performance metric for automatic metadata extraction;
(2) High adaptivity. Since massive scholarly documents have diverse formatting layouts, the extraction approaches must adapt to different documents and have universal high performance.

Therefore, a standard dataset can not only provide a real test data for performance evaluation, but also serve as a baseline to setup a fair and reproducible comparison among different extraction approaches.

Unfortunately, the PDF specification only defines the basic logical structure to describe the texts, paragraphs, and other layout objects. The accuracy and efficiency of metadata extraction are affected mainly by the following factors:

(1) Implementation variations of visual formatting in PDF documents from different computer programs. The structure and sometimes the source code of document elements is different although they have the same visual appearance, due to the implementation difference of formatting elements (such as paragraphs, segmentations, tables, columns, etc.) and complying with PDF specifications. The missing of standard for metadata and tags in PDF documents makes it very difficult even impossible to process and extract massive documents automatically without human manipulations.
(2) Individual style differences from different authors. For an instance, considering a paper with authors from two different affiliations, the double-column segment of author names and affiliations can be implemented by two columns, or two-column table in single column, or single column with manual alignment. Although they have the same visual appearance, the output documents have different binary source files. Even if a journal or publisher has a formatting template, different authors can meet the requiring formats by their own different means of typesetting and layouts.
(3) Source of PDF documents. Some PDF documents are born digital, some are generated by scanned images. The scanned-PDF documents must undergo the Optical Character Recognition processing before metadata extraction.
(4) Errors in PDF document itself. Some authors do not comply with the formatting template of the journal or publisher due to different writing behaviors, careless mistakes, personal styles or cultural background. Sometimes even the documents from the same journal issue have different formatting layouts or compilation errors due to mistakes in publishing process or digital preservation.

However, the creation of such standard datasets for layout analysis and metadata extraction is a costly process in terms of data selection, acquisition, and annotation [4–6]. Such cost of acquisition and annotation of real datasets sometimes forces the use of synthetic data. The research community devoted a big effort to the generation of public dataset for document analysis, such as document imaging, page analysis, and graphics recognition [7–10]. However, the existing datasets are for general purpose imaged document analysis, not suitable for metadata extraction.

It is ideal that the dataset contains real, representative, and comprehensive documents from different sources. However, in order to collect enough page layouts from different documents, researchers must browse documents as widely as possible to fulfill the realistic and comprehensive goal. Since different institutions have different accessibilities to different sources of scholarly documents due to institutional subscription or publicly access, such dataset must also be extended to make it more comprehensive when new layouts are found and added [11–14].

In this paper we present a dataset, namely, PARDA(Pdf Analysis and Recognition DAtaset), for performance evaluation and analysis of scholarly documents, especially on metadata extraction, such as title, authors, affiliation, author-affiliation-email matching, year, date, etc. We collect 147 real scholarly documents from the published journals, magazines, and conference proceedings. The dataset covers computer science, physics, life science, management, mathematics, and humanities. And each document has distinct layouts and appearance in terms of formatting of metadata. We also construct the ground truth metadata in xml file associated this dataset.

We identify different occurrences of formatting types in real corpus are summarized, including 6 types of titles, 14 types of author names, and 30 types of author-affiliation combinations. This summary can serve as a reference template database and baseline for general purpose metadata extraction and implementation. Moreover, various frequently occurred words in headers and affiliations are summarized to improve the accuracy of document segmentation and metadata extraction. These frequently occurred words can be used extensively if they are accompanied with domain-specific words and semantics from other sources.

The remainder of the paper is organized as follows: In Sect. 2 we give the metadata extraction workflow. In Sect. 3 we give the dataset description based on layout categorization of scholarly documents. In Sect. 4 we provide the ground truth of the dataset. We conclude the paper in Sect. 5.

2 Metadata Extraction Workflow

In order to extract metadata from scholarly documents, both character stream (i.e., pure texts) and formatting stream (line height, font type, font size, character location, etc.) are extracted in parallel. When a PDF document is being processed, explicit and implicit formatting semantics are used for segmentation and metadata extraction. The targeted pages are segmented into header, footnote, title, authors, affiliations, and address (if any). Each segment may have multiple elements. The element identification (images, tables, figures, etc.) and resolution identification including line spaces, line heights, and columns will be done before metadata extraction. The procedure is illustrated in Fig. 1 as algorithm I.

420   T. Fan et al.

Algorithm I: Metadata extraction workflow

```
Input: D // the original PDF document
Output: arrAuth<authorList array>, arrAuthMark<marks array of author names>
    arrAffi<affiliationList array>, arrAffiMark<marks array of affiliations array>
    arrMatch<mapping array of author names to their corresponding affiliation>
for each document D do
get_resolution(line_spaces, line_heights, columns);//resolution identification
Lmn=gridding();initialize parameters of page layouts to 2 dimensional array Lmn
while (metadata is in the current page && the metadata is not repeated metadata) do
    markFlag=Y; //Mark the current page with Y flag;
    MetaDoc.append(currentpage);// Extract pages with Y flags into a new document;
    pagenext(); //Move to next page;
end while
for each page in MetaDoc do
    while (there exists a horizontal rectangle spanning the column) do
        hrect=getHoriRectangle();//get the horizontal rectangles;
        nextLine(); //Move to next line;
    end while
    for each horizontal rectangle in hrect do
        hsect=segmentationBetweenRect();//Extract between horizontal rectangles;
        moveNextHRect();//Move to next horizontal rectangle;
    end for
    for each section in hsect do
        if(getColumnNo(hsect)>1) do  //current horizontal section has>1 columns
            while (VertRectangle()!=empty) do // vertical rectangle between columns
                vrect = getVertRectangle(); //get the vertical rectangles;
            end while
            moveNextColumn(); //Move to next column;
            for each vertical rectangle in vrect do
                vsect=concat(currSection);//concat contents of vertical rectangles;
                moveNextVRect();//Move to next vertical rectangle;
            end for
        end if
    end for
    for each section in vsect do
        arrAuth=getAuthors(); arrAuthMark=getAuthMark();
        arrAffi=getAffi();  arrAffiMark=getAffiMark();
    end for
end for
MetaDoc.nextPage();// move to next metadata page
for each element in arrAuth, arrAuthMark, arrAffi, arrAffiMark do
    arrMatch=getMapping(arrAuth,arrAuthMark,arrAffi,arrAffiMark);//Match metadata;
end for
end for
```

Fig. 1. Metadata extraction algorithm

In the preprocessing stage, the document is preprocessed, including when a document is loaded. Usually the first page (or multiple pages if the document has longer section of authors and affiliations) will be truncated into the targeted pages for postprocessing, especially the metadata extraction. In our approach, the metadata are extracted based on formatting template database, explicit semantics, and implicit semantics. And the authors are matched with their affiliations according to the marks or implicit semantics. To improve the accuracy, the metadata are verified by redundant information in different segments. For example, author affiliation may appear after the paper title and before the abstract, and it may also be located in the footnote. Such redundant information can verify the author and affiliation matching automatically by extra verification process.

3   Dataset Description

3.1   Layout Categorization Methodology

There are many journals, magazines, and proceedings of different publishers that publish a large number of scientific articles, most of them have similar sections, such as headers, titles, authors, affiliations, abstract, footnote, body texts, the references, figures and tables, etc. However, different scholarly documents may have different formatting styles and layouts, although they have similar reading order and logical metadata. This makes it difficult to extract and parse metadata widely using the same formatting templates or by machine learning techniques unless the machine has exhaustive templates or training datasets. To make the dataset as pervasive as possible, we classify the formatting layouts of existing scholarly documents by sections and try to cover as many as possible layouts from our collections and observations. We list the categorization in Table 1.

Table 1. Layout categorization.

Section	Containing elements(if any)
Header	Publisher, journal type, journal name, publishing dada of papers, paper status, date, URL, DOI, special symbols, embedded image
Title	Main title, subtitle, equations, symbols, special characters, different font types, font sizes, line heights
Authorship	Multiple authors, single column, multiple columns
Author name	Different blocks of first name, middle name, and last name, special characters, diacritics and dialects
Affiliation	Full name, abbreviation, multiple lines, phone number, country, state/province, city, zip code
Email	{ }, "lastname", "firstname", embedded image
Visual order	Relative order of Authorship, affiliation, abstract, and footnote
Footnote	Affiliation, conference location, date paper submission and processing details

We select the dataset documents according to the existence and formatting style of each element of each section and group them into different categories.

3.2 Templates of Title and First Page

Please note that although some researchers in the same academic domain tend to use similar formatting styles, there are no dominant or prevalent formatting styles or patterns in all the research fields. Actually the formatting patterns are scattered and occurred across different research fields. This requires the scalable and extensible approach to extract metadata from such papers other than universal and fixed templates. We select from the publicly accessed and our institutional subscribed scholarly documents to construct the dataset. The selected documents come from various academic fields, including computer science, physics, life science, management, mathematics, and humanities from publishers such as ACM, IEEE, Springer, Elsevier, arXiv, etc. These documents vary from journals, magazines to conference proceedings. We list some examples in the following figures. For example, some journals of Elsevier, like FGCS, JPDC, JSA, the journal name has larger font size than paper title. In order to adapt to more scholarly documents, we collect a comprehensive formatting templates from real published documents including title, author name affiliation, and address.

In Fig. 2 we list most used title templates.

Parallelizing Data Race Detection

(a) Simple title(single line or multiple

lines with normal characters)

K-shell photoionization of ground-state Li-like carbon ions $[C^{3+}]$: experiment, theory and comparison with time-reversed photorecombination

(b) Multi-line with superscripts and symbols

Study of the $\eta \to e^+ e^- \gamma$ Decay Using WASA-at-COSY Detector System

(c) Title with equation

Reconfigurable Asynchronous Logic Automata

(RALA)

(d)Title with short subtitle

A Simple, Verified Validator for Software Pipelining

(verification pearl)

(e) Title with punctuation and subtitle

Orchestration by Approximation

Mapping Stream Programs onto Multicore Architectures

(f) Title with normal length subtitle

Disambiguation of Finite-State Transducers

N. Smaili and P. Cardinal and G. Boulianne and P. Dumouchel
Centre de Recherche Informatique de Montréal.
{nsmaili, pcardinal, gboulian, Pierre.Dumouchel}@crim.ca

(g)same font size in title and authors

Squibs and Discussions

Real versus Template-Based Natural Language Generation: A False Opposition?

(h) title accompanied by subtitle

Fig. 2. Frequently used titles

In Fig. 3 we list some layout examples from real documents.

Fig. 3. Sample layouts from real documents.

We only list a handful of the real documents that have different layouts in Fig. 3.

However, many documents have diverse layouts and may have combination of multiple layouts on header, title, authors, affiliation, abstract, footnote, etc.

For example, the title of a scientific paper may have the following formatting layouts except normal titles:

(a) The title has multiple lines with superscripts and symbols
(b) The title has equation in it

(c) The title has subtitle

(d) The title has special characters and punctuations

Moreover, the abstract section is easier to extract if it has preceding word like "abstract" and "summary" and the abstract section has uniform formatting layouts (at least 3 consecutive lines). Even if the paper has many authors and affiliations and the abstract is not on the first page, the abstract section can still be extracted if they have these preceding words. In some cases if the paper has no such preceding words but does have abstract section, we can still extract the abstract section according to the following two criteria: (1) There are at least 3 consecutive lines with uniform formatting layouts; and (2) In these lines there are words or phrases that merely appear in author names or affiliations, such as "we", "recently", "this paper", "proposed", review", etc. Such collection can be extended easily for further and newly added documents. In this paper we locate the beginning of the abstract if: (1) one line is not belonging to affiliation (according to feature words of affiliation), (2) its length is greater than 40, and (3) the following consecutive lines are not belonging to affiliation. Note that here the length 40 is empirically set by observations and can be tuned to other values. Since abstract is the concise summary of the whole paper using descriptive words and usually has no overlapping words with affiliation, the abstract can be identified by the formatting layouts and their changes.

3.3   Header Templates

The first line is title if a paper has no header. However, there are many papers that have headers (mostly in single column). Although the contents in headers vary in different papers, they can be divided into images and pure texts.

As for the images in header, it can be identified and filtered by the binary values of the parsed text stream. Usually they are not normal ASCII characters or the file has special pointer to the image objects. Therefore, the forgoing input can be regarded as header and then filtered until there are consecutive ASCII characters. When it comes to header of pure texts, the occurrence of feature words can be identified and the line can be regarded as header and filtered. Some feature words are summarized in Table 2.

Table 2. Frequently occurred feature words and symbols in pure text headers

Class	Examples
Publisher	IEEE, ACM, arXiv, Publishing, Company
Journal type	Journal, J., Proc., Proceedings, Conferences Workshop, Symposium, Letters, Lett., Transaction, Trans.
Journal name	Complete names and abbreviations of terms, Sci., Tech., Med., Com., Inf.
Publishing data	Volume, Vol., Issue, No., page, pp., article
Paper status	Manuscript, preprint, accepted, submitted, publication, pub.
Date and time	Year and month, January to December, Jan. to Dec.
Special format string	Partial or complete website URL, beginning and end of page number, DOI digits, date
function word	on, and, in, of, for
Special symbol	&, /, ©, ®

Although Table 2 is not a complete list of feature words in header, it can be easily extended and contain newly observed words. In this paper we use this list to identify and filter header texts and achieve high accuracy for most scholarly documents. Moreover, data in header and footnote can mutually be verified and improve the accuracy of metadata extraction.

3.4 Authorship Templates

In order to extract and parse the metadata, the fundamental work is to locate the header, title, authors, affiliation, abstract, and the footnote. Specifically, if the header and the abstract section are located, the metadata, such as title, author, affiliation, and address must be between the header and the abstract for normal document and can be extracted by their formatting templates respectively. Therefore, the content positioning and segmentation is the first step before metadata extraction. Since most of the metadata is located between the running header and the abstract, the metadata can be located as long as the running header and abstract is detected and identified.

The authorship section is another important source of metadata. But different publisher has different styles for authorship. For example, some journals require single-column authorship. Some conference proceedings requires multiple column authorship if the authors have more than one affiliation. In order to extract author names, the scholarly documents can be simply categorized into two classes: author names with symbols or marks, and author names without any symbol or mark. If all the author names have no symbol or mark, all the authors may belong to the same affiliation (if the paper has only one affiliation), or authors belong to multiple affiliations separated by columns. Or if at least one author has symbol or mark, her affiliation may also have symbol or mark.

If the authorship is single column, it still can have multiple formatting layouts like:

(a) Multiple separated authors belong to one affiliation and authors names in different line from affiliation;
(b) Multiple authors without separators belong to one affiliation and author names in different line from affiliation;
(c) Multiple separated authors belong to multiple affiliations, each author name in same line with its affiliation
(d) There are other symbols or marks in the authorship, like "Jr.", comma, paren-thesis, "and", and email address in the same line or different line with affiliation
(e) Authors are only separated by white spaces.

However, in most scholarly documents, if the authorship section is formatted in multiple columns, it is indicating that the paper has more than one author and maybe multiple affiliations. In this situation, each author may belong to different affiliation, or all the authors belong to the same affiliation, or some authors belong to the same affiliation and the remaining authors belong to other affiliation. Then the authorship may have the following variations:

(a) Multiple authors belonging to one affiliation and they are in the same column;
(b) Multiple authors belonging to one affiliation and they are in the different columns, each column has its own affiliation name;
(c) Multiple authors belonging to one affiliation and they are in the different columns, all column sharing their affiliation name;
(d) Multiple authors belonging to multiple affiliations respectively.

In many cases, if one paper has multiple affiliations, it can also be achieved by single column formatting with marks in superscripts locations in author names and affiliations avoiding multiple columns formatting. The introduction of marks can result in many variations of authorship layouts of single column, such as:

(a) Authors are numbered by digital, lower case characters, upper case characters, special symbols, Greek symbols, or embedded images;
(b) One author has more than one marks and one of them indicating correspondence author or co-first-author;
(c) Multiple affiliations in different lines or the same line, and the author belonging to first affiliation has no mark;
(d) Multiple affiliations in one line and each affiliation has a mark, and author mark is preceding the comma separator;
(e) Affiliation name is after the author name and in a parenthesis;
(f) Five affiliations with marks of digitals, characters and symbols of correspondence author;
(g) Marks are preceding the author names.

Sometimes papers jointly use multiple columns and marks for segmentation of author names and their affiliations. Such examples of multiple columns formatting with marks in author names and affiliations as:

(a) Two affiliations, two columns, one mark for the only one author, the remaining authors belong to the same affiliation without marks;
(b) Three affiliations, each affiliation has one mark, combination of single column and two columns;
(c) Four affiliations, only one author has mark for correspondence authors, combination of single column and two columns;
(d) Four affiliations, each author name separated in two lines.

We list some authorship examples in Fig. 4.

In some research fields such as life science and high energy physics, international cooperation results in a huge number of authors and affiliations. It's difficult for the existing approach to extract authors and their affiliations with high accuracy. We collect the dataset that covers the entire above mentioned formatting layout from real documents. It reflects the breadth of real documents and can serve as the basic testing data for in-depth performance evaluation.

Due to copyright constraints, rewriting all the real documents as their appearance and distribute all the rewritten PDF files can make this dataset publicly accessible, the rewritten files may contain different compiling codes as the original documents. Therefore, the rewritten documents are useful for OCR based approaches after they are

Karl E. Kazor, Haneen S. Alzehli, Allison N. Zindell, Lung W. Lau, Fotios M. Andreopoulos, Brant D. Watson, Jeffrey L. Goldberg

(1) Single column authorship with marks and separators, all authors first and all affiliations together

Automatically Patching Errors in Deployed Software

Jeff H. Perkins, Sunghun Kim, Sam Larsen, Saman Amarasinghe, Jonathan Bachrach, Michael Carbin, Carlos Pacheco, Frank Sherwood, Stelios Sidiroglou, Greg Sullivar, Weng-Fai Wong, Yoav Zibin, Michael D. Ernst, and Martin Rinard
MIT CSAIL, HKUST, VMware, BCG, EBAE AIT, NUS, Come2Play, U. of Washington
jhp@csail.mit.edu, mernst@cs.washington.edu, rinard@csail.mit.edu

(2) Numbering with Greek symbols and multiple affiliations in one line

JOHN TALBURT and THERESE L. WILLIAMS, University of Arkansas at Little Rock
THOMAS C. REDMAN, Navesink Consulting Group
DAVID BECKER, Mitre Corporation

(3) Author in same line with affiliation

Complete Information Flow Tracking from the Gates Up

Mohit Tiwari   Hassan M G Wassel   Bita Mazloom   Shashidhar Mysore   Frederic T Chong   Timothy Sherwood
Department of Computer Science, University of California, Santa Barbara
{tiwari,hwassel,betamaz,shashmc,chong,sherwood}@cs.ucsb.edu

(4) Four-blocks authorname without separator, author name in different line from affiliation

In-Network Coherence Filtering: Snoopy Coherence without Broadcasts

Niket Agarwal, Li-Shiuan Peh, and Niraj K. Jha
Department of Electrical Engineering, Princeton University
Department of Electrical Engineering and Computer Science, Massachusetts Institute of Technology
{niketa@princeton.edu, peh@csail.mit.edu, jha@princeton.edu}

(5) Mark preceding the author name

Patrick Ruch
SIM, University Hospital of Geneva
24 Micheli du Crest
1201 Geneva, Switzerland
and
LITH, Swiss Federal Institute of Technology
1015 Lausanne, Switzerland
patrick.ruch@sim.hcuge.ch

(6) single column authorship   one author belonging to two affiliations without marks

Paul A. Lightsey
Ball Aerospace & Technologies Corp.
P. O. Box 1062
Boulder, Colorado 80306
E-mail: plightse@ball.com

Charles Atkinson
Northrop Grumman Aerospace Systems
One Space Park
Redondo Beach, California 90278

Mark Clampin
Lee D. Feinberg
NASA
Goddard Space Flight Center
Greenbelt, Maryland 20771

(7) single column authorship with author-affiliation block one by one

Kees van Deemter   Emiel Krahmer
University of Aberdeen   Tilburg University

Mariët Theune
University of Twente

(8) Multi-column authorship with marks

KARIN HARBUSCH   GERARD KEMPEN
Computer Science Department   Cognitive Psychology Unit
University of Koblenz-Landau   Leiden University, and
PB 201602, 56016 Koblenz/DE   Max Planck Institute, Nijmegen/NL
harbusch@uni-koblenz.de   kempen@fsw.leidenuniv.nl

(9) multi-column authorsship with fully captitalized names

Highly Efficient Techniques for Network Forensics

Miroslav Ponec   Paul Giura   Hervé Brönnimann   Joel Wein
mpx@cis.poly.edu   pgiura@cis.poly.edu   hbr@poly.edu   wein@poly.edu
Department of Computer and Information Science
Polytechnic University, Brooklyn, New York

(10) Multiple authors belonging to one affiliation and they are in the different columns, all column sharing their affiliation name

Scalable Speculative Parallelization on Commodity Clusters

Hanjun Kim   Arun Raman   Feng Liu   Jae W. Lee   David I. August
Departments of Electrical Engineering and Computer Science   Parakinetics Inc.
Princeton University   Princeton, USA
Princeton, USA   david@parakinetics.com
{hanjunk, rarun, fengliu, august}@princeton.edu

(11) Two affiliations, two columns, one mark for the only one author, the remaining authors belong to the same affiliation without annotation

Fig. 4. Authorship examples of single and multiple columns formatting with/without marks

scanned as images for post-processing and extraction. In order to make this dataset equally standard for original compilation based metadata extraction, such as PDFBox [15], we write an alternative file containing all the URLs of the selected documents to be publicly downloaded.

The corresponding document can be downloaded according to the institutional accessibility of each individual. If some documents can't be downloaded or accessed, the performance evaluation can also be conducted as long as the missing document ID is stated so that the evaluation on the subset of PARDA can still be comparable.

4   Groundtruthing

The availability of high accuracy metadata archives of standard PDF documents becomes the key issue for successful implementation of metadata extraction software. It is a very difficult task for collecting a large number of high quality PDF documents by using traditional methods to meet all the requirements for automatic metadata extraction process. We select the scholarly documents from the publicly accessed and our institutional subscribed database to construct the dataset. We choose XML as the PARDA ground-truth format for metadata extraction performance evaluation and comparison. The XML format is compatible with other established metadata description formats. However, the existing metadata specification formats do not have any explicit metadata entry of connection of authors and their affiliations. The CERIF (Common European Research Information Format) contextual metadata covers persons, organizations, projects, products, publications, patents, facilities, equipment, funding, and – most importantly – the relationships between them [16]. For example, the de-facto metadata standard, the Dublin Core(DC) standard [17], has 15 elements in a metadata of simple DC(more on qualified DC), ranging from title, creator, publisher, subject to language. In DC, the metadata landscape is currently characterized in terms of four "levels" of interoperability,i.e., Level 1 (Shared term definitions), Level 2 (Formal semantic interoperability), Level 3 (Description Set syntactic interoperability) and Level 4 (Description Set Profile interoperability). But it does not have any direct entry for connections for authors and their affiliations. The BibTex does not have any entry or field for authors and their corresponding affiliations either, although it has an "institution" field. For a paper that has multiple authors affiliated to multiple affiliations, one "institution" is not sufficient to present the authorship correctly.

Therefore, in order to make the ground truth file compatible with the Dublin Core standard, we use an extended sub-element "affiliation" of creator provide the connection for authors and their affiliations. If an author has multiple affiliations, the creator can also have multiple "affiliation" entries as they appear in the original paper. Moreover, we use the description entry to store the abstract.

We give an example record of the ground true file(part) in DC format in Fig. 5.

```xml
<?xml version="1.0"?>
<metadata
  xmlns="http://example.org/myapp/"
  xmlns:xsi="http://www.w3.org/2001/XMLSchema-instance"
  xsi:schemaLocation="http://example.org/myapp/
http://example.org/myapp/schema.xsd"
  xmlns:dc="http://purl.org/dc/elements/1.1/"
  xmlns:dcterms="http://purl.org/dc/terms/">
  <dc:title>
    Automatically Patching Errors in Deployed Software
  </dc:title>
  <dc:subject>
    Error Handling and Recovery,Monitors
  </dc:subject>
  <dc:subject>
    Corrections,Enhancement
  </dc:subject>
  <dc:subject>
    Invasive Software
  </dc:subject>
<dc:creator>
Jeff H. Perkins
 <affiliation>
MIT, Cambridge, MA, USA
 </affiliation>
  </dc:creator>
<dc:creator>
Sunghun Kim
 <affiliation>
HKUST, Hong Kong
 </affiliation>
  </dc:creator>
<dc:creator>
Sam Larsen
 <affiliation> VMWare, Redwood, CA, USA </affiliation>
  </dc:creator>
  <dc:description>
    We present ClearView, a system for automatically......
  </dc:description>
  <dc:publisher>ACM </dc:publisher>
  <dc:identifier xsi:type="dcterms:URI">
    http://dl.acm.org/citation.cfm?id=1629575.1629585
  </dc:identifier>
</metadata>
```

Fig. 5. Sample ground truth file of metadata in DC format

Alternatively, we also provide a dedicated BibTex file with institution field for each document which containing the affiliations that corresponds to authors as they appear in the author field. In order to make sure that each author is correctly connected with their affiliation, every author in the author field must have a string in the institution field, even if the institution is null. We use semicolon(;), not "and" in the institution field to separate multiple affiliations, instead of "and" in author field. We give an example record of the ground true file(part) in BibTex format in Fig. 6.

```
@inproceedings{Paper001,
   author    = {Jeff H. Perkins and
               Sunghun Kim and
               Samuel Larsen......},
   institution={MIT,   Cambridge,   MA,   USA;HKUST,   Hong
Kong;VMWare, Redwood, CA, USA;......}
   title     = {Automatically patching errors in deployed
software},
   booktitle = {Proceedings of the 22nd {ACM} Symposium on
Operating Systems Principles 2009, {SOSP} 2009, Big Sky,
Montana, USA, October 11-14, 2009},
   pages     = {87--102},
   year      = {2009},
   url                                                      =
{http://doi.acm.org/10.1145/1629575.1629585},
   doi       = {10.1145/1629575.1629585}
}
```

Fig. 6. Sample ground truth file of metadata in BibTex format

5 Conclusion Remarks

In this paper we presented a new dataset, PARDA, for performance evaluation of metadata extraction from scholarly documents. Although there are some datasets for layout analysis and performance evaluation, they are not suitable for metadata extraction due to their coverage of variations in sections including title and authorship. We selected scholarly documents widely from publicly accessed and our university subscribed sources. PARDA provides comprehensive and accurate ground truth description file and associated metadata for a wide variety of layouts that have complex combinations of titles, authors, and affiliations, address, and emails (if any).

The original URL of each document is collected in independent files. The ground truth files of metadata are both in Dublin Core and BibTex format.

We are currently rewriting all the real dataset documents with forged stuff according to their layouts, especially focusing on the complex combinations of titles, authors, and affiliations, address, and emails so that the dataset can be freely downloaded without charge of copyright or permissions. Note that the newly rewritten PDF documents are more useful for OCR based metadata extraction approaches because our rewritten documents do not keep it exactly same with the original PDF documents as they are in the publisher databases.

Acknowledgment. The funding support of this work by Natural Science Fund of China (No. 61472109, No. 61572163, No. 61672200, and No. 61772165) is greatly appreciated.

References

1. Lipinski, M., Yao, K., Breitinger, C., Beel, J., Gipp, B.: Evaluation of header metadata extraction approaches and tools for scientific PDF documents. In: JCDL 2013 Indianapolis, Indiana, USA, 22–26 July 2013, pp. 385–386 (2010)
2. Do, H.H.N., Chandrasekaran, M.K., Cho, P.S., Kan, M.Y.: Extracting and matching authors and affiliations in scholarly documents. In: JCDL 2013, Indianapolis, Indiana, USA, 22–26 July 2013, pp. 219–228 (2013)
3. Jiang, C., Liu, J., Ou, D., Wang, Y., Yu, L.: Implicit semantics based metadata extraction and matching of scholarly documents. J. Database Manag. (JDM) **29**, 1–22 (2018). https://doi.org/10.4018/JDM.2018040101
4. Tkaczyk, D., Szostek, P., Bolikowski, Ł.: GROTOAP2—the methodology of creating a large ground truth dataset of scientific articles. **20**(11/12) (2014)
5. Märgner, V., El Abed, H.: Tools and metrics for document analysis systems evaluation. In: Doermann, D., Tombre, K. (eds.) Handbook of Document Image Processing and Recognition, pp. 1011–1036
6. Antonacopoulos, A., Bridson, D., Papadopoulos, C., Pletschacher, S.: A realistic dataset for performance evaluation of document layout analysis. In: 10th International Conference on Document Analysis and Recognition, ICDAR 2005 (2005)
7. Nartker, T.A., Rice, S.V., Lumos, S.E.: Software tools and test data for research and testing of page-reading OCR systems. In: SPIE and IS&T (2005)
8. Todoran, L., Worring, M., Smeulders, A.W.M.: The UvA color document dataset. IJDAR **7**, 228–240 (2005)
9. Becker, C., Duretec, K.: Free benchmark corpora for preservation experiments: using model-driven engineering to generate data sets. In: JCDL 2013, pp. 349–358 (2013)
10. Caragea, C., et al.: CiteSeer[x]: a scholarly big dataset. In: de Rijke, Maarten, et al. (eds.) ECIR 2014. LNCS, vol. 8416, pp. 311–322. Springer, Cham (2014). https://doi.org/10.1007/978-3-319-06028-6_26
11. Antonacopoulos, A., Karatzas, D., Bridson, D.: Ground truth for layout analysis performance evaluation. In: IAPR International Workshop on Document Analysis Systems, DAS 2006 (2006)
12. Tkaczyk, D., Czeczko, A., Rusek, K., Bolikowski, L., Bogacewicz, R.: GROTOAP: ground truth for open access publications. In: JCDL 2012, pp. 381–382 (2012)
13. Tao, X., Tang, Z., Xu, C., Gao, L.: Ground-truth and performance evaluation for page layout analysis of born-digital documents. In: 2014 11th IAPR International Workshop on Document Analysis Systems, DAS 2014, pp. 247–251 (2014)
14. Valveny, E.: Datasets and annotations for document analysis and recognition. In: Doermann, D., Tombre, K. (eds.) Handbook of Document Image Processing and Recognition, pp. 983–1009
15. http://pdfbox.apache.org
16. Jeffery, K.G., Houssos, N., Jörg, B., Asserson, A.: Research information management: the CERIF approach. Int. J. Metadata Semant. Ontol. **9**, 5–14 (2014)
17. http://dublincore.org/

New Cross-Domain QoE Guarantee Method Based on Isomorphism Flow

Zaijian Wang[1(✉)], Chen Chen[1], Xinheng Wang[2] ⓘ, Lingyun Yang[1], and Pingping Tang[1]

[1] Anhui Normal University, Wuhu, Anhui, China
wzj0553@foxmail.com, Alice-Cr@ahnu.edu.cn,
{lingyun716,pphysicstpping}@126.com
[2] University of West London, London W5 5RF, UK
Xinheng.Wang@uwl.ac.uk

Abstract. This paper investigates the issue of Quality of Experience (QoE) for multimedia services over heterogeneous networks. A new concept of "Isomorphism Flow" (iFlow) was introduced for analyzing multimedia traffics, which is inspired by the abstract algebra based on experimental research. By using iFlow, the multimedia traffics with similar QoE requirements for different users are aggregated. A QoE evaluation method was also proposed for the aggregated traffics. Then a new cross-domain QoE guarantee method based on the iFlow QoE is proposed in this paper to adjust the network resource from the perspective of user perception. The proposed scheme is validated through simulations. Simulation results show that the proposed scheme achieves an enhancement in QoE performance and outperforms the existing schemes.

Keywords: Diffserv networks · Quality of experience · Multimedia traffic

1 Introduction

With the increasing demands of high quality personalized services and large number of smart devices such as smartphones and smart TVs being used for Internet of Things (IoT), a large volume of multimedia data is delivered over the heterogeneous networks, such as WiFi networks, Differentiated Services (DiffServe) networks, Long Term Evolution (LTE) networks and Bluetooth networks [1–4]. Each user/device within these heterogeneous networks requires very different Quality of Experience (QoE), and the services could be delivered through the routes with different features to meet their QoE requirements with the lowest costs [6]. However, bandwidth constraints and the resulted delay and packet loss may have an adverse impact on the delivered multimedia quality [1]. To guarantee the QoE of multimedia traffic still remains a challenge for multimedia communications.

Existing research efforts on QoE are focusing on three aspects: (1) development of QoE-driven frameworks for multimedia applications [1, 5, 6]; (2) QoE evaluation [7–9]; and (3) the influence of QoE features on the user's QoE level [10–13]. However, little work is done for cross-domain QoE guarantee, and very little efforts are made on differentiated traffics from QoE perspective. At the same time, the existing QoE

H. Gao et al. (Eds.): CollaborateCom 2018, LNICST 268, pp. 432–447, 2019.
https://doi.org/10.1007/978-3-030-12981-1_30

evaluation methods still need to be improved to effectively provide cross-domain QoE guarantee. The reason is the user' preferences are missed in evaluating the QoE.

Figure 1 demonstrates a typical application scenario of multimedia communications via a heterogeneous network, where multimedia traffics will tranverse three typical networks (WiFi, DiffServe, and LTE). Among these three networks, each network will provide its own service guarantee mechanisms to guarantee the quality of services. For example, the WiFi network prioritizes the multimedia traffic by adopting four Access Categories (AC): voice (AC_VO), video (AC_VI), best effort (AC_BE), and background (AC_BK). The DiffServ network, on the other hand, guarantees the quality of traffics by processing different traffic classes according to their DiffServ Code Point (DSCP) values. The LTE network, however, guarantees the quality of traffics based on traffic differentiation and prioritization of data flows. In this case, the users are exposed to a complex and diverse heterogeneous network environment. When these three networks cannot effectively interconnect with each other, the user's QoE cannot be guaranteed. The effectiveness of the network is greatly weakened.

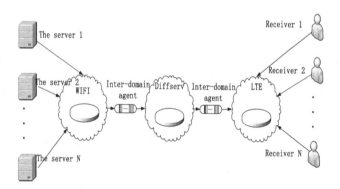

Fig. 1. A typical scenario of multimedia communication

As mentioned above, the recent developments on QoE can't solve the problem to provide cross-domain QoE guarantee for multimedia traffics over heterogeneous networks. In order to tackle this problem, a new cross-domain QoE guarantee method is proposed in this paper, in which users obtain their personalized services by differentiating multimedia traffics at a fine-grained QoE level. To differentiate appropriately multimedia traffics from QoE perspective, a new concept of "Isomorphism Flow (iFlow)" is introduced in this paper after analyzing four types of QoE features of multimedia traffics from real world applications. Based on the QoE features, the multimedia traffics with similar QoE requirements are aggregated into a same iFlow category. Meanwhile, an improved QoE evaluation method is proposed, which considers user's preference. To the best of our knowledge, this is the first work on exploiting QoE related features to provide cross-domain QoE guarantee for multimedia traffics over heterogeneous networks.

The key contributions of this paper are as follows:

(1) A new concept: this paper, for the first time, introduces a new concept of iFlow based on the QoE features, by which the multimedia traffics are appropriately classified to provide differentiated services for users from the perspective of user perception.

(2) A new model: according to our experiment, a typical QoE evaluation model was improved to make its evaluation results closer to the real value.

(3) A new method: we propose a new cross-domain QoE guarantee method based on iFlow and improved QoE evaluation method, in which the network resource is allocated according to user's QoE requirements.

The rest of this paper is organized as follow. The related work is described in Sect. 2. Section 3 introduces typical QoE features and iFlow concept. Section 4 describes a new cross-domain QoE guarantee method based on iFlow. In Sect. 5, the simulation results are presented. Finally, Sect. 6 concludes this paper and also provides suggestions for future work.

2 Related Work

QoE includes two main aspects [14]: Quality of Service (QoS) and human perception. QoS mechanism is mainly responsible for the business management from the viewpoint of network and is to provide business diversity. Human perception is subjective in nature and is internal to the user, thus not directly observable to the experimenter, which generally exhibits the effects of hysteresis and recency.

The main features of QoE depend on the user's emotion, hobbies, etc. The aim of our future multimedia network communications is to meet the personalized user satisfaction with the needs and expectations.

As mentioned before, QoE guarantee frameworks and QoE evaluations are the most important aspects of QoE research. In this section, the state-of-the-art research work in these two areas is described.

2.1 QoE Guarantee Method

For multimedia communications in IoT, authors in [1] introduce a new concept of Quality of Things (QoT), and propose a new quality aware IoT architecture based on QoT for multimedia applications to ensure the quality of multimedia content to be collected, processed and delivered appropriately in such applications. authors in [5] propose a QoE-driven framework named Smart Media Pricing (SMP) to price the QoE for IoT multimedia services, which is translated to a game theoretical QoE maximization problem. Authors in [6] propose a novel vehicle network architecture for the smart city scenario, in which a joint resource management scheme is proposed to mitigate the network congestion with the joint optimization of caching, networking and computing resources.

Based on the centrality of nodes, authors in [7] propose a suboptimal dynamic method that is suitable for the IoT with frequent content delivery, and a green resource allocation algorithm based on Deep Reinforcement Learning (DRL) to improve the accuracy of QoE in an adaptive manner. The model proposed in [7] can capture the network cost and the influencing factors of IoT user services according to the conditions of the IoT, and pay attention to the issues of cache allocation and transmission rate. Under this content-centric IoT, the goal is to allocate cache capacity between content-centric computing nodes and process transmission rates within the total network cost and Mean Opinion Score (MOS) limits for the entire IoT. A 5G QoE system capable of extracting video metadata and stream QoS metrics is proposed in [8]. Authors in [9] present an IoT-based architecture for multi-sensorial media delivery to TV users in a home entertainment scenario. In [10] a computational offloading scheme is formulated to model the competition among IoT users and allocate the limited processing power of fog nodes efficiently. Each user aims to maximize its own QoE, which reflects its satisfaction of using computing services in terms of the reduction in computation energy and delay. Through numerical studies, it evaluates the users' QoE as well as the equilibrium efficiency. It reveals that by utilizing the proposed mechanism, more users benefit from computing services in comparison with an existing offloading mechanism. It further shows that the proposed mechanism significantly reduces the computation delay and enables low-latency fog computing services for delay-sensitive IoT applications.

These papers all indicate that there are some unreasonable or waste of resources in the process of network resource scheduling. We need to propose new schemes to make the network more optimized and the QoE higher.

2.2   QoE Evaluation Method

According to different classification standards, the QoE evaluation methods can be classified into three different categories, according to a comprehensive survey [15], including:

(1) subjective evaluation method: QoE is obtained from subjective test, where human viewers evaluate the quality of tested traffics under a controlled environment;
(2) objective evaluation method: objective quality models are developed to predict QoE based on objective QoS parameters; and
(3) data-driven QoE analysis method: this method adopts measurable QoE metrics, e.g., viewing time, probability of turns, etc.

Subjective evaluation method refers to the evaluation given in a specific and controlled environment according to people's feeling, and a Mean Opinion Score (MOS) of multiple testers is finally obtained as the benchmark for the quality of each sequence. At present, ITU-T has launched a corresponding subjective quality assessment standard for different video services [16]. Typical subjective evaluation methods include Double Stimulus Continuous Quality Scale (DSCQS), Double Stimulus Impairment Scale (DSIS) and Single Stimulus Continuous Quality Scale (SSCQE) [17]. Objective evaluation method is mainly to establish the mapping relation between the objective QoS parameters and user QoE by using the relevant information of multimedia, so as to make the result as close as possible to the subjective. In addition, objective evaluation methods based on input parameter types can be divided into: parameter planning model, packet layer model, bitstream layer model, mixed layer model, and media layer model [18]. These models are applicable to different situations. Data-driven QoE analysis method carries out large-scale measurement studies in various services.

A QoE predictive assessment scheme that can be applied to real-world network environments with real-time processing requirements is proposed in [8]. A model of user's QoE is given in [9]:

$$QoE_Q = \alpha e^{-\beta QoS} + \gamma \tag{1}$$

where α, β and γ are the parameters constraining the quantization of QoE, QoS represents the QoS a user can obtain. It mainly evaluates the user's QoE based on various network parameters.

Paper [10] studies the influence of odor type on the user's QoE level, and suggests adding olfactory sense to improve the user's QoE. Paper [11] defines the user satisfaction level of video streaming through the function formula, which utilizes emotions to predict the user's QoE and puts forward to customize the personalized content through the viewer's emotional feedback so as to improve the method of video QoE user experience. Paper [12] discusses some environmental factors parameters of user QoE modeling.

In our works, user's preferences and tags are very important in real-time communications. Our focus is not only on all network parameters, but also the user's preferences for either whether to change the user experience or whether the scheme we built based on this can meet the requirements of user evaluation or not. Therefore, users' geographical location, gender, network parameters and preferences will be taken into account in our real-time communication software.

3   Typical QoE Features and Isomorphic Flow Concept

To consider QoE features in QoE evaluation and garantee is still at its infancy, and there is still great room for development. The selected QoE features should be a good indicator of user experience or engagement, and easy to track and monitor in real-time [15]. By surveying 50 volunteers, we obtain the distributions of age and gender, shown in Fig. 2. It is obvious that the users' age and gender will affect their preference for traffics. Furthermore, their further preference for different traffics are obtained as shown in Table 1. Meanwhile, we also investigate hobbies and business categories, which affect user's preference for traffics. This paper mainly focuses on four typical QoE features and provides some meaningful results.

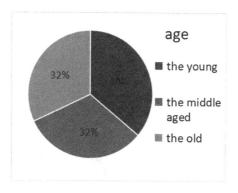

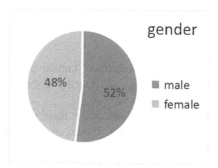

Fig. 2. Distribution of age and gender

Table 1. The effect of interest on the degree of business preference

Traffic	Medical (%)	Game	Household	Message
Traveling	36%	14%	22%	30%
Reading	18%	22%	36%	22%
Drawing	22%	38%	18%	20%
Music	24%	36%	24%	28%

Typical QoE Features

The four typical QoE features are as follows.

(1) Gender: the gender difference of users is one of the primary factors to be considered in our personalized service since there are obviously gender difference in physical characteristics and hobbies between male and female in most cases. The percentage of gender preference for four kinds of traffics is shown in Fig. 3.

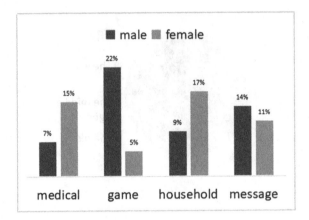

Fig. 3. The percentage of gender preference for four kinds of traffics

(2) Age group: as far as users are concerned, human beings love different things at different age. A person will change and develop his/her preferences when growing older, so we also consider them.

(3) Hobbies: users' hobbies largely determine their favorite businesses. They are closely related to users' personalities. If we can assign priority of different businesses according to users' interests before evaluation, the evaluation results will be more accurate. Table 1 shows that different traffic preferences caused by different users' hobbies. It indicates that users with different hobbies have different uses for social software.

(4) Traffic categories: the traffics with similar QoE requirement can be classified into the same category from QoE perspective, which has a globally unique label with corresponding scheduling priority.

After surveying 50 volunteers, it shows that the QoE requirements are not completely stochastic. The users with similar age generally have similar preference on traffic categories. Furthermore, the users with similar age and gender generally have more similar preference on traffic categories. For example, women prefer to use video and text services, while men are more likely to enjoy voice services and pictures.

Figure 4 indicates that the frequency of old users enjoying medical traffics is higher than that of young people, however, the young and middle-aged users prefer online gaming and household traffics than old users.

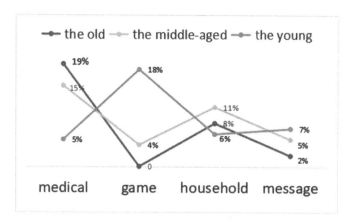

Fig. 4. The effect of age on the degree of traffic preference

The results of above observation and analysis inspired us that similar QoE requirements may mean similar geometric spatial structure in higher-dimensional QoE space, which is comprised of QoE metrics. In other words, multimedia traffics may be represented by QoE metrics in higher-dimensional QoE space. The multimedia traffics with similar QoE requirements can be aggregated, and provided with differentiated services by similar network operator to guarantee end-to-end QoE for different users.

Isomorphic Flow Concept

According to the concept of graphic isomorphism in abstract algebra, this paper introduces a new concept of "Isomorphism Flow" (iFlow) for evaluating multimedia traffic, which is generated by aggregating the multimedia traffics with similar QoE requirements.

Different from typical traffic/QoS classes or aggregation flow, the iFlow is generated according to QoE metrics. The multimedia traffics belonged to the same traffic/QoS classes may be different iFlow categories. Even if the same multimedia traffic may be divided into different iFlow categories when users with different background have different QoE requirements. For the same user, the same multimedia traffic may be divided into different iFlow categories when the users' preference changes with circumstance. Meanwhile, different multimedia traffics may be divided into the same iFlow category when the users' preferences are identical. It is obviously that multimedia traffic is divided into corresponding iFlow from the perspective of QoE.

To express easily, a higher-dimensional QoE space is comprised of QoE metrics. In QoE space, the multimedia traffics belonged to the same iFlow categories have similar geometric structures. However, for different users, the same traffics may have different geometric structures with different preference. Each of iFlow categories has a sole label. Based on users' QoE, the traffics with the same users' QoE and different users have the same priority and network operations. Therefore, the iFlow can reflect users' preference and help utilize the network resources efficiently by classifying the network multimedia traffics into different iFlow categories according to users' QoE. For example, when user A prefers to gaming and user B is inclined to choose household, if

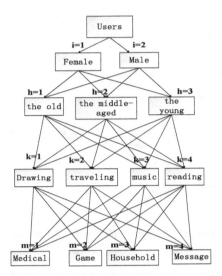

Fig. 5. User characteristics and traffic association diagrams

Table 2. Definitions of various parameters

Characteristics	Meaning
Gender	i = 1 stands for female, i = 2 stands for male
Age	h = 1 stands for the old, h = 2 stands for the middle age, h = 3 stands for the young
Hobby	k = 1 stands for drawing, k = 2 stands for traveling, k = 3 stands for music, k = 4 stands for reading
Traffic	m = 1 stands for medical, m = 2 stands for game, m = 3 stands for household, m = 4 stands for message

users A and B have priorities for their traffics, the gaming traffic of user A and the household traffic of user B belong to the same iFlow category. Otherwise, if users A and B have different priorities for their traffics, the gaming traffic of user A and the household traffic of user B belong to the different iFlow category. In this paper, the selected traffics are divided into four categories (from 1 to 4) to easily explain, for which the value is larger and the priority is higher, the iFlow with higher priority will be assigned with a higher label value.

As shown in Fig. 5 and Table 2, users can be divided into two genders, respectively, and each of the genders can be further divided into three categories in different age groups (the old, the middle and the young). Each age category has different hobbies. Through investigating typical Chinese families, we select four typical activities (drawing, traveling, music and reading) for hobbies. Users with different hobbies have different preference for different traffics (medical, game, household and message).

The priority of traffic is different among users with different tags, the equation of traffic priority is given as follows.

$$D_j = [A_h^i, T_k^m] \tag{2}$$

where D_j denotes the jth priority, A_h^i denotes a user with different gender i and age h, for which the meaning are shown in Table 2, and T_k^m denotes the traffic with m and k. The detailed finding from 50 volunteers is provided in the appendix A, from which the highest priority group D_1 is provided as follows.

$$D_1 = \{A_1^1, T_1^2; A_1^1, T_3^1; A_1^1, T_3^4; A_1^1, T_4^3; A_2^1, T_1^2; A_2^1, T_2^1; A_2^1,$$
$$T_3^4; A_2^1, T_4^3; A_3^1, T_1^2; A_3^1, T_1^3; A_3^1, T_2^3; A_3^1, T_3^1; A_1^2, T_1^3, A_1^2$$
$$T_4^1; A_1^2, T_4^2; A_1^2, T_4^4; A_2^2, T_1^2; A_2^2, T_3^4; A_2^2, T_4^1; A_2^2, T_4^3;$$
$$A_3^2, T_1^2; A_3^2, T_1^3; A_3^2, T_3^1; A_3^2, T_3^4\}$$

From D_1, the same traffics have different priorities for different groups of users. For example, (A_1^1, T_3^1) and (A_3^2, T_3^4) belong to the same iFlow with same priority in this proposed method. However, (A_1^1, T_3^1) represents that the older female with music preference like medical of home traffics; (A_3^2, T_3^4) represents that the young men who like music preferred real-time messaging of home traffics.

4 A New Cross-Domain QoE Guarantee Method Based on iFlow

As shown in Fig. 6, the whole process of the proposed method can be divided into three modules. In module A, multimedia traffics are transmitted. In module B, the multimedia traffics are classified according to QoE characteristics. According to the users' preference from our survey, the corresponding traffics in the queue should be sorted and prioritized. According to the definition of iFlow, homogeneous flow scheduling process is started by setting roughly 50 users and 4 priorities for 4 types of traffics over heterogeneous networks. Since the users have different preferences, the users are divided into different priorities. The user with higher preference degree has higher priority by providing the queue with higher priority. Then the corresponding mapping is provided according to the order of priority access to the queue in the network.

The module C is the evaluation module, in which an improved model is utilized to calculate the corresponding user's MOS value. The evaluation includes subjective and objective evaluations, in which the MOS value from objective evaluation model is compared with that from subjective evaluation model. After the comparison, the results are used to verify the accuracy of our improved model.

The proposed method comprises of two sections including isomorphic flow scheduling process and QoE evaluation. In isomorphic flow scheduling process sections, the isomorphic flow is introduced. In QoE evaluation section, an improved QoE evaluation process is described. The following figure shows the scenario assessment framework under our architecture.

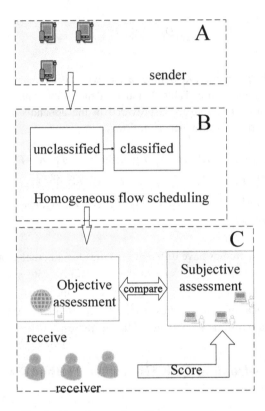

Fig. 6. Experience of quality assessment process

Isomorphic Flow Scheduling Process

The detailed isomorphic flow scheduling process is provided in this section. As shown in Fig. 7, within each network of heterogeneous networks there have different QoS/traffic classifications for different multimedia traffics. $D_i(i = 1, 2, \cdots, n)$ represents the priority of the corresponding queue i. When the traffics with different priorities are scheduled into different queues in heterogeneous networks, the queue with higher priority has higher probability to be transmitted. The traffics belonging to the same iFlow category are scheduled into the same queue as shown in Fig. 7.

QoE Evaluation

A typical QoE evaluation model [9] shown in Eq. (1) considers the influences of various network parameters, however, neglects user's preferences so that users' perception can't be reflected. Therefore, this paper tries to improve this model by introducing preference impact factor to increase the weight of user's interest and enhance the precision of this typical model. M' is selected as the range of preference influencing factors $(0, 1)$, for which the smaller the value is, the more consistent with the use of traffic of the user's interest is.

This paper assigns different weights and normalized the QoS parameters (resolution, delay and packet loss rate). Q represents the normalized network influence parameter, which is the x-coordinate of the model proposed as follows.

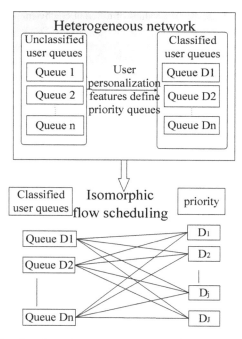

Fig. 7. The effect of age on the degree of business preference

$$Q = \text{resolution} * C1 + \text{delay} * C2 + \text{loss rate} * C3$$
$$(Q = 0 \sim 1) \tag{3}$$

where C1 $\approx$ −0.00017, C2 $\approx$ 0.01220. C3 $\approx$ −0.0000001.
The improved model is as follows:

$$QoE = a - MQoE_{QoS} \tag{4}$$

where QoE_S denotes the QoE value from Eq. (1), $M = M' + b$, where b is the corrected parameter. This paper classifies the preferences of the volunteers and identified four preference factors M', which are defined as M' = 0.1, 0.3, 0.6 and 0.9. In order to show it more visually, M is calculated by adding an influence factor and a parameter b.

5 Experiments

In order to demonstrate the effectiveness of the proposed method, the proposed method is compared with existing schemes in bandwidth utilization performance. Meanwhile the improved QoE evaluation model is analyzed by whether to consider the preference influencing factors or not.

B represents the bandwidth utilization as follows.

Table 3. The values of different coefficient

β	α	γ	a	b	M
−2.02	−0.32	0.6	8.65	8.42	M' + 8.42

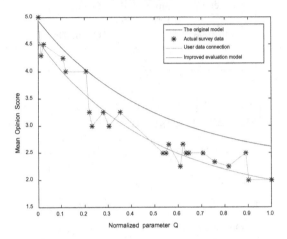

Fig. 8. The comparison between the original model and the present model and our research results

$$B = Y1/Y2 * 100\% \tag{5}$$

where $Y1$ is the bandwidth loss of the user and $Y2$ is the total bandwidth of the user. In this paper, the bandwidth utilization is used to calculate the improvement of this proposed scheme compared with the traditional ones.

In the simulation environment, 50 volunteers are selected. According to their preferences, the multimedia traffics are divided into medical, gaming, household, and massage.

According to Eq. (4), the values of different coefficient are obtained as shown in Table 3. The value range of M' is at [0, 1].

To verify the effectiveness of the improved QoE evaluation method, the proposed QoE model is evaluated when $M' = 0$ and $M' = 1$, respectively. $M' = 0$ means that the preference influencing factor isn't considered; $M' = 1$ means that the preference influencing factor is considered. The definition of x coordinate parameter Q is given in formula (3). The results of comparison are shown in Fig. 8. Based on Eq. (4), Table 3 and subjective evaluation, the QoE level can be obtained as follows:

$$\begin{cases} QoE = 2.688e^{-2.02QoS} + 6.3916 & M' = 0 \\ QoE = 2.9664e^{-2.02QoS} + 1.60478 & M' = 1 \end{cases} \tag{6}$$

After normalizing the network parameters, this paper compares the results of evaluation among three models. To facilitate observation, the average MOS value is utilized in x-coordinate. As shown in Fig. 8, it is observed that the results of subjective evaluation are closer to the improved model than that of typical model. The simulation results indicate that the MOS value of typical model is higher than that of subjective evaluation since the typical model neglects users' preferences.

When M' selects 0.1, 0.3, 0.6 and 0.9, respectively, Eq. (7) is obtained according to Eq. (4) as follows.

$$
\begin{cases}
QoE = 2.71872e^{-2.02QoS} + 2.19304 & M' = 0.1 \\
QoE = 2.77376e^{-2.02QoS} + 2.06232 & M' = 0.3 \\
QoE = 2.85632e^{-2.02QoS} + 1.86624 & M' = 0.6 \\
QoE = 2.93888e^{-2.02QoS} + 1.67016 & M' = 0.9
\end{cases}
\tag{7}
$$

The computing result of Eq. (7) is shown in Fig. 9. It indicates that those different traffics have different influence degrees for the same user. The user has higher preference to medical traffic, the MOS value is higher.

To verify the effectiveness of the new cross-domain QoE guarantee method, the proposed QoE guarantee method is compared with Aggregate flow method and mapping table [19] in bandwidth utilization performance. Based on iFlow, the simulation is carried out and the results are shown in Fig. 10. Figure 10 indicates that the broadband utilization ratio of the new cross-domain QoE guarantee method is significantly higher than that of the other method.

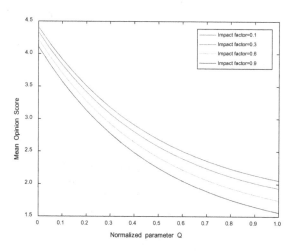

Fig. 9. Shows the curves obtained by the four preference factors of the present model

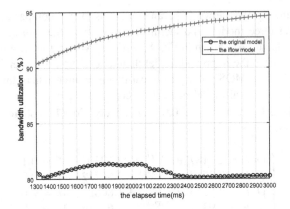

Fig. 10. Bandwidth utilization comparison chart

6 Conclusions

In this paper, a new cross-domain QoE guarantee method based on iFlow is presented to provide user with good perception and acquire high utilization ratio of network resources for multimedia traffic in IoT. After investigating the behavior of multimedia traffic and analyzing typical QoE features of multimedia traffics, a new concept of Isomorphism for multimedia traffic, iFlow, is introduced. iFlow is generated by aggregating different traffics with similar QoE requirements. Furthermore, an improved QoE evaluation method is proposed, in which the user's interests have the very high weight. The simulation studies are given to demonstrate the effectiveness of the proposed method.

Acknowledgment. This work was supported in part by National Natural Science Foundation of China (No. 61401004).

References

1. Karaadi, A., Sun, L., Mkwawa, I.-H.: Multimedia communications in Internet of Things QoT or QoE. In: 2017 IEEE International Conference on Internet of Things (iThings) and IEEE Green Computing and Communications (GreenCom) and IEEE Cyber, Physical and Social Computing (CPSCom) and IEEE Smart Data (SmartData), pp. 23–29 (2017)
2. Wang, Z., Dong, Y., Mao, S., Wang, X.: Internet multimedia traffic classification from QoS perspective using semi-supervised dictionary learning models. IEEE/CIC China Commun. **14**(10), 202–218 (2017)
3. Wang, Z., Mao, S., Yang, L., Tang, P.: A survey of multimedia big data. IEEE/CIC China Commun. **15**(1), 155–176 (2018)
4. Naserian, E., Wang, X., Dahal, K., Wang, Z., Wang, Z.: Personalized location prediction for group travellers from spatial-temporal trajectories. Future Gener. Comput. Syst. **24**(1), 1–15 (2018)
5. Wang, W., Wang, Q.: Price the QoE, not the data: SMP-economic resource allocation in wireless multimedia Internet of Things. IEEE Commun. Mag. **56**(9), 74–79 (2018)

6. Li, M., Si, P., Zhang, Y.: Delay-tolerant data traffic to software-defined vehicular networks with mobile edge computing in smart city. IEEE Trans. Veh. Technol. (Early Access) **67**, 1–14 (2018)

7. He, X., Wang, K., Huang, H., Miyazaki, T., Wang, Y., Guo, S.: Green resource allocation based on deep reinforcement learning in content-centric IoT. IEEE Trans. Emerg. Top. Comput. (Early Access), 1 (2018)

8. Nightingale, J., Salva-Garcia, P., Calero, J.M.A., Wang, Q.: 5G-QoE: QoE modeling for ultra-HD video streaming in 5G networks. IEEE Trans. Broadcast. **64**(2), 621–634 (2018)

9. Charonyktakis, P., Plakia, M., Tsamardinos, I., Papadopouli, M.: On user-centric modular QoE prediction for VoIP based on machine-learning algorithms. IEEE Trans. Mob. Comput. **15**(6), 1443–1456 (2016)

10. Murray, N., Lee, B., Qiao, Y., Miro-Muntean, G.: The impact of scent type on olfaction-enhanced multimedia quality of experience. IEEE Trans. Syst. Man Cybern.: Syst. **47**(9), 2503–2515 (2017)

11. Tao, X., Dong, L., Li, Y., Zhou, J., Ge, N., Jianhua, L.: Real-time personalized content catering via viewer sentiment feedback: a QoE perspective. IEEE Netw. **29**(6), 14–19 (2015)

12. Scott, M.J., Guntuku, S.C., Lin, W., Ghinea, G.: Do personality and culture influence perceived video quality and enjoyment. IEEE Trans. Multimed. **18**(9), 1796–1807 (2016)

13. Mitra, K., Zaslavsky, A., Åhlund, C.: Context-aware QoE modelling, measurement, and prediction in mobile computing systems. IEEE Trans. Mob. Comput. **14**(5), 920–936 (2015)

14. Chen, B.-W., Ji, W., Jiang, F., Rho, S.: QoE-enabled big video streaming for large-scale heterogeneous clients and networks in smart cities. IEEE Access **4**(1), 97–107 (2016)

15. Chen, Y., Kaishun, W., Zhang, Q.: From QoS to QoE: a tutorial on video quality assessment. IEEE Commun. Surv. Tutor. **7**(2), 1126–1165 (2015)

16. ITU-T Recommendation P.913. Methods for the subjective assessment of video quality, audio quality and audiovisual quality of Internet video and distribution quality television in any environment (2014)

17. ITU-R Recommendation BT.500-11. Methodology for the subjective assessment of the quality of television pictures (2002)

18. Takahashi, A., Hands, D., Barriac, V.: Standardization activities in the ITU for a QoE assessment of IPYV. IEEE Commun. Mag. **46**(2), 78–84 (2008)

19. Wang, Z.J., Dong, Y.N., Wang, X.: A dynamic service class mapping scheme for different QoS domains using flow aggregation. IEEE Syst. J. **9**(4), 1299–1310 (2015)

Extracting Business Execution Processes of API Services for Mashup Creation

Guobing Zou[1,2], Yang Xiang[1,2], Pengwei Wang[3], Shengye Pang[1], Honghao Gao[1], Sen Niu[4(✉)], and Yanglan Gan[3(✉)]

[1] School of Computer Engineering and Science, Shanghai University, Shanghai, China
guobingzou@gmail.com, yangxiang618@gmail.com
[2] Shanghai Institute for Advanced Communication and Data Science,
Shanghai University, Shanghai, China
[3] School of Computer Science and Technology, Donghua University, Shanghai, China
{wangpengwei,ylgan}@dhu.edu.cn
[4] School of Computer and Information Engineering,
Shanghai Polytechnic University, Shanghai, China
sens306314@gmail.com

Abstract. Mashup services creation has become a new research issue for service-oriented complex application systems. During the mashup service creation, how to extract business execution processes among APIs plays an important role when a mashup service developer receives a bunch of recommended API services. However, it does not exist an effective way to perform mashup recommendation with the support of extracting API business execution processes. In this paper, we propose a novel approach for automated extraction of API business execution processes for mashup creation. Based on the proposed word-domain matrix model, API annotation in a mashup service is transformed as a bipartite graph problem that is solved by the maximum bipartite matching algorithm to semantically annotate involved APIs. Then, directed dependency network among APIs is constructed by analyzing path dependencies and evaluating the compound polarity. Finally, API business execution processes in a mashup service can be extracted. The advantage of the work is that it generates business execution processes instead of a list of independent APIs, which can significantly facilitate mashup service creation for software developers. To validate the performance, we conduct extensive experiments on a large-scale real-world dataset crawled from ProgrammableWeb. The experimental results demonstrate the feasibility and effectiveness of our proposed approach.

Keywords: Service-oriented computing · API service ·
Mashup creation · Business execution processes · API annotation

1 Introduction

With the advancement of network technology and increasing demands on service-oriented application integration, more and more service providers publish their

Published by Springer Nature Switzerland AG 2019. All Rights Reserved
H. Gao et al. (Eds.): CollaborateCom 2018, LNICST 268, pp. 448–466, 2019.
https://doi.org/10.1007/978-3-030-12981-1_31

software on the Internet in the form of web APIs. It accelerates the interoperable machine-to-machine interaction and greatly promotes the procedure of service discovery, optimum selection, automatic composition and recommendation. As of May 2018, the world's largest online service repository ProgrammableWeb recorded more than 19,000 API services and approximately 8,000 mashup services. Especially, developing a mashup service for software engineers who use multiple individual existing APIs as components to create a value-added composite service becomes a popular software development schema in service-oriented environment [12]. Mashup services integrate the data and functionality from more than one APIs that enriches the applicability of web services. Currently, most existing mashup services are created by software developers who manually choose appropriate APIs and compose them together as a whole to a service management platform. As a result, it tends to be a labor-intensive challenging task for mashup service developers to select their desired web APIs from multiple functionally equivalent candidate ones in a large service repository.

To address the provision of web APIs, correlative research efforts have been made to improve the effectiveness of mashup creation. The mainstream method includes semantic-based, social network-based and machine learning-based service recommendation. The semantic-based methods [5,6,8,12] mainly focus on using LDA probabilistic topic model to calculate semantic similarity between mashup request and API description. Another way [1,11,12] is to leverage social network techniques to mine user's social features and interests from usage historical logging, where candidate APIs are recommended according to their high similarity of the social aspects with users. Moreover, machine learning algorithms [9,10,13] such as clustering and matrix factorization are recently exploited to more effectively enhance API recommendation.

Although the above investigation can assist and facilitate the procedure of recommending appropriate APIs from a large-scale web service repository, the deficiency of the existing approaches is that they are still difficult and time-consuming for software developers to create a mashup service. The reason is that they need to further understand the functionality of the provided web APIs and their corresponding business invocation relationships, when these APIs are programmed and integrated into a mashup service. Therefore, how to design a novel approach for automatically and effective extraction of business execution processes among APIs has been a key research issue to be solved in mashup service creation.

An ideal way of overcoming the above problem is to reason out the business execution processes for a set of APIs that are recommended to mashup developers. To this end, we propose a novel framework for automated extraction of API business execution processes when developing a mashup service. Given a mashup service repository, a word-domain matrix is firstly modeled through calculating the semantic similarity between word and domain by WordNet. In such case, we then transform an API annotation problem to a weighted bipartite graph, where the maximum bipartite matching algorithm is employed to optimally find a solution to semantically annotate APIs in a mashup functional description. Afterwards, a directed dependency network is constructed among APIs by analyzing path dependencies and evaluating the compound polarity via Stanford CoreNLP parser. Finally, business execution processes among APIs can be extracted by network maximum flow algorithm. The advantage of the work is that it generates API business execution processes based on an existing service recommendation approach that only produces a list of independent APIs. Therefore, it can significantly facilitate mashup service creation for software developers. To validate the feasibility and effectiveness of our approach, we conduct extensive experiments on a real-world dataset crawled from ProgrammableWeb. The experimental results demonstrate that our approach outperforms the competing ones in terms of six evaluation metrics.

The main contributions of this paper are summarized as follows:

- We propose a novel API annotation approach that semantically maps highly correlative words to their corresponding APIs in mashup functional description, where word-domain matrix is constructed to provide weights in the modeled bipartite graph.
- On the basis of API annotation, we propose a novel approach for extracting API dependency network in mashup service by analyzing path dependencies between APIs and evaluating their compound polarity.
- We design and implement a prototype system and conduct extensive experiments on a large-scale real-world dataset crawled from ProgrammableWeb. The experimental results validate the feasibility and effectiveness of our proposed approach for business execution processes extraction.

The reminder of this paper is organized as follows. The problem is formulated in Sect. 2. Section 3 elaborates our approach for extracting API business execution processes. Section 4 presents extensive experiments and analyzes the performance. Section 5 reviews the related work. Finally, Sect. 6 concludes the paper.

2   Problem Formulation

Definition 1 (API Service). A web API can be denoted as a two-tuple $api = \langle W^{(a)}, D^{(a)} \rangle$, where $W^{(a)} = \{w_1, w_2, \cdots\}$ is a functional description, and $w_i (i = 1, 2, \cdots)$ is the i-th word in the description. $D^{(a)} = domain_a$ corresponds to a domain tagged in api.

Definition 2 (Mashup Service). A mashup service, M, is represented as a three-tuple $M = \langle W^{(m)}, L^{(m)}, D^{(m)} \rangle$, where $W^{(m)} = \{w_1, w_2, \cdots\}$ is a functional description. $L^{(m)} = \{api_1, api_2, \cdots\}$ is a list of APIs, where api_i is the i-th API involved in M. $D^{(m)} = domain_m$ corresponds to a domain tagged in M.

Definition 3 (Atomic Grammatical Dependency). Given a mashup service $M = \langle W^{(m)}, L^{(m)}, D^{(m)} \rangle$, the atomic grammatical dependency of any two words w_s and w_t in $W^{(m)}$ is reflected by a set of directed paths denoted as $dep(w_s, w_t)$

$$dep(w_s, w_t) = \{w_s \xrightarrow{td_{z1}} w_{z1} \xleftarrow{td_{z2}} w_{z2} \xrightarrow{td_{z3}} \ldots \xrightarrow{td_{zn}} w_t\} \tag{1}$$

Where w_{zi} is the i-th dependency bridge word. td_{zj} represents a binary dependency relationship of the two adjacent words.

Note that the arrow direction of the dependency relationship indicates the order of dependency or domination between two adjacent words. The forward arrow $\mathbf{w_s} \rightarrow \mathbf{w_t}$ states the dependency of w_s on w_t, or w_t is dominated by w_s. Conversely, the reverse arrow $\mathbf{w_s} \leftarrow \mathbf{w_t}$ states the dominance of w_s on w_t, or w_t depends on w_s.

Definition 4 (Grammatical Dependency Set). Given a mashup service $M = \langle W^{(m)}, L^{(m)}, D^{(m)} \rangle$, the set of grammatical dependencies $C^{(m)}$ in $W^{(m)}$ can be expressed as

$$C^{(m)} = \{dep(w_s, w_t) | w_s, w_t \in W^{(m)}\} \tag{2}$$

Definition 5 (Mashup Functionality Annotation). A functional description $W^{(m)}$ of a mashup service M corresponds to a markup description $SW^{(m)}$, expressed by

$$SW^{(m)} = \{\langle w_1, \{api_{11}, \cdots\} \rangle, \langle w_2, \{api_{21}, \cdots\} \rangle, \cdots\} \tag{3}$$

Where $\{w_1, w_2, \cdots\}$ are words in the description of $W^{(m)}$. $\{api_{k1}, \cdots\}$ states the set of APIs annotated by w_k.

Definition 6 (Business Execution Processes Extraction). Given a mashup service $M = \langle W^{(m)}, L^{(m)}, D^{(m)} \rangle$, the task of extracting business execution processes of APIs in M is defined as

$$g(SW^{(m)}, C^{(m)}) := G' \tag{4}$$

Where $SW^{(m)}$ is a semantically annotated functional description of $W^{(m)}$; $C^{(m)}$ is the set of atomic grammatical dependencies in $W^{(m)}$; g is an effective approach that derives a generated graph G', corresponding to the desired business execution processes of APIs in M.

It is observed that given a mashup service M or a mashup functional description with a set of recommended APIs, we mainly focus on how to semantically annotate its APIs from $W^{(m)}$ to $SW^{(m)}$ and design an effective approach g for business execution processes extraction.

3 Automated Extraction of Business Execution Processes

3.1 Framework of the Approach

Figure 1 illustrates the overall framework of our proposed approach. From the perspective of task functionality, it goes through three crucial stages, including word-domain model construction, mashup functionality API annotation, and dependency network extraction.

In the stage of word-domain model construction, all the mashup services are aggregated to form a word bank. Domains are derived from the partitioning of original API and mashup service repository. WordNet is then applied to calculate the semantic similarity degree of a pair of word and domain. In the stage of mashup functionality API annotation, the similarity between a word and an API is evaluated by word-domain matrix and API-domain concurrence matrix. Furthermore, we transform a mashup annotation problem to a bipartite graph and adopt the maximum bipartite graph matching algorithm to annotate APIs in mashup service. In the stage of dependency network extraction, we generate a set of semantic relationship trees for an annotated mashup description via Stanford CoreNLP parser. By evaluating the polarity of invocation relationships among APIs based on analyzing path dependencies, we construct an API dependency network where network maximum flow algorithm is applied to detect start and end points for business execution processes extraction.

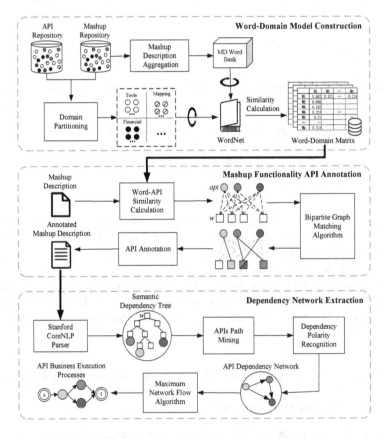

Fig. 1. The framework of our approach.

3.2   Word-Domain Model Construction

To best match feasible words for an API in a mashup service, the similarity calculation between them becomes a key factor. Since domain and API concurrency matrix can be available from service description, word and API relationships can be directly derived if we have word and domain matrix model.

Definition 7 (Word-Domain Matrix). The word-domain model is denoted by an $m * n$ matrix M_{d_w}, where m is the number of all service domains and n is the number of words collected from all mashup functional descriptions.

$$M_{d\_w} = \begin{array}{c} \\ d_1 \\ d_2 \\ \vdots \\ d_m \end{array} \overset{\begin{array}{cccc} w_1 & w_2 & \dots & w_n \end{array}}{\left(\begin{array}{cccc} sem_{11} & sem_{12} & \dots & sem_{1n} \\ sem_{21} & sem_{22} & \dots & sem_{2n} \\ \vdots & \vdots & \ddots & \vdots \\ sem_{m1} & sem_{m2} & \dots & sem_{mn} \end{array} \right)} \tag{5}$$

Each entry sem_{ij} represents the semantic similarity degree between d_i and w_j, ranging from 0 to 1. All the domains $D = \{d_1, \dots, d_m\}$ are accumulated by domain partitioning from API and mashup service repository, while all the words $W = \{w_1, \dots, w_n\}$ are collected and preprocessed from mashup service repository.

We use WordNet as a lexical database to measure the semantic similarity between domain and word. Domains and mashup functional description words are mapped into a hierarchical semantic tree in WordNet representation, where the similarity degree of two nodes can be calculated based on their path distance. Given a domain d_i and a mashup functional description word w_j, the semantic similarity degree sem_{ij} is calculated by

$$sim\,(d_i, w_j) = \frac{2 * depth\,(lso\,(d_i, w_j))}{len\,(d_i, w_j) + 2 * depth\,(lso\,(d_i, w_j))} \tag{6}$$

Where, $lso\,(d_i, w_j)$ represents the deepest common parent between d_i and w_j. $depth\,(lso\,(d_i, w_j))$ is the depth of $lso\,(d_i, w_j)$. $len\,(d_i, w_j)$ represents the shortest path length between d_i and w_j.

Due to polysemy, a mashup functional description word may correspond to multiple concepts in semantic dictionary. In order to eliminate the ambiguity between two words, an improved similarity calculation algorithm is used to maximize the semantic matching degree. Given a domain d_i and a word w_j, the updated semantic similarity degree sem_{ij} is calculated by

$$sim'\,(d_i, w_j) = \max_{c_x \in synsets(d_i), c_y \in synsets(w_j)} sim(c_x, c_y) \tag{7}$$

Where, $synsets\,(d_i)$ and $synsets\,(w_j)$ represent the collection of concepts corresponding to d_i and w'_j respectively.

3.3 Mashup Functionality API Annotation

In this section, we describe how to map the words in a mashup functionality description to the corresponding involved APIs. Given a mashup service $M = \langle W^{(m)}, L^{(m)}, D^{(m)} \rangle$, API annotation is to match the most mashup appropriate functional description words for each API that belongs to M. It converts original mashup functional description $W^{(m)}$ to the annotated one $SW^{(m)}$, which is formally expressed by

$$f(W^{(m)}) = SW^{(m)} \tag{8}$$

$$W^{(m)} = \{w_1, w_2, \cdots\}$$
$$\Downarrow f \tag{9}$$
$$SW^{(m)} = \{\langle w_1, \{api_{11}, \cdots\}\rangle, \langle w_2, \{api_{21}, \cdots\}\rangle, \cdots\}$$

Where function f performs two steps, including the task of semantic similarity calculation between API and word (f_a) and the task of optimally matching an API to its semantically correlative words (f_b). Thus, mashup functionality API annotation can be decomposed as

$$f\left(W^{(m)}\right) = f_b\left(f_a\left(W^{(m)}\right)\right) \tag{10}$$

(1) f_a: semantic similarity calculation between API and word. Derived from API service repository, the concurrency tagging between an API api_i and a domain d_j indicates that whether api_i belongs to d_j. Here, another API-domain matrix denoted as M_{a_d} reflects the relationship.

$$M_{a\_d} = \begin{array}{c} \\ api_1 \\ api_2 \\ \vdots \\ api_l \end{array} \overset{\begin{array}{cccc} d_1 & d_2 & \dots & d_m \end{array}}{\begin{pmatrix} tag_{11} & tag_{12} & \dots & tag_{1m} \\ tag_{21} & tag_{22} & \dots & tag_{2m} \\ \vdots & \vdots & \ddots & \vdots \\ tag_{l1} & tag_{l2} & \dots & tag_{lm} \end{pmatrix}} \tag{11}$$

Where each row and column in the matrix represents an API and a domain, respectively. Each entry is either equal to 0 or 1. If the domain tagging of api_i is marked by d_j, tag_{ij} equals 1, while the rest of the values in M_{a_d} are 0.

Based on the API-domain matrix M_{a_d} and constructed word-domain matrix M_{d_w}, the weighting matrix M_{a_w} between API and mashup functional description word can be directly produced with the multiplication of M_{a_d} and M_{d_w}.

$$M_{a\_w} = \begin{array}{c} \\ api_1 \\ api_2 \\ \vdots \\ api_l \end{array} \overset{\begin{array}{cccc} w_1 & w_2 & \dots & w_n \end{array}}{\begin{pmatrix} wt_{11} & wt_{12} & \dots & wt_{1n} \\ wt_{21} & wt_{22} & \dots & wt_{2n} \\ \vdots & \vdots & \ddots & \vdots \\ wt_{l1} & wt_{l2} & \dots & wt_{ln} \end{pmatrix}} \tag{12}$$

Taking the above matrices, given a mashup service $M = \langle W^{(m)}, L^{(m)}, D^{(m)} \rangle$, the semantic similarity degree between an API and a mashup functional description word can be calculated. Formally, two submatrices $M_{a\_d}^{(m)}$ and $M_{d\_w}^{(m)}$ are intercepted to deduce semantic similarity matrix $Sim_{a\_w}(m)$.

$$Sim_{a\_w}(m) = M_{a\_d}^{(m)} \times M_{d\_w}^{(m)} \tag{13}$$

Where $M_{a\_d}^{(m)}$ represents a submatrix of M_{a_d} whose rows are composed of APIs involved in $L^{(m)}$. Similarly, $M_{d\_w}^{(m)}$ represents a submatrix of M_{d_w} whose columns are composed of words involved in $W^{(m)}$. As a result, $Sim_{a\_w}(m)$ is a submatrix of M_{a_w} and each entry reflects the weighting between an API and a word in M.

(2) f_b: optimally matching an API to its semantically correlative words. By applying the generated similarity matrix $Sim_{a\_w}(m)$, API annotation problem for a mashup service $M = \langle W^{(m)}, L^{(m)}, D^{(m)} \rangle$ is transformed to a fully connected and weighted bipartite graph $G = \langle V, E \rangle$. Specifically, API vertices $V_a \subset V$ originates from all of the APIs in $L^{(m)}$; word vertices $V_w \subset V$ originates from all of the mashup functional description words in $W^{(m)}$; the weighting wt_{ij} of each edge in E corresponds to an entry in $Sim_{a\_w}(m)$. The transformed bipartite graph for API annotation of mashup functionality is illustrated in Fig. 2.

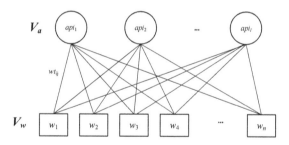

Fig. 2. The transformed weighted bipartite graph for API annotation.

In this way, the solution to a mashup functionality API annotation problem is formally equivalent to best finding a partition of the bipartite graph G. Here, we apply a threshold-based API annotation algorithm called T-WDM and an API annotation algorithm called G-WDM based on bipartite graph maximum matching. For the T-WDM algorithm, if an edge weighting wt_{ij} in G is greater than predefined threshold θ, then api_i is annotated by w_j. Based on bipartite graph maximum matching, G-WDM is an improvement of Kuhn-Munkres method, which optimizes the matching between APIs and words.

Note that API annotation is a content-based matching problem like LDA topic modeling, which can be thought as classifying each word into a category of APIs. Since the words that actually express the API has low frequency in the entire large-scale service repository, it can easily occur inaccuracy with high error on mapping words to API tags using LDA modeling. To avoid this application scenario, we leverage an external lexical database WordNet for similarity calculation between mashup description words and API tags.

From the maximum matching solution to the bipartite graph, we mark the original mashup functional description $W^{(m)}$ to its semantically annotated one $SW^{(m)}$, by replacing the words with their matched APIs.

3.4 Dependency Network Extraction

In this section, we generate API business execution processes based on dependency network, which can be extracted by parsing mashup description and analyzing the path dependency relationships.

Given an annotated mashup service description $SW^{(m)}$, Stanford CoreNLP parser [2] is applied to further generate a set of semantic dependency trees, each of which represents a sentence in $SW^{(m)}$. An edge in a semantic dependency tree states a unique binary relationship by a dependency type $r\ (w_a, w_b)$. r represents a specific dependency type; w_a and w_b represent a dominant word and a dependent word in the relationship, respectively. Taking an annotated service description $SW^{(m)}$ as input, we mark an API to its corresponding position in semantic dependency tree. For example, given a mashup functional description *"See where the latest news is happening in the UK"*, its semantic dependency tree is illustrated in Fig. 3.

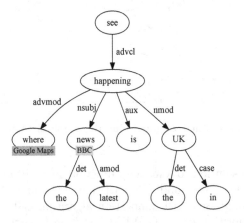

Fig. 3. Semantic dependency tree is extracted from a mashup functionality description. CoreNLP tool is used to analyze the functionality description and derive its corresponding semantic dependency tree of a mashup service. In the figure, those words in the eclipse come from mashup service description; those words around the arrows represent the dependency relationships; those words in the rectangles below the circles are tags marked for involved APIs.

As shown in Fig. 3, there are multiple dependency types among words in a semantic dependency tree. The binary dependency modification between two words for a dependency type is defined as below.

Definition 8 (Binary Dependency Modification). Given a dependency type $r(w_a, w_b)$, the binary dependency modification between w_a and w_b holds three different kinds of possibilities:

(1) If w_a directly modifies w_b on r, it is denoted as $w_a \xrightarrow{r} w_b$;
(2) If w_a is reversely modified by w_b on r, it is denoted as $w_a \xleftarrow{r} w_b$;
(3) If w_a and w_b are mutually modified on r, it is denoted as $w_a \xleftrightarrow{r} w_b$.

Based on above definition, all dependency types are classified into three categories, including **positive**, **negative** and **neutral**.

Definition 9 (Dependency Relationship Polarity). Given a dependency type $r(w_a, w_b)$, its dependency relationship polarity can be identified by a piecewise function $H(r)$

$$H(r(w_a, w_b)) = \begin{cases} positive, & \text{if } w_a \xrightarrow{r} w_b \text{ is satisfied} \\ neutral, & \text{if } w_a \xleftrightarrow{r} w_b \text{ is satisfied} \\ negative, & \text{if } w_a \xleftarrow{r} w_b \text{ is satisfied} \end{cases} \quad (14)$$

By using $H(r)$, dependency polarity of two APIs in a semantic dependency tree can be recognized via multiplicative chain rule. Given two APIs api_i and api_j, assume that it has a reachable path from api_i to api_j, denoted as $dep(api_i, api_j) = \{api_i \xrightarrow{td_{z1}} w_{z1} \xleftarrow{td_{z2}} w_{z2} \xrightarrow{td_{z3}} \dots \xrightarrow{td_{zn}} api_j\}$, the dependency polarity of these two APIs is calculated by

$$L(dep(api_i, api_j)) = \prod_{(w_i, w_j)} \delta_{(w_i, w_j)} \cdot H(r(w_i, w_j)), \quad (w_i, w_j) \in dep(api_i, api_j)$$

(15)

Where $\delta_{(w_i, w_j)}$ is a symbol term indicating the dependency direction in the pathway chain of $dep(api_i, api_j)$. $H(r(w_i, w_j))$ is the dependency relationship polarity for a dependency type $r(w_i, w_j)$ in $dep(api_i, api_j)$.

Performing the calculation of dependency polarity between every pair of APIs in a mashup service, we extract an API dependency network.

Definition 10 (API Dependency Network). Given a mashup service $M = \langle W^{(m)}, L^{(m)}, D^{(m)} \rangle$, its API dependency network is a directed graph $G' = \langle V', E' \rangle$. $V' = L^{(m)}$ and an edge $e' \in E'$ satisfies the conditions:

(1) $E' = \{e' | e' = \langle api_i, api_j \rangle, api_i, api_j \in L^{(m)}\}$;
(2) The dependency polarity of $L(dep(api_i, api_j))$ is positive.

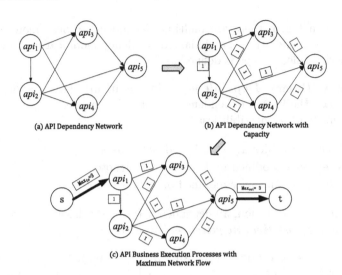

(a) API Dependency Network

(b) API Dependency Network with Capacity

(c) API Business Execution Processes with Maximum Network Flow

Fig. 4. Extracted API dependency network and business execution processes.

When extracting API dependency network, if the two APIs (api_i, api_j) has positive dependency polarity, an edge $e' = \langle api_i, api_j \rangle$ is added to E'; if it has negative dependency polarity, an edge $e' = \langle api_j, api_i \rangle$ is added to E'; if it has neutral dependency polarity, above two edges are both added to E'. An API dependency network is shown in Fig. 4(a).

As shown in Fig. 4(a), the extracted API dependency network G' can be regarded as a candidate of business execution processes before a starting and ending point are chosen, respectively. To pick them out, the capacity of each edge in G' is set as 1 as shown in Fig. 4(b). Under this setting, the maximum network flow algorithm [3] is applied to check the entire network traffic value of G'. When it reaches the maximum traffic value, the reliance level arrives at the optimum state. The starting and ending points of the maximum flow corresponds to the ones where the sum of in-degree and the sum of out-degree are the maximum. Consequently, business execution processes of APIs in a mashup service can be extracted as shown in Fig. 4(c).

4   Experiments

4.1   Experimental Setup and Dataset

We developed a prototype system and all modules are implemented in Java. It integrates WordNet[1] for word-domain matrix construction and Stanford CoreNLP parser for API dependency network extraction. Meanwhile, four competing approaches are integrated in our prototype system. All the experiments

---

[1] https://wordnet.princeton.edu/.

have been carried out on a PC with an Intel Dual Core 2.8 GHz processor and 4 GB RAM in Windows 10.

The dataset used in the experiment was collected from the largest online service management platform ProgrammableWeb.com[2]. As of May 2018, ProgrammableWeb recorded more than 19,000 API services and approximately 8,000 mashup services. We crawled the information of APIs and mashup services, including name, functional description and domain. After the preprocessing, we obtained a collection of 13,869 API services and 6,254 mashup services. The statistics of experimental dataset is shown in Table 1.

Table 1. The statistics of experimental dataset crawled from ProgrammableWeb.

Dataset item	Value
Total number of mashup services	6,254
Total number of API services	13,869
Total number of domains	474
Average number of mashups in a domain	13.927
Average number of APIs in a domain	2.121
Total number of words in mashup descriptions	112,987

All the mashup services, including two or more than two API services are selected from Table 1, to conduct the experiments. We classify these mashups based on the number of API that mashup contains. Each class randomly extracted 100 samples as experimental data. Because the data on the ProgrammableWeb does not contain the API execution process sequence, we invite experienced web development experts to manually determine the execution process of each mashup service. For each mashup record we only keep the mashup identification number (including), natural language text description, API list and domain. The API set as experimental data is directly using all the APIs that we collected. For each API record we keep the API ID, natural language text description and domain.

4.2 Case Study of Business Execution Processes Extraction

To validate the applicability, we show a case study of three crucial stages for API business execution processes. Figure 5 illustrates a specific case of API business execution processes extraction for mashup *"BBC News Map"*. Its functional description is described as *"See where the latest news is happening in the UK"*. Two involved APIs are invoked for the implementation of mashup functionality, including *Google Maps* in domain *Mapping* and *BBC* in domain *Media*. There are 10 tokens in this description except punctuation. After removing the nonsensical

---

[2] https://www.programmableweb.com.

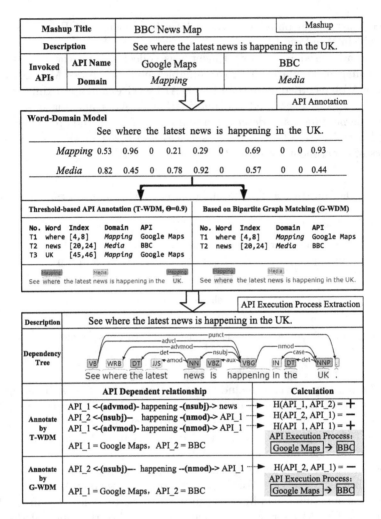

Fig. 5. The experimental result of extracting API business execution processes from a mashup service requirement.

prepositions and particles (*the*, *is*, and *in*), there are 6 remaining tokens. After the preprocessing, it goes through three steps as below.

(1) The word-domain matrix is constructed to evaluate the similarity between 6 words and 2 domains. The generated word-domain matrix is shown in the second part of Fig. 5.

(2) For API annotation, we can find the most similar word to the first domain *Mapping* from the word-domain matrix. Suppose we use the constant-threshold method (T-WDM) method. Under the threshold 0.9, we can find the two words of *where* (Similarly 0.97) and *UK* (0.93). For another domain

media, we can find a word *news* (0.97). In this way, we will give the corresponding API tags to these words we find.

(3) In the dependency network extraction, we invoke Stanford CoreNLP to analyze mashup functionality description and obtain a parser tree, where it consists of 10 basic Stanford dependency types. In these parse result, related to the tagged APIs is *happening* → *where* = *advmod*(negative), and *happening* → *news* = *nsubj*(positive). Using the proposed multiplicative chain rule, we can calculate the dependency relationship polarity: *where* → *news* = *positive*, which is $H\,(Google\ Maps, BBC) = positive$. Calculate all tagged API pairs in this method, then we can extract API execution business processes: $Google\ Maps \Rightarrow BBC$.

4.3   Competitive Methods and Evaluation Metrics

To demonstrate the effectiveness of our approach for API business execution processes extraction, we compare our two self-developed methods with two baseline ones. Here, the differences among these competing methods lie in API annotation.

(1) LED [7]: Levenshtein edit distance is an annotation algorithm based on the edit distance similarity calculation. This method measures the minimum number of edit operations required to convert from one string to another.
(2) STEM: It is an annotation algorithm based on stem similarity calculation. This method extracts stems from two words and calculates their similarity degree using string comparison strategy.
(3) T-WDM: This method constructs a word-domain matrix for semantic similarity degree calculation, and then transforms API annotation problem to a bipartite graph model. It identifies those edges that reach or exceed the threshold for semantic annotation of APIs in a mashup service.
(4) G-WDM: Based on T-WDM, this method annotates API service by applying the maximum matching in weighted bipartite graph. In light of the mapping among words and APIs, it performs API annotation in a mashup service.

We evaluate the effectiveness of above approaches in terms of two aspects, including API annotation and business execution processes extraction in mashup service. To test the performance of API annotation, three evaluation metrics are used including API hit rate *HitRate*, API average tagged times *AvgTag* and API cover rate *CoverRate*. *HitRate* is defined as the ratio of the sum of annotated APIs and the total number of APIs involved in a mashup service. *AvgTag* is defined to measure the average number of times that an API was tagged in a mashup service. *CoverRate* is defined as the ratio of the sum of words used to annotate more than one API service and the total number of words used to annotate APIs in a mashup service.

To test the performance of business execution processes extraction in mashup, *Recall*, *Precision* and *F−measure* are used in the experiments. *Precision* is defined as the ratio of the number of correctly extracted business execution processes and the total number of extracted business execution processes. *Recall* is defined as the ratio of the number of mashup services where business execution processes are accurately extracted and the total number of mashup services. *F−measure* is a comprehensive indicator based on *Precision* and *Recall*.

4.4 Comparative Results and Analyses

In API annotation experiments, we test the performance of four competing methods on the evaluation metrics *HitRate*, *AvgTag* and *CoverRate*. The experimental results on API annotation are shown in Fig. 6.

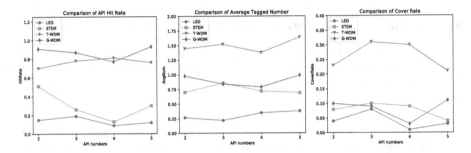

Fig. 6. Experimental results on API annotation among four competing approaches.

The horizontal axis represents the number of APIs invoked by a mashup service and the vertical axis represents the performance on each evaluation metric. Overall, three competing approaches based on semantic similarity calculation (T-WDM, G-WDM and STEM) are better than LED on all three-evaluation metrics. The main reason is that the style of mashup functional description words has many variants, while LED does not take into account semantics and can only establish logical connections among mashup and API services that use the same vocabulary.

More specifically, our two proposed approaches G-WDM and T-WDM outperform STEM and LED on *HitRate*, because latent topics have been applied to calculate semantic similarity degree based on WordNet. Regarding *AvgTag*, our approach T-WDM reaches the highest performance, while G-WDM is superior to another two competing approaches. The main reason is that a bunch of words can be matched with an API when the threshold is set as a small value in T-WDM, while an API can be approximately annotated by a word in G-WDM by the maximum matching of bipartite graph. Conversely, low similarity degree leads to a smaller number of matched words on average for an API in STEM and LED. As for *CoverRate*, our approach T-WDM has the highest value, while other three competing approaches are much lower than T-WDM. The underlying reason is that they either can only match approximately a mashup functional description word for an API in G-WDM or less than that in STEM and LED.

In the experiment of extracting business execution processes from a mashup, we compare the performance of the four competing approaches on *precision*, *recall* and *F−measure*. The experimental results are shown in Fig. 7.

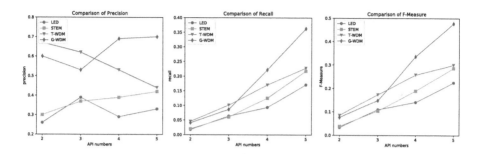

Fig. 7. Experimental results on business execution processes extraction.

From the experimental results in Fig. 7, we conclude that with the increase of the number of APIs invoked by a mashup service, our two proposed approaches T-WDM and G-WDM are better than STEM and LED. Due to the loosely relational selection strategy, the precision of T-WDM becomes smaller as the increasing number of APIs involved in a mashup service. On the contrary, the precision of G-WDM becomes bigger as the number of APIs increases in a mashup service, counting on the effective annotation by bipartite graph maximum matching. Generally, the precision of T-WDM and G-WDM exceeds more than 50% no matter how the number of APIs varies in a mashup service, whereas STEM and LED are both less than 45%. In conclusion, the experimental results validate the feasibility and effectiveness of our proposed approach.

4.5   Performance Impact of Parameters

The proposed approach T-WDM takes a threshold θ as the constraint during API annotations. This parameter directly affects the effectiveness of API annotation. In order to test its influence, we set the value of θ from 0.7 to 0.9 with a step size of 0.1 and compare the performance with G-WDM on *HitRate*, *AvgTag* and *CoverRate*. The experimental results are illustrated in Fig. 8.

It can be observed that the effectiveness of T-WDM becomes worse along with the increasing number of θ. The explanation is that as the threshold of semantic similarity degree increases, the number of matched words for an API obtained by T-WDM decreases.

For our proposed two approaches, T-WDM is superior to G-WDM in terms of *AvgTag* and *CoverRate*, regardless of the variations of θ in the experimental setting. Note that once a bipartite graph is modeled for API annotation, the results by G-WDM keep unchanged on three evaluation metrics, since the mapping from an API to its annotated words are found by the maximum matching algorithm. Therefore, when θ becomes large enough, the values of *AvgTag* and

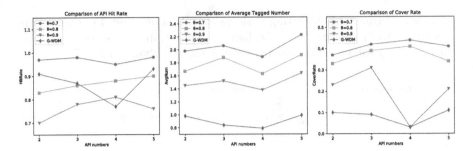

Fig. 8. Experimental results on parameter impact of API annotation.

CoverRate in T-WDM could be lower than that in G-WDM. The reason is that the value of these two metrics tends to be 0, if the threshold is so large that no appropriate words can be matched for an API.

5 Related Work

In this section, we mainly review the recent advancements on service recommendation and mashup creation that is highly related with our work.

To assist mashup developer's API selection and improve the efficiency of mashup creation, the authors in [1,11] extracted user's social attribute and interests' portrait to recommend candidate APIs for mashup service creation. The authors in [14] proposed a dynamic mashup recommendation system, where service evolution has been taken into account by exploiting LDA topic model and time series prediction. The authors in [10] enriched service recommendation results for mashup creation by employing variant K-means. This can enhance service categorization and restrain candidate services from each category.

Recently, the authors in [9] proposed an API recommendation method for mashup development using matrix factorization where mashup services are clustered through a two-level topic model. The authors in [12] proposed a new technique to fast and accurately build an API network using semantic similarity construction and community detection. By doing so, mashup developers are freed from the exhausting search phase to find their desired APIs. The authors in [4] proposed a novel service set recommendation framework for mashup creation by applying an improved clustering algorithm vKmeans and hypergraph modeling. It solves the problem of redundant service recommendation and ignored cooperation relations among services. The authors in [13] proposed a probabilistic matrix factorization approach to discover implicit co-invocation patterns between APIs, finding more accurate API rankings for mashup recommendation.

From the above investigation, we observe that the existing methods mainly focus on how to accurately and efficiently find appropriate APIs for mashup creation. Due to lacking business execution processes of these recommended APIs, it is still a challenging and time-consuming task for software developers to create a new mashup service.

6   Conclusion

In this paper, we propose a novel approach to extract API business execution processes for mashup creation. It goes through three crucial stages including word-domain model construction, mashup description API annotation and dependency network extraction. Extensive experiments conducted on large-scale real-world APIs and mashup services crawled from ProgrammableWeb validate the feasibility and effectiveness of the proposed approach. By providing the invocation relationships among APIs, it could be potentially applied to assist software developers in expediting the procedure of mashup creation. In the future work, we will consider using a greater number of criteria, including API functionality, reliability, and a range of non-functional features such as cost, performance, and API provider reputation, when recommending a set of web APIs with business execution processes.

Acknowledgement. This work was partially supported by Shanghai Natural Science Foundation (No. 18ZR1414400 and 17ZR1400200), National Natural Science Foundation of China (No. 61772128 and 61303096), Shanghai Sailing Program (No. 16YF1400300), and Fundamental Research Funds for the Central Universities (No. 16D111208).

References

1. Cao, B., Liu, J., Tang, M., Zheng, Z., Wang, G.: Mashup service recommendation based on user interest and social network. In: IEEE International Conference on Web Services (ICWS), pp. 99–106. IEEE (2013)
2. De Marneffe, M.C., Manning, C.D.: Stanford typed dependencies manual. Technical report, Stanford University (2008)
3. Edmonds, J., Karp, R.M.: Theoretical improvements in algorithmic efficiency for network flow problems. In: Jünger, M., Reinelt, G., Rinaldi, G. (eds.) Combinatorial Optimization — Eureka, You Shrink!. LNCS, vol. 2570, pp. 31–33. Springer, Heidelberg (2003). https://doi.org/10.1007/3-540-36478-1_4
4. Gao, W., Wu, J.: A novel framework for service set recommendation in mashup creation. In: IEEE International Conference on Web Services (ICWS), pp. 65–72. IEEE (2017)
5. Gao, Z., et al.: SeCo-LDA: mining service co-occurrence topics for recommendation. In: IEEE International Conference on Web Services (ICWS), pp. 25–32. IEEE (2016)
6. Jain, A., Liu, X., Yu, Q.: Aggregating functionality, use history, and popularity of APIs to recommend mashup creation. In: Barros, A., Grigori, D., Narendra, N.C., Dam, H.K. (eds.) ICSOC 2015. LNCS, vol. 9435, pp. 188–202. Springer, Heidelberg (2015). https://doi.org/10.1007/978-3-662-48616-0_12
7. Levenshtein, V.: Binary codes capable of correcting spurious insertions and deletion of ones. Probl. Inf. Transm. **1**(1), 8–17 (1965)
8. Li, C., Zhang, R., Huai, J., Sun, H.: A novel approach for API recommendation in mashup development. In: IEEE International Conference on Web Services (ICWS), pp. 289–296. IEEE (2014)

9. Rahman, M.M., Liu, X., Cao, B.: Web API recommendation for mashup development using matrix factorization on integrated content and network-based service clustering. In: IEEE International Conference on Services Computing (SCC), pp. 225–232. IEEE (2017)

10. Xia, B., Fan, Y., Tan, W., Huang, K., Zhang, J., Wu, C.: Category-aware API clustering and distributed recommendation for automatic mashup creation. IEEE Trans. Serv. Comput. **8**(5), 674–687 (2015)

11. Xu, W., Cao, J., Hu, L., Wang, J., Li, M.: A social-aware service recommendation approach for mashup creation. In: IEEE International Conference on Web Services (ICWS), pp. 107–114. IEEE (2013)

12. Yang, X., Cao, J.: A fast and accurate way for API network construction based on semantic similarity and community detection. In: Shi, X., An, H., Wang, C., Kandemir, M., Jin, H. (eds.) NPC 2017. LNCS, vol. 10578, pp. 75–86. Springer, Cham (2017). https://doi.org/10.1007/978-3-319-68210-5_7

13. Yao, L., Wang, X., Sheng, Q.Z., Benatallah, B., Huang, C.: Mashup recommendation by regularizing matrix factorization with API co-invocations. IEEE Trans. Serv. Comput. (2018). https://doi.org/10.1109/TSC.2018.2803171

14. Zhong, Y., Fan, Y., Huang, K., Tan, W., Zhang, J.: Time-aware service recommendation for mashup creation. IEEE Trans. Serv. Comput. **8**(3), 356–368 (2015)

An Efficient Quantum Circuits Optimizing Scheme Compared with QISKit (Short Paper)

Xin Zhang[1], Hong Xiang[1,2(✉)], and Tao Xiang[3]

[1] School of Big Data and Software Engineering, Chongqing University,
Chongqing, China
xianghong@cqu.edu.cn
[2] Key Laboratory of Dependable Service Computing in Cyber Physical Society,
Chongqing University, Ministry of Education, Chongqing, China
[3] School of Computer Science, Chongqing University, Chongqing, China

Abstract. Recently, the development of quantum chips has made great progress – the number of qubits is increasing and the fidelity is getting higher. However, qubits of these chips are not always fully connected, which sets additional barriers for implementing quantum algorithms and programming quantum programs. In this paper, we introduce a general circuit optimizing scheme, which can efficiently adjust and optimize quantum circuits according to arbitrary given qubits' layout by adding additional quantum gates, exchanging qubits and merging single-qubit gates. Compared with the optimizing algorithm of IBM's QISKit, the quantum gates consumed by our scheme is 74.7%, and the execution time is only 12.9% on average.

Keywords: Quantum computing · Quantum circuit ·
Circuit optimizing

1 Introduction

Quantum computing has attracted increasing attention because of its tremendous computing power [7,11,12] in recent years. There are more and more companies and scientific research institutions who devote themselves to developing quantum chips with more qubits and higher fidelity. While most theoretical studies assume that interactions between arbitrary pairs of qubits are available, almost all these realistic chips have certain constraints on qubit connectivity [6,8]. For example, IBM's 5-qubit superconducting chips *Tenerife* and *Yorktown* [1] adopt neighboring connectivity. [14] uses a 4-qubit superconducting chip, in which four qubits are not directly connected, but are connected by a central resonator. That is, the layout of this chip is central. In addition, CAS-Alibaba Quantum Laboratory's 11-qubit superconducting chip [4] and Tsinghua University's 4-qubit NMR chip [13] both reduce the fully connectivity to the linear

H. Gao et al. (Eds.): CollaborateCom 2018, LNICST 268, pp. 467–476, 2019.
https://doi.org/10.1007/978-3-030-12981-1_32

nearest-neighbor connectivity. Distinctly, this non-fully connected connection sets additional barriers for implementing quantum algorithms and programming quantum programs.

As early as 2007, Cheung et al. made a discussion about the non-fully connected physical layout [6]. By adding SWAP gates, they turned illegal CNOT operations into legitimate operations and proved that the star-shaped or the linear nearest-neighbor connectivity could be able to utilize additional $O(n)$ quantum gates to complete the adjustment, where n stands for the number of qubits. In 2017, IBM developed a quantum information science kit, namely QISKit [3], which contains an algorithm that can adjust and optimize quantum programs according to any layout. Recently, in order to find more efficient solutions, IBM organized the QISKit Developer Challenge [2].

The paper is organized as follows: Sect. 2 briefly introduce the necessary conceptions. In Sect. 3, the design concept of our optimizing scheme is presented in detail. We next compare the cost and efficiency of our scheme with QISKit's optimizing method in Sect. 4. The conclusion and future research can be found in Sect. 5.

2   Common Solutions

Before introducing the common solutions, we need to point out the main obstacles for hindering the execution of quantum programs:

- Obstacle-1: the direction of CNOT gate is illegal, as shown in the red line in Fig. 1(a);
- Obstacle-2: the connectivity between two specific qubits is illegal, as shown in the blue line.

(a) Given Layout   (b) Actual Layout

Fig. 1. An example of Obstacle-1 and Obstacle-2. (Color figure online)

For Obstacle-1, a common solution is to flip the direction by 4 additional H gates:

$$H_2 \times \text{CNOT}_{(q_1,\ q_2)} \times H_2 = \text{CNOT}_{(q_2,\ q_1)}. \tag{1}$$

As for Obstacle-2, the basic idea is exchanging the states of qubits by SWAP gates. For example, although $cnot(q_1, q_4)$ is illegal in Fig. 1(a), we can use another way to accomplish the same task, such as the circuit shown in Fig. 2.

However, the additional overhead of this solution is costly, especially for sparse physical layouts. Specifically,

$$cost = 2m \times cost_{\text{SWAP}}, \tag{2}$$

where m stands for the number of intermediate nodes on the shortest path between the control-qubit and the target-qubit, $cost_{\text{SWAP}}$ stands for 3 CNOT gates and 4 H gates.

(a) $cnot(q_1, q_4)$ (b) $SWAP(q_0, q_4)$

Fig. 2. Equivalent circuits of $cnot(q_1, q_4)$ and $SWAP(q_0, q_4)$.

3   Our Optimizing Scheme

Our optimizing scheme is an efficient general solution. Specifically, we design the following three steps to adjust and optimize quantum programs.

3.1   The Global Adjustment of Qubits

This step can be described as Algorithm 1. In Algorithm 1, we extract all CNOT gates from the quantum program separately and traverse them from front to back. Once encountering an illegal CNOT gate, we try to find an available qubits' mapping to adjust the whole Open-QASM code without converting the traversed CNOT gates illegal. At each adjustment, we have $(d_{cq} \times d_{tq} - t)$ available mappings to choose, where t stands for the number of mappings which make some traversed CNOT gates illegal, d_{cq} and d_{tq} stand for the number of adjacent qubits of control-qubit and target-qubit in the given layout, respectively. The traversal terminates when there is no illegal CNOT gate or $(d_{cq} \times d_{tq} - t) = 0$.

Suppose that there are M possible mappings, where M is related to the given layout and the connectivity of quantum programs. At this point, we need to estimate the cost of solving Obstacle-2 in the program adjusted according to these $(M + 1)$ mappings (M mappings and one empty mapping) respectively. Then take the smallest one as the global adjustment mapping. The reason for estimation, rather than accurate calculation, and the estimation process are explained in the next part. Finally, we adjust the qubits of the original Open-QASM code according to the global mapping. As for the classical register, which stores the results of the measurement, does not need to be modified. For example, $cnot(q_1, q_4)$ is illegal in Fig. 1 and it can be adjusted by the global mapping $\{1 : 3, \ 3 : 1\}$, as shown in Fig. 3.

Algorithm 1. Global Adjustment

Input: The set of CNOT in QP, C; the set of legal CNOT, A; the record of all possible costs, *costs*; the record of all possible mappings, *maps*; the current mapping, *amap*;

Output: The mapping of qubits' ID, *map*

```
 1  GlobalAdjust(costs, maps, amap)
 2  |   costs ←[ ], maps ←[ ] and amap ←[ ];
 3  |   Adjust(C, A, amap, costs, maps);
 4  |   i ←getIndexofMinValue(costs);
 5  |_  return maps[i];

 6
 7  Adjust(C, A, amap, costs, maps)
 8  |   alternativeMap ← [ ];
 9  |   for CNOT c in C do
10  |   |   if c not in A then
11  |   |   |   cq ← c[0] and tq ← c[1];
12  |   |   |   cqAdj ← getAdjacentQubit(cq) and tqAdj ← getAdjacentQubit(tq);
13  |   |   |   tMaps ← {cq : tqAdj, tq : cqAdj};
14  |   |   |   for map m in tMaps do
15  |   |   |   |   tempC ← C;
16  |   |   |   |   change qubits' ID in tempC according to m;
17  |   |   |   |   if no illegal CNOT in tempC then
18  |   |   |   |   |_  add m to alternativeMap;
19  |   |   |_  break;
20  |   if alternativeMap == [ ] then
21  |   |   cost ← estimateCost();
22  |   |_  add cost to costs and add amap to maps;
23  |   for map am in alternativeMap do
24  |   |   tempC ← C and add am to amap;
25  |   |   change qubits' ID in tempC according to am;
26  |   |   if no illegal CNOT in tempC then
27  |   |   |_  add amap to maps and add 0 to costs;
28  |   |   else
29  |   |_  |_  Adjust(C, A, amap, costs, maps);
```

3.2 The Local Adjustment of Qubits

Compared with the basic solution described in Sect. 2, our scheme has the following differences:

- There is no need to use SWAP gates again to restore the state.
- The effect of exchanging control-qubit or target-qubit with intermediate qubits by SWAP gates is completely different for the subsequent code.

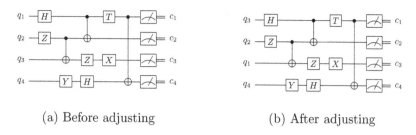

(a) Before adjusting   (b) After adjusting

Fig. 3. Adjust the circuit according to $\{1 : 3, \ 3 : 1\}$ and (b) can be executed on Fig. 1(a)

However, it is difficult to accurately calculate the costs of these two cases in the second difference. During the calculation, we will encounter several illegal CNOT gates, and for each illegal CNOT, we have two solutions. Actually, the solution space is a binary tree whose height is n and the number of leaf nodes is approximately $O(2^n)$, where n stands for the number of illegal CNOT gates. Obviously, we have to estimate the cost by greedy ideas. With the increase in the scale of programs, the manifestation of this greedy choice is more obvious, which can be seen in Sect. 4.

The cost of adjusting the Open-QASM code $qasm$ is estimated by

$$cost_{qasm} = \sum_{i=1}^{n}[(\frac{n-i}{n})^2 \cdot m_i \cdot cost_{\text{SWAP}}], \tag{3}$$

where m_i stands for the number of intermediate qubits between the control-qubit and the target-qubit of the ith illegal CNOT. Among the various estimation formulas we tried, the result obtained by Eq. (3) is optimal. The reason for adding the correction factor $(\frac{n-i}{n})^2$ in Eq. (3) is that the later the CNOT gate is executed, the easier it is influenced by the previous adjustments. That is, estimation is not reliable for the later CNOT gates. Multiplying the factor, which will continue to decrease as the estimation progress, with the estimation results can have a certain correction effect.

For improving the accuracy of estimation, we accurately calculate the top 4 layers of the binary tree, and estimate the cost of the subsequent gates of the 2^4 cases respectively, where 4 is the optimal value determined after repeated trials. Then add the estimated result and the calculated result together and choose the smallest one among the 16 cases as our choice.

Specifically, we traverse the Open-QASM code. Whenever encountering an illegal CNOT, we call Algorithm 2 to adjust it and then update the subsequent code and the classical register until the traversal terminates. It can be seen from Algorithm 2 that the mapping generated by *Adjust* function only affects the subsequent code of *illC* and that is why we call this step *Local adjustment*.

At this point, there is no Obstacle-2 in quantum programs. Then we traverse the new Open-QASM code again to handle Obstacle-1 by Eq. (1).

Algorithm 2. Local Adjustment

Input: The Open-QASM code of the quantum program, $qasm$; the first illegal CNOT, $illC$; the rest CNOTs after $illC$ in $qasm$, Cs; the record of all possible costs, $costs$; the cost in the current case, $cost$; the record of all possible mappings, $maps$; the current mapping, $amap$; the depth of recursion, d

Output: The adjusted Open-QASM code, $qasm$

```
 1  LocalAdjust(qasm, illC, Cs)
 2  │   cost ← 0, costs ←[ ], amap ←[ ], d ← 1 and maps ←[ ];
 3  │   Adjust(illC, Cs, cost, costs, amap, maps, d);
 4  │   i ←getIndexofMinValue(costs);
 5  │   add SWAP gates to qasm according to maps[i];
 6  │   change qubits'ID in qasm according to maps[i];
 7  └   return qasm;

 8
 9  Adjust(illC, Cs, cost, costs, map, maps, d)
10  │   interQs ← getIntermediateNode(illC[0], illC[1]);
11  │   cost ← cost + 34×interQs.length;
12  │   for qubit q in illC do
13  │   │   tc ← cost;
14  │   │   if q is control-qubit then
15  │   │   └   tc ← tc + 4;
16  │   │   tMap ← constructMapBetweenQ(interQs,q);
17  │   │   change qubits' ID in cnots according to tMap;
18  │   │   nIllC ← getFirstIllegalCnot(cnots);
19  │   │   restC ← getAllCnotAfterNewIllC(cnots);
20  │   │   if map != [ ] then
21  │   │   └   tMap ← map;
22  │   │   if nIllC == None then
23  │   │   └   add tc to costs and tMap to maps;
24  │   │   else if d == 4 then
25  │   │   │   tc ← tc + estimateCost();
26  │   │   └   add tc to costs and add tMap to maps;
27  │   │   else
28  │   └   └   Adjust(nIllC, restC, tc, costs, tMap, maps, d + 1);
```

3.3   The Mergence of Single-Qubit Gates

In this step, we will reduce the circuit depth by merging single-qubit gates. At first, we need to determine which kind of single-qubit gates can be merged.

The random quantum circuit shown in Fig. 4(a) contains three CNOT gates and these gates divide the execution processes of q_0, q_1, q_2 into three parts respectively. Obviously, single-qubit gates in these parts can be merged and we can reduce Fig. 4(a) to (b). Based on this example, we can draw a conclusion that for any qubit q, the n multi-qubit gates with q involved can divide the execution process of q into $n+1$ subintervals and the single-qubit gates in each subintervals can be merged into one gate.

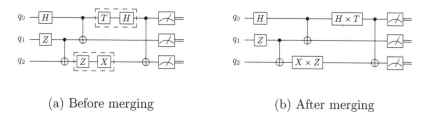

(a) Before merging   (b) After merging

Fig. 4. The change of a quantum random circuit before and after merging single-qubit gates.

As mentioned before, all single-qubit gates in Open-QASM belong to $\{u1, u2, u3\}$. Therefore, merging single-qubit gates actually contains 9 different cases: $u1 \times u1$, $u1 \times u2$, $u1 \times u3$, $u2 \times u1$, $u3 \times u1$, $u2 \times u2$, $u3 \times u2$, $u2 \times u3$ and $u3 \times u3$. In order to handle these cases, we need to do **Z-Y decompositions** [9] for $u1$, $u2$ and $u3$. For the first five cases, we can directly merge them by $R_z(\lambda) \times R_z(\phi) = R_z(\lambda + \phi)$ [5]. As for the last four cases, we have:

$$
\begin{aligned}
& R_z(\phi_1) \cdot R_y(\theta_1) \cdot R_z(\lambda_1) \cdot R_z(\phi_2) \cdot R_y(\theta_2) \cdot R_z(\lambda_2) \\
& = R_z(\phi_1) \cdot [R_y(\theta_1) \cdot R_z(\lambda_1 + \phi_2) \cdot R_y(\theta_2)] \cdot R_z(\lambda_2) \\
& = R_z(\phi_1) \cdot [R_z(\alpha) \cdot R_y(\beta) \cdot R_z(\gamma)] \cdot R_z(\lambda_2) \\
& = R_z(\phi_1 + \alpha) \cdot R_y(\beta) \cdot R_z(\gamma + \lambda_2) \\
& = u3(\beta, \phi_1 + \alpha, \gamma + \lambda_2).
\end{aligned}
\tag{4}
$$

The key of this kind of merging lies in how to transform the **Y-Z decomposition** of a quantum gate to the **Z-Y decomposition**. And we use QISKit's merge method proposed in [10] to solve this problem.

4   Numerical Results

In this section, we use the method proposed in the QISKit Developer Challenge to count the cost of gates:

$$
cost = n_2 \times 10 + n_1 \times 1,
\tag{5}
$$

where n_2 and n_1 stand for the number of CNOT gates and single-qubit gates in optimized quantum circuit, respectively.

The experiments are designed as follow: for the 14 cases of qubits number from 3 to 16, we generate 10 different random quantum circuits respectively for 16 cases with circuit depth from 1 to 16 respectively. That means, in total,

$14 \times 16 \times 10 = 2240$ circuits are generated. Then we chose four common connected graphs (linear, central, neighboring and circular) and use our optimizing scheme and QISKit's algorithm to adjust and optimize these 2240 random circuits according to these layouts, respectively. That is, each algorithm handles 8960 (2240×4) quantum circuits. Finally, the optimized quantum programs are executed by QASM-simulator. If the result of our scheme is consistent with QISKit's result, we count the cost and the execution time of each circuit.

Comparison with QISKit's Optimizing Method

Table 1 shows the quantum gates consumption of the 2240 original random quantum circuits, and the average cost of gates and compiler time required to adjust and optimize these 2240 circuits by our scheme and QISKit. Obviously, the quantum gates consumed by our scheme is 74.7% of QISKit, and the execution time is only 12.9%.

Table 1. The overall statistical

	Time (s)	Gate cost
Original circuit	0	3084391
Our scheme	16472.48	6703061
QISKit	127751.99	8974717

Specifically, the performance of our scheme varies for different scales of quantum circuits. Figure 5(a) and (b) illustrate the ratio of QISKit and our scheme about the cost of quantum gates and efficiency with various qubits q and circuit depths d, respectively. The two formulas are shown as follows:

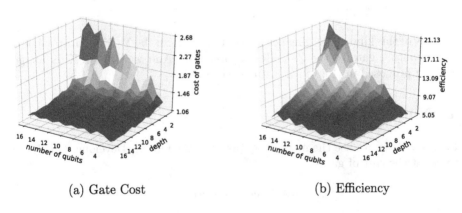

(a) Gate Cost   (b) Efficiency

Fig. 5. Experimental results

$$\text{cost}_{(n,d)} = \frac{qc_{(n,d)}}{c_{(n,d)}}, \quad \text{efficiency}_{(n,d)} = \frac{qt_{(n,d)}}{t_{(n,d)}}, \tag{6}$$

where qc and qt stand for the gate cost and execution time of QISKit's algorithm, and c and t indicate those of our method. Figure 6 shows that in all cases we executed, our algorithm can use fewer quantum gates to adjust and optimize the original circuits in less time. In the worst case (more qubits and more circuit depth), we can use 6% less gates and the efficiency is about 5 times; in optimal case (more qubits and less circuit depth), we can use 63% less gates and the efficiency is about 20 times.

Performance in Different Physical Layouts
For the four layouts we have chosen, there are also significant differences in costs of quantum gates and execution time. In order to deal with different scales of circuits in a fair manner and avoid the statistical result being dominated by large-scale circuits, we no longer directly sum up the gate costs in different cases (as used in Table 1). Specifically, the statistical method is as follows:

$$\text{cost}_{l,c} = \frac{1}{2240}[\sum_{i=1}^{2240}(\frac{c_i}{o_i})], \quad \text{efficiency}_l = \frac{1}{2240}[\sum_{i=1}^{2240}(\frac{qt_i}{ot_i})]. \tag{7}$$

where $l \in \{Linear, Circle, Center, Neighbour\}$, $c \in \{oc, qc\}$, o_i, qc_i and oc_i stand for the gate cost of the ith original circuit, the ith circuit adjusted by QISKit and our scheme respectively, qt_i and ot_i stand for the time required to compile the ith circuit by QISKit and our scheme respectively.

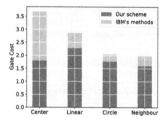
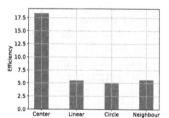

(a) Costs of four layouts   (b) Efficiency of four layouts

Fig. 6. Experimental results of four different layouts

Figure 6(a) shows that for the *central* layout, our scheme requires 1.80 times the gate consumption of the original circuit, and the optimizing method of QISKit requires 3.68 times; for the *linear* layout, the gate cost of our scheme is 2.28 times as many as the original cost and the cost of QISKit is about 2.86 times; as for the *circle* and *neighbour* layouts, our scheme need to use 1.77 times and 1.60 times the gate cost respectively, while QISKit's method need 2.05 times and 2.01 times. Figure 6(b) illustrates that for the four different layouts, our scheme is at least 4 times faster than QISKit; especially for *central* layout, the efficiency is about 17.3 times as fast as QISKit's method.

5   Conclusions

Considering the cost of physical implement, layouts of most existing quantum chips are not fully connected, which sets additional barriers for implementing quantum algorithms and programming quantum programs. We propose a general optimizing scheme to accomplish the task by adding additional logic gates, exchanging qubits in the quantum register and merging single-qubit gates. Compared with QISKit's optimizing method, the quantum gates consumed by our scheme is 74.7% and the execution time is only 12.9% overall. For circuits with more qubits and less circuit depth, this advantage is more obvious. In addition, several common connected graphs (linear, central, neighboring and circular) are compared as well. In these four cases, our scheme has advantages. Especially for the central layout, we can use only 49% gates and 5.8% execution time of QISKit's optimizing algorithm to adjust and optimize the original quantum circuits.

Acknowledgments. The work is supported by National Key R&D Program of China (NO. 2017YFB0802000).

References

1. The backend information of IBM quantum cloud. https://github.com/QISKit/qiskit-backend-information/
2. QISKit developer challenge. https://qx-awards.mybluemix.net/
3. QISKit Python API. https://qiskit.org/
4. The url of alibaba's quantum cloud platform. http://quantumcomputer.ac.cn/index.html
5. Barenco, A., et al.: Elementary gates for quantum computation. Phys. Rev. A **52**(5), 3457 (1995)
6. Cheung, D., Maslov, D., Severini, S.: Translation techniques between quantum circuit architectures. AAPT (2007)
7. Grover, L.K.: A fast quantum mechanical algorithm for database search. In: Proceedings of the Twenty-Eighth Annual ACM Symposium on Theory of Computing, pp. 212–219. ACM (1996)
8. Linke, N.M., et al.: Experimental comparison of two quantum computing architectures. In: Proceedings of the National Academy of Sciences, p. 201618020 (2017)
9. Nielsen, M.A., Chuang, I.: Quantum Computation and Quantum Information (2002)
10. QISKit: The code of merging two u3 gates. https://github.com/QISKit/qiskit-sdk-py/blob/master/qiskit/mapper/_mapping.py
11. Shor, P.W.: Polynomial-time algorithms for prime factorization and discrete logarithms on a quantum computer. SIAM Rev. **41**(2), 303–332 (1999)
12. Simon, D.R.: On the power of quantum computation. SIAM J. Comput. **26**(5), 1474–1483 (1997)
13. Xin, T., et al.: NMRCloudQ: a quantum cloud experience on a nuclear magnetic resonance quantum computer. Sci. Bull. **63**, 17–23 (2017)
14. Zhong, Y., et al.: Emulating anyonic fractional statistical behavior in a superconducting quantum circuit. Phys. Rev. Lett. **117**(11), 110501 (2016)

Feature-based Online Segmentation Algorithm for Streaming Time Series (Short Paper)

Peng Zhan[1], Yupeng Hu[1(✉)], Wei Luo[1], Yang Xu[2], Qi Zhang[1], and Xueqing Li[1(✉)]

[1] School of Software, Shandong University, Jinan, Shandong, China
{huyupeng,xqli}@sdu.edu.cn
[2] School of Computer Science and Technology, Shandong University, Qingdao, Shandong, China

Abstract. Over the last decade, huge number of time series stream data are continuously being produced in diverse fields, including finance, signal processing, industry, astronomy and so on. Since time series data has high-dimensional, real-valued, continuous and other related properties, it is of great importance to do dimensionality reduction as a preliminary step. In this paper, we propose a novel online segmentation algorithm based on the importance of TPs to represent the time series into some continuous subsequences and maintain the corresponding local temporal features of the raw time series data. To demonstrate the advantage of our proposed algorithm, we provide extensive experimental results on different kinds of time series datasets for validating our algorithm and comparing it with other baseline methods of online segmentation.

Keywords: Data mining · Streaming time series ·
Online segmentation · Algorithm

1 Introduction

Nowadays, a great number of intelligent devices in extensive fields are continuously producing streaming time series. Due to the high-dimensional, large amount, continuous and other related properties, it is unrealistic to do further data mining research on the raw streaming time series directly. Accordingly, the online segmentation for streaming time series should be done to reduce both the space and the computational cost in the first place. Online segmentation approach for streaming time series, which is aimed for not only providing the segmentation continuously, but also ensure the corresponding results retain the main temporal features of the raw data.

- The similarity-based matching and pattern recognition of time series data first need to discover several "primitive shapes" [1] or "frequent patterns" [2] subsequences, which can be used for reducing the complexity of the following similarity measurement steps.

H. Gao et al. (Eds.): CollaborateCom 2018, LNICST 268, pp. 477–487, 2019.
https://doi.org/10.1007/978-3-030-12981-1_33

- In time series outlier detection tasks, the segmentation approach can improve the efficiency of eliminating those normal time sequences.
- The typical prototypes [3] should be created for the predefined classes when doing time series classification tasks, which could be generated by the segmentation approach as a preprocessing step.
- In time series clustering tasks, meaningful temporal feature time sequences instead of raw data points, produced by segmentation process, would improve the convergence ability [4] of clustering algorithms, such as K-means.

In this paper, we aim to produce approximate representation which contains the main temporal features and process streaming time series efficiently. The Corresponding contributions could be summarized as follows.

1. We propose an online segmentation algorithm for streaming time series, called feature-based online segmentation algorithm (FOS), which subdivides the time series by a set of TPs, which do reflect the corresponding local temporal features.
2. We evaluate the different importance of TPs by standing on a more holistic view and selecting the most important TP to preform backward and forward segmentation to maintain a high similarity between the series of segments and the raw time series.
3. Comprehensive experiments have been conducted on both open source and different types of the UCR time series datasets in comparison with other baseline methods to demonstrate the advantages of our proposed algorithm.

2 Related Work

Scholars have already proposed a large number of time series segmentation methods, including Discrete Fourier Transform (DFT) [5,6], Discrete Wavelet Transform (DWT) [7], Singular Value Decomposition (SVD) [8], Piecewise Aggregate Approximation (PAA) [9], Piecewise Linear Representation (PLR) [10] and Symbolic Aggregate approXimation (SAX) [11].

Piecewise Linear Representation (PLR) refers to the approximation of a time series T, of length n, with K connected straight lines [12], which is in line with human visual experience, and lower dimension and faster calculation speed of PLR makes the storage, transmission of the data more efficient [1,3,13]. Therefore, PLR is more suitable for segmenting and approximatively representing streaming time series. The segmentation based on PLR can be described as follow:

For a given time series $T = (a_1, a_2, \ldots, a_i, \ldots, a_j, \ldots, a_n)$ of length n, where n can be a constant value or continues to grow without restriction. The T will be divided into sequences $S = (S_1, S_2, \ldots, S_k)$ while $(1 \leq k \leq n - 1)$ and be represented by a series of connected straight lines. Overall, PLR methods can be categorized into two classes: Offline PLR and Online PLR, which is an important distinction because many data mining applications in real world are inherently dynamic. In general, the offline PLR methods segment the whole time series data sequence, and the online PLR methods segment data sequences based on the data seen so far.

2.1 Offline PLR

Offline PLR algorithms segment the whole time series data sequence, that is to say, the whole datasets should be collected before PLR conducting. Although these Offline PLR methods have different implementation details, they can be grouped into one of the following two categories.

- Top-Down algorithm based on PLR (PLR-TD) [14]: The main idea of PLR-TD is considering every possible partitioning of the data sequence and segmenting at the best location according to some user-specified threshold. Both subsegments are then verified to see whether their representation error is below the threshold, if not, PLR-TD recursively splits the subsegments until the stopping criterion is met.
- Bottom-Up algorithm based on PLR (PLR-BU) [15]: PLR-BU is the natural complement to PLR-TD. PLR-BU begins with $n - 1$ segments, and then it begins to iteratively merge the lowest cost two adjacent segments until a stopping criteria is met.

2.2 Online PLR

Onine PLR algorithms mainly concentrate on PLR for streaming time series, which segment data sequences based on the data seen so far. The upcoming data sequence will be acquired and piecewisely approximated at the same time rather than gathering the whole data sequence at the very beginning.

One classic Online PLR algorithm is Slide Windows algorithm based on PLR (PLR-SW). It works by initializing the first data point of time series as the initial segmentation point (i.e., the left endpoint) of a segment and trying to find the right endpoint of the segment by put one more data point into the segment in each step [16]. Still and all, the main problem of Online PLR methods is lacking the global view of its offline counterparts, so that the fitting error of segmentation is usually less than satisfactory. To solve this problem, Keogh et al. [12] introduces an approach in which they hold the online nature of Sliding Windows (SW) and retain the superiority of Bottom-Up (BU) called SWAB (Sliding Window and Bottom-Up) to improve the fitting precision of SW method. In order to improve computing efficiency, Liu et al. [17] proposes a new concept of segmentation criterion called feasible space to reach the farthest segmenting point of each segment, and then introduces two Online PLR methods, which are the Feasible Space Window (FSW) method and the Stepwise Feasible Space Window (SFSW) method. These two methods greatly improve the computing efficiency of the segmentation, but the fitting error is larger than SWAB in most cases due to the lack of overall understanding on the temporal characteristics.

According to the comparative analysis of the existing classic Online PLR algorithms, Online PLR methods are able to do continuous segmentation, but the major drawback of them is the fitting precision of representation can not be guaranteed, compared to the Offline PLR methods.

3 Preliminary

3.1 The Definition of Turning Points

In order to divide the streaming time series T into continuous segments more reasonably, it is preferable to find those segmenting data points of special significance, in other words, the approximate straight lines by connecting those segmenting data points would reserve the variation trend features of raw time series. In this paper, those data points denote the variation trends, called the Turning Points (TPs) will be defined in Definition 1.

Definition 1 (TP). *For a streaming time series TS with n data points, which is growing continuously, could be expressed as $T = \{a_1, a_2, \ldots, a_{i-1},$ $a_i, a_{i+1} \ldots, a_n\}$, where $1 \leq i \leq n$, element $a_i = (t_i, v_i)$ indicates the recorded value v_i arrives at the distinct timestamp t_i. Considering the time-order in T is obvious $(i < i + 1)$, which could be simplified as $T = \{v_1, v_2, \ldots, v_{i-1}, v_i, v_{i+1} \ldots, v_n\}$. If v_i satisfies one of the following two inequations, v_i can be defined as a TP.*

$$v_{i-1} < v_i > v_{i+1} \text{ or } v_{i-1} < v_i = v_{i+1} \text{ or } v_{i-1} = v_i < v_{i+1} \tag{1}$$

$$v_{i-1} > v_i < v_{i+1} \text{ or } v_{i-1} > v_i = v_{i+1} \text{ or } v_{i-1} = v_i > v_{i+1} \tag{2}$$

According to the above definition, all the TPs in T could be found completely. In order to make Definition 1 more intuitively, time series T of GunPoint dataset [18] has been taken for example and shown in Fig. 1. In this Figure, it is not difficult to find that all the local extreme points, such as TP_2, TP_3, and the inflection point (TP_5) have already been selected as TPs in T. However, each TP in T does has different degree of importance in T, in other words, each TP has a disparate contribution to preserve the local temporal features and maintain the global temporal trend of T. Therefore, it is necessary to sort all the TPs based on their own TP importance (TPI) from high to low, preparing for the subsequent online segmentation. Without loss of generality, according to the previous research work [19], the traditional vertical distance (VD) and the mean value of the current T could be utilized to sort the TPI of TPs in T orderly. The definition of TPI is described as follow.

Definition 2 (TPI). *For a streaming time series TS, the mean value of T, named MT, could be calculated by the following equation. The vertical distance (VD) between TP_i in T and MT could be defined as the importance of TP_i, denoted as TPI_i. When TP_i has the maximum $VD(MVD)$, TP_i is the most important TP in T.*

$$MT = \frac{\sum_{i=1}^{N} v_i}{N} \tag{3}$$

$$TPI_i = \sqrt{(v_i - MT)^2} \tag{4}$$

In Fig. 1, all the TPIs of TPs in T have been obtained by calculating VD in Eq. 4. TP_5 with the maximum VD (1.8) could be identified as the most important TP in T.

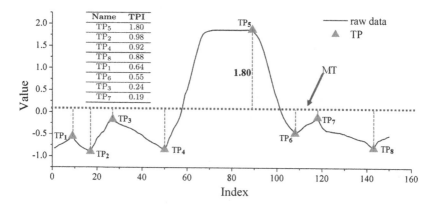

Fig. 1. Intuitive example of TPs definition and importance

3.2 The Slope Calculation and Segmentation Criteria

To ensure the fitting precision of FOS, a segmentation criterion need to be introduced for a potential segment, which we call the Maximum Error for Single Point (ME_SP). ME_SP is used to evaluate the fitting error of a single data point in a potential segment. In order to improve the computing efficiency, the FSW method subsitute the slope calculation (SC) for the calculation of the maximum vertical distance (MVD) [17]. Similarly, in our algorithm, we adopt slope calculation to speed up segmentation, and combine with finding TPs. Table 1 illustrates some definitions of the slope calculation, as follow.

In particular, for a time series T, whose ME_SP could be specified by users and be denoted as σ, where $\sigma > 0$.

Table 1. The Definitions of slope calculation

Name	Description
$line(a_i, a_j)$	The straight line connected by point a_i and a_j
$sline(a_i, a_j)$	The slope of the straight line connected by point a_i and a_j
$slow(a_i, a_j)$	The slope of the straight line connected by point a_i and $a_i - \sigma$
$sup(a_i, a_j)$	The slope of the straight line connected by point a_i and $a_i + \sigma$

If $sline(a_i, a_k)$ satisfies the Inequation 5, the MVD between a_j and $line(a_i, a_k)$ will not exceed the σ(ME_SP). According to the segmentation criteria, every time a new data point arrives, we simply compare the slope of the new line $sline()$ with $slow()$ and $sup()$ of the current segment and update them to find $maxslow_{(i:j)}$ (the maximum value of $slow()$) and $minsup_{(i:j)}$ (the minimum value of $sup()$). The corresponding equations are listed in Eqs. 6 and 7.

$$slow(a_i, a_j) \leq sline(a_i, a_k) \leq sup(a_i, a_j) \tag{5}$$

$$maxslow_{(i:j)} = max_{i<t<j}slow(a_i, a_t) \tag{6}$$

$$minsup_{(i:j)} = min_{i<t<j}sup(a_i, a_t) \tag{7}$$

The current segmentation will not end until such condition:$maxslow_{(i:j)} > minsup_{(i:j)}$ is satisfied, and then to repeat the above operation from the current segmenting point until the entire streaming time series data has been processed.

4   Algorithm

According to the above definitions, FOS can be subdivided into two major steps, as follow.

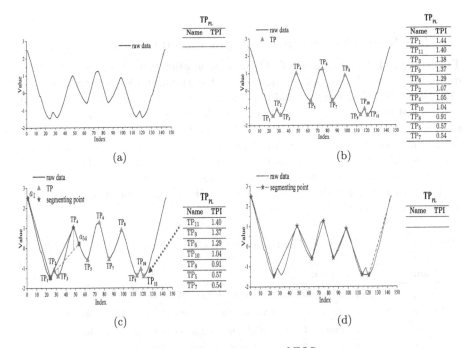

Fig. 2. The major steps of FOS

4.1   TP Selection and Evaluation

In the beginning, a buffer named buf should be created for storing the upcoming steaming time series T, and the setting of buf is same as SWAB [12]. Along with the data of T is constantly flowing into buf, TP in T could be identified according to the definition of TP in Sect. 3. After the buf is full, all the TPs in buf would be sorted based on their own degree of importance from high to low. In order to illustrate the above process more clearly, the TPs selection and evaluation on time series in Plane dataset [18] has been taken for example and shown in Fig. 2. Figure 2(a) and (b) demonstrate this process in detail. The green triangle points denote all the TPs in current buf and all the TPs have also been sorted in accordance with their own TPI from high to low and stored into the TP priority list, named TP_{PL}, in Fig. 2(b).

4.2   Adaptive Stepwise Segmentation by SC and TPS

After the above process, the most important TP (TP_1) in TP_{PL} has been identified in Fig. 2(b). Different from traditional FSW, SFSW and SWAB, which treat each data point in T equally and subdivide T in buf from the starting point, FOS performs SC-based forward and backward segmentation operation from TP_1. Due to TP_1 is selected from buf by standing on the "global" view, the corresponding forward and backward segmentation operation will become more meaningful. As shown in Fig. 2(c), the SC-based forward and backward segmentation operation would start at TP_1, the backward segmentation ends at point a_1 and the forward segmentation ends at point a_x. To preserve the basic trend of time series more rationally, the forward segmentation between TP_1 and point a_x, as shown in green dotted line in Fig. 2(c), would be refined by measuring the VD of TP_2, TP_3 and TP_4 mentioned in Sect. 3. After the corresponding calculation, TP_4 would be selected as the final segmenting point in the current forward segmentation, shown in red dotted line in Fig. 2(c), TP_1, TP_2, TP_3 and $TP4$ would be removed from TP_{PL}. Subsequently, the current most important TP (TP_{11}) in TP_{PL}, should be selected and the corresponding forward and backward segmentation would be performed at TP_{11}. So circulates, until TP_{PL} is empty. The final segmentation in current buf is shown in Fig. 2(d). After the final segmentation in current buf has been finished completely, except the rightmost subsegment, as shown in red dotted line in Fig. 2(d), all the subsegments would be removed from buf and the new follow-up data of T would flow into buf for the next segmentation until the entire T has been processed completely.

According to the final segmentation result in current buf, it is obviously that all the subsegments are formed by TPs, which could not only preserve the basic trend of time series more rationally, but also maintain high degree of similarity between the processed segments and the raw data sequence. The corresponding comparison and explanation would be given in detail in Sect. 5.

5   Experiment and Analysis

5.1   Dataset and Evaluation Metrics

In order to perform the experiment, we select some kinds of typical time series datasets of different fields, including finance, signal processing, industry provided by UCR Time Series Archive [18], and we also choose some representative industrial streaming time series including the monitoring data of Dong Fang Hong satellite (DFHS) from January 2015 to June 2015, which is the Chinese satellite dataset provided by China Academy of Space Technology, the Hang Seng Index (HSI) from 4th January 2016 to 30th December 2016 from the Yahoo Financial web site, and the monitoring data of Jinan municipal steam heating system(JMSHS) from December 2014 to March 2017.

Since our algorithm choose those important TPs as potential segmenting points, which can reflect the variation trend of the data sequence, the similarity between approximation representation and the raw data is relatively high. That is to say, each subsegment could not only reflect the basic trend of time series intuitively, but also minimize the holistic representation error as much as possible. Therefore, we use the representation error (RE) based on ME_SP to evaluate the performance of segmentation for streaming time series.

5.2   Comparison with Baseline Methods on Representation Error

In order to compare the corresponding segmentation performance more objectively, we compare FOS with three baseline methods, which are SWAB, FSW and SFSW, using the identical ME_SP. To make the experimental results more credible, we define two conditions in advance before the experiments.

For one thing, we adopt the Maximum Error Percentage for Single Point (MEPP) proposed by Liu et al. [17], which can reduce the sensitivities of different time series datasets to ME_SP by choosing appropriate ME_SP values for each dataset. For another, the results of SWAB with MEPP are considered as the benchmark (i.e., each result of SWAB is set as 1), and then we normalize the results of other methods according to the benchmark method. Table 2 illustrates the normalized representation error (NRE) results of four Online PLR methods on the above listed datasets.

In Table 2, the NRE results of SWAB on the above datasets are set as the benchmark (1), whose original NRE results are also listed in this Table. By comparing the specific NRE between FOS and FSW, SFSW on all the above datasets, it is not difficult to find that the NRE results of FOS are much smaller than that of FSW and SFSW by its global feature-based segmentation. Through the comparison between FOS and SWAB on the same datasets, we could also find that all the NRE results of FOS are smaller that of SWAB on all the datasets except DFHS. Through the corresponding analysis on DFHS, we find that the NRE of FOS is affected by the distribution of TPs in some cases. For instance, due to the concentrated distribution of TPs in DFHS dataset, the relatively more important TPs would be removed from the TP_{PL} in the previous forward

Table 2. NRE results of four methods

Dataset	SWAB		FSW	SFSW	FOS
Plane	1	(28.83)	2.63	1.89	0.94
Mallat	1	(298.72)	1.56	1.29	0.89
Strawberry	1	(124.09)	0.85	1.05	0.39
OSULeaf	1	(73.67)	2.99	2.04	0.97
Car	1	(113.71)	2.67	1.58	0.57
JMSHS	1	(786.32)	2.43	2.39	0.89
DFHS	1	(8751.86)	2.21	2.17	1.11
HSI	1	(96632.69)	1.64	1.21	0.59
Average	1		2.12	1.70	0.79

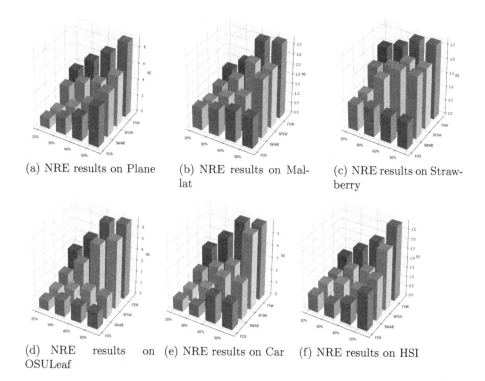

(a) NRE results on Plane

(b) NRE results on Mallat

(c) NRE results on Strawberry

(d) NRE results on OSULeaf

(e) NRE results on Car

(f) NRE results on HSI

Fig. 3. The comparison of NRE on different datasets

and backward segmentation, and the subsequent operations could only perform the corresponding segmentation based on TPs with a relatively less importance, which would lead to the NRE result of FOS is bigger than SWAB. Finally, according to the average NRE results of the above four methods on all the datasets, it is obvious that FOS can provide more accurate segmentation than other three methods in general.

In order to further analyze the segmentation performance of FOS on different datasets, extensive experiments would be conducted on the above 6 datasets by varying the MEPP from 20% to 50%. Moreover, In order to distinguish the differences between the four methods more clearly, the NRE results on these 6 datasets based on MEPP (20%) by SWAB are set as the benchmark (1) and the corresponding normalized NRE results of the four methods on 6 datasets have been shown in Fig. 3. In this figure, it is not difficult to find that NRE results on all the datasets rise gradually along with MEPP increases. Moreover, due to the lack of a more comprehensive view of segmentation, the NRE results of FSW and SFSW are much larger than SWAB and FOS in general. Although both SWAB and FOS perform online segmentation from a global perspective, SWAB treats all data points equally, while FOS selects the current most important TP to preform backward and forward segmentation. Therefore, the NRE result of FOS is much smaller than that of other three methods, in other words, a relative high similarity between the approximate representation and the raw data could be maintained by FOS.

6   Conclusion

In this paper, we propose a novel feature-based online segmentation algorithm (FOS) which reserves the main characteristic of time series and performs well on diverse streaming time series datasets. The extensive experimental results demonstrate that FOS can guarantee more accurate approximate representation of streaming time series. In future, we plan to use FOS for time series retrieval and anomaly detection.

References

1. Chiu, B., Keogh, E., Lonardi, S.: Probabilistic discovery of time series motifs. In: Proceedings of the Ninth ACM SIGKDD International Conference on Knowledge Discovery and Data Mining, pp. 493–498. ACM (2003)
2. Lonardi, J., Patel, P.: Finding motifs in time series. In: Proceedings of the 2nd Workshop on Temporal Data Mining, pp. 53–68 (2002)
3. Bagnall, A., Lines, J., Hills, J., Bostrom, A.: Time-series classification with COTE: the collective of transformation-based ensembles. IEEE Trans. Knowl. Data Eng. **27**(9), 2522–2535 (2015)
4. Fayyad, U.M., Reina, C., Bradley, P.S.: Initialization of iterative refinement clustering algorithms. In: KDD, pp. 194–198 (1998)
5. Agrawal, R., Faloutsos, C., Swami, A.: Efficient similarity search in sequence databases. In: Lomet, D.B. (ed.) FODO 1993. LNCS, vol. 730, pp. 69–84. Springer, Heidelberg (1993). https://doi.org/10.1007/3-540-57301-1_5
6. Rafiei, D., Mendelzon, A.: Efficient retrieval of similar time sequences using DFT. arXiv preprint cs/9809033 (1998)

7. Chan, F.K.-P., Fu, A.W.-C., Yu, C.: Haar wavelets for efficient similarity search of time-series: with and without time warping. IEEE Trans. Knowl. Data Eng. **15**(3), 686–705 (2003)

8. Ravi Kanth, K.V., Agrawal, D., Singh, A.: Dimensionality reduction for similarity searching in dynamic databases. In: ACM SIGMOD Record, vol. 27, pp. 166–176. ACM (1998)

9. Keogh, E., Chakrabarti, K., Pazzani, M., Mehrotra, S.: Dimensionality reduction for fast similarity search in large time series databases. Knowl. Inf. Syst. **3**(3), 263–286 (2001)

10. Keogh, E., Chu, S., Hart, D., Pazzani, M.: Segmenting time series: a survey and novel approach. In: Data Mining in Time Series Databases, pp. 1–21. World Scientific (2004)

11. Lin, J., Keogh, E., Lonardi, S., Chiu, B.: A symbolic representation of time series, with implications for streaming algorithms. In: Proceedings of the 8th ACM SIGMOD Workshop on Research Issues in Data Mining and Knowledge Discovery, pp. 2–11. ACM (2003)

12. Keogh, E., Chu, S., Hart, D., Pazzani, M.: An online algorithm for segmenting time series. In: Proceedings IEEE International Conference on Data Mining, ICDM 2001, pp. 289–296. IEEE (2001)

13. Hu, Y., Ji, C., Jing, M., Li, X.: A K-motifs discovery approach for large time-series data analysis. In: Li, F., Shim, K., Zheng, K., Liu, G. (eds.) APWeb 2016. LNCS, vol. 9932, pp. 492–496. Springer, Cham (2016). https://doi.org/10.1007/978-3-319-45817-5_53

14. Keogh, E.J., Pazzani, M.J.: An enhanced representation of time series which allows fast and accurate classification, clustering and relevance feedback. In: KDD, vol. 98, pp. 239–243 (1998)

15. Park, S., Lee, D., Chu, W.W.: Fast retrieval of similar subsequences in long sequence databases. In: Proceedings of the 1999 Workshop on Knowledge and Data Engineering Exchange (KDEX 1999), pp. 60–67. IEEE (1999)

16. Qu, Y., Wang, C., Wang, X.S.: Supporting fast search in time series for movement patterns in multiple scales. In: Proceedings of the Seventh International Conference on Information and Knowledge Management, pp. 251–258. ACM (1998)

17. Liu, X., Lin, Z., Wang, H.: Novel online methods for time series segmentation. IEEE Trans. Knowl. Data Eng. **20**(12), 1616–1626 (2008)

18. Chen, Y., et al.: The UCR time series classification archive, July 2015. www.cs.ucr.edu/~eamonn/time_series_data/

19. Si, Y.W., Yin, J.: OBST-based segmentation approach to financial time series. Eng. Appl. Artif. Intell. **26**(10), 2581–2596 (2013)

MalShoot: Shooting Malicious Domains Through Graph Embedding on Passive DNS Data

Chengwei Peng[1,2], Xiaochun Yun[1,3(✉)], Yongzheng Zhang[3], and Shuhao Li[3]

[1] Institute of Computing Technology, Chinese Academy of Sciences, Beijing, China
[2] University of Chinese Academy of Sciences, Beijing, China
[3] Institute of Information Engineering, Chinese Academy of Sciences, Beijing, China
{pengchengwei,yunxiaochun,zhangyongzheng,lishuhao}@iie.ac.cn

Abstract. Malicious domains are key components to a variety of illicit online activities. We propose `MalShoot`, a graph embedding technique for detecting malicious domains using passive DNS database. We base its design on the intuition that a group of domains that share similar resolution information would have the same property, namely malicious or benign. `MalShoot` represents every domain as a low-dimensional vector according to its DNS resolution information. It automatically maps the domains that share similar resolution information to similar vectors while unrelated domains to distant vectors. Based on the vectorized representation of each domain, a machine-learning classifier is trained over a labeled dataset and is further applied to detect other malicious domains. We evaluate `MalShoot` using real-world DNS traffic collected from three ISP networks in China over two months. The experimental results show our approach can effectively detect malicious domains with a 96.08% true positive rate and a 0.1% false positive rate. Moreover, `MalShoot` scales well even in large datasets.

Keywords: Domain reputation · Graph embedding ·
Domain representation · Malicious domains detection

1 Introduction

The Domain Name System (DNS) servers as one of the most fundamental Internet components and provides critical naming services for mapping domain names to IP addresses. Unfortunately, it has been abused by miscreants for various illegal attack campaigns (*e.g.*, directing victims to malicious Web sites [1], exploiting algorithmically generated domains to circumvent the take-down [2,3]). Cisco 2016 annual security report [4] measured that 91.3% malware abused the DNS to achieve their evil intentions.

To mitigate these threats, tremendous efforts have been devoted in the last decades to establish domain reputation and blacklisting systems. The general approaches [5–8] extract multiple domain features (*e.g.*, TTL, lookup patterns,

H. Gao et al. (Eds.): CollaborateCom 2018, LNICST 268, pp. 488–503, 2019.
https://doi.org/10.1007/978-3-030-12981-1_34

number of IPs) from DNS records and then build a classifier over some labeled datasets. However, many of the features used are shown to be not robust [9] and can be easily altered by adversaries to evade the detection. Several recent techniques [10,11] propose to utilize graph methods to establish similarity between domains. These methods treat each domain as a vertex and add an edge between two domains if they exist an association (*e.g.*, hosted on a same IP [10]). Next, they use graph theories to calculate each domain's marginal probability distribution and infer its property (*i.e.*, malicious or benign). Comparing with previous works, graph-based methods exploit global associations of the DNS data to identify malicious domains, which are more robust. Unfortunately, graph-based methods cost a large amount of calculations, which making they not suitable for large scale passive DNS database (*e.g.*, millions of vertices).

In this paper, we propose MalShoot, a lightweight and robust technique for detecting malicious domains from passive DNS database. Our work is based on the fundamental intuition that domains sharing a similar resolution data (*e.g.*, hosted on some same IPs) are strongly associated and tend to have same property, namely malicious or benign. Inspired of the great success of embedding techniques in nature language processing, we treat a domain's DNS resolution data (rdata) as its context information and embed it into a low-dimensional vector. The domains that share similar context information are finally embedded into similar vector while. Based on the feature representation, a machine-learning classifier is trained over a labeled dataset and is further applied to detect other malicious domains. We evaluate MalShoot using real-world DNS traffic collected from three large ISP networks in China over two months under three popular machine learning algorithms (RandomForest, XGBoost and Deep Neural Network). MalShoot achieves 96.08% detection rate with an approximately 0.1% false positive rate with a 10-fold cross-validation when using RandomForest.

In summary, our paper makes the following contributions:

- We develop MalShoot, a lightweight and robust approach to detect malicious domains through graph embedding technique on passive DNS database.
- We design a novel domain representation technique that can automatically represent every domain into a feature vector while maintaining their DNS resolution information.
- We perform a comprehensive evaluation of MalShoot using two months real-world DNS traffic collected from three large ISP networks in China, demonstrating its effectiveness for detecting malicious domains.

We organize our paper as follows. Section 2 presents the background of passive DNS data and related works. Section 3 elaborates on the technical details of the proposed approach. Section 4 describes the datasets. Experiment setup and results analysis are reported in Sect. 5. We discuss a few issues of our approach in Sect. 6 and conclude the paper in Sect. 7.

2 Background and Related Work

2.1 Passive DNS Data

Passive DNS replication captures inter-server DNS messages through sensors that are voluntarily deployed by contributors in their DNS infrastructures. The captured DNS messages are further processed and then stored in a central passive DNS (PDNS) database which can be queried for various purposes [12].

```
## From ISP1

{"rrname":"api.device.xiaomi.net", "rrtype":"A",

"rdata":"111.13.142.31", "count":66

"time_first":1481877769, "time_last":1485527818}
```

Fig. 1. A sample record collected from ISP_1

A typical record in a PDNS database is represented as a tuple: (*rrname, rrtype, rdata, t_f, t_l, count*), where the *rrname* is a domain name, *rrtype* represents the type of resource record (RR) returned by DNS servers, *rdata* is the data field in the RR, t_f and t_l denote the time when an individual *rdata* is first and last seen, and *count* is the number of DNS queries that receive the *rdata* in response. Figure 1 shows a sample record in our dataset. The *rdata* field is an IP address, which represents that the *rrname* ever was hosted on this IP.

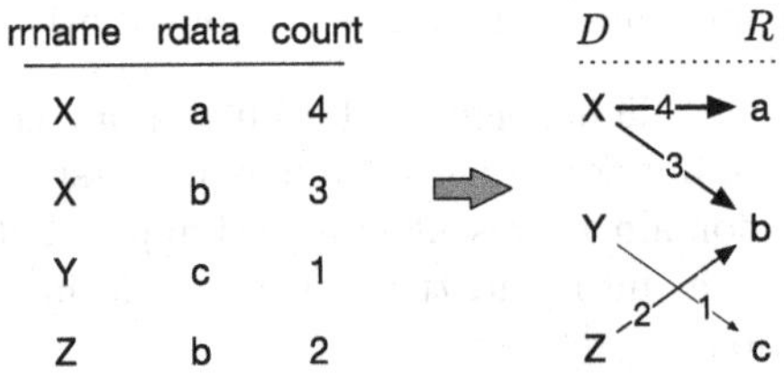

Fig. 2. Domain-resolution graph

Typically, we represent a passive DNS database as a domain-resolution bipartite graph $G = (D, R, E)$ by formatting each DNS record (*rrname, rrtype, rdata, t_f, t_l, count*) as an edge $e_{ij} = (rrname \rightarrow rdata)$ with weight $w_{ij} = count$, where D is the set of rrnames, R is the set of rdatas and E is the set of edges. Figure 2 shows an illustration for constructing a domain-resolution graph from DNS records.

2.2   Malicious Domain Detection

A wealth of research has been conducted on detecting malicious domains. Notos [5] is a pioneer work for establishing a dynamic reputation system to detect malicious domains. It use three categories of features to check a domain d, namely (i) network-based (*i.e.*, IPs associated with d); (ii) zone-based (*i.e.*, subdomains under d) and (iii) evidence-based (*i.e.*, malware samples contacting d). Bilge *et al.* proposed Exposure [6] with original time-based features, which requires less training time and data. On the other hand, Exposure overcomes some limitations of Notos, as it is able to identify malicious domains and addresses that were never seen in malicious activities before. Antonakakis *et al.* developed Kopis [7]) that aims at detecting malicious domains using the DNS traffic collected at the upper DNS hierarchy level (*i.e.*, Top Level DNS servers). The vantage point enables Kopis the *global* visibility. Moreover, Kopis can detect malware domains even when no IP reputation information is available. However, multiple features used in these detection systems, such as TTL and temporal patterns tend to be relatively brittle and allow attackers to take advantages of these features to evade detection.

Rahbarinia *et al.* proposed Segugio [8] for efficiently tracking the occurrence of new malware-control domain names in very large ISP networks. Their fundamental intuition is that infected machines tend to query new malware-control domains, moreover, machines infected with the same malware, or malware family, tend to query the same (or a partially overlapping) set of malware-control domains. On the other hand, benign machines have no reason to query malware-control domains. Manadhata *et al.* [13] proposed to identify malicious domains through host-domain query graph in an enterprise network. However, these efforts require the private information about individual users, which tends to be very sensitive.

Khalil *et al.* [10] and Peng *et al.* [11] proposed to discover malicious domains through the domain-resolution graphs. Compared to the host-domain graphs, domain-resolution graphs are constructed with publicly available DNS replication and without privacy concern. Khalil *et al.* [10] build domain-association graph by adding an edge between two domains if they hosted on same IPs for a period of time. The weight of the edge is decided on the number of IP they share. Then, they proposed a path-based inference to compute the global association with a set of malicious seeds for each unknown domain. Peng *et al.* [11] proposed a malicious domain detection method through DNS CNAME graph and focused on domains that are not resolved to IP addresses directly, but only appear in DNS CNAME records. The basic intuition is that domains connected by CNAME resource records share intrinsic relations and are likely to be in similar reputation. Unfortunately, these works are graphical analysis methods that cost complex calculation on the built domain-resolution graph when computing a domain's reputation score, which causes not scale well for large dataset. For example, [10] takes $O(|D|^2)$ steps to build the corresponding domain graph where $|D|$ is the number of domains. Our method first automatically learn the low-dimensional feature representation of every domain, which is linear with the number of records (or, edges, in $O(|E|$ time). Afterwards, `MalShoot` calculates a domain's reputation only depending on the domain's low-dimensional representation, which is independent from the graph. Therefore, our method can scale well even with millions of domains.

2.3 Graph Embedding

Recent years have seen a surge of research on node embeddings on the graphs. Formally, these works aim to learn a mapping function that encodes each node on the graph to a low-dimensional vector. Early methods for learning representations for nodes largely focused on matrix-factorization approaches [14,15]. Many recent successful methods learn the node embeddings based on random walk statistics. DeepWalk [16] preserves higher-order proximity between nodes by maximizing the probability of observing the last k nodes and the next k nodes in the random walk centered at v_i, i.e. maximizing $\log Pr(v_{i-k}, \cdots, v_{i-1}, v_{i+1}, \cdots, v_{i+k})$. Node2vec [17] preserves higher-order proximity between nodes by maximizing the probability of occurrence of subsequent nodes in fixed length random walks. LINE [18] defines two functions, one each for first- and second-order proximities, and minimizes the combination of the two. `MalShoot` preserves the second-order proximity on the domain-resolution graph to embed every domain node into a low-dimensional feature vector.

3   Proposed Approach

In this section, we present our design of `MalShoot`. `MalShoot` is a lightweight method for identifying malicious domains using passive DNS database. It consists of three modules:

1. Representation Module: The representation module is designed for representing every individual domain name in PDNS database as a low-dimensional vector through graph embedding technique.
2. Training Module: The training module is responsible for training a malicious domain detection classifier using the learned vector representations over some labeled domains.
3. Classification Module: The classification module classifies remained unknown domains using the trained classifier.

Figure 3 provides an overview of `MalShoot`'s architecture, of required inputs, of outputs, and of the way `MalShoot` processes data internally. We describe the three modules in detail in the following.

3.1   Representation Module

A domain name consists of a set of strings separated by a period. Representation module is responsible for embedding every individual domain into a low-dimensional (*e.g.*, 128 dimensions) vector used for a downstream prediction task.

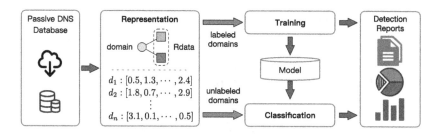

Fig. 3. Abstract illustration of the architecture of `MalShoot`

We formulate representation learning in our approach as a optimization problem. Let $G = (D, R, E)$ be the domain-resolution bipartite graph constructed from a given PDNS database, where $D = \{d_1, d_2, \cdots, d_n\}$ is the set of domains, $R = \{r_1, r_2, \cdots, r_m\}$ is the set of rdatas and E is the set of edges. Each edge, $(d_i, r_j) \in E$, represents a DNS record that domain d_i ever mapped to rdata r_j.

Let $f : D \to \mathbb{R}^d$ be the mapping function from domain nodes to d-dimensional vectors and $g : R \to \mathbb{R}^d$ be the mapping function from rdata nodes to d-dimensional vectors, where $d \ll |R|$ and $d \ll |D|$. Our goal is to map the domains that share a similar context information into similar vectors while the unrelated domains into distant vectors in the embedding space $\mathbb{R}^d$.

Denote $u_i = f(d_i)$ be the low-dimensional representation of domain d_i and $v_j = g(r_j)$ be the low-dimensional representation of rdata r_j. We first define the conditional probability of mapping to rdata r_j when giving domain d_i as:

$$p(r_j|d_i) = \frac{\exp(v_j^T \cdot u_i)}{\sum\limits_{r_k \in R} \exp(v_k^T \cdot u_i)} \tag{1}$$

To preserve the context information in the embedding space, we should make the conditional distribution of the contexts $p(\cdot|d_i)$ specified by the low-dimensional representation be close to the empirical distribution $\hat{p}(\cdot|d_i)$. Therefore, we minimize the following objective function:

$$O = \sum_{d_i \in D} \lambda_i d(\hat{p}(\cdot|d_i), p(\cdot|d_i)), \tag{2}$$

where $d(\cdot, \cdot)$ is the distance between two distributions and λ_i indicates the importance or bias of domain d_i, which can be measured by occurrence times.

The empirical distribution $\hat{p}(\cdot|d_i)$ is defined as

$$\hat{p}(r_j|d_i) = \frac{w_{ij}}{W_i}, W_i = \sum_{r_k \in N(d_i)} w_{ik},$$

which w_{ij} is the weight of edge (d_i, r_j) and $N(d_i)$ is set of rdatas that a domain, d, ever mapped on the graph, G. In this paper, for simplicity we set $\lambda_i = W_i$

and we adopt KL-divergence as the distance function. Therefore, the objective function in Eq. (2) is as:

$$O = \sum_{d_i \in D} \lambda_i d(\hat{p}(\cdot|d_i), p(\cdot|d_i)) \tag{3}$$

$$= \sum_{d_i \in D} W_i \cdot - \sum_{r_j \in N(d_i)} \frac{w_{ij}}{W_i} \log \frac{p(r_j|d_i)}{\hat{p}(r_j|d_i)} \tag{4}$$

$$= \sum_{d_i \in D} \sum_{r_j \in N(d_i)} [-w_{ij} \log p(r_j|d_i) + w_{ij} \log \hat{p}(r_j|d_i)] \tag{5}$$

$$= \sum_{(d_i, r_j) \in E} [-w_{ij} \log p(r_j|d_i) + w_{ij} \log \hat{p}(r_j|d_i)] \tag{6}$$

Due to the w_{ij} and $\hat{p}(r_j|d_i)$ are constants after the domain-resolution graph is given, we omit these constants. Therefore, our objective function is to minimize:

$$O = - \sum_{(d_i, r_j) \in E} w_{ij} \log p(r_j|d_i) \tag{7}$$

By learning $\{u_i\}_{i=1\cdots|D|}$ and $\{v_j\}_{j=1\cdots|R|}$ that minimize this objective, we are able to represent every domain d_i with a d-dimensional vector u_i.

However, optimizing objective (7) is computationally expensive, which requires the summation over the entire rdata set of R when calculating the conditional probability $p(\cdot|d_i)$. To address this problem, we adopt the approach of negative sampling proposed in [19], which samples multiple negative edges according to some noisy distribution for each edge (d_i, r_j). More specifically, it specifies the following objective function for each edge (d_i, r_j):

$$w_{ij} \log \sigma(v_j^T \cdot u_i) + \sum_{k=1}^{K} E_{r_n \sim P_n(d_i)} \left[w_{in} \log \sigma(-v_n^T \cdot u_i) \right], \tag{8}$$

where $\sigma(x) = 1/(1 + \exp(-x))$ is the sigmoid function. The first term models the positive edges, the second term models the negative edges drawn from the noise distribution and K is the number of negative edges. We set $P_n(d_i) \approx W_i^{3/4}$ as proposed in [19]. We use sigmoid function in Eq. (8) is considered on that the derivation of sigmoid function can be easily computed, $\sigma(x)' = \sigma(x)(1 - \sigma(x))$. Therefore, minimizing objective function (8) is equal to minimize the $v_j^T \cdot u_i$ for positive edge (d_i, r_j) and maximize the $v_n^T \cdot u_i$ for negative edge (d_i, r_n).

We adopt the asynchronous stochastic gradient algorithm (ASGD) [20] for optimizing Eq. (8). In each step, the ASGD algorithm samples a mini-batch of edges and then updates the model parameters. Notice that, MalShoot can directly operate on the edges to learn the feature representations. In practical, we do not need to construct the domain resolution graph.

3.2 Training Module

As MalShoot is based on supervised learning classifiers, it requires training with labeled data. The training module implements training of classifiers and requires the input of benign domains and malicious domains. We obtain malicious domains from various sources, including Malware Domains List [21], Phishtank [22], Openphish [23]. To obtain an as clean as possible set of benign domains, we choose domains that are consistently ranked among the top 20 thousands in the world according to Alexa [24]. Section 4 describes how we collect benign and malicious domains.

The output of training module is a well-trained model, ready to be used for classification of unknown domains in the classification module.

3.3 Classification Module

The classification module classifies arbitrary domains into *benign* and *malicious* based on a model trained from the training module and pre-learned vector representation.

4 Dataset

4.1 Malicious Domains

We consistently collected malicious domains from multiple sources, including Malware Domains List [21], Phishtank [22], Openphish [23] everyday from Jan. 03, 2017 to Oct. 14, 2017. In addition, we also use the Zeus Block List [25] and the list of domains that are generated by the DGAs of Conficker [26]. These malicious domains lists represent a wide variety of malicious activity, including botnet command and control servers, drive-by download sites, phishing pages, scam sites that are found in spam mails and ransomware malware domains. Domains listed in Openphish and Phishtank are operated on URLs that are submitted by users. Hence, while most URLs in these repositories are malicious, not all of them are. We submit these domains to Google Safe Browsing [27] and only reserve the confirmed malicious ones.

4.2 Benign Domains

We collected legitimate domains according to Alexa [24]. We chose domains that are consistently ranked among the top 20 thousands from Jan. 16, 2015 to Mar. 5, 2017 (513 days). In addition, we manual filter out domains that allow for the "free registration" of subdomains, such as popular blog-publishing services or dynamic DNS domains (*e.g.*, wordpress.com and dyndns.com), as their subdomains are often abused by attackers. Finally, this produced a list of 9,216 popular domains.

4.3   Passive DNS Traffic

Thanks for CNCERT/CC [28], we accessed the passive DNS traffic of three large ISP networks in China. The three ISP networks are located in the provinces of Anhui, Guangdong and Shanghai respectively. We refer to these ISP networks simply as ISP_1, ISP_2 and ISP_3. Notice that this paper is part of an IRB-approved study; appropriate steps have been taken by our data provider to minimize privacy risks for the network users.

By inspecting the DNS traffic between the ISPs' customers and their local resolvers over two months (Dec 5, 2016 - Feb 5, 2017), we collected about 530 millions DNS queries, roughly 200 millions queries in ISP_1, 130 millions in ISP_2 and 200 millions in ISP_3. Due to the privacy concerns, we only preserved the data in network layer. We extracted the DNS RRs from the DNS response packets. Each RR is formated as $\{rrname, rrtype, rdata, ts\}$, the $rrname$ is the domain name, $rrtype$ and $rdata$ represent the type and data of the RR and the ts is the timestamp when observing this RR.

5   Experiment

In this section, we present the evaluation of MalShoot on the datasets collected from thee ISP networks. We first define the evaluation metrics and describe the experiments settings. Next, we compare the overall performance of three different classifiers on the three datasets. Then, we evaluate MalShoot on unknown datasets. Finally, we compare the performance to other two domain-resolution graph based works [10].

5.1   Evaluation Metrics

To quantify to performance of MalHunter, we define following three metrics:

– *True Positive Rate (TPR)*: the ratio of number of true positives of the total number of domains that identified as malicious. $TPR = \frac{N_{TP}}{N_{TP}+N_{FN}}$.
– *False Positive Rate (FPR)*: the ratio of number of true positives to the total number of domains that are actually malicious. $FRP = \frac{N_{FP}}{N_{FP}+N_{TN}}$.
– *Area Under the ROC Curve (AUC)*: the area under the receiver operating characteristic curve, which is compromise between TPR and FPR.

where N_{TP} is the number of malicious domains that are correctly identified as malicious, N_{FP} is the number of benign domains that are falsely identified as malicious, N_{FN} is the number of malicious domains that are falsely identified as benign and N_{TN} is the number of benign domains that are correctly identified as benign. Our goal is to achieve as high as TPR while maintaining low FPR.

5.2   Experiment Setting

We conducted experiments using the two-month DNS traffic collected from the three large ISP networks. For each dataset, we first constructed a domain-resolution graph and then applied the unsupervised feature learning module, described in Sect. 3.1, to represent every domain to a low-dimensional feature vector. We tried different choices of the dimension $d \in \{64, 128, 256\}$ and found the performances were very similar, therefore, we set $d = 128$ in the follow-up experiments. Based on the collected domain blacklists and whitelists, we obtained some known malicious and benign domains in our datasets, i.e., ground truth. Last, we performed standard 10-fold cross-validations based the labeled domains and their low-dimensional representations. Specifically, we partition the ground truth into ten fold, train the classifier using nine fold and test it on the remain one fold. We repeat the process for each fold and compute the average performance. For simplicity, we only focused on the A, AAAA and CNAME records and discard the other entries. Table 1 describes the detail statistics of the three domain-resolution graphs.

Table 1. Data description in the three ISPs. Each row in the table represents the ISP network of data source, the number of domains, rdatas, edges (records) in the domain-resolution graph, the known malicious and benign domains in the ISP.

ISP	Domains	RDatas	Edges	Malicious	Benign
ISP_1	2,001,117	411,720	2,518,641	4,674	3,651
ISP_2	1,542,334	559,338	1,767,760	4,587	4,659
ISP_3	1,841,241	486,946	2,485,603	3,538	5,383

We adopt three popular supervised machine learning algorithms: Random-Forest, XGBoost [29] and Deep Neural Network (DNN) as the classifiers to evaluate the performances.

1. RandomForest: We implement RandomForest using the scikit-learn [30] machine-learning library. The parameter settings are $n\_estimator = 200$, $min\_samples\_split = 11$ and $max\_features =$ 'sqrt'. The others are as default.
2. XGBoost: XGBoost [29] is an optimized distributed gradient boosting machine learning algorithms designed to be highly efficient, flexible and portable. We implement XGBoost with the open repository in Python. The parameter settings are $max\_depth = 6$ and $num\_boost\_round = 100$. The others are as default.
3. DNN: We implement a four layer perceptron model in PyTorch. Besides the input layer (receiving low-dimensional representations) and output layer (indicating the domain's reputation score), we add two hidden layers. The architecture is as follow: $Dense(D_{in}, nh_1) \rightarrow Relu(\cdot) \rightarrow Dense(nh_1, nh_2) \rightarrow Relu(\cdot) \rightarrow Dense(nh_2, 2) \rightarrow softmax(\cdot)$, where the $D_{in} = d = 128$ is

the length of features, $Dense(n, m)$ is a full connected layer with n input nodes and m output nodes, $Relu(\cdot)$ is a non-linear activation function, $Relu(x) = \max(x, 0)$ and $softmax(\cdot)$ is a normalized function to ensure the sum of the output to be 1. We empirically set $nh_1 = 128$ and $nh_2 = 32$. We optimize the model using ASGD [20] with $batch\_size = 32$ and $cross\_entropy$ loss for 100 epochs.

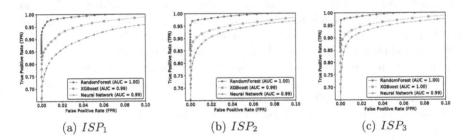

(a) ISP_1 (b) ISP_2 (c) ISP_3

Fig. 4. Performance comparison of classifiers under 10-fold cross-validation.

5.3 Experimental Results

We test the effectiveness of our detector over the ground-truth datasets through the standard 10-fold cross-validation. We compare three mostly used machine-learning classification algorithms, including RandomForest, XGBoost and Neutral Network. Figure 4 illustrates the receiver operating characteristic (ROC) curves of these classifiers, when using three PDNS database collected from three ISPs. The x-axis shows the false positive rate (FPR) and the y-axis shows the true-positive rate (TPR). We observe that all classifiers can achieve promising accuracy on the three data sources. To reach a 90% detection rate, the maximum FRP is always less than 4% for all classifiers, suggesting that MalShoot can effectively detect malicious domains. RandomForest outperforms the other classifiers in all cases. We achieves a 96.08% true positive rate with an approximately 0.1% false positive rate when using RandomForest.

5.4 Evaluation on Unknown Dataset

We now evaluate MalShoot on unknown dataset to examine whether we can accurately detect other unknown malicious domains based on the trained classifier. We focus on the best performing classifier RandomForest only and use it to for all follow-up experiments. We first use the full labeled dataset to train our detection model and then apply it to unknown domains. Due to the space limit, we only present the results on dataset of ISP_1 (results on other two ISPs have a similar distribution) in the rest of evaluations.

Among the 1,992,792 unknown domains in ISP_1 dataset (Table 1), `MalShoot` reports 173,279 malicious domains. Since this dataset is unlabeled, we have to validate the result through manual investigation. We use following two rules to consider a domain as a true positive (1) if it is hosted on a black IP address, and (2) if its second level domain (SLD) is reported as malicious (*e.g.*, if `abc.com` is reported as malicious, we treat its all subdomains as malicious). Notice that, we are conservative to judge an IP address as a black IP. We treat an IP as black only if it ever hosted enough malicious domains, (*e.g.*, 10 in our rule), which can reduce the false positives. Rule (1) confirms 168,002 as true positives and rule (2) confirms 1,219 of the left 5,277 as true positives. For the remain 4,058 not matched domains, we randomly select 100 domains and manually validate them. We find 34 domains host web content and most of them can be classified under gambling and sex categories. Therefore, `MalShoot` can effectively discover newly malicious domains with very low false positive rate.

5.5   Comparison

We compare `MalShoot` to one previous domain-resolution graph method [10].

1. Khalil *et al.* [10]:
   (a) First phase: constructing domain association graphs from DNS A records by adding an edge between two domains if they share common IPs.
   (b) Second phase: computing the global association scores with a given set of malicious seeds for every unknown domain through path-based inference.
2. `MalShoot`:
   (a) First phase: embedding every domain into a low-dimensional feature vector while maintaining its context information.
   (b) Second phase: training a classifier over a labeled dataset based on the feature representations and then applying it to detect other unknowns.

We first compare the time complexity of these two methods. For a regular domain-resolution graph $G = (D, R, E)$, the time complexity is listed in Table 2. Due to the complexity of training classifier relies on the machine-learning algorithm, we only analyze it for RandomForest.

In the first phase, approach in [10] computes the weight of every two domains if they share common IPs, therefore it costs about $O(|D|^2)$ steps. `MalShoot` updates model parameters edge by edge using Eq. (8), which costs $O(|E|)$ steps. Notice that $|D| \approx |E|$ in domain-resolution graphs (detail numbers are listed in Table 1). In the second phase, `MalShoot` works independently from the domain-resolution graph while method in [10] still needs to run complex calculation (*e.g.*, find shortest path) on the graph. Therefore, `MalShoot` can detect malicious domains without constructing domain-resolution graph or complex graphical calculation, which endows it scales well in large dataset.

We implement the method [10] and run it on the three datasets. Figure 5 shows the performances of comparing with our method. We observe that `MalShoot` outperforms the Khalil *et al.* [10] in the three datasets. The weight

Table 2. Time complexity analysis of `MalShoot` and [10]. Where $|D|$, $|E|$ is the number of domains and edges in the domain resolution graph. M is the number of trees used in RandomForest and N is the number of training samples. $|S|$ is the number of malicious seeds and $|E'|$ is the number of edges in domain graph, which could be as large as $|D|^2$

Method	First phase	Second phase
`MalShoot`	$O(|E|)$	Training: $O(MN \log N)$ Predicting: $O(M \log N)$
Khalil *et al.* [10]	$O(|D|^2)$	$O(|S|(|E'| + |D| \log |D|))$

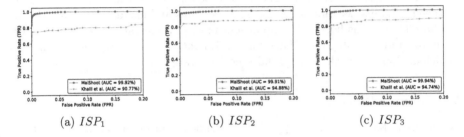

(a) ISP_1 (b) ISP_2 (c) ISP_3

Fig. 5. Performance comparison to [10] and [11]

between the two domains in [10] is defined as $w(d_i, d_j) = 1 - \frac{1}{1+|asn(ip(d_i) \cap ip(d_j))|}$, where $ip(d_i)$ is the set of IPs that domain d_i is resolved to and $asn(I)$ is the set of ASNs that the IPs in I belong to. Notice that each domain-IP pair is treated with same weight, neglecting the preferences. For example, domain d may be typically hosted on ip_1 while temporarily on ip_2, however, (d, ip_1) and (d, ip_2) are treated the same in [10], which causes it not robust for noisy resolutions (*e.g.*, fake resolution information). `MalShoot` takes a fine-grained consideration on the weight (*e.g.*, w_{ij}) of different domain-rdata pairs, which makes it robust for noisy resolutions.

6   Discussion and Future Work

In this section, we discuss some practical issues of our method.

First, `MalShoot` is a graph embedding method to detect malicious domains. It embeds every domain into a low-dimensional vector based on its context information. One practical issue is how to accurately embed domains with limited context information. For example, it is very hard to accurately infer a domain's representation if it never shares rdatas with others or only maps to a few rdatas. Notice that `MalShoot` only extract the *second-order* proximity in the domain-resolution graph. An intuitive solution to this is also preserving the *first-order* proximity, *i.e.*, maintaining the association between domain and rdata, when embedding. Therefore, if a domain maps to IPs listed in blacklists, we can also detect it.

Second, `MalShoot` is trained based on historical DNS data. Therefore, another practical issue is how to find the representation of a new domain. For a new domain d_i, if it maps to the existing rdatas, we can obtain the empirical distribution $\hat{p}(\cdot|d_i)$ over existing rdatas. To obtain the embedding of the new domain, according to the objective function Eq. (7), a straightforward way is to minimize the following objective function

$$\sum_{r_j \in N(d_i)} w_{ij} \log p(r_j|d_i)$$

by updating the embedding of the new domain and keeping the embeddings of existing rdatas. If the rdata that the new domain maps is also new, we must resort to other information, such as the lookup pattern behavior of the domain and we leave it as our future work.

7   Conclusion

In this paper, we propose a graph embedding based technique to discover malicious domains through public DNS records. We treat the set of rdatas that a domain ever mapped as its context and assume that domains sharing a similar context information are strongly associated. We design a unsupervised feature learning module that automatically represent every individual domain into a low-dimensional vector while maintaining their context information. Based on the learned features, a classifier is built over a labeled dataset and further be applied for detecting other unknown malicious domains. Experimental results show that our technique can achieve high true positive rates with low false positive rates. Compared to previous works, our approach scales well in large datasets.

Acknowledgments. The research leading to these results has received funding from the National Key Research and Development Program of China (No. 2016YFB0801502) and National Natural Science Foundation of China (No. U1736218). We thank the CNCERT/CC for providing the DNS data used in our experiments. The corresponding author is Xiaochun Yun.

References

1. Grier, C., Thomas, K., Paxson, V., Zhang, M.: @ spam: the underground on 140 characters or less. In: Proceedings of the 17th ACM Conference on Computer and Communications Security, pp. 27–37. ACM (2010)
2. Plohmann, D., Yakdan, K., Klatt, M., Bader, J., Gerhards-Padilla, E.: A comprehensive measurement study of domain generating malware. In: USENIX Security Symposium, pp. 263–278 (2016)
3. Antonakakis, M., et al.: From throw-away traffic to bots: detecting the rise of DGA-based malware. In: Presented as Part of the 21st USENIX Security Symposium (USENIX Security 2012), pp. 491–506 (2012)
4. Cisco 2016 annual security (2016). http://www.cisco.com/c/m/en_us/offers/sc04/2016-annual-security-report/index.html

5. Antonakakis, M., Perdisci, R., Dagon, D., Lee, W., Feamster, N.: Building a dynamic reputation system for DNS. In: USENIX Security Symposium, pp. 273–290 (2010)
6. Bilge, L., Sen, S., Balzarotti, D., Kirda, E., Kruegel, C.: Exposure: a passive DNS analysis service to detect and report malicious domains. ACM Trans. Inf. Syst. Secur. (TISSEC) **16**(4), 14 (2014)
7. Antonakakis, M., Perdisci, R., Lee, W., Vasiloglou II, N., Dagon, D.: Detecting malware domains at the upper DNS hierarchy. In: USENIX Security Symposium, vol. 11, pp. 1–16 (2011)
8. Rahbarinia, B., Perdisci, R., Antonakakis, M.: Segugio: efficient behavior-based tracking of malware-control domains in large ISP networks. In: 2015 45th Annual IEEE/IFIP International Conference on Dependable Systems and Networks, pp. 403–414. IEEE (2015)
9. Stinson, E., Mitchell, J.C.: Towards systematic evaluation of the evadability of bot/botnet detection methods. WOOT **8**, 1–9 (2008)
10. Khalil, I., Yu, T., Guan, B.: Discovering malicious domains through passive DNS data graph analysis. In: Proceedings of the 11th ACM on Asia Conference on Computer and Communications Security, pp. 663–674. ACM (2016)
11. Peng, C., Yun, X., Zhang, Y., Li, S., Xiao, J.: Discovering malicious domains through alias-canonical graph. In: 2017 IEEE Trustcom/BigDataSE/ICESS, pp. 225–232. IEEE (2017)
12. Weimer, F.: Passive DNS replication. In: FIRST Conference on Computer Security Incident, p. 98 (2005)
13. Manadhata, P.K., Yadav, S., Rao, P., Horne, W.: Detecting malicious domains via graph inference. In: Kutyłowski, M., Vaidya, J. (eds.) ESORICS 2014. LNCS, vol. 8712, pp. 1–18. Springer, Cham (2014). https://doi.org/10.1007/978-3-319-11203-9_1
14. Cao, S., Lu, W., Xu, Q.: Grarep: learning graph representations with global structural information. In: Proceedings of the 24th ACM International on Conference on Information and Knowledge Management, pp. 891–900. ACM (2015)
15. Ou, M., Cui, P., Pei, J., Zhang, Z., Zhu, W.: Asymmetric transitivity preserving graph embedding. In: Proceedings of the 22nd ACM SIGKDD International Conference on Knowledge Discovery and Data Mining, pp. 1105–1114. ACM (2016)
16. Perozzi, B., Al-Rfou, R., Skiena, S.: DeepWalk: online learning of social representations. In: Proceedings of the 20th ACM SIGKDD International Conference on Knowledge Discovery and Data Mining, pp. 701–710. ACM (2014)
17. Grover, A., Leskovec, J.: Node2vec: scalable feature learning for networks. In: Proceedings of the 22nd ACM SIGKDD International Conference on Knowledge Discovery and Data Mining, pp. 855–864. ACM (2016)
18. Tang, J., Qu, M., Wang, M., Zhang, M., Yan, J., Mei, Q.: Line: large-scale information network embedding. In: Proceedings of the 24th International Conference on World Wide Web, pp. 1067–1077. International World Wide Web Conferences Steering Committee (2015)
19. Mikolov, T., Sutskever, I., Chen, K., Corrado, G.S., Dean, J.: Distributed representations of words and phrases and their compositionality. In: Advances in Neural Information Processing Systems, pp. 3111–3119 (2013)
20. Recht, B., Re, C., Wright, S., Niu, F.: Hogwild: a lock-free approach to parallelizing stochastic gradient descent. In: Advances in Neural Information Processing Systems, pp. 693–701 (2011)
21. Malware domain block list (2018). http://www.malwaredomains.com

22. Phishtank (2018). http://www.phishtank.com
23. Openphish (2018). https://openphish.com
24. Alexa top 1 million (2017). http://s3.amazonaws.com/alexa-static/top-1m.csv.zip
25. Zeus domain blocklist (2016). https://zeustracker.abuse.ch/blocklist.php
26. Porras, P.A., Saïdi, H., Yegneswaran, V.: A foray into Conficker's logic and rendezvous points. In: LEET (2009)
27. Google safe browsing (2018). https://www.google.com/transparencyreport/safebrowsing/diagnostic/
28. CNCERT/CC (2018). https://www.cert.org.cn
29. Chen, T., Guestrin, C.: XGBoost: a scalable tree boosting system. In: Proceedings of the 22nd ACM SIGKDD International Conference on Knowledge Discovery and Data Mining, pp. 785–794. ACM (2016)
30. Pedregosa, F., et al.: Scikit-learn: machine learning in Python. J. Mach. Learn. Res. **12**, 2825–2830 (2011)

Learning from High-Degree Entities
for Knowledge Graph Modeling

Tienan Zhang[1], Fangfang Liu[1(✉)], Yan Shen[1], Honghao Gao[1,2],
and Jing Duan[1]

[1] School of Computer Engineering and Science, Shanghai University, Shanghai, China
`tinanoro@163.com, 1652009609@qq.com,`
`{ffliu,gaohonghao,duanjing}@shu.edu.cn`
[2] Computing Center, Shanghai University, Shanghai, China

Abstract. Knowledge base (KB) completion aims to infer missing facts based on existing ones in a KB. Many approaches firstly suppose that the constituents themselves (e.g., head, tail entity and relation) of a fact meet some formulas and then minimize the loss of formula to obtain the feature vectors of entities and relations. Due to the sparsity of KB, some methods also take into consideration the indirect relations between entities. However, indirect relations further widen the differences of training times of high-degree entities (entities linking by many relations) and low-degree entities. This results in underfitting of low-degree entities. In this paper, we propose the path-based TransE with aggregation (*PTransE-ag*) to fine-tune the feature vector of an entity by comparing it to its related entities that linked by the same relations. In this way, low-degree entities can draw useful information from high-degree entities to directly adjust their representations. Conversely, the overfitting of high-degree entities can be relieved. Extensive experiments carried on the real world dataset show our method can define entities more accurately, and inferring is more effectively than in previous methods.

Keywords: KB completion · Entity degree · Indirect relation · Entity prediction · Relation weakening

1 Introduction

Knowledge bases (KBs), such as Freebase [1], WordNet [2] and DBPedia [3] have recently grown in popularity since they are useful for various tasks, including information extraction [4], semantic parsing [5] and question answering [6]. These KBs contain large collections of facts about things, people and places that mostly in the form of triples (e.g., (*Bill Gates, FounderOf, Microsoft*)). A KB can be encoded as a graph, as shown in Fig. 1(a), where the nodes and edges represent entities and relations, respectively. While these KBs have been very large, they still miss large percentages of facts about common or popular entities. The lack of enough facts makes these KBs difficult to fulfill their potentials. However,

H. Gao et al. (Eds.): CollaborateCom 2018, LNICST 268, pp. 504–517, 2019.
https://doi.org/10.1007/978-3-030-12981-1_35

manually enriching KBs with all possible facts is impossible. Thus, researchers have devised techniques to automatically fill in missing facts by examining the facts already in the KB, which is formally known as KB completion.

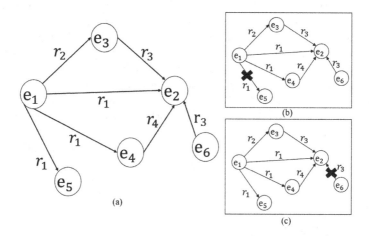

Fig. 1. (a) shows the origin knowledge base G in the form of graph; (b) demonstrates result of modeling G with PTransE, where correlation between e_1 and e_5 is weakened, even eliminated; (c) demonstrates another result that correlation between e_2 and e_6 is eliminated.

Latent feature models [7,8] are popular for performing knowledge base completion, which embed entities and relations of a KB into a continuous vector space. TransE [7] is a typical latent feature model that represents a relation with a translation vector so that the pair of embedded entities in a triple (h, r, t) (h, r and t are the head entity, relation and tail entity respectively.) can be connected by $\mathbf{r}$ with a low error. However, because of KB sparsity, the number of direct relations is small. Only utilizing the direct relations, TransE may tend to make the representations of two different entities become the same one. PTransE [9] incorporates into TransE the idea from graph feature models [10] that the relation between entities can be inferred by the indirect relations (i.e., sequences of relations) between them. In the following, direct relations and indirect relations are both referred to as path. Hence, PTransE treats each path as correlation between entities. Since high-degree entities are linked by more paths, their vector representations can be trained jointly with many entities and relations. Meanwhile, indirect relations do not bring equivalent number of paths to low-degree entities. This causes the training proportion of low-degree entities to be smaller. In addition, since vectors of entities and relations meet some formulas, the vectors of relations are also affected by the high-degree entities. Take entities e_1, e_2 and e_5 in Fig. 1(a) for example. There are three paths from e_1 to e_2: r_1, $r_2 \rightarrow r_3$ and $r_1 \rightarrow r_4$ and only one from e_1 to e_5: r_1. The quantitative differences on the paths make the correlation between e_1 and e_2 stronger and the correlation between e_1 and e_5 weaker. In extreme cases, the correlation between e_1 and e_5 will completely disappear. As shown in Fig. 1(b), resulting model of the KB in Fig. 1(a) may lose the correlation between e_1 and e_5. Similarly, in term of e_2, e_3, e_6 and r_3, the correlation between e_2 and e_6 may also be weakened.

Consider entity a being linked by relation r to entity b and c, namely, two triples (a, r, b) and (a, r, c). In terms of basic translation model, the smaller the difference between vectors of b and c is, the less information the two triples lose. Motivated by this raw idea, we propose PTransE-ag to adjust the vector representations of related entities like the above. In fact, the nature of our method is to let entities directly learn information from each other. The effectiveness of PTransE-ag is verified on one real-world, large-scale KB: Freebase. The experimental results show that PTransE-ag substantially outperforms the baselines on missing entity prediction.

In the remainder of this paper, PTransE-ag and its implementation details are discussed in Sect. 2. The experiments and analyses are listed in Sect. 3. The related works are discussed in Sect. 4. Section 5 presents the conclusion and plans for future work.

2 Our Approach

Our method is based on PTransE [9], and utilizes its many formulas. So, we introduce PTransE briefly in Sect. 2.1. PTransE-ag will be presented in Sect. 2.2. Before proceeding, let us define our mathematical notation. We denote the knowledge base as $G = (E, R, S)$, where $E = \{e_1, \cdots, e_{|E|}\}$ is the set of entities composed of $|E|$ different entities. $R = \{r_1, r_2, \cdots, r_{|R|}\}$ is set of relations composed of $|R|$ different relations, and $S \subseteq E \times R \times E$ is the set of triples in the knowledge base.

2.1 Background

PTransE [9] broadens the correlations between entities by implementing path based translation. Path Ranking Algorithm [10] assembling sequential relations to get a path proves effective. For example, triples *(A, ParentOf, B)* and *(B, ParentOf, C)* can form triple *(A, [ParentOf, ParentOf], C)*. *[ParentOf, ParentOf]* corresponds to *GrandparentOf*. Obviously, composed relations can reflect the correlation between *A* and *C*. Hence, PTransE utilizes some paths for each pair of entities to strengthen their correlations. Firstly, paths whose lengths are less than 3 are preserved. Then, path-constraint resource allocation algorithm (PCRA) computes the reliability of relation paths. Finally, reliable paths are selected for representation learning.

PCRA associates a certain amount of resources with the head entity h and then distributes resource along the given path p. The resource that eventually flows to the tail entity t is the reliability of the path p, which is denoted as $R(p|h, t)$. The number of resources flowing to t is defined in [9] as follows:

$$R_p(t) = \sum_{n \in S_{i-1}(\cdot, t)} \frac{1}{|S_i(n, \cdot)|} R_p(n), \tag{1}$$

where $S_i(n, \cdot)$ is the direct successors of $n \in S_{i-1}$, following the relation r_i, and $R_p(n)$ is the number of resources flowing to entity n.

Composition methods of relations include: ADD, MUL and RNN. ADD is an addition operation $p = r_1 + r_2 + \cdots + r_l$. MUL is cross product $p = r_1 \times r_2 \times \cdots \times r_l$. RNN refers to recurrent neural networks. Since its performance is weak, our method will not use it.

Following TransE, PTransE defines energy function for a multi-relation path triple (h, p, t) as $E(h, p, t) = ||h + p - t||$. Since $||h + r - t||$ has been minimized to make sure $r \approx t - h$, the loss function of (h, p, t) can be transformed to $E(h, p, t) = ||p - (t - h)|| = ||p - r|| = E(p, r)$, which is expected to be low when the multiple-relation path p is consistent with the direct relation.

2.2   PTransE-ag

As shown in Fig. 1(a), there are three paths from e_1 to e_2: $r_1, r_2 \to r_3$ and $r_1 \to r_4$ and only one from e_1 to e_5: r_1. The quantitative differences of paths make the correlation between e_1 and e_2 stronger and the correlation between e_1 and e_5 weaker. In extreme cases, the correlation between e_1 and e_5 will completely disappear. The resulting model of the KB in Fig. 1(a) may become Fig. 1(b). In a word, the relations between low-degree entities and other entities are weakened. We call this problem the *relation weakening problem*.

To address the relation weakening problem, we utilize the fact that two entities being both related to another entity by the same relation means that these two entities have some similarities. Given three entities a, b and c, if a is related to b by relation r and b is similar to c, then there also should be relation r between a and c. Figure 2(a) demonstrates the weakening of the relation between e_1 and e_5, where the entities and relations are represented as vectors to better display the translation. The result of the translation on e_1 is far away from e_5. To make e_5 closer to $e_1 + r_1$, our method reduces the distance between e_2 and e_5 (as shown in Fig. 2(b)), which is equivalent to increasing their similarities. Since our method corresponds to forming aggregations of entities and is based on PTransE, it is named as PTransE-ag. In addition, experiments show that directly applying aggregation on TransE would not improve the efficiency. This suggests that considering the similarities between entities modeled by few correlation information makes no sense.

Optimization Objective. Note that we will not judge whether some relations between entities are weakened. Instead, we construct a valid triple during the training of triple (h, r, t), and then directly increase the similarity between the component and its replacement to reach the goal of strengthening relations. For the sake of understanding, the valid triple is denoted as (h, r, t'') which means that it is constructed by replacing t by t''. PTransE-ag aims to ensure that the loss of (h, r, t'') will not be too large when minimizing the loss of (h, r, t). The larger the loss of (h, r, t'') is, the weaker the correlation between h and t'' is. Because the only difference between (h, r, t) and (h, r, t'') is the tail entity and

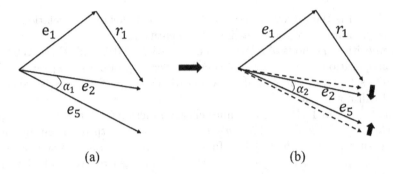

Fig. 2. (a) illustrates the outcome of modeling two triples (e_1, r_1, e_2) and (e_1, r_1, e_5), where e_5 is too far away from $e_1 + r_1$. (b) demonstrates the method to make e_5 closer to $e_1 + r_1$, i.e., reducing the distance between them $(\alpha_2 < \alpha_1)$.

the loss of (h, r, t) has been minimized, the loss of (h, r, t'') can be reduced by reducing the distance between t and t''. In short, PTransE-ag balances the losses of (h, r, t) and (h, r, t'') to reduce the global loss of the KB. The optimization objective of PTransE-ag is defined as

$$L(S) = \sum_{(h,r,t)\in S} [L(h,r,t) + L_1(h,r,t) + \frac{1}{Z} \sum_{p\in P(h,t)} R(p|h,t)L(p,r)], \quad (2)$$

where components except $L_1(h, r, t)$ are defined in PTransE [9]. Therefore, we just list their definitions without detailed explanation. $Z = \sum_{p\in P(h,t)} R(p|h,t)$ is a normalization factor, and $P(h,t)$ is the paths set between h and t. Following TransE, $L(h,r,t)$ and $L(p,r)$ are loss functions with respect to the triple (h,r,t) and the pair (p,r):

$$L(h,r,t) = \sum_{(h',r',t')\in S'} [\gamma + E(h,r,t) - E(h',r',t')]_+, \quad (3)$$

and

$$L(p,r) = \sum_{(h,r',t)\in S'} [\gamma + E(p,r) - E(p,r')]_+. \quad (4)$$

where $[x]_+ = max(0, x)$ returns the maximum between 0 and x, γ is the margin, S is the set of valid triples in KB. S' is the set of invalid triples. $E(h,r,t) = ||h+r-t||_1$ and $E(p,r) = ||p-r||_1$ are energy functions. And Formula $L_1(h,r,t)$ is defined as

$$L_1(h,r,t) = \begin{cases} 0, ||h - h''||^2 < \beta \text{ and } ||t - t''||^2 < \beta \text{ and } ||r - r''||^2 < \beta \\ \sum_{(h'',r'',t'')\in S''} ||h - h''||^2 + ||r - r''||^2 + ||t - t''||^2, \text{otherwise} \end{cases} \quad (5)$$

$\beta > 0$ is the threshold of the distance between the entities or relations. S'' is the set of valid triples constructed by replacing one of the three components of a triple. In Eq. (5), the error does not exist when the distances between the corresponding components of (h, r, t) and (h'', r'', t'') are all less than β (Note that there always be only one difference between (h, r, t) and (h'', r'', t'').). We use Eq. (5) to realize the aggregation. Here, the aggregation is extended to relation. We think that if two relations link the same head and tail entity, then they should also have some similarities. If the distance between a component and its replacement exceeds β, the distance between them should be reduced, such as with e_2 and e_5 in Fig. 1(a). In fact, our method adds the term $L_1(h, r, t)$ into PTransE optimization objective.

Implementation Detail. Before proceeding, the idea of the margin-based loss is worth discussing. Ideally, the loss of each triple is expected as small as possible. But explicitly specifying how small the loss should be is infeasible. Hence, the margin-based loss is employed to make the loss of invalid triple at least one margin larger than the loss of valid triple. Only when the loss difference is less than margin does the error exist, and then, parameter updating is executed.

Algorithm 1. Learning PTransE-ag

Input: Training set $S_{(h,r,t)}$, entities and rel. sets E and L; path sets P; path reliability
    set R; learning rate λ, margin γ, embeddings dim. k, threshold β.
1: **initialize** $r \leftarrow uniform(-\frac{6}{\sqrt{k}}, \frac{6}{\sqrt{k}})$ for each relation $r \in L$,
        $e \leftarrow uniform(-\frac{6}{\sqrt{k}}, \frac{6}{\sqrt{k}})$ for each entity $e \in E$
2: **loop**
3:     $e \leftarrow \frac{e}{||e||}$ for each $e \in E$
4:     $r \leftarrow \frac{r}{||r||}$ for each $r \in L$
5:     $S_{batch} \leftarrow sample(S, b)$ //sample a minibatch of size b
6:     $T_{batch} \leftarrow \emptyset$ //initialize the set of triplets of triples
7:     **for** $(h, r, t) \in S_{batch}$ **do**
8:         $(h', r', t') \leftarrow sample(S'_{(h,r,t)})$ //sample a invalid triple
9:         $(h'', r'', t'') \leftarrow sample(S''_{(h,r,t)})$ //sample a valid triple
10:        $T_{batch} \leftarrow T_{batch} \bigcup \{((h, r, t), (h', r', t'), (h'', r'', t''))\}$
11:    **end for**
12:    Update embeddings w.r.t.
13:    $\sum_{((h,r,t),(h',r',t'),(h'',r'',t'')) \in T_{batch}} [\nabla L(h, r, t) \quad + \quad \nabla L_1(h, r, t) \quad +$
        $\frac{1}{Z} \sum_{p \in P(h,t)} R(p|h, t) \nabla L(p, r)]$
14: **end loop**

The detailed optimization procedure is described in Algorithm 1. Algorithm 1 is similar to that of PTransE [9], with the only difference that PTransE-ag needs an extra valid triple set, denoted as S''(Line 9, Algorithm 1), to reduce the distance between similar entities. For optimization, we employ the stochastic gradient descent (SGD) with constant learning rate to minimize the loss function. All embeddings for entities and relations are first initialized following the random procedure proposed in [11]. At each main iteration of the algorithm, the embeddings are first normalized. Then, a small set of triples is sampled from the training set, and will serve as the training samples of the minibatch. For each training sample (h, r, t), randomly select a component to be replaced. For the sake of description, we take t as example. Then, the updating (step 13 in Algorithm 1) performs the following steps:

> **Step-1.** Construct an invalid triple (h, r, t'). If **Condition-1** (The loss of training sample (h, r, t) is not at least one margin smaller than the loss of invalid triple (h, r, t').) is met, the embeddings of h, r, t and t' will be updated.
> **Step-2.** Construct a valid triple (h, r, t''). Note that (h, r, t'') may not exist. If **Condition-2** $((h, r, t'')$ exists and the distance between the embeddings of t and t'' exceeds threshold $\beta)$ is met, the embeddings of t and t'' will be updated. This step is unique to PTransE-ag.
> **Step-3.** Construct an invalid triple (h, r', t). This step involves the path-based translation. Like **Step-1**, for each path p between h and t, if **Condition-3** (The loss of (p, r) is not at least one margin smaller than the loss of (p, r').) is met, the embeddings of r, r' and relations in path p will be updated. Note that no matter which component in training sample (h, r, t) is replaced, Step-3 always replaces r of (h, r, t). This is because the path-based translation only uses relation and path.

Among three steps above, **Step-2** is our work integrated into PTransE. Therefore, the difference between PTransE-ag and PTransE is that PTransE-ag will take into account other valid triples when training a triple.

Evaluation Function. The evaluation function of PTransE is directly used as ours. In TransE, the loss function of a triple also works as its evaluation function. Similarly, the evaluation function of PTransE-ag can also be derived from its loss function. It is defined as

$$S(h, r, t) = G(h, r, t) + G(t, r^{-1}, h), \tag{6}$$

where $G(h, r, t)$ is defined as

$$G(h, r, t) = E(h, r, t) + \frac{1}{Z} \sum_{p \in P(h,t)} Pr(r|p) R(p|h, t) E(p, r). \tag{7}$$

The inversion of the relation (e.g., r^{-1}) is needed in paths and learned in the path-based translation. $Pr(r|p) = \frac{Pr(r,p)}{Pr(p)}$ is the global correlation between r and p, where $Pr(x)$ is the number of x in the KB.

3   Experiments and Analysis

In this section, experiments on *entity prediction* is performed. Given an entity e and a relation r, *entity prediction* discovers the entities which are most likely to be related to e by relation r.

Dataset. To make a direct comparison to PTransE [9], we evaluate our method on the dataset used in PTransE, that is, a dataset extracted from Freebase, FB15K [7]. The statistics of FB15K are listed in Table 1.

Table 1. Statistics of dataset

Dataset	#Relation	#Entity	#Train	#Valid	#Test
FB15k	1,345	14,951	483,142	50,000	59,071

Evaluation Metrics. For each testing triple (a.k.a., seeded triple), we construct a set of triples by replacing one component of seeded triple and then compute scores of these triples including seeded triple with evaluation function. These triples are sorted in ascending order to evaluate the performance of an approach. Here, we concentrate on two evaluation metrics [7]: $Hits@n$ and $Mean$. $Hits@n$ records the proportion of seeded triples ranking in top n and $Mean$ records the mean of seeded triples' ranks. For $Mean$, the smaller the figure is, the better the performance of a method is. For $Hits@n$, it is quite the contrary. These two metrics are defined as follows:

$$Hits@n = \frac{num\ of\ seeded\ triples\ ranking\ in\ top\ n}{num\ of\ seeded\ triples} \tag{8}$$

$$Mean = \frac{\sum_{triple\ in\ testing\ set} rank\ of\ triple}{num\ of\ seeded\ triples} \tag{9}$$

However, the method of replacing one component is flawed when a constructed triple that is not in testing set ends up being valid in the KB. For example, one of our testing triples is ($NewYork$, $locatedIn$, USA). Then, during prediction, the triple ($Chicago$, $locatedIn$, USA) is constructed, which is obviously not the original testing triple but is also valid in the KB. This kind of triples will be regarded as invalid because in the evaluation only the ranks of the seeded triples are the concern. This is not reasonable. Therefore, it is necessary to filter out those undesirable valid triples during the evaluation. We name the raw evaluation setting mentioned before as Raw, the filtering setting as $Filter$.

Baselines. Although many recent works are referred to in Sect. 4, we only pick some early variants of TransE as our baselines because the aim of comparison is to verify if our modification is efficient. The employed baselines include SE [12], TransE [7], TransH [8], TransR [13] and PTransE [9].

Parameters Configurations. The optimal configurations of PTransE-ag are $\lambda = 0.001$, $\gamma = 1$, $k = 100$, and $\beta = 0.05$ and we take L_1 as dissimilarity of the loss function. λ is the learning rate of SGD, γ is the margin between loss of a valid triple and the loss of its corresponding invalid one, k is the dimensionality of entity and relation embeddings and β is the threshold of the distance between entities or relations. The number of training epochs over all training triples is set to 500.

Entity Prediction. In entity prediction, the missing head or tail entity of a triple is inferred. Given a seeded triple, construct triples by replacing tail entity by each member of entity set E. Because searching path is of high memory-consumption, we first employ evaluation function of TransE to select newly constructed triples ranking in top 500. These top 500 triples are then sorted according to scores computed by evaluation function of PTransE-ag in ascending order. Finally, record the rank of the seeded triple (Usually, seeded triple is in top 500). Having iterated over all seeded triples, we can compute values of *Hits@n* and *Mean*.

Experiment Analysis. Results on entity prediction are demonstrated in Table 2, where four metrics are listed: the *Raw* and *Filter* version of *Mean* and *Hits@10*. For PTransE, we list its results with different relation composition operations and step length. For example, PTransE(ADD,2-step) means that the composition operation is addition and the length of the step is not more than 2. For PTransE-ag, we only list the results of the ADD and MUL composition operation because RNN works worse than the other two composition operations in PTransE. Moreover, due to the complexity of the cross product of vectors, only (ADD,3-step) is listed. Aggregation is also applied on TransE, which is TransE-ag in Table 2. TransE-ag's performance is worse than TransE's. This is because TransE only takes into consideration the direct relations between entities. Direct relations are not enough to model an entity, let alone to judge if two entities have similarities. The best result for each metric is shown in bold font.

Table 2 shows that PTransE-ag consistently outperforms baselines including PTransE. This indicates that preventing the information of direct relations from being overwhelmed by paths can better define an entity. No matter whether PTransE or PTransE-ag is used, (ADD,2-step) always outperforms its counterparts on most of the metrics. This indicates that the addition composition operation is effective and too long paths provide little information on entities. In addition, PTransE with RNN obtains the worst performance among three kinds of composition operations. This suggests that complex models unnecessarily outperform simple models.

Tables 3 and 4 demonstrate the performance of PTransE and some baselines with respect to different types of relations. Relations can be categorized into four classes according to the cardinalities of their head and tail arguments: 1-to-1, 1-to-N, N-to-1 and N-to-N. On all types of relations, PTransE-ag achieves the best results. It appears that predicting entities on the "side 1" is easier (e.g., predicting the head entities in 1-to-N relations and tail entities in N-to-1 relations). However, in the other hand, it can be observed that N-to-1 relations in head entity prediction and 1-to-N relations in tail entity prediction always obtain the worst performance in all methods and they perform much worse than other

Table 2. Evaluation results on entity prediction

Metric	Mean rank		Hits@10(%)	
	Raw	Filter	Raw	Filter
SE	273	162	28.8	39.8
TransE	243	125	34.9	47.1
TransE-ag	252	133	33.2	45.9
TransH	212	87	45.7	64.4
TransR	198	77	48.2	68.7
PTransE(ADD, 2-step)	200	54	51.8	83.4
PTransE(MUL, 2-step)	216	67	47.4	77.7
PTransE(RNN, 2-step)	242	92	50.6	82.8
PTransE(ADD, 3-step)	207	58	51.4	84.6
PTransE-ag(ADD, 2-step)	182	**45**	**53.9**	**87.8**
PTransE-ag(MUL, 2-step)	205	56	52.7	87.7
PTransE-ag(ADD, 3-step)	**180**	46	53.2	82.1

Table 3. Head prediction by mapping properties of relations. (%)

Tasks	Predicting head entities(Hits@10)			
Relation Category	1-to-1	1-to-N	N-to-1	N-to-N
SE	35.6	62.6	17.2	37.5
TransE	43.7	65.7	18.2	47.2
TransH	66.8	87.6	28.7	64.5
TransR	78.8	89.2	34.1	69.2
PTransE(ADD, 2-step)	91.0	92.8	60.9	83.8
PTransE(MUL, 2-step)	89.0	86.8	57.6	79.8
PTransE(RNN, 2-step)	88.9	84.0	56.3	84.5
PTransE(ADD, 3-step)	90.1	92.0	58.7	86.1
PTransE-ag(ADD, 2-step)	91.4	**96.3**	**64.2**	88.9
PTransE-ag(MUL, 2-step)	**92.6**	95.7	63.4	**89.4**
PTransE-ag(ADD, 3-step)	90.0	94.6	58.0	82.2

types of relations. This reflects the inherent problem of TransE-series methods that non-1-to-1 relations are incompatible with the translation operation.

4 Related Work

The task of knowledge base completion has seen a lot of attention in recent years. Statistical relational learning (SRL) is widely applied on KB completion. We will touch on the latent feature models. Approaches of latent feature

Table 4. Tail prediction by mapping properties of relations. (%)

Tasks	Predicting tail entities(Hits@10)			
Relation Category	1-to-1	1-to-N	N-to-1	N-to-N
SE	34.9	14.6	68.3	41.3
TransE	43.7	19.7	66.7	50.0
TransH	65.5	39.8	83.3	67.2
TransR	79.2	37.4	90.4	72.1
PTransE(ADD, 2-step)	91.2	74.0	88.9	86.4
PTransE(MUL, 2-step)	87.8	71.4	72.2	80.4
PTransE(RNN, 2-step)	88.8	68.4	81.5	86.7
PTransE(ADD, 3-step)	90.7	70.7	87.5	88.7
PTransE-ag(ADD, 2-step)	90.1	74.2	**94.8**	**90.7**
PTransE-ag(MUL, 2-step)	**92.0**	**74.3**	92.7	90.7
PTransE-ag(ADD, 3-step)	89.2	67.3	93.5	85.0

models usually learn an embedded representation of entities and relations in low-dimensional spaces to capture the correlation between the entities/relations using latent variables. Our approach PTransE-ag also fits in this line of work.

Some earliest works include collective matrix factorization models represented by RESCAL [14] and energy-based frameworks represented by SE [12]. However, these methods acquire great expressivity at the expense of substantial increases in model complexity.

To achieve better trade-offs between accuracy and scalability, TransE [7] represented each entity with a constant vector regardless of the relation type linking this entity. TransH [8] and TransR [13] argued that an entity should behave diversely when linking different relations, and thus proposed to transform the representation of an entity based on current relation before translation. TranSparse [15] proposed to substitute sparse matrices for dense matrices of TransR to deal with the heterogeneity and the imbalance of KB. TransG [16] assumed that each relation corresponds to various semantics, each of which can be revealed by the entity pairs associated with triples. KR-EAR [17] distinguished relation types and classified them into two classes, i.e., relations and attributes. The former indicates the relationship between entities. The other one represents the properties of entities. Similar methods that tried to discovered geometric structure of the embedding space also include TransD [18], TransA [19] and TransCoRe [20]. TransD learned projection matrix by considering the interaction among relations and entities. TransA introduced Mahalanobis distance into the energy function of TransE because original L_1 or L_2 distance is sort of simple and treats each dimension of representations equally. TransCoRe further employed SVD to find out that a small number of dimensions can capture most information of a relation, and thus converted the problem of learning the embedded relation matrix into learning two low-dimensional matrices. In this way, each relation can be represented by less dimensions with a shared basis.

Although innovative and efficient, above methods only tried to exploit more information from relation-based triples. In fact, relation paths can also reflect the correlations among entities and relations. PTransE [9] learned the vector representations of paths to enrich the number of triples and thus obtained high performance on knowledge base completion. DPTransE [21] computed the contribution of paths to a certain relation by employing a graph feature model, and then learned the representations of knowledge base based on a modified TransE model. However, to obtain the contribution of paths, DPTransE needed predefined embeddings of relations in KB. RPE [22] embedded entities and relations into different low-dimensional spaces with semantics of relation paths. That is, RPE simultaneously embedded each entity into two types of latent spaces. Other works will also consider logic rules. TARE [23] integrated knowledge triples and logic rules and emphasized the importance of transitivity and asymmetry of logic rules to order the relation types. All these latent feature models tried to minimize the margin-based loss. However, they ignored the problem that some other valid triples are likely to be discarded while optimizing current triple.

5 Conclusion and Future Work

Our method aims to address the problem that indirect relations weaken correlations between some entities. PTransE obtains significant performance improvement but it ignores the side effect paths bring. However, it is the side effect that guides us to the workaround. It is found that high-degree entities are trained much more than low-degree entities do, which means more information are embedded in high-degree entities. Tracking down the basic idea of translation model, we proposed PTransE-ag that allows low-degree entities to directly learn from high-degree entities. And experiments also prove the effectiveness of PTransE-ag.

In addition, there are some shortcomings of our method. Firstly, the training time is an issue due to the extra time for finding related entities. This can be improved by optimizing the searching algorithm. In fact, the running time matters the most, which remains the same as PTransE's. Secondly, the relation weakening problem is from our intuition. Although we follow this intuition and propose PTransE-ag that surely improves performance, concrete evidences still remain to be proposed. Our future work will explore more detailed experiments. Lastly, PTransE-ag simply shrinks the difference between the vector of similar entities. It overlooks the motivation of low-dimensional vector representation that the features of an entity can be distributed represented. It is noteworthy that each dimension of an entity usually plays a different role when this entity interacts with different relations. Therefore, our future work will center on the distinguishing of dimensionality. For example, SVD [24] can be employed to learn the primary component of a vector. This may guide the direction along which entities should be closed to each other. In addition, we will further extend our method to the relation prediction task to examine and improve the universality of PTransE-ag.

Acknowledgements. This work is supported by National Key Research and Development Plan of China under Grant No. 2017YFD0400101, and National Natural Science Foundation of China under Grant No. 61502294, and Natural Science Foundation of Shanghai under Grant No. 16ZR1411200.

The url of the source code is https://github.com/IdelCoder/PTransE-ag.

References

1. Evans, C., Paritosh, P., Sturge, T., Bollacker, K., Taylor, J.: Freebase: a collaboratively created graph database for structuring human knowledge. In: Proceedings of the 2008 ACM SIGMOD International Conference on Management of Data, pp. 1247–1250 (2008)
2. Miller, G.A.: WordNet: a lexical database for English. Future Gener. Comput. Syst. **38**(11), 39–41 (1995)
3. Jakob, M., Mendes, P.N., Bizer, C.: DBpedia: a multilingual cross-domain knowledge base. In: Proceedings of Language Resources and Evaluation, pp. 1813–1817 (2012)
4. Zhou, M., Nastase, V.: Using patterns in knowledge graphs for targeted information extraction. In: KBCOM 2018 (2018)
5. Gesmundo, A., Hall, K.: Projecting the knowledge graph to syntactic parsing. In: Proceedings of Conference of the European Chapter of the Association for Computational Linguistics, pp. 28–32 (2014)
6. Singh, K., Diefenbach, D., Maret, P.: WDAqua-core1: a question answering service for RDF knowledge bases. In: WWW 2018 Companion (2018)
7. Usunier, N., Garcia, A., Weston, J., Bordes, A., Yakhnenko, O.: Translating embeddings for modeling multi-relational data. In: Proceedings of International Conference on Neural Information Processing Systems, pp. 2787–2795 (2013)
8. Zhang, J., Feng, J., Wang, Z., Chen, Z.: Knowledge graph embedding by translating on hyperplanes. In: Proceedings of AAAI Conference on Artificial Intelligence, pp. 1112–1119 (2014)
9. Liu, Z., Luan, H., Sun, M., Rao, S., Lin, Y., Liu, S.: Modeling relation paths for representation learning of knowledge bases. In: Proceedings of Conference on Empirical Methods in Natural Language Processing, pp. 705–714 (2015)
10. Mitchell, T., Lao, N., Cohen, W.W.: Random walk inference and learning in a large scale knowledge base. In: Proceedings of Conference on Empirical Methods in Natural Language Processing, pp. 27–31 (2011)
11. Glorot, X., Bengio, Y.: Understanding the difficulty of training deep feedforward neural networks. Mach. Learn. **9**, 249–256 (2010)
12. Weston, J., Collobert, R., Bordes, A., Bengio, Y.: Learning structured embeddings of knowledge bases. In: Proceedings of AAAI Conference on Artificial Intelligence, pp. 301–306 (2011)
13. Liu, Z., Lin, Y., Zhu, X.: Learning entity and relation embeddings for knowledge graph completion. In: Proceedings of AAAI Conference on Artificial Intelligence, pp. 2187–2195 (2015)
14. Tresp, V., Nickel, M., Kriegel, H.P.: A three-way model for collective learning on multi-relational data. In: Proceedings of International Conference on Machine Learning, pp. 809–816 (2011)

15. Liu, K., He, S., Ji, G., Zhao, J.: Knowledge graph completion with adaptive sparse transfer matrix. In: Proceedings of AAAI Conference on Artificial Intelligence, pp. 985–991 (2016)
16. Huang, M., Xiao, H., Zhu, X.: TransG: a generative model for knowledge graph embedding. In: Proceedings of the 54th Annual Meeting of the Association for Computational Linguistics, pp. 2316–2325 (2016)
17. Liu, Z., Lin, Y., Sun, M.: Knowledge representation learning with entities, attributes and relations. In: Proceedings of International Joint Conference on Artificial Intelligence, pp. 2866–2872 (2016)
18. He, S., Xu, L., Liu, K., Ji, G., Zhao, J.: Knowledge graph embedding via dynamic mapping matrix. In: Proceedings of the 53rd Annual Meeting of the Association for Computational Linguistics, pp. 687–696 (2015)
19. Huang, M., Yu, H., Xiao, H., Zhu, X.: TransA: an adaptive approach for knowledge graph embedding (2015)
20. Jia, Y., Zhu, J., Qiao, J.: Modeling the correlations of relations for knowledge graph embedding. J. Comput. Sci. Technol. **33**(2), 323–334 (2018)
21. Wang, Q., Xu, W., Li, W., Zhang, M., Sun, S.: Discriminative path-based knowledge graph embedding for precise link prediction. In: Pasi, G., Piwowarski, B., Azzopardi, L., Hanbury, A. (eds.) ECIR 2018. LNCS, vol. 10772, pp. 276–288. Springer, Cham (2018). https://doi.org/10.1007/978-3-319-76941-7_21
22. Liang, Y., Giunchiglia, F., Feng, X., Lin, X., Guan, R.: Relation path embedding in knowledge graphs. Neural Comput. Appl. 1–11 (2018)
23. Rong, E., Zhuo, H., Wang, M., Zhu, H.: Embedding knowledge graphs based on transitivity and asymmetry of rules. xplan-lab.org (2018)
24. Kalman, D.: A singularly valuable decomposition: the SVD of a matrix. Coll. Math. J. **27**(1), 2–23 (1996)

Target Gene Mining Algorithm Based on gSpan

Liangfu Lu[1], Xiaoxu Ren[1], Lianyong Qi[2(✉)], Chenming Cui[3], and Yichen Jiao[3]

[1] School of Mathematics, Tianjin University, Tianjin, China
[2] School of Information Science and Engineering, Qufu Normal University, Rizhao, China
lianyongqi@gmail.com
[3] School of Software, Tianjin University, Tianjin, China

Abstract. In recent years, the focus of bioinformatics research has turned to biological data processing and information extraction. New mining algorithm was designed to mine target gene fragment efficiently from a huge amount of gene data and to study specific gene expression in this paper. The extracted gene data was filtered in order to remove redundant gene data. Then the binary tree was constructed according to the Pearson correlation coefficient between gene data and processed by gSpan frequent subgraph mining algorithm. Finally, the results were visually analyzed in grayscale image way which helped us to find out the target gene. Compared with the existing target gene mining algorithms, such as integrated decision feature gene selection algorithm, our approach enjoys the advantages of higher accuracy and processing high-dimensional data. The proposed algorithm has sufficient theoretical basis, not only makes the results more efficient, but also makes the possibility of error results less. Moreover, the dimension of the data is much higher than the dimension of the data set used by the existing algorithm, so the algorithm is more practical.

Keywords: gSpan gene mining algorithm · Gene expression data · Data mining · Visual analysis

1 Introduction

1.1 A Subsection Sample

With the rapid development of high-throughput technology, various types of biology research mass data have been produced. Bioinformatics and computational biology have been developing corresponding theories and technologies to analyze the information. Moreover, as the focus of human genome research shifts to functional genome, the emphasis of bioinformatics research has quietly turned from the accumulation of biological data to the processing and information extraction of biological data. And it has become an urgent problem to be solved in [1]. Similarly, it is still a difficult problem to understand and explain complex life phenomena. The process of life activity and the factors involved in it are a complex network system. The study of biological networks is a key to understanding complex life activities [2]. Among the

H. Gao et al. (Eds.): CollaborateCom 2018, LNICST 268, pp. 518–528, 2019.
https://doi.org/10.1007/978-3-030-12981-1_36

various types of networks, of special relevance are collaborative networks. Collaborative networks have been used in many cases to develop and implement software in different domains that must jointly identify problems and provide solutions [3]. And collaborative networks have also been widely used in manufacturing successfully [4]. In this paper, we use the cooperative mutual information between two sets to calculate the correlation between gene data. And we designed a target gene mining algorithm based on gSpan to solve above problems. The data used in the experiment was divided into two parts, the experiment group and the test group. Data cleaning algorithm was applied to the all the data for primary dimensionality reduction. Then, the binary tree was processed by gSpan frequent subgraph mining algorithm after calculating the Pearson correlation coefficient between different data samples, which was constructed by the filtered data set. Finally, target gene was analyzed with the support of visual methods, which were included line chart and grayscale image and other algorithms.

2 Target Gene Mining Algorithm Based on gSpan

2.1 Gene Data Sources and Features

When extracting the gene data used in the paper, we compare the gene probe on a gene probe chip with a corresponding gene fragment of the sample, and we can obtain a value representing the difference between the gene probe and the gene fragment. And taking a logarithm of 2 as the base, a gene data can be received.

Table 1 is a sample of a gene dataset. Where the numbers in the first row represent the number of that data. In the following, each row represents the gene data measured with a specific gene probe chip for each gene sample fragment. The first column in the table shows the names of the gene probes, such as "TC01003440.hg.1" and "TC01003573.hg.1".

According to gene data, they were divided into experimental group and control group. The experimental group were similar in character, while the control group had the opposite character in group.

2.2 Data Cleaning Based on the Overall Characteristics of Gene Samples

Considering that not all the genes in the data sample are target genes, we need to clean the genes to reduce the number of redundant genes [5–7].

Data Cleaning Between Different Groups: Different samples from different groups are thought to have great diversity in gene expressions, which can be measured by variance [8]. For a gene fragment, the variance among all the samples is:

$$\sigma^2 = \frac{\sum (X - \mu)^2}{N} \tag{1}$$

Where σ is the variance and X represents the number of the amount of all these gene fragments in a sample. μ denotes the mean and N is the total sample number.

Table 1. An example of gene data sets.

Number of samples	1	2	3	4	5	6
TC01003440.hg.1	3.773364	4.266670	4.701382	4.891576	4.373340	3.786559
TC01003573.hg.1	1.979416	2.225050	2.472456	1.904527	2.572532	2.624649
TC01003581.hg.1	2.411289	2.630495	3.164683	2.468128	1.821613	0.894983
TC01003634.hg.1	1.023536	4.366745	1.049543	1.032603	0.694951	0.805963
TC01003635.hg.1	3.908017	4.654112	4.519364	3.662154	3.416480	3.878956
TC01003707.hg.1	4.680764	4.819676	5.480835	5.273236	4.406693	4.900424
TC01003855.hg.1	2.900651	4.433520	4.448808	3.992489	4.582560	3.164090
TC01003992.hg.1	3.537443	4.958187	4.264466	3.472608	3.246787	3.903415
TC01005205.hg.1	3.519913	3.387307	4.837730	4.734122	4.124148	3.688145
TC01005809.hg.1	3.091624	3.081775	4.138366	4.133202	3.486166	3.385050
TC02000261.hg.1	4.983322	4.684757	5.213353	5.376272	4.915276	5.093583

Data Cleaning in Every Group: In terms of gene expression for studying traits, there is a small difference between the same set of samples. Similar to group cleaning, in this part, variance can also be used to measure differences in groups. Variance can also be used to measure differences within a group. In this paper, we set a threshold, if the variance is greater than the threshold gene fragment, which indicates that the gene fragment is not similar to the same group of samples, and it does not conform to the principle of small differences between the target gene fragment within the group sample. So these gene fragments are cleaned from all the gene fragments.

Gene Filtering: The threshold was set to the result of above two data cleaning. And those gene fragments of low variance were filtered, which means these gene fragments were similar for all the samples and didn't show different gene expressions between different groups. On the contrary, those gene fragments of high variance were filtered.

2.3 Data Cleaning Based on the Characteristics of the Specific Sample

After preliminary cleaning of genetic data using variance, according to the authenticity of data samples among individuals, a more accurate and detailed method is adopted to sort out the selected data samples.

First, consider that for the same trait, there is a high probability that two of the samples exhibiting the same or similar trait will have the same gene expression pattern when the sample size is large [9]. Thus, Pearson correlation coefficient was calculated in all the couples after coupling the samples in the same group [10–12].

For two random scalars X and Y, the Pearson correlation coefficient between them is:

$$\rho = \frac{cov(X, Y)}{\sqrt{DX}\sqrt{DY}}, \tag{2}$$

$$cov(X, Y) = E((X - E(X)) \cdot (Y - E(Y))). \tag{3}$$

In this case, genes with high similarity in low correlation combinations are more likely to contain target genes in [13]. And the union of similar gene fragments in every couple was included in the set of gene fragments to construct the graph. Similarly, considering the nature between two different groups of sample individuals, paired combinations of data samples from all different groups with high correlation can highlight the target genes with low similarity. And we select the more dissimilar gene fragments from these combinations and merge them as another part of the final composition of the gene fragment set [14].

For two random variables, mutual information can be seen as reducing the uncertainty of one variable by knowing the value of another variable. The average mutual information is calculated by

$$I(X; Y) = H(X) + H(Y) - H(XY) \tag{4}$$

$$H(X) = -\sum_{p(x)} p(x) \log p(x) \tag{5}$$

$$H(XY) = -\sum_{x} \sum_{y} p(xy) \log p(xy) \tag{6}$$

where $I(X; Y)$ represents the average mutual information of random variables X and Y, which are gene data of two samples. The $H(X)$ and $H(Y)$ represent the entropies of X and Y. The $H(XY)$ is the joint entropy of X and Y. The $p(x)$ represents the probability distribution of X. The $p(xy)$ is the joint probability distribution of X and Y.

3 The Construction of the Graph

3.1 Basis of Construction

For a dataset that has n samples and the selected sample is P, GA and GB are the two gene fragments needed to be calculated. The mutual information $MI(n)$ of GA and GB and their corresponding gene data $GA(n)$ and $GB(n)$, was calculated firstly. Then, the gene data of sample P on gene fragments GA and GB were removed from $GA(n)$ and $GB(n)$, getting gene data $GA(n-1)$ and $GB(n-1)$ and calculate the mutual information $MI(n-1)$ between them. When the mutual information $MI(n)$ is higher than $MI(n-1)$, which means that the gene data added to the sample P lead to the increase of the amount of mutual information between $GA(n)$ and $GB(n)$ and also means the gene data GA of samples has close relationship with the gene data GB of sample P.

Based on this, MIP, which is calculated by the difference between $MI(n-1)$ and $MI(n)$, is used as a criterion to measure the correlation between gene data of sample P on GA and GB. The larger the MIP, the greater the correlation between the two gene fragments. And the smaller the MIP, the smaller the correlation between the two gene fragments.

3.2   Construction Procedure

To simplify the calculation, gene data was constructed to be a binary tree. The fragment that has the smallest variance in the group after data cleaning was placed as the root [15]. The root of a node's left subtree was the most correlative gene fragment to the node, and the root of the node's right subtree was the second most correlative gene fragment to the node [16]. All the gene fragments were inserted in the binary tree based on breadth-first principle.

4   gSpan Algorithm

The gSpan algorithm is the most widely used by the subgraph mining algorithm in the world, which was proposed by Yan and Han in [17].

4.1   Definition

Frequent subgraph: given a graph set $D = [G_1, G_2, \ldots, G_n]$ and a graph g, The number of the graph g included in set D is called G's support and recorded as support(g). For a given minimum threshold minSup, if $support(g) \geq minSup$, g is called a frequent subgraph of D. DFS Lexicographic Order: let $\{Z = code(G, T)| T \text{ is a DFS tree of graph } G\}$. Assuming there is a linear sequence Q in a label set, then the lexicographic combination of T and Q is a linear sequence in set $ET \times L \times L \times L$.

The definition of DFS lexicographic order is that for $a = code(G_a, T_a) = (a_0, a_1, \ldots, a_n)$, $b = code(G_b, T_b) = (b_0, b_1, \ldots, b_n)$ and a, b belong to Z, we conclude $a \leq b$ if and only if the following condition is true:

(1)   there exists a t, $0 \leq t \leq min(m, n)$, $a_k = b_k$, $k < t$, the lexicography combination of a_t and b_t is the mentioned above linear sequence.
(2) $a_k = b_k$, $0 \leq k \leq m$ and $m \leq n$.

DFS code: gSpan algorithm uses five parameters to code the edge in the graph by the way like $(i, j, l_i, l_{(i,j)}, l_j)$, in which l_i and l_j are the vertexes of edge $l_{(i,j)}$.

Smallest DFS code: for a given graph G, $Z = \{code(G, T)| T \text{ is a DFS tree of graph } G\}$, $min(Z(G))$, according to DFS lexicographic order, which is called the smallest DFS code of G.

DFS code tree: in DFS, each node represents a DFS code, the relationship between the parent node and child node obey the abovementioned parent-child relationship. Relationships between brothers and sisters are consistent with DFS lexicographic order, which means the preorder traversal of DFS code tree obeys DFS lexicographic order.

4.2   The gSpan Algorithm

The thinking in the gSpan algorithm is shown in Tables 2 and 3 as fake codes.

Table 2. gSpan main program.

Algorithm 1. GraphSet_Projection (D, S).
1: Sort the labels of vertexes and edges in D by frequency;
2: Delete infrequent vertexes and edges;
3: Remark the remaining vertexes and edges
4: Save the frequent edges of D into set S^1;
5: Sort S^1 by DFS lexicographic order;
6: $S \leftarrow S^1$;
7: **for** each edge e that belongs to S^1**do**;
8. Use e to initialize s, putting all the graphs that include e into set D;
9. Subgraph_Mining (D, S, s);
10. $D \leftarrow D - e$;
11. **if** $|D| <$ minSup;
12. **break;**

Table 3. gSpan subprogram.

Subprogram 1 Subgraph_Mining(D, S, s).
1: **if** $s \neq min(s)$
2: **return;**
3: $S \leftarrow S \cup \{s\}$;
4: Enumerate s in all the graphs that belongs to set D and count the amount of its subgraph;
5: **for each** e which is the subgraph of s **do**
6: **if** $support(e) \geq minSup$;
7: $s \leftarrow e$;
8: Subgraph_Mining (D_s, S, s);

4.3   Description of Target Gene Mining Algorithm Based on gSpan

The gSpan frequent subgraph mining algorithm was applied to the graph sets which is constructed by experiment group and test group to get their frequent subgraphs. Then the set of target gene fragment was got by analyzing two groups' frequent subgraphs.

5   Visual Analysis of Gene Data

5.1   The Decision with Visual Analysis

An appropriate threshold was needed while doing gene cleaning in every group and between groups. Line chart was used to help us to make the decision quickly and properly by analyzing the result of data cleaning when threshold changed. The inflection points in the threshold's line chart were considered to be possible choices of threshold values based on the characteristic that the inflection point in a line chart always represented the critical state.

5.2 Grayscale Image of Gene Data

Grayscale image was applied to the gene data to make the visual analysis process more convenient and intuitive, which started with mapping all the raw gene data to a grayscale interval that was from 0 to 1. The mapping procedures are as follows:

(1) Selecting the biggest gene data M from all the raw gene data;
(2) Rounding up M to get an integer N;
(3) Dividing all the original gene data by integer N, and get the gray value after mapping.

Table 4. Examples of mapping raw gene data to grayscale value.

Raw gene data	Grayscale values
3.773364	0.7546728
1.979416	0.3958832
2.411289	0.4822578
1.023536	0.2047072
3.908017	0.7816034
4.680764	0.9361528
2.900651	0.5801302
3.537443	0.7074886
3.519913	0.7039826
3.091624	0.6183248
4.983322	0.9966644

Table 4 shows some raw gene data and their grayscale values after mapping.

Then a single column vector that contained all the grayscale values was inserted into an $N * N$ matrix and N was an integer which was got by rounding up the square root of the data number. The blank areas in the matrix were filled with 0. Table 5 was the matrix filled with the grayscale values in Table 4.

The grayscale matrix was used as an input value to get a grayscale image. And Fig. 1 was an example of grayscale images.

Table 5. The example of grayscale value filling.

0.7546728	0.7816034	0.6183248	0
0.3958832	0.9361528	0.9966644	0
0.4822578	0.5801302	0	0
0.2047072	0.7074886	0	0

Fig. 1. An example of grayscale images

6 Experiment Results and Analysis

6.1 Experiment Results

Dental caries is one of the most common chronic diseases, and it is easy for individuals to suffer from this disease throughout their lives. In recent years, many researchers have studied the prevention of dental caries and some oral health mechanisms [18, 19]. And the gene data used in the experiment was selected from the University of California, Los Angeles, which was extracted to study the pathogenic and resistance gene about dental caries in the human body. And the data consist of 21 samples, which are divided into two groups. One group is of high S.mutans and high caries, abbreviated as HSHC in the following, which has 10 samples. Another group is of high S.mutans and low caries, abbreviated as HSLC in the following, which has 11 samples. Data which were selected from 70523 gene probe chips were included in the raw gene data and each gene probe chip corresponded to a gene fragment.

Some frequent subgraphs are obtained in this experiment by using the gSpan algorithm. Considering that some frequent subgraphs are meaningless due to the default value of the algorithm in the process of constructing gene fragment graphs. After removing these meaningless subgraphs, we can obtain two frequent subgraphs, which are shown as Figs. 2 and 3. The relationships between nodes in the frequent subgraphs and serial numbers of gene probe chips were listed in Table 6. The gene fragments corresponding to the nodes were the result of this experiment.

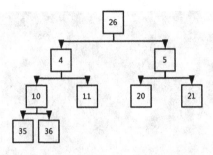

Fig. 2. Frequent subgraph of group HSLC

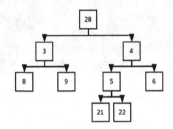

Fig. 3. Frequent subgraph of group HSHC

Table 6. Relationships between nodes in the frequent subgraphs and serial numbers of gene probe chips

Group HSLC		Group HSHC	
Nodes	Serial numbers	Nodes	Serial numbers
4	TC01000938.hg.1	3	TC01000711.hg.1
5	TC01001103.hg.1	4	TC01000938.hg.1
10	TC01001464.hg.1	5	TC01001103.hg.1
11	TC01001809.hg.1	6	TC01001120.hg.1
20	TC01003427.hg.1	8	TC01001143.hg.1
21	TC01003428.hg.1	9	TC01001291.hg.1
26	TC01003573.hg.1	21	TC01003428.hg.1
35	TC02000261.hg.1	22	TC01003431.hg.1
36	TC02000500.hg.1	28	TC01003634.hg.1

After verifying, nodes 4, 5, 21 in group HSLC (e.g. the gene fragments corresponding to gene probe chips number "TC01000938.hg.1" "TC01001103.hg.1" "TC01003428.hg.1"), were the target gene fragments to determine the gene fragment of dental caries in this experiment. Thus, the coverage rate to dental caries was 100% and dental caries gene occupied 33.3% of the results, which meant the experiment finished with good consequence.

6.2   Experiment Result Analysis

Comparing with existing target gene mining algorithms, there were two advantages of gSpan target gene mining algorithm:

(1) Higher accuracy. Although some existing algorithms also have 100% coverage rate to dental caries, the dental caries gene can only occupy for 15%–20% of the results. By constructing the gene data into graph during data process creatively and using subgraph mining algorithm, which makes the result can be more accurate and target gene can occupy a higher percentage of the result.

(2) Higher data dimensions. Existing algorithms always have dimension under 10,000 and extract some uncommon situations. The dataset used in this experiment came from raw gene data with a dimension of 70523, which is much higher than the dimension used by existing algorithms and is also much more practical.

7   Conclusion

The gSpan target gene mining algorithm was proposed in this paper in order to help mine target gene from a huge amount of gene data. And this paper focused on the following aspects:

(1) We mainly introduced the data cleaning algorithm, graph construction algorithm and gSpan frequent subgraph mining algorithm. And a target gene mining algorithm based on gSpan was proposed on the basis of the algorithms mentioned above.

(2) To verify the effectiveness of algorithm, the gene data about human dental caries extracted by the University of California, Los Angeles was used as data set. According to the experiment, the results' coverage rate to dental caries was 100%, which was the same as existing algorithms. And dental caries gene occupied 33.3% of the results, which was higher than existing algorithms which showed that the new algorithm had the better effect.

(3) Grayscale image and line chart were introduced to help visually analyze the result of the algorithm and make the decision.

And the edges of the graph only had two statuses, existing or not. Thus, the data can be constructed into weighted undirected graphs, in which the weight of each edge represents the correlation between two node genes. And the gSpan algorithm can be replaced by algorithms that can process weighted undirected graphs. Moreover, network models can also be introduced to help us find new ways to do the filtering, construction and target gene finding work [20]. Thus, a lot of work can be done to optimize the target gene mining algorithm in the future.

Acknowledgments. This work was partially supported by the National Natural Science Foundation of China under No. 51877144 and No. 61872219.

References

1. Michihiro, K., George, K.: Gene classification using expression profiles: a feasibility study. Int. J. Artif. Intell. Tools **14**(04), 641–660 (2001)
2. Lee, I., Blom, U.M., Wang, P.I., et al.: Prioritizing candidate disease genes by network-based boosting of genome-wide association data. Genome Res. **21**(7), 1109 (2011)
3. Sabau, G., Bologa, R., Bologa, R., et al.: Collaborative network for the development of an informational system in the SOA context for the university management. In: International Conference on Computer Technology and Development, pp. 307–311. IEEE (2009)
4. Shuman, J., Twombly, J.: Collaborative Business. In: Collaborative Networks Are The Organization: An Innovation in Organization Design and Management, 8 vols. The Rhythm of Business, Inc., Newton (2009)
5. Alon, U., Barkai, N., Nootterman, D.A., et al.: Broad patterns of gene expression revealed by clustering analysis of tumor and normal colon tissues probed by oligonucleotide arrays. Science **96**(12), 6745–6750 (1999)
6. Jie, Z., Cheng-quan, G., Jun-rong, C., Li-xin, G.: Tumor identification based on gene expression profiles and the search about extraction of the feature genes. Math. Pract. Theory **41**(14), 67–79 (2011)
7. Ya-ning, Z., Yan-hui, Z.: Extraction of tumor gene and its classification based on SNR. J. Xiangfan Univ. **32**(8), 13–16 (2011)
8. Quan-jin, L., Ying-xin, L., Xiao-gang, R.: Cancer information gene identification based on statistical method. J. Beijing Univ. Technol. **31**(2), 122–125 (2005)
9. Yongxiu, C.: Understanding of correlation coefficient (7), 15–19 (2011)
10. Hong-bin, L., Guang-zhong, H., Qiu-ting, G.: Similarity retrieval method of organic mass spectrometry based on the Pearson correlation coefficient. Chem. Anal. Meterage **24**(3), 33–37 (2015)
11. Niyogi, X.: Locality preserving projections. In: Neural Information Processing Systems, vol. 16, p. 153 (2004)
12. Yong-chao, W.: A novel D-S combination method of conflicting evidences based on pearson correlation coefficient. Telecommun. Eng. **52**(4), 466–471 (2012)
13. Jie, L., Li-jun, D., Sheng-nan, T.: Refinement procedure for Eigen genes of colon carcinoma based on BB-SIR. World SCI-Tech R&D **33**(4), 588–591 (2011)
14. Shoujue, W., Lingfei, Z.: Gene selection for gene expression data analysis. Micro Comput. Inf. **24**(3–3), 193–194 (2008)
15. Jing-jing, S., Li-bo, W., Wei, L.: Gene selection for cancer diagnosis. Comput. Eng. Appl., 218–220 (2010)
16. Jun, W.: Method of effective DNA microarray data feature extraction. Modern Electron. Tech. **37**(13), 95–98 (2014)
17. Yan, X., Han, J.: gSpan: graph-based substructure pattern mining. In: ICDM. IEEE (2002)
18. Lin, T.H., Lin, C.H., Pan, T.M.: The implication of probiotics in the prevention of dental caries. Appl. Microbiol. Biotechnol. **102**(2), 577–586 (2018)
19. Philip, N., Suneja, B., Walsh, L.J.: Ecological approaches to dental caries prevention: paradigm shift or Shibboleth? Caries Res. **52**(1–2), 153–165 (2018)
20. Liu, H., Bebu, I., Li, X.: Microarray probes and probe sets. Front. Biosci. **2**(1), 325 (2010)

Booter Blacklist Generation Based on Content Characteristics

Wang Zhang[1,2], Xu Bai[1,2], Chanjuan Chen[3], and Zhaolin Chen[4(✉)]

[1] Institute of Information Engineering, Chinese Academy of Sciences, Beijing, China
zhangwang@iie.ac.cn
[2] School of Cyber Security, University of Chinese Academy of Sciences,
Beijing, China
[3] China National Machinery Industry Corporation, Beijing, China
[4] Nanjing University of Aeronautics and Astronautics, Nanjing, China
zhaolin_in_chen@hotmail.com

Abstract. Distributed Denial of Service (DDoS) attacks-as-a-service, known as Booter or Stresser, is convenient and low-priced for ordinary people to launch DDoS attacks. It makes DDoS attacks even more rampant. However, until now there is not much research on Booter and little acquaintance with their backend infrastructure, customers, business, etc. In this paper, we present a new method which focuses on the content (text) characteristics on Booters websites and selects more discriminative features between Booter and non-Booter to identify Booters more effectively in the Internet. The experimental results show that the classification accuracy of distinguishing Booter and non-Booter websites is 98.74%. In addition, our method is compared with several representative methods and the results show that the proposed method outperforms the classical methods in 66% of the classification cases on three datasets: Booter websites, 20-Newsgroups and WebKB.

Keywords: Booter service · Feature selection · Text classification

1 Introduction

Distributed Denial of Service (DDoS) attacks, which create a huge volume of illegitimate traffic to jam the network and interrupt the network resource, is one of the biggest menaces for network security. DDoS attacks have existed for many years and continuously grown in both frequency and power. In 2014, CloudFlare reported a 400 Gbps NTP amplification attack on one of their customers [10]. Recently, Arbor Networks reported a 1.7 Tbps memcached amplification attack on an unnamed customer of a US-based service provider [4]. It is believed that Booters account for a large portion of the attack traffic in such mega attacks in recent years [3].

Activity of DDoS-as-a-service or DDoS-for-hire websites, also called Booter or Stresser, is not an accident. According to [12], it is the fact that (1) booters

H. Gao et al. (Eds.): CollaborateCom 2018, LNICST 268, pp. 529–542, 2019.
https://doi.org/10.1007/978-3-030-12981-1_37

provide a friendly interface and remove the need of technical skills to perform attacks, (2) booters are public in the Internet and easy to find by using Google or Bing and (3) they usually offer very affordable prices due to fierce commercial competition. Thus, Booters are also considered to be the indication of new period of the DDoS attack evolution. Despite the serious threat of Booters to the Internet, until now there is not much research on Booter and we know little about the ecosystem of these Booter services. Prior work points out that Booter blacklist generation is a promising approach to mitigate the challenge of the Booter services and show the effectiveness of the blacklists [15]. The prior work developed a Booter blacklist generation system containing three components: The crawler firstly collects suspect Booter URLs in the Internet; Secondly, the scraper acquires the suspect Booter URL information based on fifteen proposed characteristics; Finally, the classifier identifies whether a suspect URL is a Booter website on account of the scraped URL information. We observe that Booter websites often use similar content (text) in their webpages and we consider that content (text) characteristics on Booters websites are also effective to identify Booters. Therefore, we present a new method which classifies Booters based on content (text) characteristics. Also, we propose a new feature selection algorithm to improve the performance of text classification. Our main contributions are listed as follows:

- We develop a new Booter classifier based on content (text) characteristics which enrich the methods of identifying Booters.
- We propose a feature selection algorithm, which selects more discriminative features with the minimal number, to improve the performance of text classification.

The rest of this paper is organized as follows. The related work is discussed in Sect. 2. The details of our approach is described in Sect. 3. The experimental results and discussion are presented in Sect. 4. Finally, the paper is concluded in Sect. 5.

2   Related Work

Santanna et al. [15] designed a methodology for Booter blacklist generation and demonstrated the value of the Booter blacklist. Until now, their methodology has already found 519 Booters [13], which is of great benefits to the mitigation of Booter services. Karami et al. [5] investigated underlying technical and business structure of Booter services from the leaked data of three major booters and the payment obstruction to their services in cooperation with PayPal. Krämer et al. [6] designed a novel honeypot that can simulate amplifiers and be of assistance to monitor amplification DDoS attacks. Due to the important location of amplifiers, many methods of the mitigation of amplification DDoS attacks can be explored based on the honeypot amplifiers. Krupp et al. [7] developed methods to uncover the infrastructures behind amplification DDoS attacks by using fingerprint to the scanners and TTL-based trilateration techniques, which is also beneficial to the detection of back-end infrastructures of Booter services. Krupp et al. [8] construct a novel method that can attribute DDoS attacks to the honeypot operators including Booter services based on their honeypot amplifiers. Noroozian et al. [9] analysed the data captured from their honeypot amplifiers and provided us an in-depth investigation and explanation of victimization patterns, which is of assistance to understand the ecosystem of commoditized DDoS attacks. Santanna et al. [14] subscribed DDoS attacks from fourteen Booters to capture the real attack data and performed an analysis of attack characteristics of fourteen Booter services. The above works are very insightful and significant, but we also need more novel and in-depth research about the mitigation of Booter services or amplification DDoS attacks.

3   The Proposed Approach

We firstly describe the overall structure of our Booter list generation system in Sect. 3.1. Then, we describe the details of our feature selection method in Sect. 3.2.

3.1   Booter List Generation System

Our system contains two components (see Fig. 1): a crawler and a classifier. The crawler collects the suspect Booter URLs and related webpages. The classifier identifies whether a suspect URL is a Booter website based on the content (text) characteristics of the webpage. The crawler firstly collects the suspect Booter URLs from Google search engine by using relevant keywords. The total number of suspect Booter URLs is 718, which contain 51 Booter URLs. Then, the crawler acquires webpages based on the suspect Booter URLs. Sometimes, the webpage of a URL is missing, in this case, the crawler acquires webpages from web cache, which is always provided by search engines. The classifier contains three steps: feature preprocessing, feature selection and classification. In the step of feature preprocessing, we extract the content (text), remove stop words and use bag-of-words model to preprocess the above webpages. However, the feature vector of every document (webpage) using the bag-of-words model is sparse and high dimensional. Therefore, feature selection is a very important step for text classification and it ensures that the features which are most relevant to particular class labels can be picked out for model training. In the step of classification, we use Linear Support Vector Machine (LSVM) and Multinomial Naïve Bayes (MNB), which are efficient classifiers in text categorization, to classify Booters.

3.2   Feature Selection Method

Our method is a filter-based feature selection method, which just relies on the properties of the data and independent of any classification algorithm. There are some commonly used feature selection methods such as Information Gain [11], improved Gini Index [16] and Chi-square [19]. Information Gain and Chi-square

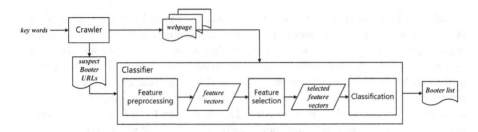

Fig. 1. The overview of Booter list generation system

are the two most effective feature selection methods [19]. Improved Gini index is an improved feature selection based on Gini index and it is reported that improved Gini Index perform more effective than Information Gain and Chi-square [16]. The feature selection methods usually consider the probability of class c_i when term t_k is present or absent, and select the representative terms of a class. However, they may ignore the differences in the distribution of different categories on a feature (term). Inspired by [17], we use centroid u_{ik} and standard deviation sd_{ik} as the representative of the distribution of class c_i on a feature (term) t_k. Mathematically, we define global inter-category distance as:

$$GD_k = \frac{1}{\sum_{i=1}^{N} sd_{ik}} \sum_{i=1}^{N} \sum_{j=i+1}^{N} |u_{ik} - u_{jk}| \tag{1}$$

where N is the number of categories. We now present the algorithm based on global inter-category distance as follows (see Algorithm 1).

Algorithm 1. Global inter-category distance algorithm

Input: D - the preprocessed data set, K - the requested number of
          features

Output: S - the selected feature subset

1 **foreach** *class c_i* **do**
2   **foreach** *term t_k* **do**
3   obtains the centroid u_{ik} and standard deviation sd_{ik} of class c_i ;
4   **end**
5 **end**
6 **foreach** *term t_k* **do**
7   calculates the GD_k of term t_k by using Equation (1);
8 **end**
9 arranges all terms in descending order based on their GD_k;
10 selects top-K terms into S;
11 return S;

Global inter-category distance algorithm firstly obtains centroid u_{ik} and standard deviation sd_{ik} for each class, then calculates the sum of the distance between different category pairs (Eq. (1)), and finally selects top-K features (terms) based on the score of our metric method. However, the above method may have a problem that sometimes a class is lack of their representative features and is difficult for the classifier to distinguish it. The global inter-category distance method may neglect the distance between a specific category and others, and cause an imbalance problem in text categorization [18]. Thus, it is necessary to ensure the balance of representative features for each class. To solve this problem, We define type-based inter-category distance as:

$$TD_{ik} = \frac{1}{\sum_{i=1}^{N} sd_{ik}} \sum_{j=1}^{N} |u_{ik} - u_{jk}| \tag{2}$$

For each class c_i, we calculate the distance TD_{ik} between this class and others, then average the requested number of features to each class to ensure the balance of their representative features. It ensures that every class obtains equal and enough representative features. We now prestent the feature selection algorithm based on type-based inter-category distance as follows (see Algorithm 2).

Algorithm 2. Type-based inter-category distance algorithm

    Input: D - the preprocessed data set, K - the requested number of
           features
    Output: S - the selected feature subset
 1 averages the requested number of features and sets the selected number of
   each class c_i as n_i;
 2 **foreach** *class* c_i **do**
 3   **foreach** *term* t_k **do**
 4   obtains the centroid u_{ik} and standard deviation sd_{ik} of class c_i ;
 5   **end**
 6 **end**
 7 **foreach** *class* c_i **do**
 8   **foreach** *term* t_k **do**
 9   calculates the TD_{ik} of term t_k by using Equation (2);
10   **end**
11   arranges all terms in descending order based on their TD_{ik};
12   selects top-n_i terms into S;
13 **end**
14 return S;

The feature selection algorithm based on type-based inter-category distance ensures the balance of representative features for each class. However, we also want to pick out the features that are discriminative for all of the categories besides selecting the balanced and representative features for each class. Thus, we combine global distance with type-based distance, and define combined inter-category distance as:

$$CD_{ik} = \frac{2GD_k}{N(N-1)} + \frac{TD_{ik}}{N-1} \tag{3}$$

We replace the Eq. (2) in Algorithm 2 with Eq. (3) to get another feature selection algorithm and compare these three methods in Chap. 4.

4   Experiments

In this Section, we use three datasets to fully verify the presented feature selection algorithm, and show the experiment results on Booter websites, 20-Newsgroups and WebKB datasets in Sects. 4.1, 4.2 and 4.3, respectively. Finally, we discuss the above experiments in Sect. 4.4.

4.1   Booter Websites

The total number of the collected suspect Booter URLs is 718, which contain 51 Booter URLs. We also acquired webpages based on the suspect Booter URLs. We extracted the content (text), removed stop words and used bag-of-words model to preprocess the webpages. After that, the dimension of the features is 66448. This dataset is small, thus, we adopted LeaveOneOut in this experiment. According to [15], we define classification accuracy metrics as following:

- True positive (T_P): The number of Booter websites are correctly classified as Booter
- True negative (T_N): The number of non-Booter websites are correctly classified as non-Booter
- False positive (F_P): The number of non-Booter websites are incorrectly classified as Booter
- False negative (F_N): The number of Booter websites are incorrectly classified as non-Booter.

$$CAR = \frac{T_P + T_N}{n} \tag{4}$$

$$FP_{er} = \frac{F_P}{n} \tag{5}$$

$$FN_{er} = \frac{F_N}{n} \tag{6}$$

Where n is the total number of the collected suspect Booter websites. CAR is classification accuracy rate, FP_{er} is false positive error rate, FN_{er} is false negative error rate. In order to evaluate the performance of the proposed method, we used Linear Support Vector Machine (LSVM) and Multinomial Naïve Bayes (MNB), which are efficient classifiers in text categorization.

The performance curves of LSVM classifier are drawn in Fig. 2. We compare global distance method with Information Gain, improved Gini Index and Chi-square. This data set has only two categories, and it's no need to use type-based distance method or combined distance method, which are suitable for multi-category tasks. Figure 2(a) shows that the CAR performance of using global distance method is superior to other feature selection methods when the number of selected features is 50 and greater than 1000. It acquires the highest value, 97.91%, when the number of selected features is 5000. Figure 2(b) indicates that FP_{er} of using global distance method is less than other feature selection methods when the number of selected features is 50 and greater than 1000. It reaches 0.69%, the lowest value, when the number of selected features is 5000. Figure 2(c) shows FN_{er} performance based on global distance method is less than other feature selection methods when the number of selected features is greater than 800. It reaches 1.25%, the lowest value, when the number of selected features is 6000. Thus, the experiments show that global distance method using LSVM classifier produces highest CAR values in 7 out of 12 cases, lowest FP_{er} values in 7 out of 12 cases, and lowest FN_{er} values in 7 out of 12 cases.

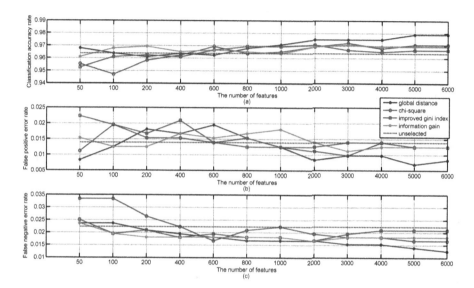

Fig. 2. The performance curves of LSVM classifier on Booter websites. (a) The curves of classification accuracy rate; (b) The curves of false positive error rate; (c) The curves of false negative error rate

The performance curves of MNB classifier are drawn in Fig. 3. Figure 3(a) shows that the CAR performance of using global distance method is superior to other feature selection methods except when the number of selected features is 6000. It acquires the highest value, 98.74%, when the number of selected features is 800. Figure 3(b) indicates that FP_{er} of using global distance method is less than other feature selection methods in all cases. It reaches 0.0%, the lowest value, when the number of selected features is from 600 to 6000. Figure 3(c) shows FN_{er} performance based on global distance method is less than or equal to other feature selection methods when the number of selected features is 400, 600, 800, 3000, 4000. It reaches 1.25%, the lowest value, when the number of selected features is 600. Thus, the experiments show that global distance method using MNB classifier produces highest CAR values in 11 out of 12 cases, lowest FP_{er} values in 12 out of 12 cases, and lowest FN_{er} values in 5 out of 12 cases.

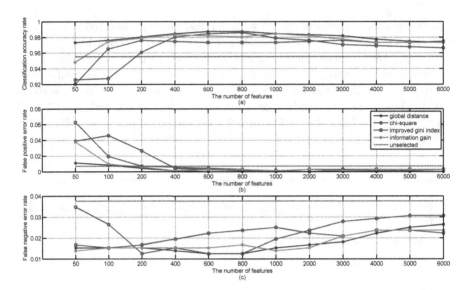

Fig. 3. The performance curves of MNB classifier on Booter websites. (a) The curves of classification accuracy rate; (b) The curves of false positive error rate; (c) The curves of false negative error rate

4.2   20-Newsgroups

The 20-Newsgroups [2] dataset collects about 20,000 newsgroup documents and is evenly divided into 20 different categories. It is a popular data set for experiments in text categorization. In this experiment, we used bydate version of the data set, which contains 18846 documents and is sorted by date into training (60%) and test (40%) sets. We removed stop words and used bag-of-words model to preprocess the data set. After that, the dimension of the features is 129326. Macro-F1 and Micro-F1 were used to evaluate the performance of different feature selection methods.

The performance curves of LSVM classifier on 20-Newsgroups are drawn in Fig. 4. Figure 4(a) shows that the macro-F1 performance of using combined distance method is superior to the three classical feature selection methods when the number of selected features is greater than 1000. Among the three distance methods, combined distance method and type-based distance method are always superior to global distance method. Combined method is a bit superior to type-based method when the number of selected features is small, and there is no obvious difference between the two methods when the number of selected features is large. Figure 4(b) shows that the micro-F1 performance of using combined distance method is superior to other three feature selection methods when the number of selected features is greater than 2000. Among the three distance methods, combined distance method and type-based distance method are superior to global distance method except when the number of selected features is 100, 200 and 800. Combined method is a bit superior to type-based method

when the number of selected features is small, and there is no obvious difference between the two methods when the number of selected features is large.
Thus, the experiments show that distance method using LSVM classifier produces highest macro-F1 values in 10 out of 16 cases and highest micro-F1 values
in 9 out of 16 cases.

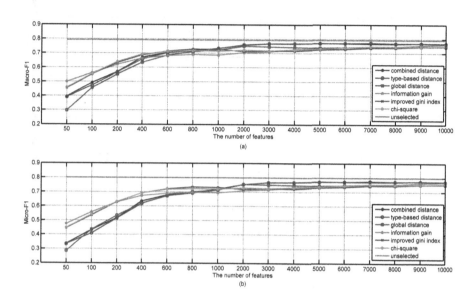

Fig. 4. The performance curves of LSVM classifier on 20-Newsgroups. (a) The curves
of Macro-F1; (b) The curves of Micro-F1

The performance curves of MNB classifier on 20-Newsgroups are drawn in
Fig. 5. Figure 5(a) shows that the macro-F1 performance of using combined distance method outperforms other three feature selection methods when the number of selected features is greater than 4000. Among the three distance methods,
combined distance method and type-based distance method outperform global
distance method except when the number of selected features is 600, 800 and
1000. Combined method is a bit superior to type-based method when the number of selected features is small, and there is no obvious difference between the
two methods when the number of selected features is large. Figure 5(b) shows
that the micro-F1 performance of using combined distance method is superior
to other three feature selection methods when the number of selected features
is greater than 4000. Among the three distance methods, CD method and TD
distance method outperform GD method except when the number of selected
features is 100, 200, 600, 800 and 1000. Combined method is a bit superior to
type-based method when the number of selected features is small, and there is
no obvious difference between the two methods when the number of selected
features is large. Thus, the experiments show that distance method using MNB

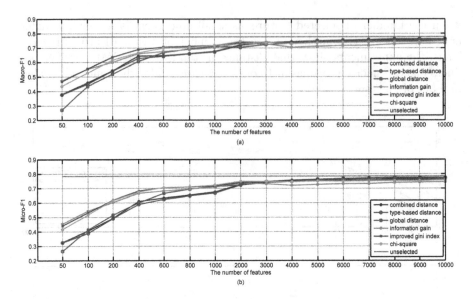

Fig. 5. The performance curves of MNB classifier on 20-Newsgroups. (a) The curves of Macro-F1; (b) The curves of Micro-F1

classifier produces highest macro-F1 values in 7 out of 16 cases and highest micro-F1 values in 7 out of 16 cases.

4.3   WebKB

The WebKB [1] dataset is also a popular data set for experiments in text categorization, which collects 8282 webpages from four different college websites. These webpages are unevenly divided into 7 categories: student (1641), faculty (1124), staff (137), department (182), course (930), project (504), other (3764). In the experiment, we just selected 4 categories: course, faculty, project and student. We removed stop words and used bag-of-words model to preprocess the data set. After that, the dimension of the features is 48909. Macro-F1 and Micro-F1 were used to evaluate the performance of different feature selection methods. 10-fold validation was adopted in this experiment.

The performance curves of LSVM classifier on WebKB are drawn in Fig. 6. It can be seen from Fig. 6(a) that the macro-F1 curve of using combined distance method is always higher than other three classical feature selection methods except that the number of selected features is 100. Among the three distance methods, these curves are indented and intertwined. However, averaged macro-F1 value of TD method is higher than GD method, and CD method is higher than TD method. Figure 6(b) shows the same situation as Fig. 6(a). Thus, the experiments show that distance method using LSVM classifier produces highest macro-F1 values in 9 out of 10 cases and highest micro-F1 values in 9 out of 10 cases.

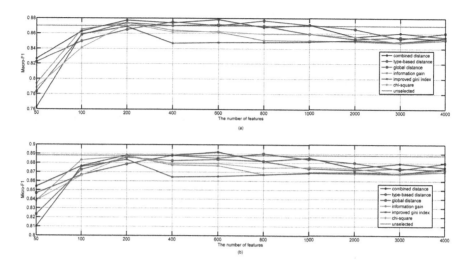

Fig. 6. The performance curves of LSVM classifier on WebKB. (a) The curves of Macro-F1; (b) The curves of Micro-F1

The performance curves of MNB classifier on WebKB are drawn in Fig. 7. It can be seen from Fig. 7(a) that the macro-F1 curve of using combined distance method is higher than other three classical feature selection methods except that the number of selected features is 2000, 3000, 4000. The macro-F1 curves of the three distance methods are also indented and intertwined. However, averaged macro-F1 value of TD method is higher than GD method, and CD method is higher than TD method. Figure 7(b) also shows the same situation as Fig. 7(a). Thus, the experiments show that distance method using MNB classifier produces highest macro-F1 values in 7 out of 10 cases and highest micro-F1 values in 7 out of 10 cases.

4.4   Discussion

The results of Booter websites, 20-Newsgroups and WebKB show that our method outperforms the other metrics in 68.05%, 51.56% and 80.00% cases, respectively. In general, our method produced the highest F1 values in 66% of the classification cases. In the experiment of Booter websites, MNB classifier is more effective than LSVM classifier, and it acquired the highest CAR value, 98.74%. In the experiment of balanced dataset like 20-Newsgroups, we observe that the distance method is not very effective compared with the classical algorithms when the number of selected features is small, however, the distance method perform more effectively and get close to the upper unselected curves earlier when the number of selected features increases. In the experiment of skewed dataset lisk WebKB, we observe that the distance method is very effective in most cases. Among three distance methods, combined distance method and type-based distance method outperform global distance method in most

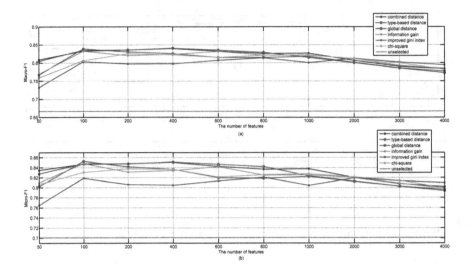

Fig. 7. The performance curves of MNB classifier on WebKB. (a) The curves of Macro-F1; (b) The curves of Micro-F1

cases especially when the number of selected features is very small, and they improve the imbalance problem. In general, combined distance method is also a bit superior to type-based distance method.

5   Conclusion

Booter is increasingly becoming a popular way to launch DDoS attacks, however, there is not much research on Booter and we know little about the ecosystem of these Booter services. In this paper, we develop a new Booter classifier based on text characteristics, which is different from previous work and enrich the methods of identifying Booters. The experiments show that the Booter classifier based on text characteristics has a classification accuracy of 98.74%. We also propose a new feature selection algorithm, which uses the distance between the different categories on a term and select more discriminative features, to improve the performance of text classification. The proposed method is superior to the several classical methods on Booter websites, 20 newsgroups and WebKB dataset in 66% of the classification cases.

Acknowledgement. This paper is Supported by National Key Research and Development Program of China under Grant No. 2017YFB0803003 and National Science Foundation for Young Scientists of China (Grant No. 61702507).

References

1. The 4 universities data set (1998). http://www.cs.cmu.edu/afs/cs.cmu.edu/project/theo-20/www/data/. Accessed 4 June 2018
2. Home page for 20 newsgroups data set (2008). http://www.qwone.com/~jason/20Newsgroups/. Accessed 4 June 2018
3. Akamai: Third quarter 2016 state of the internet/security report (2016). https://www.akamai.com/us/en/about/news/press/2016-press/akamai-releases-third-quarter-2016-state-of-the-internet-security-report.jsp. Accessed 4 July 2018
4. Goodin, D.: US service provider survives the biggest recorded DDoS in history (2018). https://arstechnica.com/information-technology/2018/03/us-service-provider-survives-the-biggest-recorded-ddos-in-history/. Accessed 4 July 2018
5. Karami, M., Park, Y., McCoy, D.: Stress testing the booters: understanding and undermining the business of DDoS services. In: Proceedings of the 25th International Conference on World Wide Web, pp. 1033–1043. International World Wide Web Conferences Steering Committee (2016)
6. Krämer, L., et al.: AmpPot: monitoring and defending against amplification DDoS attacks. In: Bos, H., Monrose, F., Blanc, G. (eds.) RAID 2015. LNCS, vol. 9404, pp. 615–636. Springer, Cham (2015). https://doi.org/10.1007/978-3-319-26362-5_28
7. Krupp, J., Backes, M., Rossow, C.: Identifying the scan and attack infrastructures behind amplification DDoS attacks. In: Proceedings of the 2016 ACM SIGSAC Conference on Computer and Communications Security, pp. 1426–1437. ACM (2016)
8. Krupp, J., Karami, M., Rossow, C., McCoy, D., Backes, M.: Linking amplification DDoS attacks to booter services. In: Dacier, M., Bailey, M., Polychronakis, M., Antonakakis, M. (eds.) RAID 2017. LNCS, vol. 10453, pp. 427–449. Springer, Cham (2017). https://doi.org/10.1007/978-3-319-66332-6_19
9. Noroozian, A., Korczyński, M., Gañan, C.H., Makita, D., Yoshioka, K., van Eeten, M.: Who gets the boot? Analyzing victimization by DDoS-as-a-Service. In: Monrose, F., Dacier, M., Blanc, G., Garcia-Alfaro, J. (eds.) RAID 2016. LNCS, vol. 9854, pp. 368–389. Springer, Cham (2016). https://doi.org/10.1007/978-3-319-45719-2_17
10. Prince, M.: Technical details behind a 400 Gbps NTP amplification DDoS attack (2014). https://blog.cloudflare.com/technical-details-behind-a-400gbps-ntp-amplification-ddos-attack/. Accessed 4 July 2018
11. Quinlan, J.R.: Induction of decision trees. Mach. Learn. 1(1), 81–106 (1986)
12. Santanna, J.J.: DDoS-as-a-Service: investigating booter websites. Ph.D. thesis. University of Twente, Enschede, The Netherlands (2017). https://doi.org/10.3990/1.9789036544290
13. Santanna, J.J.: Booters (black)list and ecosystem analysis (2018). https://jjsantanna.github.io/booters_ecosystem_analysis/. Accessed 4 July 2018
14. Santanna, J.J., et al.: Booters—an analysis of DDoS-as-a-Service attacks. In: 2015 IFIP/IEEE International Symposium on Integrated Network Management, IM, pp. 243–251. IEEE (2015)
15. Santanna, J.J., de Vries, J., de O. Schmidt, R., Tuncer, D., Granville, L.Z., Pras, A.: Booter list generation: the basis for investigating DDoS-for-hire websites. Int. J. Netw. Manag. 28(1), e2008 (2018)
16. Shang, W., Huang, H., Zhu, H., Lin, Y., Qu, Y., Wang, Z.: A novel feature selection algorithm for text categorization. Expert Syst. Appl. 33(1), 1–5 (2007)

17. Yan, J., et al.: OCFS: optimal orthogonal centroid feature selection for text catego-
    rization. In: Proceedings of the 28th Annual International ACM SIGIR Conference
    on Research and Development in Information Retrieval, pp. 122–129. ACM (2005)
18. Yang, J., Qu, Z., Liu, Z.: Improved feature-selection method considering the imbal-
    ance problem in text categorization. Sci. World J. **2014**(3) (2014)
19. Yang, Y., Pedersen, J.O.: A comparative study on feature selection in text catego-
    rization. In: ICML, vol. 97, pp. 412–420 (1997)

A 2D Transform Based Distance Function for Time Series Classification

Cun Ji[1,4(✉)], Xiunan Zou[1], Yupeng Hu[2(✉)], and Shijun Liu[2,3(✉)]

[1] School of Information Science and Engineering, Shandong Normal University,
Jinan, China
`jicun@sdnu.edu.cn, Parker_nan@163.com`
[2] School of Software, Shandong University, Jinan, China
`{huyupeng,lsj}@sdu.edu.cn`
[3] Engineering Research Center of Digital Media Technology,
Ministry of Education, Jinan, China
[4] Shandong Provincial Key Laboratory of Software Engineering,
Shandong University, Jinan, China

Abstract. Along with the arrival of Industry 4.0 era, time series classification (TSC) has attracted a lot of attention in the last decade. The high dimensionality, high feature correlation and typically high levels of noise that found in time series bring great challenges to TSC. Among TSC algorithms, the 1NN classifier has been shown as effective and difficult to beat. The core of the 1NN classifier is the distance function. The large majority of TSC have concentrated on alternative distance functions. In this paper, a two-dimensional (2D) transform based distance (2DTbD) function is proposed. There are three steps in 2DTbD. Firstly, we convert time series to 2D space by turing time series around the coordinate origin. Then we calculate distances of each dimension. Finally, we ensemble distances in 2D space to get the final time series distance. Our distance function raises the accuracy rate through the fusion of 2D information. Experimental results demonstrate that the classification accuracy can be improved by 2DTbD.

Keywords: Internet of Things · Data mining ·
Time series classification · 2D transform · Distance function

1 Introduction

The Internet of things (IoT) is made up of small sensors and actuators embedded in objects with internet access [20]. It plays a key role in solving challenges faced in today's society [22,34]. Usually, sensors in an IoT system collect data with equal intervals. Data collection in an IoT system is time series data.

Time series is always considered as a whole instead of individual numerical field. Time series has attracted significant interests in the data mining community [30,40]. A time series analysis foresees tasks such as: indexing, representation, pattern discovery, clustering, classification, anomaly detection [13,15].

© ICST Institute for Computer Sciences, Social Informatics and Telecommunications Engineering 2019
Published by Springer Nature Switzerland AG 2019. All Rights Reserved
H. Gao et al. (Eds.): CollaborateCom 2018, LNICST 268, pp. 543–559, 2019.
https://doi.org/10.1007/978-3-030-12981-1_38

As a fundamental research, time series classification (TSC) has been studied extensively. In TSC, an unlabeled time series is assigned to one of two or more predefined classes. The high dimensionality, high feature correlation and typically high levels of noise bring great challenges to TSC [21,23,39]. Now, TSC arises in many real world fields [29], such as: electrocardiogram classification, fault detection and identification of physical systems, automotive preventive diagnosis, gesture recognition, alarm interpretation of telecommunication networks, data sensor analysis, speaker identification and/or authentication, aerospace health monitoring.

A lot of TSC algorithms have been proposed. Among TSC algorithms, the 1NN classifier with dynamic time warping (DTW, [6]) has been shown as effective and difficult to beat [5,12,36]. The core of the 1NN classifier is the distance function. The large majority of TSC have concentrated on alternative distance functions [1,3].

In this paper, a new distance function based on 2D transform is proposed. This distance function raises the accuracy rate through the fusion of 2D information. The contributions of this paper can be summarized as follows:

1. We introduce a 2D transform method for time series. The 2D transform method can transform time series into a 2D space.
2. We propose a 2D transform based distance (2DTbD) function. The 2DTbD function calculates distance between two time series using information after 2D transform.
3. We evaluate 2DTbD on 43 data sets from UCR Time Series Classification Archive [9]. The experimental results show that our distance function is more accurate.

The rest of this paper is structured as follows. Section 2 discusses some related work on TSC. In Sect. 3, we describe how to classification time series using 1NN classifier with 2DTbD, 2D transform is also given in this section. Experimental results are presented in Sect. 4, and our conclusions are given in Sect. 5.

2 Related Work

In recent years, many new distance functions are proposed to measure similarity between two time series [10]. These distance functions can be divided into two categories: time domain distance functions and differential distance functions.

Suppose there are two time series, T and R of length m as (1) (2), the distance $d(T, R)$ between them can be measured by distance functions. Next, we'll describe how to calculate distance $d(T, R)$.

$$T = (t_1, t_2, \cdots, t_i, \cdots, t_m) \tag{1}$$
$$R = (r_1, r_2, \cdots, r_i, \cdots, r_m) \tag{2}$$

2.1 Time Domain Distance Functions

2.1.1 Euclidean Distance Function

A benchmark distance function is Euclidean distance (EU, [14]). The function of EU is described as (3). EU is only used to calculate the distance between two time series whose lengths are equal [32]. It is sensitive to outliers.

$$d_{EU}(T, R) = \sqrt{\sum_{i=1}^{m}(t_i - r_i)^2} \tag{3}$$

Base on EU, L_p norm distance (L_p norm, [37]) function is proposed. The function of L_p norm is described as (4). EU is a special case of L_p norm when p is 2. L_p norm is also sensitive to outliers.

$$d_{L_p norm}(T, R) = \sqrt[p]{\sum_{i=1}^{m}(t_i - r_i)^p} \tag{4}$$

2.1.2 Dynamic Time Warping Function

An other benchmark distance function is DTW. DTW is not sensitive to distortions in time dimension. The function of DTW is described as (5), (6) and (7). In (5), n is the length of T, m is the length of R. In (6) and (7), i and j should meet the conditions in (8).

$$d_{DTW}(T, R) = \sqrt{f(n, m)} \tag{5}$$
$$f(i, j) = (t_i - t_j)^2 + min\left(f(i, j-1), f(i-1, j), f(i-1, j-1)\right) \tag{6}$$
$$f(0, 0) = 0, \quad f(i, 0) = f(0, j) = \infty \tag{7}$$
$$0 < i \leq n \& 0 < j \leq m \tag{8}$$

The time complexity of DTW is $O(n^2)$. By using some constraint techniques, such as Sakoe–Chuba Band [31] and Itakura Parallelogram [18], the time complexity of DTW can be reduced [19]. Some lower bounding functions are introduced to speed up DTW, such as LB_Kim [26], LB_Yi [38], LB_Keogh [24]. Salvador and Chan introduce FastDTW [33], which is an accurate approximation of DTW that runs in linear time and space.

2.1.3 Other Time Domain Distance Functions

Besides EU and DTW, there are some alternative techniques taken from other fields [3], such as edit distance with real penalty (ERP, [7]) and longest common subsequence (LCSS, [11]). Marteau proposes the time warp edit (TWE) distance [28]. TWE is an elastic distance metric, which includes characteristics from LCSS and DTW. Stefan et al. propose the Move-Split-Merge (MSM) distance [35]. MSM is similar to other edit distance based distance function. MSM uses three fundamental operations: Move, Split, and Merge. These operations can be used to transform a time series into a target series.

2.2   Differential Distance Functions

Usually, the differential distance functions base on the values in the time domain and the difference domain. The first order differences of time series $T = (t_1, t_2, \cdots, t_i, \cdots, t_m)$ are calculated as (9).

$$t_i' = t_i - t_{i+1}, i = 1, 2, \cdots, m - 1 \tag{9}$$

2.2.1   Complexity Invariant Distance Function

Batista et al. propose complexity invariant distance (CID) [4]. CID uses the sum of squares of the first differences as a measure of complexity. The function of CID is described as (10), (11) and (12). In (10), $d(T, R)$ can be EU or DTW. In (11) and (12), t_i' and r_i' are calculated as (9).

$$d_{CID}(T, R) = d(T, R) * \frac{max(CE(T), CE(R))}{min(CE(T), CE(R))} \tag{10}$$

$$CE(T) = \sqrt{\sum_{i=1}^{m-1} t_i'} \tag{11}$$

$$CE(R) = \sqrt{\sum_{i=1}^{m-1} r_i'} \tag{12}$$

2.2.2   Derivative Distance Function

Górecki and Łuczak propose derivative distance (DD) [16]. DD uses a weighted combination of raw time series and first order differences. The function of DD is described as (13). In (13), T' and R' are the first order differences of time series T and R, respectively. The values in T' and R' is calculated as (9). In (13), the dist function for raw time series or first order differences is basic distance function, such as EU, DTW.

$$d_{DD}(T, R) = \alpha * d(T, R) + (1 - \alpha) * d(T', R') \quad (0 \le \alpha \le 1) \tag{13}$$

2.2.3   Derivative Transform Distance Function

Based on derivatives and transforms of time series, Górecki and Łuczak propose derivative transform distance (DTD) [17]. DTD is an extension of DD. The function of DTD is described as (14).

$$d_{DTD}(T, R) = \alpha * d(T, R) + (1 - \alpha) * d(f(T), f(R)) \quad (0 \le \alpha \le 1) \tag{14}$$

In (14), $f(T)$ and $f(R)$ are the transform of time series T and R, respectively. In addition to first order differences, DTD can use cosine transform, sine transform or Hilbert transform. For $T = (t_1, \cdots, t_i, \cdots, t_m)$, the transform is represented as $f(T) = (f(t_1), \cdots, f(t_k), \cdots, f(t_m))$. For $f(t_k)$, cosine transform, sine transform and Hilbert transform are calculated as (15), (16) and (17), respectively.

$$f_{cos}(t_k) = \sum_{i=1}^{m} t_i * cos\left[\frac{\pi}{m} * \left(i - \frac{1}{2}\right) * (k - 1)\right] \tag{15}$$

$$f_{sin}(t_k) = \sum_{i=1}^{m} t_i * sin\left[\frac{\pi}{m} * \left(i - \frac{1}{2}\right) * k)\right] \tag{16}$$

$$f_{Hilbert}(t_k) = \sum_{i=1, i \neq k}^{m} \frac{t_i}{k - i} \tag{17}$$

3   1NN Classifier with 2DTbD

We select the 1NN classifier with our distance function to classify time series. As Fig. 1 shows, there are mainly two processes to classify one time series: (1) 2D transform and (2) classification.

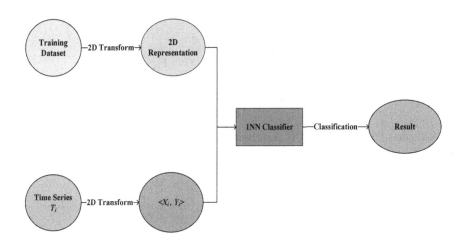

Fig. 1. Processes of classification based on 2D transform

3.1   2D Transform

Recently, many researchers convert the shapes into time series (read [5,8,25] for detail). The distance from each point to the center of gravity is calculated as value of time series. A demo of how convert a shape into time series is shown in Fig. 2. This demo refers to [25].

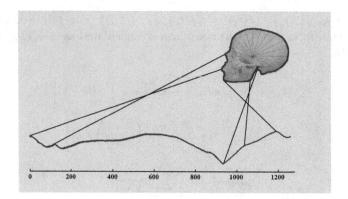

Fig. 2. A demo of how convert a shape into time series

2D transform acts in a diametrically opposite way. 2D transform turns time series around the coordinate origin. In this way, time series $T = (t_1, \cdots, t_i, \cdots, t_m)$ is converted into a 2D space. We use 2D representation $< X, Y >$ to represent T. The value x_i in $X = (x_1, \cdots, x_i, \cdots, x_m)$ is calculated as (18), the value y_i in $Y = (y_1, \cdots, y_i, \cdots, y_m)$ is calculated as (19). In (18) and (19), m is the length of time series T.

$$x(i) = t_i * cos\left[\frac{2 * \pi}{m} * (i - 1)\right] \qquad (18)$$

$$y(i) = t_i * sin\left[\frac{2 * \pi}{m} * (i - 1)\right] \qquad (19)$$

A demo of 2D transform is shown in Fig. 3. In Fig. 3(a), there are two time series, T_1 and T_2. Figure 3(b) shows 2D representation $< X_1, Y_1 >$ of T_1 and $< X_2, Y_2 >$ of T_2.

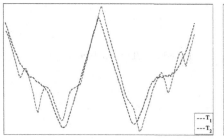

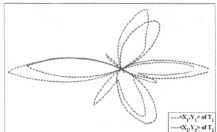

(a) Two time series, T_1 and T_2 (b) 2D representation for T_1 and T_2

Fig. 3. A demo of 2D transform

3.2 1NN Classifier with 2DTbD

After 2D transform, we use 1NN classifier with 2DTbD to classify the 2D representation of time series. 1NN classifier for 2D representation is shown in Algorithm 1. In Algorithm 1, we input 2D representation $< X, Y >$ of time series T and 2D representation of the training data set $2DTrain$. We calculate the dist between $< X, Y >$ and every 2D representation in $2DTrain$. We record the minimum distance $minDist$ and the corresponding class label C_T. Finally, the class label C_T is return as the classification result.

Algorithm 1. 1NN classifier for 2D representation

Input: 2D representation of time series T: $< X, Y >$, 2D representation of training
 data set: $2DTrain$
Output: Class label of T: c_T
1: $miDist = +\infty$
2: **for** each $(< X_i, Y_i >, c_i)$ in $2DTrain$ **do**
3:   $dist = d_{2DTbD}(< X, Y >, < X_i, Y_i >)$;
4:   **if** $(dist < mixDist)$ **then**
5:    $minDist = dist$
6:    $c_T = c_i$
7:   **end if**
8: **end for**
9: **return** c_T

In line 3 of Algorithm 1, 2DTbD is calculated. Calculation processes for 2DTbD are shown in Fig. 4. In Fig. 4, there are two time series, T_i and T_j. The 2D representation of them are $< X_i, Y_i >$ and $< X_j, Y_j >$, respectively. As Fig. 4 shows, there are mainly two steps to calculate 2DTbD:

Step 1: Calculate distance of each dimension. Each dimension is viewed as a new time series, we calculate $d(X_i, X_j)$ in X dimension and $d(Y_i, Y_j)$ in Y dimension by time series distance function, such as EU, L_p norm, DTW, ERP, CID.

Step 2: Calculate 2DTbD by ensemble dimension distances. As (20) shows, we use the means of $d(X_i, X_j)$ in X dimension and $d(Y_i, Y_j)$ in Y dimension as the distance of time series.

$$d_{2DTbD}(T_i, T_j) = \frac{d(X_i, X_j) + d(Y_i, Y_j)}{2} \qquad (20)$$

4 Experiments

4.1 Experimental Setup

– **Data sets.** We performed experiments on 43 data sets from the UCR Time Series Classification Archive [9]. We used the UCR Time Series Classification

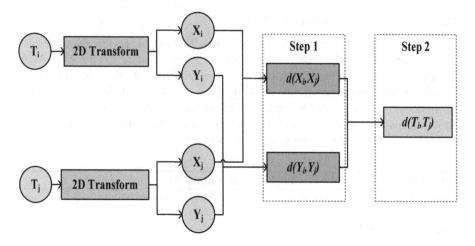

Fig. 4. Calculation processes for 2DTbD

Archive for two reasons [22,27]: (1) This archive has a large number of publicly accessible data sets; (2) These data sets cover a wide range of domains, from environmental monitoring to medical diagnosis.

- **Evaluation criterion.** We use error rate err as an evaluation criterion. The err is calculated as (21). In (21), n is the number of time series in test data set, n_{err} is the number of time series which is divided into an error class. The smaller err is, the better classifier effects.

$$err = \frac{n_{err}}{n} \tag{21}$$

- **Comparison distance functions.** We select CID, ERP and DTW as comparison distance functions. CID is presentation for differential distance functions. DTW and ERP is representant for time domain distance functions. Aslo, DTW is a benchmark distance function for time series.
- **Algorithm code.** We implemented our algorithm based on code that is freely accessible from an online repository [2]. **In order to promote reproducibility, our code and detailed results are open**[1]. Our code is carried out in Java using MyEclipse with JDK 1.8.

4.2   Contrast Experiments Between CID and 2DTbD$_{CID}$

When 2DTbD uses CID for each dimension, we call it 2DTbD$_{CID}$. In this subsection, we will contrast CID with 2DTbD$_{CID}$. As (10) in Sect. 2.2.1 shows, CID is based on EU or DTW, we call them CID$_{EU}$ or CID$_{DTW}$. Our distance function uses CID$_{EU}$ or CID$_{DTW}$ for each dimension, then we get 2DTbD$_{CIDEU}$ or 2DTbD$_{CIDDTW}$.

---

[1] Web page for our code: https://github.com/sdujicun/XY.

4.2.1 Contrasting CID$_{EU}$ with 2DTbD$_{CIDEU}$

Table 1 lists the classification error rates of 1NN classifier with CID$_{EU}$ or 2DTbD$_{CIDEU}$. The lower error rate for each data set is given in bold. As Table 1 shows, 1NN classifier with 2DTbD$_{CIDEU}$ produced better accuracy on 26 data sets, whereas 1NN classifier with CID$_{EU}$ was better on 10 and these two classifiers tied on the other 7 data sets.

To show the differences better, the data in Table 1 is drawn in Fig. 5. In Fig. 5, the points at the bottom left of the blue line indicate cases where 2DTbD$_{CIDEU}$ achieves a lower error rate than CID$_{EU}$. Most points is in the bottom left of the blue line.

Table 1. The error rates of 1NN classifier with CID$_{EU}$ or 2DTbD$_{CIDEU}$

Data set	CID$_{EU}$	2DTbD$_{CIDEU}$	Data set	CID$_{EU}$	2DTbD$_{CIDEDEU}$
Adiac	**0.371**	0.376	Lightning7	0.479	**0.411**
Beef	**0.367**	**0.367**	Mallat	0.078	**0.074**
Car	**0.267**	**0.267**	MedicalImages	0.308	**0.301**
CBF	0.018	**0.017**	MoteStrain	0.248	**0.221**
Chlorine	0.355	**0.351**	NonThorax1	0.160	**0.133**
CinCECG	0.112	**0.074**	NonThorax2	0.120	**0.108**
Coffee	**0.000**	**0.000**	OliveOil	**0.133**	**0.133**
CricketX	0.400	**0.390**	OSULeaf	**0.413**	0.430
CricketY	0.492	**0.418**	Plane	**0.029**	**0.029**
CricketZ	0.451	**0.415**	SonySurface1	**0.160**	0.180
DiatomSize	**0.059**	0.062	SonySurface2	0.114	**0.111**
ECGFiveDays	**0.246**	0.249	StarCurves	**0.041**	0.053
FaceAll	0.287	**0.221**	SwedishLeaf	0.126	**0.120**
FaceFour	**0.205**	0.250	Symbols	0.088	**0.062**
FacesUCR	0.266	**0.223**	Synthetic	0.073	**0.067**
FiftyWords	0.338	**0.330**	Trace	0.130	**0.110**
Fish	**0.217**	**0.217**	TwoLeadECG	**0.229**	**0.229**
GunPoint	0.080	**0.073**	TwoPatterns	0.157	**0.114**
Haptics	**0.562**	0.571	Wafer	**0.008**	0.009
InlineSkate	0.615	**0.613**	WordSyn	0.361	**0.354**
ItalyPower	0.042	**0.035**	Yoga	**0.165**	0.168
Lightning2	0.328	**0.213**			

The results in Table 1 and Fig. 5 demonstrate that 2DTbD$_{CIDEU}$ works better than CID$_{EU}$.

4.2.2 Contrasting CID$_{DTW}$ with 2DTbD$_{CIDDTW}$

Table 2 lists the classification error rates of 1NN classifier with CID$_{DTW}$ or 2DTbD$_{CIDDTW}$. The lower error rate for each data set is given in bold. As

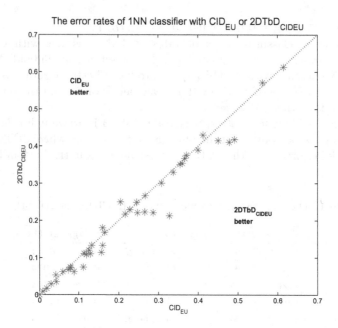

Fig. 5. The error rates of 1NN classifier with CID$_{EU}$ or 2DTbD$_{CIDEU}$ (Color figure online)

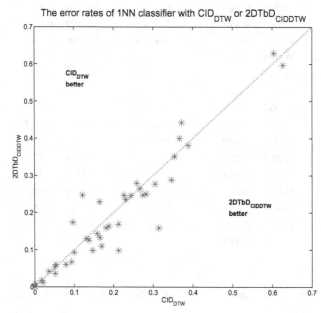

Fig. 6. The error rates of 1NN classifier with CID$_{DTW}$ or 2DTbD$_{CIDDTW}$ (Color figure online)

Table 2. The error rates of 1NN classifier with CID_{DTW} or 2DTbD_{CIDDTW}

Data set	CID_{DTW}	2DTbD_{CIDDTW}	Data set	CID_{DTW}	2DTbD_{CIDDTW}
Adiac	0.389	**0.381**	Lightning7	0.274	**0.247**
Beef	**0.367**	0.400	Mallat	**0.054**	0.060
Car	0.283	**0.250**	MedicalImages	**0.259**	0.279
CBF	**0.001**	0.008	MoteStrain	0.189	**0.164**
Chlorine	0.354	**0.351**	NonThorax1	0.213	**0.169**
CinCECG	0.314	**0.159**	NonThorax2	0.132	**0.130**
Coffee	**0.000**	**0.000**	OliveOil	0.167	**0.133**
CricketX	**0.231**	0.236	OSULeaf	**0.372**	0.442
CricketY	0.267	**0.264**	Plane	**0.000**	**0.000**
CricketZ	**0.244**	0.246	SonySurface1	0.213	**0.098**
DiatomSize	**0.036**	0.042	SonySurface2	**0.122**	0.247
ECGFiveDays	**0.226**	0.247	StarCurves	0.079	**0.060**
FaceAll	0.139	**0.126**	SwedishLeaf	0.171	**0.110**
FaceFour	0.182	**0.159**	Symbols	**0.051**	0.054
FacesUCR	0.100	**0.093**	Synthetic	**0.017**	**0.017**
FiftyWords	0.305	**0.277**	Trace	**0.000**	**0.000**
Fish	**0.166**	0.229	TwoLeadECG	**0.097**	0.174
GunPoint	0.093	**0.067**	TwoPatterns	**0.000**	0.002
Haptics	0.627	**0.597**	Wafer	0.021	**0.012**
InlineSkate	**0.604**	0.629	WordSyn	0.346	**0.288**
ItalyPower	0.052	**0.036**	Yoga	0.160	**0.144**
Lightning2	0.148	**0.098**			

Table 2 shows, 1NN classifier with 2DTbD_{CIDDTW} produced better accuracy on 24 data sets, whereas 1NN classifier with CID_{DTW} was better on 15 and these two classifiers tied on the other 4 data sets.

To show the differences better, the data in Table 2 is drawn in Fig. 6. In Fig. 6, the points at the bottom left of the blue line indicate cases where 2DTbD_{CIDDTW} achieves a lower error rate than CID_{DTW}. Most points is in the bottom left of the blue line.

The results in Table 2 and Fig. 6 demonstrate that 2DTbD_{CIDDTW} works better than CID_{DTW}.

4.3 Contrast Experiments Between ERP and 2DTbD_{ERP}

When 2DTbD uses ERP for each dimension, we call it 2DTbD_{ERP}. In this subsection, we will compare 1NN classifier with ERP to 1NN classifier with 2DTbD_{ERP}. In our experiments, the gap g for ERP is set to 0.5, the maximum allowed distance to the diagonal $bandSize$ is set to 0.5.

Table 3 lists the classification error rates of them. The lower error rate for each data set is given in bold. As Table 3 shows, 1NN classifier with 2DTbD_{ERP} produced better accuracy on 24 data sets, whereas 1NN classifier with DTW was better on 14 and these two classifiers tied on the other 5 data sets.

Table 3. The error rates of 1NN classifier with ERP or 2DTbD$_{ERP}$

Data set	ERP	2DTbD$_{ERP}$	Data set	ERP	2DTbD$_{ERP}$
Adiac	0.389	**0.373**	Lightning7	0.247	**0.192**
Beef	**0.367**	**0.367**	Mallat	0.087	**0.078**
Car	**0.200**	0.233	MedicalImages	0.329	**0.305**
CBF	0.033	**0.009**	MoteStrain	0.142	**0.131**
Chlorine	**0.340**	0.344	NonThorax1	**0.172**	0.173
CinCECG	0.276	**0.157**	NonThorax2	**0.107**	0.114
Coffee	**0.000**	0.036	OliveOil	**0.133**	**0.133**
CricketX	**0.236**	0.244	OSULeaf	0.430	**0.384**
CricketY	0.315	**0.249**	Plane	0.019	**0.010**
CricketZ	0.285	**0.274**	SonySurface1	0.225	**0.210**
DiatomSize	**0.046**	0.056	SonySurface2	**0.163**	0.174
ECGFiveDays	0.146	**0.084**	StarCurves	0.148	**0.142**
FaceAll	0.215	**0.200**	SwedishLeaf	0.138	**0.118**
FaceFour	**0.170**	**0.170**	Symbols	**0.075**	0.081
FacesUCR	0.071	**0.060**	Synthetic	**0.060**	**0.060**
FiftyWords	0.310	**0.273**	Trace	**0.050**	0.120
Fish	**0.097**	0.126	TwoLeadECG	**0.082**	0.215
GunPoint	**0.067**	0.080	TwoPatterns	**0.000**	**0.000**
Haptics	0.581	**0.565**	Wafer	0.010	**0.005**
InlineSkate	**0.565**	0.611	WordSyn	0.359	**0.321**
ItalyPower	0.061	**0.036**	Yoga	0.155	**0.143**
Lightning2	0.131	**0.115**			

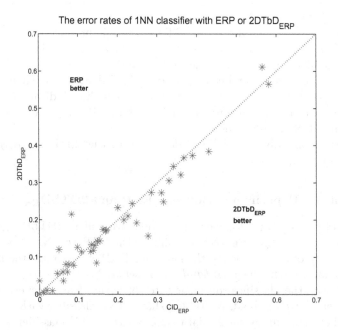

Fig. 7. The error rates of 1NN classifier with ERP or 2DTbD$_{ERP}$ (Color figure online)

To show the differences better, the data in Table 3 is drawn in Fig. 7. In Fig. 7, the points at the bottom left of the blue line indicate cases where $2DTbD_{ERP}$ achieves a lower error rate than ERP. Most points is in the bottom left of the blue line.

The results in Table 3 and Fig. 7 demonstrate that $2DTbD_{ERP}$ works better than ERP. This proves that the accuracy can be improved by 2DTbD.

4.4   Contrast Experiments Between DTW and 2DTbD$_{DTW}$

When 2DTbD uses DTW for each dimension, we call it $2DTbD_{DTW}$. In this subsection, we will compare 1NN classifier with DTW to 1NN classifier with $2DTbD_{DTW}$.

Table 4 lists the classification error rates of them. The lower error rate for each data set is given in bold. As Table 4 shows, 1NN classifier with $2DTbD_{DTW}$ produced better accuracy on 21 data sets, whereas 1NN classifier with DTW was better on 17 and these two classifiers tied on the other 5 data sets.

To show the differences better, the data in Table 4 is drawn in Fig. 8. In Fig. 8, the points at the bottom left of the blue line indicate cases where $2DTbD_{DTW}$ achieves a lower error rate than DTW. Most points is in the bottom left of the blue line.

Table 4. The error rates of 1NN classifier with DTW or 2DTdD$_{DTW}$

Data set	DTW	2DTbD$_{DTW}$	Data set	DTW	2DTbD$_{DTW}$
Adiac	0.396	**0.389**	Lightning7	0.274	**0.233**
Beef	0.367	**0.333**	Mallat	**0.066**	0.077
Car	**0.267**	**0.267**	MedicalImages	**0.263**	0.287
CBF	**0.003**	0.029	MoteStrain	0.165	**0.134**
Chlorine	0.352	**0.350**	NonThorax1	0.210	**0.188**
CinCECG	0.349	**0.185**	NonThorax2	0.135	**0.131**
Coffee	**0.000**	**0.000**	OliveOil	0.167	**0.133**
CricketX	0.246	**0.226**	OSULeaf	**0.409**	0.455
CricketY	**0.256**	0.272	Plane	**0.000**	**0.000**
CricketZ	0.246	**0.241**	SonySurface1	**0.275**	0.296
DiatomSize	**0.033**	0.042	SonySurface2	**0.169**	0.170
ECGFiveDays	**0.232**	0.239	StarCurves	0.093	**0.073**
FaceAll	**0.192**	0.193	SwedishLeaf	0.208	**0.130**
FaceFour	0.170	**0.159**	Symbols	**0.050**	0.061
FacesUCR	**0.095**	0.098	Synthetic	**0.007**	0.013
FiftyWords	0.310	**0.279**	Trace	**0.000**	**0.000**
Fish	**0.177**	0.229	TwoLeadECG	**0.096**	0.182
GunPoint	0.093	**0.060**	TwoPatterns	**0.000**	0.001
Haptics	0.623	**0.607**	Wafer	0.020	**0.011**
InlineSkate	**0.616**	0.658	WordSyn	0.351	**0.292**
ItalyPower	0.050	**0.036**	Yoga	0.163	**0.145**
Lightning2	**0.131**	0.131			

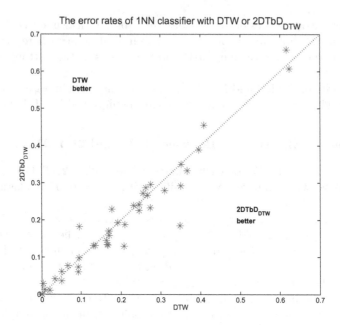

Fig. 8. The error rates of 1NN classifier with DTW or 2DTdD$_{DTW}$ (Color figure online)

The results in Table 4 and Fig. 8 demonstrate that 2DTbD$_{DTW}$ works slightly better than DTW. This proves that the accuracy can be slightly improved by 2DTbD.

4.5   Summary of Experimental Results

All results of our experiments are shown in Fig. 9. As Fig. 9 shows, 2DTbD performs better on all comparison experiments.

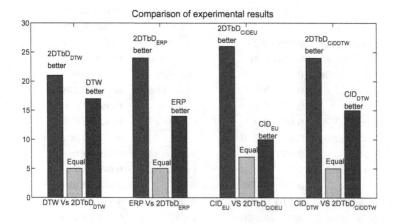

Fig. 9. Comparison of experimental results

5   Conclusion

TSC has attracted a lot of attention in the last decade. Among TSC algorithms, the 1NN classifier has been shown as effective and difficult to beat. The core of 1NN classifier is the distance function. In this paper, a new distance function 2DTbD is proposed. 2DTbD calculates distance by merging distances in 2D space. Our experimental results demonstrate that the classification accuracy can be improved by 2DTbD.

Acknowledgments. This work was supported by the National Natural Science Foundation of China (61872222, 91546203), the National Key Research and Development Program of China (2017YFA0700601), the Major Program of Shandong Province Natural Science Foundation (ZR2018ZB0419), the Key Research and Development Program of Shandong Province (2017CXGC0605, 2017CXGC0604, 2018GGX101019).

References

1. Bagnall, A., Bostrom, A., Large, J., Lines, J.: The great time series classification bake off: an experimental evaluation of recently proposed algorithms. Extended version. arXiv preprint arXiv:1602.01711 (2016)
2. Bagnall, A., Bostrom, A., Lines, J.: The UEA TSC codebase (2016). https:// bitbucket.org/aaron_bostrom/time-series-classification
3. Bagnall, A., Lines, J., Bostrom, A., Large, J., Keogh, E.: The great time series classification bake off: a review and experimental evaluation of recent algorithmic advances. Data Min. Knowl. Disc. **31**(3), 606–660 (2017)
4. Batista, G.E., Keogh, E.J., Tataw, O.M., De Souza, V.M.: CID: an efficient complexity-invariant distance for time series. Data Min. Knowl. Disc. **28**(3), 634–669 (2014)
5. Batista, G.E., Wang, X., Keogh, E.J.: A complexity-invariant distance measure for time series. In: Proceedings of the 2011 SIAM International Conference on Data Mining, pp. 699–710. SIAM (2011)
6. Berndt, D.J., Clifford, J.: Using dynamic time warping to find patterns in time series. In: KDD Workshop, Seattle, WA, vol. 10, pp. 359–370 (1994)
7. Chen, L., Ng, R.: On the marriage of Lp-norms and edit distance. In: Proceedings of the Thirtieth International Conference on Very Large Data Bases, vol. 30, pp. 792–803. VLDB Endowment (2004)
8. Chen, Y., Hu, B., Keogh, E., Batista, G.E.: DTW-D: time series semi-supervised learning from a single example. In: Proceedings of the 19th ACM SIGKDD International Conference on Knowledge Discovery and Data Mining, pp. 383–391. ACM (2013)
9. Chen, Y., et al.: The UCR time series classification archive (2015). http://www. cs.ucr.edu/~eamonn/time_series_data
10. Chhieng, V.M., Wong, R.K.: Adaptive distance measurement for time series databases. In: Kotagiri, R., Krishna, P.R., Mohania, M., Nantajeewarawat, E. (eds.) DASFAA 2007. LNCS, vol. 4443, pp. 598–610. Springer, Heidelberg (2007). https://doi.org/10.1007/978-3-540-71703-4_51
11. Das, G., Gunopulos, D., Mannila, H.: Finding similar time series. In: Komorowski, J., Zytkow, J. (eds.) PKDD 1997. LNCS, vol. 1263, pp. 88–100. Springer, Heidelberg (1997). https://doi.org/10.1007/3-540-63223-9_109

12. Ding, H., Trajcevski, G., Scheuermann, P., Wang, X., Keogh, E.: Querying and mining of time series data: experimental comparison of representations and distance measures. Proc. VLDB Endowment **1**(2), 1542–1552 (2008)
13. Esling, P., Agon, C.: Time-series data mining. ACM Comput. Surv. **45**(1), 12 (2012)
14. Faloutsos, C., Ranganathan, M., Manolopoulos, Y.: Fast subsequence matching in time-series databases, vol. 23. ACM (1994)
15. Fu, T.: A review on time series data mining. Eng. Appl. Artif. Intell. **24**(1), 164–181 (2011)
16. Górecki, T., Łuczak, M.: Using derivatives in time series classification. Data Min. Knowl. Disc. **26**(2), 310–331 (2013)
17. Górecki, T., Łuczak, M.: Non-isometric transforms in time series classification using DTW. Knowl.-Based Syst. **61**, 98–108 (2014)
18. Itakura, F.: Minimum prediction residual principle applied to speech recognition. IEEE Trans. Acoust. Speech Signal Process. **23**(1), 67–72 (1975)
19. Jeong, Y.S., Jeong, M.K., Omitaomu, O.A.: Weighted dynamic time warping for time series classification. Pattern Recognit. **44**(9), 2231–2240 (2011)
20. Ji, C., et al.: A self-evolving method of data model for cloud-based machine data ingestion. In: 2016 IEEE 9th International Conference on Cloud Computing, pp. 814–819. IEEE (2016)
21. Ji, C., Liu, S., Yang, C., Pan, L., Wu, L., Meng, X.: A shapelet selection algorithm for time series classification: new directions. Procedia Comput. Sci. **129**, 461–467 (2018)
22. Ji, C., Zhao, C., Pan, L., Liu, S., Yang, C., Wu, L.: A fast shapelet discovery algorithm based on important data points. Int. J. Web Serv. Res. **14**(2), 67–80 (2017)
23. Keogh, E., Kasetty, S.: On the need for time series data mining benchmarks: a survey and empirical demonstration. Data Min. Knowl. Disc. **7**(4), 349–371 (2003)
24. Keogh, E., Ratanamahatana, C.A.: Exact indexing of dynamic time warping. Knowl. Inf. Syst. **7**(3), 358–386 (2005)
25. Keogh, E., Wei, L., Xi, X., Lee, S.H., Vlachos, M.: LB_Keogh supports exact indexing of shapes under rotation invariance with arbitrary representations and distance measures. In: Proceedings of the 32nd International Conference on Very Large Data Bases, pp. 882–893. VLDB Endowment (2006)
26. Kim, S.W., Park, S., Chu, W.W.: An index-based approach for similarity search supporting time warping in large sequence databases. In: Proceedings of 17th International Conference on Data Engineering, pp. 607–614. IEEE (2001)
27. Li, D., Bissyandé, T.F., Klein, J., Le Traon, Y.: DSCo-NG: a practical language modeling approach for time series classification. In: Boström, H., Knobbe, A., Soares, C., Papapetrou, P. (eds.) IDA 2016. LNCS, vol. 9897, pp. 1–13. Springer, Cham (2016). https://doi.org/10.1007/978-3-319-46349-0_1
28. Marteau, P.F.: Time warp edit distance with stiffness adjustment for time series matching. IEEE Trans. Pattern Anal. Mach. Intell. **31**(2), 306–318 (2009)
29. Prieto, O.J., Alonso-González, C.J., Rodríguez, J.J.: Stacking for multivariate time series classification. Pattern Anal. Appl. **18**(2), 297–312 (2015)
30. Raza, A., Kramer, S.: Ensembles of randomized time series shapelets provide improved accuracy while reducing computational costs. arXiv preprint arXiv:1702.06712 (2017)
31. Sakoe, H., Chiba, S.: Dynamic programming algorithm optimization for spoken word recognition. IEEE Trans. Acoust. Speech Signal Process. **26**(1), 43–49 (1978)

32. Sakurai, Y., Yoshikawa, M., Faloutsos, C.: FTW: fast similarity search under the time warping distance. In: Proceedings of the Twenty-Fourth ACM SIGMOD-SIGACT-SIGART Symposium on Principles of Database Systems, pp. 326–337. ACM (2005)

33. Salvador, S., Chan, P.: Toward accurate dynamic time warping in linear time and space. Intell. Data Anal. **11**(5), 561–580 (2007)

34. Sampaio, A., Lima Jr., R.C., Mendonça, N.C., Filho, R.H.: Implementation and empirical assessment of a web application cloud deployment tool. Int. J. Cloud Comput. **1**, 40–52 (2013). http://hipore.com/stcc/2013/IJCC-Vol1-No1-2013.pdf#page=46

35. Stefan, A., Athitsos, V., Das, G.: The move-split-merge metric for time series. IEEE Trans. Knowl. Data Eng. **25**(6), 1425–1438 (2013)

36. Wang, X., Mueen, A., Ding, H., Trajcevski, G., Scheuermann, P., Keogh, E.: Experimental comparison of representation methods and distance measures for time series data. Data Min. Knowl. Disc. **26**(2), 1–35 (2013)

37. Yi, B.K., Faloutsos, C.: Fast time sequence indexing for arbitrary Lp norms. VLDB (2000)

38. Yi, B.K., Jagadish, H., Faloutsos, C.: Efficient retrieval of similar time sequences under time warping. In: Proceedings of 14th International Conference on Data Engineering, pp. 201–208. IEEE (1998)

39. Zhang, Z., Cheng, J., Li, J., Bian, W., Tao, D.: Segment-based features for time series classification. Comput. J. **55**(9), 1088–1102 (2012)

40. Zhang, Z., Wen, Y., Zhang, Y., Yuan, X.: Time series classification by modeling the principal shapes. In: Bouguettaya, A., et al. (eds.) WISE 2017. LNCS, vol. 10569, pp. 406–421. Springer, Cham (2017). https://doi.org/10.1007/978-3-319-68783-4_28

Research on Access Control of Smart Home in NDN (Short Paper)

Rina Wu, Bo Cui[✉], and Ru Li

Inner Mongolia Key Laboratory of Wireless Networking and Mobile Computing,
College of Computer Science, Inner Mongolia University,
Hohhot 010021, China
wrn@mail.imu.edu.cn, {cscb,csliru}@imu.edu.cn

Abstract. Named Data Networking (NDN) is one of the future Internet architectures and can support smart home very well. There is a large amount of private data with lower security level in smart home. Access control is an effective security solution. However, the existing NDN's access control mechanisms that can be applied to smart homes don't reasonably use the cache in NDN and take into account users' authorization cancellation phase. Therefore, we designed an access control mechanism for smart homes in NDN. We mainly consider the process of the user requests permission, user requests data and user permission cancellation. By using the Cipher Block Chaining (CBC) symmetric encryption algorithm, identity-based encryption, and proxy re-encryption, the cache in NDN is effectively utilized, and the counting Bloom Filter is used to filter ineffective Interest packets and complete the user's privilege cancellation phase. Experimental results show that the access control mechanism designed in this paper can effectively reduce the total time which starts from user requests the permission to decrypt data and reduce the time overhead of the NDN routers in the process of user privileges cancellation after using the counting Bloom Filter.

Keywords: Named Data Networking · Access control · Smart home · Encryption

1 Introduction

Smart home is a recent research hot spot of the Internet of Things and has a great influence on people's daily life. It is composed of a large number of low-power resource constrained devices, and in the communication process it involves large amounts of small data exchange and so on. So these features lead to obvious differences between smart home and TCP/IP in design concept and construction system [1]. For example, the communication of TCP/IP is connection-oriented, making it difficult to maintain the communication in the smart home. Named Data Networking (NDN) can solve the above problems [2]. For example, NDN can use namespace to solve home devices which require a lot of IP address.

NDN can solve many problems of smart home in TCP/IP, but NDN still has many shortcomings in solving the problem of smart home security. Therefore, in NDN, the

H. Gao et al. (Eds.): CollaborateCom 2018, LNICST 268, pp. 560–570, 2019.
https://doi.org/10.1007/978-3-030-12981-1_39

security of smart home is crucial. Access control is an important solution to NDN-smart home security. It restricts users' access to the protected resources and ensures that private data is only used by legitimate users [3].

According to the characteristics of NDN, many kinds of access control mechanisms are designed to enhance the security of NDN communication. As the Zhang team at UCLA proposes that data can be protected in the communication process through encryption as long as the naming mechanism and the key representation are accurate [4]. Zhang et al. [5] explain the design of the naming mechanism in detail. The access control mechanism of the existing NDN can be divided into the following aspects: based on ordinary encryption, based on attribute encryption, based on ambiguous name, and access control mechanism combined in many ways [6]. Chen et al. [7] encrypt data using a symmetric encryption algorithm, encrypt data keys using asymmetric encryption algorithms, but without making reasonable use of the NDN cache feature. Hamdane et al. [8] proposed identity-based encryption access control, although it is guaranteed that private keys will no longer be allocated using public key certificates, Simplifying public key management and saving computing and communication costs, but cannot guarantee the security of key distribution. Attribute-based encryption is mainly based on users' attributes [9]. The mechanism includes a set of attributes composed of multiple attributes and integrates the access structure into the property set. This mechanism causes a large amount of encryption/decryption overhead and a lack of attribute recovery mechanism. Wood et al. [10] use proxy re-encryption method to design and implement the secure content transmission in order to ensure the security of the content itself without considering the data consumer's identity information and the stage of consumer permission application logout.

The main work of this paper is to make use of the NDN cache feature in the process of user requesting data to cancel the user privileges and reduce the total delay (from permission application to decryption) and improve the user logout mechanism.

The rest of this paper is organized as follows. Section 2 introduces system model design, namespace design and overall flow design of access control. Section 3 deals with experimental testing and performance analysis. Finally, Sect. 4 summarizes the full work and discusses future work.

2 NDN-Smart Home Access Control Design

2.1 System Model

In smart home, the home manager is responsible for managing all the devices. In this system, home manager is defined as the home administrator who performs the functions that grant users privileges. Figure 1 shows the NDN-smart home model. And this system includes five entities: home manager, user, intelligent gateway, home cloud and smart home devices. We assume that all five entities have very high security. The routers are NDN routers, and the security of the NDN routers is greatly improved. The research focus on the parts labeled ① and ② in Fig. 1, namely, the user application/revocation authority and user request data phase.

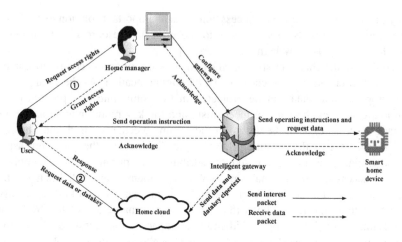

Fig. 1. The system model of NDN-smart home

2.2 NDN-Smart Home Namespace

Figure 2 shows the design of namespace by using a name tree to represent the composition of the namespace. In this paper, /ndn/homeID is used as the common prefix in smart home. /ndn indicates that all communication processes in smart home are performed in NDN. /homeID represents the home manager. The namespace is divided into user sub-namespace: /user, task sub-namespace: /task, and key sub-namespace: /key for three different service models. /location and/sensor are the correspondence of the physical location of the device. /userID represents the identity of the requesting user.

2.3 Overall Flow of Access Control Mechanism

The access control mechanism designed in this paper needs to be implemented in combination with symmetric encryption, identity-based encryption, proxy re-encryption and counting Bloom Filter.

The access control mechanism studied is the part of ① and ② of Fig. 1, corresponding to Fig. 3. The access control mechanism is divided into four stages: initialization stage shown as the part ① in Fig. 3, the user application permission stage shown as the part ② in Fig. 3, the user access data stage shown as the part ③ in Fig. 3 and the user logout stage, the logout process is similar as the user application process. The following is a detailed introduction to each phase:

Initialization Phase

In the stage of data encryption, we use CBC to encrypt the data generated by the device. Secondly, the private key generator in the identity-based encryption algorithm is used to generate the private key corresponding to the identity public key for the home manager and users.

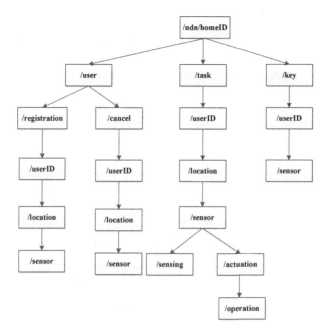

Fig. 2. NDN-smart home namespace

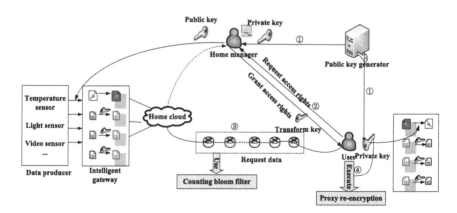

Fig. 3. Access control mechanism

User Applies Permission Phase

When users apply for access, $user_i$ must send an Interest packet signed by his private key to the home manager and indicate the time of application, if the user does not set the time, the time is set by the home manager to the default value. After successful authentication, the home manager will add $user_i$ information to the user registry. The user registry are listed in Table 1.

Figure 4 shows the message sequence chart of requesting permission for users. After successfully verifying the identity of users, the home manager will generate the

Table 1. User registry

User	Public key	Public key digest	Data type	Time (month)
Alice	Pk(Alice)	SHA256(Pk(Alice))	Light	6
Bob	Pk(Bob)	SHA256(Pk(Bob))	Temperature	12
John	Pk(John)	SHA256(Pk(John))	Light	6
Eva	Pk(Eva)	SHA256(Pk(Eva))	Electricity	24
...	...	...	...	...

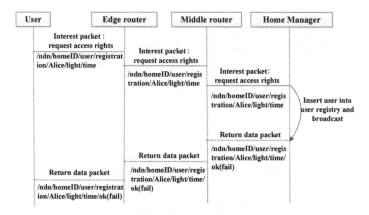

Fig. 4. MSC of user request permission process

transform key using the re-encryption key generation algorithm of proxy re-encryption. It is returned to users in the registration confirmation data packet, which is used as the certificate for users to register successfully.

User Requests Data of Data Key Phase

In the stage of user request data, there are four processes: user request data, user request data key, decrypt data key cipher text and decrypt data cipher text. The four processes will be explained in detail in this section.

Users can access the data in two ways:

One is the intermediate routers don't cache the data and data keys cipher text required by the authorized user. Figure 5 is the message sequence chart in which the user requests data from the data provider (i.e. home cloud) is shown.

The other is intermediate routers which have cached the data and data key cipher text needed by authorized users. Figure 6 is the message sequence chart, which makes reasonably use of the cache characteristic of NDN.

User Logs off Permission Phase

There are two different logout situations in this mechanism:

Figure 7 shows the active cancellation. The passive cancellation is the home manager which will delete the users in the registered user table according to the time in

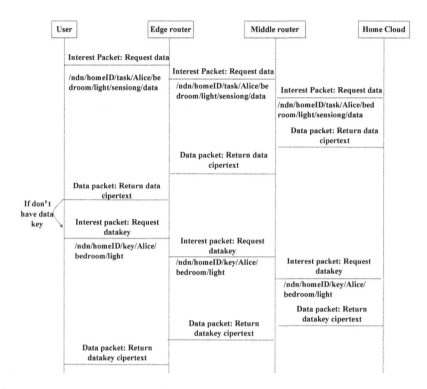

Fig. 5. MSC of user request permission process

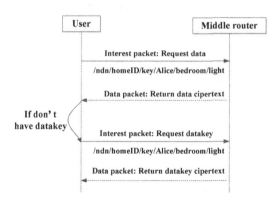

Fig. 6. MSC of user request permission process

the registry within a certain period of time and broadcast the deleted users to the intermediate routers. And the middle routers will update the counting Bloom Filters in time.

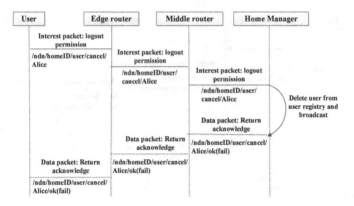

Fig. 7. MSC of user requests to cancel authority

3   Experimental Results and Performance Evaluation

3.1   Reference [7]'s Access Control Mechanism

In reference [7] the user first needs to send the private key signed Interest packet to the producer to apply for access privilege, and record it in the user registry after the data producer has verified successfully. It is used for intermediate forwarding nodes to generate Bloom Filter to filter Interest packets sent by unauthorized users. Secondly, the producer encrypts the data generated by using symmetric key and encrypts the data key with the public key of each registered user. When the user obtains the data key, he decrypts the data key with his own private key, and then decrypts the data with the data key.

3.2   Index of Performance Testing

This experiment aims at the designed access control mechanism and simulates the whole process using ndnSIM2.4. Performance measurement is the time a user takes from the request for permission to successfully decrypt the data, expressed in terms of T_{Total}, which is computed according to the following formula:

$$T_{\text{Total}} = T_{\text{Authority}} + T_{\text{DataKey}} + T_{\text{Data}} \tag{1}$$

For the access control mechanism proposed in this paper, $T_{\text{Authority}}$, T_{DataKey} and T_{Data} are computed according to the following formulas:

$$T_{\text{Authority}} = T_{\text{TransformKey}} + T_{\text{Response}} \tag{2}$$

$$T_{\text{DataKey}} = T_{\text{Response}} + T_{\text{Re\_Enc}} + T_{\text{Decrypt}} \tag{3}$$

$$T_{\text{Data}} = T_{\text{Response}} + T_{\text{Decrypt}} \tag{4}$$

Access control mechanisms proposed in reference [7], $T_{Authority}$, $T_{DataKey}$, the formula is as follows:

$$T_{Authority} = T_{Response} \tag{5}$$

$$T_{DataKey} = T_{Response} + T_{Pub\_Enc} + T_{Decrypt} \tag{6}$$

The meaning for each time variable in the formula is shown in Table 2:

Table 2. The meaning of the time variable of the formula

Formula symbol	Representative meaning
$T_{Authority}$	Time of users successfully obtained permission
$T_{DataKey}$	Time of users successfully obtained data key
T_{Data}	Time of users successfully obtained data
$T_{Response}$	Time of users successfully obtained data packet
$T_{TransformKey}$	Time of the permission provider generated the transform key
T_{Re_Enc}	Re-encryption time
$T_{Decrypt}$	Time of users successfully decrypted data
T_{Pub_Enc}	Time of encrypting data key

Experimental Results and Performance Evaluation

Figure 8(a) shows the time with the length of plaintext in different methods. We can see that the time used in re-encryption is not proportional to the length of plaintext. With the increase of plaintext length, the curve tends to be more and more peaceful. In public key encryption algorithm, the time of public key encryption increases with the length of plaintext. When the length of encrypted plaintext is 90 KB, the time of re-encryption is less than the public key encryption algorithm.

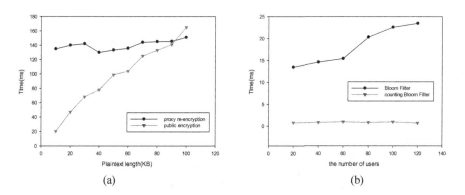

Fig. 8. Comparison between encryption and identity filtering mechanism

As Fig. 8(b) shows the time with different number of users in different methods. As you can see from Fig. 8(b), it takes much longer to regenerate the Bloom Filter than to counting Bloom Filter to perform only delete operations, and it takes more and more time to generate the Bloom Filter as the number of users' increases. The counting Bloom Filter is not affected by the number of users.

Experimental Scene and Simulation Experiment

Figure 9(a) shows the network topology used by the simulation. The topology uses a single link with multiple user sources, with 55 nodes, with three user nodes: Node A, Node B, Node C; a privileges provider: node P1; a data provider: node P2. Node A, node B, node C sends the authority Interest packet to the node P1 in turn. After the user receives the confirmation data packet, user A, user B and user C in turn send the Interest packets requesting the data key and data to P2.

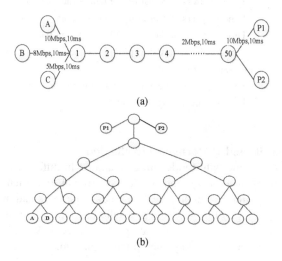

Fig. 9. Simulation topology structure

Figure 9(b) shows the tree topology used by the simulation. The topology with 34 nodes, with two user nodes: Node A, Node B, a privileges provider: node P1, a data provider: node P2. The T_{Total} of User B is calculated according to user A distance P1 and P2 position (that is, the number of nodes between user A and P1 and P2).

The length of transform key is 256 bit, the data segment size is 4 KB, the data key length is 128 bit, the forwarding route policy is the best route strategy, the cache policy is the least recently used, the packet size is 1024 KB.

Figure 10(a) shows the T_{Total} of node A. It can be seen that because node A is the node that firstly sends the request Interest packet, the data needed by node A isn't cached in the intermediate nodes, so the Interest packet is returned by node P2. Therefore, we can see that when the cache of intermediate nodes is not used the T_{Total} is slightly higher than that in reference [7], about 14%. Figure 10(b) shows the T_{Total} of node B. As can be seen that because the content of user B request is the same as that of user A request, the intermediate forwarding nodes cache the copy of user A request data. Therefore, user B can retrieve the data in the cache of intermediate nodes, and when node A is two hops from node P2, the T_{Total} is lower than reference [7]. And the longer distance between node A and node P2, the better for user B.

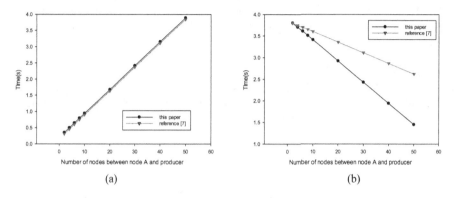

(a)   (b)

Fig. 10. T_{Total} for node A and B to get data in the dumbbell topology

Figure 11(a) shows the T_{Total} of node C. It can be seen that node C is affected by the location of node B. The time of node C to make full use of NDN cache is obviously lower than that of reference [7], about 45%.

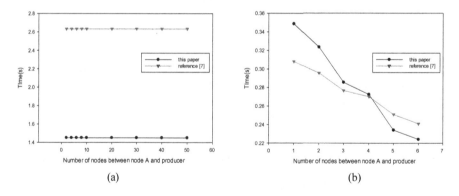

(a)   (b)

Fig. 11. T_{Total} for node C and T_{Total} for node B

Figure 11(b) shows in the tree network topology, the time when user B successfully acquired the data. When user A is four nodes away from node P2, The scheme presented in this paper is lower than that in reference [7] in terms of calculation.

4   Conclusion and Future Work

This paper is mainly to design and implement the access control mechanism of smart home in NDN and design the process from user application permission stage to user logout stage. It can effectively reduce the time from registering permission to successfully decrypting the data, and improve the identity filtering mechanism and user logout mechanism. The following work deploys the proposed access control mechanism in the smart home and tested the performance.

Acknowledgment. This paper is supported by the National Natural Science Foundation of China (Grant No. 61751104) and Natural Science Foundation of Inner Mongolia (Grant No. 2018MS06028) and Research Project of Higher Education School of Inner Mongolia Autonomous Region under Grant NJZY16020.

References

1. Shang, W., Yu, Y., Droms, R., et al.: Challenges in IoT networking via TCP/IP architecture. Technical report NDN-0038. NDN Project (2016)
2. Datta, S.K., Bonnet, C.: Integrating named data networking in Internet of Things architecture. In: IEEE International Conference on Consumer Electronics-Taiwan, pp. 1–2. IEEE (2016)
3. Sandhu, R.S., Samarati, P.: Access control: principle and practice. IEEE Commun. Mag. **32** (9), 40–48 (1994)
4. Zhang, L., Estrin, D., Burke, J., et al.: Named data networking (NDN) project. Technical report NDN-0001, 157–158 (2010)
5. Zhang, Z., Yu, Y., Afanasyev, A., et al.: NAC: name-based access control in named data networking. In: 4th ACM Conference on Information-Centric Networking on Proceedings, pp. 186–187. ACM (2017)
6. Chaabane, A., De Cristofaro, E., Kaafar, M.A., et al.: Privacy in content-oriented networking: threats and countermeasures. ACM SIGCOMM Comput. Commun. Rev. **43** (3), 25–33 (2013)
7. Chen, T., Lei, K., Xu, K.: An encryption and probability based access control model for named data networking. In: Performance Computing and Communications Conference, pp. 1–8. IEEE (2014)
8. Hamdane, B., Serhrouchni, A., El Fatmi, S.G.: Access control enforcement in named data networking. In: 8th International Conference for Internet Technology and Secured Transactions, pp. 576–581. IEEE (2013)
9. Qiao, Z., Liang, S., Davis, S., Jiang, H.: Survey of attribute based encryption. In: International Conference on Software Engineering, Artificial Intelligence, Networking and Parallel/Distributed Computing, pp. 1–6. IEEE (2014)
10. Wood, C.A., Uzun, E.: Flexible end-to-end content security in CCN. In: 11th Consumer Communications and Networking Conference, pp. 858–865. IEEE (2014)

The Realization of Face Recognition Algorithm Based on Compressed Sensing (Short Paper)

Huimin Zhang[1,2(✉)] , Yan Sun[3], Haiwei Sun[3], and Xin Yuan[3]

[1] University of Michigan, Ann Arbor, MI 48105, USA
lizzyww@umich.edu
[2] Shanghai Jiao Tong University, Shanghai 200240, China
[3] Jiangsu University, Zhenjiang 212013, Jiangsu, China
614564957@qq.com, 329788350@qq.com, jund85@163.com

Abstract. Once the sparse representation-based classifier (SRC) was raised, it achieved a more outstanding performance than typical classification algorithm. Normally, SRC algorithm adopts l_1-norm minimization method to solve the sparse vector, and its computation complexity increases correspondingly. In this paper, we put forward a compressed sensing reconstruction algorithm based on residuals. This algorithm utilizes the local sparsity within figures as well as the non-local similarity among figure blocks to boost the performance of the reconstruction algorithm while remaining a median computation complexity. It achieves a superior recognition rate in the experiments of Yale facial database.

Keywords: Compressed sensing · Face recognition ·
Feature extraction · Sparse representation classification ·
Image reconstruction

1 Introduction

Face recognition technology, as one of the most significant and successful applications of image analysis and understanding, has now become a research focus in computer vision field. A potential issue one may face is that some features may be lost during data collection and compression. To solve this problem, Donoho and Cande et al. [1] put forward a compressed sensing algorithm that combined sampling and compression. They performed a non-adaptive linear projection to input signal sampling, and reconstructed the original signal using corresponding reconstruction algorithms. This method helped decrease the size of data as well as offered possibility to realize a better restoration even in the case of small sampling data. Based on this method, our paper raised a compressed sensing reconstruction algorithm based on residuals to deal with the large data volume in image signal processing.

H. Gao et al. (Eds.): CollaborateCom 2018, LNICST 268, pp. 571–580, 2019.
https://doi.org/10.1007/978-3-030-12981-1_40

2   Sparse Representation-Based Classifier

Sparse representation-based classifier (SRC) theorem supposes that each class of testing sample has enough training samples. Then, the testing data can be linear represented by training data, and other categories of samples has zero contribution to the reconstruction of this testing samples. Therefore, a common signal classification problem has been transformed into a sparse representation problem. Through computing the category of minimal reconstruction error between testing sample and training sample, we are able to judge the class of testing figures.

The mathematics model of SRC algorithm is as follow:

Suppose n training sample belongs to c classes separately, namely $\{(b_i, g_i)|(b_i \in \chi \subseteq R^m, g_i \in \{1, 2, ..., c\}, i = 1, 2, ..., n\}$ where g_i is the classification label of b_i, m is the dimension of the space, χ and c is the number of all categories. Suppose the alignment of ith class of training sample is the column of matrix $D_i = \{b_{i,1}, b_{i,2}, ..., b_{i,n_i}\} \in R^{m \times n_i}, i = 1, 2, ...c$, where $b_{i,j}$ represents samples in i^{th} class and n_i is the number of training samples in i^{th} category. Then the dictionary matrix can be represented as:

$$D = \{D_1, D_2, ...D_c\} \in R^{m \times n} \tag{1}$$

where $n = \sum_{i=1}^{c} n_i$.

According to SRC theorem, the testing sample can be linearly represented by the dictionary atoms as:

$$b = D\alpha \tag{2}$$

where $\alpha \in R^n$ represents the coefficient vector of atoms in the linear combination.

Suppose the testing sample b belongs to j^{th} class, then the elements in coefficient vector α are all zero except that part relevant to j^{th} class, which can be written as:

$$\alpha = [0, ..., 0, \alpha_{j,1}, ..., \alpha_{j,n_j}, 0, ..., 0]^T \tag{3}$$

where $\alpha_{j,i} \in R$ is the corresponding coefficient of training sample $b_{j,i}$.

Consequently, coefficient α is sparse, and the testing sample b can be represented by linear combination of training data in j^{th} class. The problems of seeking for sparse coefficient vector α can be represented as:

$$\min_{\alpha} \|\alpha\|_0 \quad s.t. \quad b = D\alpha \tag{4}$$

This is a NP-hard problem, and one may only attain an approximate solution efficiently. The problems in Eq. (4) can be approximated as:

$$\min_{\alpha} \|\alpha\|_1 \quad s.t. \quad b = D\alpha \tag{5}$$

where $\|\alpha\|_1$ denotes l_1-norm. Take environmental noise into consideration, Eq. (5) can be transformed as:

$$\min_{\alpha} \|\alpha\|_1 \quad s.t. \quad \|b - D\alpha\|_2 \leq \epsilon \tag{6}$$

For each class i, suppose δ_i is the eigenfunction that selects the coefficient associated with i^{th} category, which is defined as:

$$\delta_i(\alpha_j) = \alpha_j, \quad if \quad g_j = i \tag{7}$$

By exacting the coefficient containing the information of ith class, δ_i can be represented by a new vector:

$$\delta_i = [\delta_i(\alpha_1), \delta_i(\alpha_2), ..., \delta_i(\alpha_n)]^T \tag{8}$$

Finally, by minimizing the reconstruction error, we are able to obtain the class that testing sample b belongs to:

$$identity(b) = \underset{i=1,...,c}{argmin}\, r_i(b) = \|b - D_i\delta_i\|_2 \tag{9}$$

3   Face Recognition Algorithm Based on Compressed Sensing

3.1   Compressed Sensing Reconstruction Algorithm Based on Residuals

Compressed sensing algorithm performed a linear projecting of signal $x \in R^N$ to a $M \times N$ measurement matrix ϕ , $M \ll N$,

$$y = \phi x \tag{10}$$

where $y \in R^M$ is a measurement vector. The obtained subrate can be defined as M/N, and the sparse matrix is named ψ. To solve the reconstruction, one need to solve the following optimization problem:

$$\hat{x} = \underset{x \in R^N}{argmin} \|\psi x\|_1 \quad s.t. \quad y = \phi x \tag{11}$$

According the Restricted Isometry Property (RIP), if M is big enough, ϕ and ψ would satisfy the incoherence and isometric requirements in compressed sensing reconstruction.

Documents [2,3] have made tremendous efforts in reducing the computation complexity in compressed sensing reconstruction algorithm as well as improving the quality of image reconstruction. However, due to the multidimensional characteristics of image or video data, these two reconstruction methods exert heavy load on storage and computation. Besides, measurement matrix ϕ is large, and requires a larger storage space. To alleviate these problems, document [4] raises the block compressed sensing (BCS) method, in which images are divided into $\sqrt{N_a} \times \sqrt{N_a}$ size non-overlapping blocks, and can realize block-by-block sensing independently. That means $y_i = \Phi_a x_i$, where x_i is i^{th} image block, and Φ_a is a $M_a \times N_a$ measurement matrix. Document [2] raises the BCS-SPL algorithm. It is realized through doing image reconstruction to each image block:

$$\hat{x}_i = BCS - SPL(y_i, \Phi_a) \tag{12}$$

where $BCS - SPL(\cdot)$ is a smooth projection Landweber compressed sensing reconstruction algorithm based on blocking, which ensures the local sparsity. Document [5] suggests adding image block prediction into compressed sensing reconstruction algorithm. It enhances the reconstruction quality through implicitly increasing the compressibility of signals, and will not make any changes to signal sampling process. In this algorithm, the prediction of current image block is based on adjacent image blocks during reconstruction process.

Suppose existing an image block x_i and its measured value $y_i = \Phi_a x_i$. $\tilde{x}_i$ is the prediction of x_i derived from its adjacent image blocks. Then the residual in measurement domain can be derived from $r_i = y_i - \Phi_a \tilde{x}_i$. The final reconstruction calculation method is expressed as:

$$\hat{x}_i = \tilde{x}_i + BCS - SPL(r_i, \Phi_a) \tag{13}$$

Since residual (the difference between x_i and $\tilde{x}_i$) is more compressible (sparse) than image block itself, we can reconstruct a better approximated signal through compressed sensing theory.

Our paper will depict how to apply sparse representation in over-complete dictionary to the algorithm efficiently. Suppose there is a image X with size $\sqrt{N} \times \sqrt{N}$, and it is divided into K pieces of $\sqrt{N_s} \times \sqrt{N_s}$ non-overlapping blocks, and realizes block-by-block sensing independently. From mathematical perspective,

$$y_i = \Phi_s x_i (i = 1, 2, ...K) \tag{14}$$

where $x_i \in R^{N_s}$ is the vector representation of ith image block, $y_i \in R^{M_s}$ is a measurement vector and Φ_s is a $M_s \times N_s$ measurement matrix. Notably, all the image blocks were sampled using the same sub-rate, meaning the global sampling rate is M_s/N_s.

If one try to recover the whole image X through reconstructing image blocks given measurement value y_i, the first thing is to seek out a best prediction. One method to settle this problem is solving the following minimization problem by using some image prior knowledge:

$$\hat{X} = \underset{P \in R^N}{argmin} \|X - P\|_2 + \lambda \Theta(P) \tag{15}$$

where $\|X - P\|_2$ is l_2-norm data fidelity term, $\Theta(P)$ represents the regularized item of the prior image, and λ is the normalized parameter.

The proposed algorithm did not seek out proper prediction image P in Eq. (15) directly. Instead, it realizes the sparse representation of image blocks through improving local sparsity and non-local self-similarity of image blocks, and therefore finds out a best prediction. In short, it makes prediction to figures based on group sparse representation.

Suppose image P is divided into H overlapping image blocks with size $\sqrt{N_p} \times \sqrt{N_p}$. Each small block is represented by vector $p_i \in R^{N_p}(i = 1, 2, ...H)$. Then pile up the best matching blocks p_i in $W \times W$ window to form a $N_p \times C$ matrix based on Euclidean distance. Denote it as $B_i \in R^{N_p \times C}$. Each matrix $B_i(i = 1, 2, ...H)$ contains all the image blocks possessing similar structures. Define the operator to extract matrix B_i from P as $G_i(\cdot)$. $B_i = G_i(P)$. Since the image blocks are overlapped, one can restore image P from B_i as:

$$P = \sum_{i=1}^{H} G_i^T(B_i) \cdot / \sum_{i=1}^{H} G_i^T(E_{N_p \times C}) \tag{16}$$

in which $G_i^T(\cdot)$ is the operator to put each small block B_i back to reconstructed image, otherwise it is zero. The operator $\cdot/$ means dividing element by element. $E_{N_p \times C}$ is an identity matrix with size $N_p \times C$. Equation (16) shows that the reconstructed figures are derived from taking the average value of all the overlapped blocks. Using overlapped blocks can ensure that the obtained prediction will not be affected by the blocking artifacts, and therefore improves the prediction quality of images.

Suppose each group of similar blocks B_i can be linearly represented by some atoms from over-complete dictionary D. Notably, the dictionary structure based on sparse group representation differs from the dictionary form based on sparse block representation. Suppose $D = [d_1, d_2, ...d_M]$. Each atom d_j is a $(N_p \times C) \times M$ matrix, and have the same size as B_i. Given dictionary D with M atoms, seeking out the sparse representation of each B_i for D can be equate to finding sparse vector $\hat{\alpha}_i \in R^M$, that is $\hat{B}_i \simeq \sum_{j=1}^{M} \hat{\alpha}_{i,j} d_j$ where $\hat{\alpha}_{i,j}$ is the jth element in sparse vector α_i. Then, the sparse coding of B_i in dictionary D is:

$$\hat{\alpha} = \underset{\alpha_i \in R^M}{argmin} \|B_i - \sum_{j=1}^{M} \alpha_{i,j} d_j\|_2 + \lambda\|\alpha_i\|_0 \tag{17}$$

where λ is the regularization parameter. The sparsity is measured by l_0-norm of α_i, and the definition of B_i has taken account of the similarity of image blocks. Based on Eq. 16, reconstructing the whole image P from sparse vector $\alpha_i(i = 1, ..., H)$ can be represented as;

$$P \simeq D \odot \hat{\alpha} = \sum_{i=1}^{H} G_i^T(\hat{B}_i) \cdot / \sum_{i=1}^{H} G_i^T(E_{N_p \times C}) \tag{18}$$

where $\hat{\alpha}$ represents the cascade of all $\hat{\alpha}_i$, and the symbol $D \odot \hat{\alpha}$ is used to simplify following equations.

Based on Eqs. (15) and (17), the image prediction based on sparse representation can be expressed as: $\tilde{X} = D \cdot \tilde{\alpha}$. Therefore,

$$\tilde{\alpha} = \underset{\alpha}{argmin} \|X - D \odot \alpha\|_2 + \lambda\|\alpha\|_0 \tag{19}$$

Since X is unknown during the compressed sensing reconstruction procedure, one may not obtain the solution of Eq. (19). This paper uses iterative process to generate best prediction image. Each iteration includes two stages, the first stage is to solve Eq. (20):

$$\tilde{\alpha}^{[k]} = \underset{\alpha}{argmin} \|\tilde{X}^{[k]} - D \odot \alpha^{[k]}\|_2 + \lambda\|\alpha^{[k]}\|_0 \tag{20}$$

Since l_0 is a non-convex optimization, finding solution with respect to Eq. (20) is NP-hard. This problem can be solved by method provided in document [6]. Therefore, the prediction obtained in k^{th} iteration can be represented as $\tilde{X}^{[k]} = D \odot \tilde{\alpha}^{[k]}$.

The second stage employs residual reconstruction algorithm to recover the image. Divide the predicted image $\tilde{X}^{[k]}$ into K non-overlapping blocks $\tilde{x}_i^{[k]}(i = 1, 2, ..., K)$ with size $\sqrt{N_s} \times \sqrt{N_s}$. Use $\tilde{y}_i^{[k]} = \Phi_s\tilde{x}_i^{[k]}$ to perform block sampling, and use $r_i^{[k]} = y_i^{[k]} - \tilde{y}_i^{[k]}$ to calculate reconstruction residual. Then, the computational method of recovering image block is expresses as:

$$\hat{x}_i^{[k]} = \tilde{x}_i^{[k]} + BCS - SPL(r_i^{[k]}, \Phi_s) \tag{21}$$

Finally, merging all the reconstructed non-overlapping blocks to obtain the reconstructed image $X^{[\hat{k}+1]}$. Improve the reconstruction quality through iterative generating prediction and refactoring residuals.

The basic procedures of compressed sensing reconstruction algorithm based on residuals are as follow:

Input: measurement matrix Φ_s, measurement value $y_i(i = 1, 2, ...K)$, window size W based on best Euclidean distance matching, regularization parameter λ, overlapping block size N_p and non-overlapping block size N_s.

Output: reconstructed image $\hat{X}$.

Initialization: $k = 0$ and $\hat{X}^{[0]} = BCS - SPL(y_i^{[k]}, \Phi_s)$

Repeat the following five steps:

Step 1: Solve $\tilde{\alpha}^{[k]} = \underset{\alpha}{argmin} \|\tilde{X}^{[k]} - D \odot \alpha^{[k]}\|_2 + \lambda\|\alpha^{[k]}\|_0$.

Step 2: Calculate the predicted image $\tilde{X}^{[k]} = D \odot \tilde{\alpha}^{[k]}$.

Step 3: Divide $\tilde{X}^{[k]}$ into K non-overlapping image blocks $[\tilde{x}_i^{[k]}]_{i=1}^K$.

Step 4: From $i = 1$ to K, calculate both $r_i^{[k]} = y_i^{[k]} - \Phi_s\tilde{x}_i^{[k]}(i = 1, 2, ...K)$ and $\hat{x}_i^{[k]} = \tilde{x}_i^{[k]} + BCS - SPL(r_i^{[k]}, \Phi_s)$.

Step 5: Place $[\hat{x}_i^{[k]}]_{i=1}^K$ back to the whole image plane $X^{[\hat{k}+1]}$

Stop iteration until $\|\hat{X}^{[k+1]} - \hat{X}^{[k]}\|_2 \leq 0.001$.

3.2   Improved Uniformly Blocking SRC Algorithm

During the face recognition procedure, dividing the image into blocks to reconstruct and solve sparse vectors can efficiently reduce the computation complexity. The idea of uniform partitioning is to divide facial image into 2×2, 3×3 and 4×4 image blocks, as is shown in Fig. 1.

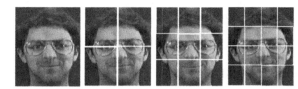

Fig. 1. Uniformly blocking figure

Firstly, uniformly blocking SRC algorithm divides the facial image into K image blocks with same size. Then, it performs SRC algorithm to each image block, and gets the category of each image block with minimal reconstruction error. Finally, the category of all the image blocks is based on majority vote; therefore one can infer the category of the whole facial image.

Combing with the compressed sensing reconstruction algorithm based on residual, it optimizes the uniformly blocking SRC algorithm in solving sparse vector. The procedures of improved uniformly blocking SRC face recognition algorithm are given below.

(1) Input n training facial figures with c classes.
(2) Divide each training figure into q blocks with equal size according to a certain method. Then, transform each image block to the corresponding column vector to form the sub-sample matrix A_i, i=1,2,...q.
(3) Divide the testing facial figure t according to the same method. Then, transform each figure block into column vector to get sub-testing facial figure blocks t_i, i=1,2,...q.
(4) For each sub-block t_i, choose its corresponding sub-sample matrix A_i, and gain the reconstructed image blocks by solving corresponding sparse vector. Use the compressed sensing reconstruction algorithm based on residuals.
(5) Calculate the reconstruction error between reconstructed image blocks and original testing image blocks, and categorize each image block based on minimal reconstruction error.
(6) The category of the whole image is based on majority principle. Ideally, the majority category of image blocks is the actual category among q image blocks. Therefore, one can judge the category of the whole face figure.

4   Experiment Analysis

To verify the recognition performance of the algorithm proposed in our paper, we did simulated analysis based on Yale face database. This experiment applied imresize function to resize each face image to 128×128 pixel and chose both 4×4 and 8×8 dividing algorithm. By comparing with popular classifiers SVM, SRC, and ASRC algorithm described in document [7], we can verify the performance of the algorithm.

4.1 Experiment Environment

Hardware environment: a 64-bit win10 PC with 8 GB RAM and Core i5 processor.

Software environment: MATLAB 7.0.

4.2 Experiment Results and Analysis

In this experiment, we select each category of face image with $m = 3,4,5,6$ from Yale face database as training samples. Considering the rationality of random sampling, repeat each algorithm for ten times by obtaining different quantity of training data. Use the average value as the final result. The identification rate of each algorithm in Yale face database is listed in Table 1, where 4×4 and 8×8 represent using 4×4 uniformly blocking method and 8×8 uniformly blocking method.

Table 1. Identification rate of each algorithm in Yale face database

Training size	Identification rate (%)				
	SVM	SRC	ASRC	4×4	8×8
3	77.46	81.13	85.92	86.83	87.67
4	82.24	85.42	86.67	89.14	90.38
5	86.67	88.46	90.19	91.22	92.78
6	88.67	90.53	91.74	93.45	94.75

According to the data in Table 1, when the training size of samples is 6, the 8×8 uniformly blocking algorithm has the highest identification rate at 97.75%. It makes a 4.22% improvement compared to traditional SRC algorithm. By analyzing the experimental data in Yale face database, one may find that as the training size increases, the two blocking algorithms performs better than other three algorithms. Therefore, the experiment verifies the accuracy of the proposed algorithm.

In the efficiency measurement, we compared three different algorithms: PCA combined with SVM, PCA combined with SRC, and uniform blocking algorithm. We divided 100 experimental data into 10 testing set, and measured the average classification time per set. The experiment result is shown in Fig. 2.

Generally, the uniform blocking algorithm has a medium classification efficiency, with average rate between 1.8 and 2.2 s. It is faster than PCA combined with SVM (between 2.4 and 2.8) and a little slower than PCA combined with SRC (between 1.4 and 1.8). As one can seen, its computation complexity did not increase too much due to its accuracy in image reconstruction.

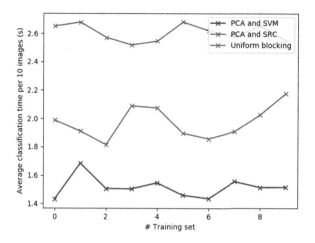

Fig. 2. Efficiency comparison between PCA combined with SVM, PCA combined with SRC, and Uniform blocking algorithm.

5 Conclusion

This paper utilizes the local sparsity within figures and the non-local similarity among image blocks to improve the performance of reconstruction and optimize the problems of solving minimal l_1-norm with respect to sparse coefficient in traditional SRC algorithm. By comparing the minimal error between testing sample figures and reconstructed sample figures, the algorithm categorizes image blocks based on majority vote, and finally realizes the recognition of face images. Experimental results show that the improved uniformly blocking SRC algorithm has an obvious improvement in face recognition rate.

References

1. Donoho, D.L.: Compressed sensing. IEEE Trans. Inf. Theory **52**(4), 1289–1306 (2006)
2. Fowler, J.E., Mun, S., Tramel, E.W.: Multiscale block compressed sensing with smoothed projected landweber reconstruction. In: Signal Processing Conference, Barcelona, pp. 564–568 (2011)
3. Liu, Y., Zhang, C., Kim, J.: Disparity-compensated total-variation minimization for compressed-sensed multiview image reconstruction. In: IEEE International Conference on Acoustics, Speech and Signal Processing, South Brisbane, pp. 1458–1462 (2015)
4. Mun, S., Fowler, J.E.: Block compressed sensing of images using directional transforms. In: IEEE International Conference on Image Processing, p. 547. IEEE (2010)
5. Tramel, E.W., Fowler, J.E.: Video compressed sensing with multihypothesis. In: Snowbird: Data Compression Conference, pp. 193–202. IEEE Computer Society (2011)

6. Zhang, J., Zhao, D., Gao, W.: Group-based sparse representation for image restoration. IEEE Trans. Image Process. **23**(8), 3336–3351 (2014)
7. Wang, J., Lu, C., Wang, M., et al.: Robust face recognition via adaptive sparse representation. IEEE Trans. Cybern. **44**(12), 2368–2378 (2014)

An On-line Monitoring Method for Monitoring Earth Grounding Resistance Based on a Hybrid Genetic Algorithm (Short Paper)

Guangxin Zhang[1], Minzhen Wang[1(✉)], Xinheng Wang[2],
Liying Zhao[1], and Jinyang Zhao[3]

[1] Changchun Institute of Technology, Changchun 130000, Jilin, China
Shilin008@sina.com
[2] School of Computing and Engineering, University of West London,
London, UK
[3] State Grid Fushun Power Supply Company, Fushun 113000, Liaoning, China

Abstract. In this paper, a method for measuring the grounding resistance of the tower without disconnecting all the down conductors is proposed for the first time in view of the shortage of manual measurement of the grounding resistance of the tower. This paper introduces the measurement model of single or multiple down conductors, and uses a hybrid genetic algorithm to comprehensively calculate the grounding resistance of all towers in the closed loop, which greatly improves the measurement accuracy. Through simulation analysis and actual measurement, it proves that the method is simple and convenient to measure, does not need to disconnect the grounding wire, and has high measurement accuracy. Compared with the clamp ammeter method, the accuracy is improved by 30%. The method is applied to the on-line monitoring system of the tower grounding resistance, which can reduce the labor intensity of the line maintenance personnel, greatly improve the work efficiency and provide a basis for discovering the fault in time.

Keywords: Grounding resistance · Grounding wire · Measurement ·
Hybrid genetic algorithm

1 Introduction

The grounding resistance of the transmission line tower [1] is an important parameter of the tower grounding device. It is very important for the stable operation of transmission line. When there is a lightning accident, the lightning current flows through the grounding device and flows into the ground. If the grounding resistance is too high, it will produce over-voltage counterattack and cause a trip accident of the circuit [2, 3]. Therefore, it is one of the important measures to ensure the operation reliability of the transmission line to measure the grounding resistance of the tower regularly and make it conform to the power industry standards [4].

At present, measurement methods mainly include fall-of-potential method [5], three-pole method [6], different-frequency method [7] and clamp ammeter method [8]. The fall-of-potential method requires many measurements to draw curve, this method is

H. Gao et al. (Eds.): CollaborateCom 2018, LNICST 268, pp. 581–591, 2019.
https://doi.org/10.1007/978-3-030-12981-1_41

heavy work and difficult to operate. Three pole method is accurate, but the operation is cumbersome, ant it is necessary to arrange the voltage pole and the current pole. The grounding down conductor must be disconnected during the measurement, which greatly increases the labor intensity of the staff and has low efficiency. The different-frequency method is to inject non-power frequency signals on the basis of the three-pole method, which can effectively eliminate the power frequency interference. The injection current is small and the wiring strength is low, but it is still offline measurement, and the measurement error is greatly affected by the frequency of the input signal. The megohm meter method is simple and convenient to measure. It can be measured by clamping the grounding down conductor with a jaw. When the pole has a grounding wire, it is not necessary to disconnect the grounding down conductor. However, when there is multiple grounding down conductors, it still needs to be disconnecting other grounding down conductors and retains the measured line only, which brings inconvenience to the measurement and causes a large measurement error [9]. The common shortcoming of these methods is that manual field measurement is required. When the measurement is performed, the grounding down conductor is disconnected, which consumes a lot of manpower and material resources, and is easy to cause loose bolts or poor contact, resulting in an increase in the grounding resistance of the tower. Therefore, this paper studies a real-time monitoring method of grounding resistance that does not disconnect all grounding down conductors and has high measurement accuracy.

2 Tower Grounding Resistance Measurement Model and Measurement Method Without Disconnecting the Grounding Down Conductor

When the transmission line has a lightning protection line and is directly connected to the tower to access the earth, all the towers in the same line form a parallel network through the lightning protection line, and each tower is a branch of the parallel network. The principle of measuring the unconnected grounding down conductor is to install a grounding resistance detector with the same number of grounding conductors for each tower, measure the grounding resistance of all the towers in the parallel network in time-sharing, and perform unified analysis and calculation, so as to obtain the ground resistance with higher accuracy.

The following is an example of measuring a base tower to introduce a measurement model and method for a single tower and multiple grounding down conductors.

2.1 Static Oblique Parabolic Model

The schematic diagram and equivalent model of the grounding resistance measurement of the single tower grounding down conductor are shown in Figs. 1 and 2, respectively. The measured tower and the overhead line, the adjacent tower and the grounding down conductor form a closed loop [10]. In the figure, R_1 is the grounding resistance of the tower to be tested, $R_2, R_3 \cdots R_n$ are the grounding resistance of other towers in the closed loop; $R_{p1}, R_{p2} \cdots R_{pn}$ is the resistance of the tower itself, $L_{p1}, L_{p2} \cdots L_{pn}$ is the self-reactance of the tower; $R_{l1}, R_{l2} \cdots R_{ln}$ is used to avoid lightning resistance, $L_{l1}, L_{l2} \cdots L_{ln}$ is the lightning line reactance; U_1 is the output voltage of the grounding resistance detector, and I_1 is the induced loop current.

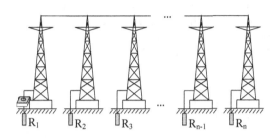

Fig. 1. Single grounding wire measurement diagram

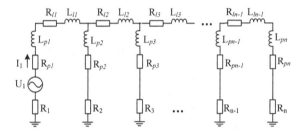

Fig. 2. Single grounding wire equivalent model

Since the lightning protection line and the resistance and reactance of the tower itself are small compared with the resistance of the tower to be tested, the measurement can be neglected, so the equivalent circuit can be simplified to Fig. 3, at this time, the loop resistance:

$$R_1' = R_1 + R_0 = \frac{U_1}{I_1} \tag{1}$$

Where R_0 is the parallel value of the other tower grounding resistance, i.e. $R_0 = R_2 // R_3 // \cdots // R_n$.

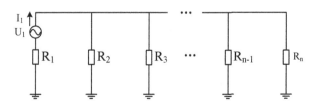

Fig. 3. Simplified equivalent model

585 G. Zhang et al.

Single grounding down the line, you only need to attach the grounding resistance detector directly to the grounding line of the tower, you can measure the grounding resistance in the circuit, and then get the tower grounding resistance. The grounding resistance detector is composed of a voltage coil, a current coil and a wireless trans-mission module. The measuring principle is to adopt the law of electromagnetic induction, the voltage coil provides an excitation signal to the circuit under test, and induces a pulse potential U on the circuit to be tested, at the potential U. Under the action, the current I will be generated in the circuit under test, U and I will be measured in real time, and the resistance value of the whole measurement circuit will be cal-culated according to Eq. (1).

According to the specification DL/T887-2004, when the number of parallel towers meets the requirements, the parallel value of other towers adjacent to the tower to be tested is far less than the grounding resistance of the tower under test, and is ignored in the calculation., the grounding resistance of the tower to be tested is:

$$R_1 \approx \frac{U_1}{I_1} \tag{2}$$

2.2 Multiple Grounding Down Conductor Measurement Models

In order to realize that there is multiple grounding down conductors in the tower, it is not necessary to disconnect the grounding down conductor. In this paper, a grounding resistance detector is installed for each grounding down conductor. When measuring, each detector is connected in parallel with each other. The power supply is supplied so that the induced voltages generated by each of the grounding down conductors are exactly equal. Under the premise that the internal resistance of the grounding of the tower is the same, the induced current generated by each grounding wire is exactly the same. Figures 4 and 5 are schematic diagrams and equivalent circuit diagrams for measuring the grounding resistance of four grounded down-conductor towers.

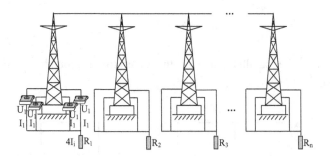

Fig. 4. Multiple grounding wire measurement schematic

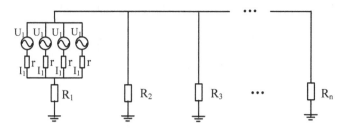

Fig. 5. Multiple grounding wire equivalent model

In Fig. 4, since the induced voltage and current generated by the four grounding down conductors are exactly the same, it is only necessary to measure the induced current of one of the down conductors. Therefore, among the four detectors, only one main detector is needed, which is the same as the principle of Sect. 2.1. It is responsible for supplying voltage to the grounding down conductor and measuring voltage and current. The other three are auxiliary detectors, which are responsible for guiding other grounding. The line provides power. In order to ensure the same internal resistance of each grounding wire, the upper and lower ends of the detectors to which the grounding wires are connected are respectively connected by wires, so that each grounding wire is limited to a fixed area.

It can be seen from Fig. 5 that, under the premise the specification is satisfied, the method has the same voltage U as the method for measuring a single down-conductor tower, and the current I flowing through the tower resistance R is four times the measured current. Therefore, the grounding resistance $R_1 \approx \frac{U_1}{4I_1}$ of the tower to be tested is $R_1 \approx \frac{U_1}{mI_1}$ if there are m grounding down conductors.

3 Calculation Method of Tower Grounding Resistance Measured Without Disconnecting the Grounding Down Conductor

Since the above measurement method ignores the lightning protection line in the loop, the tower itself and other parallel pole tower grounding resistance, there will be some error in the measurement results. In addition, in the actual measurement, there may be a local resistance increase caused by the open circuit of the ground, which also increases the measurement error of the ground resistance of the other towers. In order to reduce the error and improve the measurement accuracy, this paper considers the mutual influence between the grounding resistance of each pole in the loop, and adopts a new calculation method to analyze and calculate the grounding resistance of all the towers in the closed loop.

Measure the grounding resistance of each tower separately and bring it into Eq. (1).

$$
\begin{cases}
R'_1 = R_1 + \dfrac{1}{\frac{1}{R_2}+\frac{1}{R_3}+\cdots+\frac{1}{R_i}+\cdots+\frac{1}{R_n}} \\
R'_2 = R_2 + \dfrac{1}{\frac{1}{R_1}+\frac{1}{R_3}+\cdots+\frac{1}{R_i}+\cdots+\frac{1}{R_n}} \\
\quad\cdots\cdots \\
R'_i = R_i + \dfrac{1}{\frac{1}{R_1}+\cdots\frac{1}{R_{i-1}}+\frac{1}{R_{i+1}}+\cdots+\frac{1}{R_n}} \\
\quad\cdots\cdots \\
R'_n = R_n + \dfrac{1}{\frac{1}{R_1}+\frac{1}{R_2}+\cdots+\frac{1}{R_i}+\cdots+\frac{1}{R_{n-1}}}
\end{cases}
\tag{3}
$$

Where: R'_i is the measured value of the grounding resistance of the ith base tower in the parallel network. When the tower has one grounding down conductor, $R'_i = \frac{U_i}{I_i}$; when the tower has m grounding down conductors, $R'_i = \frac{U_i}{mI_i}$; U_i, I_i are the voltage and current detected by the ground resistance detector; R_i is the value of the tower grounding resistance to be calculated.

By solving the Eq. (3), the tower grounding resistances $R_1, R_2 \cdots R_n$ can be obtained. Equation (3) is a system of nonlinear equations with n variables and n equations $(n \geq 4)$. It is very difficult to solve directly. It needs to be transformed into extreme value problems. Classical algorithms (such as Newton method, gradient method and steepest descent Method, etc.) or genetic algorithm for calculation are used. The classical algorithm has strong local search ability and fast convergence speed, and can obtain the local optimal solution. However, its convergence is related to the selection of the initial point. The initial point quality directly affects the accuracy of the algorithm, but the initial selection is good. The point is very difficult. Genetic algorithm [11] (GA) is a randomized search method for simulating the evolutionary process of biological survival of the fittest. It has a strong global search ability and can quickly obtain the optimal solution range, but its local convergence ability is weak. Equation (3), genetic algorithm is not dominant compared with the classical algorithm, usually only find the suboptimal solution of the problem.

Combining the advantages and disadvantages of classical algorithm and genetic algorithm, this paper proposes a hybrid genetic algorithm [12] which combines classical algorithm (conjugate gradient method [13]) and genetic algorithm to solve nonlinear Eq. (3). The algorithm fully inherits the global search ability of the genetic algorithm and the local search and fast convergence ability of the classical algorithm, which can effectively improve the convergence speed and the accuracy of the solution, and quickly and accurately find the global optimal solution.

For the convenience of calculation, the Eq. (3) can be simply expressed as:

$$
\begin{cases}
f_1(R_1, R_2, R_3, \cdots, R_n) = R'_1 \\
f_2(R_1, R_2, R_3, \cdots, R_n) = R'_2 \\
\quad\cdots\cdots \\
f_i(R_1, R_2, R_3, \cdots, R_n) = R'_i \\
\quad\cdots\cdots \\
f_n(R_1, R_2, R_3, \cdots, R_n) = R'_n
\end{cases}
\tag{4}
$$

Where, $f_i(R_1, R_2, R_3, \cdots, R_n) = R_i + \dfrac{1}{\frac{1}{R_1} + \cdots \frac{1}{R_{i-1}} + \frac{1}{R_{i+1}} + \cdots + \frac{1}{R_n}}$

The idea of using a hybrid genetic algorithm to solve the Eq. (4) is: First, construct the objective function of the genetic algorithm, and transform the Eq. (4) into the extremum problem, that is, find an R, so that the value of the Eq. (4) is the smallest. When the minimum value approaches to 0, the corresponding R is the solution of the system of equations, and the objective function is shown in Eq. (5). Then, the selection, crossover and mutation operations of the genetic algorithm are performed to find a point near the most advantageous point (population center point). Finally, the population center point obtained by the genetic algorithm is used as the initial point of the conjugate gradient method for secondary optimization. Find the minimum value of the objective function and find the optimal solution. The specific steps are shown in Fig. 6.

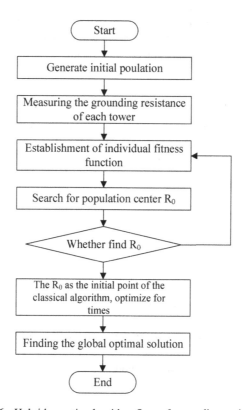

Fig. 6. Hybrid genetic algorithm flow of grounding resistance

$$\begin{cases} find : R = (R_1, R_2, R_3, \cdots, R_n) \\ s.t. : minf(R) = min\sqrt{\sum_{i=1}^{n} \left(f_i(R) - R'_i \right)^2} \end{cases} \quad (5)$$

4 Model Simulation and Application

In order to verify the accuracy of the method for measuring the grounding resistance of the tower and the accuracy of using the hybrid genetic algorithm to calculate the grounding resistance, a grounding resistance measurement simulation model was built. As shown in Figs. 3 and 5, five towers were built. In the simulation, the excitation voltage is set to 1 V and the frequency is 1582 Hz.

4.1 Simulation Analysis of Grounding Resistance Measurement Method Without Disconnecting Grounding Wire

For the case that the tower has a single root and multiple grounding down conductors, the traditional method - the clamp ammeter method and the unconnected ground down conductor measurement method are used to measure the grounding model parameters U_i and I_i, and calculate according to Eq. (2). The grounding resistance is approximated by R'_i, and the measurement results are shown in Table 1.

Table 1. Comparison of traditional methods and measured values of this research method

Grounding pole number	Single ground wire		Multiple grounding wires	
	Clamp ammeter method	Do not disconnect the ground wire	The clamp ammeter method	Do not disconnect the ground wire
1	6.35	6.35	4.18	4.18
2	8.71	8.70	7.25	7.24
3	12.3	12.31	5.32	5.32
4	5.60	5.60	10.51	10.5
5	6.35	6.34	7.26	7.25

According to the comparison results in Table 1, the grounding resistance values of the towers measured by the two methods are basically the same, that is, in the same environment, the resistance value measured by the grounding resistance measurement method of the tower without disconnecting the grounding down conductor can be compared with the clamp ammeter method. Comparable, and there is no need to disconnect the ground lead.

4.2 Accuracy Analysis of the Calculation Method of the Grounding Resistance of the Tower Without Measuring the Grounding Wire

Simulation analysis at Sect. 4.1 is only for the purpose of verifying the accuracy of the measurement method and directly using the comparative analysis of the measurement results. In this section, the direct measurement results are compared with the results calculated by the hybrid genetic algorithm, and the accuracy of the calculation results is verified. The error comparison is shown in Table 2.

Table 2. Comparison of error calculation results using/without genetic algorithm

Grounding pole number	Theoretical value (Ω)	Unused genetic algorithm		Used genetic algorithm	
		Calculated (Ω)	Error (%)	Calculated (Ω)	Error (%)
1	9	11.55	28.33	9.14	1.56
2	8	9.21	15.13	8.03	0.37
3	10	11.37	13.70	10.01	0.10
4	7	8.62	23.14	7.02	0.29
5	13	15.87	22.08	13.21	1.62

In order to more intuitively represent the error situation, the error curve of the mixed and used genetic algorithm is drawn using Matlab as shown in Fig. 7.

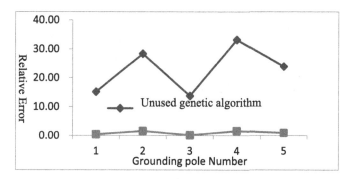

Fig. 7. Relative error curve of ground resistance

It can be seen from Fig. 6 that the grounding resistance error is relatively large without using the genetic algorithm, and the error of the resistance value calculated by the hybrid genetic algorithm is greatly reduced. In the unconnected grounding down-line measurement model, the hybrid genetic algorithm is used to calculate the grounding. The resistance can greatly improve the measurement accuracy of the tower grounding resistance.

The method for measuring the grounding resistance of the poles of the uninterrupted grounding wire studied in this paper has been applied to the real-time monitoring system of the ground resistance of the transmission line, and it has been put into use in the state grid Yanbian power supply company 66 kV Yanxijiayi line 2#–11#, and the state grid Dandong power supply company 66 kV Langqian line 1#–6#. Since the installation, the operation has been stable, and several abnormalities in the grounding resistance of the tower have been found. For example, Langqian line 3# tower grounding pole grounding resistance being very high, nearly 300 Ω, and other grounding resistance values are normal, which indicates that there is a bad contact condition in the grounding pole of the 3# pole tower. The staff found the hidden danger of the line in time according to the measurement result and avoided the occurrence of lightning strikes. The long-term operation results show that the method is convenient to measure, does not need to disconnect the grounding wire, and has high precision, which can completely replace the traditional pole tower grounding resistance measurement method. It provides great convenience for line maintenance personnel and provides technical support for timely detection of hidden dangers.

5 Conclusion

In this paper, the measurement method of the grounding resistance of the transmission line tower is studied, and the grounding resistance of the tower is measured without any disconnection. The method has obvious advantages for the measurement of the tower with multiple grounding down conductors. In order to improve the measurement accuracy, the mutual influence between adjacent towers in the same parallel network is considered, the grounding resistance of each tower is measured, the grounding resistance equations are constructed, and the grounding resistance is calculated by the hybrid genetic algorithm, which greatly improves the measurement accuracy. Through simulation analysis and practical application, the method studied in this paper is simple in operation and high in measurement accuracy. It can be used in online monitoring system, replacing traditional manual measurement methods, greatly improving the labor efficiency of workers, and the application prospect is very broad.

References

1. Lin, J.: Three - pole method and clamp - meter method for measuring earthing resistance of transmission line. Electr. Eng. Autom. **30**, 1–2 (2016)
2. Liao, F., Huang, W.: Study on new model and test method of ground parameter of line pole tower. Power Electr. Eng. **29**(4), 1–4 (2009)
3. Xu, W., Li, X.: Based on ATP-EMTP, the calculation model of impact grounding resistance of tower ground body. Electr. Power Constr. **31**(5), 22–25 (2010)
4. Wu, H.: Accurate measurement method and experimental study of earthing resistance of poles and towers, pp. 1–2. Chongqing University (2016)
5. Wu, Y., Xie, B.: Effect of the length of the test line on the measurement of grounding resistance by potential drop method. New Technol. New Prod. China **1**(2), 32–33 (2016)
6. Yang, M.: Research on measurement method of ground resistance of transmission line poles and towers. New Technol. New Prod. China (9), 78 (2015)
7. Jia, C., Hu, Z.: Measurement of grounding resistance of grounding grid by multiple synchronous frequency. Power Autom. Equip. (4), 167–172 (2015)
8. Zhou, Q.: Comparison and analysis of ground resistance measurement of two commonly used transmission line poles and towers. Electr. Measur. **12**(9), 48–49 (2012)
9. Galliana, F., Capra, P.P.: Traceable technique to calibrate clamp meters in AC current from 100 to 1 500 A. IEEE Trans. Power Syst. **61**(9), 2512–2513 (2012)
10. Guo, K.: Study on measuring method of ground resistance of transmission line tower, pp. 11–15. North China Electric Power University (2008)

11. Tian, Q., Gu, Z.: Solving nonlinear equations based on hybrid genetic algorithm. Comput. Technol. Dev. **17**(3), 10–12 (2007)
12. Xing, H., He, G.: Application of hybrid genetic algorithm in ground resistance measurement. J. Electro. Measur. Instrum. **30**(9), 1389–1396 (2016)
13. Li, J., Wang, Y.: Fast convergence of hybrid genetic algorithm. Comput. Eng. Des. **35**(2), 686–689 (2014)

Cloud Technology and Applications

How Good is Query Optimizer in Spark?

Zujie Ren[1(✉)], Na Yun[1], Youhuizi Li[1], Jian Wan[2], Yuan Wang[3], Lihua Yu[3],
and Xinxin Fan[3]

[1] School of Computer Science, Hangzhou Dianzi University, Hangzhou, China
renzju@gmail.com
[2] Department of Software Engineering, Zhejiang University of Science
and Technology, Hangzhou, China
[3] Key Enterprise Research Institute of NetEase Big Data of Zhejiang Province,
Netease Hangzhou, Network Co. Ltd., Hangzhou, China

Abstract. In the big data community, Spark plays an important role
and is used to process interactive queries. Spark employs a query optimizer, called Catalyst, to interpret SQL queries to optimized query execution plans. Catalyst contains a number of optimization rules and supports cost-based optimization. Although query optimization techniques
have been well studied in the field of relational database systems, the
effectiveness of Catalyst in Spark is still unclear. In this paper, we investigated the effectiveness of rule-based and cost-based optimization in
Catalyst, meanwhile, we obtained a set of comparative experiments by
varying the data volume and the number of nodes. It is found that even
when applied query optimizations, the execution time of most TPC-H
queries were slightly reduced. Some interesting observations were made
on Catalyst, which can enable the community to have a better understanding and improvement of the query optimizer in Spark.

Keywords: Spark SQL · Catalyst · Query optimization

1 Introduction

With the emergence of various types of big data frameworks, a group of data
query processing systems have been developed, such as Apache Hadoop [1],
Google Dremel [2], Cloudera Impala [3], and Apache Spark [4]. Spark supports
processing structured data using either Spark SQL or DataFrame API [5–7]. Like
relational database management systems, Spark implements a query optimizer,
called Catalyst, which converts SQL-like queries into logical execution plans.

Query optimization techniques, including rule-based and cost-based optimization, have attracted a large number of scholars to study it [8–11]. However, few people have evaluated the effectiveness of query optimizer in Spark.
Although query optimizer in relational databases can significantly accelerate the
execution of SQL queries [12–15], the performance of query optimizer in Spark is
still unclear. With the rapid development of Spark, Catalyst supports both rule-
based and cost-based optimization since the version of Spark 2.2. A systematic
evaluation of Catalyst will contribute to optimize the performance of Spark.

© ICST Institute for Computer Sciences, Social Informatics and Telecommunications Engineering 2019
Published by Springer Nature Switzerland AG 2019. All Rights Reserved
H. Gao et al. (Eds.): CollaborateCom 2018, LNICST 268, pp. 595–609, 2019.
https://doi.org/10.1007/978-3-030-12981-1_42

In this paper, we investigated the query execution efficiency for different optimization rules. A group of queries in TPC-H [16–18] are selected to evaluate rule-based and cost-based optimization. In the experiments, we varied both data volume and cluster scale to observe the query execution time. We found that the execution time were accelerated slightly for most query optimization rules. Optimization rules has slight effect on the optimization of SQL query executions.

2   Related Work

Query optimization has attracted plenty of research attention [19–22]. Many researchers focused on improving the effectiveness of optimization techniques. Lei *et al.* [23] investigated the quality of cardinality estimator in query optimizers of a group of DBMS, and found that all estimators routinely produce large errors. They found that exhaustive enumeration techniques can improve performance despite the sub-optimal cardinality estimates.

Kocsis *et al.* [24] proposed *Hylas*, a tool for automatically optimizing Spark queries in the source code by semantics-preserving transformation strategy. Liu *et al.* [25] proposed a prototype of query optimization based on cost model, and defined cost models for the common operations in relational queries. Zhang *et al.* [26] proposed an optimization scheme of partial bloom filter, it can reduce the amount of data in the shuffle stage and effectively improve the performance of equivalent connection.

Yang *et al.* [27] decided to enhance Spark SQL optimizer with detailed statistics information. This scheme is able to filter out most of the records in advance, which can reduce the amount of data in the shuffle stage and effectively improve the performance of equivalent connection.

Although a few research efforts have been put on query optimizers in Spark, the above papers are based on the improvement of optimization techniques or tools, and there is no systematic study on the optimization effect of Catalyst, it is still in infant stage. In this paper, we characterized the effectiveness of the query optimization in Spark, aiming to derive some design implications for improving the query optimizer in Spark.

3   Experimental Results

TPC-H benchmark are chosen to evaluate the query optimization performance of Catalyst. During the experiments, we selected a subset of TPC-H queries based on the optimization rules. Those queries include Q2, Q3, Q5, Q7, Q9, Q12, Q14, Q16, Q18, Q19 and Q22. The master and slave nodes in Spark cluster are configured with 128GB memory and 40 CPU cores.

We compared the execution time and tasks in cluster environments between optimization rules are used and not used, so as to observe the effectiveness of rule-based optimization and cost-based optimization framework in Catalyst.

3.1   Overview of Catalyst

Catalyst follows a typical structure of query optimizers. The main components of Catalyst and their functions are described as follows (Fig. 1).

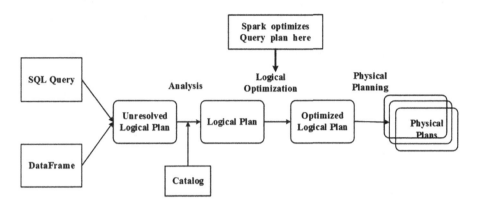

Fig. 1. The architecture of Catalyst.

- **SQLParser**–parses SQL statements, generates a syntax tree, and forms unresolved logical plans.
- **Analyzer**–combines the unresolved logic plan generated in the previous step with the data dictionary to bind and generate analyzed logical plans.
- **Optimizer**–applies rules to logical plans and expressions, merge and optimize tree nodes to obtain the optimized logical plans.
- **SparkPlanner**–transforms optimized logical plans into physical programs that can be recognized by processing.
- **CostModel**–selects the best physical execution plan based on some performance data.

As the kernel of Catalyst, Optimizer processes SQL queries based on the rules defined in the batches [6], including *CombineFilters*, *PushDownPredicate*, *LikeSimplication*, *CombineLimits*, *CombineUnions*, *ConstantFolding* and *NullProPagation* optimization rules.

However, the query plans automatically chosen by the Spark optimizer are not optimal, especially on the cost. In order to improve the quality, Yang *et al.* [27] decided to enhance Spark SQL optimizer with detailed statistics information. So that we can better estimate the number of output records and output size for each database operator.

3.2   Evaluation of Rules

CombineFilters. *CombineFilters* rule can recursively merge adjacent filter conditions. If this rule is not applied, the filter statements are carried out one by one, as defined in the SQL queries. *Q2, Q3* and *Q18* in TPC-H are selected to drive the target system and observe the performance changes caused by *CombineFilters* rule. The results are shown in Table 1 and Fig. 2. (The prefix "U_" represents that use of the optimization rules, and the prefix of "UN_" means no use of optimization rules.) For Q2, there is only a slight differences in the number of stages and tasks, but for Q3 and Q18, they are completely identical.

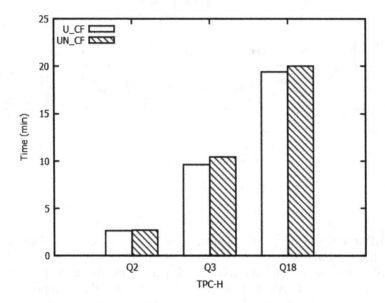

Fig. 2. Execution time changes when applying *CombineFilters*

Table 1. The results when applying *CombineFilters* and not.

Experiment cases	Division of stages	Number of tasks
U-Q2	0~16	2618
UN-Q2	0~17	2620
U-Q3	0~4	3377
UN-Q3	0~4	3377
U-Q18	0~7	6149
UN-Q18	0~7	6149

For *CombineFilters* optimization rule, there are slight differences on the processing time of SQL statements (Fig. 2). However, I/O fluctuates and disk transfers are much frequent in the condition without *CombineFilters* rule. *CombineFilters* rule can reduce disk interaction in the optimization of *Q18* (Fig. 3).

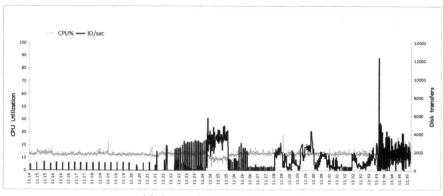

(a) Q18 with *CombineFilters* rule

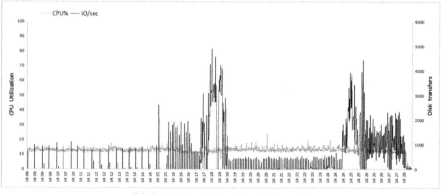

(b) Q18 without *CombineFilters* rule

Fig. 3. The resource utilization with and without *CombineFilters*.

PushDownPredicate. *PushDownPredicate* optimization rule can push the predicate in SQL statements into the subqueries, thereby reduce the number of subsequent data processing. We selected *Q5*, *Q7*, *Q16* of TPC-H to carry on experiments. For the same SQL statements, the results are shown in Table 2. For Q5, Q7, Q16, the number of stages and tasks is exactly the same when applying *PushDownPredicate* and not.

As shown in Fig. 4, the time consumed when not using *PushDownPredicate* rule is more than that of using the optimization rule in the optimization process for *Q5*. However, the processing time of SQL statements are almost same for *Q7* and *Q16*.

LikeSimplification. *LikeSimplification* optimization rule can simplify *"LIKE"* expression to avoid the full scan of tables with extra calculation burden. For example, it can optimize the sentence *"%N"* (*%N* represents the demo beginning with *N*) to *"StartsWith"* for operations. *Q2*, *Q9* and *Q14* of TPC-H are selected to drive experiments.

Table 2. The results when applying *PushDownPredicate* and not.

Experiment cases	Division of stages	Number of tasks
U-Q5	0~11	4186
UN-Q5	0~11	4186
U-Q7	0~10	4184
UN-Q7	0~10	4184
U-Q16	0~0(Job0) 1~5(Job 1)	5(Job0) 1038(Job1)
UN-Q16	0~0(Job0) 1~5(Job 1)	5(Job0) 1038(Job1)

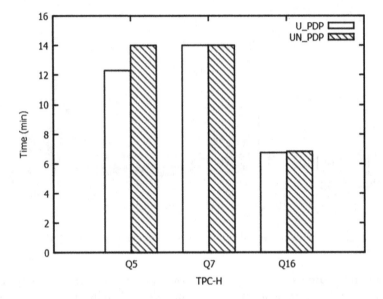

Fig. 4. Execution time changes when using *PushDownPredicate*.

Table 3. The results when applying *LikeSimplification* and not.

Experiment cases	Division of stages	Number of tasks
U-Q2	0~16	2618
UN-Q2	0~16	2618
U-Q9	0~11	4548
UN-Q9	0~11	4548
U-Q14	0~3	2647
UN-Q14	0~3	2647

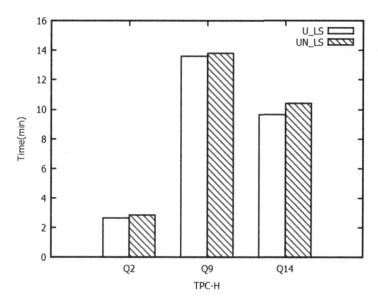

Fig. 5. Execution time changes when using *LikeSimplification* ("LS" refers to *LikeSimplification* rule).

Stages and tasks remain unchanged during the processing of performing *Q2*, *Q9*, and *Q14* (Table 3), Fig. 5 depicts the results for *Q2*, *Q9*, and *Q14*. The suffix of "LS" refers to *LikeSimplification* rule. The "*%N*" involved in SQL statements are optimized to "*StartsWith*" for operations when using *LikeSimplification* optimization rule. Figure 5 shows that the execution efficiency is slightly improved when using LikeSimplication.

3.3   Evaluation with Special Queries

In this section, we focused on the optimization strategies of other rules. TPC-H benchmark do not contain these rules in SQL statement. Same principles as those mentioned above, we selected representative SQL statements to do experiments, those queries include *CombineLimits*, *CombineUnions*, *ConstantFolding* and *NullPropagation*. The query are executed in cluster environments that use the corresponding optimization rules and do not use.

CombineLimits rule compares adjacent "*Limit*" statements in SQL, the small one retains and returns as a result, it can avoid counting "*Limit*" statements many times during the process of calculation. *CombineUnions* rule recursively merges adjacent "*Union*" statements. *ConstantFolding* rule can calculate expressions that are calculated directly in advance, there is no need to put expressions into the physical execution to generate objects to operate. *NullPropagation* rule replaces "*Null*" value, expressions that determine the value of "*Null*" are calculated at the logical stage, can avoid propagation of "*Null*" values on syntax trees.

Table 4. The results when applying optimization rules.

Experiment cases	Division of stages	Number of task
U-*CombineLimits*	0∼3(Job0) 4∼6(Job1)	639(Job0) 2447(Job1)
UN-*CombineLimits*	0∼3(Job0) 4∼7(Job1)	639(Job0) 2647(Job1)
U-*CombineUnions*	0∼2(Job0)	2904(Job0)
UN-*CombineUnions*	0∼1(Job0) 2∼2(Job1) 3∼3(Job2)	2904(Job0) 4(Job1) 17(Job2)
U-*ConstantFolding*	0(Job0)	1(Job0)
UN-*ConstantFolding*	0(Job0)	1(Job0)
U-*NullPropagation*	0∼1(Job0)	2373(Job0)
UN-*NullPropagation*	0∼1(Job0)	2373(Job0)

We executed the same SQL statements in cluster environments when the optimization rules are using and not. The results are shown in Table 4, more tasks are needed to perform under the condition that *CombineLimits* or *Combine Unions* rule is not used, but stages and tasks remain unchanged when applying *CombineUnions* and *NullPropagation* rule (Each job gets divided into smaller sets of tasks called stages that depend on each other, similar to the map and reduce stages in MapReduce).

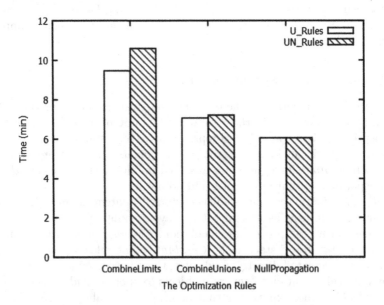

Fig. 6. Execution time changes when using optimization rules.

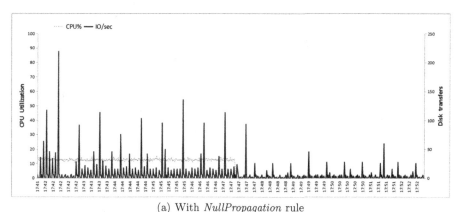

(a) With *NullPropagation* rule

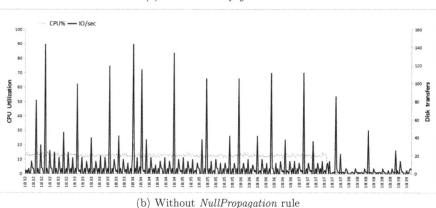

(b) Without *NullPropagation* rule

Fig. 7. The resource utilization with and without *NullPropagation*.

More time are needed to perform under the condition that *CombineLimits* rule is not used, and there are slight differences for *CombineUnions* and *NullPropagation* (Fig. 6). But as far as resource consumption is concerned, more CPU and I/O resources are needed to process the same SQL statements without using the corresponding optimization rules (Fig. 7).

3.4 Varying Data Sizes

Spark implements cost-based optimization framework to improve the quality of query execution plan. In this section, we analyzed the optimization effects of CBO and RBO under different sizes of data.

The scala factor *(SF)* was set as 10 and 100, respectively. Evaluation queries include Q2, Q3, Q5, Q7, Q9, Q12, Q14, Q16, Q18, Q19 and Q22. The results are shown in Fig. 8. Meanwhile, we set SF = 10 and 100 when RBO is applied. Experiments are carried out on *CombineFilters* (Fig. 9a), *PushDownPredicate* (Fig. 9b) and *LikeSimplication* (Fig. 9c) rules.

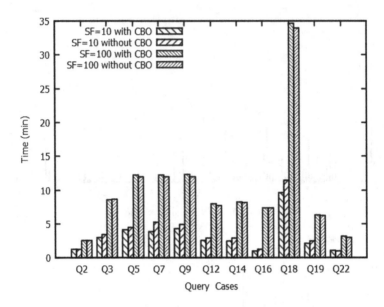

Fig. 8. Execution time changes with and without CBO.

The results are shown in Fig. 9. With the increase of the data volume, the processing time for the same SQL statements is increased correspondingly. For the same data scale, the execution time reductions are still slight.

3.5 Varying Cluster Scale

In this section, we compared the optimization effects of CBO and RBO under different cluster scales. At the same time, we guaranteed that the amount of data processed on each slave node is up to 10G.

The number of slave nodes are ranged from 1 to 15. The rules of *Combine-Filters*, *PushDownPredicate* and *LikeSimplication* are applied. The processing time results are shown in Fig. 10, which shows that the improvement achieved by *CombineFilters* rule for Q3 is slight, and there is a downward trend for Q9 with the increase of cluster scales. For Q7, the execution time is reduced if not applying optimization rule. Less time is spent without using the optimization rule.

Similarly, SQL queries with and without CBO framework are executed. The results of experiments are shown in Fig. 11. For Q12, the expansion of cluster scales has limited effect. For Q5, the SQL processing time has a downward trend without the usage of CBO framework. However, with the increase of cluster scales, the time needed to use CBO optimization rule is small for Q9.

When the number of slave nodes varies from 1, 5, 10 to 15, neither rule-based optimization nor CBO framework have much effect. Rule-based optimization and CBO framework have different optimization effects for different SQL statements. However, the differences are not obvious.

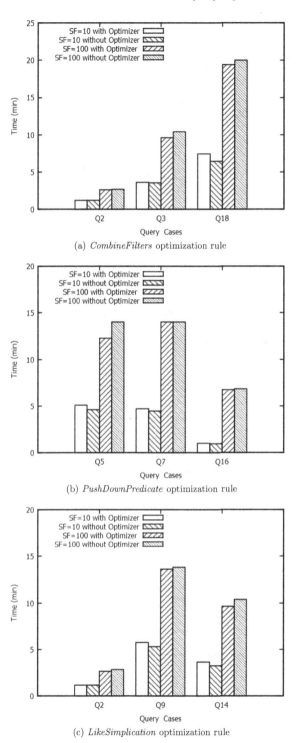

(a) *CombineFilters* optimization rule

(b) *PushDownPredicate* optimization rule

(c) *LikeSimplication* optimization rule

Fig. 9. Execution time with different data volumes.

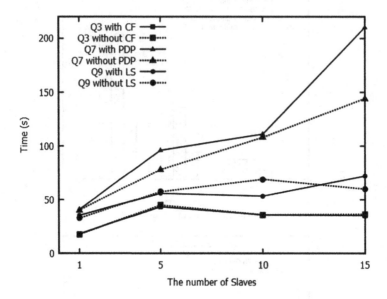

Fig. 10. Execution time changes when using rule-based optimization.

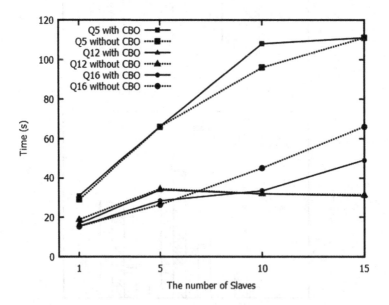

Fig. 11. Execution time changes when using cost-based optimization.

4   Discussion

Based on the experimental results, the resource consumption by Spark SQL in runtime can be realized and choose the optimization strategy better, so that we can further decrease the system overhead and query time. To achieve that, we must understand the optimization strategy of optimization rules and its behaviors. The written SQL statements should be standardized, and conform to the syntax requirements of the optimization method. Thus, faster and more accurate query optimization of SQL statements can be achieved.

As the kernel of Catalyst, optimizer is responsible for optimizing the syntax tree, it contains many rules defined in the batches, including *CombineFilters*, *PushDownPredicate*, *LikeSimplication*, *CombineLimits*, *CombineUnions*, *ConstantFolding* and *NullProPagation* optimization rules. The corresponding optimization rules are summarized in Table 5.

Table 5. The list of optimization rules.

The optimization rules	Introduction of corresponding optimization strategies
CombineFilters	Recursively merge adjacent filter conditions
PushDownPredicate	Push the predicate in SQL statements into the subquery, reduce the number of subsequent data processing
LikeSimplication	Simplify "LIKE" expression to avoid the full scan of tables
CombineLimits	Compare adjacent "Limit" statements, and return the small one.
CombineUnions	Recursively merge adjacent "Union" statements
ConstantFolding	Calculate expressions in advance that are calculated directly
NullPropagation	Replace "Null" value

After evaluating the Catalyst optimizer, we investigated the effectiveness of the optimization rules and cost-based optimization in Catalyst. We derived the following implications:

- The query optimizer has little effect on execution time reductions. Different SQL statements correspond to different optimization rules. However, optimization strategies are not always the optimal choice in optimizer.
- For different SQL statements, rule-based optimization and CBO framework have little effect under different cluster scales.
- For the same SQL statements, the processing time grows with the increase of the workload data volume. However, even if the amount of data grows, the reduction of execution time will not become obvious.

5   Conclusion

In this paper, the optimization effects of rule-based and cost-based optimization framework in Catalyst optimizer in Spark were studied. We evaluated their
optimization performance under various queries. At the same time, some comprehensive validation experiments was carried out by varying the data volume
and cluster scale. The results show that even if query optimization rules are
applied, the execution time of most benchmark queries were slightly reduced,
and optimization rules have slight effect on the executing of SQL statements.

Acknowledgement. This work is supported by Key Research and Development Program of Zhejiang Province (No. 2018C01098), and the Natural Science Foundation of
Zhejiang Province (NO. LY18F020014).

References

1. Taylor, R.C.: An overview of the Hadoop/MapReduce/HBase framework and its
   current applications in bioinformatics. BMC Bioinform. **11**, S1 (2010)
2. Melnik, S., et al.: Dremel: interactive analysis of web-scale datasets. Proc. VLDB
   Endow. **3**(1–2), 330–339 (2010)
3. Ducarme, P., Rahman, M., Brasseur, R.: IMPALA: a simple restraint field to simulate the biological membrane in molecular structure studies. Proteins Struct. Funct.
   Bioinform. **30**(4), 357–371 (1998)
4. Zaharia, M., Chowdhury, M., Franklin, M.J., Shenker, S., Stoica, I.: Spark: cluster
   computing with working sets. In: USENIX Conference on Hot Topics in Cloud
   Computing, p. 10 (2010)
5. Salloum, S., Dautov, R., Chen, X., Peng, P.X., Huang, J.Z.: Big data analytics on
   apache spark. Int. J. Data Sci. Anal. **1**(3–4), 145–164 (2016)
6. Armbrust, M., et al.: Spark SQL: relational data processing in spark. In: SIGMOD
   2015, pp. 1383–1394. ACM (2015)
7. Zaharia, M., et al.: Apache spark: a unified engine for big data processing. Commun. ACM **59**(11), 56–65 (2016)
8. Ma, J., et al.: Logical query optimization for cloudera impala system. J. Syst.
   Softw. **125**, 35–46 (2017)
9. Naacke, H., Curé, O., Amann, B.: SPARQL query processing with apache spark.
   arXiv preprint arXiv:1604.08903 (2016)
10. Graefe, G.: The cascades framework for query optimization. IEEE Data Eng. Bull.
    18(3), 19–29 (1995)
11. Esawi, A.M.K., Ashby, M.F.: Cost-based ranking for manufacturing process selec-
    tion. In: Batoz, J.L., Chedmail, P., Cognet, G., Fortin, C. (eds.) Integrated Design
    and Manufacturing in Mechanical Engineering, pp. 603–610. Springer, Dordrecht
    (1999). https://doi.org/10.1007/978-94-015-9198-0_74
12. Wu, J.-M., Zhou, J.: Research of optimization rule of SQL based on oracle database.
    J. Shaanxi Univ. Technol. (2013)
13. Antoshenkov, G., Ziauddin, M.: Query processing and optimization in oracle RDB.
    VLDB J. Int. J. Very Large Data Bases **5**(4), 229–237 (1996)
14. Chaudhuri, S.: An overview of query optimization in relational systems. In: Pro-
    ceedings of the seventeenth ACM SIGACT-SIGMOD-SIGART Symposium on
    Principles of Database Systems, pp. 34–43. ACM (1998)

15. Herodotou, H., Babu, S.: Profiling, what-if analysis, and cost-based optimization of mapreduce programs. Proc. VLDB Endow. **4**(11), 1111–1122 (2011)
16. Chiba, T., Onodera, T.: Workload characterization and optimization of TPC-H queries on apache spark. In: IEEE International Symposium on Performance Analysis of Systems and Software (ISPASS), pp. 112–121. IEEE (2016)
17. Liang, W., Zheng, Y.: TPC-H analysis and test tool design. Comput. Eng. Appl. (2007)
18. Transaction processing performance council. http://www.tpc.org
19. Ioannidis, Y.E.: Query optimization. ACM Comput. Surv. (CSUR) **28**(1), 121–123 (1996)
20. Roy, P., Seshadri, S., Sudarshan, S., Bhobe, S.: Efficient and extensible algorithms for multi query optimization. ACM SIGMOD Rec. **29**, 249–260 (2000)
21. Graefe, G., DeWitt, D.J.: The EXODUS Optimizer Generator, vol. 16. ACM (1987)
22. Barbas, P.M.: Database query optimization, 21 January 2014. US Patent 8,635,206
23. Leis, V., Gubichev, A., Mirchev, A., Boncz, P., Kemper, A., Neumann, T.: How good are query optimizers, really? Proc. VLDB Endow. **9**(3), 204–215 (2015)
24. Kocsis, Z.A., Drake, J.H., Carson, D., Swan, J.: Automatic improvement of apache spark queries using semantics-preserving program reduction. In: Proceedings of the 2016 on Genetic and Evolutionary Computation Conference Companion, pp. 1141–1146. ACM (2016)
25. Liu, C.: Research on SparkSQL query optimization based on cost model (2016)
26. Zhang, L.: Research on query analysis and optimization based on spark system (2016)
27. Wang, Z.: Spark issue. https://issues.apache.org/jira/browse/SPARK-16026

An Optimized Multi-Paxos Protocol with Centralized Failover Mechanism for Cloud Storage Applications

Wenmin Lin[1], Hao Jiang[1], Nailiang Zhao[2(✉)], and Jilin Zhang[2]

[1] School of Computer Science and Technology, Hangzhou Dianzi University,
Hangzhou, China
linwenmin@hdu.edu.cn, Jianghaokobe@163.com
[2] Network and Information Center, Hangzhou Dianzi University,
Hangzhou, China
{znl,jilin.zhang}@hdu.edu.cn

Abstract. For typical Multi-Paxos protocol running on a cloud storage application, the failover mechanism is complex in terms of implementation. When the leader fails within a replica group, a new leader should be elected by broadcasting prepare requests over the replica group. Moreover, repairing new leader's missing log entries requires broadcasting prepare request as well. This introduces too much network cost and increase the latency to restore normal storage service at the same time. In view of this challenge, an optimization for Multi-Paxos protocol with centralized failover mechanism for cloud storage applications is proposed in this paper. Compared with typical Multi-Paxos protocol, failover mechanism and normal client requests handling logic are split, and been handled by two clusters respectively: A coordinator cluster is dedicated to handle failover issues as a central manager; while a data cluster only takes charge of data replication and storage regarding client commands. With the centralized failover mechanism in the new design, the centralized coordinator cluster maintains real-time status information of each replica group. And a replica with largest apply index value is elected as the new leader by coordinator cluster; while repairing missing log entries can be achieved with limited replica's bitmap information maintained by coordinator cluster as well. Comparison between two protocols is implemented and analyzed to prove the feasibility of our proposal.

Keywords: Centralized failover mechanism · Multi-Paxos · Replica group ·
Leader election · Leader repair

1 Introduction

Nowadays, increasing amount of applications are deployed in cloud, due to the convenience of "pay as you go" manner of using IT infrastructure. Among those applications, cloud storage is one of the most popular one. Cloud storage applications enable users to store data of their applications on cloud, instead of building their own storage infrastructures [1, 2]. As a typical distributed computing application, cloud storage

H. Gao et al. (Eds.): CollaborateCom 2018, LNICST 268, pp. 610–625, 2019.
https://doi.org/10.1007/978-3-030-12981-1_43

systems take advantage of replica technique to achieve fault tolerance and high availability, by storing user's data on multiple disks over the network, so as to make sure the data won't be lost as long as majority disks works probably [3].

As a typical distributed computing application, a cloud storage system can be treated as a set of distributed servers belong to one cluster. The servers work as a whole to handle client commands (i.e., write or read operations to store data and read stored data) [4]. Each sever can be described as a deterministic state machine that performs client commands in sequence. The state machine has a current state, and it performs a step by taking as input a client command and producing an output and a new state. The core implementation of a cloud storage system is to guarantee all servers execute the same sequence of state machine commands [5]. As a result, every cloud storage system can be modeled as a replicated state machine as shown in Fig. 1.

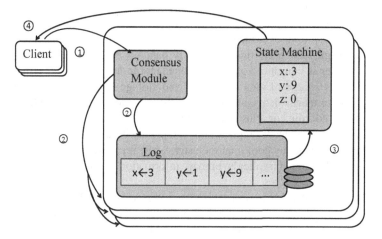

Fig. 1. Replicated state machine architecture [5].

Replicated state machines are typically implemented using a replicated log [4, 5]. Each server stores a log containing a series of client commands, which its state machine executes in sequence. Each log contains the same commands in the same order, so each state machine processes the same sequence of commands. Since the state machines are deterministic, each computes the same state and the same sequence of outputs. Keeping the replicated log consistent is the job of the consensus algorithm [16]. The consensus module on a server receives commands from clients and adds them to its log. It communicates with the consensus modules on other servers to ensure that every log eventually contains the same requests in the same order, even if some servers fail. Once commands are properly replicated, each server's state machine processes them in log order, and the outputs are returned to clients. As a result, the servers appear to form a single, highly reliable state machine.

There have been numerous researches on the consensus algorithm for replicated state machines. Among which Paxos is the dominated one over last decades: most implementations of consensus are based on Paxos or influenced by it. Representative algorithms include Multi-Paxos [4], E-Paxos [6], as well as Raft [5]. The difference between Paxos and its variants vs. Raft is: Raft is strongly based on leadership mechanism, all client commands are handled by leader replica and other replicas work as followers; while for Multi-Paxos, leader is not necessarily required, but it always employs a distinguished leader to guarantee liveness of the algorithm; Moreover, E-paxos is totally leaderless to guarantee client latency for handling client commands in wide area environment. In this paper, we mainly focus on the optimization of Multi-Paxos regarding its failover mechanism.

For cloud storage systems running typical Multi-Paxos protocol, when the leader fails within a replica group, prepare requests are broadcast over the replica group to elect a new leader; and for each missing log entry in the new leader, repairing it requires broadcasting prepare requests to learn the missing log entry as well. This is both time consuming and introducing too much network cost. In view of this challenge, rather than electing a new leader in a distributed manner, we introduce a centralized failover mechanism to improve system performance of Multi-Paxos protocol in this paper. Briefly, we split failover mechanism and normal client commands handling logic in the new design, and each functionality is handled by a cluster respectively: A coordinator cluster is introduced as a central manager to handle failover issues; A data cluster only takes charge of data replication and storage regarding client commands. Moreover, failover mechanism consists of two phases: leader election and leader repair. The centralized coordinator cluster maintains real-time status information of each replica group. When the leader replica fails, a replica with largest apply index value is elected as the new leader by coordinator cluster; while repairing missing log entries can be achieved with limited replica's bitmap information maintained by coordinator cluster as well.

The reminder of this paper is organized as follows: Sect. 2 discusses related work on consensus algorithm for cloud storage applications. Section 3 highlights the problem of original failover mechanism with typical Multi-Paxos protocol. The details of centralized failover mechanism to optimize Multi-Paxos protocol is presented in Sect. 4. Section 5 compares our proposal and typical Multi-Paxos protocol with respect to message delay and message cost. Section 6 evaluate the performance of optimized Multi-Paxos protocol and typical Multi-Paxos protocol in terms of commit throughput. And Sect. 7 concludes the paper.

2   Related Work

Regarding distributed computing systems such as cloud storage applications [17, 18], the core of implementation is the consensus algorithm, to make sure each server belongs to the same cluster executes client commands in the same sequence [11–13]. There have been numerous researches related to consensus algorithms over last decades [14, 15], from which Paxos is the dominated one. Most implementations of consensus are based on Paxos or influenced by it. Among those consensus algorithms, they can be categorized as follows: (1) Lamport's Paxos [4, 8, 9], and its variants such as Multi-Paxos, Elaborations paxos (E-paxos) [6]; (2) Raft protocol [5], which is based on strong leadership mechanism.

The main difference between those consensus algorithm is the leadership mechanism: (1) Multi-Paxos does not necessarily requires a leader; and when there's no leader in a replica group, Multi-Paxos degrades to Basic-Paxos [10]. (2) E-Paxos is totally leaderless, which is designed to reduce remote client latency. It is a good candidate for wide-area data storage applications. (3) Moreover, Raft uses a strong form of leadership than other two consensus algorithms.

When failover happens, Multi-Paxos, E-paxos and Raft will behave differently. (1) For typical Multi-Paxos, a new leader will be elected by broadcasting prepare request in a replica group. And the leader is elected randomly, which is the first replica receives Prepare OK from majority replicas. Then missing log entry repair is conducted for leader by learning it from Prepare request as well. (2) For E-Paxos, since there's no leader in the replica group, when failover happens, a replica may only need to learn the decision for an paxos instance, since it has to execute commands that depend on that instance. The data repair process is similar to Multi-Paxos, so missing log entries with a replica is learnt from Prepare request as well. (3) For Raft, a leader must be elected before the system can handle more client request, that's because the leader handles all client requests (if a client contacts a follower, the follower redirects it to the leader). Raft uses randomized times to elect leaders, which adds a small amount of mechanism to heartbeats. The implementation simplifies the management of replicated log, and makes Raft easier to understand when comparing with other 2 protocols.

Our work is to optimize Multi-Paxos protocol in terms of system performance when replica failure happens. Compared with typical Multi-Paxos protocol, in this paper, we split the original distributed cluster to coordinator cluster and data cluster. The coordinator cluster is a central manager, which only takes charge of failover issues; while data cluster is only for handling client requests of data storage. This simplifies the implementation of Multi-Paxos protocol. Also, to avoid single point of failure, we made coordinator as a replica group as well, where existing consensus component is applied, so as to reduce complexity.

3 Preliminary Knowledge

3.1 How Multi-Paxos Protocol Works

Multi-Paxos is an optimization of basic Paxos protocol, which is similar to 2-phase commit protocol (i.e., the protocol consists of prepare phase and accept phase). When a replica R_i within a replica group receives a client command C_k, the two phases of basic Paxos protocol work as follows:

Prepare Phase: R_i first record C_k as the k-th client command in its local log, then broadcast *prepare_C_k* requests with proposal number R_i-k within the replica group. On receiving the *prepare_C_k* request for each replica R_j, it will send back *prepare_C_k_OK* response to R_i after checking it's ok to log C_k as the k-th log entry locally. If R_i receives *prepare_C_k_OK* response from majority replicas, it will enter Accept phase to make C_k as the k-th log entry in majority replicas.

Accept Phase: R_i initiates $Accept\_C_k$ requests and broadcast it within the replica group. On receiving $Accept\_C_k$ requests for each replica R_j, it will record C_k as the k-th log entry, and send back $Accept\_C_k\_OK$ response after it checks there's no proposal number larger than R_i-k for the k-th log entry. Similarly, when R_i receives $Accept\_C_k\_OK$ responses from majority replicas, it will mark C_k as committed; and broadcast $Commit\_C_k$ requests. Once R_j receives $Commit\_C_k$ request, it will mark C_k as committed if it has recorded C_k as the k-th log entry as well.

After a command get committed, it can be applied to state machine as long as it has no dependency on other commands, or all its dependency are resolved probably. Therefore, a response will be send back to client to indicate the success of executing C_k by the cloud storage application.

Compared with basic-Paxos protocol, a distinguished replica is elected as leader for Multi-Paxos protocol to improve system's performance by reducing 2-phase commit protocol to 1-phase commit protocol. As shown in Fig. 2, compared with basic Paxos protocol, "Prepare phase" is omitted in Multi-Paxos protocol, since only the leader replica makes proposal in the system. And there's only one phase(i.e., "Accept phase") during the execution of consensus algorithm.

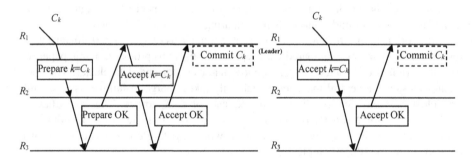

Fig. 2. The difference between basic-Paxos and Multi-Paxos

Multi-Paxos protocol could be treated as an optimization for basic Paxos protocol to address the live lock issue with basic Paxos protocol [4]. The live lock issue means for a same log entry (e.g., the k-th log entry), more than one replica issues $Prepare\_C_k$ requests within the replica group. In this scenario, according to the basic Paxos design, it's with great possibility that no command will be chosen as the k-th log entry.

Let's take the scenario in Fig. 3 to describe how Multi-Paxos protocol works. A client sends 3 commands C_1, C_2 and C_3 at the same time to the leader replica R_1, i.e., $\{C_1: "x = v_1", C_2: "y = v_2", C_3 = "x^* = v_3"\}$. C_1 and C_3 are updating the same key x; while C_2 is updating key y. Then R_1 will log C_1, C_2, and C_3 in sequence at its local log firstly, then broadcast $Accept\_C_1$ messages regarding each command to each follower in the replica group. On receiving the $Accept\_C_1$ request from R_1, R_2 and R_3 will record the C_1 in its local log; then send back $Accept\_C_1\_OK$ message to R_1. Once R_1 receives Accept OK messages from at least follower replica, it will mark C_1 as committed, and broadcast $Commit\_C_1$ request to all followers. And on receiving a $Commit\_C_1$ message, a follower replica will mark C_1 as committed if it has already record C_1 in its local log. Once C_1 is committed, it can be applied to the state machine and sends back to client that C_1 has already been recorded correctly. For C_2 and C_3, the workflow is similar to C_1.

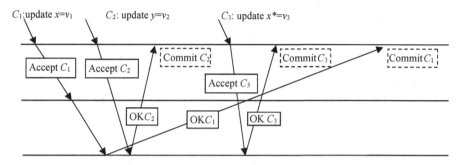

Fig. 3. A Multi-Paxos workflow example

As depicted in Fig. 3, the 3 commands (i.e., C_1, C_2 and C_3) are committed in out-of-order manner (i.e., the committing sequence is $\{C_2, C_3, C_1\}$), since the network delay may results the "*Accept_C₂_OK*" and "*Accept_C₃_OK*" messages arrives R_1 before "*Accept_C₁_OK*" message. And according to the protocol design, the applying sequence of three commands will be: $\{C_2, C_1, C_3\}$, since C_3 has dependency on C_1.

3.2 Problem Statement

Regarding the typical Multi-Paxos protocol design, when the leader replica fails, failover mechanism will be triggered to elect a new leader. And before new leader is elected, Multi-Paxos protocol degrades to basic Paxos: client requests should go through both prepare and accept phases to get committed and applied in the system. The new leader is elected during processing new client requests C_k: On receiving a client request C_k, a replica R_j will first checks whether itself is the leader, if yes it will skip prepare phase, and enter Accept phase directly. Otherwise, R_j will execute prepare phase and accept phase in sequence: it will first broadcast a *Prepare_C_k* request to check whether there's any other proposal regarding the k-th log entry. Once it receives "*Prepare_C_k_OK*" responses from majority replicas within the replica group, it will initiate "*Accept_C_k*" request among the replica group. Once R_j receives "*Accept_C_k_OK*" response from majority replicas, R_j will promote itself to leader. Otherwise, it will learn which replica is the new leader when it receives *Commit_C_k* request later.

The problem with failover mechanism in typical Multi-Paxos includes 3 parts: (1) Huge network cost: electing a new leader requires broadcasting prepare request over the replica group; (2) Reduced system performance: Multi-Paxos degrades to basic Paxos during the failover period, and it is with great possibility that no leader will be elected, when each replica tries to issue a prepare request regarding the same log entry due to the live lock issue [4]. (3) Data syncing on leader would increase client latency if the new leader has large missing items: after a new leader is elected, the number of missing items on the new leader would be very large compared with other follower nodes, since the leader is elected randomly. As a result, data syncing on leader node would be quite time consuming, so the client latency of writing operations would be increased.

In view of those challenges, we propose a centralized failover mechanism for Multi-Paxos protocol in this paper. Instead of electing new leader by broadcasting Prepare requests over the cluster, we introduce a designated coordinator taking charge of failover when there's node fails happens in the cluster. With the central coordinator, the 3 problems we analyzed above could be solved accordingly: (1) communication cost is saved since the new leader is elected by coordinator; (2) a new leader will always be elected as long as the majority nodes are not failed; (3) the coordinator will try to elect a follower node with most items as new leader as possible. As a result, the cost of data syncing is saved, so as to reduce client latency on writing operations.

4   A Centralized Failover Mechanism for Multi-Paxos Protocol in Cloud Storage Applications

Motivated by the problem discussed in Sect. 3, the optimized Multi-Paxos protocol is discussed in details in this section. In our proposal, instead of electing the new leader by broadcasting Prepare requests in the distributed cluster, we apply a centralized failover mechanism to optimize the system performance for Multi-Paxos protocol.

4.1   The Architecture of Centralized Failover Mechanism for Multi-Paxos Protocol

The architecture of our optimized Multi-Paxos protocol is depicted in Fig. 4. The implementation of cloud storage are split into two parts: Data Cluster and Coordinator Cluster respectively. Data Cluster is for handling normal data storage logic (i.e., log replication and data storage); while Coordinator Cluster is for failover issues handling.

Definition 1 (Coordinator cluster). Coordinator Cluster works as a centralized manager to handle failover issues. By collecting status report from each replica group, it maintains the status of each replica group, thus it an detect the running status of each replica, and trigger failover mechanism when leader replica fails.

The design of the centralized coordinator is inspired with 2-Phase Commit protocol as discussed in [7]. However, original 2 Phase Commit protocol faces the challenge of typical single point of failure. To achieve high availability, we make the coordinator as a cluster consisting of $2F' + 1$ nodes. Moreover, each node is running consensus algorithm to achieve fault tolerance as well.

Definition 2 (Data cluster). Data cluster is a collection of physical hosts for handling data storage requests, where replicated state machine is implemented, to make sure client requests are handled in the same sequence over several replicas.

As shown in Fig. 4, a data cluster consists of x physical machines, and for each machine p_i, there're a set of multiple processes running consensus algorithm for data storage. A piece of data is stored on $2F + 1$ physical machines as replicas to achieve fault tolerance. Moreover, each $2F + 1$ processes consists of a replica group as shown in Definition 3.

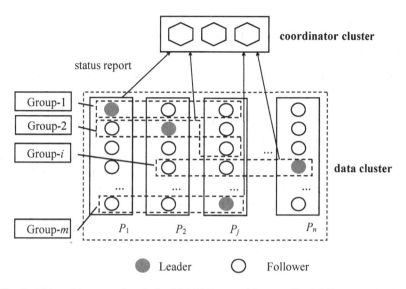

Fig. 4. The architecture of optimized Multi-Paxos with centralized failover mechanism

Definition 3 (Replica group). A replica group consists of $2F + 1$ processes from $2F + 1$ physical hosts. A process is a backup for each other within the same replica group, which is running Multi-Paxos protocol. At one moment, there's one leader elected by coordinator in the group, and other replica works as followers.

The replicas of each group is deployed on different physical machines, so as to make sure exception of one physical host has least impact on the cloud storage system. Also, each replica sends its running status periodically to the coordinator for leader election.

4.2 A Centralized Failover Mechanism for Multi-Paxos Protocol

In this section, the centralized failover mechanism for Multi-Paxos protocol is introduced in details. Table 1 lists some key terms and the definition.

Table 1. Key terms and notification for optimized Multi-Paxos protocol.

Term	Definition
G_i	The i-th replica group
G_i-R_j	The j-th replica of the i-th replica group
C_k	The k-th client request
G_i-R_i-$AppIndex$	The apply index of replica G_i-R_j
G_i-$StatusSet$	The status report collection of the i-th replica group
G_i-R_j-$Bitmap$	The bitmap of log entries existence for G_i-R_j
t	Timeouts for replica group status probing
F	The maximum number of failed replicas within a replica group

Definition 4 (Apply index G_i-R_i-AppIndex). R_i-AppIndex is the index of a replica R_i evolves in a Multi-Paxos protocol. It indicates that commands $C_1, C_2, \ldots C_{Ri-AppIndex}$ are already applied from local log to the state machine.

Definition 5 (Status report G_i-R_j.Status). G_i-R_j.status is the status report of replica R_j from G_i, it can be formulated as G_i-Rj.status = <i, j, role, G_i-R_i-AppIndex, health status>. i is the replica group number, j is the replica number, role indicates whether the replica is a leader or follower, G_i-R_i-AppIndex is the apply index of G_i-R_j, and health status indicates whether the replica running properly.

The state diagram of the coordinator is shown in Fig. 5. When the system starts, coordinator will enter probing state to collect each replica's status report from each replica group. If it detects there's no leader in current replica group, it will trigger failover mechanism, which consists of two phases: leader election and leader repair.

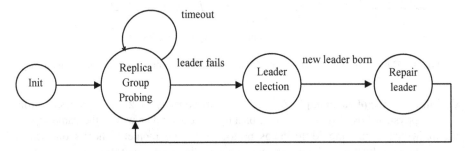

Fig. 5. The state machine of centralized coordinator

4.2.1 New Leader Election

There're three cases when new leader election happens: (1) When the system starts: all replicas within a same group are default to be follower at the beginning. Leader election is triggered to elect a leader for each replica group. Since at this moment, all replicas are the same, the coordinator will randomly assign a replica as the leader. (2) a leader replica report unhealthy status during system running, such as shortage of memory, to indicate it can't perform properly as a leader anymore. (3) a leader does not send status report to leader within timeout t. For case (2) and case (3) the coordinator need to elect a new replica with largest apply index as the new leader. This is to make sure the new leader has as much log entries as possible. This is to save time cost to learn all possible missing log entries. As a result, the replica group will take least time to recovery data storage service to clients.

Please be noted that if a follower reports unhealthy status report or lose connection to the coordinator, new leader election won't triggered. The distributed cloud storage system works fine as long as there's quorum replica works fine within a replica group. Otherwise, the system will break if over F replicas are failed.

Algorithm 1 summarizes the new leader election algorithm. Take the case in Fig. 6 for example. A replica group G_i has 3 replicas R_1, R_2 and R_3, where R_1 is the leader. If R_1 reports unhealthy status report or lose connection during the system running, new leader election is triggered. Since R_2's apply index R_2-AppIndex = 5, while R_3's apply index = 3, R_2 will be elected as the new leader. Since both R_2 and R_3 are working properly, the storage service will be restored once R_2 get repaired with all missing log entries.

Algorithm 1. New leader election

---

1. **foreach** t timeouts:
2.   **foreach** replica group G_i:
3.   check whether G_i-$StatusSe$t is collected from each replica
4.   if yes:
5.   **foreach** status report in G_i-$StatusSe$t:
6.   check the health status of each replica G_i-R_j:
7.   case 1: G_i-R_j is running OK
8.   keep probing
9.   case 2: G_i-R_j has health problem
10.   if G_i-R_j is leader:
11.   elect replica with largest R_j-$AppIndex$ as the new leader
12.   **endforeach**
13.   if no:
14.   check which replica loses the status report
15.   if the leader status is missing and majority replicas are healthy:
16.   elect the replica with largest R_j-$AppIndex$ as the new leader
17.   **end foreach**
18. **endforeach**

4.2.2   Repair New Leader with Missing Log Entries

When a new leader is elected, we need to repair the new leader to fill all missing log entries before restoring client request handling service.

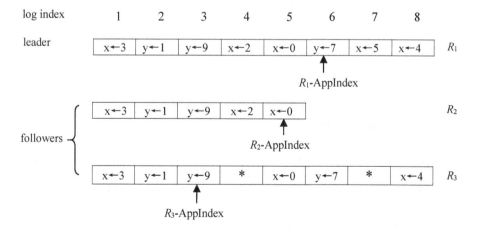

Fig. 6. Example for log entries when failover is triggered

Definition 6 (Bitmap of a replica's log entries G_i-R_j-Bitmap): G_i-R_j-Bitmap is the bitmap of replica's log entries. For i-th bit in G_i-R_j-Bitmap, the Boolean indicates whether R_j has the i-th log entry or not.

Definition 7 (logEntry summary G_i-logEntry): For a replica group G_i, G_i-logEntry is the log entry summary in G_i. It is an array consisting of $2F + 1$ entries, and G_i-logEntry $[i]$ means for the i-th log index, which replica has the log record.

When a new leader is elected, some log entries may be missing due to network delay or missing sync messages from former leader. Before restoring cloud storage service, we need to make sure all committed client commands should be ready in the new leader. As a result, the coordinator should calculate which replica to find the missing log entries. We introduce a bitmap for each replica R_j, where i-th bit indicates whether R_j has the i-th client command. With bitmap from majority replicas, the coordinator can calculate the global G_i-logEntry as a summary for log storage within G_i. Moreover, here only majority replicas' bitmap is required due to the design of Multi-Paxos: a command can only be committed after it is accepted by majority replicas in the group. Therefore, the new leader can always obtain the missing log entry once it get committed by former leader.

Algorithm 2. repair new leader with missing log entries in replica group G_i

---

1. coordinator send bitmap request to $F+1$ replicas within G_i (except the failed former leader)
2. with the $F+1$ bitmaps, coordinator calculates the value of G_i-logEntry
3. coordinator send G_i-logEntry to the new leader
4. **foreach** missing log entry $record_k$ in the new leader's log:
5.   check G_i-logEntry to get replica R_j, and R_j has $record_k$ in its log
6.   send a request to R_j for $record_k$
7.   fill the missing log entry with R_j's response
8. **end foreach**

Algorithm 2 summaries the algorithm to repair a new elected leader with missing log entries. Take the scenario in Fig. 5 for example, when R_1 fails, R_2 will elected as the new leader. With bitmap information from both $R_2 = \{1, 1, 1, 1, 1, 0, 0, 0\}$ and $R_3 = \{1, 1, 1, 0, 1, 1, 0, 1\}$, G_i-logEntry $= \{R_2, R_2, R_2, R_2, R_2, R_3, NULL, R_3\}$. Compared with former leader R_1, R_2's missing log entry is $record_6$. And with G_i-logEntry, it can obtain $record_6$ from R_3.

5 Comparison Analysis

In this section, we evaluate our proposal (*OMP*) by comparing it with the typical Multi-Paxos protocol (*MP*) with respect to when failover is triggered. As introduced in Sect. 4, when the coordinator detects there's exception with current leader in a group, failover mechanism is triggered to elect a new leader and repair log entries for the new leader. Two factors are considered in the comparison: message delay to restore normal service; as well as the message cost to repair the new leader with missing log entries.

5.1   Comparison of Message Delay

The message delay means how many round trips is required for the coordinator to choose a new leader and repair missing log entries for the new leader.

For our optimized Multi-Paxos protocol, message delay consists of following parts:

(a) 0.5 round trip to obtain heartbeat messages sent from coordinator to all nodes;
(b) 1 round trip to get bitmap messages required by coordinator;
(c) 1 round trip to get missing log entries, since leader already know where to find missing log entries from G_i-logEntry.

As a result, the message delay of the optimized Multi-Paxos protocol is a *const* as listed in formula (1):

$$messageDelay(OMP) = 2.5 \tag{1}$$

While for typical Multi-Paxos protocol, message delay consists of following parts:

(a) $\sum_{i=0}^{m} \alpha^i$ round trips to elect a new leader. α is the probability that conflict happens when electing a new leader. m is the total times of conflict. In optimal case, there's only 1 round trip to elect a new leader, if majority nodes replies with Prepare OK for the first replica initiating Prepare request.
(b) n round trip of Prepare requests to obtain the missing log entries on leader, to broadcast Prepare request to all replicas within the same group.

As a result, the message delay of the typical Multi-Paxos protocol is $n + 1$ as listed in formula (2):

$$messageDelay(MP) = n + \sum_{i=0}^{m} \alpha^i \tag{2}$$

5.2   Comparison of Message Cost

Suppose there're n missing log entries in the new leader node. Message cost include the message produced when a new leader is elected and missing log entries are repaired.

For our proposed optimized Multi-Paxos protocol, the message cost consists of following 4parts:

(a) $2F + 1$ heartbeat messages, from which the coordinator detects leader failure;
(b) $F + 1$ bitmap messages from majority replicas, with which the coordinator decide which replica to be new leader;
(c) 1 log entry summary message (i.e., G_i-logEntry) merged with $F + 1$ bitmap messages in (b) is sent to the new leader;
(d) n request messages made by the new leader, to require missing log entries from G_i-logEntry in (c);

Combined with (a)–(d), the message produced during failover is $(2F + 1) + (F + 1) + 1 + n = 3F + n + 3 = 3 * (F + 1) + n$.

Furthermore, the message produced for optimized Multi-Paxos could be reduced for step (d) when $n > F$. Since we already know the missing log entry exists in one of the $F + 1$ majority nodes, the maximum request messages in step (d) is $F + 1$. Therefore, the message cost for OMP is $(2F + 1) + (F + 1) + 1 + (F + 1) = 3(F + 1)$ when $n > F$.

$$messageCost(OMP) = 3 * (F + 1) + n \text{ if } n \leq F \qquad (3)$$

$$messageCost(OMP) = 3 * (F + 1) \quad \text{if } n > F \qquad (4)$$

For typical Multi-Paxos protocol, the message cost includes 2 parts:

(a) $2 * F * \sum_{i=0}^{m} \alpha^i$ Prepare requests to elect a new leader. Similar to formula (1), α is the probability that conflict happens when electing a new leader. m is the total times of conflict.
(b) $2 * F * n$ requests to repair n missing log entries in the new leader.

Combined (a) and (b), the total message produced by failover mechanism with typical Multi-Paxos protocol is $2 * F * \sum_{i=0}^{m} \alpha^i + 2 * F * n = 2F * \left(\sum_{i=0}^{m} \alpha^i + n \right)$:

$$messageCost(MP) = 2 * F * \left(\sum_{i=0}^{m} \alpha^i + n \right) \qquad (5)$$

Table 2 summaries the comparison result, which indicates our optimized Multi-Paxos protocol works better than the typical Multi-Paxos protocol, in terms of both message delay and message cost.

Table 2. Comparison summary of difference between OMP vs. MP

Protocol	Message delay	Message cost
Multi-Paxos (MP)	2.5	$3 * (F + 1) + n$ if $n \leq F$ $3 * (F + 1)$ if $n > F$
Optimized Multi-Paxos (OMP)	$n + \sum_{i=0}^{m} \alpha^i$	$2 * F * \left(\sum_{i=0}^{m} \alpha^i + n \right)$

6   Evaluation

We evaluated the optimized Multi-Paxos protocol against typical Multi-Paxos protocol, using three replicas for each replicated state machine. The protocols are implemented with Golang [19] and running on Mac OS 10.13.16. For the coordinator node, we apply the existing open source library etcd (which implements Raft protocol) [20] as the centralized manager to monitoring data cluster and electing leader replica.

A client on a separate instance sends batched requests to both three-replica group in loop. And the client requests are initiated by using a replicated key-value store where client requests are updates (i.e., write operations). For each protocol, the evolution of commit throughput in the three-replica setup that experiences the failure of one replica is recorded, as depicted in Fig. 7.

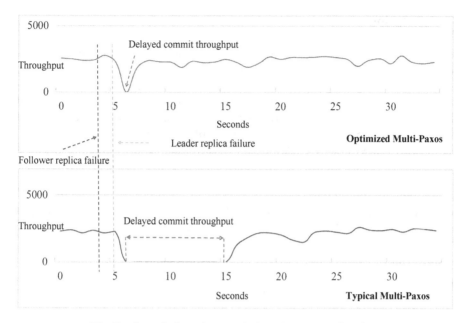

Fig. 7. Commit throughput evolution when one replica fails

As shown in Fig. 7, under normal cases, the commit throughput of both optimized Multi-Paxos protocol and typical Multi-Paxos protocol are almost identical; Moreover, a follower replica fails has no impact on the system's performance. This is due to both protocols are using a stable leader to handle client requests. Furthermore, both protocols suffer from availability issue when the leader replica fails. This is reasonable as well, since a distributed system running either protocol can't process client requests until a new leader is elected.

The difference between two protocols is the impact on commit throughput when the leader of three replicas fails. In our implementation, optimized Multi-Paxos takes about 1 s to elect a new leader and recovery client request handling service; while Multi-Paxos protocol takes about 10 s to restore the service. And the reason for this difference is: when failover happens, for our proposed optimized Multi-Paxos protocol, a new leader is elected by the coordinator node when it loses heartbeat information of the leader, which takes 1 round of message; while in typical Multi-Paxos protocol, new leader is elected during broadcasting prepare requests, which takes at least 1.5 round of message loop among each replica pair within the group. Please be noted, as discussed previously, it's of great opportunity that no leader can be elected in Multi-Paxos protocol due to the mutual stomping issue [4]. Under such circumstances, the commit throughput of typical Multi-Paxos protocol will be delayed infinitely.

7   Conclusion

In this paper, we proposed an optimization with centralized failover mechanism for Multi-Paxos protocol, so as to improve performance of cloud storage applications. Compared with original design of typical Multi-Paxos protocol, failover mechanism and data handling logic are split to different clusters. A coordinator cluster is introduced as a central manager to handle failover issues; while data cluster only takes charge of log replication for data storage. In the new design of failover mechanism, a replica with largest apply index value is elected as new leader; and repair missing log entries is conducted with limited replica's bitmap information. Finally, comparison between two protocols is analyzed to prove the feasibility of our proposal.

Acknowledgement. This paper is supported by The National Key Research and Development Program of China (No. 2017YFB1400601), National Natural Science Foundation of China (No. 61872119), Natural Science Foundation of Zhejiang Province (No. LY12F02003).

References

1. Zeng, W., et al.: Research on cloud storage architecture and key technologies. In: Proceedings of the 2nd International Conference on Interaction Sciences: Information Technology, Culture and Human, pp. 1044–1048. ACM, Korea (2009)
2. Arokia, R., Shanmugapriyaa, S.: Evolution of cloud storage as cloud computing infrastructure service. IOSR J. Comput. Eng. 1(1), 38–45 (2012)
3. Ousterhout, J., Agrawal, P., Erickson, D., et al.: The case for RAM cloud. Commun. ACM 54, 121–130 (2011)
4. Lamport, L.: Paxos made simple. ACM SIGACT News 32(4), 18–25 (2001)
5. Ongaro, D., Ousterhout, J.: In search of an understandable consensus algorithm. In: Proceedings of the ATC 2014, Usenix Annual Technical Conference, pp. 1–18 (2014)
6. Moraru, I., Andersen, D.G., Kaminsky, M., There is more consensus in Egalitarian parliaments. In: SOSP, pp. 358–372 (2013)
7. Gray, J., Lamport, L.: Consensus on transaction commit. ACM Trans. Database Syst. 31(1), 133–160 (2006)
8. David, M.: Paxos Made Simple. http://www.scs.stanford.edu/~dm/home/papers/paxos.pdf
9. Chandra, T., Griesemer, R., Redstone, J.: Paxos made live - an engineering perspective. In: ACM PODC, pp. 1–16 (2007)
10. Lamport, L.: Fast Paxos. https://www.microsoft.com/en-us/research/wp-content/uploads/2016/02/tr-2005-112.pdf
11. Rao, J., Shekita, E.J., Tata, S.: Using paxos to build a scalable, consistent, and highly available datastore. Proc. VLDB Endow. 4(4), 243–254 (2011)
12. Ailijiang, A., Charapko, A., Demirbas, M.: Consensus in the cloud: paxos systems demystified. In: 2016 25th International Conference on Computer Communication and Networks, pp. 1–10 (2016)
13. Marandi, P.J., et al.: The performance of Paxos in the cloud. In: Proceedings of the 2014 IEEE 33rd International Symposium on Reliable Distributed Systems, pp. 41–50 (2014)
14. Kirsch, J., Amir, Y.: Paxos for system builders: an overview. In: Proceedings of the 2nd Workshop on Large-Scale Distributed Systems and Middleware, pp. 1–5 (2008)

15. Wang, C., Jiang, J., Chen, X., Yi, N., Cui, H.: APUS: fast and scalable Paxos on RDMA. In: Proceedings of the 2017 Symposium on Cloud Computing, pp. 94–107 (2017)
16. Lamport, L., Malkhi, D., Zhou, L.: Reconfiguring a state machine. SIGACT News **41**(1), 63–73 (2010)
17. Xu, X., et al.: An IoT-oriented data placement method with privacy preservation in cloud environment. J. Netw. Comput. Appl. **124**, 148–157 (2018)
18. Xu, X., Fu, S., et al.: Dynamic resource allocation for load balancing in fog environment. Wirel. Commun. Mob. Comput. **2018**, 15 (2018)
19. GoLang. https://github.com/golang/go
20. Etcd. https://github.com/etcd-io/etcd

A Resource Usage Prediction-Based Energy-Aware Scheduling Algorithm for Instance-Intensive Cloud Workflows

Zhibin Wang[1,2], Yiping Wen[1,2(✉)], Yu Zhang[1,2], Jinjun Chen[1,3], and Buqing Cao[1,2]

[1] School of Computer Science and Engineering, Hunan University of Science and Technology, Xiangtan, China
ypwen81@gmail.com, Jinjun.Chen@gmail.com,
cao6990050@163.com

[2] Key Laboratory of Knowledge Processing and Networked Manufacturing, Hunan University of Science and Technology, Xiangtan, China

[3] Swinburne Data Science Research Institute, Swinburne University of Technology, Melbourne, Australia

Abstract. The applications of instance-intensive workflow are widely used in e-commerce, advanced manufacturing, etc. However, existing studies normally do not consider the problem of reducing energy consumption by utilizing the characters of instance-intensive workflow applications. This paper presents a resource usage Prediction-based Energy-Aware scheduling algorithm, named PEA. Technically, this method improves the energy efficiency of instance-intensive cloud workflow by predicting resources utilization and the strategies of batch processing and load balancing. The efficiency and effectiveness of the proposed algorithm are validated by extensive experiments.

Keywords: Energy · Instance-intensive · Scheduling · Cloud workflow · Batch processing · Prediction

1 Introduction

With the development of cloud computing and software technology, workflow applications in the field of science and engineering have grown steadily in variety and scale. As a typical application type in cloud computing environment, instance intensive cloud workflow usually exists in electronic commerce, advanced manufacturing and other fields. Unlike complex scientific workflow, instance intensive workflow has a large number of potential and relatively simple concurrent instances, in which instance is a single execution event of workflow at a particular time. For example, while processing bank cheques, millions of cheques are processed simultaneously every day, and each check transaction is a fairly simple workflow that takes only a few steps to complete.

Workflow scheduling is the key to managing workflow execution efficiency. In order to achieve high execution efficiency, the performance of instance intensive cloud workflow needs to achieve high throughput, high load balance and high resource utilization. High throughput allows a large number of workflow events to start and

H. Gao et al. (Eds.): CollaborateCom 2018, LNICST 268, pp. 626–642, 2019.
https://doi.org/10.1007/978-3-030-12981-1_44

complete in a set of time periods. Load balancing allows for balancing requests from users and providing users with better quality of service. Resource utilization can effectively manage resources. Up to now, several instance-intensive cloud workflow scheduling algorithms have been proposed. Unfortunately, most studies do not take energy into account, as energy has become one of the main problems of clouds and has received increasing attention due to environmental and financial considerations [17].

On the other hand, several researches have shown that predicting the future of users' demands and cloud resource usage can be applied to handle the energy problem [3]. Besides, it takes considerable time for configuring the virtual machines (VMs) according to the requirements of the application in cloud computing platforms [24]. If the future requirements of resources can be predicted beforehand, a large number of instance-intensive clouds workflow instances can be processed by the already configured VMs, and a high utilization of cloud resources can be maintained to reduce the energy consumption. That is, extra time to launch and configure new VMs can be saved, by which higher throughput may be achieved. Extra energy consumption caused by low utilization of cloud resources can also be reduced.

In addition, the combination of scheduling and batch decision can improve the efficiency of batch jobs instead of dealing with them alone [18]. Methods and prototype systems that support automatic batch execution in workflows have been proposed in [5, 6, 19]. However, there are few researches on workflow scheduling considering batch execution of several workflow instances to reduce energy consumption. For instance-intensive workflows, it does not have a dedicated energy-aware scheduling algorithm. Therefore, the resource prediction-based energy-aware scheduling method for developing instance-intensive cloud workflows has practical significance.

With these observations, this paper presents a resource usage Prediction-based Energy-Aware scheduling algorithm for instance-intensive cloud workflows, named PEA. It uses the technology of predicting resources utilization and the strategies of batch processing and load balancing to reduce energy consumption. Our contributions are three folds. Firstly, a formal concept of combining scheduling with batch processing and resource utilization prediction is proposed. Secondly, a scheduling method based on resource utilization prediction is designed for instance-intensive cloud workflow. Finally, comprehensive experiments and simulations are conducted to demonstrate the validity of the proposed method.

2 System Models and Architecture

Our problem consists in scheduling the instance-intensive workflow meeting the specified makespan in such a way that the energy consumption are minimized. In this section, we describe the energy model and system architecture underneath our approach. For ease of understanding, we summarize the major notations and their meanings used throughout of this paper in Table 1.

Table 1. Key notations and descriptions

Notation	Description
w_i	The i-th instance-intensive workflow
t_{ij}	The j-th workflow activity of wi_i
t_{ijk}	The k-th instance of the workflow activity t_{ij}
p_m	The m-th physical machine
c_m	The calculate ability of p_m
vm_n	The n-th type of virtual machine (VM)
vc_n	The calculate ability of vm_n
r_m	The number of VMs on p_m at time t
$U_m(t)$	The CPU utilization of p_m at time t
φ_m	The basic energy consumption rate of p_m

2.1 Concepts and Definitions

For better introducing PEA and related concepts, we first give some definitions which will be used later.

Definition 1 (Instance-Intensive Workflow). Instance-Intensive Workflow can be defined as $W = \{w_1, w_2, \ldots, w_I\}$, where I is the number of Instance-Intensive workflow, and w_i could be expressed as $w_i = <T_i, E_i, OD_i >$, where

(1) T_i is a set of workflow activities, and a workflow activity could be expressed as $t_{ij} = <ID_{ij}, Type_{ij}, W_{ij}, SD_{ij}, GC_{ij} >$, where ID_{ij} is the activity number, which is unique, $Type_{ij}$ is the execution type of the activity, which can be divided into two types: normal activity and batch-processing activity, W_{ij} is calculation workload, SD_{ij} is the deadline for this activity and GC_{ij} stands for the grouping characteristics values of t_{ij}. $t_{ij} \in T_i, T_i = \{t_{i1}, t_{i2}, \ldots, t_{iJ}\}$, where J is the number of workflow activities.

(2) E_i is the set of directed edges between the workflow activities to represent dependency, which can be expressed as $E_i = \{ <t_{ia}, t_{ib} > \mid <t_{ia}, t_{jb} > \in T \times T\}$.

(3) OD_i is the time constrained (i.e. overall deadline).

Definition 2 (Activity Instance). t_{ijk} is the k-th instance of the workflow activity t_{ij}, $1 \leq k \leq K$, where K is the number of instances of j-th activity of i-th workflow.

Definition 3 (Cloud Resource). $P = \{p_1, p_2, \ldots, p_M\}$ is a set of physical machines (PMs), where M is the number of PMs. The PMs provide the hardware infrastructure for creating virtualized resources to meet service demands. $VM = \{vm_1, vm_2, \ldots, vm_N\}$ is the set of N types of virtual machine (VM). A VM type vm_n is specified by the characteristic of computing performance vc_n in million instructions per second.

2.2 Energy Model

The energy consumption for PMs is composed of CPU, memory, disk, power supply, etc. Various research results in the literature show that CPU utilization significantly affects energy consumption [1, 2, 4]. Therefore, this study focuses on the influence of CPU utilization on the overall energy consumption of the system and ignores the influence of other components.

Hsu et al. [4] proposed a simplified energy consumption model of PM. The energy consumption rate at time instant t for the p_m, denoted as PE_m, which can be calculated by Eq. 1.

Where φ_m is the basic energy consumption rate of p_m, $U_m(t)$ is CPU utilization rate of p_m at time instant t and α_m is a constant, which could be calculated as $\alpha_m = \varphi_m/7$.

$$PE_m = \begin{cases} \varphi_m & \text{if} \quad U_m(t) = 0 \\ \varphi_m + \alpha_m & \text{if} \quad 0 < U_m(t) \leq 0.2 \\ \varphi_m + 3\alpha_m & \text{if} \quad 0.2 < U_m(t) \leq 0.5 \\ \varphi_m + 5\alpha_m & \text{if} \quad 0.5 < U_m(t) \leq 0.7 \\ \varphi_m + 8\alpha_m & \text{if} \quad 0.7 < U_m(t) \leq 0.8 \\ \varphi_m + 11\alpha_m & \text{if} \quad 0.8 < U_m(t) \leq 0.9 \\ \varphi_m + 12\alpha_m & \text{if} \quad 0.9 < U_m(t) \leq 1 \end{cases} \quad (1)$$

We assume that CPU utilization is the ratio of resources required by the VMs to the PM (Mainly for computing resources). Therefor, $U_m(t)$ could be calculated by Eq. 2.

$$U_m(t) = \sum_{n=1}^{N} \sum_{l=1}^{r_{n,l}} vc_{n,l}/c_m \quad (2)$$

Where c_m is the computing performance of p_m, $r_{n,l}$ represents the number of VMs of type vm_n running on the p_m at time t and $vc_{n,l}$ is the computing performance of vm_n.

Integral to PE_m can be obtained the total energy consumption of p_m, denoted as E_m, could be calculated by Eq. 3.

$$E_m = \int_{t \in \omega_m} PE_m(U_m(t))dt \quad (3)$$

Where ω_m is the total operating time of p_m.

2.3 System Architecture

The scheduling architecture of PEA is shown in Fig. 1. It consists of three layers: user layer, scheduling layer and resource layer. The scheduler consists of batch processing, resource monitor, resource predictor and energy-aware resource allocator. Batch processing is used to merge some activity instances to generate an activity execution instance. Resource monitor detects the resource usage of PMs and updates the CPU utilization information of each PM. Resource predictor predicts subsequent resource usage by using resource usage information obtained from the resource monitor and controls the opening and closing of the resource to avoid the invalid waste of the energy. Energy-aware resource allocator allocates appropriate resources to execute the instance through the strategy of load balancing.

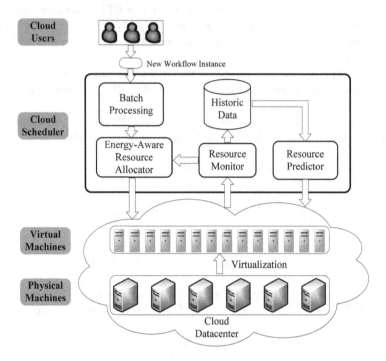

Fig. 1. The scheduling architecture of PEA

The overview of the scheduling process for this architecture is as follows. When new active instances arrive, they first enter the batch processing module, and some of instances are merged into new instances. On the other hand, the resource predictor prepares the resources needed by the instance in advance. Finally, energy-aware resource allocator put these instances into the resources prepared in advance.

The main characteristics of PEA include three points: batch strategy, resource prediction and load balancing. The benefits of this algorithm are summarized below.

- The strategy of batch processing could reduce the energy waste caused by computation processing and repeated transmission of data.
- The technology of resource prediction can adapt to the rapid increase of instance-intensive workflow. Reduce energy consumption caused by the untimely resource allocation and closure.
- The strategy of load balancing allows open PMs to operate at lower energy rates, which reduces the overall energy consumption.

3   Algorithm Implementation

The proposed PEA algorithm is capable of reducing energy consumption while meeting the makespan. It consists of four parts, such as batch processing, resource monitor, resource predictor and energy-aware resource allocator. The implementation of batch processing and resource monitor have been mentioned in our previous work. Detailed introductions of the mechanism of these are referred to [27]. In this section, we will focus on the implementation of resource predictor and energy-aware resource allocator.

3.1   Resource Predictor

Instance-intensive workflow has the characteristics of short-term rapid growth. A large number of task instances require a large allocation of resources in a short period of time. These tasks are often time - constrained, and exceeding them can have a huge impact. In the stock market, for example, failure to deal with it in time can lead to huge economic consequences. Therefore, more idle PMs are usually opened in the process of traditional resource allocation. However, if we keep the resources in the idle state for a long time, this will be extremely energy consuming. We use the method of resource usage prediction to allocation and recovery the PM in advance, so as to achieve the purpose of energy saving.

The model of resource predictor involves a number of steps as shown in Fig. 2. In preprocessing step, first, preprocess the historical data, which consists of three steps: feature selection, construction sequence and data partitioning. Then we use the processed historical data to train the DBN to get the model. Finally, we input the current data into the model to get the forecast information of the future resource utilization to guide the allocation or recovery of the resources.

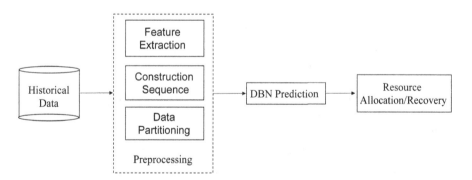

Fig. 2. The structure of resource predictor

Algorithm 1 specifies the process of resource utilization prediction and pre-opened on the physical machine according to the conditions.

Algorithm 1. Resource Prediction Algorithm RPA

Input: The set of cloud Resource history D.

Output: the information of Pre-opened PM.

01: Initialize Weight$_{ij}$ of the predictive model

02:   set $W_{ij} \leftarrow$ **Weight**$_{ij}$

03: select feature F in D

04: for $i \leftarrow$ length(F)

05: Δt time serialize (Fi)

06: foreach training model **do**

07:   Update ΔW_{ij}

08: $W_{ij} = W_{ij} + \Delta W_{ij}$

09: P_{t+1}=prediction model (W_{ij})

10: if P_{t+1} exceeds the set threshold

11:   Pre-open PM

12: return the information of Pre-opened PM

As shown in Algorithm 1, it describes process of forecasting in resource predictor. The input of model is a historical dataset of the data center in the cloud computing environment and the output is resource utilization value in the future. Firstly, model initializes and sets weights (lines 1–2). Then, feature selection has been done (line 3). Time serialization of feature data at Δt time granularity (lines 4–6). Training the prediction model and updating the weight of the model (lines 7–9). Finally, Pre-open the physical machine according to conditions (lines 10–11).

Preprocessing of Resource Predictor. Because the original data in the historical data set is huge and has many features, the direct use of the model will cause the problems such as large error and poor interpretability. Therefore, a series of data processing processes are carried out to improve the accuracy of prediction results. The main steps of data preprocessing include feature extraction, reconstruction sequence and data partition.

Feature Extraction. The resources in cloud computing environment mainly include CPU utilization, content utilization, disk and bandwidth. According to different cloud resource forecast requirements, the selected characteristics are different. In the stage of data analysis, the early analysis of feature selection is done. This paper mainly focuses on the prediction of CPU utilization ratio, so the historical CPU utilization factor is used as input feature in feature selection process.

Construction Sequence. Owing to the high correlation of host load data in the adjacent time interval, [24] proposes to use host load monitoring tool to record workload data into one-dimensional time series for predictive network training and good prediction results can be achieved. So this paper synthetically considers the practical significance of model input and prediction effect, and formats it according to the present time interval from the selection feature (in this paper, the granularity is per hour, the time interval is set length according to the specific problem). The time series of cloud resources are constructed and the time series data are taken as the input parameters of the depth confidence network in order to improve the prediction accuracy.

Data Partitioning. The prediction model is a model that describes the mapping relationship between the historical data feature F_t and the first period prediction value Y_{t+1}, which can be expressed as $F_t \rightarrow Y_{t+1}$. The purpose of data partition is to select the appropriate t value so as to predict cloud resources better.

DBN Prediction. In [20], they used an unsupervised learning model, the deep belief network (DBN). The structure of DBN can be described as two layers. The lower layer is composed of multiple restricted Boltzmann machines (RBM). The upper layer is a BP neural network. The training process of the deep belief network is divided into two parts, the unsupervised learning part corresponding to the RBM network in the lower layer and the supervised learning part corresponding to the fine-tuning of the BP neural network in the upper layer. We use this method to predict the utilization rate of cloud resources. The specific process is shown in the Fig. 3.

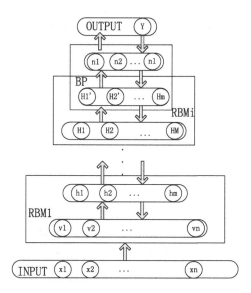

Fig. 3. The structure of DBN

3.2   Energy-Aware Resource Allocator

The main idea of energy-aware resource allocation is to balance the resource usage of open physical machines and limit the resource utilization of each host to a specified threshold. The specific steps can be described as follows:

(1) Specify a suitable VM type for all instances. This VM type should be the minimum VM type that guarantees that the instance can be completed within the deadline.
(2) The current CPU utilization of the PMs obtained in the resource monitor is sorted in ascending order.
(3) The VM type obtained from (1) is mapped to the sorted PM one by one until the CPU utilization of PM after VM loading is lower than or equal to the threshold value.
(4) If no PM meets the requirements, then assign the instance to a new PM that has been pre-opened.
(5) Return (2) until all instances are assigned resources.

Algorithm 2 Resource Allocation Based on CPU Utilization RA

Input: The current resource usage CRU

the pending instances PI

Output: The final resource allocation policies

01: for each PI [i] is not empty

02:   Assign a suitable vm_k to a PI [i]

03: DPM←sort(PMs) by the CPU utilization in CRU

04: for each PI [i] is not empty

05:   **for** i=1 to M

06:   **if** DPM[i] allocate to PI [i],it does not exceed the threshold

07:   PI [i] ←DPM[i]

08: if PIQ[i] did not get resources

09:   PI [i] ←Pre-opened PM

Algorithm 2 specifies the process of physical machine resource allocation. It is to show the steps mentioned above in the form of pseudo-code. The appropriate virtual machine types is arranged for each instance (lines 1–2). Sort current resources based on CRU (line 3). These sorted resources are in turn attempted to map virtual machine type. If the CPU threshold is met, schedule the current resource to calculate the instance (lines 4–7). If no resource satisfies the condition, this instance is calculated from the pre-opened resource (lines 8–9).

4 Experimental Evaluation

In this section, we conducted a series of comprehensive experiments to evaluate the performance of our proposed PEA. For comparative analysis, we performed comparison experiments with other methods to verify the effectiveness of our proposed PEA method.

4.1 Experimental Context

In this experiment, VM scheduling in the cloud environment will be simulated and tested by cloud simulator CloudSim [26]. The hardware environment used in the experiment is Intel(R) Core(TM) i5-6500 CPU @3.2 GHz, 8 GB memory. The software environment is Eclipse3.5 for Windows7, and cloudsim-3.0.3 is configured to complete the experiment.

In the process of verifying the proposed method, three types of physical machines of different specifications were mainly used to construct the cloud simulation environment. The specific configuration of the physical machine and related energy consumption settings are shown in Table 2. Set the basic power consumptions of the HP ProLiant ML110 G4 and HP ProLiant ML110 G5 to 86 W and 93.7 W based on the energy consumption values of them. Then based on the operating energy specifications for the single-processor HP ProLiant BL460c G6 in the HP white paper, the basic power consumption is set to 192 W.

Table 2. Parameter settings

Physical machine hardware configuration	Basic energy consumption (W)
HP ProLiant ML110 G4 (Intel Xeon 3040, dual-Processor clocked at 1860 MHz, 4 GB of RAM)	86
HP ProLiant ML110 G5 (Intel Xeon 3075, dual-Processor clocked at 2660 MHz, 4 GB of RAM)	93.7
HP ProLiant SL390s G7 (Intel Xeon 5649, dual-Processor clocked at 3060 MHz, 16 GB of RAM)	192

4.2 Performance Evaluation

In this section, we have carried out resource utilization prediction comparison experiments and scheduling method comparison experiments to verify our proposed method.

Resource Usage Prediction Comparison Experiment. In order to get closer to the complexity of the cloud computing environment, this article uses the real data of Google Cloud Data Center for simulation and verification. In May 2011, Google publicly released a 29-day historical dataset and documentation from the data center that detailed the semantics, formats, and patterns. This workload consists of more than 12,000 heterogeneous physical hosts running 4,000 different types of applications and a large amount of data for approximately 1.2 billion rows of resource usage data. We have selected the information of 40 physics machines for 29 days to carry on the experiment.

In this resource usage prediction experiment, we compared other algorithms such as back propagation (BP), support vector regression (SVR), radial basic function (RBF) and multivariable linear regression (MLR). The evaluation indicators selected are commonly used indicators in the prediction model, including mean absolute error (MAE), mean squared error (MSE), and mean absolute percentage error (MAPE). The specific formula for the evaluation index selected is as follows

$$MAE = \frac{1}{N} \sum_{i=1}^{N} |yt_i - yp_i| \tag{4}$$

$$MSE = \frac{1}{N} \sum_{i=1}^{N} (yt_i - yp_i)^2 \tag{5}$$

$$MAPE = \frac{1}{N} \sum_{i=1}^{N} \left| \frac{yt_i - yp_i}{yt_i} \right| \tag{6}$$

Where N is the total number of test sets, yt_i is the actual value, and yp_i is the output value of the network. MAE is the average absolute of the actual value and the predicted value. Compared with the average error, the average absolute error is absolutized because of the deviation, and there is no positive and negative offset. Therefore, the average absolute error can better reflect the actual situation of the predicted value error. MSE is very sensitive to a set of very large or very small errors in measurement. It can well reflect the precision of measurement. MAPE uses the same unit dimension to reflect the extent of the deviation of the measurement result from the true value. They evaluate the results from different angles, and the smaller the value, the higher the prediction accuracy (Figs. 4, 5 and 6).

The intraday average of the three evaluation indicators is shown in Table 3. The experimental results show that the DBN prediction method proposed in this paper is the best compared with the comparison method, and the DBN prediction ability is more stable with the increase of the prediction window. The main reason why the DBN method is significantly better than other prediction methods is that the features extracted by the RBM network can better reflect the complex characteristics of the entire data center workload data, and thus can stably improve the prediction effect.

Scheduling Algorithm Comparison Experiment. We conduct Comparison experiments on energy consumption with others. To reveal the advantages of our PEA algorithm in reducing energy consumption, we compare an energy-aware virtual machine scheduling [7] method is proposed, which is referred to as EVMS. The main idea of EVMS is to migrate activities to low-energy physical machines to reduce energy consumption, and then migrate some activities on low-energy physical machines to higher-energy virtual machines to speed up activity execution time. In this experiment, EVMS is used as the benchmark algorithm for comparison.

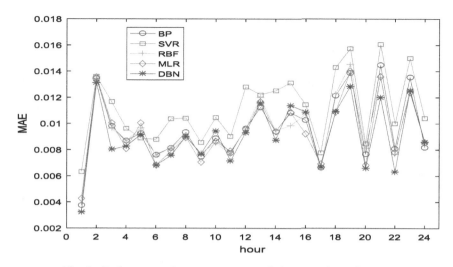

Fig. 4. Performance of resource usage prediction experiment in MAE

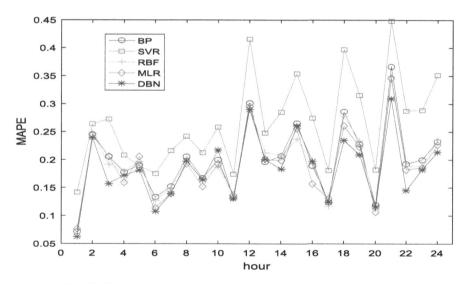

Fig. 5. Performance of resource usage prediction experiment in MAPE

Figure 7 plots the energy consumption results of three algorithms and Table 4 shows the ratio of PEA to the energy consumption of EVMS. From the results we can see that our PEA algorithm has the lower energy consumption. This is because the resource utilization prediction technology in PEA algorithm and two strategies can greatly reduce energy consumption. The technology of resource utilization prediction can effectively reduce energy waste caused by untimely opening and closing of resources. Batch processing strategy can combine multiple examples to reduce the energy loss caused by repeated calculation. The energy consumption is related to the

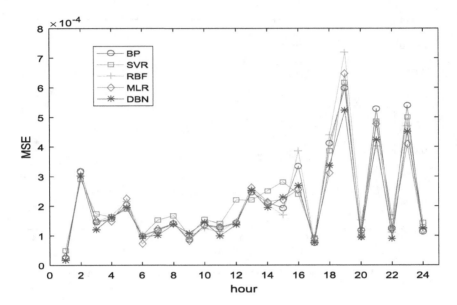

Fig. 6. Performance of resource usage prediction experiment in MSE

Table 3. Comparison of forecasting methods

	MAE	MSE	MAPE
SVR	0.0111	2.2466e−04	0.2660
BP	0.0094	2.1655e−04	0.1996
RBF	0.0095	2.1744e−04	0.1955
MLR	0.0094	2.0469e−04	0.1912
DBN	0.0089	1.9517e−04	0.1847

characteristics of activities. The load balancing strategy with CPU utilization threshold limits ensures that the system works at a low energy rate without affecting the running time.

5   Related Work

In cloud computing, any reduction in energy consumption can bring huge economic savings because the data center contains a large number of computer clusters. So there has been a lot of research on how to reduce energy consumption.

The energy consumption model of computer systems is the first problem that needs to be solved. Aliza et al. [1] lists the impact of various hardware and software on the energy consumption of computer systems. They found that the CPU is the component that has the greatest impact on system energy consumption among all components. Lien et al. [2] found that physical machine CPU utilization and energy consumption are

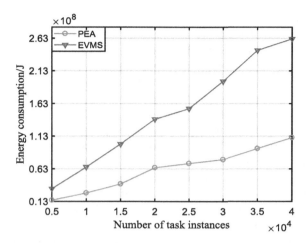

Fig. 7. Comparison experiments in energy consumption.

Table 4. Improvements of energy consumption with PEA compared to each comparison algorithm

	Number of task instances							
	5000	10000	15000	20000	25000	30000	35000	40000
EVMS	45.62%	39.34%	39.49%	46.56%	45.88%	39.19%	38.45%	42.25%

not linear. They collect data on power and CPU utilization, propose a power consumption model based on CPU utilization, and design a virtual instrument software module. Real-time measurement of the power consumption of the streaming server. These observations are used in this paper.

Some researchers use Resource forecasting method, like Kimura et al. [21] proposed a resource allocation model based on regression method, estimating the amount of resources in the virtual computing infrastructure. It predicts the number of vCPUs and the capacity of the required RAM with a nonlinear exponential regression model which allows the better selection of the configuration and the number of virtual machine and reduces the cost of small cloud providers. Ardagna et al. [22] presented workload predition model based on moving average. And a distributed solution was proposed that incorporated workload prediction and distributed non-linear optimization techniques. Roy et al. [23] proposed a forecasting model using Auto Regressive Integrated Moving Average model. A discussed the challenges involved in auto scaling in a cloud environment. Rahmanian et al. [25] proposed a learning automata-based ensemble resource usage prediction algorithm which combines state of the art prediction models in cloud computing environment. This algortithm determines the weights of each component model to achieve accurate prediction according to different situations. Faruk et al. [26] presented iOverbook, which is an autonomous, online and intelligent framework to calculate overbooking rate. It analyzes historical data of datacenter host CPU utilization and uses neural network to predict future CPU utilization. Specifically, it predicts the average CPU utilization over the specified time interval of the physical host and then calculates the overbooking rate of the CPU on the next hour. Finally, perfoming on the data of real Google cloud computing environment, the experiment shows that iOverbook can help Cloud service providers improve their resource utilization by an average of 12.5% and save 32% power in the datacenter.

Many efficient workflow scheduling techniques for the purpose of reducing the energy consumption have been researched [9–12, 15]. Kim et al. [13] discussed an energy credit scheduler for estimating power consumption in VM based on the number of workloads performed on VM. Based on the estimation model, the scheduling algorithm of virtual environment is designed, and the resource computing task based on minimum energy consumption and minimum budget is realized, and it is implemented in Xen virtualization system. Yassa et al. [14] described the scheduling strategy of DVFS based particle swarm optimization (PSO) algorithm for practical and scientific workloads. To reduce power consumption by using different levels of voltage to supply the workload by sacrificing clock frequency. This multiple voltage involves a tradeoff between the mass and energy of the schedule. The main disadvantages of evolutionary algorithms are slow convergence and long computation time, which are not suitable for instance intensive workflow.

6   Conclusion

In this paper, we present a resource usage Prediction-based Energy-Aware scheduling algorithm, named PEA. The method is promoted with strategies to merge several activity instances, predict the resource usage and balance resource utilization of physical machines to improve energy efficiency in instance-intensive cloud workflows. For processing instance-intensive workflows, our goal is to reduce the overall energy consumption of the system as much as possible under the premise of the activity deadline. Experimental evaluations have been performed to verify the efficiency and effectiveness of our proposed method.

Acknowledgment. This paper was supported by National Natural Science Fund of China (No. 61772193, 61402167, 61702181, 61572187, 61873316 and 61872139), Innovation Platform Open Foundation of Hunan Provincial Education Department of China (No. 17K033), Hunan Provincial Natural Science Foundation of China (No. 2017JJ2139, 2017JJ4036, 2016JJ2056 and 2017JJ2098), and the Key projects of Research Fund in Hunan Provincial Education Department of China (No. 15A064).

References

1. Alizai, M.H., Kunz, G., Landsiedel, O., Wehrle, K.: Promoting power to a first class metric in network simulations. In: International Conference on Architecture of Computing Systems, pp. 1–6 (2010)
2. Lien, C.-H., Liu, M.F., Bai, Y.-W., Lin, C.H., Lin, M.-B.: Measurement by the software design for the power consumption of streaming media servers. In: IEEE Instrumentation and Measurement Technology Conference Proceedings, pp. 1597–1602 (2006)

3. Rahmanian, A.A., Ghobaei-Arani, M., Tofighy, S.: A learning automata-based ensemble resource usage prediction algorithm for cloud computing environment. Future Gener. Comput. Syst. **79**, 57–71 (2017)
4. Hsu, C.-H., Slagte, K.D., Chen, S.-C., Chung, Y.-C.: Optimizing energy consumption with activity consolidation in clouds. Inf. Sci. **258**, 452–462 (2014)
5. Liu, J., Jinmin, H.: Dynamic batch processing in workflows: model and implementation. Future Gener. Comput. Syst. **23**, 338–347 (2007)
6. Liu, J., Wen, Y., Li, T., Zhang, X.: A data-operation model based on partial vector space for batch processing in workflow. Concurrency Comput. Pract. Experience **23**, 1936–1950 (2011)
7. Dou, W., Xiaolong, X., Meng, S., Yang, J.: An energy-aware virtual machine scheduling method for service QoS enhancement in clouds over big data. Concurrency Comput. Pract. Experience **29**, e3909 (2016)
8. Xu, R., Wang, Y., Huang, W., Yang, Y.: Near-optimal dynamic priority scheduling strategy for instance-intensive business workflows in cloud computing. Concurrency Comput. Pract. Experience **29**, e4167 (2017)
9. Rahman, M., Hassan, R., Ranjan, R., Buyya, R.: Adaptive workflow scheduling for dynamic grid and cloud computing environment. Concurrency Comput. Pract. Experience **25**, 1816–1842 (2013)
10. Moreno, M., Mirandola, R.: Dynamic power management for QoS-aware applications. Sustain. Comput. Inf. Syst. **3**, 231–248 (2013)
11. Ma, Y., Gong, B., Sugihara, R., Gupta, R.: Energy-efficient deadline scheduling for heterogeneous systems. J. Parallel Distrib. Comput. **72**, 1725–1740 (2012)
12. Changtian, Y., Jiong, Y.: Energy-aware genetic algorithms for activity scheduling in cloud computing. In: Chinagrid Conference IEEE, pp. 43–48 (2012)
13. Kim, N., Cho, J., Seo, E.: Energy-credit scheduler: an energy-aware virtual machine scheduler for cloud systems. Future Gener. Comput. Syst. **32**, 128–137 (2014)
14. Yassa, S., Chelouah, R., Hubert, K., Granado, B.: Multi-objective approach for energy-aware workflow scheduling in cloud computing environments. Sci. World J. **2013**, 13 (2013)
15. Tang, X., Chen, C., He, B.: Green-aware workload scheduling in geographically distributed data centers. In: IEEE International Conference on Cloud Computing Technology and Science Proceedings, pp. 82–89 (2013)
16. Cui, L., Zhang, T., Xu, G., Yuan, D.: A scheduling algorithm for multi-tenants instance-intensive workflows. Appl. Math. Inf. Sci. **7**, 99–105 (2013)
17. Li, Z., Ge, J., Haiyang, H., Song, W., Hao, H., Luo, B.: Cost and energy aware scheduling algorithm for scientific workflows with deadline constraint in clouds. IEEE Trans. Serv. Comput. **11**, 713–726 (2018)
18. Potts, C.N., Kovalyov, M.Y.: Scheduling with batching: a review. Eur. J. Oper. Res. **120**, 228–249 (2000)
19. Pufahl, L.: Modeling and executing batch activities in business processes. University of Potsdam (2018)
20. Zhang, W., Duan, P., Yang, L.T., Yang, S.: Resource requests prediction in the cloud computing environment with a deep belief network. Softw.: Pract. Experience **47**, 473–488 (2017)
21. Kimura, B., Yokoyama, R.S., Miranda, T.O.: Workload regression-based resource provisioning for small cloud providers. In: 2016 IEEE Symposium on Computers and Communication (ISCC), pp. 295–301. IEEE (2016)
22. Ardagna, D., Casolari, S., Colajanni, M.: Dual time-scale distributed capacity allocation and load redirect algorithms for cloud systems. J. Parallel Distrib. Comput. **72**, 796–808 (2012)

23. Roy, N., Dubey, A., Gokhale, A.: Efficient autoscaling in the cloud using predictive models for workload forecasting. In: 2011 IEEE 4th International Conference on Cloud Computing, pp. 500–507. IEEE (2011)
24. Sunirma, K., Manna, M.M., Mukherjee, N.: Prediction-based instant resource provisioning for cloud applications. In: IEEE/ACM International Conference on Utility and Cloud Computing, pp. 597–602. IEEE (2015)
25. Rahmanian, A.A., Ghobaei-Arani, M., Tofighy, S.: A learning automata-based ensemble resource usage prediction algorithm for cloud computing environment. Future Gener. Comput. Syst. **79**, 54–71 (2017)
26. Caglar, F., Gokhale, A.: iOverbook: intelligent resource-overbooking to support soft real-time applications in the cloud. In: IEEE International Conference on Cloud Computing, pp. 538–545. IEEE (2014)
27. Wang, Z., Wen, Y., Chen, J., Cao, B., Wang, F.: Towards energy-efficient scheduling with batch processing for instance-intensive cloud workflows. In: International Symposium on Parallel and Distributed Processing with Applications (2018)
28. Calheiros, R.N., Ranjan, R., Beloglazov, A., De Rose, C.A.F., Buyya, R.: CloudSim: a toolkit for modeling and simulation of cloud computing environments and evaluation of resource provisioning algorithms. Softw. Pract. Experience **41**, 23–50 (2011)

Web Service Discovery Based on Information Gain Theory and BiLSTM with Attention Mechanism

Xiangping Zhang, Jianxun Liu, Buqing Cao$^{(\boxtimes)}$, Qiaoxiang Xiao, and Yiping Wen

Key Laboratory of Knowledge Processing and Networked Manufacturing, Hunan University of Science and Technology, Xiangtan, Hunan, China
zxpkpnm@gmail.com, ljx529@gmail.com, buqingcao@gmail.com, 18390219693@163.com, ypwen81@gmail.com

Abstract. Web service discovery is an important problem in service-oriented computing with the increasing number of Web services. Clustering or classifying Web services according to their functionalities has been proved to be an effective way to Web service discovery. Recently, semantic-based Web services clustering exploits topic model to extract latent topic features of Web services description document to improve the accuracy of service clustering and discovery. However, most of them don't consider deep and fine-grained level information of description document, such as the weight (importance) for each word or the word order. While the deep and fine-grained level information can be fully used to argument service clustering and discovery. To address this problem, we proposed a Web service discovery approach based on information gain theory and BiLSTM with attention mechanism. This method firstly obtains the effective words through information gain theory and then adds them to an attention-based BiLSTM neural network for Web service clustering. The comparative experiments are performed on ProgrammableWeb dataset, and the results show that a significant improvement is achieved for our proposed method, compared with baseline methods.

Keywords: Web service clustering · Mashup creation · Information gain · Attention layer · BiLSTM

1 Introduction

With the wide adoption of Service-Oriented Architecture (SOA), the quantity and diversity of published web services on the Internet have been rapidly growing [1]. For example, programmableweb.com, the largest API services repository, has collected almost 19000 API services with various functionalities. This provides a convenient way for developers to build up software by using and compositing existing services. However, developers have to spend a lot of time for searching suitable Web services to complete the development process of software if they don't know what the functionalities of the Web services is [2]. In order to reduce software development cycle,

H. Gao et al. (Eds.): CollaborateCom 2018, LNICST 268, pp. 643–658, 2019.
https://doi.org/10.1007/978-3-030-12981-1_45

mashup technology has emerged as a promising Web services development method, which allows Web service developers to create new or value-added Web services with existing Web APIs [3]. The key challenge of creating a new mashup is that find appropriate web services according to user's complex functional requirements.

Web service discovery is to identify the most relevant services in response to a requester's query by comparing Web services and the requester's requirement [21]. Clustering or classifying Web services according to their functionalities has been proved to be an effective way to Web service discovery. The Web services are grouped into clusters if they are similar in functionality aspect, which can improve the retrieval efficiency and avoid to return a set of Web services not similar to user's query term. But the difficulty of Web services discovery is still existing, that service providers and requesters have different perspectives and knowledge of the same service. For example, a service was classified as "education" by the provider while a requester may send query term "teaching", this may make the discovery engine can't return a satisfying searching result. However, it's impractical to expect that service providers and requesters share an identical understanding of a Web service.

To solve this problem, several semantic-based Web service discovery frameworks are proposed. They consider that the contextual information of Web service description documents to improve Web service discovery. For example, [4] exploits Latent Dirichlet Allocation (LDA) to extract the latent topic information of Web service description documents for Web service discovery. Several of them have integrated functional documents and user-contributed tagging information to enhance the ability of LDA for service clustering and mining [4]. [21] proposes a sentence representation model to consider both the word-level semantics and the sentence-level semantics with BiLSTM for text classification. [24] have propose a hierarchical attention network for document classification. However, most of them don't consider deep and fine-grained level information of description document, such as the weight (importance) for each word or the word order, the word order information of the documents. We consider that the deep and fine-grained level information can be exploited to improve the performance of service clustering. In our prior work [10], we use the accurate word clusters information extracted from the original description to enhance the ability of LDA model. On this basis, we propose a Web service discovery method based on information gain theory and BiLSTM with attention mechanism, named as IGBA. To be our best knowledge, this is the first work combines information gain theory and BiLSTM with attention mechanism for Web service clustering. The contributions of this paper are summarized as follows:

- We perform information gain theory to extract the importance of each word in the description document. And we rank them according to the value size to make an effective words list. Each word of Web service description document will be assigned a score by information gain what can be considered as a weight represents the importance to the description document, and an effective words list is archived.
- We exploit an attention-based BiLSTM to argument the performance of Web service clustering. The model combines the original Web service description documents and the effective words list together for modeling, it can capture the deep

information, such as the weight for each word and the word order in description documents which is valuable for Web service clustering.
- We conduct comparative experiments on a real-world dataset which is crawled from programmableweb.com. The experimental results indicate that the proposed approach indeed improve the accuracy of Web services discovery.

The rest of this paper is organized as follows: Sect. 2 presents related work on Web services discovery technologies. Section 3 describes our approach in details. Section 4 presents experimental evaluation and results. Finally, Sect. 5 concludes the paper and discusses some future works.

2   Related Work

Web services discovery is a process of retrieving appropriate Web services from service repository to satisfy users' requirement. Web services providers or developers publish their Web services in services repository with their description documents. Then Web services search engine can use the information in which the description documents contain to match the users' requirements. Generally speaking, existing literatures can be roughly classified into two categories: keyword-based Web services discovery methods [7], semantic-based Web services discovery methods [6].

Keyword-based Web services discovery methods depend on selecting appropriate keywords and making a query that matches the selected keywords with the Web service descriptions [7]. [25] which leverage key features being mined from the WSDL documents to represent the functionalities of a service. Due to the different knowledge background between providers and requesters it is difficult for them to select suitable keywords. Besides, keywords can't capture the latent semantics of Web services description documents, which may lead to some irrelevant searching results.

Semantic-based Web services discovery methods usually extract some important the information from Web services description through topic model, such as Latent Dirichlet Allocation (LDA) topic model for Web services clustering [8]. Liu and Fulia [22] incorporated user, topic, and service related latent factors into service discovery and recommendation by combining topic model and matrix factorization. Cao et al. [3] propose a Web service clustering method based on an integration of service content and network via exploiting a two-level topic model. Chen et al. [5] integrates tagging data and WSDL documents through augmented LDA to model Web services for clustering. Shi et al. [10] leverages the accurate word clusters information obtained by Word2vec to enhance the ability of LDA topic model then cluster Web services together if they are similar. However, due to the description documents of Web services usually contain limited numbers of terms which are even not useful or valuable words, these approaches may lead to low clustering results [11]. Actually, the latent semantic correlation behind the terms of service document can be exploited to improve the accuracy problem. In addition, LDA-based clustering methods are inappropriate for modeling short text which the description documents of Web services are.

Recently, many deep learning methods have been proposed to solve the text classification task [23]. [21] propose a model for extracting a sentence representation that considers both the word-level semantics and the sentence-level semantics with BiLSTM for text classification. Our work differs from them in that we firstly use information gain theory to capture the top-N words which have contain most useful and valuable information from the original Web service description documents to enhance the performance of Web service discovery. In this paper, we model the original Web service documents and the effective words together by using BiLSTM neural network with attention mechanism that can capture the word with a high value weight and the information of word order. The deep and fine-grained level information can improve the performance of service clustering effectively.

3   Methodology Overview

This section consist of four sub-sections, respectively describes the architecture, pre-process, information gain theory and neural network model of the proposed method with details.

3.1   The Architecture of Web Service Discovery

The overall architecture of our Web service discovery method is shown in Fig. 1. In this architecture, we first crawl the web service data which contain the web service name, description and category from programmableweb.com. Then the Web services description documents for each web services are extracted and the information gain algorithm are performed for them to distill the effective words which contains more useful and valuable information for Web services clustering. Then, the original document and the effective words are integrated as the input of the attention-based BiLSTM neural network model. Finally, the web services with similar functionality are classified into the same cluster.

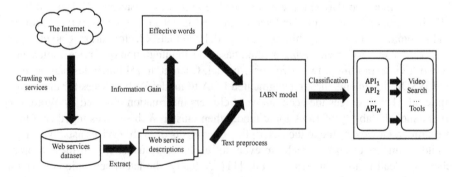

Fig. 1. The architecture of web services discovery approach

3.2   Web Service Document Preprocess

The Web service developer usually provides a brief description document about the Web services' function when publishing it on service repository, such as, programmableweb.com. As we can see in Fig. 2, it's a structure diagram of a Web service, including its name, description document and category.

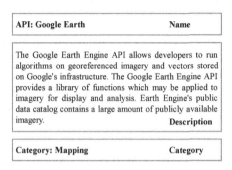

Fig. 2. API structure diagram

However, the Web service description documents always contain lots of noise which negatively affects text analysis. We should clear the description documents first. We extract all Web service description documents from the crawled dataset and concatenate them to a text file. Then we denote it by $D = \{d_1, d_2, \ldots, d_n\}$, n is the number of documents. In order to get a better performance, we perform a text preprocess for it, which contains below steps:

- Tokenization. Chopping a sentence into pieces, each piece is a word or a punctuation mark.
- Remove stop words. There are some common short function words which contain little lexical meaning but occur frequently in the Web services description documents. Those words can't afford useful information for web service discovery, such as, *the, in, a, an, with,* those words should be removed.
- Stemming. For grammatical reasons, documents have to use different forms of a word, such as *provide, providing, provides.* The common word endings for English words, such as *es, ed* and *ing* should be removed. Then *providing* become *provid.*

After performing text preprocessing, we obtain the processed Web services documents for further steps.

3.3   Information Gain

As shown in the original Web services description documents in the Fig. 2, those words, such as *"the"*, *"to"*, *"and"*, which can't afford enough information for classifying the API *"Google Earth"* into category Mapping obviously. By contrast, when we observe those words, such as *"earth"*, *"engine"*, *"display"*, we conjecture the API

"*Google Earth*" can be classified into category Mapping naturally. Information gain (IG) is the difference of the information entropy that a characteristic word appears or does not appear in the text documents [12]. The IG score is greater means that the information carried by the characteristic word is greater. IG score for each word is calculated using the formula below:

$$IG(w) = -\sum_{i=1}^{M} P(C_i)logP(C_i) + P(w)\sum_{i=1}^{M} P(C_i|w)logP(C_i|w) + P(\bar{w}) \qquad (1)$$

where M is the number of categories, $P(C_i)$ is the probability of class C_i, $P(w)$ and $P(\bar{w})$ are respectively the probabilities of presence and absence of word w, $P(C_i|w)$ and $P(C_i|\bar{w})$ are the conditional probabilities of class C_i given presence and absence of word w, respectively. Then we can get the effective words for augmenting the model we proposed. We set up an experiment to study how to select the number of effective words appropriately.

3.4   The Neural Network Model of Web Service Clustering

Inspired by the success of neural network model work on text classification [20], we present an attention-based BiLSTM approach to classify Web services into different clusters bases their description documents. In this section, we first give an overview of our attention-based BiLSTM model for web service clustering. The architecture of our model is illustrated in Fig. 3, which contains Input layer, Embedding layer, LSTM layer, Attention layer, and Output layer.

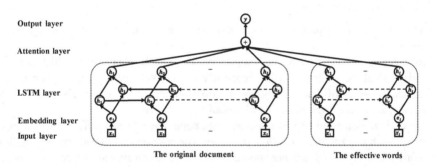

Fig. 3. The architecture of IGBA model

(1) *Input layer:* the original Web service description document which have been preprocessed and the extracted effective words are connected together as input data of BiLSTM model in the input layer.

(2) *Embedding layer:* we concatenate the Web service description document $d_i = \{x_{i1}, x_{i2}, \ldots, x_{iL}\}$ and its effective words $E_i = \{x'_{i1}, x'_{i2}, \ldots, x'_{il}\}$ as a sentence S_i. We use the pretrained model from Wikipedia corpus to map each word into a

fixed length vector by word2vec [19]. For each word x_{ij} in S_i, we transform into its word embedding e_{ij}. Then S_i is feed into the next layer as a real-valued vector $emb_i = \{e_{i1}, e_{i2}, \ldots, e_{i(L+l)}\}$.

(3) *LSTM layer:* LSTM units are firstly proposed to overcome gradient vanishing problem. The main idea of it is to introduce an adaptive gating mechanism, which decides the degree to which LSTM units keep the previous state and memorize the extracted features of current data input. The flow of data is shown in Fig. 4 [13].

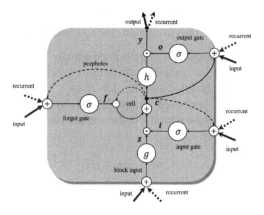

Fig. 4. LSTM unit

Let e_{ij} be the input vector of S_i, N is the number of LSTM blocks and M is the number of inputs. Then, we have the following weights for an LSTM unit.

1. Input Weights: $W_z, W_s, W_f, W_o \in \mathbb{R}^{N \times M}$.
2. Recurrent Weights: $R_z, R_s, R_f, R_o \in \mathbb{R}^{N \times M}$.
3. Peephole Weights: $p_s, p_f, p_o \in \mathbb{R}^N$.
4. Bias Weights: $b_z, b_s, b_f, b_o \in \mathbb{R}^N$.

Then the vector formulas for a LSTM layer can be written as follow:

$$z^t = g(W_z x^t + R_z y^{t-1} + b_z) \qquad \text{\textit{block input}}$$
$$i^t = \sigma(W_i x^t + R_i y^{t-1} + p_i \odot c^{t-1} + b_i) \qquad \text{\textit{input gate}}$$
$$f^t = \sigma(W_f x^t + R_f y^{t-1} + p_f \odot c^{t-1} + b_f) \qquad \text{\textit{forget gate}}$$
$$c^t = z^t \odot i^t + c^{t-1} \odot f^t \qquad \text{\textit{cell}}$$
$$o^t = \sigma(W_o x^t + R_o y^{t-1} + p_o \odot c^t + b_o) \qquad \text{\textit{output gate}}$$
$$y^t = h(c^t) \odot o^t \qquad \text{\textit{block output}}$$

Where σ, g, h are pointwise nonlinear activation functions and $\sigma(x) = 1/(1+e^{-x}), g(x) = h(x) = tanh(x)$. $\odot$ is present pointwise multiplication of two vectors.

The whole LSTM layer contains two sub-layers for feature selection of two different text respectively [14]. The output of the kth word in LSTM layer is shown in the following equation:

$$h_k = \left[\overrightarrow{h_k} \oplus \overleftarrow{h_k}\right] \tag{2}$$

Here, we use element-wise sum to combine the forward and backward pass outputs.

(4) *Attention layer:* Since not all words contribute equally to the representation of the sentence meaning, we use attention mechanism to extract such words that are important to the web service clustering. Let H be a matrix consisting of output vectors $[h_1, h_2, \ldots, h_T]$ generated by the LSTM layer, where $T = L + l$ is the sentence length. The representation r of the sentence is formed by a weighted sum of these output vectors:

$$M = tanh(H) \tag{3}$$

$$\alpha = softmax(w^T M) \tag{4}$$

$$r = H\alpha^T \tag{5}$$

We obtain the final sentence-pair representation, that is used for web services clustering from [14]:

$$h^* = tanh(r) \tag{6}$$

(5) *Output layer:* In this model, we use a softmax classifier to predict category $\hat{y}$ from a discrete set of classifications Y for a Web service document [17]. The classifier takes the hidden state h^* as input:

$$\hat{p}(y|D) = softmax\left(W^{(D)}h^* + b^{(D)}\right) \tag{7}$$

$$\hat{y} = arg\, max_y\, \hat{p}(y|D) \tag{8}$$

The cost function is the negative log-likelihood of the true category $\hat{y}$:

$$J(\theta) = -\frac{1}{m}\sum_{i=1}^{m} t_i \log(y_i) + \lambda||\theta||_F^2 \tag{9}$$

Where $t \in \Re^m$ is the one-hot represented ground truth and $y \in \Re^m$ is the estimated probability for each class by softmax (m is the number of target classes), and λ is an L2 regularization hyper-parameter which prevent the model from overfitting the training data.

4 Evaluation and Results

4.1 Experiment Datasets

To evaluate the performance of different Web service discovery method, we have crawled 12919 Web APIs and their related information from programmableweb.com during Oct. 2016. We select top 10 categories which involve 4351 web services for experimental evaluation. The detailed distribution data of the top 10 Web services categories is shown in Table 1.

We also use English Wikipedia corpus for mapping each word in Web services description documents into 300 dimensions vector by using gensim [15] which is a python natural language process library. The latest English Wikipedia corpus can be downloaded from https://dumps.wikimedia.org/enwiki/.

Table 1. The distribution of web services in top-10 categories

Category	Number	Category	Number
Tools	790	Messaging	388
Financial	586	Payments	374
Enterprise	487	Government	306
eCommerce	435	Mapping	295
Social	403	Science	287

4.2 Evaluation Metrics

In this section, we evaluate the proposed approach by using precision, recall, purity and entropy. Suppose that $AC = \{AC_1, AC_2, \ldots, AC_K\}$ represents the standard classification of Web services in top K categories. We denote the predicted Web services classification results as $PC = \{PC_1, PC_2, \ldots, PC_M\}$. The precision and recall metrics calculated as follows:

$$precision(PC_i) = \frac{|AC_i \cap PC_i|}{|PC_i|} \tag{10}$$

$$recall(PC_i) = \frac{|AC_i \cap PC_i|}{|AC_i|} \tag{11}$$

where $|AC_i|$ is the number of Web services which category is AC_i, $|PC_i|$ is the number of Web services that are classified into the category PC_i, and $|AC_i \cap PC_i|$ is the number of Web services in PC_i that are classified into AC_i correctly.

The purity of PC is calculated as follow:

$$purity(PC_i) = \frac{\max(|PC_i \cap AC_j|)}{|PC_i|}, 1 \leq j \leq K \qquad (12)$$

$$purity(PC) = \sum_{i=1}^{top_k} \frac{|PC_i|}{N} \times purity(PC_i) \qquad (13)$$

where N is the number of Web services in AC, and top_k represents top $k(1 \leq k \leq M)$ clusters in prediction clusters. The entropy of PC is calculated as follow:

$$entropy(PC_i) = -\sum_{j=1}^{K} \frac{|PC_i \cap AC_j|}{|PC_i|} \times log_2\left(\frac{|PC_i \cap AC_j|}{|PC_i|}\right) \qquad (14)$$

$$entropy(PC) = \sum_{i=1}^{top_k} \frac{|PC_i|}{N} \times entropy(PC_i) \qquad (15)$$

For each predicted cluster PC_i, we calculate their recall, precision, purity and entropy, respectively.

4.3   Baseline Methods

To demonstrate the effectiveness of the proposed method, we compare with several competitive approaches which is related to our work:

- TF-IDF [16]: The similarity calculation between Web services is based on the term frequency and inverse document frequency. Then it exploits the K-means algorithm to cluster all Web services.
- LDA-K [3]: The similarity calculation between services is based on the document-topic vector which obtained by LDA model. The number of topics needs manual adjustment. Then it adopts K-means algorithm to cluster all Web services.
- HDP-K [17]: The similarity calculation between Web services is based on the document-topic vector which obtained by Hierarchical Dirichlet process. The number of topics can be unbounded and learnt from the Web service description documents. Then it performs K-means algorithm on Web services to cluster them.
- WE-LDA [9]: This method leverages the high-quality word vectors to improve the performance of Web services clustering. The word vectors are obtained by word2vec.
- WT-LDA [5]: This method integrates tagging data and WSDL documents to augment Latent Dirichlet Allocation. Then it uses K-means algorithm to cluster all web services.
- BiLSTM [18]: This approach divides all Web services documents into two parts, i.e., train set and test set. It firstly captures the most important semantic information in the Web service description document-based LSTM on the train set and then predicts the Web service category on the test set.
- IGBA: The proposed method in this paper, which uses the effective words that are selected by information gain to argument attention-based BiLSTM neural network training process and improve the clustering performance of Web services.

4.4   Evaluation Results

In this section, we firstly investigate the impact of the parameter of λ which is the L2 regularization hyper-parameter and study the effect of the number of effective words. Then the performance of the proposed approach is compared with other Web services discovery approaches.

(1)   *The impact of λ and hidden units*

This experiment studies the impact of the hyper-parameter λ on Web services classifying in our model. During this experiment, we change the value of λ from 0.02 to 0.1, and the steps is 0.02. Then we calculate the values of precision, recall, purity and entropy in different hidden units which vary from 100 to 1000. The experimental results are shown in Fig. 5. It can be seen from those figures, the values of precision, recall and purity are becoming bigger and the value of entropy is decreasing while the number of hidden units are increasing from 100 to 900. This is because more hidden units result in more effective information in the neural network, which are used for classifying Web services. And it is over-fitting when the hidden units vary from 900 to 1000, the values of these metrics are decreasing. We can also know that when λ = 0.04, the performance of our approach reaches the peak point in most instances. The λ is added into the cost function that prevents the model from over-fitting the training data. It can encourage all parameters to become smaller. But there is not an automatic algorithm for selecting the value of λ. So, we choose λ = 0.04, the number of hidden units is 900 for the next experiment.

(2)   *The impact of the number of effective words*

In this experiment, we study the impact of the number of effective words on Web services classifying. We set the number of effective words from 2 to 10, and the steps is 2. According to the previous section, we set the number of hidden units is 900, and λ = 0.04. Then we calculate the four metrics, precision, recall, purity and entropy.

The results of our proposed method are shown in Fig. 6. It can be seen from Fig. 6 (a), when the number of effective words increasing from 2 to 4, the precision of our proposed method is becoming better. This is because those words carry more useful and valuable information to augment the attention layer to catch more effective information. We can also observe that recall and purity is increase while the number of effective words is increasing. Then the model can get better performance of Web service classification. When the number of effective words increase from 4 to 10, the performance of our approach is becoming worse, such the entropy is getting bigger, since the information of the too much additional words which we call noise make the semantic of Web services description documents becoming indistinct. So, we consider the best number of effective words of our dataset is 4 for next experiment.

(3)   *The comparison of Web services discovery methods*

In order to investigate the performance of different Web services discovery approaches, we compare our method with other five methods. We choose the best result of all methods to compare their performance. Table 2 presents the performances of all

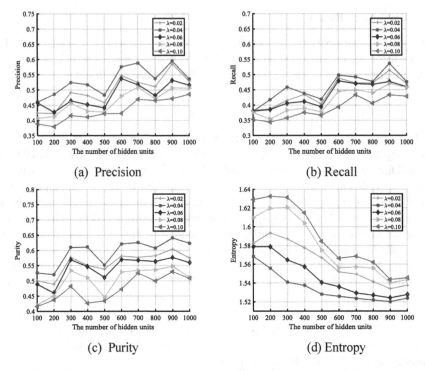

Fig. 5. The performance with the change of λ and the number of hidden units

Web services discovery methods on top 10 categories of our dataset. The bigger Precision, Recall, Purity and the smaller Entropy demonstrate that the method is better. Specifically, we have the following observations:

- The performance of our model is significantly superior to all other methods. Our model IGBA has an average precision improvement of 512% over the TF-IDF, 30.9% over the LDA-K, 16.6% over the WT-LDA, 12.1% over the WE-LDA, 12.7% over the BiLSTM. The reason is that IGBA integrates the original description documents and the effective words together and use an attention-based BiLSTM neural network to model them. The effective words and the attention mechanism promote to capture the latent semantic information for classifying Web services. This model considers deep and fine-grained level information of description document, such as the importance for each word and the information of word order. The performance of the original BiLSTM is worse than our method because the attention layer of our approach assigns different weight to each word in the Web service description documents. The recall metric of IGBA is also higher than other methods significantly that can retrieve more correct results than other methods.

- The topic model-based methods, LDA-K, HDP-K, WT-LDA and WE-LDA show a significant improvement of the precision compared with the lexical matching-based method TF-IDF. The reason is that TF-IDF fails to catch the latent semantic information in the Web services description. It only uses the term-based vector to

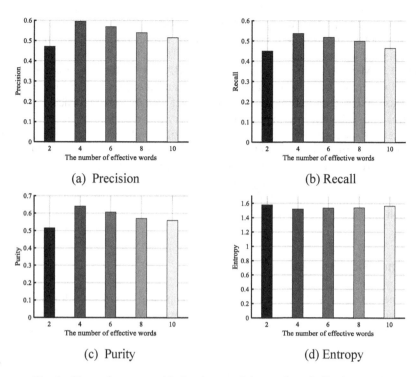

(a) Precision (b) Recall

(c) Purity (d) Entropy

Fig. 6. The performance with the change of the number of effective words

Table 2. The performances of all Web services discovery methods

Methods	Precision	Recall	Purity	Entropy
TF-IDF	0.1037	0.3123	0.1815	2.6735
LDA-K	0.4853	0.5022	0.5347	1.5996
HDP-K	0.5372	0.5211	0.5107	1.5736
WT-LDA	0.5449	0.5306	0.5517	1.5463
WE-LDA	0.5579	0.5321	0.5439	1.5288
BiLSTM	0.5637	0.5407	0.5672	1.5319
IGBA	**0.6352**	**0.5766**	**0.6608**	**1.5101**

represent the functional features of Web services without the latent semantic which the description documents contain. We also observe that the recall of TF-IDF method is unexpectedly low, because the distributions of Web services are uneven that can be proved in Table 1. LDA-K, WT-LDA and WE-LDA exploits the LDA technique to mine the latent functional information from the description documents so they obtain the better results than TF-IDF method. We can also observe that WT-LDA and WE-LDA are better than LDA-K, because those methods exploits the additional information which is considered as function summary to augment LDA model. The additional information can improve the accuracy of Web services discovery. The performances of WE-LDA are better WT-LDA, because the word cluster obtain by word2vec can provide more information for LDA modeling to capture the latent semantic.

- The LSTM-based methods, BiLSTM and IGBA have a better performance compared with other traditional methods. IGBA has a better performance than BiLSTM because IGBA uses information gain to extract effective words which carry more useful and valuable information for Web services clustering. Those words are exploited to augment the attention mechanism of neural network to catch the latent classifying information. The attention mechanism will assign high weights to the relevant words and low weights to the irrelevant words. For example, it is not the word earth than the word library can afford more useful information for classifying the Web service Google Earth into category earth. And the word earth is assigned to a high weight.

5   Conclusion and Future Work

This paper presents a Web service discovery approach based on information gain theory and attention-based Bidirectional neural network. We extract the effective words from the Web service description documents based on information gain theory. And we use an attention-based BiLSTM neural network for catching important information for Web service classifying. The comparative experiments performed on ProgrammableWeb dataset demonstrate the effectiveness of the proposed approach. The results show that a significant improvement of the clustering accuracy compared with other approaches and illustrates that the information which is carried by the effective words can greatly improve the performance of Web service clustering indeed. In the future work, we will develop new method based on integrated deep neural network model for extracting the multi-functionality information and context of Web service to create novel mashup application.

Acknowledgements. The work was supported by the Hunan Provincial Natural Science Foundation of China under grant No. 2017JJ2098, 2017JJ4036, 2018JJ2139, 2018JJ2136, Open Foundation of State Key Laboratory of Networking and Switching Technology (Beijing University of Posts and Telecommunications) under grant No. SKLNST-2016-2-26, National Natural Science Foundation of China under grant No. 61572187, 61772193, 61702181, 61872139, 61873316, Innovation Platform Open Foundation of Hunan Provincial Education Department of China under grant No. 17K033.

References

1. Xia, B., Fan, Y., Tan, W., et al.: Category-aware API clustering and distributed recommendation for automatic mashup creation. IEEE Trans. Serv. Comput. **8**(5), 674–687 (2015)
2. Samanta, P., Liu, X.: Recommending services for new mashups through service factors and top-k neighbors. In: ICWS 2017, pp. 381–388 (2017)

3. Cao, B., Liu, X., Li, B., et al.: Mashup service clustering based on an integration of service content and network via exploiting a two-level topic model. In: ICWS 2016, pp. 212–219 (2016)
4. Li, C., Zhang, R., Huai, J., et al.: A probabilistic approach for web service discovery. In: ICWS 2013, pp. 101–108 (2013)
5. Chen, L., Wang, Y., Yu, Q., Zheng, Z., Wu, J.: WT-LDA: user tagging augmented LDA for web service clustering. In: Basu, S., Pautasso, C., Zhang, L., Fu, X. (eds.) ICSOC 2013. LNCS, vol. 8274, pp. 162–176. Springer, Heidelberg (2013). https://doi.org/10.1007/978-3-642-45005-1_12
6. Rodriguez Mier, P., Pedrinaci, C., Lama, M., et al.: An integrated semantic web service discovery and composition framework. IEEE Trans. Serv. Comput. **9**(4), 537–550 (2016)
7. Cheng, B., Zhao, S., Li, C., et al.: A web services discovery approach based on mining underlying interface semantics. IEEE Trans. Knowl. Data Eng. **99**, 1–18 (2017)
8. Lu, Y., Mei, Q., Zhai, C.: Investigating task performance of probabilistic topic models: an empirical study of PLSA and LDA. Inf. Retrieval **14**(2), 178–203 (2011)
9. Shi, M., Liu, J., Zhou, D., Cao, B., et al.: WE-LDA: a word embeddings augmented LDA model for web services clustering. In: ICWS 2017, pp. 9–16 (2017)
10. Chen, F., Lu, C., Wu, H., et al.: A semantic similarity measure integrating multiple conceptual relationships for web service discovery. Expert Syst. Appl. Int. J. **67**(C), 19–31 (2017)
11. Zhu, L., Wang, G., Zou, X.: Improved information gain feature selection method for Chinese text classification based on word embedding. In: ICSCA 2017, pp. 72–76 (2017)
12. Greff, K., Srivastava, R.K., Koutnik, J., et al.: LSTM: a search space odyssey. IEEE Trans. Neural Netw. Learn. Syst. **28**(10), 2222–2232 (2017)
13. Zhou, P., Shi, W., Tian, J., et al.: Attention-based bidirectional long short-term memory networks for relation classification. In: ACL 2016, pp. 207–212 (2016)
14. Řehůřek, R., Sojka, P.: Software framework for topic modelling with large corpora. In: Proceedings of LREC 2010 Workshop New Challenges for NLP Frameworks (2010)
15. Chen, L., et al.: WTCluster: utilizing tags for web services clustering. In: Kappel, G., Maamar, Z., Motahari-Nezhad, H.R. (eds.) ICSOC 2011. LNCS, vol. 7084, pp. 204–218. Springer, Heidelberg (2011). https://doi.org/10.1007/978-3-642-25535-9_14
16. Tian, G., He, K., Sun, C., et al.: Ontology learning from web service descriptions. J. Front. Comput. Sci. Technol. **9**(5), 575–585 (2015)
17. Huang, Z., Xu, W., Yu, K.: Bidirectional LSTM-CRF models for sequence tagging. Comput. Sci. (2015)
18. Mikolov, T., Chen, K., Corrado, G., et al.: Efficient estimation of word representations in vector space. Comput. Sci. (2013)
19. Wang, Z., Hamza, W., Florian, R.: Bilateral multi-perspective matching for natural language sentences (2017)
20. Cao, B., Liu, X., Rahman, M.D., Li, B., Liu, J., Tang, M.: Integrated content and network-based service clustering and web APIs recommendation for mashup development. IEEE Trans. Serv. Comput. https://doi.org/10.1109/tsc.2017.2686390. Accepted 22 Mar 2017
21. Wu, Z., Zheng, X., Dahlmeier, D.: Character-based text classification using top down semantic model for sentence representation (2017)
22. Liu, X., Fulia, I.: Incorporating user, topic, and service related latent factors into web service recommendation. In: ICWS 2015, pp. 185–192 (2015)
23. Zhang, X., Zhao, J., Lecun, Y.: Character-level convolutional networks for text classification, pp. 649–657 (2015)

24. Yang, Z., Yang, D., Dyer, C., et al.: Hierarchical attention networks for document classification. In: Conference of the North American Chapter of the Association for Computational Linguistics: Human Language Technologies, pp. 1480–1489 (2017)
25. Elgazzar, K., Hassan, A., Martin, P.: Clustering WSDL documents to bootstrap the discovery of web services. In: ICWS 2010, pp. 147–154 (2010)

Neighborhood-Based Uncertain QoS Prediction of Web Services via Matrix Factorization

Guobing Zou[1], Shengye Pang[1], Pengwei Wang[2], Huaikou Miao[1,3], Sen Niu[4], Yanglan Gan[2(✉)], and Bofeng Zhang[1(✉)]

[1] School of Computer Engineering and Science, Shanghai University, Shanghai, China
guobingzou@gmail.com, shengyepang@gmail.com, bfzhang@shu.edu.cn
[2] School of Computer Science and Technology, Donghua University, Shanghai, China
{wangpengwei,ylgan}@dhu.edu.cn
[3] Shanghai Key Laboratory of Computer Software Evaluating and Testing, Shanghai, China
[4] School of Computer and Information Engineering, Shanghai Polytechnic University, Shanghai, China
sens306314@gmail.com

Abstract. With the rapidly overwhelming number of services on the internet, QoS-based web service recommendation has become an urgent demand on service-oriented applications. Since there are a large number of missing QoS values in the user historical invocation records, accurately predicting these missing QoS values becomes a hot research issue. However, most existing service QoS prediction research assumes that the transactional process of the service was stable, and its QoS doesn't change as time goes. In fact, service invocation process is usually affected by many factors (e.g., geographical location, network environment), leading to service invocations with QoS uncertainty. Therefore, QoS prediction based on traditional methods can not exactly adapt to the scenarios in real-world applications. To solve the issue, combined with the collaborative filtering and matrix factorization theory, we propose a novel approach for prediction of uncertain service QoS under the dynamic Internet environment. Extensive experiments have been conducted on a real-world data set and the results demonstrate the effectiveness and applicability of our approach for QoS prediction.

Keywords: Service-oriented computing · Uncertain QoS prediction · Collaborative filtering · Matrix factorization

1 Introduction

Web services are self-contained and self-describing computational Web components designed to support machine-to-machine interaction by programmatic Web method calls [2]. With the development of Web services on the Internet, Quality

© ICST Institute for Computer Sciences, Social Informatics and Telecommunications Engineering 2019
Published by Springer Nature Switzerland AG 2019. All Rights Reserved
H. Gao et al. (Eds.): CollaborateCom 2018, LNICST 268, pp. 659–675, 2019.
https://doi.org/10.1007/978-3-030-12981-1_46

of Services (QoS) has become a very important criterion as it can distinguish services with the same functionality. In general, QoS criteria can be divided into user-independent and user-dependent properties. User-independent QoS criteria (e.g., price, popularity) are usually defined by service providers, which are identical to different service requesters. Due to the influence of unpredictable network connections and heterogeneous user environments, QoS values of those user-dependent criteria (e.g., failure probability, response time, throughput) can fluctuate widely among different service requesters or different invocations by the same service requester.

QoS as nonfunctional property plays an important role in many research branches of services computing, such as service selection under QoS constraints [5,7,8], dynamic composition of web services with QoS optimality [17], and QoS prediction for service recommendation [4,9]. However, it is difficult and sometimes impossible to trigger actual service invocation transactions on the client-side. Moreover, it is also impractical to release QoS information from service providers or third-communities when publishing their web services on the Internet for use. Therefore, there are usually a large number of missing QoS values in the user-service historical invocation records and how to effectively predict these missing service QoS has become solid foundations of further service-oriented applications.

In recent years, existing QoS-aware approaches have been done by applying matrix factorization theory for QoS prediction of web services. The traditional matrix factorization based methods decompose user-service transactional QoS matrix formed by the historical invocations into two characteristic sub-matrices, thereby predicting the missing values in the original QoS matrix [10]. On the basis of the traditional matrix factorization method, there are researchers who have made modifications on QoS matrix with external heuristic information to improve the accuracy of service QoS prediction. By calculating user similarity, some works combined user neighborhood with traditional matrix factorization to more accurately predict service QoS values [6,14,15]. Besides considering similar users, another group of works further considered similar services to optimize matrix factorization process for more precise QoS prediction [19].

However, most existing approaches mainly focused on how to accurately implement QoS matrix factorization and they rarely took the uncertainty of QoS transactions into consideration for effective service recommendation. During actual service invocation processes, users often make a lot of invocations to a same service over a long period of time. As a result, a pair of user-service combination always generates multiple QoS transactional records. Therefore, it is mandatory to design a novel approach for effectively solving the research issue on service QoS prediction with uncertainty. To solve the above issue, we have fully considered the features of uncertain QoS of web services and proposed a new method to achieve more accurate uncertain service QoS prediction satisfying the demands on real-world service-oriented applications.

The main contributions of this paper are threefold as below.

- First, user uncertain QoS model is structured as a three-layer tree leveraging the historical QoS transaction logs, which depicts the QoS uncertainty of users' invoking web services many times under a dynamic application environment.
- Second, considering the feature of QoS uncertainty, we propose a new similarity calculation method to identify the neighborhood in terms of user side and service side, respectively. Furthermore, by fusing the similar users and services into a unified matrix factorization framework in an uncertain service invocation environment, we propose three QoS prediction strategies called U_UMF S_UMF and US_UMF.
- Third, we implement a prototype system for QoS prediction with uncertainty and conduct extensive experiments on a large-scale real-world data set that has more than 1.5 million QoS transaction logs from service invocations of users among 27 countries. The experimental results validate the effectiveness of the proposed approach for uncertain QoS prediction.

The remainder of this paper is organized as follows. Section 2 gives a motivating example. Section 3 elaborates our uncertain QoS prediction approach. Section 4 shows extensive experiments and analyzes the results. Section 5 reviews the related work and Sect. 6 concludes the paper.

2 Motivating Example

In this section, we give a motivating example to illustrate the uncertainty of service QoS during user invocation process. It is observed from Fig. 1 that there are a set of services and users in the service-oriented application environment. Each user has invoked a subset of services at different times, generating uncertain service QoS transaction logs. The nonfunctional QoS values (e.g., response time) are observed by each service requester.

In this scenario, let's take James as an example. As a service requester, James has invoked service 2, service 3 and service 4 for 31, 16 and 23 times, respectively. Those invocations of the same service reflect different variations on response time in an uncertain application environment. Now we aim to predict his missing QoS values for service 5. In traditional matrix factorization methods, they mostly consider the situation where each user invokes a service only once. However, in real-world service-oriented applications, a user may invoke a web service a bunch of times, each of which consists of multiple QoS invocation records. Based on above hypothesis, we should take the QoS uncertainty of web services into consideration so as to improve prediction accuracy and usability for real-world application demands.

3 Uncertain QoS Prediction of Web Services

In this section, we first illustrate the overall framework of our approach for uncertain QoS prediction of web services. Then, we detailedly present each component in the framework.

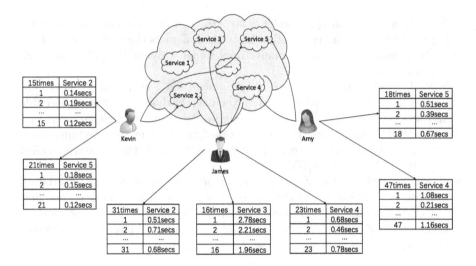

Fig. 1. The motivating scenario of service invocations with QoS uncertainty

3.1 Framework of the Approach

We design an approach for uncertain QoS prediction of web services via improved matrix factorization integrated with neighborhood information of services and users. The overall framework is shown in Fig. 2.

The whole framework is composed of three key steps, including uncertain QoS user modeling, similar neighborhood mining, and uncertain QoS prediction. Initially, we build up uncertain QoS user model leveraging the historical QoS transaction logs. On the basis of nonfunctional QoS criteria modeling of a service user, we evaluate the neighborhood relationship between all of the users and services. Then a neighborhood set can be mined for an active user or target service by the similarity computation among uncertain QoS user models. Finally, we fuse user neighborhood and/or service neighborhood into traditional matrix factorization algorithm. Consequently, we propose three different uncertain QoS prediction strategies: U_UMF (User_Uncertain Matrix Factorization), S_UMF (Service_Uncertain Matrix Factorization) and US_UMF (User Service_Uncertain Matrix Factorization).

3.2 Uncertain QoS User Modeling

It is observed that a service user may invoke a set of web services, each of which corresponds to multiple QoS transaction logs that can be formalized as a QoS matrix with uncertainty. Formally, an uncertain QoS user model is defined as a four-tuple $\langle Auser, Lservices, Smatrices, f \rangle$. $Auser$ represents an active user; $Lservices$ is a list of all the services which the active user has ever invoked; $Smatrices$ consists of a number of different matrices where each matrix includes all of the QoS transaction logs invoked by the active user on a web service in

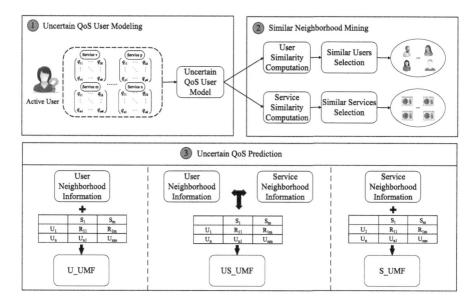

Fig. 2. The framework of QoS prediction of web services with uncertainty

Lservices; f is a mapping function from a service to its corresponding uncertain QoS matrix denoted by $f : Lservices \rightarrow Smatrices$.

We visualize uncertain QoS user model of web services as a tree with three layers. It can be illustrated in Fig. 3, including user layer, invocation service layer and QoS transaction matrixes layer.

3.3   Similar Neighborhood Mining

To integrate external heuristic information with uncertainty into a matrix factorization framework, the neighborhood set with similar users or services needs to be identified for making QoS prediction.

User Neighborhood Mining. Given an active user a, its neighborhood set can be mined by evaluating the similarity between a and each candidate user u with their corresponding uncertain QoS user model. Given an uncertain QoS transaction matrix, it is transformed into a vector by averaging the invocation QoS values within each corresponding column. To simplify the calculation, we only take the ith QoS criterion into consideration.

$$\overline{Val(a,s)} = \frac{\sum\limits_{j=1}^{n} V(q_{ji})}{n} \tag{1}$$

Where n counts the number of invocation times on web service s by user a, $V(q_{ji})$ is the QoS value on the ith criterion in the jth invocation on service s by user a.

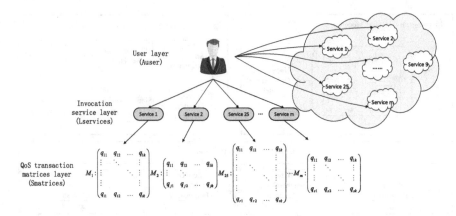

Fig. 3. Uncertain QoS user model of web services

After the transformation, a modified Pearson Correlation Coefficient is employed to calculate the similarity between an active user a and a candidate user u. Here, two weighting factors that correspond to user a and u are calculated as below.

$$\lambda_a = \frac{N_a(s)}{N_a(s) + N_u(s)} \qquad \lambda_u = \frac{N_u(s)}{N_a(s) + N_u(s)} \qquad (2)$$

Where $N_a(s)$ counts the number of invocation times on web service s by user a, $N_u(s)$ counts the number of invocation times on web service s by user u .

$$Sim(a, u) = \frac{\sum\limits_{s \in S(\cap)} \lambda_a(\overline{Val(a, s)} - Ave(\overline{Val(a)})) * \lambda_u(\overline{Val(u, s)} - Ave(\overline{Val(u)}))}{\sqrt{\sum\limits_{s \in S(\cap)} (\lambda_a(\overline{Val(a, s)} - Ave\overline{Val(a)}))^2} * \sqrt{\sum\limits_{s \in S(\cap)} (\lambda_u(\overline{Val(u, s)} - Ave(\overline{Val(u)})))^2}} \qquad (3)$$

Where $S(a)$ and $S(u)$ represent web services that a and u have invoked, respectively. $S(\cap) = S(a) \cap S(b)$ denotes services that both a and u have invoked, $\overline{Val(a, s)}$ represents the average QoS on s invoked by a and $\overline{Val(u, s)}$ represents the average QoS on s invoked by u. $Ave(\overline{Val(a)})$ represents the average QoS on all the services invoked by user a and $Ave(\overline{Val(u)})$ represents the average QoS on all the services invoked by user u.

Although the similarity from the modified Pearson Correlation Coefficient calculation is evaluated by the difference of co-invoked web services between two users, it may still incur overestimation on the similarity calculation as there exists such a situation where both users invoke very small amount of services with high QoS similarity. Based on this observation, the similarity calculation can be further improved by a weighting factor that devalues the overestimated similarity.

$$Sim'(a, u) = \frac{2 * |S(a) \cap S(u)|}{|S(a) \cup S(u)|} * Sim(a, u) \qquad (4)$$

By doing so, if an active user provides more QoS transaction logs, it is probably associated with more accurate neighborhood set. Along this way, similar neighborhood set can be mined by the traditional Top-K algorithm as below.

$$T(a) = \{u | u \in U \wedge u \in Top\text{-}K(a), u \neq a\} \tag{5}$$

Where $T(a)$ is a set of top K similar users for the active user a.

Service Neighborhood Mining. Given two web services s and v , their similarity is evaluated based on the established uncertain QoS user model. To that end, we modify Pearson Correlation Coefficient to calculate the similarity degree by the following two weighting factors, indicating the importance on each web service.

$$\lambda_s = \frac{N_u(s)}{N_u(s) + N_u(v)} \qquad \lambda_v = \frac{N_u(v)}{N_u(s) + N_u(v)} \tag{6}$$

Where $N_u(s)$ counts the number of invocation times on web service s by user u, and $N_u(v)$ counts the number of invocation times on web service v by user u.

$$Sim(s,v) = \frac{\sum\limits_{u \in U(\cap)} \lambda_s(\overline{Val(u,s)} - Ave(\overline{Val(s)})) * \lambda_v(\overline{Val(u,v)} - Ave(\overline{Val(v)}))}{\sqrt{\sum\limits_{u \in U(\cap)} (\lambda_s(\overline{Val(u,s)} - Ave\overline{Val(s)}))^2} * \sqrt{\sum\limits_{u \in U(\cap)} (\lambda_v(\overline{Val(u,v)} - Ave\overline{Val(v)}))^2}} \tag{7}$$

Where $U(s)$ and $U(v)$ represent the users who have invoked service s and service v, respectively. $U(\cap) = U(s) \cap U(v)$ denotes the users who have both invoked service s and v, $\overline{Val(u,s)}$ represents the average QoS on s invoked by u and $\overline{Val(u,v)}$ represents the average QoS on v invoked by u. $Ave(\overline{Val(s)})$ represents the average QoS on service s invoked by all of the users and $Ave(\overline{Val(v)})$ represents the average QoS on service v invoked by all of the users.

To further improve the reliability, an enhanced PCC for the similarity calculation between two web services is used to avoid the overestimation case.

$$Sim'(s,v) = \frac{2 * |U(s) \cap U(v)|}{|U(s) \cup U(v)|} * Sim(s,v) \tag{8}$$

After the above adjustment, similar neighborhood set can be mined by Top-K algorithm.

$$T(s) = \{v | v \in S \wedge v \in Top - K(S), v \neq s\} \tag{9}$$

Where $T(s)$ is a set of top K similar services for the target service s.

3.4   Uncertain QoS Prediction

On the basis of similar neighborhood mining with QoS uncertainty, we apply the idea of collaborative filtering to improve the traditional matrix factorization algorithm and propose three kinds of QoS prediction strategies: U_UMF (User_Uncertain Matrix Factorization), S_UMF (Service_Uncertain Matrix Factorization) and US_UMF (User Service_Uncertain Matrix Factorization)

U_UMF QoS Prediction. In collaborative filtering based recommender systems, the interactive experience of service users inside a neighborhood should be highly similar. As a result, they contribute the similar patterns on web services invocations. Based on this intuition, we improve the traditional matrix factorization prediction algorithm as U_UMF (User_Uncertain Matrix Factorization), considering similar neighborhood set of active user based on uncertain QoS of web services.

First, we define user relational regularization terms.

$$EU_{iu} = \frac{Sim'(i, u)}{\sum\limits_{g \in T(i)} Sim'(i, g)} \tag{10}$$

$$min \sum_{i=1}^{m} \left\| U_i - \sum_{u \in T(i)} EU_{iu} * U_u \right\|_F^2 \tag{11}$$

Where $T(i)$ is a set of top K similar neighborhood users for the user i. $Sim'(i, u)$ represents the similarity between user i and u. U_i represents the eigenvector of user i. The goal of this paradigm is to minimize the intrinsic behavioral commonality between the user i and its corresponding similar neighborhood users $T(i)$. That is given similar neighborhood set, the eigenvector of i is similar with the average eigenvector of all users. After that, we combine the paradigm with the traditional matrix factorization, forming a new objective function for uncertain QoS prediction model [10].

$$\mathcal{L}_U(R, U, S) = \frac{1}{2} \sum_{i=1}^{m} \sum_{j=1}^{n} I_{ij}(R_{ij} - U_i^T S_j)^2 + \frac{\lambda_1}{2} \|U\|_F^2$$

$$+ \frac{\lambda_2}{2} \|S\|_F^2 + \frac{\alpha_1}{2} \sum_{i=1}^{m} \left\| U_i - \sum_{u \in T(i)} EU_{iu} * U_u \right\|_F^2 \tag{12}$$

Where $R = U^T S$ is the user-service matrix. $I_{i,j}$ is the indicator function that is equal to 1 if user i invoked web service j and is equal to 0 otherwise. $\|\cdot\|_F^2$ denotes the Frobenius norm. α_1 controls the importance of this constraint paradigm in the U_UMF matrix factorization model. Two regularization terms related to U and S are involved to avoid the problem of overfitting, where λ_1 and λ_2 are the learning rates. In many recommendation systems, this formula was widely adopted.

To solve the modeled uncertain QoS prediction problem, we leverage the most commonly used gradient descent algorithm to find the optimum value of the objective function.

$$\frac{\partial \mathcal{L}_U}{\partial U_i} = \sum_{j=1}^{n} I_{i,j}(R_{i,j} - U_i^T S_j)(-S_j) + \lambda_1 U_i + \alpha_1 (U_i - \sum_{u \in T(i)} EU_{iu} * U_u) \quad (13)$$

$$\frac{\partial \mathcal{L}_U}{\partial S_j} = \sum_{i=1}^{m} I_{i,j}(R_{i,j} - U_i^T S_j)(-U_i) + \lambda_2 S_j \quad (14)$$

S_UMF QoS Prediction. From the perspective of web services, similar neighborhood services with the target service can be combined with traditional matrix factorization to improve the accuracy of the service QoS prediction. We propose an improved matrix factorization prediction algorithm called S_UMF (Service_Uncertain Matrix Factorization), considering similar services with QoS uncertainty.

It is observed that similar services share high similarity when invoked by different users. Under this assumption, the regularization of service relations can be defined as below.

$$ES_{jv} = \frac{Sim'(j, v)}{\sum\limits_{h \in T(j)} Sim'(j, h)} \quad (15)$$

$$min \sum_{j=1}^{n} \left\| S_j - \sum_{s \in T(j)} ES_{js} * S_s \right\|_F^2 \quad (16)$$

Where $T(j)$ is a set of top K similar neighborhood services for the service j. $Sim'(j, v)$ represents the similarity between service j and v. S_j represents the eigenvector of service j. The goal of this paradigm is to minimize the intrinsic behavioral commonality between the service j and its corresponding similar neighborhood services $T(j)$. In the same way, we combine the paradigm with the traditional matrix factorization, forming a new objective function for uncertain QoS prediction model.

$$\mathcal{L}_U(R, U, S) = \frac{1}{2} \sum_{i=1}^{m} \sum_{j=1}^{n} I_{ij}(R_{ij} - U_i^T S_j)^2 + \frac{\lambda_1}{2} \|U\|_F^2$$

$$+ \frac{\lambda_2}{2} \|S\|_F^2 + \frac{\alpha_2}{2} \sum_{j=1}^{n} \left\| S_j - \sum_{s \in T(j)} ES_{js} * S_s \right\|_F^2 \quad (17)$$

Where α_2 controls the importance of this constraint paradigm in the S_UMF matrix factorization model.

Finally, gradient descent algorithm is applied to solve the modeled uncertain QoS problem and find the optimum value of the objective function.

$$\frac{\partial \mathcal{L}_S}{\partial U_i} = \sum_{j=1}^{n} I_{i,j}(R_{i,j} - U_i^T S_j)(-S_j) + \lambda_1 U_i \tag{18}$$

$$\frac{\partial \mathcal{L}_S}{\partial S_j} = \sum_{i=1}^{m} I_{i,j}(R_{i,j} - U_i^T S_j)(-U_i) + \lambda_2 S_j + \alpha_2(S_j - \sum_{s \in T(j)} EU_{js} * S_s) \tag{19}$$

US_UMF QoS Prediction. When comprehensively considering both similar users and services, we propose an improved matrix factorization prediction algorithm called US_UMF (User Service_Uncertain Matrix Factorization) with the consideration of uncertain QoS. Combining formula (12) and (17), the objective function on QoS prediction problem for US_UMF is as below.

$$\mathcal{L}_U(R, U, S) = \frac{1}{2} \sum_{i=1}^{m} \sum_{j=1}^{n} I_{ij}(R_{ij} - U_i^T S_j)^2 + \frac{\lambda_1}{2} \|U\|_F^2 + \frac{\lambda_2}{2} \|S\|_F^2 +$$

$$\frac{\alpha_1}{2} \sum_{i=1}^{m} \left\| U_i - \sum_{u \in T(i)} EU_{iu} * U_u \right\|_F^2 + \frac{\alpha_2}{2} \sum_{j=1}^{n} \left\| S_j - \sum_{s \in T(j)} ES_{js} * S_s \right\|_F^2 \tag{20}$$

Where α_1 and α_2 control the importance of similar user and service, respectively. As with the above two methods, the gradient descent algorithm is used to derive an optimum solution to the uncertain QoS prediction problem.

$$\frac{\partial \mathcal{L}_U}{\partial U_i} = \sum_{j=1}^{n} I_{i,j}(R_{i,j} - U_i^T S_j)(-S_j) + \lambda_1 U_i + \alpha_1(U_i - \sum_{u \in T(i)} EU_{iu} * U_u) \tag{21}$$

$$\frac{\partial \mathcal{L}_S}{\partial S_j} = \sum_{i=1}^{m} I_{i,j}(R_{i,j} - U_i^T S_j)(-U_i) + \lambda_2 S_j + \alpha_2(S_j - \sum_{s \in T(j)} EU_{js} * S_s) \tag{22}$$

4   Experimental Evaluation

To validate the effectiveness and applicability of our proposed approach for uncertain QoS prediction, we conduct a set of experiments on a large-scale real-world service data set.

4.1   Experimental Settings and Data Set

The experiments are carried on a PC with Intel(R) core(TM) i5-5200U processor 2.20 GHz and 8G RAM in Windows 10 operating system. Our large number of data set of QoS transaction logs is from WS-DREAM[1], collecting approximately

---

[1] http://wsdream.github.io.

1.5 million historical QoS invocation records from multiple execution processes of 101 web services. Furthermore, 150 service requesters from more than 20 countries participated in the service invocation processes of these services. The distributions of users and services in different countries is illustrated in Fig. 4. More specifically, Table 1 shows the situation of a user access to each service with multiple QoS transaction logs.

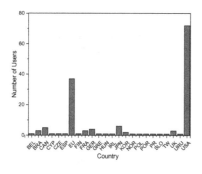 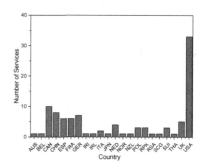

Fig. 4. Data distributions of users and services in different countries

Table 1. Uncertain QoS transaction logs for a user invoking a set of web services

UserIP	WSID	Response time	DataSize	HttpCode	HttpMessage
35.9.27.26	1521	1101	1457	200	Bad types
35.9.27.26	1521	2032	1457	200	Bad types
35.9.27.26	1521	1408	1457	200	Bad types
35.9.27.26	6405	415	620	200	OK
35.9.27.26	6405	470	620	200	OK
35.9.27.26	8953	20009	2624	−1	Timed out
35.9.27.26	8953	20002	2624	−1	Timed out
35.9.27.26	8953	20024	2624	−1	Timed out

4.2   Competitive Methods and Evaluation Metrics

We carried out experiments on four different methods for QoS prediction of web services including the traditional matrix factorization method and the three improved ones in support of uncertain Internet application environment. They are described as below.

(1) MF (Matrix Factorization): The most primitive matrix factorization prediction algorithm.
(2) U_UMF (User_Uncertain Matrix Factorization): An improved matrix factorization prediction algorithm for QoS prediction that combines similar neighborhood users with uncertainty and the traditional matrix factorization model.

(3) S_UMF (Service_Uncertain Matrix Factorization): An improved matrix factorization prediction algorithm for QoS prediction that fuses similar neighborhood services with uncertainty and the traditional matrix factorization model.

(4) US_UMF (User Service_Uncertain Matrix Factorization): An improved matrix factorization prediction algorithm for QoS prediction that integrates both similar neighbor users and services with uncertainty into the traditional matrix factorization model.

In order to measure the accuracy on QoS prediction among different approaches, Mean Absolute Error(MAE) and NMAE are used as the evaluation metrics. They are defined as below.

$$MAE = \frac{\sum_{i,j} |R_{i,j} - \hat{R}_{i,j}|}{N} \tag{23}$$

Where $R_{i,j}$ represents the real QoS value and $\hat{R}_{i,j}$ represents the predicted QoS value, when user i invokes service j. Note that NMAE is a normalized form of MAE.

$$NMAE = \frac{MAE}{\sum_{i,j} R_{i,j}/N} \tag{24}$$

4.3   Experimental Results and Analysis

In order to make the experiments closer to the actual situation, we preprocess the QoS transactions by randomly pruning invocation records from user-service QoS matrix to imitate real-world service-oriented application scenario. We dilute uncertain QoS matrix density to 5%, 10%, 15%, 20% and 25%, respectively. The experiments on uncertain QoS prediction of web services are conducted among four competitive approaches. The experimental results are shown in Table 2 and Fig. 5, respectively.

Table 2. Experimental results of uncertain QoS prediction among four competitive service approaches at three different matrix densities

	Density=5%		Density=15%		Density=25%	
	MAE	NMAE	MAE	NMAE	MAE	NMAE
MF	1085.744	0.7828	841.346	0.6043	719.8431	0.5109
U_UMF	1084.241	0.782	838.5726	0.6011	714.051	0.5099
S_UMF	1083.203	0.7812	832.8425	0.5901	710.5599	0.5092
US_UMF	**1080.589**	**0.7791**	**814.4709**	**0.5851**	**706.9142**	**0.5087**

From the experimental results, three observations can be concluded in Table 2 and Fig. 5. Furthermore, among them US_UMF method shows the best accuracy

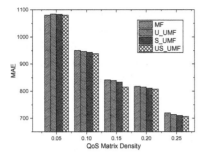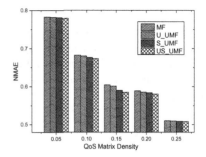

Fig. 5. Experimental results on MAE and NMAE among four competitive service QoS prediction approaches at five different matrix densities

in QoS prediction, because more information is taken into account. The experimental result validates our theory well.

To further verify the effectiveness and applicability of the improved matrix factorization approach integrated with similar user and services for uncertain QoS prediction we adjust three crucial parameters involved in the approach and test them how to influence the performance on prediction accuracy. These parameters include the number of similar neighborhood users selected for an active user (TOP-K_U), the number of similar neighborhood services selected for a target service (TOP-K_S), and the number of hidden topics in the matrix factorization framework (Dimensionality). We performed three sets of experiments on US_UMF approach each of which aims to adjust one of the three parameters.

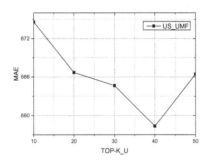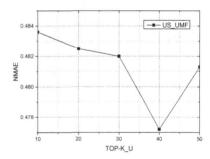

Fig. 6. The results of MAE and NMAE along with the changes of TOP-K_U

In experiment one we set the uncertain QoS matrix sparsity to 25%, Dimensionality to 10, and TOP-K_S to 10, while TOP-K_U varies from 10 to 50 with 10 interval. We can find from the experimental results in Fig. 6 as the number of similar users increases from 10 to 40, the MAE and NMAE of US_UMF gradually decrease and they reach the best when TOP-K_U equals 40. That is, the prediction accuracy of uncertain service QoS becomes better and better. However, when TOP-K_U reaches 50, the effectiveness of QoS prediction begins to decline. The main reason is that we have selected some users with low similarity in the neighborhood set for an active user, which reduces the uncertain QoS prediction accuracy. Therefore, as the number of similar neighborhood users increases, the performance on QoS prediction becomes better and better within a certain range.

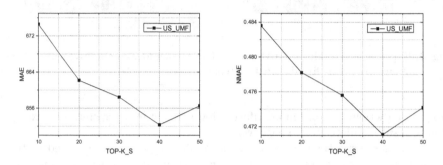

Fig. 7. The results of MAE and NMAE along with the changes of TOP-K_S

In experiment two we set the uncertain QoS matrix sparsity to 25%, Dimensionality to 10, and TOP-K_U to 10, while TOP-K_S varies from 10 to 50 with 10 interval. The results in Fig. 7 demonstrate that as the number of similar users increases from 10 to 40, the MAE and NMAE of US_UMF gradually decrease and they reach the best when TOP-K_S arrives at 40. In other words, the prediction accuracy of uncertain service QoS becomes better and better. However, when TOP-K_S reaches 50, the effectiveness of QoS prediction begins to decline. The main reason is that we have selected some services with low similarity in the neighborhood set for a target service, which reduces the uncertain QoS prediction accuracy. Therefore, as the number of neighborhood users increases, performance on QoS prediction becomes better and better within a certain range.

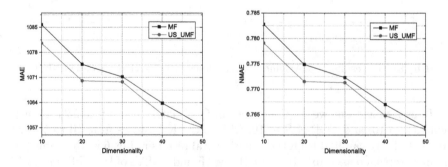

Fig. 8. The results of MAE and NMAE along with the changes of TOP-K_S

Dimensionality indicates how many feature factors are considered in matrix factorization model and it is an important parameter that influences the prediction accuracy. In experiment three we set the uncertain QoS matrix sparsity to 25%, Top-K_S to 10, and TOP-K_U to 10, while Dimensionality varies from 10 to 50 with 10 interval. We can observe from Fig. 8 that as the number of Dimensionality increases, performance on QoS prediction becomes better and better within a certain range.

5   Related Work

In recent years, QoS-aware services recommendation based on the prediction of missing QoS values and the technology of collaborative filtering and matrix factorization has gained a lot of attentions [12, 16, 18].

There are two kinds of collaborative filtering method for QoS prediction of web services: neighborhood-based and model-based. The neighborhood-based methods can be further divided into similar-user based [3], similar-service based [11], and the combination of them [13]. Neighborhood-based approaches often apply PCC as the calculation method when evaluating the relationship between two users or services, since it shows excellent performance in similarity measurement [1]. Different with the neighborhood-based method, model-based method usually train a predefined model with large-scale service repository. By using the trained model, it can recommend similar users or services for an active user or a target service. In more detail, clustering and classification algorithms are the most commonly used machine learning methods for model-driven collaborative filtering service recommendation [20].

In recent years, matrix factorization methods have been proposed for QoS prediction of web services. These methods focus on using the historical QoS transaction logs to model them as a QoS matrix that is decomposed by two characteristic submatrices. As a result, those missing values can be predicted in the original QoS matrix. Recently, some researchers tried to combine the techniques of collaborative filtering and matrix factorization together to make better QoS prediction for service recommendation. Zheng et al. integrated similar neighborhood users to traditional matrix factorization [19]. Besides considering similar users, Wei et al. further applied similar neighborhood services to optimize the process of matrix factorization [14].

However, most existing approaches mainly count on the QoS transaction logs without the consideration of uncertainty, which may reduce the prediction accuracy and its applicability on service-oriented systems.

6   Conclusion

In this paper, we fully consider the QoS uncertainty of real-world service invocations in dynamic Internet environment. To solve QoS prediction problem with uncertainty, we propose an approach consisting of three steps. First, uncertain QoS user model is constructed by the representation of three-layer tree. Second, we evaluate the similarity among uncertain QoS user models and mine similar neighborhood users and services. Finally, we integrate the generated similar users and services with QoS uncertainty into traditional matrix factorization model and present three QoS prediction strategies, including User_Uncertain Matrix Factorization (U_UMF), Service_Uncertain Matrix Factorization (S_UMF), and User Service_Uncertain Matrix Factorization (US_UMF). Comprehensive experiments conducted on large-scale real-world web services validate the effectiveness and applicability of the proposed approach for service-oriented systems.

Acknowledgement. This work was partially supported by Shanghai Natural Science Foundation (No. 18ZR1414400, 17ZR1400200), National Natural Science Foundation of China (No. 61772128, 61303096), Shanghai Sailing Program (No. 16YF1400300), and Fundamental Research Funds for the Central Universities (No. 16D111208).

References

1. Alshamri, M.Y.H., Alashwal, N.H.: Fuzzy-weighted similarity measures for memory-based collaborative recommender systems. J. Intell. Learn. Syst. Appl. **6**(1), 1–10 (2014)
2. Bichier, M., Lin, K.J.: Service-oriented computing. Computer **39**, 99–101 (2006)
3. Breese, J.S., Heckerman, D., Kadie, C.: Empirical analysis of predictive algorithms for collaborative filtering. Uncertainty Artif. Intell. **98**(7), 43–52 (2013)
4. Deng, S., et al.: A recommendation system to facilitate business process modeling. IEEE Trans. Cybern. **47**(6), 1380–1394 (2016)
5. Deng, S., Wu, H., Hu, D., Zhao, J.L.: Service selection for composition with QoS correlations. IEEE Trans. Serv. Comput. **9**(2), 291–303 (2016)
6. Ding, S., Li, Y., Wu, D., Zhang, Y., Yang, S.: Time-aware cloud service recommendation using similarity-enhanced collaborative filtering and ARIMA model. Decis. Support Syst. **107**, 103–115 (2018)
7. Hadad, J.E., Manouvrier, M., Rukoz, M.: TQoS: Transactional and QoS-aware selection algorithm for automatic web service composition. IEEE Trans. Serv. Comput. **3**(1), 73–85 (2010)
8. Haddad, J.E., Manouvrier, M., Ramirez, G., Rukoz, M.: QoS-driven selection of web services for transactional composition. In: IEEE International Conference on Web Services, pp. 653–660 (2008)
9. Kuang, L., Xia, Y., Mao, Y.: Personalized services recommendation based on context-aware QoS prediction. In: IEEE International Conference on Web Services, pp. 400–406 (2012)
10. Salakhutdinov, R., Mnih, A.: Probabilistic matrix factorization. In: International Conference on Neural Information Processing Systems, pp. 1257–1264 (2007)
11. Sarwar, B., Karypis, G., Konstan, J., Riedl, J.: Item-based collaborative filtering recommendation algorithms. In: International Conference on World Wide Web, pp. 285–295 (2001)
12. Shao, L., Zhang, J., Wei, Y., Zhao, J., Xie, B., Mei, H.: Personalized QoS prediction forweb services via collaborative filtering. In: IEEE International Conference on Web Services, pp. 439–446 (2007)
13. Wang, J., De Vries, A.P., Reinders, M.J.T.: Unifying user-based and item-based collaborative filtering approaches by similarity fusion. In: ACM SIGIR Conference on Information Retrieval, pp. 501–508 (2006)

14. Wei, L., Yin, J., Deng, S., Li, Y., Wu, Z.: An extended matrix factorization approach for QoS prediction in service selection. In: IEEE International Conference on Services Computing, pp. 162–169 (2012)
15. Wu, X., Cheng, B., Chen, J.: Collaborative filtering service recommendation based on a novel similarity computation method. IEEE Trans. Serv. Comput. **10**(3), 352–365 (2017)
16. Xu, Y., Yin, J., Deng, S., Xiong, N.N., Huang, J.: Context-aware QoS prediction for web service recommendation and selection. Expert Syst. Appl. **53**, 75–86 (2016)
17. Yilmaz, A.E., Karagoz, P.: Improved genetic algorithm based approach for QoS aware web service composition. In: IEEE International Conference on Web Services, pp. 463–470 (2014)
18. Zheng, Z., Ma, H., Lyu, M.R., King, I.: QoS-aware web service recommendation by collaborative filtering. IEEE Trans. Serv. Comput. **4**(2), 140–152 (2011)
19. Zheng, Z., Ma, H., Lyu, M.R., King, I.: Collaborative web service QoS prediction via neighborhood integrated matrix factorization. IEEE Trans. Serv. Comput. **6**(3), 289–299 (2013)
20. Zou, G., Li, W., Zhou, Z., Niu, S., Gan, Y., Zhang, B.: Clustering-based uncertain QoS prediction of web services via collaborative filtering. Int. J. Web Grid Serv. **13**(4), 403–424 (2017)

Runtime Resource Management for Microservices-Based Applications: A Congestion Game Approach (Short Paper)

Ruici Luo[1,3], Wei Ye[2,3], Jinan Sun[2,3(✉)], Xueyang Liu[2,3], and Shikun Zhang[2,3]

[1] School of Electronics Engineering and Computer Science,
Peking University, Beijing, China
[2] National Engineering Research Center for Software Engineering,
Peking University, Beijing, China
[3] Key Laboratory of High Confidence Software Technologies,
Ministry of Education, Beijing, China
{luoruici,wye,sjn,liuxueyang,zhangsk}@pku.edu.cn

Abstract. The term "Microservice Architecture" has sprung up in recent years as a new style of software design that gains popularity as cloud computing prospers. In microservice-based applications, different microservices collaborate with one another via interface calls, but they may also compete for resources when an increase of users' need renders the resources insufficient. This poses new challenges for allocating resources efficiently during runtime. To tackle the problem, we propose a novel approach based on Congestion Game in this paper. Firstly, we use a weighted directed acyclic graph to model the inter-relationship of the microservices that compose an application. Then we use $M/G/1$ Queue in Queue Theory to describe the arrival process of access requests, and combine it with the above graph to calculate the arrival rate of access requests to each microservice, which in turn is used to estimate response time in a newly-designed microservice revenue function. Finally, we define resources competing problem as a congestion game where each microservice is a player aiming to maximize its revenue, and propose an algorithm to find Nash equilibrium in polynomial time. Experiment results show that our approach can effectively improve the overall performance of the system with limited resources, and outperform Binpack and Spread, two scheduling strategies used in Docker Swarm.

Keywords: Microservice architecture · Resource management · Game theory

1 Introduction

The popularity of cloud computing technology not only promotes the development of computer hardware and system software architectures, but also brings

© ICST Institute for Computer Sciences, Social Informatics and Telecommunications Engineering 2019
Published by Springer Nature Switzerland AG 2019. All Rights Reserved
H. Gao et al. (Eds.): CollaborateCom 2018, LNICST 268, pp. 676–687, 2019.
https://doi.org/10.1007/978-3-030-12981-1_47

about changes in the way software is developed and used. The idea of IT resource servitization is becoming increasingly popular, leading to the trend of "X as a service." The service model represented by IaaS, PaaS and SaaS has been widely adopted. In the open, dynamic and complex cloud computing environment, software systems need continuous online evolution [19] to respond quickly to users' need, therefore the complexity of software is ever growing. Considering the principles, methods, and techniques for modeling and controlling complexity in software engineering, the basic idea can be summarized as separation of concerns [14]. Microservice Architecture [7] is a design principle that aims to fight against the increasing complexity of software in the cloud environment. The core idea is to separate an application into a series of distinct microservices, such that each of them addresses a separate business logic and can run in a separate environment. It can make the boundaries between services clear and enable them to adopt lightweight mechanism to communicate. As a result, it forms a highly cohesive and loosely-coupling architecture.

In a large-scale application system based on microservice architecture, such properties as large amount of microservices, continuous online evolution and complex dependencies among microservices pose new challenges for runtime resource management. On one hand, microservices need to accomplish a specific business logic by collaboration; on the other hand, they may also compete for resources in a constrained runtime environment.

Game theory has been successfully applied to many computer resource-related optimization problems such as online price setting, flow and congestion control, network routing optimization, etc. [2]. Nash Equilibrium [13] in game theory is the most common solution: it is a state where for any participant in the game, he cannot get more benefits by changing his strategy without changing the strategies of other participants. At this point the strategy combination of all participants constitutes the Nash equilibrium state.

Considering the collaboration and competition among microservices, we propose to use game theory to model the runtime resource management problem as a congestion game, and optimize resource allocation by finding the Nash Equilibrium state of the Game, where each microservice is considered as a player to maximize its revenue. More specifically, we make the following contributions in this paper:

1. We establish a microservice application model in which we quantify call relationships among microservices based on runtime microservice interaction information.
2. We design a microservice revenue function based on the compliance level with quality of service (QoS) requirements specified in Service Level Agreement (SLA).
3. We define the competition for resources among microservices as a congestion game model and provide a polynomial-time algorithm for solving resource management optimization problem.

The rest of the paper is organized as follows. Section 2 summarizes related works. Section 3 provide some background information regarding resource man-

agement under microservices scenario. Section 4 presents our proposed congestion game model of resource management for microservices. Section 5 discusses
the algorithm to find the Nash Equilibrium of the congestion game. Section 6
presents the results of experiments done to validate our model, and finally Sect. 7
concludes the paper.

2   Related Works

The methods of resource planning, scheduling and management in cloud computing environment can be divided into three categories: optimization method,
adaptive method and game theory method.

Optimization is a crucial method to solve the scheduling and allocation problem of computing resources in a cloud environment. [18] solved deployment optimization problem by greedy algorithm under the scenario where a service joins
in and leaves dynamically. [11] tried to minimize the cost of computing resources
during service deployment by studying dynamic backpack problem in which the
goal is to minimize the sum of the cost of all backpacks. [6] studied the scenario of multiple IaaS and targeted at minimizing the overall consumption, and
proposed to solve virtual machine deployment optimization problem by random
integer programming method.

A classic MAPE-K feedback loop can be formed by monitoring and analyzing
the runtime data of an application, planning the resources the application needs
and then executing, combined with a shared knowledge base [9]. A self-adaptive
software using such method usually consists of two parts: the managed element
and the managing element. The former refers to the application logic that can be
dynamically adjusted during runtime; the latter refers to the adaptive logic that
can regulate the application logic through a feedback loop. Considering that the
applications in a cloud environment are usually deployed in a mixed operating
environment of IaaS and Paas, [4] proposed a scheduling method for two kinds
of virtualization resources (virtual machine instance of IaaS layer and container
of PaaS layer) through a cybernetic feedback loop.

Because of the resemblance between the resource competition behavior
among applications in a cloud computing environment and the economic competition behavior in a free market, game theory can be used to describe the
competitive relationship in resource management. In existing literatures, it is
common to consider resource-related roles as players in a game where each player
gets the corresponding resources by adopting a certain strategy to optimize its
own revenue/cost. [3] studied the scenario where multiple SaaS providers run
applications in the same IaaS. After establishing a mathematical model to measure the benefits and costs of SaaS and defining the decision space of IaaS and
SaaS in the game, the authors found the optimal solution for IaaS/SaaS resource
pricing/acquisition by calculating the Nash equilibrium. [20] described the competitive characteristics of parallel computing tasks on resources at the business
level by game theory and proposed a scheduling algorithm based on the dual constraints of completion time and cost, considering both optimization and fairness.

Most existing game theory-based methods focus on scheduling of infrastructure (virtual machine) resources, but do not consider more granular scheduling units and their collaboration at the application level.

3   Background

Different microservices have different requirements for computing resources, load, and QoS. Take a social application for example. The activity feed service displays contents such as topics, articles, and videos of interest to users, and is used to display advertisements. It is the service that has the greatest impact on user experience and application revenue. In comparison, the user service stores a huge amount of social relationship data, which is important for data analysis and recommendation tasks, but is less important than the activity feed service from the perspective of application revenue. It is conceivable that the application runtime resource management needs to consider the importance of each service from the business perspective.

In addition, the satisfaction level of SLA will affect the application revenue as well. The response time of a user's access request is the most important factor to measure the satisfaction level. The shorter the response time, the higher the SLA satisfaction level, and the higher the revenue (the revenue agreed in the SLA, the revenue from user experience, etc.). The longer the response time, the lower the SLA satisfaction level, and the lower the revenue (default penalty, user loss, etc.).

Therefore, taking both the business importance and response time into account, we come up with the following revenue function for one access request to microservice i:

$$\theta_i = v_i + m_i r_i \tag{1}$$

where v_i is the revenue when response time is zero, and r_i is the actual response time of the access request. Note that the slope of the function $m_i < 0$, which means that the shorter the response time, the higher the revenue and vice versa. For each microservice i, a different v_i and m_i can be set to reflect its business importance. For example, an activity feed microservice in a social application, corresponding to a smaller primary function slope, indicates that the smaller the response time, the more revenue it will receive than the benefits of other services.

4   Microservice Oriented Model for Resource Management Issue

Therefore in this section, we will (1) build a microservice application model based on the runtime interaction information of microservices; (2) design a microservice revenue model based on the revenue function defined in Sect. 3 (Eq. (1)); (3) define a congestion game model for microservice runtime resource management.

4.1   Microservice Application Model

An **Application** is a triplet (S, E, T) where:

- S is the collection of microservice that make up an application. For any microservice $s \in S$, there is a collection of access endpoints $E_s = \{e_1, e_2, \ldots, e_n\}$.
- $E = \bigcup_{s \in S} E_s$ is the collection of access endpoints for all microservices.
- T represents the interaction between endpoints, $\forall t \in T, t = <e_o, e_q, p>$, $e_o, e_q \in E, p \in \mathbb{R}^+$

Essentially, the definition above can be regarded as a directed acyclic graph (DAG) composed of an endpoint set and a call request set. For each edge in the graph, it associates two endpoints to represent a call relationship, and uses a positive real number to represent the expected number of accesses that a access to the source endpoint will cascade to the target endpoint. $p < 1$ means only some requests will trigger sub-request (e.g. A branch judgement occurs in the program). $p \geq 1$ means a request will trigger more than one sub-requests on average (e.g. Loops, branches or other situations occur in the program).

4.2   Microservice Revenue Model

The number of microservice requests per unit time has several properties: (1) the number of requests is large enough; (2) a single request has little impact on the overall system performance and resource consumption; (3) all requests arrive independently. Therefore, the number of access requests for microservice per unit time can be described by Poisson distribution:

$$P(X = k) = \frac{e^{-\lambda} \lambda^k}{k!} \qquad (2)$$

Where λ represents the average number of microservice access requests that arrive per unit time. In order to cope with a large number of access requests, each logical microservice can physically have multiple instances (containers) running at the same time, distributed on different virtual machines. Provided that access requests are balanced to each microservice running instance, we can use a queuing system to describe how each microservice processes its access requests, assuming that the following properties hold:

- The request arrival time is in accordance with the Poisson distribution, i.e. the exponential probability density distribution.
- Process time for each request is the same.
- For requests that arrive at the same time, the microservice processes them with time-sharing policy.

Therefore, processing access requests by each microservice accords with the condition of M/G/1 Queue [5]. For microservice i, the expectation of access request response time γ can be calculated as:

$$E[\gamma_i] = \frac{1}{C_i \mu_i - \lambda_i} \qquad (3)$$

- C_i is the maximum computing resource that the corresponding microservice container can consume.
- μ_i is the service efficiency of the corresponding microservice container, which is the number of requests processed per unit time per unit of computing resource.
- λ_i is the access request arrival rate at each container, which is equivalent to the total request arrival rate of microservice i divided by its number of physical units, i.e. containers.

For the parameter λ_i required in Eq. (3), we need to make predictions based on history data. Using Microservice Application Model defined in Sect. 4.1, $\forall i \in S$, the arrival rate collection is defined as $\omega_i = \{\lambda_{ie_1}, \lambda_{ie_2}, \ldots, \lambda_{ie_n}\}$, where $e_1, e_2, \ldots, e_n \in E_i$. The total arrival rate of microservice i can be represented as $\lambda_i = \sum_{e \in E_i} \lambda_{ie}$. For any microservice, it is possible to cascade its access requests to the microservices it depends on. Using the call graph T in Microservice Application Model, we can easily derive the T-based arrival rate update algorithm by traversing the graph.

Assuming that all microservices run on a finite resource collection $R = \{1, \ldots, r\}$, and the access request arrival rate of microservice i on resource r per unit time is λ_{ir}, the total number of microservices that occupy resource r is x_r, the microservice revenue from resource r per unit time can be written as follows:

$$d_r(x_r) = \lambda_{ir}\theta_i \tag{4}$$

Substitute θ_i with Eq. (1) from Sect. 3, and we have:

$$d_r(x_r) = \lambda_{ir}(\nu_i + m_i E[\gamma_i]) \tag{5}$$

Note that we have used the expected value of γ_i to approximate γ_i. Substitute $E[\gamma_i]$ with Eq. (3), and we have:

$$d_r(x_r) = \lambda_{ir}(\nu_i + \frac{m_i}{\frac{C}{x_r}\mu_i - \lambda_{ir}}) = \lambda_{ir}\nu_i + \frac{m_i}{\frac{C\mu_i}{x_r\lambda_{ir}} - 1} \tag{6}$$

Here we have substituted C_i in Eq. (3) with $\frac{C}{x_r}$, where we assume that all containers on resource r share the computing resource equally, and that each resource has the same constant computing capacity C.

4.3   Microservice Congestion Game Model

Congestion games are used to describe scenarios where players share resources in a game, in which every player maximizes its own revenue by strategically selecting resources. The revenue generated by the resource is related to the number of players who choose this resource, which means that the more players that have chosen this resource, the less revenue each player can earn from this resource. The formal definition of a congestion game is as follows:

- A finite set of players $M = \{1, \ldots, n\}$

- A finite set of congestible resources $R = \{1, \ldots, r\}$
- A finite set of strategies Σ_i for each player, where each strategy $P \in \Sigma_i$ is a subset of resource set R. We use $\Sigma = \prod_{i=1}^{n} \Sigma_i$ to denote the joint strategy space and $\sigma = (\sigma_1, \ldots, \sigma_n) \in \Sigma$ is a strategy vector in which the player i chooses the strategy σ_i
- For each resource $r \in R$ and a strategy vector $\sigma = (\sigma_1, \ldots, \sigma_n) \in \Sigma$, the load (i.e. congestion number, or the number of times this resource is selected) $x_r(\sigma) = \#\{i : r \in \sigma_i\}$, where $\#$ means the size of the set.
- For each resource $r \in R$, a revenue function $d_r : \mathbb{N} \to \mathbb{R}$ describes the relationship between the number of times this resource is selected x_r and the revenue every player can earn. d_r is a monotonically decreasing function on x_r.
- For a given strategy vector $\sigma = (\sigma_1, \ldots, \sigma_n) \in \Sigma$, player i's total revenue $S_i = \sum_{r \in \sigma_i} d_r(x_r(\sigma))$. For Congestion Game Model, a strategy vector $\sigma^* = (\sigma_1^*, \ldots, \sigma_n^*)$ is a Nash Equilibrium of the congestion game if and only if

$$\sum_{r \in \sigma_i^*} d_r(x_r(\sigma^*)) \geq \sum_{r \in \sigma_i'} d_r(x_r(\sigma')), \forall i \in N, \forall \sigma_i \in \Sigma_i, \sigma' = (\sigma_i, \sigma_{-i}^*) \quad (7)$$

We further apply Microservice Revenue Model in Sect. 4.2 to the congestion game. For any microservice i and its non-empty decision vector $\sigma = (\sigma_1, \ldots, \sigma_n) \in \Sigma$, its revenue function is defined as follows:

$$S_i(\sigma) = \sum_{r \in \sigma_i} d_r(x_r(\sigma)) \quad (8)$$

$$d_r(x_r(\sigma)) = \lambda_{ir} \nu_i + \frac{m_i}{\frac{C \mu_i}{x_r(\sigma) \lambda_{ir}} - 1} \quad (9)$$

We can see that $d_r(x_r)$ is a monotonically decreasing function on x_r (note that $m_i < 0$), which satisfies the conditions of Congestion Game Model.

5   Nash Equilibrium of the Congestion Game

The existence of Nash equilibrium can be shown by constructing a potential function [15] that assigns a value to each outcome. Moreover, the construction will also show that iterated best response finds a Nash equilibrium.

To solve the Nash equilibrium of the congestion game, we propose an algorithm that adopts an incremental optimization scheme. We set up an empty set as the strategy vector initially. At each iteration, only one player is allowed to change its current strategy and choose its best response against the strategy vector. For n microservices, there are n steps to achieve the Nash equilibrium, where in each step only one other player enters. When no player can change his strategy solely to gain more utility, the Nash equilibrium in the step is achieved.

In general, we consider the nth step, where former $n-1$ players have achieved equilibrium and their strategy vector is $\sigma(n-1) = (\sigma_1, \sigma_2, \ldots, \sigma_{n-1})$. It is interesting to find out, after the nth player enters, how will the system regain the equilibrium. The player n will choose his best response strategy against the former $n - 1$ players' strategies in equilibrium, which must congest some of the resources and affect the strategy vector $\sigma(n - 1)$. Each affected player changes its current strategy and chooses the best response like the nth player. The Nash equilibrium is achieved at last. Formally, $S_n(\sigma_n, \sigma(n-1))$ is denoted as the utility of the player n, where player n chooses the strategy σ_i and the former $n - 1$ players choose the strategy tuple $\sigma(n - 1) = (\sigma_1, \sigma_2, \ldots, \sigma_{n-1})$.

To regain the Nash equilibrium strategy vector of n players, we propose Algorithm 1:

Algorithm 1. Regain to equilibrium(n)

Require: n-1 players' strategy vector $\sigma(n) = (\sigma_1, \sigma_2, \ldots, \sigma_{n-1})$
Ensure: n players' strategy vector $\sigma(n) = (\sigma_1, \sigma_2, \ldots, \sigma_n)$;
 1: calculate the nth player's best strategy σ_n^*
 2: initialize $\sigma(n) = (\sigma(n - 1), \sigma_n^*)$
 3: $i = 0$
 4: **while true do**
 5:    **if** $i == n$ **then**
 6:       break;
 7:    **end if**
 8:    **if** $\forall \sigma_i \in \Sigma_i, S_i(\sigma(n)) \geq S_i(\sigma_i, \sigma_{-i}(n))$ **then**
 9:       $i = i + 1$;
10:    **else**
11:       calculate the ith player's best strategy σ_i^*
12:       replace the ith players strategy: $\sigma(n)[i] = \sigma_i^*$
13:       $i = 0$;
14:    **end if**
15: **end while**

For every player, the time complexity of calculating best strategy is $O(r * n)$, where r is the number of resources and n is the number of players. To obtain all players' Nash equilibrium state, the iteration in Algorithm 1 would be executed at most $n * r$ times. In a word, to obtain the final strategy vector, the time complexity of the algorithm is $O(n^2 r^2)$.

6   Evaluation

6.1   Experiment Setting

We conducted experiments on an open-source project called Pwitter [1], which is a social-networking application resembling Twitter. It is a three-layer application developed in python that runs on Gunicorn and uses Redis and MySQL for data storage. We modified and extended Pwitter to microservice architectural style. After conversion, our version of Pwitter has a network of 30 microservices, and each of them is exposed to between 10 to 20 API endpoints via HTTP. We run these microservices on virtual machine instances provided by Aliyun (a cloud provider in China). The specification of each instance is ecs.c5.x2large with 8 core CPU and 16G memory.

Docker is installed on each virtual machine instance, and each microservice runs in the form of a Docker Container. We use Swarm to administrate all the microservices, which is an official cluster management tool of Docker. To deploy a microservice, we can simply initiate a request to the Manager Node, which will place its corresponding runtime container on a suitable virtual machine instance based on the scheduling results of the chosen resource management algorithm to maximize the microservice revenue.

Docker Swarm has three inherent strategies for cluster scheduling, namely:

- Spread, the default Strategy, which picks the Worker node that currently has the least resource (CPU, memory etc.) consumption, so as to prioritize on fair usage of resources.
- Binpack, a strategy contrary to Spread, which chooses to fill up a Work node as much as possible first, so as to keep more nodes available.
- Random, which picks a Worker node at random.

To verify the effectiveness of our proposed scheduling strategy based on Congestion Game, we used this strategy to deploy the 30 microservices of Pwitter and compare the performance with that of using Spread and Binpack. After deployment, we simulated http requests and gradually increased the frequency from 1000 requests per second to 5000 requests per second at 1000 interval. To verify the effectiveness of different strategies under different resource constraints, we repeated the above experiment on 5, 10, 15, 20 and 30 virtual machine instances respectively.

6.2   Experiment Results

We use average request response time, ratio of request failure and microservice revenue as three metrics to compare the performance of each strategy.

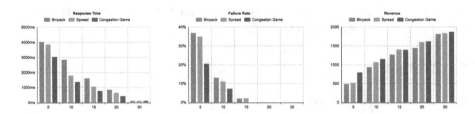

Fig. 1. Average request response time, failure rate and revenues of each strategy using different number of virtual machine instances

As shown in Fig. 1, all three strategies have relatively large response delay when only 5 virtual machine instances are used. The average response time using Spread or Binpack is close to 4000 ms, while the average response time of Congestion Game Scheduling Strategy is 3025 ms, about 25% less. As the number of virtual machine instances increased, our strategy still has an edge compared to the other two, though the gap narrows gradually. All three strategies have roughly the same average response time when 30 virtual machine instances are used.

Congest Game Scheduling strategy also has the lowest request failure ratio compare to the other two when only 5 virtual machine are used. Its failure ratio is about 20% while Binpack has the highest failure ratio of 37%, an increase of 17%. When the number of virtual machine instances increased to 15, our strategy has no request failure at all while the other two still have about 2% failure ratio. When more than 15 virtual machine instances are used, none of the three strategies have request failure, which indicates that the virtual machine resources have satisfied the need at 5000 requests per second.

In the end, Congestion Game scheduling strategy has far more microservice revenue than the other two strategies when only 5 virtual machine instances are used. Similarly, the advantage closed out as more virtual machine instances are used. When the number reaches 30, the three strategies basically have the same revenue.

From the above results of experiments, we can see that when the number of virtual machine instances is limited, the Congestion Game scheduling strategy can optimize the performance of the system and largely outperform Binpack or Spread provided by Docker Swarm. Such gap in performance shrinks as the number of virtual machine instances increases since each instance is less pressured and more microservice containers can be run to decrease the request response time.

7   Conclusion

This paper proposes a congestion game-based resource management method under the scenario of internal resource competition among microservices in a cloud environment. Firstly, we construct a model for microservice-based applications that captures the runtime dependency among microservices that compose an application. Secondly, we propose a microservice revenue function, and then we define the problem of internal resource competition as a congestion game where each microservice is a player that tries to maximize its revenue. Finally we propose a polynomial-time algorithm to find the Nash Equilibrium of the game to solve the problem. We conducted experiments to verify the effectiveness of our approach, and results show that our proposed congestion game-based scheduling method can effectively increase the overall performance of the microservice-based application under computing resource constraints, outperforming existing strategies used by Docker Swarm.

References

1. Affetti, L.: Pwitter. https://github.com/deib-polimi/pwitter
2. Altman, E., Boulogne, T., El-Azouzi, R., Jiménez, T., Wynter, L.: A survey on networking games in telecommunications. Comput. Oper. Res. **33**(2), 286–311 (2006). https://doi.org/10.1016/j.cor.2004.06.005
3. Ardagna, D., Panicucci, B., Passacantando, M.: Generalized nash equilibria for the service provisioning problem in cloud systems. IEEE Trans. Serv. Comput. **6**(4), 429–442 (2013). https://doi.org/10.1109/TSC.2012.14
4. Baresi, L., Guinea, S., Leva, A., Quattrocchi, G.: A discrete-time feedback controller for containerized cloud applications. In: Proceedings of the 2016 24th ACM SIGSOFT International Symposium on Foundations of Software Engineering, FSE 2016, pp. 217–228. ACM, New York (2016). https://doi.org/10.1145/2950290.2950328
5. Bolch, G., Greiner, S., de Meer, H., Trivedi, K.S.: Queueing Networks and Markov Chains: Modeling and Performance Evaluation with Computer Science Applications. Wiley-Interscience, New York (1998)
6. Chaisiri, S., Lee, B.S., Niyato, D.: Optimal virtual machine placement across multiple cloud providers. In: 2009 IEEE Asia-Pacific Services Computing Conference (APSCC), pp. 103–110 (2009). https://doi.org/10.1109/APSCC.2009.5394134
7. Dragoni, N., Lanese, I., Larsen, S.T., Mazzara, M., Mustafin, R., Safina, L.: Microservices: how to make your application scale. In: Petrenko, A.K., Voronkov, A. (eds.) PSI 2017. LNCS, vol. 10742, pp. 95–104. Springer, Cham (2018). https://doi.org/10.1007/978-3-319-74313-4_8
8. Gupta, A., Garg, R.: Load balancing based task scheduling with ACO in cloud computing. In: 2017 International Conference on Computer and Applications (ICCA), pp. 174–179 (2017). https://doi.org/10.1109/COMAPP.2017.8079781
9. Hoenisch, P., Schulte, S., Dustdar, S., Venugopal, S.: Self-adaptive resource allocation for elastic process execution. In: 2013 IEEE Sixth International Conference on Cloud Computing, pp. 220–227 (2013). https://doi.org/10.1109/CLOUD.2013.126
10. Kansal, S., Kumar, H., Kaushal, S., Sangaiah, A.K.: Genetic algorithm-based cost minimization pricing model for on-demand IaaS cloud service. J. Supercomput. (2018). https://doi.org/10.1007/s11227-018-2279-8
11. Li, Y., Tang, X., Cai, W.: Dynamic bin packing for on-demand cloud resource allocation. IEEE Trans. Parallel Distrib. Syst. **27**(1), 157–170 (2016). https://doi.org/10.1109/TPDS.2015.2393868
12. Ling, Y., Yi, X., Bihuan, C., Xin, P., Wenyun, Z.: Towards runtime dynamic provision of virtual resources using feedforward and feedback control. J. Comput. Res. Dev. **52**(4), 889–897 (2015)
13. Maskin, E.: The theory of implementation in Nash equilibrium: a survey. In: Social Goals and Social Organization, pp. 173–204 (1985)
14. Mei, H., Huang, G., Zhang, L., Zhang, W.: ABC: a method of software architecture modeling in the whole lifecycle. Scientia Sinica Informationis **44**(5), 564–587 (2014)
15. Monderer, D., Shapley, L.S.: Potential games. Games Econ. Behav. **14**(1), 124–143 (1996)
16. Pahl, C., Jamshidi, P.: Microservices: a systematic mapping study. In: Proceedings of the 6th International Conference on Cloud Computing and Services Science, CLOSER 2016, vol. 1 and 2, pp. 137–146. SCITEPRESS - Science and Technology Publications, LDA, Portugal (2016). https://doi.org/10.5220/0005785501370146

17. Sheikholeslami, F., Navimipour, N.J.: Service allocation in the cloud environments using multi-objective particle swarm optimization algorithm based on crowding distance. Swarm Evol. Comput. **35**, 53–64 (2017). https://doi.org/10.1016/j.swevo.2017.02.007, http://www.sciencedirect.com/science/article/pii/S221065021730130X

18. Stolyar, A.L., Zhong, Y.: An infinite server system with general packing constraints: asymptotic optimality of a greedy randomized algorithm. In: 2013 51st Annual Allerton Conference on Communication, Control, and Computing (Allerton), pp. 575–582 (2013). https://doi.org/10.1109/Allerton.2013.6736576

19. Wang, H.M., Shi, P.C., Ding, B., Yin, G., Shi, D.X.: Online evolution of software services. Jisuanji Xuebao (Chin. J. Comput.) **34**(2), 318–328 (2011)

20. Wei, G., Vasilakos, A.V., Zheng, Y., Xiong, N.: A game-theoretic method of fair resource allocation for cloud computing services. J. Supercomput. **54**(2), 252–269 (2010). https://doi.org/10.1007/s11227-009-0318-1

CPN Model Based Standard Feature Verification Method for REST Service Architecture

Jing Liu[(✉)], Zhen-Tian Liu, and Yu-Qiang Zhao

Inner Mongolia University, Hohhot 010021, China
liujing@imu.edu.cn

Abstract. The representational state transfer (REST) service architecture is widely used in large-scale and scalable distributed web systems. If the REST service architecture does not comply with its standard feature constrains, it can result in degraded performance or low scalability of the REST-based web systems. Therefore, in order to enhance the quality of system designing, it is necessary to verify whether the system design meets the standard feature constrains of the REST service architecture. In this paper, we propose a standard feature constrains verification method for REST service architecture based on Colored Petri Nets (CPN) model. Firstly, five standard feature constrains of the REST service architecture are modeled using the CPN. Then a verification method is proposed based on synchronized matching of the execution paths in model state space. Lastly, we validate the usability and validity of the proposed verification method using a practical course management web system based on the REST service architecture. Experimental results show that our method can effectively confirm whether the web application system design based on REST service architecture conforms to the standard feature constrains of the REST service architecture. Besides, it can also provide intuitive and feasible execution data when the standard feature constraints are not met, which can facilitate the defects location and correction of the following design of application systems.

Keywords: REST service architecture · colored Petri nets model · Verification of standard features

1 Introduction

In 2000, Fielding first proposed the representational state transfer (REST) service architecture [1]. It refers to a new style abstracted in combination with the design principles of the hyper text transfer protocol (HTTP) standard and the uniform resource identifier (URI) standard, which is resource-oriented and emphasizes resource-centricity. At present, REST service architecture is widely used in collaborative web systems. Many web application systems are developed based on REST service architecture, such as Amazon shopping website

© ICST Institute for Computer Sciences, Social Informatics and Telecommunications Engineering 2019
Published by Springer Nature Switzerland AG 2019. All Rights Reserved
H. Gao et al. (Eds.): CollaborateCom 2018, LNICST 268, pp. 688–707, 2019.
https://doi.org/10.1007/978-3-030-12981-1_48

and Google search engine [2]. The advantages of the REST service architecture include the use of a browser as a client to simplify software requirements, the use of caching mechanisms to increase access speed, the use of stateless communication to increase server scalability, and reducing the complexity of the web system development to improve the scalability.

Now, some web application systems applying REST service architecture do not comply the standard feature constraints of REST service architecture, thus causing many corresponding problems. For example, failure to meet stateless constraints will damage the scalability of the system, which will affect system load balancing. Failure to meet client-server constraints will increase the overhead of the system server and increase response time. Failure to meet cacheable constraints will result in more time overhead, because each time you retrieve a resource, you need to request it from the server [3]. Therefore, in order to prevent the above problems, when designing a web application system based on the REST service architecture, it is necessary to verify whether the system design meets the standard feature constrains of the REST service architecture. So that, we can improve the quality of R&D of web systems based on REST service architecture.

There are several formal methods to verify whether REST service architecture complys standard feature constrains, such as finite state machine (FSM) based method and communicating sequential processes (CSP) based method. The FSM-based method does not support tiering and cache acknowledgment, while the CSP-based method uses a higher degree of abstraction and a more complex description. Therefore, in view of the advantages of the colored Petri nets (CPN) model in visualization, hierarchical modeling, complex data description, concurrent behavior description and dynamic execution [4–6], we propose a CPN model based standard feature constrains verification method for REST service architecture. Firstly, CPN modeling is performed on the standard feature constraints of the REST service architecture, including client-server constrain, cacheable constrain, stateless constrain, layered constrain, and uniform interface constrain, etc. Secondly, the verification of path synchronization matching based on the model state space is implemented. That is, based on the CPN model of the application system and the CPN model of the standard feature constraints, the respective execution paths in the model state space are synchronously matched. If the path can be executed synchronously, the application system meets the REST standard feature constraints. Lastly, we use the course management web system based on REST service architecture as an example to verify the availability and effectiveness of the above verification methods. The experimental results show that the verification method we proposed can effectively confirm whether the web application system design based on REST service architecture conforms to the standard feature constraints of REST service architecture. In addition, this method also can provide intuitive and feasible execution data when the standard feature constraints are not met, so as to facilitate the defects location and correction of the following design of application systems.

This paper is organized as follows. Section 2 introduces related research. Section 3 gives the CPN modeling process of five standard feature constraints in the REST service architecture. Section 4 elaborates the core idea and concrete algorithm of the verification method based on the model state space execution path synchronization matching. Section 5 applies verification methods to specific web systems, so as to verify their availability and effectiveness. Section 6 concludes the paper.

2   Relevant Technology

2.1   REST Service Architecture

The REST architecture is resource-centric, so resources are the most critical abstraction in the REST architecture, and any unit can be a resource. At the same time, all resources must have a uniform resource identifier (URI), the operation of the resource does not change the resource identifier, and all operations are stateless. RESTful web services mainly use four methods in the HTTP protocol, including POST, GET, PUT, and DELET. Among them, the POST method is to add new data, that is, adding a resource without an ID. The GET method is to read the data and get an existing resource. The PUT method is to update the data, update a resource or add a resource without an ID, and replace the current state of the resource with the given representation information. The DELETE method is to delete a resource, and the deletion is idempotent which is an important attribute. Idempotent is that sending multiple requests has the same impact on resource status as sending one request [7].

The main elements of the REST architecture include data unit, connector, and component. The data unit is mainly composed of resources, resource identifiers, indicators, presentation metadata, resource metadata and control data. The connector acts as a unified interface for each component to communicate with each other and access resources. It is mainly composed of client, server, cache, parser and channel. The connector encapsulates the underlying implementation and communication mechanism of the resource. Components primarily include user agent, origin server, and intermediary, which are divided based on their role in the application.

2.2   CPN Method

We use CPN technology to model the REST service architecture. The experimental tool is CPN Tools, which can effectively support the verification analysis of the model. CPN is a formal modeling method that evolved from the traditional Petri Net, so we can say that CPN is a high-level Petri Net. CPN has strong mathematical modeling ability, which is closely related to mathematics. Besides, it is often used for modeling and analysis of complex and concurrent systems. The CPN modeling language has a mathematical definition that combines both grammar and semantics. The verification method involves mathematical formula attributes and computer-aided proofs, which are implemented by the model.

The CPN verification method we used includes the following two methods, simulation method and state space method. The simulation method verifies the state transition of each step in the system, and verifies whether the system model meets the expectations [8]. The state space verification method generates a corresponding state space after the system simulation is executed. The state space is the executable path of the system. It shows all the reachable state and state changes of the CPN model with a directed graph, where the node represents the state, the arc represents the occurred event. The state space can be automatically generated. Based on the above characteristics, we use the CPN method to model the REST service architecture application. By simulating the resource changes of the application service through state transitions, it can be effectively verified.

CPN is defined as a nine-tuple, CPN $= (P, T, A, \Sigma, V, C, G, E, I)$ [9]. The definition of each element is shown in Table 1. And the CPN method we used is defined strictly in accordance with the standard.

Table 1. Definition of CPN elements

Name	Definition	Name	Definition
P	Set of places	T	Set of transitions
A	Set of arcs	Σ	Set of colour sets
V	Set of variables	C	Colour set function
G	Guard function	E	Arc expression function
I	Initialisation function		

2.3   Related Work

Based on the notion of MROP, Sergio et al. present a metamorphic testing approach for the automated detection of faults in RESTful Web APIs [13]. Irum et al. explore the usage of formal application of Event-B on the REST architectural style [15]. And they successfully address inconsistency design issue, model checking of service specifications and the state-explosion problem that may arise due to a large number of resources. Costa et al. proposed a method, tool and guiding principle for evaluating REST architecture [7]. They evaluated their method in the architecture trade off analysis method (ATMM) scenario, considering various attributes and verifying the correctness of the method. Xi et al. mainly used the CSP method to formally model the REST architecture [10]. Firstly, they analyzed the calling process of the resource, abstracting four main process components, including user agent, intermediary, origin server, and resource. Then they showed the communication of four processes. Secondly, they analyzed and validated the standard feature constraints of the REST service architecture based on the Process Analysis Toolkit (PAT) model verification tool and sequential logic description. Ting et al. also used CSP methods to model and analyze the RESTful web services [11]. They abstracted the REST architecture model into three modules, client, server, and resource. Then the process in the REST architecture and its specific method behavior were described by CSP. Finally, the first-order logic was used to describe the stateless attributes of the web service and verified based on the PAT tool. In addition, Adhipta et al. used hierarchical CPN to simulate the behavior of the web services system model [12]. They performed functional verification based on the generated state space, proving that the web services extension model can improve the communication transmission performance of information. From the above research, we known that it is feasible to model, analyze and verify the web application system using the CPN model.

In summary, the current verification work on the standard features of the REST service architecture is mainly focused on the CSP-based method, but this type of verification method has a high degree of abstraction and a complicated description. Therefore, we make full use of the advantages of CPN modeling technology, and propose a standard feature verification method for REST service architecture based on CPN model. This method can effectively confirm whether the web application based on the REST service architecture conforms to the standard feature constraints of the REST service architecture. When the standard feature constraints are not met, it can also provide intuitive and feasible execution data, which can facilitate the defects location and correction of the following design of application systems.

3   Standard Feature Constraint Modeling of REST Service Architecture Based on CPN Model

3.1   Process View of the REST Service Architecture

The REST service architecture emphasizes the resource invocation process. Everything is resource-centric. Therefore, the process view of the REST service architecture is used to describe the interaction of REST architecture resources, showing the interaction between different components. Referring to Jensen et al., Fig. 1 shows an example of the interaction of the four main components in the REST service architecture process view.

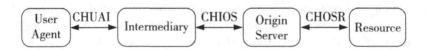

Fig. 1. Four main parts of the REST service architecture application model

The process view of the REST service architecture mainly includes four components, user agent, intermediary, origin server and resource. The interaction between components is through channels and interfaces, and all have a unified interface. User agents, intermediary and origin server have an internal caching mechanism [8]. The channels between each other are described as CHIOS, CHOSR, and CHUAI, etc., which implement information transmission and reception.

Specifically, when a user agent (i.e., a client) sends a request message, it first requests its internal cache to get the resource. If the resource exists in its internal cache, it is directly returned to the user agent. If the resource does not exist in its internal cache, then a request message is sent to the external network intermediary. Here, the internal channel between the two is defined as CHUAI. The request message can be described as a four-tuple (GET, PUT, POST, DELETE) [14], and all messages are represented in the same four-tuple form. The specific meaning of the elements in the four-tuple is described in Sect. 2.1. Intermediary is mainly composed of proxy or gateway and also has caching function. The main purpose of intermediary is to forward messages and transfer information. The user agent sends the request information to the intermediary, and the intermediary has two ways to query the resources. One is to request resources from its internal cache, and the other one is to request resources from the origin server, where it communicates via the internal channel CHIOS. The resources required by the user agent are stored on the origin server, which is the only component that can communicate with the resource. The user agent can communicate with the origin server through the intermediary. After receiving the request resource information, the origin server checks its cache. If the cache does not have the resource, the origin server sends the request information to the resource and returns the requested resource to the intermediary. Communication between the origin server and the resource takes place via the CHOSR channel.

3.2   CPN-Based Standard Feature Constraint Modeling

Client-Server Constrain. The user agent and origin server act as two separate components that are separated by a unified interface. The client-server constraint applies the C/S architecture feature to standardize the REST architecture. REST is a typical C/S architecture, which guarantees that communication can only be initiated unilaterally by the client in the form of request - response. The REST architecture emphasizes the thin server, the server only handles resource-related operations, and all display work should be on the client. The user agent sends request resource information to its internal cache or origin server, ignoring the absence of resources. The information requested by the user agent must exist in its internal cache or origin server, and all request messages sent by the user agent will be replied to by its cache or origin server. Figure 2 shows the CPN model of the client-server standard feature constraints in the REST service architecture. Firstly, the client sends a request for resource information msg, which is described as a variable of type Msg 1, Msg 1 is described as a record type in CPN modeling:

colset Msg1=record m:MSG * f:FORMAT * s:SENDER * r:RECEIVER;

The four elements are all string types, the MSG describes the content of the request resource, the FORMAT describes the format of the request resource, the SENDER describes the sender of the request message, and the RECEIVER describes the sender of the response message. Secondly, we should query whether the resource information exists in the client's internal cache. If the resource is in its cache (exemplified by the first element component m = "1" in expression on the output arc of the RequestUC transition), the response information is returned by the cache to the user agent. If the request resource does not exist in the cache (exemplified by the first element component m = "no" in expression on the output arc of the RequestUC transition), then the resource needs to be requested again from the origin server. Finally, the resource information requested by the client is returned to the user agent.

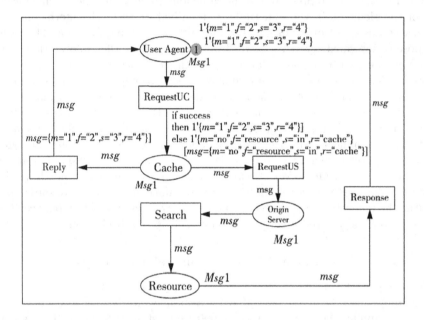

Fig. 2. CPN model with client-server constraints

Cacheable Constrain. User agent, intermediary and origin server all have a caching mechanism, and request resource information can be stored in the buffer, which can improve the inefficiency caused by stateless features. Cachable constraints are used to verify whether the user agent, intermediary and origin server all have caching capabilities, and response information can be retained in these three internal caches. Cacheable attributes effectively improve access performance, reduce system response time, and facilitate user agent. In this paper we only consider cacheable request information. If the user agent sends the request information for the first time, there is no information in the cache, so the resource information should be requested from the origin server. Otherwise, the user agent gets the resources directly from its internal cache without having to access the server. If the two request resource information functions are the same, the second one can directly access the cache to obtain resource information.

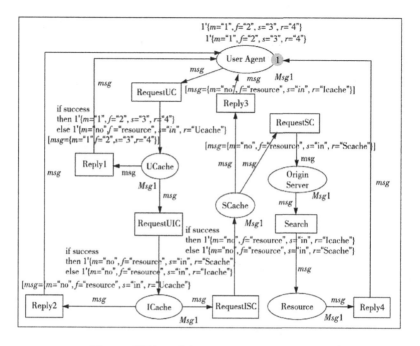

Fig. 3. CPN model with cachable constraints

Figure 3 shows the cacheable standard feature constraint model for the REST service architecture. Firstly, the user agent sends request resource information, and the request resource information msg is described as above. Secondly, it should query whether the resource information exists in the cache of the user agent. If the resource exists in its internal cache (exemplified by the first element component m = "1" in expression on the output arc of the RequestUC transition, namely RequestUserAgentCache), the information is returned directly to the user agent by its internal cache. If the request resource does not exist in the internal cache of the user agent (exemplified by the first element component m = "no" in expression on the output arc of the RequestUC transition), then the request information needs to continue to be sent to the network intermediary. If the resource information stored in its cache (exemplified by the fourth element component r = "Ucache" in expression on the output arc of the RequestUIC transition, namely RequestUserIntermediaryCache.), it is returned to the user agent. If the request resource information does not exist in the intermediary cache (exemplified by the fourth element component r = "Icache" in expression on the output arc of the RequsetUIC transition), the request information needs to be sent to the origin server. If the resource information exists in the origin server cache(exemplified by the fourth element component r = "Icache" in expression on the input arc of the RequestSC transition, namely RequestUserAgentServer-Cache), it is returned to the user agent. Finally, if the resource information does not exist in the origin server cache (exemplified by the fourth element compo-

nent r = "Scache" in expression on the input arc of the RequestSC transition),
it is necessary to request information from the data resource, and finally return
a response message to the user agent.

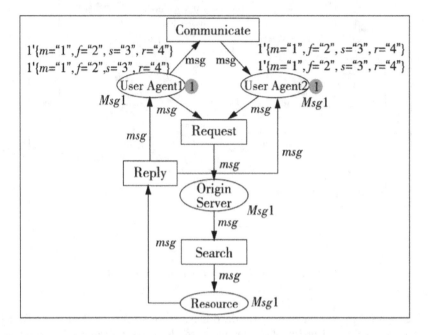

Fig. 4. CPN model with stateless constraints

Stateless Constrain. The server in the REST service architecture does not
store any session state information with the client. All status information only
exists in the communication message, that is, the request message sent by the
user agent to the server must contain all information to understand the message.
Stateless means that session state information remains in the user agent and the
server is stateless. If the request information comes from different user agents at
the same time, but the request resource information of the multiple user agents
is the same, the origin server feeds back the same resource information to the
user agents. The state of the REST service architecture refers to the state of the
client. The representation of each resource on the client is a state of the client.
The status information can be described as a triplet (id, data, oper), id is the
id of the resource identifier, data is the content of the information, and oper is
the specific operation, such as GET, PUT, POST, and DELETE.

Figure 4 shows the stateless standard feature constraint model of the REST
architecture. First, the communication content between the two user agents is
included in the request information, and the user agent only saves the communication content of both. Second, the user agent sends the request resource
information to the origin server through the channel Request, and then returns

the requested resource to the user agent. If the resource information requested by multiple user agents is the same, the response information obtained must also be consistent (the response information obtained by the two user agents is {m = "1", f = "2", s = "3", r = "4"}), indicating that the REST architecture server is stateless.

Layered Constrain. The layered constraint mainly checks whether the REST service architecture application conforms to the three-tier architecture. Layered constraints increase the independence between the layers and improve the scalability of the system. In a REST service architecture web application system, a component can only communicate with its neighboring components. That is, if the user agent wants to send the request information, it can only send it to its internal cache or intermediary, and cannot directly send it to the origin server. Similarly, the origin server cannot directly return a response message to the user agent. This constraint breaks down the REST architecture into layers of several levels. The mutual communication between other components is also the same. In the layered constraint, only the three-tier REST application system is considered in the REST architecture, namely the user agent layer, the middleware layer and the server layer.

Figure 5 shows the layered standard feature constraint model of the REST architecture. Firstly, the REST architecture is a standard three-tier architecture application. Secondly, the user agent can only send the request resource information to the intermediary (the interaction between the user agent and the intermediary is performed through the channel CHUAI), and then the intermediary continues to send the request information to the origin server (the interaction between the intermediary and the origin server is performed through the channel CHIOS), and finally returns the requested resource information to the user agent through the above interface. Among them, the three components are divided into three layers by the channel CHUAI and the channel CHIOS.

Uniform Interface Constrain. The unified structure constraint guarantees the consistency of the message format between component communication, that is, checking whether the interface of the REST architecture application is consistent, and improving the interactivity and reusability of the system. In this constraint, the request message sent by the user agent and the message format returned by the origin server must be consistent, that is, the identifiers of the resources are consistent. The request message is described as a quad representation {msg, r_format, sender, receiver}, where msg represents the requested resource, r_format represents the format of the resource, sender represents the request sender of the resource, and receiver represents the request recipient of the resource.

Figure 6 shows the unified interface standard feature constraint model for the REST architecture. The request information sent by the user agent to the origin server is consistent with the format of the response information of the server (exemplified by the first element component m = "1" in expression on the

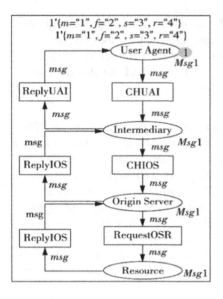

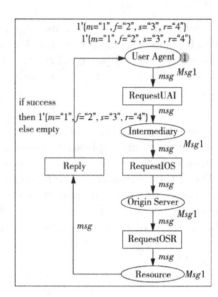

Fig. 5. CPN model with layered constraints

Fig. 6. CPN model with uniform interface constraints

output arc of the Reply transition). The information of the sender and receiver should focus on the same resource identifier, which reflects the unified interface standard features of the REST architecture.

4   REST Service Architecture Standard Feature Verification Method

This section proposes a standard feature verification method for REST service architecture. Based on the CPN model of the application system and the CPN model with standard feature constraints, we perform synchronous matching on the respective execution paths in the model state space. If the path can be executed synchronously, the application system meets the REST standard feature constraint. If the standard feature constraints are not met, the intuitive and feasible execution data is provided, which can facilitate the defects location and correction of the following design of application systems.

4.1   Core Idea of the Verification Method

The core idea of the verification method proposed in this paper can be summarized as constructing the CPN model of the application system and the CPN model of the standard feature constraint, respectively generating their respective state spaces, and obtaining the corresponding execution path sets of each model. We perform a synchronous path matching algorithm based on the model state space, and check whether the state space execution path of the application system model synchronizes the path containing the standard feature constraint model. If it is included, the verification is successful, otherwise there is a non-conformity. By using the state difference set to locate the application system model and the defect errors in the system design, the non-conformity status and path are found, and the modification and perfection are made to meet the REST service architecture standard feature constraints.

Specifically, performing a synchronous path matching algorithm based on a model state space is the core. First, we give a key concept, the synchronization node. Assume that a node of the REST service architecture standard feature constraint model state space is identified by M^*, and a node of the application system model state space is identified by M. If the Marking value of M^* is equivalent to the function of M, that is, the key segment data in the two node tags is the same, and the functions of the subsequent executable transition description are also the same, then the two nodes can be called a synchronization node. The synchronization of the state space execution path includes the relationship of the synchronization node and the transition path. And the execution order of the synchronization node and the transition path is also consistent and orderly. The key part of the algorithm is that the state space execution path completes the synchronous execution matching. Intuitively, from the perspective analysis of the state space execution path generation, the possible enabled transition is fired from the initial state of the application system model. After one or more transition fired, a synchronization node that can be executed simultaneously with the start node of the standard feature constraint model is obtained. Then, the synchronization node is fired. After performing one step operation, one or more transition may be fired, and again get the next synchronization node that can be executed simultaneously with the starting node of the standard feature constraint model. Matching such synchronization nodes in turn, and firing corresponding enabled transitions until reaching the termination node of the standard feature constraint model, the synchronization matching method ends. At this point, it indicates that the application system meets the feature constraint of the standard REST service architecture. If the synchronization matching fails in any intermediate node, it indicates that the application does not meet the feature constraints of the standard REST architecture. Finding non-compliant features based on the REST service architecture application system can be achieved by looking up the difference set of the path set in the state space. By comparing the path generated by the application system model state space with the path generated by the corresponding standard feature constraint model state space, it is judged which path node is terminated. Then the token information reflected by the node identifier can provide intuitive application system execution data. That is, when the application system runs to this state, there is an execution state data that does not meet the constraint, which is used to help the system designer complete the positioning and correction of the application system design defects to meet the standard REST service architecture constraints.

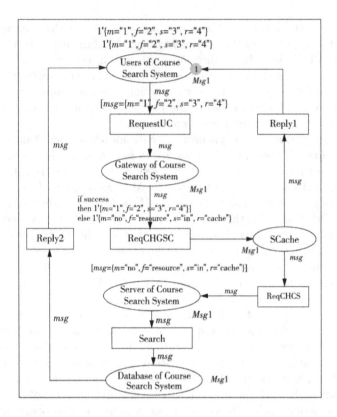

Fig. 7. CPN model for the course query subfunction

4.2 Algorithm Description of the Verification Method

Assume: Nodes* ={M0, M1, ..., Mm}, Arcs* ={A0, A1, ..., Am}

$$\text{Nodes} = \{N0, N1, ..., Nn\}, \text{Arcs} = \{B0, B1, ..., Bn\}$$

Nodes* describes the nodes and path sets of the standard feature constraint model state space, and the Nodes describes the nodes and path sets of the application system model state space. The core of the algorithm can be described as follows. Firstly, the standard model is matched within the node and path range of the application system model, and the initial synchronization nodes of the two models are found(shown in the ①). Then, finding the successor synchronization nodes of the two models. If found, the transitions of the two models each fired to start the next search (shown in the ②). If not found, the application system model continues to fired the transition, looking for a synchronization node that matches the standard feature constraint model (shown in the ③). Finally, if the synchronization node is successfully matched to the terminate synchronization node, the verification is successful, otherwise the verification fails (shown in the ④).

Algorithm 1. SynchronizedPathMatch

function *SynchronizedPathMatch*

    int m,n,i,j,k;

    if ((M0⊆Nodes)∧(A0⊆Arcs)) **then**
        Model can be synchronized;
        ①
        while i<n **do**
            if (Ni==M0 and Bi==A0) **then**
                Find the initial synchronization node;
            else
                i++;
            end if
        end while

        j =i+1;
        k =1;
        ②
        while (j≤n and k≤m) **do**
            if (Nj==Mk and Bj==Ak) **then**
            {
                Find the next synchronization node;
                k++;
                j++;
            }
              else
                ③
                while (j≤n) **do**
                    if (Nj==Mk and Bj==Ak) **then**
                    Find the synchronization node;
                  else
                    j++;
                end if
              end while
            end if
        end while
        ④
        if (k==m) **then**
            return *true*
        else
            return *false*
        end if
    end if
end function

5   The Example of the Standard Feature Verification Method for REST Service Architecture

This section takes the course management web system based on the REST service architecture as an example to verify the availability and effectiveness of the verification method given in the previous section. It is confirmed that the verification method we proposed can be used to verify whether the web application system design based on the REST service architecture conforms to the standard feature constraints of the REST service architecture.

5.1   Web Application System Modeling Based on REST Service Architecture

This section conducts CPN modeling on the subfunctions of the query course in a course management web system. The constructed CPN model of the application system focuses on resource interaction and communication in the process of querying the course. As shown in Fig. 7, the communication behavior between the course query client, the course query system gateway, the course query system server, and the course query system database is modeled and analyzed. Then we use the verification method based on the model state space to perform path synchronization matching. So that we can confirm whether the model meets the five standard feature constraints of the REST service architecture.

In the model, the query request resource information msg is sent by the user of the course query system, and the data of the request information msg is defined as: colset Msg1 = record m: MSG * f:FORMAT * s:SENDER * r:RECEIVER, where MSG, FORMAT, SENDER and RECEIVER are both string types. The request information is transmitted to the gateway of the course inquiry system through the channel ReqCHUG, and then the gateway transmits the request information to the cache of the course query system server (Server) through the channel ReqCHGSC. If the request resource information is cached in the SCache of the server (exemplified by the first element component m = "1" in expression on the output arc of the ReqCHGSC transition). the server directly returns a message to the user of the course query system through the channel Reply1. If the course query system server does not have the requested resource in the cache (exemplified by the first element component m = "0" in expression on the output arc of the ReqCHGSC transition), the request message is sent through the channel Search to the database of the course query web system. Then the request resource information is returned from the database to the system user. Figure 8 shows the state space corresponding to the CPN model of the course query subfunction.

5.2   Standard Feature Constraint Verification Example and Analysis

Based on the CPN model of the course query subfunction given in Fig. 7, it is tested by the five REST service architecture standard feature constraints in

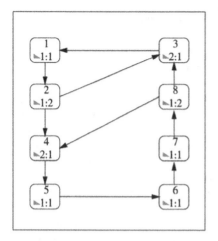 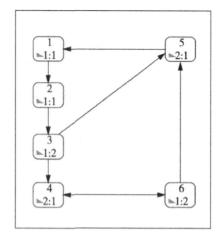

Fig. 8. State space of the course query subfunction model

Fig. 9. State space of standard client-server constraints

Sect. 4.2 to verify whether the course query subfunction web application is a standard REST architecture application.

(1) Checking the standard feature constraint of the client-server and comparing it with the state space execution path of the standard client-server constraint in Sect. 3.2. we can find that the REST architecture model does not meet the client-server constraints. The user function of the course query system is equivalent to the function of the user agent in the standard REST architecture model. The gateway function of the course query system is equivalent to the intermediary in the standard REST architecture model. The server function of the course query system is equivalent to The functionality of the origin server in the standard REST architecture model, and the database function of the course query system is equivalent to the functionality of the resources in the standard REST architecture model. After verification by the synchronous path matching algorithm, the node 1 in Fig. 8 and the node 1 in Fig. 9 are initial synchronization nodes. Then through the transition path, we find that the REST architecture application model lacks the caching capabilities of its client. When obtaining the request information, the system first checks whether the cache exists. If it does not exist, continue to request the resource information from the origin server. Therefore, the course query subfunction web system should add client caching function.

(2) Verifying the cacheable standard feature constraints, and comparing it with the state space execution path of the standard cacheable constraint model in Sect. 3.2. we can find that the REST architecture model does not meet the cacheable constraint. After verification by the synchronous path matching algorithm, it can be found that the node 1 in Fig. 8 and the node 1 in Fig. 10 are initial synchronization nodes. From the subsequent transition path, we find that the client and the gateway of the course query system lack the

caching function. Therefore, the course query subfunction web system should add a corresponding caching mechanism.

(3) The layered standard feature constraint is tested. By performing path verification on its state space, we can find that the REST architecture model satisfies the layered constraint. Through the comparison with the state space execution path of the standard layered constraint of Sect. 3.2, the course query system users can only interact through the gateway of the course query system, and the database of the course query system can only communicate with the server. The subfunction web system meets the layered standard feature constraints. At the same time, the stateless and unified interface standard feature constraints are tested. By comparing the state space execution path of the standard stateless constraint in Sect. 3.2, we find that the course query system of the REST architecture meets the stateless constraint. All information about the message can be included in the request and response. The main content is stored in the server, and the server is stateless. In addition, we compare the state space execution path of the standard unified interface constraint of Sect. 3.2, and find that the model meets the unified interface constraint. The message format of the request and response is the same, both in the form of msg. When the same request information is sent twice, the response information is the same, so the uniform interface constraint is met.

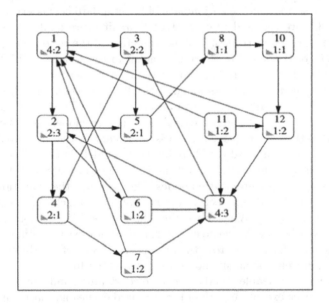

Fig. 10. State space of standard cachable constraints

Through the above analysis, Fig. 11 shows the modified CPN model of the course query subfunction application system based on REST service architecture.

After using the method we proposed, the application system meets the standard feature constraints of the REST service architecture. As can be seen from the comparative analysis of Figs. 7 and 11:

(1) Figure 11 adds the Users Cache function to Fig. 7, which can add a cache function to the client of the course management web system.
(2) Figure 11 adds the Gateway Cache feature to Fig. 7, which adds a cache function to the gateway of the course management web system.

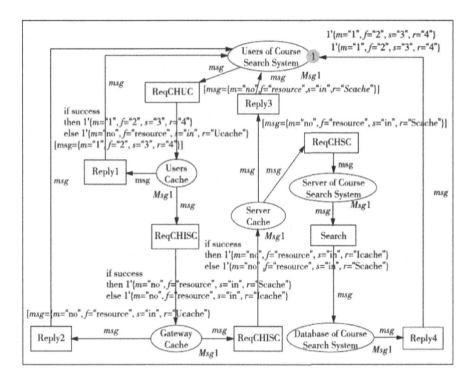

Fig. 11. Corrected CPN model of the course query subfunction

Adding the above two buffers can make the system more complete. When the client of the course management web system sends the request information, it first checks whether the resource exists in its internal cache. If the resource exists in its cache (exemplified by the fourth element component r = "4" in the expression on output arc of the ReqCHUC transition), the response message is returned directly to the client. If there is no client cache (exemplified by the fourth element component r = "Ucache" in the expression on output arc of the ReqCHUC transition), the resource needs to be requested from the gateway of the course management web system. If the resource is not in the client cache (exemplified by the fourth element component r = "Ucache" in the expression on output arc of the ReqCHUC transition), the resource needs to be requested from the gateway of the course management web system. If the resource exists in the gateway's cache (exemplified by the fourth element component r = "Ucache" in the expression on output arc of the ReqCHUG transition), the response message is directly returned to the client.

6   Conclusion

Before implementing a web system based on the REST service architecture, it is crucial to verify whether the system design meets the standard features of the REST service architecture, and effectively improve the quality of the development of the web system based on the REST service architecture. We propose a standard feature verification method for REST service architecture based on CPN model. Firstly, the CPN model description of five standard feature constraints of REST service architecture is given. Next, we propose a verification method based on model state space to perform path synchronization matching. Based on the CPN model of the application system and the CPN model with standard feature constraints, the respective execution paths in the model state space are synchronously matched. If the paths can be executed synchronously, the application system meets the REST standard feature constraints. Finally, taking the course query function system based on REST service architecture as an example, the availability of the above verification method is confirmed. Applying the verification method we proposed can effectively confirm whether the web application system design based on REST service architecture conforms to the standard feature constraints of REST service architecture. When the standard feature constraints are not met, we provide intuitive and feasible execution data to facilitate the defects location and correction of the following design of application systems. The next step is to strengthen the formal description and validation of the core process of the verification method, and apply this method to practical objects with more typical application systems based on REST service architecture, so that we can refine execution details and improve the availability of methods.

Acknowledgment. This work was supported in part by the National Natural Science Foundation of Chain (No. 61662051, No. 61262017).

References

1. Fielding, R.T.: Architectural styles and the design of network-based software architectures, p. 303. University of California, Irvine (2000)
2. Paganelli, F., Turchi, S., Giuli, D.: A web of things framework for RESTful applications and its experimentation in a smart city. IEEE Syst. J. **10**(4), 1412–1423 (2017)
3. Song, Y., Xu, K., Liu, K.: Research on web instant messaging using REST web service. In: IEEE Symposium on Web Society, pp. 497–500 (2010)

4. Liu, J., Ye, X., Zhou, J.: Colored Petri net hierarchical model of complex network software and model integration verification method. High-Tech Commun. **23**(11), 1139–1147 (2013)
5. Benabdelhafid, M.S., Boufaida, M.: Toward a better interoperability of enterprise information systems: a CPNs and timed CPNs -based web service interoperability verification in a choreography. Procedia Technol. **16**, 269–278 (2014)
6. Sun, L.: Dynamic composition modeling and validation OD web services based on hierarchical colored Petri nets. China University of Petroleum, Dongying (2011)
7. Costa, B., Pires, P.F., Merson, P.: Evaluating REST architectures-approach, tooling and guidelines. J. Syst. Softw. **112**, 156–180 (2016)
8. Jensen, K., Kristensen, L.M., Wells, L.: Coloured Petri nets and CPN tools for modeling and validation of concurrent systems. Int. J. Softw. Tools Technol. Transf. **9**(3–4), 213–254 (2007)
9. Jensen, K., Kristensen, L.M.: Coloured Petri Nets: Modeling and Validation of Concurrent System, pp. 95–188. Springer, Berlin (2009). https://doi.org/10.1007/b95112
10. Wu, X., Zhu, H.: Formalization and analysis of the REST architecture from the process algebra perspective. Future Gen. Comput. Syst. **56**, 153–168 (2016)
11. Ting, Y.: Formal Modeling and Analysis of RESTful Web Services. East Chain Normal University, Shanghai (2015)
12. Adhipta, D., Hassan, M.F., Mahmood, A.K.: Web services extension model simulation in hierarchical colored Petri net. In: International Conference on Computer & Information Science, pp. 741–746. IEEE (2012)
13. Segura, S., Parejo, J.A., Troya, J., et al.: Metamorphic testing of RESTful web APIs. IEEE Trans. Softw. Eng. **PP**(99), 1 (2017)
14. Garriga, M., Mateos, C., Flores, A., et al.: RESTful service composition at a glance. J. Netw. Comput. Appl. **60**(C), 32–53 (2016)
15. Rauf, I., Vistbakka, I., Troubitsyna, E.: Formal verification of stateful services with REST APIs using event-B. In: IEEE International Conference on Web Services, pp. 131–138. IEEE Computer Society (2018)

Crawled Data Analysis on Baidu API Website for Improving SaaS Platform (Short Paper)

Lei Yu[1(✉)], Shanshan Liang[1], Shiping Chen[2], and Yaoyao Wen[1]

[1] Department of Computer Science, Inner Mongolia University, Hohhot, China
yuleiimu@sohu.com
[2] Commonwealth Scientific and Industrial Research Organization,
Canberra, Australia

Abstract. SaaS (Software-as-a-Service) is a cloud computing model, which is sometimes referred to as "on-demand software". Existing SaaS platforms are investigated before building new distributed SaaS platform. The service data mining and evaluation on existing SaaS platforms improve our new SaaS platform. For SaaS that provide various APIs, we analysis their website data in this paper by our data mining method and related software. We wrote a crawler program to obtain data from these websites. The websites include Baidu API and ProgrammableWeb API. After ETL (Extract-Transform-Load), the obtained and processed data is ready to be analyzed. Statistical methods including non-linear regression and outlier detection are used to evaluate the websites performance, and give suggestions to improve the design and development of our API website. All figures and tables in this paper are generated from IBM SPSS statistical software. The work helps us improve our own API website by comprehensively analyzing other successful API websites.

Keywords: SaaS (Software-as-a-Service) · Baidu API · Data analysis · Regression · Micro service

1 Introduction

There are three cloud computing models: IaaS (Infrastructure-as-a-service), PaaS (Platform-as-a-service) and SaaS (Software-as-a-service). Researchers have been studying service data mining in various platforms for boosting research on service recommendations and service compositions.

However, researchers in service computing domain lack of a cloud SaaS platform hosting real-world services. Based on three models of cloud computing, we aim at building a public cloud for service data mining. The advantage of using the vertical architecture is that we can monitor SaaS applications in detail, such as their network bandwidth, CPU and memory usage, user locations and amount of sessions, etc.

© ICST Institute for Computer Sciences, Social Informatics and Telecommunications Engineering 2019
Published by Springer Nature Switzerland AG 2019. All Rights Reserved
H. Gao et al. (Eds.): CollaborateCom 2018, LNICST 268, pp. 708–716, 2019.
https://doi.org/10.1007/978-3-030-12981-1_49

2   Related Works

Researches on commercial and non-profit service orchestration platforms are discussed in this section, and then related service data mining are investigated. OpenStack Heat, Windows Azure AppFabric/MarketPlace (including AppMarket), Amazon AWS Lambda and Google App Engine are discussed below.

The combination of Windows Server and AppFabric [2] provides an easy-to-manage platform for developing, deploying, and reliably hosting middle-tier WCF/WF services. Malawski [3] have developed prototype workflow executor functions using AWS Lambda. Villamizar [4] presents a cost comparison of a web application developed and deployed using the same scalable scenarios by AWS Lambda. Abrahao [5] proposed a platform-independent monitoring middleware for cloud services. This middleware was implemented in both Microsoft Azure and Google App Engine to monitor the quality of cloud services. Using Google App Engine as a platform, Nishida [6] proposes a modeling and simulation based framework to predict the cloud performance. Basu [7] presents a performance case-study on implementing the building blocks of a privacy preserving collaborative filtering scheme in Java on the Google App Engine (GAE/J) cloud platform. Prodan [8] employs the Google App Engine (GAE) for high-performance parallel computing. Prodan [9] designed a generic master-slave framework that enables implementation and integration of new algorithms by instantiating one interface and two abstract classes.

Using frequent association mining techniques to a large-scale data set that contains descriptively narrated texts, Park [10] analyzes the association between words. Huang [11] proposes a novel dimensionality reduction method called locality-regularized linear regression discriminant analysis for feature extraction. Bravi [12] focuses on nonlinear regression problems by assuming that the process underlying the generated data can be approximated by a continuous function. They present a new feature ranking method based on the solution of instances of the global optimization problem.

3   Data Analysis on Baidu API Website

In the section, statistical methods are used to study whether the statistical variables are related. We discover what relations among these variables are. All figures and tables in this section are generated by IBM SPSS statistical software.

3.1   Nonlinear Regression

The nonlinear regression process is used to establish a nonlinear relationship between the dependent variable and a set of independent variables.

A nonlinear regression model can generally be expressed as:

$$Y = f(x, \theta) + e_i$$

$f(x, \theta)$ is an expectation function. It can be any kind of function.

The purpose of this experiment is to use the "non-linear" regression process to fit the model of the relationship between the appropriate dependent variable (Invocation times) and the independent variables (Visits, Favorites, and Comments) [13]. The following diagram is an analysis example.

The Preliminary Analysis of the Data and Parameter Settings
Firstly, we make a composite scatter plot between the independent variable (Invocationtimes) and the other three dependent variables as shown in the following figures (Fig. 1):

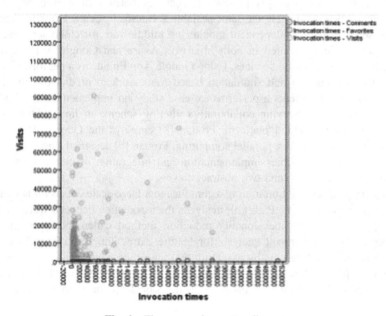

Fig. 1. The composite scatter diagram

Through observation, it is recommended to use a nonlinear model of the class with $Y = a * (b + c * EXP(d * Xe + f))$ exponential.

The Setting of the Loss Function, Looking for Whether There is a Strong Influence Point in the Data
According to this table, we can draw the following conclusions: 1, 15, 30, 34, 35, 36, 37, 90, 100, 101, 128, 153, 155, 186, 262 may be the impact points and its standardized residuals are greater than 3 (Table 1).

Table 1. Casewise diagnostics

Case number	Std. residual	Invocation times	Predicted value	Residual
1	−7.317	1744	104182.22	−102438.224
15	11.517	214748	53496.01	161251.992
30	6.670	139180	45794.64	93385.358
34	3.587	214748	164527.74	50220.257
35	−9.250	7279	136791.94	−129512.939
36	4.541	118237	54661.68	63575.322
37	−3.866	1715	55845.75	−54130.748
72	4.735	75290	8992.62	66297.379
90	5.546	79561	1907.97	77653.034
100	3.218	47408	2350.19	45057.812
101	3.225	45615	456.16	45158.841
128	4.147	63822	5757.18	58064.819
153	4.626	68278	3511.50	64766.497
155	5.899	85238	2641.63	82596.374
186	3.569	49612	−351.63	49963.628
262	3.833	105284	51616.45	53667.347

a. Dependent Variable: Invocation times

In order to reduce the influence of strong influence points, we use the least absolute deviations to calculate the residual value.

The Independent Variable is Visits

The functional form of setting and analyzing variables and models (Table 2):

Invocationtimes = 1.581 * EXP(−48.887 * Visits ** (−1/49.892) + 49.563)

Table 2. ANOVA

Source	Sum of squares	df	Mean squares
Regression	358720824316.627	4	89680206079.157
Residual	486073597544.478	691	703435018.154
Uncorrected total	844794421861.105	695	
Corrected total	805089065634.983	694	

Dependent variable: Invocation times
a. R squared = 1 − (Residual Sum of Squares)/(Corrected Sum of Squares) = .396.

The "ANOVA" table gives the structure of the analysis of variance. The R-square value is 0.396. The fitted model can account for variations in the dependent variable greater than 39.6%.

The fitting trend is shown in the following figure (Fig. 2):

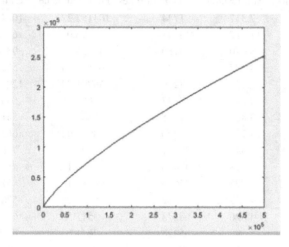

Fig. 2. Fitting trend map

The Independent Variable is Favorites

The functional form of setting and analyzing variables and models (Table 3):

Invocationtimes = 318985.678 * EXP(0.992 * Favorites2 + 4.141E − 6)

Table 3. ANOVA

Source	Sum of squares	df	Mean squares
Regression	490399653302.685	3	163466551100.895
Residual	354394768558.420	692	512131168.437
Uncorrected total	844794421861.105	695	
Corrected total	805089065634.983	694	

Dependent variable: Invocation times
a. R squared = 1 − (Residual Sum of Squares)/(Corrected Sum of Squares) = .560.

The "ANOVA" table gives the structure for analysis of the variance. The R-square value is 0.560. The fitted model can account for variations in the dependent variable greater than 56.0%.

The fitting trend is shown in the following figure (Fig. 3):

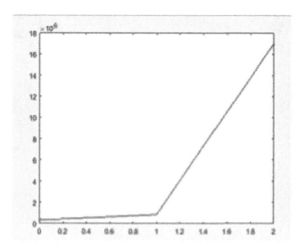

Fig. 3. Fitting trend map

The Independent Variable is Comments

The functional form of setting and analyzing variables and models is (Table 4):

Invocation times = 424303.081 * (1 − (−0.002) * EXP(116.870 * Comments − 4.761))

Table 4. ANOVA

Source	Sum of squares	df	Mean squares
Regression	618756082710.866	4	154689020677.717
Residual	226038339150.239	691	327117712.229
Uncorrected total	844794421861.105	695	
Corrected total	805089065634.983	694	

Dependent variable: Invocation times
a. R squared = 1 − (Residual Sum of Squares)/(Corrected Sum of Squares) = .719.

The "ANOVA" table gives the structure for analysis of variance. The R-square value is 0.719. The fitted model can account for variations in the dependent variable greater than 71.9%. This indicates that the fitting effect of the model is better.

The fitting trend is shown in the following figure (Fig. 4):

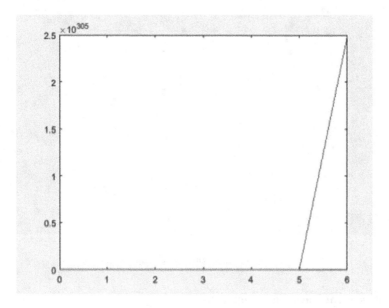

Fig. 4. Fitting trend map

3.2 Summary of Data Analysis

Statistical results show that the four variables are important factors to indicate how popular a service is. Moreover, the four variables are related to each other. Nonlinear regression methods are used to quantify their relationships. The result is that the fitted model should be improved in future to fit the service data.

4 Inspiration for Our SaaS Platform

This section shows the meaning of analyzing the crawled data. According to results of data mining and analysis above, our new platform [14] is improved in the aspect of design, development and operations. All data used in this paper can be downloaded from our website.

As mentioned earlier in this paper, we already know that invocation times of services are strongly related to visits, favorites and comments. Therefore, during designing, we extend service user privileges so that they can directly and freely invoke services in the platform and obtain results returned by service providers. Furthermore, service user in the platform can fully interact with each other to find potential co-developers, give suggestions, and even composite new services based on other users history of composing services.

5 Conclusions

Existing SaaS platforms are investigated before we build a new distributed SaaS platform. We analysis API website data by our data mining method and IBM software. Outlier detection, prediction, and statistical methods are used to evaluate the websites performance, and give suggestions to improve the design and development of our API website. The result of data analysis tells us which indicators are important to popularize a cloud service. Moreover, it helps us improve our own API website by comprehensively analyzing other successful API websites.

Acknowledgment. This work was supported by grants from Natural Science Foundation of Inner Mongolia Autonomous Region (2015BS0603) and Open Foundation of State key Laboratory of Networking and Switching Technology (Beijing University of Posts and Telecommunications, SKLNST-2016-1-01).

References

1. Couto, R.S., Sadok, H., Cruz, P., Silva, F.F.D., Sciammarella, T., Campista, M.E.M., et al.: Building an IaaS cloud with droplets: a collaborative experience with openstack. J. Netw. Comput. Appl. (2018)
2. Kaufman, S., Garber, D.: Pro Windows Server AppFabric. Apress, New York (2010)
3. Malawski, M., Gajek, A., Zima, A., Balis, B., Figiela, K.: Serverless execution of scientific workflows: experiments with hyperflow, AWS lambda and Google cloud functions. Future Gener. Comput. Syst. (2017)
4. Villamizar, M., Ochoa, L., Castro, H., Salamanca, L., Verano, M., Lang, M., et al.: Cost comparison of running web applications in the cloud using monolithic, microservice, and aws lambda architectures. SOCA **11**(2), 1–15 (2017)
5. Abrahao, S., Insfran, E.: Models@runtime for monitoring cloud services in Google App Engine. In: IEEE 13th World Congress on Services, pp. 30–35 (2017)
6. Nishida, S., Shinkawa, Y.: A performance prediction model for Google App Engine. In: IEEE International Conference on P2p, Parallel, Grid, Cloud and Internet Computing, vol.3, pp. 134–140 (2014)
7. Basu, A., Vaidya, J., Dimitrakos, T., Kikuchi, H.: Feasibility of a privacy preserving collaborative filtering scheme on the Google App Engine: a performance case study. In: Proceedings of the 27th Annual ACM Symposium on Applied Computing, pp. 447–452 (2012)
8. Prodan, R., Sperk, M., Ostermann, S.: Evaluating high-performance computing on Google App Engine. IEEE Computer Society Press (2012)
9. Prodan, R., Sperk, M.: Scientific computing with Google App Engine. Future Gener. Comput. Syst. **29**(7), 1851–1859 (2013)
10. Park, S.H., Synn, J., Kwon, O.H., Sung, Y.: Apriori-based text mining method for the advancement of the transportation management plan in expressway work zones. J. Supercomput. **74**(3), 1283–1298 (2018)
11. Huang, P., et al.: Locality-regularized linear regression discriminant analysis for feature extraction. Inf. Sci. **429**, 164–176 (2018)

12. Bravi, L., Piccialli, V., Sciandrone, M.: An optimization-based method for feature ranking in nonlinear regression problems. IEEE Trans. Neural Netw. **28**(4), 1005–1010 (2017)
13. Yu, L., Junxing, Z., Yu, P.S.: Service recommendation based on topics and trend prediction. In: Wang, S., Zhou, A. (eds.) CollaborateCom 2016. LNICST, vol. 201, pp. 343–352. Springer, Cham (2017). https://doi.org/10.1007/978-3-319-59288-6_31
14. http://www.servicebigdata.cn

Software Testing and Formal Verification

A Hardware/Software Co-design Approach for Real-Time Binocular Stereo Vision Based on ZYNQ (Short Paper)

Yukun Pan[1], Minghua Zhu[1(✉)], Jufeng Luo[2], and Yunzhou Qiu[2]

[1] Hardware/Software Co-Design Technology and Application Engineering Research Center, East China Normal University, Shanghai 200062, China
mhzhu@sei.ecnu.edu.cn
[2] Shanghai Internet of Things CO., LTD, Shanghai 201899, China

Abstract. Based on the ZYNQ platform, this paper proposes a hardware/software co-design approach, and implements a binocular stereo vision system with high real-time performance and good human-computer interaction, which can be used to assist advanced driver assistance systems to improve driving safety. Combining the application characteristics of binocular stereo vision, the approach firstly modularizes the system's functions to perform hardware/software partitioning, accelerates the data processing on FPGA, and performs the data control on ARM cores; then uses the ARM instruction set to configure the registers within FPGA to design relevant interfaces to complete the data interaction between hardware and software; finally, combines the implementation of specific algorithms and logical control to complete the binocular stereo vision system. The test results show that the frame rate with an image resolution of 640 * 480 can reach 121.43 frames per second when the FPGA frequency is 100M, and the frame rate is also high for large resolution images. At the same time, the system can achieve real-time display and human-computer interaction with the control of the graphical user interface.

Keywords: Binocular stereo vision system · Hardware/software co-design · Data interaction · Processing system · Programmable logic

1 Introduction

In recent years, autonomous driving and advanced driver assistance systems (ADAS) have become more and more important to reduce traffic accidents. The research on ADAS has reached a new craze under the promotion of computer vision and artificial intelligence. Binocular stereo vision is an important branch of computer vision [1]. The 3D scene perception method based on binocular stereo vision has many advantages in security, detection characteristics, cost and scope of application [2]. Although the accuracy of using radar for 3D scene perception is high in ADAS, the cost and difficulty of this approach are also high. Therefore, there are many researches applying binocular stereo vision to ADAS [3, 4]. The biggest advantage of binocular stereo vision is that it can achieve a certain accuracy of target recognition and ranging to realize some ADAS functions such as forward collision warning under the premise of low development cost [5]. Therefore, the binocular stereo vision system has some research significance and application value.

In order to enable binocular stereo vision to assist ADAS, the binocular stereo vision system needs real-time performance and human-computer interaction. However, the relevant algorithms of binocular stereo vision are intensive to compute and complex to implement. The traditional CPU is good at logical control and human-computer interaction, but the CPU instruction set is slow to process complex algorithms and cannot achieve real-time performance. Most researchers often use FPGA to implement complex algorithms [6, 7], which can achieve high real-time performance. However, FPGA is good at parallel computing, but has poor control and management capabilities, which makes the existing single FPGA implementation system lack human-computer interaction. At present, with the continuous development and maturity of hardware/software co-design approach, the system using hardware/software co-design approach has both the advantages of hardware's high-speed computing and the advantages of software's control and interaction. Therefore, hardware/software co-design is an effective approach for the binocular stereo vision system with real-time performance and human-computer interaction. In [8], the author uses the hardware/software co-design and embedded system to realize real-time stereo vision and focus on reducing the complexity of the processing algorithm while maintaining the accuracy of disparity images. Compared with the current state-of-the-art pure FPGA implementation, it still has advantages in processing speed. But the system in [8] lacks human-computer interaction and does not fully exploit the advantages of hardware/software co-design approach. So how to effectively combine the advantages of CPU processor and FPGA to carry out hardware/software co-design to obtain the optimization of logical control and data processing is the problem to study for the binocular stereo vision system.

The hardware/software co-design means meeting system-level objectives by exploiting the synergism of hardware and software through their concurrent design [9]. In the early years, for the problems and challenges faced by embedded system design, some researchers explored a new design methodology—hardware/software collaborative design approach [10]. Its fundamental thought is to coordinate the hardware subsystem and software subsystem in the design process, so that each step is the optimal result of hardware and software considerations. Compared with the drawbacks of designing hardware and software architecture independently in traditional methods [11], the hardware/software co-design approach comprehensively analyzes the system functions and existing resources according to the system target requirements, and maximizes the concurrency between hardware and software to collaboratively design the system architecture so that the system can achieve the best performance [12]. Embedded systems using hardware/software co-design approach can have the advantages of high computational speed, high flexibility, low cost, low power consumption, and short development cycle [8]. Therefore, the hardware/software co-design is the best choice for some systems that require complex computations and good human-computer interaction. With the continuous development of technology, the main research object of hardware/software co-design has changed from a configurable embedded computer system to a single chip integrated with embedded systems [10]. ZYNQ (Xilinx All Programmable Zynq-7000 SoC) is an embedded processor chip that combines high-performance ARM processor with high-capacity FPGA. It has both hardware and software programmable features. However, there are always some challenges in the hardware/software co-design on the ZYNQ platform [13]. Firstly, how to reasonably perform hardware/software partitioning can coordinate the software scheduling control and hardware data processing. Secondly, how to effectively manage data between hardware and software makes data to be processed quickly and accurately. Finally, how to design and implement the system's algorithms and logical control is the main problem in system construction on the ZYNQ platform.

This paper proposes a hardware/software co-design approach for real-time binocular stereo vision system. This approach solves these design difficulties on the ZYNQ platform well, and the binocular stereo vision system based on ZYNQ implemented by the co-design approach has high real-time performance and good human-computer interaction. By analyzing the application characteristics of the binocular stereo vision, the approach firstly modularizes the system's functions to perform hardware/software partitioning, then uses FPGA to implement the complex algorithms to accelerate data processing in the Programmable Logic (PL) of ZYNQ, and uses ARM processor to complete the image acquisition, program logical control, and image display in the Processing System (PS) of ZYNQ. Moreover, the approach uses the PS instruction set to configure the registers of the PL to design relevant interfaces to complete the data interaction between PL and PS, implements the system's algorithms and logical control, and fully utilizes the advantages of the ZYNQ heterogeneous multi-core processor [13] to complete the system construction, so that the stereo vision system achieves the best performance. The key contributions of this work include firstly proposing a hardware/software co-design approach for binocular stereo vision, and then correctly and efficiently realizing the data interaction between PL and PS, finally implementing the system based on the co-design approach and ensuring that the system has a certain speedup ratio and human-computer interaction in the actual test environment.

The rest of the paper is organized as follows. In Sect. 2, our hardware/software co-design approach is introduced. We describe the co-design of real-time binocular stereo vision system in Sect. 3. We implement the system and analyze experimental results and system performance in Sect. 4. And then conclude this paper in Sect. 5.

2 Hardware/Software Co-design Approach

The hardware/software co-design approach proposed in this paper solves the ZYNQ platform ARM+FPGA co-design difficulties from three aspects: hardware/software partitioning, data interaction between PL and PS and implementation of module algorithms and logical control, and builds a complete binocular stereo vision system.

The System Hardware/Software Partitioning. For binocular stereo vision, the system functions are modularized and each module is divided by considering the performance requirements, implementation cost, modifiability and nature of computation [11]. The data logical control is divided into the PS and controlled by ARM core. The complex data processing algorithms are divided into the PL and accelerated by FPGA. Such hardware/software partitioning can make the system have high computational speed and good interactivity.

Efficient Data Interaction Between PL and PS. The system designs the hardware and software relevant interfaces to complete their data interaction. This is the core thought of the hardware/software co-design approach proposed in this paper.

Figure 1 shows the PL and the PS data interaction structure. In the ZYNQ platform, system can exchange information between PL and PS through the advanced extensible interface (AXI) bus. So we design the interface of data control and transmission for the PL and the PS to complete data interaction by the AXI bus. The control interface is designed by custom registers in the PL and the PS, which has a unique physical mapped address via the AXI4_Lite bus. The PL and the PS can access each other's registers through the system's general port AXI (AXI_GP) and physical mapped address, and then generate interactive signals by reading and writing registers' value to achieve the communication of the control interface. The data transmission interface is implemented in the PL by the system's high performance AXI (AXI_HP), and is implemented in the PS by the system's video for Linux 2 (V4L2) driver interface [13].

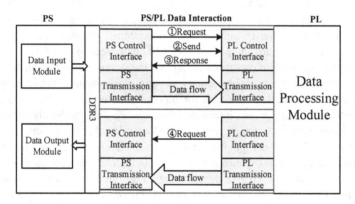

Fig. 1. Diagram of the PL and the PS data interaction structure

When the PS sends the acquired data from the double data rate (DDR3) memory to the data processing module of the PL, the PS control interface needs to request the module whether can receive data through the PL control interface, corresponding to ① in Fig. 1. After obtaining the module receivable data signal, the PS shall send the transmission signal to the PL through the PS control interface, and the PL shall give a response signal after receiving the signal through the PL control interface, corresponding to ② and ③ in Fig. 1. After a short delay waiting for the signal interaction to complete, the PL begins to receive the data of the PS through the data transmission interface. The significance of ② and ③ is to enable the system to correctly control and transmit one frame data. Otherwise, it will cause the system to lose data or receive the previous frame data during the data interaction. When the PL sends processed data to the PS, the PS control interface needs to apply the memory buffer and enable the stored signal, and then the PL control interface requests the PS control interface whether can store the processed data, corresponding to the ④ in Fig. 1. When the PL gets the storable signal, it starts to transmit data through the transmission interface, and the PS stores the received data into the memory buffer. Due to the data processing module processes and transmits the data while receiving the data, the receiving and transmission of each frame data are parallel and continuous. Therefore, there is no need for ② and ③ in the data interaction from PL to PS. In this way, the data interaction of the system between PL and PS is completed efficiently.

Implementation of the Module Algorithms and Logical Control. The hardware designs the algorithms module's intellectual property (IP) core and data flow control between the IP cores. The software completes the data logical control, including data acquisition, storage and transmission. The entire system architecture is built through the implementation of the specific module algorithms and logical control. The binocular stereo visions system's modularization design is described in detail in Sect. 3.

Applying the hardware/software co-design approach to the binocular stereo vision system can efficiently complete hardware/software partitioning, and perform data interaction between PL and PS quickly and accurately. Combining the implementation of the module algorithm and logical control can ensure the system's real-time performance and human-computer interaction. The approach can also be applied to other embedded systems for machine vision and image processing, and has good universal property and application value.

3   The Proposed Co-design System

The process of designing and implementing the real-time binocular stereo vision system mainly includes camera acquisition, camera calibration, stereo rectification, stereo matching and 3D scene application. Figure 2 shows the flow chart of the system. Camera acquisition is the system's data source. Camera calibration requires the camera's internal parameters, external parameters and distortion parameters to lay the data foundation for subsequent modules [14]. The camera parameters of the same camera are fixed. Therefore, it is convenient to carry out camera calibration offline once and then write the value of these parameters to the system. In order to achieve the best performance of the system, this paper uses the mature algorithm principle of Zhang's calibration plate calibration method [15] and the MATLAB calibration toolbox for camera calibration [16, 17]. Stereo rectification is the strict alignment of pixels on the same line of binocular images [18]. This paper uses Bouguet's stereo rectification algorithm principle [19] and encodes it based on the relevant functions of the open source computer vision library (OpenCV). Stereo matching is a technique for recovering depth information from a planar image. It calculates the position difference between corresponding pixels according to the rectified binocular images, and forms a disparity image that can obtain depth information of the 3D scene. This paper uses the stereo matching algorithm which is designed by our research group based on AD census algorithm [20] and has a good representation in binocular stereo vision system. The disparity images obtained by stereo matching can be used for 3D scene application such as autonomous vehicles and robot navigation. In the rest of this Section, we apply our approach described in Sect. 2 to introduce the co-design of binocular stereo vision system from system architecture, logic design of the PL and programming design of the PS.

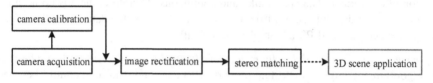

Fig. 2. A flow chart of binocular stereo vision system

3.1 System Architecture

Our goal is to design a real-time binocular stereo vision system. In order to ensure that the system has a certain speedup ratio and human-computer interaction, we combine the algorithms complexity and the characteristics of the ZYNQ platform, and use the hardware/software partitioning described in Sect. 2 to divide the system into the PL and the PS. Based on this work we designed the overall architecture of the system which is shown in Fig. 3. The system experiment platform mainly includes ZYNQ, DDR3 memory, USB driver-free binocular camera, high definition multimedia interface (HDMI) monitor, and an ordinary PC for auxiliary processing.

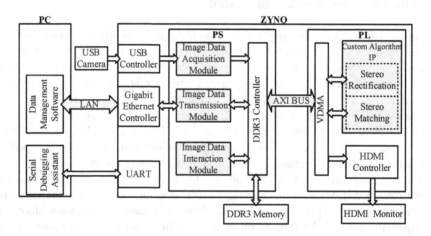

Fig. 3. Diagram of system architecture design

The PL utilizes all-purpose modular design idea in ZYNQ; it contains the following custom algorithm IP cores and Xilinx official IP cores at least:

Custom Algorithm IP. Because stereo rectification algorithm and stereo matching algorithm are complex in binocular stereo vision system, they are designed as the hardware IP cores to achieve parallel acceleration on FPGA. Because of Zynq-7000 obtains full support of Xilinx Vivado High-Level Synthesis (HLS) tool [21]. When some algorithms are designed with C language successfully, it is simple for HLS to synthesize the C language into Verilog and package into IP cores which can run on FPGA. Therefore, we can easily complete the design and synthesis of the hardware IP core through C language programming, shortening the hardware development cycle.

Data Transmission Controller. This module designed with AXI Video Direct Memory Access (VDMA) need to realize two functions. First, the image data captured by the PS is transmitted to the PL through the AXI_HP interface and corresponding control signals are generated to complete data control and interaction. Second, the processed image data by the PL is transmitted to the PS through the AXI_HP interface and corresponding control signals are generated to complete data control and interaction.

The PS needs to complete multi-task management and logical control in ZYNQ. Therefore, the following tasks need to be done in the PS:

Image Data Acquisition Module. Because the image data acquisition doesn't require complicated computation, the V4L2 video capture interface is used in the PS encoding to drive the USB controller to complete image data acquisition and storage.

Image Data Transmission Module. By using the User Datagram Protocol (UDP) communication in the PS encoding, the Ethernet port controller is driven to quickly transmit useful image data to the PC.

Image Data Interaction Module. The V4L2 drive interface is used in the PS encoding to control the VDMA of the PL to achieve the data interaction between PL and PS. This is an important module of the PS.

In addition, the system architecture also includes DDR3 memory for data storage via DDR3 controller, HDMI monitor for real-time image display and relevant control operation, and universal asynchronous receiver/transmitter (UART) interface for debugging the entire system through the serial debugging assistant.

It is worth noting that the communication of the control interface in the data interaction between PL and PS described in Sect. 2 are implemented by the instruction set in the image data interaction module configuring the registers in the Custom algorithm IP core. After the accurate communication of control signals, the AXI_HP interface executes high-performance data transmission through the VDMA of the PL.

3.2   Logic Design of the PL

Logic design of the PL mainly implements the data processing module algorithms described in Sect. 2, and completes the control of data flow in hardware part. Figure 4 shows the PL architecture of the system.

The PL architecture includes an algorithm processing acceleration channel and a real-time display channel. The DDR3 controller is used to control the reading and writing of image data in the DDR3 memory by the PL. In the algorithm processing acceleration channel, through the definition of the relevant registers in the stereo rectification IP core, the PS encoding can read and write the registers' value through the instruction configuration to achieve the communication of control signals during data interaction. This process corresponds to the PL control interface implementation of the

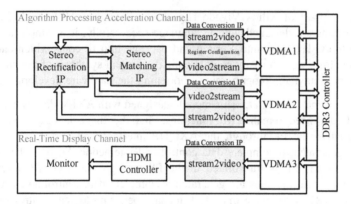

Fig. 4. Diagram of the PL architecture

data interaction between PL and PS described in Sect. 2. After correct communication, the image data in the DDR3 memory is converted into the stream data by the AXI_HP interface and the M_AXI_MM2S port of VDMA1 and VDMA2 respectively, then the data is passed to the custom data conversion IP core that converts the stream data into video data through the M_AXIS_MM2S port of VDMA, finally the data is passed to the stereo rectification IP core and stereo matching IP core. Due to the parameters such as offline calibration and image resolution are required during stereo rectification, there is corresponding register configuration sub-module in the data conversion IP core connected to VDMA1. After the video data is processed by stereo matching IP core, it is converted into the stream data through the data conversion IP core connected to VDMA1, and then sent to the VDMA1 through the S_AXIS_S2MM port, finally the stream data is converted into the memory mapped data by the VDMA1 through the M_AXI_S2MM port and is sent to the DDR3 memory by the AXI_HP interface. The stereo rectification IP core can send the processed left image of binocular images to the DDR3 memory through the data conversion IP core connected to VDMA2 and VDMA2 in the same process. In the real-time display channel, the image data in the DDR3 memory can be sent to the monitor through the VDMA3, the data conversion IP core and the HDMI controller with the same data processing method in the algorithm processing acceleration channel, and the monitor can real-time display image. It is worth noting that during the data transmission process of the PL, due to the bandwidth limitation of the DDR3, the image data in the DDR3 memory is intermittent. In order to perform data transmission correctly and efficiently between different IP cores, it is necessary to use FIFO which is a first-in, first-out data buffer and primarily used for data transfer between different clock domains for data buffering in data transmission. The entire line of image data is controlled by the FIFO buffer, so that the discontinuous data can be efficiently transmitted. Moreover, FIFO buffer reduces data interruption to quickly transmit and process data, and can effectively avoid data processing errors and data loss problems.

3.3   Programming Design of the PS

For completing the data logical control described in Sect. 2, The PS is designed to allow the user to control the execution of the system with simple button operation. In the architecture, the PS is mainly refined into the following modules as shown in Fig. 5: system initialization, image acquisition thread, data interaction thread, display control thread, and UDP processing thread. In order to achieve fast communication among threads, shared memory that implemented by memory mapping is used in the system to complete data resource sharing between threads.

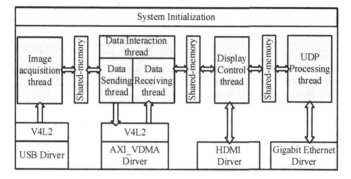

Fig. 5. Diagram of the PS architecture

System Initialization. This module mainly completes some system configuration before starting to execute each module. Firstly, the calibrated parameters are configured by using the memory mapping to write the parameters' value to register configuration sub-module of the data conversion IP core connected to VDMA1 in the PL. Secondly, because some interfaces of the PL such as USB capture interface, data input and output interface is made into a video device in the system. The video device can be operated to control the data transmission between PL and PS through the V4L2 video capture interface and the V4L2 video overlay interface. Therefore, the system initialization should have the relevant configuration of the video device. Finally, the system initialization requires some configuration such as socket definition and binding for UDP processing thread.

Image Acquisition Thread. This thread completes the binocular images data acquisition. The thread grabs the image data through the V4L2 video capture interface command VIDIOC_QBUF and puts it into the buffer queue that has been mapped to the user space, and then other threads fetch image data from the queue through the command VIDIOC_DQBUF. The loop operation of two matching interface command completes the real-time acquisition of image data.

Data Interaction Thread. The thread is divided into a data sending sub-thread and a data receiving sub-thread, corresponding to the PS control interface implementation of the data interaction between PL and PS in Sect. 2. In the PS encoding of the two sub-threads, the memory mapping is used to directly configure the custom registers of the

PL as control signals to complete the control of data interaction between PL and PS. In the data sending sub-thread, the PS encoding fetches the data from the DDR3 memory buffer to the VDMA through the V4L2 video overlay interface command VIDIOC_DQBUF, and then clears the buffer to store the next frame of image data through the command VIDIOC_QBUF. By the same principle, in the data receiving sub-thread, the PS encoding uses the command VIDIOC_DQBUF to write the received data into the DDR3 memory buffer through the AXI_HP interface and VDMA, and then clears the buffer to write the next frame of image data through the command VIDIOC_QBUF.

Display Control Thread. The thread completes the real-time display of image data and implements human-computer interaction through some buttons. The image display area and user control area of the Graphical User Interface (GUI) are designed by the PS encoding. The monitor is directly fetched the image data from DDR3 memory for display. Button operations mainly include the configuration of relevant registers during system initialization, and the control of the system's start and end.

UDP Processing Thread. The thread quickly transmits useful image data to the PC through the Ethernet driver interface, and makes data foundation for the later 3D scene application technology. In order to ensure the system's real-time performance, the thread uses a simple UDP communication for video data transmission. It is worth noting that since the maximum transmission unit is up to 1500 bytes under Ethernet, the thread requires packet sending and packet receiving for one frame of image data.

Before the end of the system, in order to ensure system security, the PS encoding needs to release some resources in system initialization, such as closing the socket, closing the video device and so on. In this way, the PS has a full structured system.

4   Implementation and Experimental Results

In order to successfully run the real-time binocular stereo vision system, this paper uses the ZC706 development board developed by Xilinx with ZYNQ7000 series as an embedded hardware board to implement the system. Figure 6 shows the system development board and peripheral interfaces. The USB interface needs to be connected to a USB free-drive binocular camera for image acquisition and peripheral keyboard and mouse for system human-computer interaction; the Ethernet interface is used to transmit data to the PC; the UART interface is used to connect the serial debugging assistant; the Joint Test Action Group (JTAG) interface is used for system co-simulation and testing; and the HDMI interface is connected to the monitor for real-time processing result display.

The system implements logic design of the PL through the Xilinx Vivado design tool, which can be used for IP core design and packaging, advanced synthesis and implementation of hardware architecture. Table 1 shows the consumption of the main system hardware resources in the PL. The consumption of the main development board resources is within the available range, which can meet the system execution requirements. The PL implements complex algorithms through FPGA parallel acceleration, which increases the system processing speed.

Fig. 6. System development board and peripheral interface

Table 1. Consumption of the system hardware resources

Resource	Utilization	Available	Utilization%
LUT	182797	218600	83.62
FF	171525	437200	39.23
BRAM	486	545	89.17
DSP	268	900	29.78

We use the QT designer tool based on the Linux operating system to complete programming design of the PS and GUI layout of this system, and transplant it to the embedded Linux system of the development board through cross-compilation. Then through the embedded Linux system's relevant configuration of the kernel driver, device tree and file system, the system's startup work is finally completed. Figure 7 shows the GUI of the system at runtime. The left part of the GUI is the image display area, including the original binocular images, the rectified image and the disparity image. The right part of the GUI is the user control area. The user can configure different cameras, image resolution and gain effect of the disparity image, and they also can control the execution of the system through the button. The GUI fully embodies the system's human-computer interaction performance.

In order to get the system's speed comparison between the architecture (FPGA 100 MHz, ARM 667 MHz) and ordinary CPU (2.50 GHz), We use binocular images with a resolution of 640 * 480 to test the processing time of stereo rectification algorithm and stereo matching algorithm several times. In our system architecture, the clock and counter are used to count the hardware processing time from the first line of one frame of image data into the PL to the last line of the frame of image data out of the PL. The software processing time is counted by using the program instruction to record the system's time difference in the PS. Table 2 shows the average processing time for the test image set. It takes nearly half a minute for the ordinary CPU to finish the two

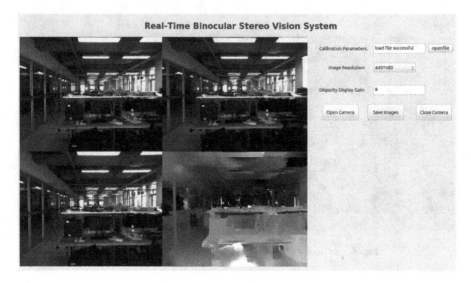

Fig. 7. The GUI of the system

algorithms. For the co-design approach of the system architecture in ZYNQ platform, the two algorithms are parallel acceleration processing. The logical control of the PS consumes 0.00473 s, and the data processing algorithms of the PL consumes 0.00350 s. The architecture only takes milliseconds to process one frame of image data, and which is thousands of times faster than the ordinary CPU. Such a high speedup ratio enables binocular stereo vision system to achieve real-time performance in actual scene application. In addition, in order to highlight the superiority of our co-design approach, we compare the system architecture in this paper and [8] in terms of processing time as shown in Table 3. It can be seen that the system architecture in [8] consumes less hardware resources, but the frame rate of the image is lower than that this paper, and our system also embodies human-computer interaction, so the hardware/software co-design approach proposed in this paper is superior to that in [8], which has high application value in the actual scene.

Table 2. Processing time of complex algorithms

Platform	Stereo rectification	Stereo matching	Total
CPU	0.231 s	29.750 s	29.981 s
ZYNQ	0.00473 + 0.00350		0.00823 s

In order to be able to further test the processing performance and execution efficiency of the system architecture, we tested frame rate through the different resolutions' binocular images. Due to the narrow bandwidth limitation of the development board's USB2.0, the camera's high-resolution transmission is not fast and the overall system's best performance cannot be tested. Therefore, we change the acquisition thread to store

Table 3. Comparison result of system processing time

Design	Device	Image size	Hardware resources	Frame rate
[8]	ZC706	640 * 480	182933 LUTs, 143223 FFs, 100 DSPs, 138 BRAMs	101
This paper	ZC706	640 * 480	182797 LUTs, 171525 FFs, 268 DSPs, 486 BRAMs	121.43

the different resolutions' binocular images in the startup card, and read these images through our co-design system for actual testing, and use the button on the GUI to control the system execution and change image resolution and other interactive work. The processing time is counted by recording the system's time difference from the completion of one frame of image data acquisition to the receiving of the processed frame of image data, and the average processing frame rate of the system is continuously measured by testing 100 frames, 1000 frames, and 10000 frames of image data. The test results are shown in Table 4. It can be seen that the frame rate with an image resolution of 640 * 480 can reach 121.43 frames per second, and the processing speed can exceed 30 frames per second for the full high definition of 1920 * 1080. If the system is applied to ADAS and combines with the signal processing control in the PS, it can help the driver to quickly make correct prediction of some driving operation commands. Therefore, the binocular stereo vision system has important significance in practical application.

Table 4. Image processing frame rate at different resolutions

Resolution	640 * 480	1280 * 720	1280 * 960	1920 * 1080
Frame rate	121.427	66.726	54.960	36.559

5 Conclusion

This paper has presented a hardware/software co-design approach for binocular stereo vision system. We firstly modularize the system's functions and combine the advantages of hardware and software to perform the hardware/software partitioning between modules, and then use the efficient data interaction to make the system have the best performance. Finally, we implement the system based on ZYNQ platform. The experimental results also show that the system has good human-computer interaction and can fully meet the real-time requirements. In the later research work, we plan to further optimize the system architecture and revelant algorithms, so that the processing speed of the system can be accelerated at high resolution, and make the system more perfect. In addition, we will apply the system's disparity images to real-time target tracking and distance measurement in real-world vehicle applications, enabling the system to truly contribute to the advanced driver assistance systems.

Acknowledgments. This work is supported by Shanghai Science and Technology Commission Project (17511106902), Shanghai Youth Science and Technology Phosphorus Project (No. 18QB1403900) and Shanghai Science and Technology Major Funding Project (No. 15DZ1100400).

References

1. Szeliski, R.: Computer Vision: Algorithms and Applications. Springer, New York (2010)
2. Woodfill, J.I., Gordon, G., Buck, R.: Tyzx DeepSea high speed stereo vision system. In: Conference on Computer Vision and Pattern Recognition Workshop, CVPRW 2004, p. 41. IEEE (2004)
3. Janai, J., Güney, F., Behl, A., Geiger, A.: Computer vision for autonomous vehicles: problems, datasets and state-of-the-art (2017). https://arxiv.org/abs/1704.05519
4. Bimbraw, K.: Autonomous cars: past, present and future a review of the developments in the last century, the present scenario and the expected future of autonomous vehicle technology. In: International Conference on Informatics in Control, Automation and Robotics, pp. 191–198. IEEE (2015)
5. Song, W., Yang, Y., Fu, M., et al.: Lane detection and classification for forward collision warning system based on stereo vision. IEEE Sens. J. **PP**(99), 1 (2018)
6. Jin, S., Cho, J., Xuan, D.P., et al.: FPGA design and implementation of a real-time stereo vision system. IEEE Trans. Circ. Syst. Video Technol. **20**(1), 15–26 (2010)
7. Pérez-Patricio, M., Aguilar-González, A.: FPGA implementation of an efficient similarity-based adaptive window algorithm for real-time stereo matching. J. Real-Time Image Process. 1–17 (2015)
8. Perri, S., Frustaci, F., Spagnolo, F., et al.: Design of real-time FPGA-based embedded system for stereo vision. In: 2018 IEEE International Symposium on Circuits and Systems (ISCAS), pp.1–5. IEEE (2018)
9. De Michell, G., Gupta, R.K.: Hardware/software co-design. Proc. IEEE **85**(3), 349–365 (1997)
10. Wolf, W.H.: Hardware-software co-design of embedded systems. Proc. IEEE **82**(7), 967–989 (1994)
11. Adams, J.K., Thomas, D.E.: The design of mixed hardware/software systems. In: Design Automation Conference Proceedings, pp. 515–520. IEEE (1996)
12. Edwards, S., Lavagno, L., Lee, E.A., et al.: Design of embedded systems: formal models, validation, and synthesis. Proc. IEEE **85**(3), 366–390 (1997)
13. Lu, J., Jiang, D., Ma, M.: Embedded system software and hardware cooperative design practical guide based on Xilinx ZYNQ. China Machine Press, Beijing (2013, Chinese)
14. Yan, Y., et al.: Camera calibration in binocular stereo vision of moving robot. In: The Sixth World Congress on Intelligent Control and Automation, WCICA 2006, pp. 9257–9261. IEEE (2006)
15. Zhang, Z.: Flexible camera calibration by viewing a plane from unknown orientations. In: The Proceedings of the Seventh IEEE International Conference on Computer Vision, vol. 1, pp. 666–673. IEEE (2002)
16. Bouguet, J.: Camera calibration toolbox for matlab (2004). http://www.vision.caltech.edu/bouguetj/calibdoc/
17. Fetić, A., Jurić, D., Osmanković, D.: The procedure of a camera calibration using camera calibration toolbox for MATLAB. In: 2012 Proceedings of the International Convention Mipro, pp. 1752–1757. IEEE (2012)

18. Tang, Y.P., Pang, C.J., Zhou, Z.S., et al.: Binocular omni-directional vision sensor and epipolar rectification in its omni-directional images. J. Zhejiang Univ. Technol. **1**, 20 (2011)
19. Bouguet, J.: The calibration toolbox for matlab, example 5: stereo rectification algorithm. Code and instructions only. http://www.vision.caltech.edu/bouguetj/calib_doc/htmls/example5.html
20. Mei, X., Sun, X., Zhou, M., et al.: On building an accurate stereo matching system on graphics hardware. In: IEEE International Conference on Computer Vision Workshops, pp. 467–474. IEEE Computer Society (2011)
21. Zynq-7000 All Programmable SoC Overview DS190 (v1.2). Xilinx (2012)

The Cuckoo Search and Integer Linear Programming Based Approach to Time-Aware Test Case Prioritization Considering Execution Environment

Yu Wong[1,2], Hongwei Zeng[1], Huaikou Miao[1,2], Honghao Gao[1,3], and Xiaoxian Yang[4(✉)]

[1] School of Computer Engineering and Science,
Shanghai University, Shanghai 200444, China
{joye_wong, zenghongwei, hkmiao, gaohonghao}@shu.edu.cn
[2] Shanghai Key Laboratory of Computer Software Evaluating and Testing,
Shanghai 200444, China
[3] Computing Center, Shanghai University, Shanghai 200444, China
[4] School of Computer and Information Engineering,
Shanghai Polytechnic University, Shanghai, China
xxyang@sspu.edu.cn

Abstract. Regression testing plays an important role in software development process. The more mature software system development is, the greater the proportion of regression testing during software life cycle takes. To this point, test case prioritization techniques are proposed to detect more faults as early as possible and improve the effectiveness of regression testing. However, it is often performed in a time constrained execution environment. This paper introduces a new method of time-aware test case prioritization. First of all, it takes advantage of the cuckoo search algorithm to reorder test suite. Then, integer linear programming model is employed to test selection in light of time budget. At last, a novel fitness function is designed focusing on code coverage that from method-call information perspective. Experimental results show that our method improves the effectiveness of fault detection compared with traditional fault detection techniques especially time is constrained.

Keywords: Test case prioritization · Time-aware · Cuckoo search

1 Introduction

Regression testing takes up a large proportion of workload during the software testing process, which should be completely executed in all stages of software development. It is expensive in most circumstances. As we known, researcher had stated that a test suite of software having 20,000 lines of code requires 7 weeks to run and check [1]. As a solution, test case prioritization (TCP) is an effective solution that aims to make test suite detect more faults as early as possible. Therefore, kinds of TCP strategies have been published, such as greedy algorithm, meta-heuristic algorithm. However, effective

H. Gao et al. (Eds.): CollaborateCom 2018, LNICST 268, pp. 734–754, 2019.
https://doi.org/10.1007/978-3-030-12981-1_51

meta-heuristic methods are not always applicable to TCP, requiring making related adjustment according to different test scenario.

Most of the existing approaches to prioritization did not incorporate a testing time budget. Li et al. [2] firstly applied hill climbing and genetic algorithm (GA) to the TCP. Though their meta-heuristic searches algorithms have no difference with the additional greedy algorithm in performance, time constraint is still not incorporated in their proposed algorithms. Walcott et al. [3] used the GA to reorder test suites in light of testing time constraints. But the effectiveness of their methods has yet to be verified. Cuckoo Search (CS) is a relatively new meta-heuristic algorithm proposed in 2009 [4, 5]. It aims to effectively solve the optimization problem by simulating parasitic brooding behavior of cuckoo. Many experimental studies [4, 5] have proved that CS is more effective than other optimization algorithms such as particle swarm optimization (PSO) algorithm. However, there is no valuable literature to demonstrate the superiority of the CS algorithm in TCP. Some existing CS approaches in testing [6, 7] have been applied for TCP, but the effectiveness of their approaches was not proved by experiments.

In response to the above issues, the TCP problem is transformed into finding an optimal solution of the test case prioritization in our method, and the performance of the method is verified by multi-level comparison experiments. Thus, this paper presents a test case prioritization technique that combine CS algorithm and the integer linear programming (ILP). The ILP is applied to selecting test cases when time is limited. A new fitness function based on code coverage and method-call information is designed to solve the multi-object problem. Through empirical evaluation, the parameter combination of CS algorithm is optimized. Then our approach is evaluated and compared with previous TCP techniques. The experimental results demonstrate that our proposed TCP algorithm detect faults more and earlier than traditional techniques and other heuristic-based prioritization algorithms especially time is constrained.

The rest of the paper is organized as follows. Section 2 discusses related work for test case prioritization techniques. Section 3 describes how to combine the integer linear programming with cuckoo search algorithm to solve the time-aware test case prioritization problem and introduces a new fitness function. Section 4 describes the design, results, and analysis of experiments. Section 5 comes conclusion and future work.

2 Related Work

Techniques for test case prioritization aim to improve the rate of fault detection through reordering test cases for execution. Many TCP strategies have been raised, the existing TCP techniques are classified into three categories: source code, requirement, and model. The TCP technologies based on source code are also divided into greedy algorithm, machine learning method, fusion expert method and others. This section describes other exiting relevant contributions in TCP strategies.

Rothermel et al. [8] firstly proposed the complete definition of the TCP problem. They empirically evaluated several test case prioritization techniques such as statement coverage prioritization, function coverage prioritization and so on. These researches focused on code-coverage TCP methods,and had been relatively mature [8, 9]. In 2001, Elbaum [10] conducted specific research for TCP metrics, including APFD and APFDc. APFD metric proclaims that all faults have the same severity and all test cases have equal costs. APFDc considers test case costs and fault severities. Their study primarily focused on white-box testing but not black-box testing.

In addition, the multi-objective is also gradually used in the TCP problem. Islam et al. [11] proposed a multi-objective test case prioritization approach based on latent semantic indexing, that is the method of information retrieval (IR). Saini and Tyagi [12] proposed a multi-objective test case prioritization algorithm (MTCPA) which is based on two objective functions. The objective functions include test case execution time used in the GA and statement coverage. The proposed method has been compared with different prioritization techniques to find the optimal solution. Experimental results showed that the proposed algorithm returns a test case suite with maximum fault coverage and minimum execution time with maximum APFD criteria as the solution.

There are many other meta-heuristic search algorithms applied to solve multi-objective TCP problem. Schultz and Radloff [13] were committed to combining PSO algorithm with multi-target TCP problems. However, they compared their own approaches with just Random by experiments. The credibility of the effectiveness of their approaches seemed not strong enough. Cuckoo Search (CS) is proposed by Yang and Deb [4, 5] in 2009. Many researches of various fields have proved that CS algorithm shows greater effectiveness than other heuristics. For example, CS was extended to solve multi-objective problems in [5]. In specific, the proposed MOCS (multi-objective cuckoo search) was tested on a subset of well-chosen test functions. And it performs better for almost all these test problems in comparison with the PSO algorithm and the GA. A few researchers have attempted to use the cuckoo algorithm in test field. Nagar et al. [6] proclaimed that they use the CS algorithm in TCP. But actually they applied the CS algorithm to test case selection, instead of the test case prioritization. Prior to them, Srivastava et al. [7] also applied CS algorithm to TCP, but the algorithm converged slowly and the effectiveness of their approach was not proved by experiments. Thus, the CS algorithm is applied to solve the time-constrained TCP problem, and its effectiveness in fault detection is verified by experiments in this paper.

In recent years, test Case Prioritization has also made progress in other aspects. During 2016, Alves and Machado et al. [14] proposed another novel refactoring-based approach, which reordered an existing test sequence utilizing a set of refactoring fault models. This approach promoted early detection of refactoring faults. Eghbali and Tahvildari [15] proposed a new heuristic for breaking ties in coverage based techniques using the notion of lexicographical ordering. This technology is a positive solution to the problem of how to choose a better one once the test cases cover the same number of statement. In 2017, Lachmann et al. [16] introduced a technique for test case prioritization of manual system-level regression testing based on supervised machine learning, and used SVM Rank to evaluate their approach by means of two subject systems. Kim et al. [17] proposed a test case prioritization method based on failure history data.

3   Time-Aware Test Case Prioritization

Test suite usually could not be run in a limited time, so the test cases that detect more faults should be run as much as possible. Although faults could not be predicted, test cases that cover more code usually have more potential to detect more faults from the perspective of code coverage. Therefore, these test cases that cover more code need to be selected to run when time is constrained. Among them, the test case that covers more code should be executed earlier. The test case prioritization problem is incorporated with time budget, and it is called time-aware test case prioritization problem. According to Walcott et al. [3], this problem is defined as follows.

Definition 1 (Time-aware Test Case Prioritization):
   Given: A test suite T, the set of permutations of T's powerset PT, the time budget $Time_{max}$, and two functions from PT to the real numbers $fit()$ and $Time()$.

Problem 1: Find the test tuple $\sigma_{max} \in$ PT such that $Time(\sigma_{max}) \leq Time_{max}$ and $\forall \sigma \in$ PT where $\sigma_{max} \neq \sigma$, $Time(\sigma) \leq Time_{max}$ and $fit(\sigma) \leq fit(\sigma_{max})$.
   In Definition 1, PT represents the collection of all possible tuples and subtuples of T. The time budget $Time_{max}$ is expected limited test case execution time in actual test scenario. The execution time of each test case is obtained in our experiments in Sect. 4. $Time_{max}$ is simulated by the percentage of total execution time of all test cases. The test tuple σ contains several test cases, $Time(\sigma)$ is total execution time of them. The function $fit()$ is usually designed according to fault-related code information, requirement information and so on. It measures the potential fault detection capabilities of test tuples.

Table 1. Test suite and faults exposed.

Test cases (execution time)	Faults									
	F_1	F_2	F_3	F_4	F_5	F_6	F_7	F_8	F_9	F_{10}
T_1 (9 min)	X	X		X	X		X	X		X
T_2 (1 min)	X									
T_3 (3 min)	X			X						
T_4 (4 min)		X	X				X			
T_5 (4 min)				X		X			X	

T_1	T_4	T_5	T_3	T_2
7 faults	3 faults	3 faults	2 faults	1 fault
9 min	4 min	4 min	3 min	1 min

(a) Fault-based prioritization

T_2	T_3	T_4	T_5	T_1
1 fault	2 faults	3 faults	3 faults	7 faults
1 min	3 min	4 min	4 min	9 min

(b) Time-based prioritization

T_2	T_1	T_5	T_4	T_3
1 fault	7 faults	3 faults	3 faults	2 fault
1 min	9 min	4 min	4 min	3 min

(c) Average-based prioritization

T_4	T_5	T_3	T_1	T_2
3 faults	3 faults	2 faults	7 faults	1 fault
4 min	4 min	3 min	9 min	1 min

(d) Time-aware prioritization

Fig. 1. Prioritizations based on different principles.

Consider an example program with 10 faults and a test suite of 5 test cases, with the faults detecting abilities as shown in Table 1. Meanwhile, the time budget is 12 min. As illustrated in Fig. 1, if test cases are prioritized based on faults, the execution order of them is $<T_1>$ and 7 faults are detected within 9 min. If test cases are prioritized based on time, the execution order of them is $<T_2, T_3, T_4, T_5>$ and 8 faults are detected within 12 min. If test cases are prioritized based on average time, the execution order of them is $<T_2, T_1>$ and 7 faults are detected within 10 min. Time-aware test case prioritization problem aims to design an intelligent method to find a great execution order that detect more faults in less time. For example, in Fig. 1(d), executing test cases in $<T_4, T_5, T_3>$ detect 8 faults within 11 min.

Moreover, definition 1 is separated into the following two definitions to design an intelligent technique in this paper.

Definition 2 (Test Case Selection in Time Budget):

Given: A test suite T, the time budget $Time_{max}$, and two functions from T to the real numbers $fit1()$ and $Time()$.

Problem 2: Find the subset $T'_{max} \subset T$ such that $Time(T'_{max}) \leq Time_{max}$ and $\forall T' \subset T$ where $T'_{max} \neq T'$, $Time(T') \leq Time_{max}$ and $fit1(T') \leq fit1(T'_{max})$.

The function $fit1()$ in Problem 2 also be designed by known fault-related code information, requirement information, or others. In experiments, method coverage information is considered in $fit1()$. More specifically, the integer linear programming (ILP) is used for test case selection in time budgets and it will be elaborated in Sect. 3.1.

Definition 3 (Test Case Prioritization of Test Subset):

Given: A subset obtained by solving Problem 2 T'_{max}, the collection of T'_{max}'s all possible tuples and sub tuples PT, and a function from PT to the real numbers $fit2()$.

Problem 3: Find the test tuple $\sigma_{max} \in PT$ such that $\forall \sigma \in PT$ where $\sigma_{max} \neq \sigma$ and $fit2(\sigma) \leq fit2(\sigma_{max})$.

In Definition 3, the fitness function $fit2()$ is designed by code information and execution time. It helps us to find the test tuple that detect more faults as soon as possible and is referred to in Sect. 3.3.

3.1 ILP-Based Test Case Selection Introduction

For the time-aware test case prioritization problem, test case selection in time budget should be first solved to obtain an optimal test case subset that run in limit time. In our software test environment, execution time of test cases and the specific methods covered by each test case are available. The test case set, execution time, and covered method meet a corresponding linear relationship. In order to select a test subset covering more methods under certain linear constraints (Eqs. 5 and 6), a linear programming model is undoubtedly suitable. In this section, test case selection in time budget is viewed as a 0/1 integer linear programming (ILP) problem to solve as follows [18].

Suppose that test suite T contains n test cases $\{T_1, T_2, \ldots, T_n\}$, the execution time of each test case is $time(T_i)$. The code unit set of the program is denoted as $C = \{c_1, c_2, \ldots, c_m\}$. A code unit may be a method, a class, or a statement block. The problem is to select a subset T'_{max} that not only covers the biggest code unit subset of C but also the sum execution time of it does not exceed the time budget.

Let Boolean variable x_i ($1 \leq i \leq n$) indicates if test case T_i is selected or not, and Boolean variable s_{ij} is defined as whether a test case T_i covers c_j. So, for the set of code units, m Boolean variables y_i ($1 \leq i \leq m$) are used to represent whether code unit c_j is covered by at least one test case. The problem is reduced to the 0/1 ILP described as follows:

0/1 variables:

$$x_i = \begin{cases} 1, & \text{if } T_i (1 \leq i \leq n) \text{ is selected} \\ 0, & \text{otherwise} \end{cases} \tag{1}$$

$$S_{ij} = \begin{cases} 1, & \text{if } T_i \text{ covers } c_j \\ 0, & \text{otherwise} \end{cases} \tag{2}$$

$$y_j = \begin{cases} 1, & \text{if one or more selected test cases cover } c_j \\ 0, & \text{otherwise} \end{cases} \tag{3}$$

A linear function to be maximized:

$$\max \sum_{j=1}^{m} y_j \tag{4}$$

Problem constraints:

$$\sum_{i=1}^{n} time(T_i) * x_i \leq Time_{max} \tag{5}$$

$$\sum_{i=1}^{n} s_{ij} * x_i \geq y_j \quad (i < j < m) \tag{6}$$

In Eq. 4, the linear function $\sum_{j=1}^{m} y_j$ amounts to the function $fit1()$ in Problem 2, and it aims to pick out a subset of test cases that cover the most code in finite time $Time_{max}$. The $time(T_i)$ is the execution time of the test case T_i. Although this test subset has reached the maximum code coverage, there may still have spare time to run unselected test cases after executing the selected ones. In order to detect more faults, the remaining unchosen test cases need to be further selected according to the remaining time. For further selection, the total number of methods that are covered by each test case is calculated, then select the maximum coverage test case that run in the remaining time. The optimal subset of test suite T is obtained by the ILP and further selection.

3.2 Test Case Prioritization Using CS

The suitable test case subset that could be executed in a limited time has been selected, but many faults detected by the test cases are duplicated. If the test case set is not prioritized, a lot of time will still be wasted. Thus, the test case subset that have potential to detect more faults should be run first. This TCP problem is absolutely considered as the global optimized problem that solved by Cuckoo Search (CS) algorithm. CS is a meta-heuristic algorithm that effectively solve optimization problem by simulating the parasitic brooding behavior of certain species of cuckoo. Based on the fitness value of each iteration, a fraction of worse nests will be abandoned, and each generation infinitely close to an optimized solution by replacing the solutions to the better ones [4, 5]. The optimal solution is based on the fitness function which measures the potential fault detect ability of the test sequence.

For simplicity in describing the CS, CS usually uses the following three idealized rules: (a) Each cuckoo lays one egg at a time, and dumps it in a randomly chosen nest; (b) The high-quality eggs will be carried over to the next generations; (c) The number of available host nests is fixed, and the egg laid by a cuckoo is discovered by the host bird with a probability p_a. In this case, the host bird either get rid of the egg, or simply abandon the nest and build a completely new nest [4, 5].

According to Yang [4], based on above three rules, the basic steps of the cuckoo search algorithm for TCP are described as Algorithm 1.

Algorithm 1   CS Algorithm for TCP [4]

1: **Begin**
2:   *Generate initial test tuple population (n host nests x_i ($i = 1, 2, ..., n$))*
3:   **while** ($t <$ *MaxGeneration*)
4:     *Get a test tuple(cuckoo) x_i randomly by Lévy flights and evaluate it;*
5:     *Choose a test tuple (nest) among n (say, j) randomly;*
6:     **if** ($f(x_i) > f(x_j)$)
7:       *replace x_j by the new solution x_i;*
8:     **end if**
9:     *Rank the solutions and find the current best;*
10:    *A fraction (p_a) of worse nests are abandoned and new ones are built to replace them;*
11:    *Keep the best solutions (or nests with quality solutions);*
12:   **end while**
13:   *Obtain the best solution.*
14: **End**

In CS algorithm for TCP, the initial population is generated randomly from the permutation of the test subset obtained by ILP. Each d-dimensional vector x_i called test tuple represents one of the ordering results of d test cases. The parameter t represents the t-th generation of nest transformation and *MaxGeneration* is set to terminated the algorithm. The objective function $f(x_i)$ is just $fit2()$ in Problem 3 and will be defined in Sect. 3.

In the loop, Lévy flights is the core of the CS, and it is performed to generate new solutions. For a nest $x_i^{(t)}$, a Lévy flight is described as follows:

$$x_i^{(t+1)} = x_i^{(t)} + \alpha \oplus \text{Lévy}(\lambda) \tag{7}$$

In (7), α is the step size, in this paper $\alpha = 1$ is setted here. The product $\oplus$ means entrywise multiplication. In test case prioritization, a test tuple is a sequence of test cases (non-numerical values), so the location numbers of test cases in a test tuple are used to form a nest. Suppose vector $\mathbf{I}$ marks the initial locations of test cases in test tuple x_i, a Lévy flight of x_i is defined as

$$\mathbf{I}^{(t+1)} = \textbf{Hash}(\mathbf{I}^{(t)} + \alpha \oplus \text{Lévy}(\lambda)) \tag{8}$$

In (8), $\alpha \oplus \text{Lévy}(\lambda)$ creates a new d-dimensional vector which elements are d random integers based on Lévy distribution. To get these d random numbers, Levy Random Number Generator (LRNG) is designed. The final results of $\mathbf{I}^{(t+1)}$ are a set of integers between 0 to d got by modulo operation. These d integers represent locations, and they are highly likely to cause hash conflicts. Hash function is applied to solve this hash conflict. It computes new sequence numbers of test cases in x_i, and quadratic probing method to solve conflict. At last, a new vector $\mathbf{I}^{(t+1)}$ is obtained and a new test tuple $x_i^{(t+1)}$ generates according to $\mathbf{I}^{(t+1)}$.

To better elaborate, an example is given to explain the specific process of Lévy flight. In Fig. 2(a), the original test tuple $x_i^{(t)} = (x_0, x_1, x_2, x_3, x_4)^{\text{T}} = (T_3, T_4, T_1, T_5, T_2)^{\text{T}}$, so $\mathbf{I}^{(t)} = (2, 4, 0, 1, 3)$, elements in I are the location of test cases in the tuple. Then update the $\mathbf{I}^{(t)}$ with the Lévy vector generated by LRNG in Fig. 2(b), but there are conflicts in the new $\mathbf{I}^{(t)}$ like "3" and "1". Then quadratic probing method is used to solve hash conflicts in Fig. 2(c). In addition, the element "n_i" in Fig. 2(c) means the i-th repetition of value "n". At last, a new subscripts vector $\mathbf{I}^{(t+1)}$ is got without conflict and the new test tuple vector $[T_5, T_4, T_3, T_1, T_2]$ is obtained according to $\mathbf{I}^{(t+1)}$ as shown in Fig. 2(d).

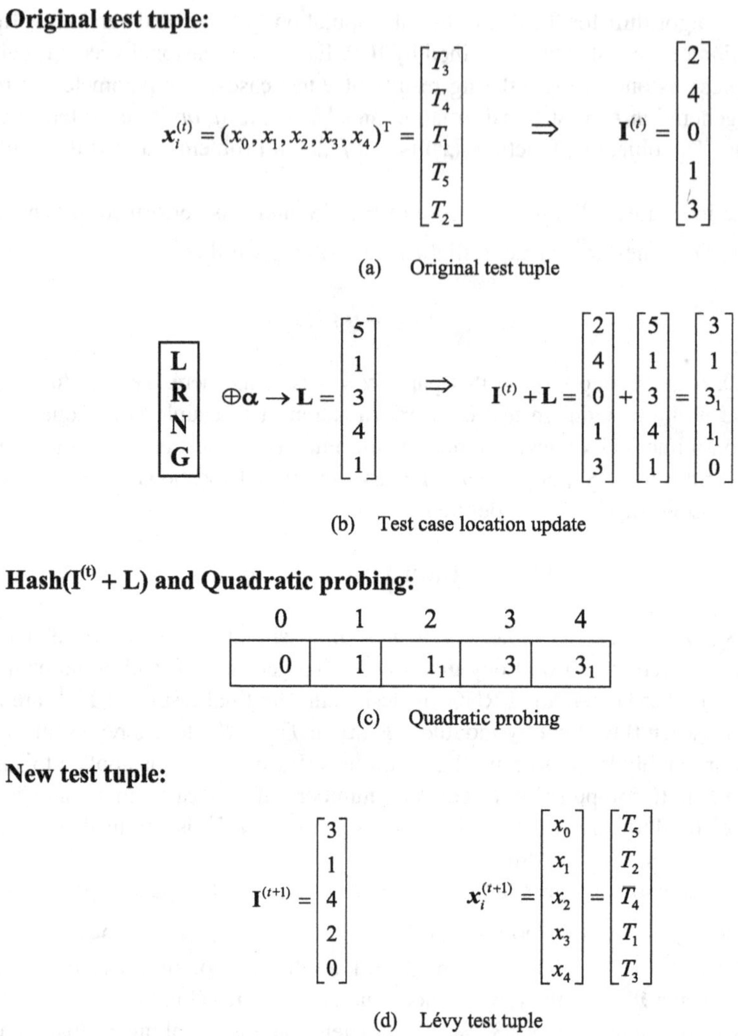

Original test tuple:

$$x_i^{(t)} = (x_0, x_1, x_2, x_3, x_4)^{\mathrm{T}} = \begin{bmatrix} T_3 \\ T_4 \\ T_1 \\ T_5 \\ T_2 \end{bmatrix} \quad \Rightarrow \quad \mathbf{I}^{(t)} = \begin{bmatrix} 2 \\ 4 \\ 0 \\ 1 \\ 3 \end{bmatrix}$$

(a)   Original test tuple

$$\begin{matrix} \mathbf{L} \\ \mathbf{R} \\ \mathbf{N} \\ \mathbf{G} \end{matrix} \oplus \alpha \to \mathbf{L} = \begin{bmatrix} 5 \\ 1 \\ 3 \\ 4 \\ 1 \end{bmatrix} \quad \Rightarrow \quad \mathbf{I}^{(t)} + \mathbf{L} = \begin{bmatrix} 2 \\ 4 \\ 0 \\ 1 \\ 3 \end{bmatrix} + \begin{bmatrix} 5 \\ 1 \\ 3 \\ 4 \\ 1 \end{bmatrix} = \begin{bmatrix} 3 \\ 3_1 \\ 3_1 \\ 1_1 \\ 0 \end{bmatrix}$$

(b)   Test case location update

Hash($\mathbf{I}^{(t)} + \mathbf{L}$) and Quadratic probing:

0	1	2	3	4
0	1	1_1	3	3_1

(c)   Quadratic probing

New test tuple:

$$\mathbf{I}^{(t+1)} = \begin{bmatrix} 3 \\ 1 \\ 4 \\ 2 \\ 0 \end{bmatrix} \quad x_i^{(t+1)} = \begin{bmatrix} x_0 \\ x_1 \\ x_2 \\ x_3 \\ x_4 \end{bmatrix} = \begin{bmatrix} T_5 \\ T_2 \\ T_4 \\ T_1 \\ T_3 \end{bmatrix}$$

(d)   Lévy test tuple

Fig. 2. Create new test tuple by the Lévy flight.

3.3   Fitness Function Design

In meta-heuristic algorithm, fitness function play an important role. To use the cuckoo search algorithm to search the best test tuple, a new fitness function of the CS is designed for TCP algorithm.

$$Fitness(\sigma, t_c, \omega_1, \omega_2) = \omega_1 F_{cover}(\sigma, t_c) + \omega_2 F_{mc}(\sigma) \tag{9}$$

The fitness of a test tuple σ is evaluated by code coverage information and method-call information, and $\omega_1, \omega_2 \in [0, 1]$ are weights that satisfy $\omega_1 + \omega_2 = 1$. In which, the code coverage information is obtained on a given test coverage adequacy criteria t_c.

$F_{cover}(\sigma, t_c)$ is related to code coverage, giving precedence to test tuples which cover more code earlier. F_{cover} is calculated in two parts: $F_{c\text{-}actual}$, $F_{c\text{-}max}$. First, $F_{c\text{-}actual}$ is computed by summing the products of execution time $time(T_i)$ and the code coverage of the sub tuple $\sigma_{\{1,i\}}$. In which, the sub tuple $\sigma_{\{1,i\}} = <T_1, T_2, \ldots, T_i>$ for each test case $T_i \in \sigma$. Formally, for each σ,

$$F_{c\text{-}actual}(\sigma, t_c) = \sum_{i=1}^{|\sigma|} \left\{ time(\langle T_i \rangle) * ccover(\sigma_{\{1,i\}}, t_c) \right\} \tag{10}$$

$F_{c\text{-}max}$ represents the maximum code coverage of the test tuple σ at maximum time limit (i.e. the maximum value that $F_{c\text{-}actual}$ takes). For each σ,

$$F_{c\text{-}max}(\sigma, t_c) = ccover(\sigma, t_c) * \sum_{i=1}^{n} time(\langle T_i \rangle) \tag{11}$$

Then,

$$F_{cover}(\sigma, t_c) = \frac{F_{c\text{-}actual}(\sigma, t_c)}{F_{c\text{-}max}(\sigma, t_c)} \tag{12}$$

The F_{cover} evaluates the code coverage of the test tuple σ, but larger code coverage may have smaller number of method calls. $F_{mc}(\sigma)$ is associated with method call number. More method calls covered by the test tuple make fault detection more effective. Similarly, $F_{mc}(\sigma)$ is also calculated in two parts. Meanwhile, for each σ,

$$F_{m\text{-}actual}(\sigma) = \sum_{k=1}^{|\sigma|} \left\{ \sum_{i=1}^{k} time(\langle T_i \rangle) * mc(\sigma_{\{1,k\}}) \right\} \tag{13}$$

$$F_{m\text{-}max}(\sigma) = mc(\sigma) * \sum_{i=1}^{|\sigma|} time(\langle T_i \rangle) \tag{14}$$

where $mc(\sigma_{\{1,i\}})$ means the method call number of the sub tuple $\sigma_{\{1,i\}} = <T_1, T_2, \ldots, T_i>$ for each test case $T_i \in \sigma$.

Then, $F_{mc}(\sigma)$ is obtained by these two parameters. Specifically, for each σ,

$$F_{mc}(\sigma) = \frac{F_{m\text{-}actual}(\sigma)}{F_{m\text{-}max}(\sigma)} * \frac{2}{|\sigma|} \tag{15}$$

where $2/|\sigma|$ is to neutralize the gap between numerator and denominator.

3.4   Algorithm Implementation About TCP Using CS

Our approach combines the CS with ILP for the test case prioritization problem under time constraint. To conclude above all, this section further describes the specific implementation process of our approach in Algorithm 2.

Algorithm 2   CSPrioritize

Input: Program P, Test suite T, s, g_{max}, p_a, p_t, t_c, ω_1, ω_2
Output: Maximum fitness tuple $F_{max} \in F$ in set σ_{max}

1: $Time_{max} \leftarrow p_t * \sum_{i=0}^{n} time(T_i)$
2: $T'_{max} \leftarrow ILP(T, Time_{max}, p_t)$
3: $POP \leftarrow Permute(T'_{max})$
4: $g \leftarrow 0$
5: $R_g \leftarrow RandomPerplr(POP, s)$
6: **repeat**
7:      $\sigma_i \leftarrow SelectOne(R_g)$
8:      $\sigma_j \leftarrow ApplyLevy(\sigma_i)$
9:      **if** $(Fitness(\sigma_j, t_c, \omega_1, \omega_2) > Fitness(\sigma_i, t_c, \omega_1, \omega_2))$
10:          $\sigma_i \leftarrow \sigma_j$
11:      $Fitness \leftarrow \phi$
12:      **for** $\sigma_k \in R_g$
13:          $Fitness \leftarrow Fitness \cup Fitness(\sigma_i, t_c, \omega_1, \omega_2)$
14:      $R_g \leftarrow Rank(R_g, Fitness)$
15:      $R_{g+1} \leftarrow ApplyLevy(R_g, p_a)$
16:      $g \leftarrow g + 1$
17: **until** $g \geq g_{max}$
18: $\sigma_{max} \leftarrow SelectBest(R_{g+1}, Fitness)$
19: **return** σ_{max}

In Algorithm 2, the inputs of the CS for TCP algorithm are the program P, each $T_i \in \{T_1, T_2, \ldots, T_n\}$, and the following user specified parameters: (1) s, maximum number of candidate test tuples generated during each iteration, (2) g_{max}, maximum number of iterations, (3) p_a, the fraction (p_a) of worse nests will be abandoned, (iv) p_t, percent of the execution time of T allowed by the time budget, (4) t_c, test coverage adequacy criteria, like class, method, block and so on, (5) ω_1, the program coverage weight, (6) ω_2, the program method calls weight, which $p_t, \omega_1, \omega_2 \in [0, 1]$, and $\omega_1 + \omega_2 = 1$.

The cuckoo search algorithm uses heuristic search to identify the test tuple $\sigma_{max} \in Permute(T'_{max})$, which T'_{max} is the subset of T and it may have the highest rate of fault detection in provided limit time. The subset T'_{max} get by the ILP. The initial test tuples get from $Permute(T'_{max})$. Finally, after the iterative process of the algorithm, the output is the best test tuple, that is, the test tuple with the greatest value. In general, any $\sigma_j \in Permute(T'_{max})$ has the form $\sigma_j = <T_1, \ldots, T_n>$ where $u \leq n$.

The first two lines of the algorithm are the key to our time-aware processing and aim to solve the Problem 2. Line 1 is the time acquisition and time constraint step. Next, the ILP is used to filter out the optimal set T'_{max} of test cases which are executed in restricted time. The next two lines are the process to generate the initial population of test case prioritization using CS. Before the algorithm run for the loop on line 6, the algorithm creates a set R_0 containing s random test tuples σ from $Permute(T'_{max})$. R_0 is the first generation of s potential "best" test tuple.

Then a test tuple is randomly chosen by $SelectOne(R_g)$ and Lévy flights is performed by $ApplyLevy(\sigma_i)$ to obtain a new solution. After that, the fitness value of them are compared and the better one is selected to stay in R_g. Once a set of test tuples is created, the *Fitness*(σ_j, t_c, ω_1, ω_2) method on line 9 will use coverage information and method-call information to calculate the fitness value of $\sigma_j \in R_g$. On line 14, the test tuples in R_g are reordered according to their fitness value. p_a of worse nests will be abandoned, and should be rebuilt by Lévy flights as well. After iterating over *MaxGeneration* times, the test tuple with the highest fitness value in the last test tuple set R_g is the global optimal solution obtained by the algorithm.

4 Empirical Evaluation and Discussion

Test case prioritization aims to detect more faults as early as possible. The APFD metrics is commonly used as a standard to evaluate this performance, and the specific meaning of it is described later in this section. Experiments are designed to compare the calculated APFD value and the number of detected faults, which proves that our method has better fault detection capability than the traditional methods.

In this section, the part one describes experiment environment, design and evaluation metrics. In the next part, it presents the parameters of our method in the next comparative experiments. Then, the first experiment compares the performance of CS with traditional techniques and the genetic algorithm. The second one compares them under time constraints.

4.1 Experiment Configuration

Test cases run on the Linux virtual machine. The execution time of them is obtained by the tool time.pl [19] in the SIR system and specifically defined as the average value of its 500 tests. All experiments are conducted on the same computer which is configured as the 64-bit Windows 7 operating systems, Pentium(R) dual-core CPU and 4 GB memory. The heuristic algorithm for each different parameter configuration is performed 200 times, and the random TCP experiment is performed 500 times to reduce the uncertainty of the experimental results. Experiments are conducted many times to avoid occasional abnormal data posing a threat to the validity of the experimental results.

Table 2. Case study application.

Apache-xml-security	
Classes	115
Methods	505
LOC	16800
Test cases	10
Seeded faults	12

Case Study. To validate the effectiveness of our approach, a Java program Apache-xml-security from the SIR infrastructure [20] is used as an analysis object. The differences between versions do not need to be considered. Version 0 is just chosen as our research object.

Table 2 shows the details of our case study. Apache-xml-security is a component library implementing XML signature and encryption standards, supplied by the XML subproject of the open source Apache project. It currently provides a mature implementation of Digital Signatures for XML, with implementation of encryption standards in progress. There are several sequential, previously-released versions of XML-security, each provided with a developer supplied JUnit test suite [20]. In each version, faults are seeded using fault seeding procedure described in Java Fault Seeding Process. Moreover, new faults are implanted with the original basis, and some faults that are not detected by any test cases or are detected by each test case should also be removed. Eventually, twelve faults are retained after screening. In addition, the number of test cases described in the table is also obtained by deleting redundancy.

Table 3. Study tools.

Tools	
Emma	A free Java code coverage tool
Source monitor	A tool for measuring code written in a variety of languages
time.pl	Calculate the time taken by test cases to execute the program, and it is used to collect timings
Lingo	An integrated tool for building and solving linear, nonlinear and integer optimization models

Implementation and Environment. The open source software program Apache-xml-security run in a Linux system environment. It is built by creating a virtual Ubuntu system on VMware. In this virtual environment, faults are injected in the source code and test cases are run on the research object.

There are tools should be used as shown in Table 3. They are related to two aspects. One is code information and the other is time constraint. In the CS algorithm, every time when the initialization or iteration executed, the fitness function of each test tuple should be calculated with test case code coverage information and the number of method calls. In which, the code coverage information is obtained by a tool called Emma. Emma instruments classes for class, method and block coverage. Emma is quite fast: the runtime overhead of added instrumentation is small (5–20%) and the byte-code instrumentor itself is fast, mostly limited by file I/O speed. Memory overhead is a few hundred bytes per Java class [21]. However, in addition to the code in the experiment coverage information, the method-call information of each test case is also indispensable. In this regard, the code metric tool Source Monitor is used to feed us back to a series of code-related information.

Meanwhile, the calculation of time cost for the test case use the tool time.pl [19] in the SIR system. This tool calculates the time taken by test cases to execute the program, and it is used to collect timings. Code coverage and test case execution time should be combined to filter out the better and more test cases that run in a limited time. This operation takes advantage of Lingo because it is easier to understand and handle than other tools when dealing with integer linear programming problems.

Evaluation Metrics. To calculate the fault detection ability, APFD (Average Percentage Fault Detection) metric [10] should be considered to apply to. It evaluates the optimization degree of test case prioritization set, and measures the effectiveness of different test case prioritization techniques under different time constrains.

Assume there is a test case set T with n test cases and m defects. Given a test case prioritization tuple, TF_i represents the location of the first test case in which fault i-th was detected. APFD is calculated as follows:

$$APFD = 1 - \frac{TF_1 + TF_2 + \ldots + TF_m}{nm} + \frac{1}{2n} \tag{16}$$

and the larger the value of APFD, the higher the efficiency of the test sorting.

At the same time, not all test cases usually should be run due to time constraints. It will most likely cause some faults might not be detected by any test case. In this regard, counting TFi = n + 1 if there are no test cases detect the i-th fault.

Take the test tuple <T_4, T_5, T_3> in Fig. 1. (d) as an example, its APFD = 1 − (3 + 1 + 1 + 2 + 3 + 2 + 1 + 6 + 2 + 6)/5 ∗ 10 + 1/2 ∗ 5 = 0.56.

Although the execution time of the test case is important, the other evaluation criteria APFDc that takes the severity of faults and time cost into account is not used as our evaluation criteria. Because, this paper puts more emphasis on detecting more faults in a limited time when comparing the different techniques under different time constraints.

4.2 Experiments and Results

Table 4. Parameters used in CS configurations.

CS parameters	
P	Apache-xml-security
(g_{max}, s)	(25, 60), (50, 30), (75, 15)
p_a	0.8, 0.5, 0.25
(ω_1, ω_2)	(1, 0), (0, 1), (0.85, 0.15)
t_c	class, method
p_t	0.85, 0.75, 0.5, 0.25

Optimal Parameters of CS Algorithm. As shown in Table 4, there are many uncertain parameters in the CS algorithm. So the fault detection effectiveness of our CS algorithm are compared under different parameter configurations. It aims to obtain a greatest parameter configuration for the next comparative experiments. Different parameter values of the four variable groups need to be combined. Finally, there are $3 * 3 * 3 * 2 * 4 = 216$ different parameter configurations.

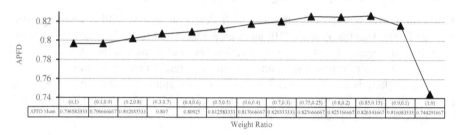

APFD Mean	(0,1)	(0.1,0.9)	(0.2,0.8)	(0.3,0.7)	(0.4,0.6)	(0.5,0.5)	(0.6,0.4)	(0.7,0.3)	(0.75,0.25)	(0.8,0.2)	(0.85,0.15)	(0.9,0.1)	(1,0)
	0.796583333	0.796666667	0.802083333	0.807	0.80925	0.812583333	0.817666667	0.820333333	0.825066667	0.825166667	0.826541667	0.816083333	0.744291667

Weight Ratio

Fig. 3. Variation trend of CS prioritization algorithm's APFD value at different weight ratios.

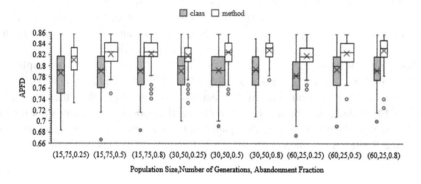

Fig. 4. Code coverage adequacy criteria comparison: method vs. class.

Table 5. Coverage adequacy criteria comparison t-test.

APFD mean		p-value	t-value
Class	Method		
0.790634	0.822273	<0.01	−31.652

Among them, the parameter combination (ω_1, ω_2) is related to fitness function calculation and the value (0.85, 0.15) is obtained by trying different weight ratios. The weight ratio is adjusted gradually by the step size of 0.1 from (0, 1) to (1, 0), then the relative optimal one is obtained. Experiments performed under each weight ratio and the results is shown in Fig. 3. According to the trend of the curve in Fig. 3, the fault detection rate of the CS algorithm get the best results when the ratio of weights is (0.85,

0.15). As is shown in Fig. 3, the TCP considers the code coverage without method calls when (ω_1, ω_2) is (0, 1). And its fault detection performance is significantly worse than the one which took method calls into consideration as well. This shows that adding the number of method invocations in fitness function gets a more rigorous fitness value, which indeed to improve the quality of test tuples.

The optimal weight ratio of the fitness function has been determined. Now combine and compare the experimental results of other uncertain parameters. First, the effect of different coverage adequacy criteria on experimental results is compared. There are 18 combinations of those 2 code coverage criteria with 9 different generations number, population size and abandonment fraction. Figure 4 illustrates box diagrams about experimental results. Table 5 shows the t test result of experiments, and the p-value and t-value are obtained by 2-tail t test at significant level $\alpha = 0.05$.

The p-value reveals the degree of difference of two targets. These two targets have difference when $p < 0.1$ and the difference is significant when $p < 0.05$. If $p > 0.1$, they have no difference. The t-value shows which is better. If p-value has told us these two targets have difference and t-value < 0, the latter one is better. According to the p-values and t-value in Table 5, fine-grained method-level experimental results are significantly better than the class-level. Although the experiment might not proceed with the level of the block, there is a great possibility of believing that the performance of the experiment might be further enhanced if the code coverage criterion is block.

The method has been chosen to be the code coverage criterion in next experiments. The white boxes in Fig. 4 are extracted and compared to determine other parameters. These parameters include the population size, number of generations and abandonment fraction. Figure 5. Shows those nine boxes and verifies that the abandonment fraction had better not choose the value of 0.25.

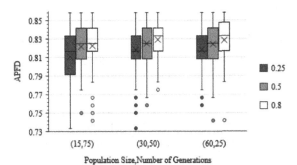

Fig. 5. Population size, generations number and abandonment fraction comparison.

In Table 6, compares to other ones, whatever the (s, g_{max}) is, the p-value is always <0.01 when $p_a = 0.25$. Though $p_a = 0.5$ shows no significant difference between $p_a = 0.8$ in Fig. 5, Table 6 proves that $p_a = 0.5$ and $p_a = 0.8$ have significant differences (p = 0.0366), and $p_a = 0.8$ is better than $p_a = 0.5$ (t = -2.467) when the (s, g_{max}) is (60, 25). The dark shadows in Table 6 show that the t test result has no significant difference when not partitioning (s, g_{max}), and it prove the $p_a = 0.8$ is better as well.

When focus on the experimental results of different (s, g_{max}) combinations in Table 7, differ from the GA, the difference is not reflected on the CS algorithm. Except (15, 75) shows obvious disadvantage over (30, 50) and (60, 25). The $(s, g_{max}) = (30, 50)$ shows there is no significant different from $(s, g_{max}) = (60, 25)$. Thus, a relatively good combination (50, 30) is chose for the next experiments. Finally, the optimal parameter is $(s, g_{max}, p_a, \omega_1, \omega_2, t_c) = (30, 50, 0.8, 0.85, 0.15, \text{method})$.

Table 6. Abandonment fraction comparison t-test.

(s, g_{max})	p_a (1)	APFD mean	p_a (2)	APFD mean	p-value	t-value
(15, 75)	0.25	0.81092	0.5	0.82175	<0.01	−3.615
	0.5	0.82175	0.8	0.82296	0.6378	−0.471
	0.25	0.81092	0.8	0.82296	<0.01	−4.074
(30, 50)	0.25	0.81854	0.5	0.8255	<0.01	−2.957
	0.5	0.8255	0.8	0.8295	0.0533	−1.938
	0.25	0.81854	0.8	0.8295	<0.01	−4.982
(60, 25)	0.25	0.81829	0.5	0.82429	<0.01	−2.805
	0.5	0.82429	0.8	0.82856	0.0366	−2.097
	0.25	0.81829	0.8	0.82856	<0.01	−4.822
Total	0.25	0.81592	0.5	0.82385	<0.01	−5.422
	0.5	0.82385	0.8	0.82706	**0.0143**	**−2.454**
	0.25	0.81592	0.8	0.82706	<0.01	−7.771

Table 7. Population size, generations number t-test.

p_a	(s, g_{max}) (1)	APFD mean	(s, g_{max}) (2)	APFD mean	p-value	t-value
0.25	(15, 75)	0.81092	(30, 50)	0.81854	<0.01	−2.596
	(30, 50)	0.81854	(60, 25)	0.81829	0.9149	0.107
	(15, 75)	0.81092	(60, 25)	0.81829	<0.01	−2.612
0.5	(15, 75)	0.82175	(30, 50)	0.8255	0.1232	−1.545
	(30, 50)	0.8255	(60, 25)	0.82429	0.5757	0.5602
	(15, 75)	0.82175	(60, 25)	0.82429	0.2828	−1.075
0.8	(15, 75)	0.82296	(30, 50)	0.8295	<0.01	−2.941
	(30, 50)	0.8295	(60, 25)	0.82856	0.694	0.3937
	(15, 75)	0.82296	(60, 25)	0.82856	0.014	−2.467
Total	(15, 75)	0.81854	(30, 50)	0.82451	<0.01	−3.992
	(30, 50)	0.82451	(60, 25)	0.82376	0.5573	0.587
	(15, 75)	0.81854	(60, 25)	0.82376	<0.01	−3.535

Alternative Prioritization Comparisons. To verify the effectiveness of our approach using integer linear programming at different time budgets, time constraint is added on the last experiments. This section compares our approach with the GA, several traditional techniques under different time constraints.

Our CS algorithm combined with the ILP model described in Sect. 3.1. The genetic algorithm is implemented according to the technique designed by Walcott et al. [3].

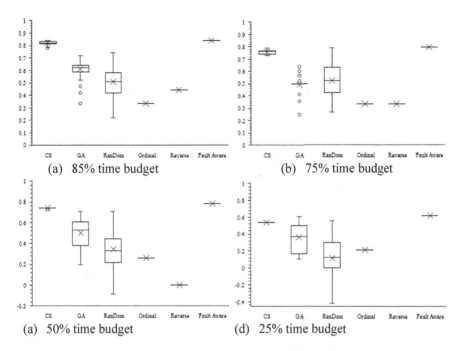

(a) 85% time budget   (b) 75% time budget

(a) 50% time budget   (d) 25% time budget

Fig. 6. CS vs other techniques APFDs under different time-constraint.

Analyzing experimental results in general according to Fig. 6. Compare with the GA and other traditional techniques, our CS algorithm obviously improves the efficiency of fault detection to a certain extent, except the reverse order algorithm due to contingency. In addition, by observing the first three boxes of 4 pictures, it may be found that APFD value of our CS algorithm is not only high but also concentrated. It shows that the fault detection performance of our approach is more stable than the latter two techniques.

In Fig. 6, the fault aware is an strategy under ideal conditions, its premise is that the faults detected by the test case are predicted in advance. This strategy runs the test cases that detect more faults as early as possible. Although it is no practical meaning, it is used as a reference to the performance of our approach. By comparing with the data diagram of this idealized technology, it shows that applying the cuckoo algorithm to TCP problem does not match the fault aware strategy. But the difference is not obvious, the CS algorithm shows good fault detection performance.

Analyzing experimental results in detail according to Fig. 6 and Table 8. In Fig. 6, our CS algorithm is superior in fault detection efficiency to the other four techniques except fault aware strategy, whether there is no time constraint (100%), loose time constraint (85%) or compact time constraint (25%). The p-values (all p-values < 0.01)

752   Y. Wong et al.

and t-values obtained by the t-test in Table 8 prove that this superiority is extremely significant. When compare with fault-aware strategy, the difference between our approach and the fault-aware is significant under most of the time constraints, but is not significant when the time constraint is 85%.

Table 8. CS vs other techniques under different time constraints and t-test.

Time percent	CS APFD mean	Detected number	Other algorithms	APFD mean	Detected number	p-value	t-value
0.85	0.82796	12	GA	0.61428	11(±1)	<0.01	33.084
			Random	0.50648	11	<0.01	27.562
			Order	0.33333	11	<0.01	30.894
			Reserve	0.44444	8	<0.01	23.846
			Fault aware	0.84259	12	**0.1602**	**−1.4096**
0.75	0.77019	11	GA	0.49486	9(+1)	<0.01	46.212
			Random	0.52204	11	<0.01	18.007
			Order	0.33333	11	<0.01	23.676
			Reserve	0.33333	8	<0.01	23.676
			Fault aware	0.7963	11	0.045	−2.0169
0.5	0.74	11	GA	0.49864	9(±1)	<0.01	18.807
			Random	0.34517	7(±4)	<0.01	23.780
			Order	0.26042	7	<0.01	158.26
			Reserve	0	6	<0.01	244.2
			Fault aware	0.78125	11	<0.01	−13.631
0.25	0.53571	9	GA	0.36057	8(+1)	<0.01	11.012
			Random	0.11802	5(±4)	<0.01	17.623
			Order	0.21429	7	<0.01	1.3E+14
			Reserve	−∞	0	<0.01	+∞
			Fault aware	0.61905	9	<0.01	−3E+13

In Table 8, the "Detected number" records the number of faults that are detected by the current technology under different time constraints. Table 8 presents that our approach always detect as many faults as the fault aware strategy, and the number of faults detected by our approach is always not less than other techniques. The more compact the time constraint, the more obvious the advantage of the CS algorithm that detects more faults.

In general, the effective of our approach has been proved by the comparison about the number of fault detections and the evaluation standard APFD in above experiments. The conclusion is that applying CS Algorithm and integer linear programming to the time constraint TCP problem not only detects more faults but also detects faults as early as possible.

5   Conclusion

This paper proposes a time-aware test case prioritization technique, using cuckoo search algorithm and integer linear programming. The integer linear programming model is used to generate the best test case subset when the time is limited. A new fitness function based on code coverage and method-call information is also designed to improve the effectiveness of fault detection. Experimental analysis demonstrates that a time-aware test case order is created by our approach. And it significantly outperforms ones obtained from other prioritization techniques, even the genetic algorithm.

In the future work, the mature industrial projects will be further selected as experimental objects to verify the feasibility and effectiveness of the algorithm. Then, block, even sentence will be considered as our code coverage criterion in the later experiments. Finally, parallel computing and test case clustering will be studied in the future because of the consumption of time and space that the test suite should be permutated dynamically.

Acknowledge. This work is supported by the National Natural Science Foundation of China under grant No. 61572306 and No. 61502294, the CERNET Innovation Project under Grant No. NGII20170513, and the Youth Foundation of Shanghai Polytechnic University under Grant No. EGD18XQD01.

References

1. Elbaum, S., Malishevsky, A.G., Rothermel, G.: Test case prioritization: a family of empirical studies. IEEE Trans. Softw. Eng. **28**(2), 159–182 (2002)
2. Li, Z., Harman, M., Hierons, R.M.: Search algorithms for regression test case prioritization. Acta Paediatrica **33**(4), 225–237 (2007)
3. Walcott, K.R., Soffa, M.L., Kapfhammer, G.M.: Time aware test suite prioritization. In: ACM/SIGSOFT International Symposium on Software Testing and Analysis, ISSTA 2006, Portland, Maine, USA, July, DBLP, pp. 1–12 (2006)
4. Yang, X.S., Deb, S.: Cuckoo search via levey flights. In: World Congress on Nature & Biologically Inspired Computing, pp. 210–214. IEEE Xplore (2010)
5. Yang, X.S., Deb, S.: Multi-objective cuckoo search for design optimization. Comput. Oper. Res. **40**(6), 1616–1624 (2013)
6. Nagar, R., Kumar, A., Singh, G.P.: Test case selection and prioritization using cuckoos search algorithm. In: International Conference on Futuristic Trends on Computational Analysis and Knowledge Management, pp. 283–288. IEEE (2015)
7. Srivastava, P.R., Reddy, D.V.P.K., Reddy, M.S.: Test case prioritization using cuckoo search. Adv. Autom. Softw. Test. Framew. Refin. Pract. **28**(2), 159–182 (2012)
8. Rothermel, G., Untch, R.H., Chu, C.: Prioritizing test cases for regression testing. IEEE Trans. Softw. Eng. **27**(10), 929–948 (2001)
9. Elbaum, S., Malishevsky, A.G., Rothermel, G.: Prioritizing test cases for regression testing. In: ACM (2000)
10. Elbaum, S., Malishevsky, A.G., Rothermel, G.: Incorporating varying test costs and fault severities into test case prioritization. In: ICSE, pp. 329–338. IEEE Computer Society (2001)

11. Islam, M.M., Marchetto, A., Susi, A.: A multi objective technique to prioritize test cases based on latent semantic indexing. In: Proceedings 16th European Conference Software Maintenance and Reengineering, pp. 21–30 (2012)
12. Saini, A., Tyagi, S.: MTCPA: multi-objective test case prioritization algorithm using genetic algorithm. In: International Journal of Advanced Research in Computer Science and Software Engineering (2015)
13. Schultz, M., Radloff, M.: Test case prioritization using multi objective particle swarm optimizer. In: International Conference on Signal Propagation and Computer Technology, pp. 390–395. IEEE (2014)
14. Alves, E.L., Machado, P.D., Massoni, T., Kim, M.: Prioritizing test cases for early detection of refactoring faults. Softw. Test. Verif. Reliab. 26, 402–426 (2016)
15. Eghbali, S., Tahvildari, L.: Test case prioritization using lexicographical ordering. IEEE Trans. Softw. Eng. 42(12), 1178–1195 (2016)
16. Lachmann, R., Schulze, S., Nieke, M.: System-level test case prioritization using machine learning. In: IEEE International Conference on Machine Learning and Applications, pp. 361–368. IEEE (2017)
17. Kim, J., Jeong, H., Lee, E.: Failure history data-based test case prioritization for effective regression test. In: Symposium on Applied Computing, pp. 1409–1415. ACM (2017)
18. Zhang, L., Hou, S.S., Guo, C.: Time-aware test-case prioritization using integer linear programming. In: Eighteenth International Symposium on Software Testing and Analysis, ISSTA 2009, Chicago, IL, USA, pp. 213–224 (2009)
19. Time.pl:a tool to collect timings. http://sir.unl.edu/content/tools.php
20. Do, H., Elbaum, S., Rothermel, G.: Supporting controlled experimentation with testing techniques: an infrastructure and its potential impact. Empir. Softw. Eng. 10, 405–435 (2005)
21. Roubtsov, V.: EMMA: a free Java code coverage tool. http://emma.sourceforge.net/

Using Hybrid Model for Android Malicious Application Detection Based on Population (Short Paper)

Zhijie Xiao[1], Tao Li[1,2(✉)], and Yuqiao Wang[1]

[1] College of Computer Science and Technology, Wuhan University of Science and Technology, Wuhan 430065, Hubei, China
544247884@qq.com, litaowust@163.com, leowon@vip.qq.com
[2] Hubei Province Key Laboratory of Intelligent Information Processing and Real-Time Industrial System, Wuhan 430065, Hubei, China

Abstract. In the Android system security issue, the maliciousness of the applications is closely related to the permissions they applied. In this paper, a population-based model is proposed for detecting Android malicious application. Which is in the view of the current disadvantages of missing report, long detection period caused by features redundancy, and the instability of detection rate lead by unbalanced data of benign and malicious samples. Drawing on the idea of population in biology, each app was labeled by preprocessing. And adaptive feature vectors were automatically selected through the feature engineering. Thus the malicious application detection is carried out in the form of hybrid model voting. The experimental results show that feature engineering can remove a large amount of redundancy before classification. And the hybrid voting model can provide adaptive detection service for different populations.

Keywords: Android security · Population · Feature engineering · Security detection

1 Introduction

The various applications running on smartphones are changing people's life and communication mode. At the same time, there are some illegal elements who use malicious programs to carry out malicious charges, remote control, privacy theft and other improper acts, which seriously affect the lives of users [1–4]. Google Bouncer in Google Play can detect malicious programs, but it is not real-time, so malicious applications have been downloaded in large quantities before being detected [5]. Part of the third party application market did not carry out any form of security check before releasing the application [6]. The increasingly severe security situation of Android operating system makes it important to improve the detection efficiency of malware.

The traditional research methods are mainly divided into two categories: static analysis [7] and dynamic detection [8]. Document [9] uses static analysis to extract the function call list of executable linked format files by using the readelf. The classification algorithm is used to classify the extracted samples, so as to achieve the purpose of detecting malware. Literature [10] implements a behavior monitoring system on the

H. Gao et al. (Eds.): CollaborateCom 2018, LNICST 268, pp. 755–766, 2019.
https://doi.org/10.1007/978-3-030-12981-1_52

Android platform, dynamically monitoring the various features and events of the Android system, and classifies it by means of decision tree and regression analysis. However, due to the limited resources and power consumption of the mobile phone system, the implementation of the scheme is rather complicated. Although the traditional dynamic detection methods have their own advantages, they cannot meet the needs of timely detection of a large number of applications.

After analyzing 1100 Android application privileges using the neural network algorithm, it is found that the Android privileges often used by these programs are only a small part [11]. Literature [12] compares the use of permissions to normal software and malware, and finds that access network, reading mobile status, access to network status, and write SD cards are widely used in malicious programs and benign programs. However, malicious programs tend to use SMS related permissions, automatic startup permissions when user starting up, and changes to WIFI status permissions, while benign programs rarely use these permissions.

The above study shows that there are obvious differences in the frequency of use of different Android permissions. Moreover, the combination of normal software and malware in the combination of permissions and the tendency of categories are also quite different. Permission mechanism is the core of Android security mechanism, and the permissions of application are corresponding to the API provided by the system. Therefore, many researchers regard permissions as important detection objects.

Document [13] proposes a multilevel integrated malware detection model which extract Dalvik instructions, permissions and API as features. A three level ensemble classifier based on J48 decision tree is constructed, which has better detection. However, the technology implementation is more complex and is not suitable for detecting large-scale data. Literature [14] extracts the rights of the APK file as the feature, and uses the information gain algorithm to filter the features to implement a Android malware detection model based on the improved random forest algorithm. It achieves better detection results for feature dimensionality reduction, but there is a deficiency in solving the data imbalance, and the detection rate of Android malware is low.

AndroidProtect [15] uses static analysis to mine mass application feature values and uses dynamic target program behavior monitoring to adjust the accuracy of evaluation. Dynamic monitoring can correct deviations, but it is inefficient in dealing with large-scale applications. The author [16] proposed the similarity calculation method combined with the Euclidean distance to evaluate the dangerous trend of the Android application. By using the minimum set of privileges as the security threshold, the distance of the application to the threshold is calculated to represent the dangerous trend of the application. However, the minimum privilege set does not exist in every type of application, and the detection rate based on Euclidean distance is not good enough. To sum up, aiming at the problems existing in the current Android malware detection technology, such as the lack of detection of unknown malware, the imbalance of data in the detection process, and the low detection efficiency, this paper proposes an integrated model based on population for Android malware detection.

2 System Framework

We propose a method of Android application security detection based on the applied population, using feature engineering and mixed model voting. The model consists of 3 main modules: Feature extraction, feature engineering and safety inspection (Fig. 1).

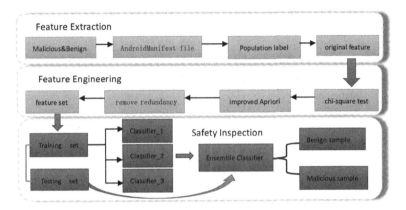

Fig. 1. The picture shows the framework of the entire hybrid detection model.

In the data preprocessing module, we optimize the code for the Scrapy frame crawler used in the article [16]. Using the application category label provided by the web site, the application is crawled by category and stored in the cloud database.

In the issue of Android system security, the permission to be applied is an important object for security analysis and evaluation. Because the same type of application implements similar functions, the required system privileges are similar. In the data preprocessing module, we annotate the collected malicious and benign samples, compare the same type of application into a population and give them a population label. Then, according to the population as a unit, the APK file is reverse processed to get the list file AndroidManifest.xml. According to the population as a unit, the APK file is reverse processed to get the list file AndroidManifest.xml. The permission information of the application is stored in the AndroidManifest.xml file. In order to improve the efficiency of application rights acquisition and carry on the batch extraction of permission, this paper uses the python program and combines the AAPT (Android Asset Packging Tool) to write the AndroidManifest.xml file parsing code. The experiment obtains the application permissions of each population according to the population, thus forming the original feature data set and storing it in the cloud database in the form of 0–1 matrix.

Chi-Square Test. The correlation of two features can be quickly calculated by chi square test. In the detection, we only need to know whether the sample features are available or not, and do not consider the number of occurrence. Therefore, it is very suitable for the processing of Android privilege characteristics. We give the definition of the population label and the specific information for each population:

Definition 1. Class $= \{C1, C2, C3 \ldots Cx\}$ *Cx are category labels for each population, such as flashlights, cameras, readers, players, social chat and so on.*

Definition 2. Population $= (Cx, Permission1, Permission2, Permission3 \ldots Permissionm)$. *Permissionm represents the m permissions feature of the population.*

We suppose two classified variables X and Y, their ranges are {Malicious sample, Benign sample} and {Contain Permissioni, Not Contain Permissioni}, For each population, we count five frequency characteristics: MP, MN, BP and BN (Table 1).

Table 1. The table describes the meaning of each item in the chi square test.

	Contain Permissioni	Not Contain Permissioni	Sum
Malicious	MP	MN	
Benign	BP	BN	
Sum			N

So we calculate the formula:

$$\chi^2 = \frac{(MP * BN)^2 * N}{(MP + MN) * (BP + BN) * (MP + BP) * (MN + BN)} \tag{1}$$

The m permissions of each population are calculated in turn to get the chi-square value χ^2. The greater the value of χ^2, the greater the possibility that the relationship between X and Y will be established. According to the check level a, find the chi square value table, get the critical value and compare it. If the lookup table value is less than the chi square value, then the permissions are redundant and need to be removed. After chi square test, a new population feature vector set D is obtained.

InG Algorithm. After the initial dimension reduction by chi square test, the information gain algorithm is applied to feature selection to further remove redundancy. In information gain, the criterion is how much information the feature can bring to the classification system. The more information it brings, the more important the feature is. For a feature, whether a system has a characteristic information quantity will change, and the difference between the front and rear information is the information quantity brought by this feature to the system. The amount of information is entropy. Information gain describes the ability of attribute X to discriminate sample Y.

We use Y to represent the random variable of the application category, Y= {Malicious, Benign}. For each permission Permissioni in a population, its information entropy H (x) is:

$$H(X) = -\sum_i P(X_i) lb P(X_i) \tag{2}$$

The conditional information entropy H (X|Y) of X after the known variable Y is:

$$H(X|Y) = -\sum_j P(y_i) \sum_i P(x_i|y_j)lbP(x_i|y_j) \tag{3}$$

Mutual information between variables X and Y is:

$$MI(X, Y) = H(X) - H(X|Y) = \sum_{x,y} P(x, y)lb\frac{P(x, y)}{P(x) * P(y)} \tag{4}$$

The greater the information gain of the privilege feature Permissioni, the greater the correlation between the feature and the category. After calculating the information gain of each privilege feature, the features are arranged in descending order according to information gain. The feature set of each population is selected adaptively through experiments to train and test the classifier. At this point, we get the data set S for each population.

3 Security Detection Algorithm

3.1 SVM Algorithm Based on Bagging

Android malicious sample is difficult to collect compared to the benign sample, so it is easy to appear the imbalance between the benign sample and the malignant sample, which makes the classifier more biased in the benign sample, and eventually leads to the low detection rate. At the same time, the SVM algorithm is sensitive to the samples at the boundary. If there are misplaced samples on the boundary, the stability of the classifier will be greatly affected.

Using Bagging to construct balanced data sets for benign and malicious samples can reduce the impact of imbalanced data on experimental results. In order to improve the detection efficiency, this paper adopts the Linear Support Vector Machine to design the SVM algorithm based on Bagging. The concrete steps are as follows:

1. Randomly divide 70% data from S as training set S_train and 30% data as test machine S_test, and the range of data set S is {Maliouse, Benign}.
2. Using Bagging to extract m benign samples and M malicious samples to form a new training data set $D_i = (X_i, Y_i)$, the digital m is generated by a random number generator, in which $X_i = (X_{i1}X_{i2}X_{i3}\ldots X_{im})$, that is, the information of an application sample. $Y_i = \{0, 1\}$, of which 0 represents benign samples, and 1 indicates malignant samples.
3. The SVM classifier is represented as:

$$\begin{cases} \min_\lambda \frac{1}{2}\sum_{i,j} \lambda_i\lambda_jy_iy_jx_i^T x_j - \sum_{i=1}^n \lambda_i \\ \sum_{i=1}^n y_i\lambda_i = 0, 0 \le \lambda_i \le \alpha, i = 1, 2, \ldots n \end{cases} \tag{5}$$

A is a penalty term. The two step programming method is used to solve the model and get the Lagrange multiplier. Then the LSVM parameter is solved as follows:

$$\omega = \sum_i \lambda_i y_i x_i \tag{6}$$

$$\lambda_i \left(y_i \sum_i \lambda_j y_j x_i^T x_j + c - 1 \right) = 0 \tag{7}$$

$$C(x) = sign \left(\sum_{i=1}^n \lambda_i y_i x_i^T + c \right) \tag{8}$$

4. Repeat 3 times steps 2 and 3, get three LSVM base classifiers, and combine 3 base classifiers into SVM ensemble classifier CC. The test sample X in S_test is put into the integrated classifier CC, and the result is cast. The voting formula is:

$$CC(x) = voting(C_1(x), C_2(x), C_3(x), \ldots C_k(x)) = \delta \left(\sum_i singn(C_i(x) = y) \right) \tag{9}$$

If $C_i(x) = y$, in that way sign(r) = 1, conversely, sign(r) = −1.
If $\sum_i singn(C_i(x) = y) > 0$, $\delta(q) = 1$, samples is malware, otherwise $\delta(q) = 0$, indicating benign.

3.2   A Classifier Based on Improved Naive Bayes

The idea of naive Bayes is to obtain a priori probability by training samples, and the posterior probability of events is obtained according to the prior probabilities and sample data information. Finally, the event is attributed to the maximum of the posterior probability. The Bias classifier is derived from the formula, so it has a stable classification efficiency, low sensitivity to real data and high algorithm efficiency.

In a population, an application of information $X = (X_1, X_2, X_3 \ldots X_k)$, C_i represents whether the application is benign or malignant. So we can get the posteriori hypothesis.

$$P(C_i|X) = \frac{P(X|C_i)P(C_i)}{P(X)} \tag{10}$$

Naive Bayes assumes that the influence of a feature on classification is independent of other attributes, so we can known that:

$$P(X|C_i) = \prod_{k=1}^n P(X_k|C_i) \tag{11}$$

However, in practical applications, permissions are independent of each other, which is not valid in Android malware detection. After multiple removal of redundancy after the feature engineering module, we get the data set S, which is very representative of the classification, so the naive Bayes can be applied to the detection scene.

$$P(C_i|X) = \frac{P(C_i) \prod_{k=1}^n P(X_k|C_i) \frac{1}{x_k^2} \sum_{i=1}^n x_i^2}{P(X)} \tag{12}$$

At the same time, in the detection scene, the extent of the influence of different permissions on malicious detection is different. The simple Bias cannot show the difference of the feature [17]. Therefore, we introduce the weight influence factor $\frac{1}{\chi_k^2}\sum_{i=1}^{n}\chi_i^2$ to the posterior probability of the Bias classification, and the influence factor represents the proportion of the influence that the authority brings to the classification.

4 Experimental Results and Analysis

4.1 Experimental Data

At present, we have climbed 62 categories and totaling 325371 Android benign applications from AnZhi [18]. Malicious samples from VirusShare [19]. For the following reasons, we chose two groups of cameras and flashlights as experimental objects. First, the two types of applications, such as cameras and flashlights, have clear functional boundaries. For a app, it is easier to distinguish whether it belongs to a flashlight or camera category from its main permission statement and the application description that is filled in when it is uploaded. Second, flashlights and cameras are widely used by users, while mobile devices are produced with flashlights and cameras, but almost every user will install another flashlight or camera app because of the individual needs.

4.2 Experimental Results

Taking Android permission meaning as background knowledge, chi square test and InG algorithm are used to perform two times of feature de redundancy. In the module of the feature engineering, we take all the rights characteristics of the population as the experimental set, and get 128 feature vectors of the flashlight, and 134 camera population characteristics. After screening, each authority is scored. The higher the score, the greater the information gain and the better the privilege of the categorization result. List 10 rights information with the highest score in two populations.

In the table, the top 10 features of the population and flashlight population information gain are listed. From the table, we can see that there are differences in the distribution of permission characteristics among the two populations, and the information gain of the same permissions in different populations is also different. It can be seen that different populations have different requirements and distributions in terms of authority, which shows that the characteristics of populations are different (Table 2).

Table 2. The top10 information gain of the flashlight and camera population.

Rank	Flashlight	InG
1	CAMERA	0.538
2	FLASHLIGHT	0.511
3	INTERNET	0.384
4	ACCESS_NETWORK_STATE	0.347
5	ACCESS_COARSE_LOCATION	0.315
6	ACCESS_WIFI_STATE	0.280
7	ACCESS_FINE_LOCATION	0.279
8	GET_TASKS	0.247
9	WAKE_LOCK	0.231
10	WRITE_SETTINGS	0.206
Rank	Camera	InG
1	WRITE_EXTERNAL_STORAGE	0.442
2	INTERNET	0.418
3	CAMERA	0.397
4	ACCESS_NETWORK_STATE	0.385
5	READ_PHONE_STATE	0.379
6	ACCESS_WIFI_STATE	0.341
7	WAKE_LOCK	0.326
8	ACCESS_COARSE_LOCATION	0.303
9	VIBRATE	0.285
10	GET_TASKS	0.247

In order to find optimal subset, we count the Accuracy and F1-score under the number of different privileges, as shown in the following figure (Fig. 2).

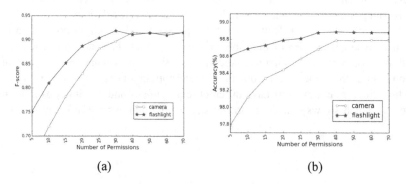

(a)   (b)

Fig. 2. (a) and (b) respectively represent the Accuracy and F1-score of two different populations when increasing the number of permissions.

From the graph, it is found that in the flashlight population, the set of the top 30 permissions is the optimal set. In the camera population, the set of the top 40 permissions is the optimal set, because at this time the two populations have reached a higher and more stable accuracy. Considering that we normally tend to select the smallest subset of permissions. Adding more permissions does not help on improving but may introduce redundant, noisy and irrelevant information (Table 3).

Table 3. The F1 score of the four classification algorithms on two populations. Top20 represents the first 20 features of the information gain rankings.

		NB	SVM	RF	Mixture
Flashlight	Top 20	82.3	88.0	88.4	88.7
	Top 30	84.2	89.2	89.7	92.0
	Top 50	88.4	93.7	90.6	91.8
	Top 90	92.3	91.5	91.0	91.2
	Data S	90.7	92.1	90.9	91.0
Camera	Top 20	81.4	86.5	85.1	83.0
	Top 40	83.6	88.1	87.6	91.5
	Top 60	88.9	90.2	89.7	91.5
	Top 90	90.5	90.9	91.1	91.3
	Data S	90.8	91.3	89.9	90.8

The table shows two groups of flashlights and cameras. The purpose is to evaluate the effect of feature engineering. The classification algorithms are naive Bayes, LSVM, RF and the hybrid voting algorithm in this paper(Mixture), in which LSVM and RF use the default parameters in the Weka tool.

The 10 cross validation method is used to train the classifier and get the result.

It can be seen from the table that the classification results of RF and mixture are better. In the flash population, when the number of permissions reaches the first 30, the F1 value gradually stabilizes in the 92.0%. In the camera population, when the number of permissions reaches 40, the F1 value is gradually stabilized at the 91.5%.

According to Occam's Razor, Entities should not be multiplied unnecessarily, for these two populations, we respectively take the top 30 and the top 40 of the rights for classification. This shows that the feature engineering screening method proposed in this paper can eliminate a large number of redundant features and improve the efficiency of detection.

For non-equilibrium data, 3 sets of data sets are designed to test the effectiveness of the proposed method. After the characteristic engineering module was processed, the flashlight population data set SF and the camera population data set SC were obtained. SF contains 300 malicious applications, 1200 benign applications. And 280 malicious applications and 1250 benign applications in SC. Three data sets of two populations, A, B, and C, are extracted randomly by no return (Table 4).

Table 4. Data distribution of data sets A, B, C in two populations. 280(M)+625(B) represents 280 malicious samples and 625 benign samples.

Population	A	B	C
Camera	280(M)+280(B)	280(M)+625(B)	280(M)+1250(B)
Flashlight	300(M)+300(B)	300(M)+600(B)	300(M)+1200(B)

Three samples of A, B and C in two populations were sampled without return. Each dataset was divided into 10 averages, of which 8 were used as training sets and 2 as test sets. Then, our algorithm and the method of Wang [16], Zhang [15] are used to classify these data sets simultaneously. For the results obtained, the classification indexes Precision, Recall, and Accuracy are calculated. Repeat the 10 cross validation to get the average value. The results are shown in the following table (Table 5).

Table 5. The results of different methods are compared to the A, B, C data sets. F represents the flashlight population, and C represents the camera population.

Data	Method	Precision		Recall		Accuracy	
		F	C	F	C	F	C
A	Mixture	96.7	96.2	98.9	98.8	97.8	98.1
	Wang	95.4	94.8	97.4	96.3	96.0	97.5
	Zhang	96.5	97.3	98.5	97.4	97.1	97.9
B	Mixture	96.8	96.5	97.9	98.5	97.6	97.7
	Wang	94.3	93.3	94.6	97.1	95.3	96.3
	Zhang	95.9	98.0	92.2	92.5	96.5	96.7
C	Mixture	96.3	93.1	98.7	98.4	97.6	97.6
	Wang	93.3	92.9	95.6	95.7	95.1	95.5
	Zhang	94.6	96.4	95.7	92.3	96.1	96.7

For the two unbalanced data sets of B and C, the detection rate of the three methods decreased when the imbalances increased, but the variation of Mixture in the detection rate was smaller and stable at a better level. For a detection method, the negative impact of malware to be detected as a benign software is far greater than that of the benign software being misrepresented as malware, so the Recall is a very important index. A slight reduction in accuracy and improvement in Recall are of great importance in the detection of Android applications.

5   Conclusion

This article is based on the idea of biological population. The static feature of Android is removed by feature engineering, so that the feature is pruned, the model training time is shortened, and the detection efficiency is improved. Then we use mixed model voting to detect malicious applications. Experiments on two commonly used flashlight and camera populations show that malware detection rates reach 98.7% and 98.4% respectively on unbalanced datasets. It is limited to detect only the permissions for malicious application detection, but the method is simple and easy to implement. It can detect a large number of applications at the same time. In the case of good detection rate, it also has a high detection efficiency.

Acknowledgement. Authors are partially supported by Major projects of the Hubei Provincial Education Department (No. 17ZD014), Hubei college students' Innovation and Entrepreneurship Training Program project (No. 201610488020), National defense pre research fund of Wuhan University of Science and Technology (No. GF201712) and Colleges and Universities in Hubei Provincial College Students' Innovation Entrepreneurial Training Program (No. 201710488027).

References

1. The development of the China Mobile Internet and its security report (2017). [EB/OL]. http://www.isc.org.cn/zxzx/xhdt/listinfo-35398.html. Accessed 17 May 2017/08 Mar 2018
2. Yi, L., Zhang, N., Liu, D.: Study on mobile malware situation and trends. Inf. Commun. Technol. **7**(2), 75–79 (2013)
3. Jiang, X., Zhou, Y.: A survey of Android malware. In: Jiang, X., Zhou, Y. (eds.) Android Malware, pp. 3–20. Springer, New York (2013). https://doi.org/10.1007/978-1-4614-7394-7_2
4. Chu, J., Zheng, L.: The security analysis of Android OS. Microcomput. Appl. **20**(7), 1–3 (2013)
5. Peng, H., Gates, C., Sarma, B., et al.: Using probabilistic generative models for ranking risks of Android apps. In: ACM Conference on Computer and Communications Security, pp. 241–252. ACM (2012)
6. Zhou, Y., Jiang, X.: Dissecting Android malware: characterization and evolution. In: IEEE Symposium on Security and Privacy, pp. 95–109. IEEE (2012)
7. Feng, Y., Anand, S., Dillig, I., et al.: Apposcopy: semantics-based detection of Android malware through static analysis. In: ACM SIGSOFT International Symposium on Foundations of Software Engineering, pp. 576–587. ACM (2014)
8. Petsas, T., Voyatzis, G., Athanasopoulos, E., et al.: Rage against the virtual machine: hindering dynamic analysis of Android malware. ACM (2014)
9. Schmidt, A.D., Bye, R., Schmidt, H.G., et al.: Static analysis of executables for collaborative malware detection on Android. In: IEEE International Conference on Communications, pp. 1–5. IEEE (2009)
10. Shabtai, A., Elovici, Y.: Applying behavioral detection on Android-based devices. In: Cai, Y., Magedanz, T., Li, M., Xia, J., Giannelli, C. (eds.) MOBILWARE 2010. LNICST, vol. 48, pp. 235–249. Springer, Heidelberg (2010). https://doi.org/10.1007/978-3-642-17758-3_17
11. Barrera, D., Oorschot, P.C.V., Somayaji, A.: A methodology for empirical analysis of permission-based security models and its application to Android. In: ACM Conference on Computer & Communications Security, pp. 73–84. ACM (2010)
12. Zhou, Y.: Dissecting Android malware: characterization and evolution. **4**(3), 95–109 (2012)
13. Zhang, W., Ben, H., Zhang, K., et al.: Malware detection techniques by mining massive behavioral data of mobile Apps. J. Integr. Technol. **5**(2), 29–40 (2016)
14. Yang, H., Xu, J.: Android malware detection based on improved random forest algorithm. J. Commun. **38**(4), 8–16 (2017)

15. Zhang, T., Li, T., Wang, H., Xiao, Z.: AndroidProtect: Android apps security analysis system. In: Wang, S., Zhou, A. (eds.) CollaborateCom 2016. LNICST, vol. 201, pp. 583–594. Springer, Cham (2017). https://doi.org/10.1007/978-3-319-59288-6_58

16. Wang, H., Li, T., Zhang, T., Wang, J.: Android apps security evaluation system in the cloud. In: Guo, S., Liao, X., Liu, F., Zhu, Y. (eds.) CollaborateCom 2015. LNICST, vol. 163, pp. 151–160. Springer, Cham (2016). https://doi.org/10.1007/978-3-319-28910-6_14

17. Peng, H.: Discussion on the selective weighted Bias classification method. Zhongshan University (2010)

18. Anzhi[EB/OL]. http://www.anzhi.com/

19. VirusShare [EB/OL]. https://virusshare.com/

Author Index